ISBN 978-1-333-79892-5
PIBN 10553924

The Cycle.

| Vol. I., No. 1. | BOSTON, MASS., 2 APRIL, 1886. | FIVE CENTS. |

 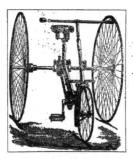

PUBLISHED EVERY FRIDAY BY ABBOT BASSETT, 22 SCHOOL ST., ROOM 19.

VOL. I.   *&* BOSTON, MASS., 2 APRIL, 1886.   NO. 1.

TERMS OF SUBSCRIPTION.

One Year, by mail, post-paid...........,;...........$1.50
Three Copies in one order..........................3.00
Club Subscriptions..................................1.00
Six Months..90
Single Copies.......................................05

Specimen Copies free.

ABBOT BASSETT . . . .   EDITOR

ALFRED MUDGE & SON, PRINTERS, 24 FRANKLIN ST., BOSTON.

All communications should be sent in not later than
Tuesday, to insure insertion the same week.

Entered at the Post-office as second-class mail matter.

WE MAKE OUR BOW.

RESPECTFULLY we make our bow. Beyond this we do not care to go at present. Promises are easily spoken and more easily broken. Deeds, not words, we care to be judged by, and we appeal to our record in the past for a promise of the future.

THE CYCLE goes forth into the wheel world to do what little good it can in a modest way. It has no enemies to punish, no gigantic wrong to right, no personal desires to advance. It will endeavor to give the news fairly and impartially, and it will aim to do this in a dignified way.

THE paramount idea in every venture of this kind is to make money for those who project the enterprise. THE CYCLE hopes to be able to fill the coffers of its publisher. Without this idea, the paper would not exist; but there is allied to it a feeling that any unfairly earned is never enjoyed, and enjoyment is our end and aim.

question uppermost in the minds of us to-day is the action of the Racing the matter of the so-called "makeurs." The best solution of the would engage the earnest attention o have the interest of the sport 'e are forced to admit that we what appears to us to be the best way out of the difficulty.

THERE are those who say we must have but two classes, the professionals and the amateurs. They are satisfied with the law as it now exists, and they demand a rigid enforcement of it. We think it safe to say that a count of League members would show nine in ten with this view of affairs.

BUT there is another class who hold strong opinions which are worthy of serious consideration. They are interested in racing, but they want to see it conducted without the environment of professional sport. They are satisfied that the promateurs have given us the fairest races; for, when a man rides to advertise a wheel, he must ride to win, and want of success means to him loss of favor with his employer, and consequent loss of salary. Those of this inclination are now found to be divided in their ideas, for while some are crying, "Down with the Racing Board, and let us return to the old order of things," others are heard to call for an intermediate class of riders which shall include the promateurs and exclude the professionals. The formation of this intermediate class is beset with difficulties, for those in its ranks would be ranked as professionals by the League, the N. C. U., and all athletic associations, and they could hope to race only with their own members. Were a movement in this direction made, it would be useless to pursue it without the co-operation of English riders, and its success would depend largely upon the wise direction of those who engineered it.

A THIRD class would do away with the amateur law altogether. They have a hopeless task; but should they, by any stroke of luck or *finesse* get the League to repeal the law, a new association would immediately spring up, with the amateur law as a cornerstone.

IT has been averred that the action of the Racing Board is illegal and without precedent. Can it be thought for a moment that the Board would take such a step without knowing just how they stood in this respect? If they were called upon, the Board could cite any number of precedents; and the courts have decided, again and again, that an association, such as the League is, has a perfect right to take such action as this. We will cite one precedent. The National Association of Amateur Oarsmen keeps a close watch on amateur oarsmen, and if it finds a man travelling about the country, participating in races, and incurring expense which it is evident he cannot afford, they immediately declare him a professional, and he remains so until he proves himself an

amateur. This goes a little further than the Racing Board.

THE question will come before the Boston meeting, and the League will be obliged to put itself on record. That it will vote by a large majority for the strict enforcement of the amateur law we do not for a moment doubt; but we believe the members will deal fairly with the promateurs, and place them in a class by themselves, if a way is provided that meets their ideas of the fitness of things. Towards a solution of the problem in this direction we believe the friends of the suspects should work.

THE Racing Board has been revising its rules for the season of 1886. Very few changes have been made, and it speaks well for the rules that this is so, for they have stood the test of several seasons, and the only important alterations are in the way of additions. The Board has added to the rules the spirit of the votes passed a few weeks since, which provides that no records on board tracks or against time shall be accepted, and those which place restrictions on the championships by providing that no prize at the meeting shall exceed $50 in value, and all entries shall be revised by the board. It is provided that the curb shall be *fixed* as well as "continuous and welldefined." The fifteen and twenty-five mile bicycle championships have been given up, and a twenty-mile bicycle and two and five mile tricycle championships have been established. It is provided that if the three watches mark the same time, that shall be the official time. If all mark different time, the intermediate time shall be taken. The start and finish will hereafter be taken by the *front* wheel instead of the driver. Two rules have been added. One defines a class race, and it reads as follows : —

A class race is open only to those who, up to date of the closing of entries, have not won one of the first three positions in a public event in the same, or better time than the class under consideration; or in relative time, judged from other distances according to the appended table.

One mile.	Two mile.	Three mile.	Four mile.
2.45	5.40	8.30	14.30
2.50	5.50	8.45	15.00
3.00	6.10	9.15	16.00
3.10	6.30	9.45	17.00
3.20	6.50	10.30	18.30

One of the greatest sources of trouble has been the races where a majority of heats won decides the final winner. It is an easy matter to determine the destination of the first prize in these, but it often happens that the second and third places are in dispute. A new rule provides that points shall be counted in these races just as they are in a lap race.

A CYCLING RETROSPECT.

BY JAM SATIS.

It is hard to realize, when one thinks of the great number and variety of bicycles and tricycles in use all over the country, that it is just ten years since the first bicycles were brought over from England and exhibited at the Centennial Exposition at Philadelphia.

It is true that we had the "bone-shaker" in 1869, but we speedily lost interest in it when we found that it was practically useless on the road, as no one but an athlete could get up a hill on it, and it caused every horse to fall into hysterics, and every driver into "cursory" remarks.

In England, however, as their roads were better, men kept on riding, and the machines were steadily improved.

James Starley was the real inventor of the modern machine, being the first to realize that the rear wheel of a bicycle was merely needed to prevent the rider from going over backward, and the less weight it carried the better the machine would go. He therefore began to make the front wheel larger, and reduced the size of the hind wheel to some twenty inches. This necessitated a step on the backbone to enable the rider to mount, and he added one accordingly.

This invention of a machine with one large wheel to carry the rider, and a small trailer behind, was all that was needed to give the trade the impetus which has carried it on to its present size and prosperity.

The machines shown at the Centennial in 1876, — though they would now be genuine curiosities, they were so clumsy and ill-proportioned, — yet really contained most of the *principles* upon which the machines of to-day are constructed. The changes in the material used, and in the proportions of the machines, and in the workmanship and finish, have made modern machines look so differently that it is hard to believe they are essentially the same.

Cycling was started in this country in 1877, chiefly by Mr. F. W. Weston, and the machines imported then by him and by a few others, were considered the best to be had in England.

It sounds incredible, but at that time ball-bearings did not exist, hollow forks were looked upon as too weak to be safe, as was also the Stanley head; and a suspension saddle as hard as a stone was a luxury.

Speaking generally, the first machines brought over had solid forks, hollow, but very heavy, backbones, open steering heads, and plain or coned bearings; the handle-bar was about eighteen inches long, and straight and solid.

The weight of a 54-inch machine was about sixty pounds until 1879, when hollow forks came into general use, and the substitution of steel for iron enabled makers, while greatly reducing the weight of their machines, to retain the requisite strength. This was especially noticeable in the backbone, which, when made of iron and of small diameter, had to be very thick, while, as soon as steel was used, the diameter was increased and the thickness greatly reduced. This gave a lighter, stronger, and greatly stiffer backbone, besides improving the looks of the machine.

Up to 1882, there were many changes and improvements in bicycles, not to mention a vast number of contrivances and rattle-traps which were finally discarded, though for a time they were used. To mention a few : —

Various "rigid wheels," spring steps, ground, spring, and back-wheel brakes; backbones with a receptacle for space spokes ; besides endless bearings of all sorts and kinds.

But by 1882, makers and riders had made up their minds pretty thoroughly as to the real requisites of a good machine, and the changes made since then have been mostly improvements in details only, — very little has been added.

The most conspicuous improvements are the use of tangent spokes and long dropped handle-bars. The tangent spoke had been used before, but the method of attachment was bad, and they fell into disfavor. As at present used, they certainly are a valuable improvement, but cannot justly be called a great change.

In order to see what changes have been made since 1882, I have made a careful comparison of the description of a popular light roadster of the highest grade, in the Indispensable of 1882, with the description of the same machine in the makers' catalogue of 1886, and find only six points of difference, viz : —

Warwick hollow rims for crescent solid ; steel hubs instead of gun-metal ; hollow dropped handle-bar instead of straight solid ; ball pedals instead of plain ; tangent instead of direct spokes ; weight of 50-inch machine, thirty-five pounds instead of thirty-eight.

The result of all these changes is a machine which is lighter, stronger, faster, and in many ways better, but it cannot be called a *different* machine, nor can much be said to have been added to it.

In short, we may say that the ordinary roadster bicycle is about as good as it can be made with the materials to be had to-day. If aluminum ever becomes cheap enough, we may see much lighter machines certainly, but I doubt if the design will change perceptibly.

In succeeding chapters I shall take up tricycles and safety machines, and trace their development.

NOTES OF A CYCLIST.

To promote the use of the wheel is made by the constitutions of many bicycle clubs one of the duties of the club. But I question if there is anything pertaining to club duties which is more generally overlooked. Of course, the force of example counts for something, and a well-ordered club produces an effect on the community. This is very well as far as it goes, but it surely does not go far enough to satisfy the spirit of such a clause. Every wheelman does a twofold good by doing more than this. If he can promote cyling by making converts, he confers a benefit upon every convert he makes, and he helps himself by making the number of cyclers larger, thus securing the advantages of numbers and influence.

Roughly speaking, there are two means to be employed to promote the cause. The most natural and common one is the force of example, and that of course must always appear. Still, I am free to assert, this form is rarely used as fully as it might be. Too many wheelmen are only "butterfly riders," — of them, more anon. The trouble in this respect is that the example is usually presented only when air and roads are fine, and Nature draws out-of-doors to exercise even the most lazy and indolent. The uninitiated think, and rightly, that anybody might ride then. The usefulness and practicability of the wheel are more clearly shown by its use. when the roads are bad ; in storm as well as sun ; and by use for such necessary purposes as business and shopping. In other words, it should be shown by constant and varied use that the wheel is a practical all-around mount.

The other way to promote the cause is the diffusion of information. What will do more than anything else to make converts among those past boyhood, and especially among ladies, is to demonstrate that it is the easiest, pleasantest, and most healthful exercise in the world. Intelligent people are waking up to the fact that out-door exercise is an absolute necessity to good health, and many are casting around for the best means to secure it.

Cycling could never have reached the development already attained, had it not promised something beside pleasure. Nearly all the older men who ride, and they number thousands, have taken it up for other reasons. Cycling is destined to grow and secure permanency according as its ranks are swelled by a good proportion of all classes. It is necessary to diffuse information required by different classes, and advance the arguments needed to convince them, is order to bring them into the ranks.

If one has a hobby, he must harp upon it. I am so firmly convinced that everybody ought to use a cycle, that I am tempted to believe that nearly every other body might be induced to do so, if they could only be convinced of its potent effects. So I am, perhaps, too prone to urge upon fellow-wheelmen the wisdom of looking upon the matter from all sides, and urge them to lay great stress upon the health argument.

When I wrote in the first paragraph the words "bicycle clubs," I felt the same twinge of regret that I always feel when I see the phrase ; but still not the indignation that I yield to when I read of "ladies' tricycle clubs." I mean that "bicycle club" implies the exclusion of ladies, and that the need of a "ladies' tricycle club" anywhere indicates that ladies are struggling against circumstances in being compelled to organize separately.

THIS is not as it should be. As an exercise for ladies, cycling is beyond all praise. To encourage them, clubs should welcome them and aid them. It is perfectly possible to arrange all club affairs so that the appearance of ladies will in no way interfere with any member's plans. Some active and growing clubs already have good-sized lady membership. Look at the three Orange ladies who last year averaged two thousand miles, and see if they do not make strong riders.

THERE is no better way to help cycling than to secure the co-operation of the ladies. Many a wife and mother has started husband or son on the wheel. It is a politic as well as a sensible and manly course to welcome ladies to club membership. · 5678.

FROM A FEMININE POINT OF VIEW.

˝ THANKS, Mr. Editor, for your kind invitation to be present at the house warming. I shall be rejoiced to take my old friend by the hand in his new domicile, and to wish unnumbered blessings upon all that it contains.

THERE can be no greater comfort, and no greater joy, than one drinks in under the shadow of his own vine and fig-tree; and I extend my congratulations and my best wishes for the realization of the fondest hopes that have been created during the building of the new house.

THE old roof has given me kindly shelter, and I have none but the kindest thoughts in regard to it. That I may find as much joy under the new thatch is my sincere desire.

THE approach of spring has given me a keen desire to be abroad, and I await with impatience the arrival of my steed for 1886. Among so many fine machines, it is no easy matter to choose the best.

I HAVE been looking at the cut of a machine that pleases me not a little. It is a bar steerer built especially for ladies. Those who think the bar steerer unfit for feminine use may change their minds when they see this, for its axle is but a few inches from the ground, and the mount is easily made. This is accomplished by depressing the axle after the manner of a herdic cab. All the chains are well covered, and there seems to be little danger of soiled dresses.

A FRIEND of mine asked me the other day for some facts concerning the membership of ladies in the League. She felt that she ought to belong to the institution, and was anxious to find out what advantage she would gain thereby. After a talk with the editor, I was able to lay before her the abstract and concrete advantages, and among the former I enumerated the privilege of wearing the League uniform. She would have been untrue to her sex if she had n't at once plied me with questions concerning the color of the uniform, the texture and the cut of the garments. Here I was at a loss, and it occurred to me that I might get from some reader of the CYCLE an idea or two in this direction.

I AM told that a light weight cloth is made for ladies' wear. Has it been tried, and with what results ? I should be glad to hear from any lady who has tried the material, for if it is a good thing, it will be worn by our coterie of riders the coming season, and should be aired for the first time on the occasion of the League Meet.

I AM more than pleased with the promises of the May gathering. I am assured that a double quartette of lady riders from New Jersey will be in Boston, mounted on the front seats of as many tandems. New York city will send not less than half a dozen, and Philadelphia will contribute a goodly number. I am inclined to believe we shall have to call upon the writers of circus posters to give us adjectives to describe the affair.

THE invitation is open for all. Boston will show the world the most numerously patronized ladies' run the world ever saw, and its fame will be sent down to posterity in the usual way by the employment of photography.

DAISIE.

DETROIT.

SEVERAL members of the Detroit Bicycle Club will participate in the Big Four tour this year.

CHIEF Consul J. H. Johnson, of Detroit, with the aid of members of the Michigan Division, is compiling a road book of the State. The routes from Detroit to Chicago will receive careful attention.

THE Detroit Club have formed a stock company, called the Detroit Bicycle Track Association, and will, as soon as the frost is out of the ground, commence the track. The ground selected is admirably located and easily reached by street cars.

A PROJECT is now on foot to form a bicycle race circuit, to include St. Louis, Chicago, Detroit, and Cleveland. It is being worked up, and will prove a great boon to racers, as they can visit the different cities with less expense, and the racing can be done with about the training it takes for one race.

CAPT. SNOW will keep an accurate record of the miles ridden by members of the club. Reports will be sent in monthly, showing weekly mileage. To the member riding the greatest number of miles, a handsome gold medal will be given.   DETROIT.

SAVE THE MILE GROUND.

BOSTON wheelmen are aroused over the proposed destruction of their best road out of the city. The proposed construction of a cable road from Brookline to Boston over Beacon street, having its termination at the corner of Beacon and Tremont streets, is meeting with an emphatic remonstrance from every one who believes that Boston should continue to possess one highway outlet unencumbered with car tracks. ˝ Prominent among the opposition are the owners of carriages and bicycles. The argument that an ordinary service railroad in a public street, and more so as a cable railway, interfere with the com-

fort and safety of riding, has passed into an axiom. A hearing on the question of granting a charter to the cable syndicate is to be held at the State House soon. Petitions of remonstrance have been placed in each of the local bicycle warerooms, and wheelmen are earnestly requested to immediately call and add their signatures to the list of remonstrants. We have a blank at this office.

DURYEA'S NEW WHEEL.

THE Post-Dispatch thus describes Mr. Duryea's new bicycle : In a rear room on the second floor of the Turner building, a peculiar looking machine was being ridden around to-day by a few wheelmen of the city. The thing had such a weird look that one beholder said it reminded him of a nightmare. A spectator observing first one man and then another get into the machine and ride off easily, could scarcely believe that he was gazing on the first spokeless and hubless bicycle ever made. But such it was, and it proved to be the one that the fertile brain of Charles E. Duryea has evolved. Mr. Duryea, up to a few months ago, was a resident of this city, and for two years studied on the original idea of making a bicycle without spokes. Last fall, after getting the details well worked out, he went to Peoria, Ill., where he has since devoted all his time to inventing, and especially to making a model of this wonderful idea. Being a practical wheelman himself, and the inventor of several bicycle appliances, including the Duryea saddle, he was not long in getting the model put together. To do this he used only the roughest kind of material, and consequently the machine, as shown to-day, weighed twice as much as it will when the gas-pipe is replaced by fine steel and the cog-wheels with chain gearing. The wheel is not only spokeless, but it is inclined away from the rider, which at first adds to its strange appearance. The wheel, as shown to-day, had a diameter of fifty-two inches. Not a spoke was in it, and the driving gearing was placed on the rim, the big wheel passing under the gearing by running on small idle-wheels. The pedals are of the regular tricycle kind. The rider's seat is placed on an iron support extending upward from the gearing, and as the wheel is inclined toward the right, the rider's seat is removed a few inches from the tire, over which one arm is thrown to grasp the handle. The rider thus presents the spectacle of a rider within his wheel, and at the same time over it. It gives one's ideas of mechanics a shock to see a rider propelling a wheel around under his arm. The equilibrium is maintained by means of a little wheel behind, as in an ordinary bicycle.

It has been ridden over granite, up and down sidewalks, and has worked to perfect satisfaction even in its crude form. No header can be taken on it, as the rider sits as in an open tricycle. Besides its other peculiarities, it is the first one-track cycle ever made that a lady could ride as easily as a man.

" COMMENDABLE enterprise " is what the Cyclist calls the action of an English maker who secured an English patent on an article put out by an American firm before the inventor could get it for himself.

Before buying your new mount for the coming season, send for price list and description of the

"NEW RAPID" BICYCLES,

——————— WITH THE ———————

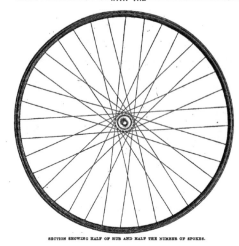

During 1885 not a single spoke broke or wheel buckled.

Universally acknowledged to be the strongest and most rigid wheel made.

SECTION SHOWING HALF OF HUB AND HALF THE NUMBER OF SPOKES.

TRUE TANGENT WHEEL.

At the Inventions Exhibition, London, 1885, the "New Rapid" was awarded *a Gold Medal*, the highest and only award for Bicycles.

PRESS OPINIONS.

"One of the best machines in the market."—The Cyclist.
"The best wheel ever built."—Bicycling News.

"The 'True Tangent' Wheel (New Rapid) is far and away the most perfect yet made."—Illustrated Sports.

SEND TEN CENTS FOR LARGE SIZE CABINET PHOTOS.

S. T. CLARK & CO.

IMPORTERS,

BALTIMORE, MD.

CONTRIBUTORS' CLUB

TO THOMAS STEVENS, WHEELING ALONE ACROSS ASIA, 1886.

Editor of the Cycle: — The following verses from a recent collection of poems by Professor H. A. Beers, of Yale ("The Thankless Muse," Houghton, Mifflin & Co., 1885), alluding to Life's circuit from youth to old age, seem to me an appropriate invocation to the dauntless bicycler who is now fighting his solitary way through the wilds of the Orient; and I therefore ask leave to address them to him through the first number of your paper : — .

> But courage still ! Without return or swerVing,
> Across the globe's huge shadow keep the track,
> Till, unperceived, the slow meridian's curving.
> That leads thee onward, yet shall lead thee back.
>
> To stand again with daybreak on the mountains,
> And, where the paths of night and morning meet,
> To drink once more of youth's forgotten fountains,
> When thou hast put the world between thy feet.

."Delhi, India, to be kept till called for,' is the address which should be inscribed on mail matter for this round-the-world tourist, — the postage rates being five cents for a half-ounce letter, two cents for a postal-card, and one cent for two ounces of printed matter. His route from Teheran, the Persian capital (which he left on 4 March, after a five months' halt), lies through Meshed, Herat, Kandahar, Quetta, Delhi, and Lucknow to Calcutta ; and in case he lives to reach Delhi, the discovery there of a goodly number of tokens that his American admirers have not lost interest in the journey, may help cheer and encourage him for the final and most desperate stage of it.

"The most remarkable and interesting exploit ever accomplished by a bicycle, or ever likely to be accomplished by one," is the characterization of Stevens's tour, from San Francisco to Teheran, which I print in "X. M. Miles on a Bi." (p. 483). I give no less than 8,000 words to the story of that tour, and it took me no less than eight days of extremely tiresome work to put them together. My enthusiastic interest in his adventure is a fact which I do not expect you (being a Boston man, and a tricycler at that) to sympathize with, or even to comprehend; but accepting it as a fact, you can at least see the advantage of proclaiming it, for the simple sake of the free advertisement involved in my thus ensuring to THE CYCLE'S first number a circulation as extensive as the globe.　　KARL KRON.

WASHINGTON SQUARE, N. Y., 24 March, 1886.

STEEL.

Editor of the Cycle: — I have experienced two severe headers from the breaking of balls in the main bearings of my bicycle. The tempering of balls to the necessary hardness must be a severe strain upon them, as the temperature is raised and lowered through several hundred degrees of heat quite rapidly.

The subjoined item from the *Industrial World* looks as though it might have a valuable bearing upon this subject, and I send it to you, hoping that it will attract the attention of the manufacturers of bicycles : —

' "Herr A. Jarolimek publishes some novel statements on the tempering of steel in *Dingler's Polytechnic.* Hitherto it has generally been considered that, to obtain a specific degree of softness, it is necessary to heat the hard steel to a particular annealing color, — that is to say, to a definite temperature, — and then to cool it rapidly. Herr Jarolimek says the requisite temper, which is obtained by momentarily raising the temperature to a particular degree, can also be acquired by subjecting the steel for a longer time to a much lower temperature."
　　　　　　　　　　　　C. E. HAWLEY.

WASHINGTON, D. C., 11 March, 1886.

TANDEMS.

Editor of the Cycle: — Everything goes to show that the tandem will be a popular machine the coming year. A number of riders out in the back woods would like to hear from the riders of these machines with a view to securing the best. Can you not get a few ideas to help us ?　　HUDSON.

CYCLETS

WHEEL ETHICS.

"TELL me, O Wheelman, are you ride away,"
I asked, " where haVe you been this Sabbath day ? "

Then the cycler replied from his lofty perch,
With gracious mien, " I haVe been to church;
I haVe been to church, though strange to tell,
I haVe heard neither parson nor tolling bell.

" 'T was a volunteer choir, and the rapturous notes
That fell on my ear, as the tiny throats
Seemed bursting with praise of the Maker's name,
Thrilled with such joy I was glad that I came.

" And the air was so pure, so fresh and sweet,
Though I sat on a softly cushioned seat, —
That I neVer once thought of going to sleep;
Nor was the sermon too dull of deep.

" I remember the text, too, ' God is loVe,' —
'T was eVerywhere written, around me, above,
On the stately columns that rose at my side,
To the vaulted arch so blue and wide.

" Upreaching to the very throne of Grace, —
'T was a grandly solemn, sacred place,
And I almost forgot how cold and drear
Is the earth, sometimes, heaven seemed so near."

Thus I hold that pure worship has no part
In the *time* or the *place*, but springs from the *heart*.
　　　　　　　　　　CHARLES RICHARDS DODGE.

WE are here.

WE ask your kind indulgence.

AND your esteemed favor in the shape of patronage.

WE have come to stay, for we feel that we will be welcome.

THE CYCLE starts out with a large circulation, and you will find it round.

OUR correspondent " 5678 " has written a little pamphlet on " The Advantages of Cycling." It is a readable little book, and a good thing to put into the hands of a beginner, or any one contemplating taking up the wheel. We are promised a few copies, and will mail one to any address on receipt of a two-cent stamp.

WHEN the League comes to Boston, the members will be entertained one evening at an improvised beer garden in Music Hall. This is a very generous move on the part of the Massachusetts wheelmen, but are they sure that the Cincinnati and Buffalo members will not sigh for home during the evening ?

THE editor of the *Bulletin* has just given us an editorial, which he heads " Snowed Under." We are also under a similar cool mantle, for our mail has been so large the past week, we find ourselves unable to attend to it without delay. For the many kind words of encouragement we have received, we are deeply grateful; and we shall feel that the debt of gratitude is increased if those who have sent us letters of congratulation will find in this paragraph an acknowledgment of their kind favor.

ST. LOUIS newspapers think the Racing Board has an especial grudge against that city, and they have the coolness to say that the Board refused to accept board-track records, because St. Louis was making them, and suspended the promateurs because a road race was on the tapis in that city. The Racing Board has no power over coincidences.

MASSACHUSETTS just holds her own at the time of election of the League consul and representatives. Fourteen representatives may be elected by ballot, but in the near future we shall have nineteen.

THE following from the Smithville *Mechanic,* which is the organ of the H. B. Smith Machine Company, gives the views of that company on the makers' amateur question: " It must be admitted that if an amateur rides for money, whether as a stake or for wages, he should be a professional; at least that would be our definition of a professional, — one who rides for money, either wages or stake, or both. We have had but few applications of the kind, and have never accepted any, nor have we ever paid a professional for racing. We think if makers and dealers will respectfully decline to *hire* amateur riders, the Racing Board will have less trouble in the matter. Amateur rules should be liberal enough to allow worthy amateurs to be helped in the way of expenses by their friends, or perhaps some of our best men who may be poor could not appear on distant tracks ; besides, the well-to-do young man would have all the advantage of travelling, training, etc., which would be unfair."

GORMULLY and Jeffery have been awarded the first prize for a collective display of bicycles at the New Orleans Exposition.

L. D. MUNGER has been taking a record at New Orleans. On 27 March, he rode twenty-five miles on the asphalt road from Lee Circle to Carrollton in 1.24.46⅖. The best previous record was 1.54.0 by W. A. Rhodes, 27 June, 1885.

MATTERS in litigation between the Pope Manufacturing Company and the Overman Wheel Company have progressed very little the past week. The Overman Wheel Company has given the required bond in the insolvency proceedings at Hartford. A hearing was set down for Wednesday last on the removal of the attachment for $73,000, but was postponed to Monday of next week at the request of the Overman Wheel Company. Several parties, who have been offered as surety, have been examined before Commissioner Hallett, and of these nearly all will be accepted by the Pope Manufacturing Company.

Adjustment in Height in Front.   Adjustment in Length.   A Comfortable Coasting Plate.
Adjustment in Height in Rear.   Adjustment in Width.   A Bifurcated Seat.

WILLIAM D. MCPHERSON, a reporter on the South Framingham *Tribune*, during the riding season, collects the local news astride a bicycle.

CHIEF CONSUL DUCKER has appointed Fred Burckes League consul for Somerville, and T. M. Cunningham for consul, Clinton.

THE Lynn Cycle Club Track Association held a meeting at the rooms of the Lynn Cycle Club Friday evening, and incorporated with the following officers: President, T. A. Carroll; vice-president, S. S. Merrill; clerk, Edwin M. Bailey; treasurer, William Forsyth; board of directors, T. A. Carroll, S. S. Merrill, W. A. Rowe, J. H. Thurman, E. G. Gordon, George Butler, George Porter, William Bond, and W. W. Stall, of Boston. The track will be in condition to race by 1 May, and will be three laps to the mile, a dead level, with raised turns, and it is expected to be as fast as any track in the world.

THE Faneuil House has been appointed League hotel for Brighton.

THE Hartford wheelmen are busy pedaling on the home tracks, and are making some excellent records. George C. Dresser recently made a quarter in 22, half in 46½, three quarters in 1.9⅓, and the mile in 1.34.

THERE is promise of a bicycle tournament in New Orleans in 1887 "to rival the 'Springfield affair,'" says the *Picayune;* and a grand effort will be made to popularize cycling in the South.

W. D. WILMOT, the fancy bicyclist, has just been presented with a handsome gold medal by the Massachusetts Bicycle Club.

THE West will support to a unit T. J. Kirkpatrick, chief consul of the Ohio Division, for the presidency of the League.

AFTER 1 April the League dues will be but seventy-five cents for the remainder of the League year, nine months.

6 MARCH, the League had 6,340 members. The largest nnmber enrolled in 1885 was 5,176.

RECORDS in the home-trainer contest have been made as follows: Joseph J. Miller, Buffalo, N. Y., 20 January, 1886, one mile, 1.51; George C. Dresser, Hartford, Conn., 23 Feb., one mile, 1.36⅗; P. J. Dukelow, Rochester, N. Y., 8 March, one mile, 1.29⅗.

HARRY A. GREEN has been nominated by the San Francisco Club for the position of consul of the California Division of the League.

AMONG the new devices shown at the Stanley Show was Wood's Non-Vibrating Steering Gear. The feature of the invention consists in substituting for the usual pinion a pair of india-rubber wheels, between which the steering-rod is made to pass. The rod has a "waved" or corrugated surface, which gives a grip to the rubbers, and being held tightly by the rubber rollers, the hand can be taken from the steering-handle when on a straight road without any fear of the machine swerving and causing an upset, whilst all tricyclists will appreciate the advantages it possesses in requiring no oiling and in its perfect noiselessness. It is adjustable in case of wear, and if the rubbers wear out, they can be replaced at a small expense.

THE reception committee for the League Meet has been enlarged by the addition of some fifty men. The original committee was composed very largely of ornamental members, but the new men have young blood in their veins. They are drawn from the clubs hereabouts, and they will attend to all the depot and hotel work that comes in their line.

THE last number of the *Phonographic Monthly* has an article describing the second ladies' run to Cape Ann, written by one of the participants.

THE last athletic entertainment of the Massachusetts Club will be held on Saturday evening next. There will be fencing and sparring, and a home-trainer race for one fourth and one mile. Mr. Ethier has sent over to Harvard College an offer to spar any athletic young man they may send to represent them on this occasion.

MR. GEO. H. DAY, who has charge of the Pope Manufacturing Co.'s works at Hartford, has gone to Havana on account of ill health.

A NEW device put out to prevent vibration of the spokes of a bicycle is the Lancaster binding ring. The system consists in affixing to the spokes on each side of the wheel a ring of No. 13 spoke wire at a distance of eight to twelve inches from the hub, according to size of wheel. This ring is placed against the outside of the spokes, and is then lashed to each one with fine wire, the lashings being secured when done with solder. The *Cyclist* says: "We can readily see that the ring would have the effect of preventing, to a great extent, the vibration of the separate spokes, and would generally hold the wheel together, whilst the makers inform us that they have thoroughly tested it over one or two seasons, and that machines that have regularly been subject to broken and stripped spoke threads and buckled wheels have been quite free from these defects since being fitted with the binding rings, and they quote in particular one 54-inch racer which buckled under a nine-stone rider, and has, since being fitted with the rings, successfully carried a thirteen-stone individual."

WE like to have good records on the books, and we will, if any racing man makes a mile in two-thirty, make a minute of it.

THE mail boy on duty at the warerooms of the Pope Manufacturing Company has been fitted out with a very gorgeous uniform, trimmed with gold cord, and bearing "Columbia Bicycle" on the front of his cap.

THE Florence Cycle Club has voted to petition the city government to change the bicycle ordinance, so that riders will be allowed to use the sidewalks for twenty-four hours after a rain storm, or when the roads are so muddy as to make wheeling bad.

MR. SINGER, head of the firm of Singer & Co., Coventry, took steamer for America on Wednesday last. He comes directly to Boston, and will spend some time in America.

THE Citizens' Club, of New York, is about to take a new departure: Mr. Richard Nelson, a member of the club, recently purchased a four-story brown-stone house, No. 328 West Sixtieth street, which he proposes to lease to the club for seven years on very favorable terms. Privilege to make the necessary alterations is also given, and the offer having been accepted, work will be begun as soon as the deed is signed. The ground floor will be converted into a large wheelroom, the partitions all being removed and iron girders substituted. This will give a clean sweep of twenty by fifty-five feet, and, if necessary, a one-story extension will be built in the yard, which will increase the depth to one hundred feet. The parlor floor will remain intact, and the back parlor converted into a billiard room. On the second floor will be the dressing and locker rooms; the third floor will be used for card and committee rooms, and the fourth floor will be fitted up for bachelor apartments, and for the use of non-resident members who may desire to use them while in town. The neighborhood is excellent, and the boulevards and Central Park are even more convenient of access than from their old headquarters. The income of the club last year was $2,500, and the treasury showed a balance at the end of the year. Mr. George R. Bidwell will occupy the old quarters with his cycling business.

A. G. SPALDING & BRO. had seven cases of Humber bicycles on the Oregon.

THE New Jersey Division of the League has interested itself in a novel test case involving the bicyclers' and tricyclers' rights on the road. About a year ago, Dr. G. F. Marsden, of Red Bank, accompanied by a friend, was riding on a double tricycle in that town. The horses, driven by Frederick Massey, of Keyport, became frightened at the strange vehicle and ran away, destroying and ruining both harness and wagon. Massey brought suit for $100 damages before Justice Warner, of Keyport, and judgment by default was secured against Marsden. Marsden has appealed the case, and it wil come up before the Common Pleas Court in Freehold next May. The Division has taken up the matter, and decided to make it a test case, to be fought, if necessary, through all the courts in the State. With a view to the protection of wheelmen's rights, a bill will be introduced into the Legislature to secure them statutory right to use public highways. During the past three years, several damage suits similar to the above have, in the lower courts, been decided against the wheelmen in that vicinity.

F. A. ELWELL'S Bermuda party arrived back in New York, 27 March. They report a most enjoyable trip. Although the season in Bermuda has been unusually cold, they were fortunate in striking a run of fine weather. The hotels and boarding-houses on the island are full to overflowing, and but for arrangements made early in the winter, the party would have been unable to secure rooms in the Hamilton Hotel. The two weeks on the islands were devoted to riding, sailing, sight-seeing, and the enjoyment of summer weather. The evenings at the hotel were very gay, dances, card parties, etc., filling the hours. On the return trip a very rough time was experienced in the Gulf Stream, unpleasant at the time, but now the subject on which the story-tellers of the party do much dilate.

THE CYCLE,

AN INDEPENDENT CYCLING PAPER.

$1.50 A YEAR.

THREE COPIES FOR THREE DOLLARS.

THE statement that bicycles were to be substituted for cavalry horses in some military operations was at first not unnaturally treated as a joke by most people. Yet in the recent manœuvres of the Austrian army, scouts mounted on bicycles and tricycles outdid cavalry in endurance, and now the cycle is formally adopted in the Austrian military establishment.

THE SPRINGFIELD GAZETTE.

THE following paragraph has been going the rounds of the papers : —

"The Overman Wheel Company placed an injunction on the undelivered copies of last week's edition of the Springfield Wheelmen's *Gazette* for alleged breach of contract in allowing the Pope Company to occupy the first page of the paper with its advertisement, when, as it is averred, the former company had a contract with the publishers which entitled them to the disputed space. Out of the trouble a discussion has arisen among the proprietors of the paper, one of them going so far as to file proceedings to dissolve the concern."

In explanation of this Mr. Ducker tells us that the Overman Wheel Company has had the first page of the *Gazette* for a long while, but its contract had expired, and in January last a contract was signed with the Pope Manufacturing Company, agreeing to give them this space beginning with the April number.

In proceeding to carry out the contract, the *Gazette* people placed the advertisement of the Pope Manufacturing Co. on the first page ; but Mr. Overman saw the papers going through the press and objected, claiming the position to be his by right. Mr. Ducker agreed to see Col. Pope, and to change the advertisement if that gentleman would release him from his contract, but he found that the colonel was in Florida, and he could not see him. Meantime Mr. Overman saw Mr. Fisk, a partner in the *Gazette*, and stated his case, and Mr. Fisk agreed to use his influence to let him have the front page. This caused trouble in the household of the *Gazette*, and an open rupture resulted. A suit was threatened and Mr. Ducker came to Boston and saw Col. Pope, who had returned, and that gentleman agreed at once to release him from his contract, and give the front page to the Overman Wheel Co., rather than stop the paper. But things had gone too far, and the result shows that the Gazette Publishing Co. is dissolved, and Mr. Ducker will at once start a new paper to be called *The Wheelmen's Gazette.*

TEAM ROAD RACING.

THE organization of the new New York and New Jersey Team Road Racing Association was perfected at a meeting held at the Citizens' club house last Saturday night. Twelve of the sixteen clubs interested in the matter were represented. The committee on a constitution presented their report, and the constitution reported was adopted, after a few modifications had been made.

The distance chosen was twenty-five miles ; teams will consist of four each ; the cup will be a perpetual challenge cup, held for six months by the winning club, and will cost not less than $250. Races will occur on Decoration and Election Days. The location of the first one was left to the executive committee.

The following officers were elected by the association for the first year : President, E. J. Shriver, of the New York Bicycle Club ; Vice-president, C. Lee Myers, of the Hudson County Wheelmen ; secretary-treasurer, M. L. Bridgeman, of the King's County Wheelmen ; executive committee, the three officers, and C. R. Zacharias, of the New Jersey Wheelmen, C. H. Luscomb, of the Long Island Wheelmen, and T. L. Bingham, of the Harlem Wheelmen.

Below is the constitution as adopted.

CONSTITUTION OF THE NEW YORK AND NEW JERSEY TEAM ROAD RACING ASSOCIATION.

ARTICLE I. — Name. — This organization shall be known as "The New York and New Jersey Team Road Racing Association."

ARTICLE II. — Object. — The object of this Association shall be the promotion of Team Road Racing between its Members.

ARTICLE III. — Members. — First. Its members shall be the following Cycle Clubs, or such of these as may hereafter qualify by subscribing to the constitution and paying initiation fee within thirty days, and such other clubs as may hereafter be admitted : Harlem Wheelmen, Brooklyn Bi. Club, Long Island Wheelmen, Citizens' Bi. Club, Pegasus Bi. Club, Hudson County Wheelmen, Orange Wanderers, New Jersey Wheelmen, New York Bi. Club, Elizabeth Wheelmen, Ilderan Bicycle Club, King's County Wheelmen, Bellerophon Wheelmen, Rutherford Wheelmen, Mt. Vernon Bi. Club, Morrisania Wheelmen.

Second. Organized clubs located within a radius of thirty miles of New York City Hall, may be admitted by a two-thirds vote of all the clubs in the Association. Applications for membership shall be made three months previous to a meeting of the Association, and referred to the Executive Committee, who shall notify each member of the Association and report at the next meeting.

Third. Each club shall be represented by two delegates.

Fourth. Each club shall have one vote in all matters pertaining to the Association.

Fifth. Due notice shall be given by letter to the Secretary of this organization, of any change in the representation of any club, by the Executive Officers of such Club.

ARTICLE IV. — Officers. — First. The officers of this Association shall be a President, Vice-President, Secretary-Treasurer, and an Executive Committee.

Second. The Executive Committee shall be composed of the President, Vice-President, Secretary-Treasurer, and three members to be elected by ballot at the annual meeting in March.

Third. The officers and members of the Executive Committee shall each be elected from a separate club.

ARTICLE V. — Duties of Officers. — First. The President will preside at all meetings of the Association and of the Executive Committee. Should the President be absent, the Vice-President shall act in his stead.

Second. The Secretary-Treasurer shall keep a correct account of all the meetings, and report the same at the next meeting. He shall send all notifications to members and delegates, and keep a correct roll of the membership. He shall care and be responsible for the funds, collect all dues, pay all bills approved by the Executive Committee. He shall keep a correct account of the financial affairs of the Association, and report the same at each business meeting.

Third. The Executive Committee shall have full management and control of all the property, effects, and assets of the Association.

ARTICLE VI. — Meetings. — First. There shall be a regular business meeting of this organization, on the first Saturday in March, at 8 P. M., and the second Saturday in September, at 8 P. M., of each year. The Executive Committee shall decide the place of all business meetings, and due notice of the same shall be given by the Secretary-Treasurer to each delegate.

Second. There shall be regular Race Meets on Decoration Day and Election Day of each year. At the regular business meeting in March and September, the place of holding the next Race Meeting shall be announced, and a Committee of Arrangements appointed by the Executive Committee.

Third. Special business meetings, when considered necessary, shall be called at the written request of five clubs, setting forth the purpose thereof. Notice of such meetings

shall state their object, and no business other than that stated shall be transacted.

Fourth. None but delegates shall be present at any business meeting.

ARTICLE VII. — Quorum. — One third of the membership shall constitute a quorum. No Voting by proxy shall be allowed.

ARTICLE VIII. — The order of business shall be : —

First. Roll call.

Second. Reading minutes of last meeting.

Third. Report of the Secretary-Treasurer.

Fourth. Report of Committees.

Fifth. Election of officers.

Sixth. Election of new members.

Seventh. Unfinished business.

Eighth. New business.

ARTICLE IX. — Initiation and Dues. — *First.* The initiation fee shall be the sum of fifteen dollars, payable on election.

Second. The regular dues of each club shall be five dollars per year, payable semi-annually in advance at each regular business meeting.

ARTICLE X. — Trophy. — *First.* There shall be a trophy, which shall be known as the New York and New Jersey Team-Road Racing Association Cup.

Second. It shall be the permanent property of the Association.

Third. It shall be held in trust by the club whose team wins at each Race Meeting until the following Race Meeting, when it shall be delivered to the Executive Committee. The winning club shall be held responsible for the trophy while in their possession.

Fourth. The date of each race, with names of club and winning team, shall be engraved on the trophy.

ARTICLE XI. — The Races. — *First.* The first race shall be run at such place and over such roads as the Association may decide.

Second. The club winning the trophy shall name the course for the next race at the regular business meeting preceding that race.

Third. If, in the judgment of the Executive Committee, the race shall be impracticable on the appointed date, they shall name an early subsequent date therefor.

Fourth. The distance named for each race shall be twenty-five miles.

Fifth. The races shall be run between such members of the Association as shall decide to enter their teams, and who notify the Executive Committee of such decisions at least thirty days previous to the Race Meeting.

Sixth. If the entries are of such number as to warrant the Executive Committee in so doing, they shall arrange for trial heats.

Seventh. Each man competing shall be distinctly numbered.

Eighth. Each Team competing shall consist of four, and be consecutively numbered.

Ninth. The first man completing the course shall count as many points as there are men competing, each man competing counting one point less than his leader at the finish, but those not finishing within one hour after the leader shall count zero.

Tenth. The member whose Team aggregates the greatest number of points shall be the Victor.

Eleventh. Every man competing must be an active member in good standing of the club he represents for a period of at least three months previous to the Race Meeting in which he competes.

Twelfth. The Rules of the League of American Wheelmen shall govern the contests.

ARTICLE XIII. — Souvenirs. — *First.* The first and second man finishing in the contest at each Race Meeting shall receive a souvenir.

Second. The souvenirs shall be provided by the Executive Committee from the Association's funds.

ARTICLE XIII. — Suspension or Expulsion. — Any club violating the provisions of this Constitution, or acting contrary to the spirit or intention of this Association, may be suspended or expelled by a two-thirds vote of the members. Ten da.,s' notice of the charges must be served upon the offending club before action.

ARTICLE XIV. — Amendments. — This Constitution may be amended at any regular meeting by a two-thirds Vote of the delegates present, providing two weeks' notice shall have been given of the proposed amendment, and a copy thereof supplied each member.

THE PATH.

John S. Prince and R. A. Neilson have agreed to run a series of races to decide the professional championship of America. The prize will be $300 a side. Articles of agreement were drawn up last Saturday for a series, and Prince, winning the toss for choice of naming the first race, put the distance at five miles. The date and track for this contest were not definitely settled, but there is a probability that it will be run about 30 May, at Lynn, on the new track now in process of construction there. The second race will be for ten miles ; and if a third is necessary, the man winning the

toss is to have the privilege of naming the distance, from one to fifteen miles.

The track is not yet selected for either of the three races, but each will be run one week after the preceding one. The races will be run under the rules of the League of American Wheelmen, with Abbot Bassett of the CYCLE as referee, and Charles S. Howard of Boston as starter, each man being allowed to select two judges. The *Globe* is final stockholder, and the first deposit of $100 a side was made by the backers of the men. The second deposit of $100 a side is to be made next Saturday, 3 April, when the dates and track for the races will be selected. The final deposit will be put up one week previous to the first race.

H. O. DUNCAN will leave Montpellier for England on 7 April, breaking his journey at Paris in order to be present at the De Civry-Gika match at Longchamps on the 11th prox. On reaching England, he goes immediately to Leicester, and will there give the finishing touches to his preparation for the twenty-mile championship that takes place on 17 April. On the following Saturday he intends riding in the fifty-mile championship, on Easter Monday in the ten-mile championship, and on the following days in the mile championship and the mile handicap at Wolverhampton. After that he returns at once to France, in order to take part in important events fixed for next day.

THE date of the fifty-mile road race of the St. Louis Wheelmen has been changed to 26 April, instead of Saturday, 24 April, owing to the latter day being in Lent.

THE CLUB.

THE Gloucester Club will reorganize this spring, and adopt a uniform of dark green.

THE Waltham Cycle Club will hold an entertainment and ball at the Waltham Skating Rink, 15 April.

THE Stoneham Club is to have an exhibition and ball on the evening of 7 April.

THE Newton Club will hold its annual dinner on the evening of 6 April. It will probably be held at the store of W. W. Stall, 509 Tremont Street.

THE Chelsea Club had a meeting last week, and the funds of the club were equally divided among the members, each receiving $5. A new club is to be organized soon, and a progressive policy is promised. Chelsea has long needed a go-ahead man to put life into its club. As a tricycle centre, the little city across the bay has made a good reputation.

ATALANTA Wheelmen, Newark, N. J., organized 11 March, 1886, with ten members. Officers: President, W. S. Gregory ; vice-president, C. A. Woodruff; secretary and treasurer, W. F. Coddington ; captain, A. W. Snow ; first lieutenant, C. G. Halsey.

THE Buffalo Bicycle Club stands third in point of membership in the New York Division of the L. A. W. The club boasts about $1,000 worth of furniture in the clubhouse, and a reserve fund of $480 in the treasury. The number of active members at present is seventy-six, and no deaths have occurred since its organization, seven years ago, for bicyclists are healthy men. Some

good records of endurance have been made by individual members during the past year. Mr. R. H. James rode 3,890 miles, and nine other members made over 1,500 miles each. The longest single ride was made by Mr. James, 206 miles in twenty-nine hours. The next longest by Mr. Rummell, 154 miles in twenty-four hours.

THE Roselle (N. J.) Ramblers are officered thus : President, H. R. Benedict ; secretary and treasurer, John L. Warner ; captain, R. L. Stewart ; lieutenant, T. H. Burnett.

THE Syracuse (N. Y.) Bicycle Club has reorganized under the name, " Syracuse Cycling Club," and has engaged rooms in the new Y. M. C. A. building. A meeting was held there last week, at which thirteen members were reported. It was decided to have uniforms of brown mixed cloth. The first trip will probably be on Decoration Day. Several of the club will attend the L. A. W. meeting at Boston.

AT a meeting of the Wilmington Wheel Club, 12 March, the following officers were elected to serve for the ensuing year : President, J. N. Robinson ; secretary, C. W. Todd ; treasurer, C. M. Sheward ; captain, R. R. Tatnall ; lieutenant, S. E. Finley; bugler, J. N. Robinson ; executive committee, C. E. Smith, C. I. Kent, and Harvey J. Wiley.

OFFICERS elect of the Northampton Wheel Club : President, E. E. Davis ; vice-president, H. R. Graves ; secretary and treasurer, L. L. Campbell ; captain, H. S. Campbell ; first lieutenant, A. A. Chabot ; second lieutenant, C. J. Shearn ; bugler, J. A. Ross.

THE Orange Wanderers have forty members, nine of whom are ladies. They use twenty-three different makes of wheels, as follows : Seven Humber tandems ; five Experts ; four Victors ; three Light Rudges ; three Sparkbrook tandems ; two Royal Mails ; two two-track Columbia tricycles ; and one each Rudge Safety, Kangaroo, Cripper, Lady's Humber, Rucker, Victor tricycle, three-track Columbia, two-track Royal Mail, Sanspariel, Humber, Star, Howe, Harvard, Yale, and Robinson & Price.

THE new house of the Philadelphia Club, to be erected at the corner of Twenty-sixth street and Pennsylvania Avenue, will be completed in about three months.

THE Buffalo Club, having found the clubhouse on Virginia street too small for their use, has decided to lease the Clifton residence on Main street, just above the street-car barns. This will give them more capacious and more accessible headquarters. They take possession 1 April.

THE Albany Wheelmen's Club is a newly formed organization in Albany, New York. It starts with a large membership and the following officers : President, Wm. C. Hickox ; vice-president, Addison J. Gallien ; secretary-treasurer, Henry Gallien ; captain, Henry E. Hawley ; lieutenant, Frank Munsell. Only a few members of the Albany Bicycle Club are with the new club. The head and front of the new movement seems to favor greater activity in cycling circles, and the club will be a member of the L. A. W., of which the Albany Club now is not, having been retired about three weeks ago.

THE TRADE.

WM. READ & SONS report a large demand for the new Royal Mail bicycle. The ball-bearing head and the Fox grip rim, together with the detachable handle-bar, are features that attract the attention of riders, and the reputation for good work which the makers enjoy, give an impetus to the sale of the machines. The new handle-bar steerer with large front wheel is daily expected. The steering arrangement of this tricycle is one that was described and especially commended in R. E. Phillips' little work on the construction of tricycles. It will be a novelty in America.

THE POPE MANUFACTURING COMPANY report larger sales of machines in March than in any previous month during their business career. There is a good demand for the new low-priced wheel, which has many parts from higher grade wheels, and sells for a very moderate price. The two-track tricycle for 1886 is on the floor. It has a larger steering wheel, and the new double grip rubbers. The light two-track will be out in two months. It will have a lighter tube, a tangent wheel, and will scale very low.

THE BOSTON SHOE is undoubtedly the most successful of all shoes made for wheelmen. It is made to fit the foot, and to conform to its motion. Strickland & Pierce are just now enlarging their facilities for manufacture, and expect a large trade the coming season. Their system of self-measurement allows them to supply wheelmen in any part of the country.

W. B. EVERETT & CO. tell us that they have sold about a dozen straight-steerer tricycles. Every person who looks at the wheel likes it, and wants to ride it. Mr. E. C.

Lee has been giving the wheel a pretty thorough test, and he pronounces it one of the easiest running wheels he ever rode. The Messrs. Everett are getting out some Springfield and some Traveller tandems. The former is much improved over last year's pattern, and the latter is one of the Humber type machines.

THE RANELAGH CLUB TRICYCLE, of the Coventry Machinists' Company, though one of the first of the bar steerers, is still very popular. Having ridden the machine over good and bad roads, up hill and down, we have found it in every way an easy running wheel, and a good hill-climber. The Marlboro' Club is one of the best of the Cripper type, and the spring in the front bar absorbs all vibration. The Coventry people are well located for trying machines, the asphalt pavement being close at hand.

MURRAY is taking in a large stock of Gormully & Jeffery's wheels, at 100 Sudbury Street. This firm makes every grade of wheel, from the low-priced youths to the new Champion, which they claim to be the equal of any imported wheel. Murray will carry a full stock of these goods in addition to the very large stock of Harvard and Yales he has now on hand in completed form and in parts.

THE STAR for 1886 is finding favor with wheelmen. The Smithville people are using the best of material this year, and much of the frame is of the best English-drawn tubing. The machine has been materially lightened, and its lines have added grace. Stall, the Boston agent, has booked large orders.

STALL'S SCREAMERS are taking with the boys, who like to make a noise. He is having one made that will be twelve feet long, and he now has one that is four feet over all.

THE LILLIBRIDGE SADDLE has always been popular, and since imitation is the sincerest flattery, it has a right to claim exceeding merit. Its easy adjustability in every direction commends it to wheelmen, and the maker has had the endorsement of some of the hardest road riders in the country.

SAMUEL T. CLARK & CO. will show us the Rapid bicycle the present year. It comes with a good record made at the shows across the water, in each of which it took a first prize. The true tangent wheel cannot buckle, and it is one of the most rigid of all wheels on the market.

DISSOLUTION OF PARTNERSHIP.— We have this day sold all right, title, and interest of the Gazette Publishing Company in *The Springfield Wheelmen's Gazette* to Chas. A. Fisk, who assumes all debts and collects all bills of said Gazette Publishing Company.　　Yours truly,
　　　　　　　　　　HENRY E. DUCKER,
　　　　　　　　　　W. C. MARSH,
　　　　　　　　　　CHAS. A. FISK,
　　　　　Proprietors Gazette Publishing Co.
SPRINGFIELD, 26 March, 1886.

TO THE READERS OF THE GAZETTE:
Relieving that *The Springfield Wheelmen's Gazette* has filled an unoccupied field in Cycling Journalism, and encouraged by the success of the paper, I have decided to issue in April a new cycling paper of 32 pages and cover, the size of *The Springfield Wheelmen's Gazette*, whose excellence has so often been pronounced upon. The paper, typography, etc., will be in keeping with former *Gazette*, while new features will be constantly added. To all of the former patrons of the *Gazette*, I would solicit a continuance of your patronage, and trust that the new paper, *The Wheelmen's Gazette*, will continue to please in the future as *The Springfield Wheelmen's Gazette* has in the past.
　　　　　Yours truly,　　HENRY E. DUCKER.
SPRINGFIELD, 29 March, 1886.

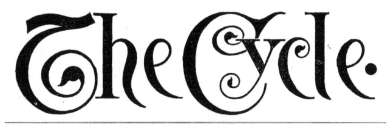

The Cycle.

Vol. I:, No. 2.   BOSTON, MASS., 9 APRIL, 1886.   FIVE CENTS.

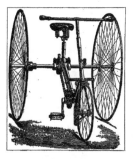

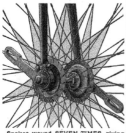

THE CYCLE

PUBLISHED EVERY FRIDAY BY ABBOT BASSETT, 22 SCHOOL ST., ROOM 19.

VOL. I. BOSTON, MASS., 9 APRIL, 1886. NO. 2.

TERMS OF SUBSCRIPTION.

One Year, by mail, post-paid......................$1.50
Three Copies in one order.........................3.00
Club Subscriptions................................1.00
Six Months.. .90
Single Copies..................................... .05

Specimen Copies free.

ABBOT BASSETT . . . . . EDITOR
W. I. HARRIS . . EDITORIAL CONTRIBUTOR

ALFRED MUDGE & SON, PRINTERS, 24 FRANKLIN ST., BOSTON.

All communications should be sent in not later than
Tuesday, to insure insertion the same week.

Entered at the Post-office as second-class mail matter.

THE BUSINESS MEETING.

SPEAKING of the mail vote now being taken by the League on the amendments to the constitution, as proposed at the spring meeting of the Board of Officers, and referring to the Boston Meet in May, the *L. A. W. Bulletin* says: "The general meeting may be done away with before that time." We must take issue with the *Bulletin* on that point. The result of the adoption of these amendments will not do away with the general meeting ; indeed, they only affect it in two important points : First, Article V. provides that the constitution shall not be altered except by a constitutional convention to be called by the president on the written application of twenty-five members. The question of abolishing the general meeting was discussed in and out of the Board meeting, and the voice of Massachusetts was very pronounced against such an interference with the rights of members, and the assumption by the Board of supreme control of League affairs. The test vote was taken on Mr. Harris's motion to insert the word "business" in Section 1 of the By-Laws, so as to make the first line read, "There shall be an annual business meeting of the League." This amendment was adopted by one majority. It was made with the intent that there should be a general meeting. The by-law is plain in its terms: "An annual business meeting of the League," not of the Board of Officers. No other construction can be placed upon it. That is what it meant, and it was so understood at the time, and any other construction would be in direct opposition to the will of the majority of the Board of Officers.

The idea of abolishing the general meeting is a pernicious one, and should not, and to our mind will not, prevail. The membership at large have little enough to say in the management of the League, without taking away this, their only rein upon the Board of Officers.

The assertion that a mail vote fully answers the object of a general meeting, is a fallacy that it hardly seems credible to us any intelligent man can hold to for a moment. The general meeting gives an opportunity for discussion that makes clearly understood such matters as may come before it, and satisfies those who are not officers, and who may have propositions to present and views to put forward on which they can get a decided expression of opinion and a yes or no vote. These gentlemen could, it is true, air the opinion through the columns of the *Bulletin* and other wheel papers, but that airing would be all they could or would accomplish.

The general meeting is part of the foundations of the League. It is a wise and necessary check upon any arrogant assumption of power by the officers, and no matter how tedious its proceedings may be, no matter how much talking may be indulged in, no matter how slow its grist may be ground, it should continue to be held as long as the League exists. Its abolishment would be the signal for a retrograde movement in the progress and usefulness of the League, and would deal a terrible blow at the principles which excuse its existence.

WE do not for a moment suppose that the business meeting will be given up. A larger vote for the measure was obtained in New York than will ever be seen again. The meeting is and should be a high court of appeal to which members can carry their grievances and where can be undone any unpopular action of any officer or committee. We do not believe it should be given up ; we do not believe it will be. If the constitutional amendment now before the League looked to the abolishment of the meeting, it would have been noticed by the cycling press before it was too late to defeat it.

IT now appears that the committee on rules anticipated the abolishment of the business meeting, and the constitution and by-laws were drawn up to provide for this. One of the results of this is that no proxy voting can be done at the Boston meeting. The right to be represented by proxy was the most important privilege held by League clubs, and now that it is gone, there is little to be gained by a club that takes its whole membership into the League. We had hoped to see a large vote on the amateur question at the League Meet in May, and wished that the large clubs at a distance might have full representation by proxy ; but we find at a late moment that this is impossible, and only those votes can be counted that are cast in person.

WE welcome to our staff this week as editorial contributor, Mr. W. I. Harris, who is too well known to call for any word of introduction from us. Mr. Harris has been a hard and an effective worker in League legislation, and we believe he will from time to time have something of interest to say to the readers of the CYCLE. We can congratulate our readers, as well as ourselves, upon this important addition to the resources of the paper.

ROLLER skating and polo are dying out, and as a natural consequence we find a great many men who lost their amateur status at these sports, who now wish to regain it. We have never believed in the idea of "once a professional always a professional," but we do believe it unwise for any athletic association to reinstate these men who lost their status with their eyes open to the results, and who now find their mistake. The ship upon which they embarked, has sunk beneath them. They were warned that its timbers were rotten. It will do them no harm to swim awhile.

A WORD to racing men : The League has the power to regulate racing, from the fact that such power has been accorded to it by the general consent of wheelmen. The outcome of the movement against the promateurs cannot at present be foreseen. It may be that the League will meet the suspended men and their friends half-way, and make some concessions. It may be that the League will adhere to the rules now on its books. We cannot tell what is before

us. But it is safe to say that the suspended men will do their cause no good if they defy the League and enter races while under suspension.

A CYCLING RETROSPECT.
BY JAM SATIS.

No. II.

TRICYCLES, though really older vehicles than bicycles, did not come into practical use until 1881 ; since then the rapidity with which the trade has advanced is very striking.

In 1881 we find four kinds of balance gear in use, on five patterns of machines out of a total of one hundred.

In 1882, out of a total of two hundred, there were nineteen driven by balance gear, and seven balance gears were in use.

To give an idea of the rapid increase in the trade I give here the number of machines described in the " Indispensable " :

In 1881 there were 100.
In 1882 there were 200,
In 1883 there were 250,
In 1884 there were 350.

I have no figures for 1885, but four hundred patterns is probably pretty near, as many old patterns are no longer made.

I have only mentioned balance geared machines in 1881 and 1882, because the various clutches and levers and other arrangements then in use are now nearly all obsolete, while a balance gear is practically in universal use on all double driving machines.

Until 1882 tricycles were experiments ; no one knew exactly what were really the requisites of a practical, good machine for general use. The makers were all trying to invent something new, and there were all sorts of rear-steerers and single-drivers and lever-actions, but Starley's balance-geared, double-driving, front-steering, " Salvo," had shown riders and makers both what really was needed ; and we find that in 1882 makers had settled on that form of machine as a standard. The season of 1883 showed this still more strongly and the number of balance-geared F. S. machines was much increased. That same year brought out the first two-track, front-steering double-driver, the " Royal Mail No. 4," and also the first T-framed, central-geared front-steerer, with bicycle cranks and pedals, — the " Markham." I never heard the " Markham " spoken of anywhere ; I do not know why, especially as the next season established central-geared F. S. machines as the favorite pattern.

The season of 1884 brought out a great number of what have since become leading patterns, viz : The " Humber Automatic Steerer," familiarly known as the " Cripper " the " Ranelagh Club," and the " Quadrant No. 8 " (the bicycle-steerer), the central-geared " Apollo," " Invincible," " Sparkbrook " and other similar patterns, besides innumerable copies of the " Humber " ordinary pattern.

By 1885 we find that makers had settled, practically speaking, upon four patterns or types as comprising everything desirable in a tricycle. These were the " Humber," " Cripper," the T-framed front-steerer with side handles, like the " Club," the " Apollo,"

" Rudge," " Quadrant No. 9," etc. ; the T-framed front-steerer, with bicycle-steering, like the " Invincible," " Ranelagh Club," " Quadrant No. 8," etc.

The season of 1886 can hardly be called open, perhaps, but it promises the " Cripper " as the leading type for the season, as nearly every maker has one machine of that pattern on his list.

I doubt if the type is as well suited to our roads as it is to the English roads, as I should think the vibration would be too great for the rider's comfort, but experience only will show whether this is so or not.

There is one very striking fact through " all this strange, eventful history," and through all the changes of patterns and new driving gears, etc., and that is that two machines have not changed at all since they were first introduced in 1881, but have steadily held their own, copying no one, and never departing from their first design. These are Coventry Rotary, — the only successful single driver, — and the Humber, which is still one of the best machines made, and probably the most copied. The Coventry Rotary has never been copied, unless the Grosvenor can be called a copy ; I should call it a caricature myself.

Both the Coventry and Humber have been changed in their details, the wheels have been made smaller, and both machines have been lightened, but the original design has always been strictly retained, and both of them remain essentially the same machines they were five years ago.

In my next I want to say a few words about methods of driving and steering, and then to take up sociables and tandems.

FROM A FEMININE POINT OF VIEW.

THE riding season is here, and soon we shall be on the road. I await with anxiety the arrival of my machine, and then farewell to dance and sociable, farewell to progressive whist and progressive euchre, and welcome the progressive wheel.

BOSTON has gone wild this winter on progressive whist, and the back country has taken to progressive euchre. Boston culture can stand nothing less than the oldest and most scholarly game, but the back country does not care to exercise its brain over cards.

THE rise and progress of this new divertisement only shows us as we have been shown a hundred times before, that the average man and woman wants a stimulus to make them interested in their pleasure beyond that which comes from the pleasure itself. This they get in the latest card games, for the prizes which are offered by the hostess are often valuable and well worth a determined effort.

MY little room at home is decorated with several souvenirs of these modern tournaments, and shall I confess it, there are a few " booby " prizes in the lot.

BUT I am wandering. Progressive whist can now be laid aside, and we may look for a better form of pleasure in the wheel. I

say this advisedly, in spite of the record of brilliant evenings I have made, and the many pleasurable moments I have enjoyed. No form of enjoyment that I have taken to can begin to compare with cycling.

I RECEIVED a call the other day from a lady friend who was out for a ride. I cannot say that she presented a pleasant appearance, for the muddy roads had been writing autographs all over her garments, and her wheel was a sight to behold. And yet she was full of enthusiasm over the glorious time she had had, and the mud was a thing that did not enter into her consideration. I confess that I envied her, for a few minutes' exercise with a clothes brush is a small price to pay for so charming an experience.

I WISH there might be established a private school for the instruction of ladies in tricycling. In the early days of roller skating a number of ladies in the city where I reside became interested in that form of exercise, and as they did not care to go to the public sessions an arrangement was made for their accommodation in the forenoon, and they used to spend this part of the day in the rink which was closed to all others at that time. The movement was a great success, and it proved a good financial venture for the rink manager.

Now why could not something of this kind be done in cycling. Not every lady wants to take her first lessons on the road, and many are deterred from trying to ride by the publicity that must needs attend their first efforts. I have used my persuasive powers to good advantage the past winter, and could I employ other means to instruct my friends I believe I could get a small army of women on to wheels. Do not think I want to be instructress. I am not in want of an occupation, but if I could say to this lady, or that, " Go to such and such a place and take a few lessons in riding, and then come and try my machine on the road," I think I could do my missionary work to better advantage.

IT is always a thankless task to sit down idly and say, Why does n't some one do this or that. Some one will do it when it is known that it will pay. I believe such a scheme as I have proposed will pay, and I hope some dealer will put it in force.

DAISIE.

THE LEAGUE TOUR.

THE following letter from the tour-master tells its own story : —

CHICAGO, March 29, 1886.

Dr. N. M. BECKWITH,
President L. A. W., New York :

Dear Sir. — Representatives of the Big Four Bicycle Tour Association held a meeting in Buffalo yesterday. It was agreed that the Association disband, with a view to resolving itself into the Touring Department of the L. A. W., to the end that all future tours that might be under the auspices of the Association be held under the auspices of the touring department of the L. A. W.

In accordance with your instructions to me, as tour-master of the L. A. W., the following gentlemen present were appointed to constitute the Touring Board, *pro tem.*, subject to your approval: George R. Bidwell, of New York; W. S. Bull, of Buffalo; F. B. Graves, of Rochester; L. W. Conkling, of Chicago; George H. Orr, of Toronto; F. G. King, of Corry, Pa.; Dr. A. G. Coleman, of Canandaigua.

Thus organized, the Board took following action: Country was divided into touring districts, Eastern, Middle, Western, and Southern, according to the regular geographical division of the United States. Canada was included in the Middle Division. Each division to have a marshal with immediate charge of the touring interests of the division, leadership of his division party in the annual tour; he to give tourists general information concerning prospective tours of individual wheelmen or parties over routes in his division, and have charge of the editing of the tour map of his division. The duties of the marshals will be generally centralized in the Chief Marshal, who will, in addition, personally lead or superintend the annual tour. A bicycle touring map of the United States will be compiled by the Board, to be in divisions as above or in one map like a railroad folder, as may develop to be best. This map will give the main or best bicycle routes to take between given points showing points passed through, in same manner as a railroad map of the United States. It will generally treat of through routes only, and will be in harmony with the division road books, in that the map will depend upon them for the details, the map practically illustrating the general work of the division road books. The map will be accompanied by touring descriptions with rail and water connections, and best lines to take between given points, and in this connection be an auxiliary to the Transportation Committee of the L. A. W.

The annual tour was set for the two weeks following Monday, 6 Sept. 1886, and is substantially over following route: Niagara Falls and Buffalo to Canandaigua, Seneca Lake, Central New York, Elmira, Northern New Jersey, and the Orange riding district to New York City. Thence ocean steamer to O'd Point Comfort, Va., and thence to Staunton, Va. From Staunton down the Shenandoah Valley, *via* Luray Cave, to Harper's Ferry, thence north to Hagerstown, Md., Gettysburg, Pa., York, Pa., and Reading, Pa., to Philadelphia, or *via* the Lehigh Valley to New York State. All details of the annual tour will be perfected, and size of party limited to the ample accommodation of tourists. Tickets will be issued during the summer, and by the purchase of same the tourist will be entitled to a place in his respective division. The price of tickets will be based on actual cost of the tour, with a slight margin for incidental expenses of organizing. A circular, giving all details of the tour, with description of the route, will be offered the *Bulletin* for publication in proper time. The Board acted upon the question of uniform, and adopted the following: The regulation L. A. W. uniform, with exception of dark brown striped seersucker Norfolk jacket and straw hat. The colors of the Touring Department will be royal purple, to consist of a narrow ribbon

tied through the buttonhole of the jacket or attached to the badge. Each division will have a distinguishing color, to be worn with the purple, and consist of a similar ribbon, as follows: Eastern, red; Middle, white; Western, blue; Southern, old gold. These colors touring members of the L. A. W. are recommended to wear on all appropriate occasions, whether on the annual tour or throughout the year. The policy of the annual tour will be that of maximum individual enjoyment with all modern conveniences and requisites, elegance of appearance and movement, and congenial companionship. The route is laid out with a view to visiting choice and characteristic sections of the country, measuring the wheeling to the ability of an average rider to perform with ease, that the participant may gather recreation on the road, knowledge of the country, and desirable acquaintances in the craft.

The Touring Board solicits the co-operation of the State divisons and individual members, and desires to be understood as placing itself at the disposition of tourists for such service as it can render.

We trust our action will meet with your approval.

Respectfully yours,
BURLEY B. AYERS,
Tour-master L. A. W.

ATHLETIC ENTERTAINMENT.

THE last athletic exhibition of the season, under the auspices of the Massachusetts Club, was given in the club gymnasium, on Saturday evening last. The interest in this class of entertainment was shown by the large crowd in attendance, every foot of room being taken by the eager throng of spectators. The entertainment was in charge of Capt. Peck, Mr. N. Ethier and Mr. John T. Williams, and the programme was carried out to the full satisfaction of the audience. A home trainer race was first in order, with John T. Williams and H. C. Getchell as entrants. After two unsuccessful attempts to tell off a mile without losing their pedals the men finished as follows: H. C. Getchell, 1.38⅔; John T. Williams, 1.47⅘. Arthur Porter, of Newton, turned off a quarter in twenty-five seconds. Mr. T. F. Martin, of Cambridge, gave an exhibition of club swinging that was highly enjoyed, and the performer was loudly applauded. Messrs. John T. Williams, N. Ethier, Mr. Dame and Mr. Teafe showed some wonderful work on the parallel bars and Mr. Teafe introduced a contortion act. Sparring bouts were given by Bangs and Lighthall, E. O. Bangs and Danielson, Osgood and Payne, and Reed and Danforth. Some very clever sparring was done, and, as large, soft gloves were used, and the boxers were all amateurs, there were no objectionable features in the exhibition, though the audience was worked up to a high pitch of excitement during the bouts, which was kept in check by the committee who would allow no remarks nor applause.

CALIFORNIA PROTESTS.

AT a meeting of the California Division, L. A. W., held 24 March, the followed resolution was offered and passed unanimously:—

"*Resolved*, That we, the amateur wheel-

men of California, assembled, desire to express our sympathy for the unfortunate position of our esteemed friend and comrade, Fred Russ Cook. That it is our heartfelt desire that he remain among us as an amateur, knowing this to be his most earnest wish. That a copy of these resolutions be forwarded to the officers of the L. A. W., and that they be urged to do all in their power to reinstate 'Our Fred'; he being one of the most valued friends to wheelmen generally, and a leading support to all that pertains to the promotion of cycling on this coast."

THE INTERNATIONAL CHAMPIONSHIP.

THE following letter has been received by the Racing Board and forwarded to Mr. Robert Todd, with the approval of the Board:—

ABBOT BASSETT, ESQ,
Chairman Racing Board L. A. W.

Dear Sir,—In reply to the letter of Robert Todd, honorary secretary N. C. U., I would say that the Springfield Bicycle Club will agree to do all in its power to assist the N. C. U. and the L. A. W. in uniting upon a plan to establish a recognized championship race of the world, and to that end it makes the following offer, which is to be extended to all countries wishing to participate:—

The Springfield Bicycle Club, through its president, Henry E. Ducker, hereby extends to the legislative bodies of the world a cordial invitation to send representatives to the fifth annual meeting of the club, to be holden at Springfield, Mass., in the month of September, 1886, and there to enter into a friendly competition for the championship of the world on such conditions as may be mutually agreed upon. The race to be for one mile, and to run as follows: The N. C. U. to have the nominating of not more than six men to compete. The L. A. W. to be limited to the same number. The Irish Cyclists' Association to choose four men; the Dutch Cyclists' Union the same number; the Australian Cyclists' Union to send two men. The race will be run as follows: The names of all the contestants to be drawn; the race will be run in heats limited to two men each,—thus numbers 1 and 2 will run the first heat, and numbers 3 and 4 will run the second, and so on till the list is exhausted. These heats will be run the first day, and the winners on the first day will compete in the final heat on the last day. The winner of the final heat to be declared the "Amateur Champion of the World." For this race the Springfield Bicycle Club will offer two valuable prizes, to be awarded, first, to the winner of the final heat; second, to the winner of the fastest heat (even though they go to the same man). The prizes are to be the absolute property of the winners.

The contestants, one and all, are to be the guests of the club, and all travelling expenses in the United States from place of landing to Springfield and return, including hotel bills for man and trainer, to be paid by the Springfield Club.

The value of the prizes will depend upon the number of contestants. The total

expense of the race not to exceed $1,000, and this appropriation must pay all the hotel and travelling expenses above referred to, and also for the prizes. In other words, we offer a committee chosen from the N. C. U. and the L. A. W. the sum of $1,000 to be expended on this race as they may deem most advisable. Our only reserve. is· that the prizes become the absolute. property of the winners; otherwise the $1,000 is at the disposal of said committee. In offering the above, the Springfield Bicycle Club feels prompted by the desire to inaugurate a series of international championship races which we hope to see transferred to other countries with each succeeding year, and to establish beyond dispute who is entitled to the championship of the world, believing that these contests, when once established, will prove a means of introducing a friendship among wheelmen unknown to any other sport. Trusting that the above will meet with the approval of the Legislative Cycling Associations of the world, and that Springfield will be the chosen ground for the first of a series of international contests, we are

Fraternally yours,

SPRINGFIELD BICYCLE CLUB,
HENRY E. DUCKER, Pres't.

CONTRIBUTORS' CLUB

A NEW DEFINITION.

Editor of the Cycle: — In the interest of the men now under suspension, I want to suggest a new rule for the League. The suspended parties will never consent to be professionals under that term, and I think it no more than right that the League should meet them half-way. I propose the following as an addition to the amateur rule.

"A promateur is one that has never contested for a money prize in any form; nor with a professional."

Then I would have the League admit "Any wheelman in good standing who is not a professional."

This would give us three classes, — the amateur who lives up to the letter and spirit of our rules, the promateur who is not an amateur nor yet a professional, and the professional. Under this rule the amateurs could race by themselves, and the promateurs would form a new class of riders that would include such men as Rowe, Hendee, and Burnham. The League would admit the promateurs to its ranks and still retain supervision of racing. Then such places as Philadelphia and Springfield, Ohio, would have pure amateur races without fear of interference from the promateurs; and such places as Hartford and Springfield could give the promateur races which would include the flyers from home and abroad. If England should not fall into this scheme, we do no doubt special sanction from the N. C. U. could be obtained for the riders who would come over. I would like to hear what wheelmen think of this.   BARNEY.

A NEW CLASS.

Editor of the Cycle: — It has been estimated that the present agitation over the amateur law may lead to the establishment of a new class of riders, who shall be neither amateur nor professional, but who will constitute a class by themselves between the two. This is a good idea, but why stop at one class? Why not have a dozen? I will suggest a few classes.

Class A will consist of the amateurs, strict and pure. They will own their own wheels, and will run for glory only. Colored ribbons to be attached to the breast by a safety pin will be the only prizes allowed.

Class B will embrace all those who leave all other business and try to make a living by riding a bicycle. They may run for what prizes they please, and win them fairly or unfairly as they see fit, for they must get their living in the easiest way.

Class C will be open to the men who live up to the amateur law so far as racing for money prizes or with professionals is concerned. They will work at their respective trades in winter, but when the racing season opens they will be allowed to make arrangements on the quiet with dealers to ride their wheels on a salary, or they may take payment for records made or races won.

Class D will include all those who ride for glory and big trophies. They will receive nothing beyond the prizes won, but their expenses will be paid by dealers, and these expenses may include suits of clothes and double-barreled shot guns.

Class E will be open to that class of pure amateurs that includes college students and the sons of millionaires. These have plenty of time and some one to pay their bills. It is not fair to put them in competition with pure amateurs who have to train after business hours.

Class F will include bicycle dealers, makers and agents. These men ride to advertise their wheels, but they pay their own expenses and avoid breaking the law. The sons of these men will be included in this class. The law will not allow a man to take money from a dealer for riding a wheel, but when the dealer is also the father it is no easy task to tell in what capacity he stands when he gives money to his son.

Class G will include all who are pure amateurs in name and act. They live up to the rule in letter and in spirit. They may work for a maker or a dealer, and it is nobody's business if they get a salary of $2,500 for doing $50 worth of work. A man may pay his clerks what he pleases.

Class H will include all cycling journalists and publishers, dealers, makers, patentees of cycling articles, etc. This will include every person who, directly or indirectly, makes a dollar out of the sport. Wheelmen who influence the sale of a machine and get a commission will go into this class.

The members of each class shall be known by a badge bearing the letter of the class, and worn on the left breast. When we get these classes established we can know where we stand.

'OSTLER JOE.

RECOGNIZED ATHLETIC SPORT.

Editor of the Cycle: — Can you inform a bewildered individual why some athletic sports are "recognized," and some are not. I can understand that the underlying idea of the amateur rule is that it is unfair to put in competition those who indulge in athletic sports as a diversion, and those who go into them as a business, for the latter have an advantage over the former in the way of training and practice, but I cannot see why the rule should cover one athletic sport and not another. A man can play base-ball, foot-ball, cricket, or tennis with or against a professional and not lose his status. Why? The college base-ball nines play with professional nines, and no one says a word. Why? I have played cricket with a club of pure amateurs and each side in the game had a paid coach with them, and yet we were still amateurs. Can you enlighten me on the point?   CRICKET.

THE sports that our correspondent mentions come under the jurisdiction of no amateur organization. The N. A. A. A. A. has several times discussed the question of taking base ball under its jurisdiction, but the motion has always been defeated. Each organization controls its own sports, and each recognizes the acts of the others. It would be out of character for the Wheelmen's or the Oarsmen's association to take jurisdiction over the sports enumerated, and so long as they have no organizations of their own, and the N. A. A. A. does not take them under its wing, the present condition of things will remain. The enforcement of the amateur law needs adjustment in many ways. — ED].

DON'T HIRE A HALL.

Editor of the Cycle: — I want to urge a very strong protest against the hiring of a hall for the League banquet. Boston has talked a great deal about her ability to give the best banquet of any city in America, and she ought to make good her boast. A banquet in a hall can never be successful. All the dishes will be cold and the wine will be hot, and the waiters will not be able to work to advantage. It will be a great mistake. Better have the dinner at a hotel, and limit the tickets. Then those who are shut out can get up little dinner parties of their own at some hotel. I belong to a club that will have its own little dinner party if the League goes to a hall for its banquet.   S. T. F.

WAIT FOR A TANDEM.

Editor of the Cycle: — My advice to the man who wants to find the best kind of a tandem, is to wait and see what is coming out this spring. At present the Humber style of tandem is a favorite with those who want speed, but it has not the element of safety in so great a degree as I desire. Nearly every other tandem puts the labor of steering and braking on the lady. This is an objection. We are promised several tandems where the lady sits behind, and the gentleman does the steering. This is what I want to see, and so I say wait. If our friend wants a machine for two gentlemen the Humber form is the thing.

BENEDICT.

NASHVILLE PLEASURES.

THE Nashville (Tenn.) Club gave an entertainment at the clubrooms, 30 March last. The exercises were introduced by the following home trainer races, contested first for half mile in the marked time:

Messrs. E. D. Fisher, 1.7; Bowman Duncan, 1.11; D. Talbot, 1.13¾; R. Vanderford, 1.15¼. Later came a home trainer race for three eighths of a mile. D. Talbot, 50½; E. D. Fisher, 49; Bowman Duncan, 51½; R. Vanderford, 53½. The following gentlemen took part in the quarter-mile races: Messrs. D. Talbot, 31½; Bowman Duncan, 30½; R. Vanderford, 32½; D. A. Palmer, 46½. Musical and literary expenses filled out the evening's programme. The prizes were gifts from the young lady friends of the club, and were as follows: —

Half mile. — E. D. Fisher, embroidered watch case.

Second mile. — Bowman Duncan, embroidered cloth tidy.

Three eighths mile. — E. D. Fisher, embroidered handkerchief case.

Quarter mile. — Bowman Duncan, linen tidy.

Mr. Canaday, one of the novitiates, received an embroidered handkerchief.

NOTES OF A CYCLIST.

APRIL ushers in the wheelmen's new year. For over four months there has been very little riding done throughout this section, say between Boston and New York. Soon after election day many wheels were housed for the winter, and along in March they were brought out again. No wonder it takes time to get into riding condition after such a rest.

I PITY the butterfly riders. They lose many of the most exhilarating rides of the year, when the air is fresh and bracing, and all nature invites to a flying spin over the hardened roads. I think I pity them even more when they get out for their first spring rides. Most wheelmen are confined by their business duties; and lack of outdoor exercise for several months has depressed and wearied them. They begin to ride in the spring weather, which is more or less debilitating to any one not in good condition. A long ride uses them up. Then a long rest and another long ride. They go on fitfully and irregularly, getting but the minimum of benefit.

MANY a man never knew what it was to enjoy good health until he took to cycling. After regular riding, they have not had a sick day. Other wheelmen, naturally more vigorous, have not gained in the same degree, but suffer from the agonies of sick headaches and such complaints. The former ride regularly, the latter fitfully. Nearly every day sees the one on his wheel. The other averages once a week or a trifle more. One begins the season feeling strong and enjoying the spring weather. The other begins wearily and is easily exhausted.

CYCLING is the most beneficial exercise in the world, if properly used. You cannot ride once a week and get much benefit. If you will, however, ride regularly and frequently, you are bound to improve.

I WISH I could induce every cyclist who rides irregularly, and who does not always feel in good physical shape, to try short daily rides. If necessary, sacrifice a little comfort to obtain the time required. A half hour's ride will do more good than a half hour's extra sleep in the morning. Breakfast fifteen minutes earlier; take fifteen minutes for a light meal instead of half an hour for a heavy one, and take the half hour gained for a spin before going to business. For a few weeks, take the ride as easily as you please. Soon you will get used to the arrangement, and can take a good lively run. I have tried the plan for two years and feel immeasurably better prepared for the day's business than I ever did before.

THESE short, daily runs are more strengthening than occasional long ones. The effect of the constantly repeated exercise is marked. When one takes infrequent, but moderately long, runs, the case is different. He gets very tired, and does not ride again until he has rested. Then he finds he has gained very little. But the man who takes regular, short runs, can take a long one and be all the stronger and more active for it the next day. Health and strength are both produced by regular, frequent exercise.

THERE is greater interest than ever in cycling if one keeps a record of his rides. The first requisite is a reliable cyclometer; the second, a small diary. Equipped with these, you can record the distance of each ride; add a line to tell where you went or any such item of interest, and note the state of the weather. Possibly it will be a little laborious at first to do this, but it will soon become as natural as your daily ride. You will find it extremely interesting for reference; you will know just what you have ridden, and whatever record you have will be accurate. It will also be an incentive to increase your riding.

AN ambition is a good thing to have, even if it is only for a riding "record." Of course, if it leads to over-exertion or any other injudicious proceedings, it should be abandoned. But if it only serves to provoke to regular riding, it should be encouraged. Any one who rides at all can cover a thousand miles in a year. For one person, this would be a fair record. From it, upwards to about three thousand miles, constitutes a good record. Few persons are so situated that they have time for over three thousand miles. Two thousand may be put down as a good average.

IF you call eight months the riding season (this is absurdly small for good roads), and deduct the Sundays from them, there are over two hundred days left. Five miles a day would give one thousand miles; ten miles a day two thousand miles. It is thus evident that when the habit of regular riding is formed, a "record" is easy to secure. Where there are macadam roads, there will be over two hundred and fifty riding days a year, exclusive of Sundays. Ten miles a day will thus easily secure a twenty-five hundred-mile record.

THIS applies to the ladies quite as much as to the gentlemen. Any one of them can, after a month or two of practice, ride an hour a day. If ridden slowly, it will give five miles, and with a little more practice, from six to eight. Every one ought to get away from household cares for an hour each day. The wheel will give the most beneficial exercise, and the "record" at the holidays will easily run from a thousand to fifteen hundred miles, and possibly even more.

5678.

CLEVELAND CARNIVAL.

THE Cleveland Club held high carnival 31 March, at the Le Grand rink. The carnival opened with a grand entry of wheelmen in fancy costume. George Collister led, in a clown suit, on a "boneshaker" of the most ancient type. Then came John T. Huntington, as Collister's partner, also in clown costume, on the smallest wheel made; Harrison Wagner, as a third clown, on an old three-wheeler; Fred Borton, dressed as "Father Time," with scythe and locks of white, his big wheel covered with linen, on which was painted a clock face. Then came Taylor Boggis, on his racer, as "Mephistopheles"; Fred Palmer in a burlesque suit, as a racing wheelman, with the mile record placarded on his back; W. P. Sargent, in a prince suit; B. F. Wade and J. H. Collister, on a tandem tricycle, in Mikado suits, drawing a child's wagon, in which sat Milton James as a baby. He enlivened the march with shrill and well counterfeited infantile cries. Other costumes were unique and pretty. A mile race on safety bicycles was won by A. E. Sprackling in 3.20; W. S. Upson, 2d. A club drill followed, in which many fine movements were given, and the glee club gave several songs. The singing was done in the centre of the rink floor, in a group made up of tricycles and bicycles, lighted by the rays of the calcium — a pretty effect that pleased the eye, while the sweet-voiced young men poured harmony into the air.

Taylor Boggis followed with an exhibition of fancy riding that surprised everybody, and earned the young athlete several great bursts of applause.

The half-mile bicycle race, in which A. E. Sprackling and W. S. Upson entered, followed, and Upson won a good race by two yards, in 1.38.

SQUIBS.

"BASSETT'S Bantling," brother Dean,
Is young, and yet has time to grow;
And bantlings, as you may have seen,
Grow old before they learn to crow!

THE Fates are favoring, the sky is clear,
For, though the editor should e'er grow lazy,
The CYCLE will be read both far and near, —
'Cause why, we've got the ever-blooming "Daisie."

A SHINY wheel with nickel plated,
A "Boston Club" man's gay salute,
A manly breast with pride elated,
A cross-eyed pug-dog — *c'était tout!*

PEDALS.

STUART C. MILLER, of the Massachusetts Bicycle Club, who was six months abroad, has returned, and is greatly improved in health by his trip. He brings with him a Traveller tandem, which is of the Humber type.

CYCLETS.

HERE we are again.

WE are blushing a little under the shower of kind words we have received, and we begin to think we have a few friends.

WE hope to prove ourselves worthy of their good wishes and to continue to deserve them.

FAST Day is the opening gate, to the riding season. It does not always show us pleasant skies, but wheelmen feel that it ought to, and unpleasant weather is looked upon only as an incident of the day.

RESIDENTS of Beacon street are organizing to protect that street from the encroachment of the cable road. Livery men and carriage men are also at work, and wheelmen are taking a hand. We don't believe the highway will be disturbed.

LAWYER DEAN has given us the law in the case, and we commend his article to the careful attention of those who say the Racing Board has done an illegal act.

WE also have an editorial contributor, and we wish it distinctly understood that he is to receive all visitors who come to us with clubs and pistols. Those who come with wedding cake will please call for the editor.

LET him who can afford a dollar a day and over in "treating" his friends try an experiment, for the next six months. Let him pay a compliment to his liver, shut down on liquid refreshment, and seek in the open air health and vigor upon the back of a horse. Ride. Dash through the Park and grow old merrily. — New York Herald.

THE Herald's advice is good as far as it goes. If it had said cycle, how much better it would sound. The horse cannot be compared with his metallic rival in health-promoting qualities.

THE World says the Racing Board reminds it of suspenders. We are glad that that journal sees fit to brace up the Board.

THE Spectator has settled on a word for a wheelman's banquet. It is "biquet" with a long e. We are glad he doesn't say "bike wet," for there comes the rub.

PRESIDENT BARTOL, of the Philadelphia Bicycle Club, has presented a novel trophy for competition among the members, to be awarded to the one who will cover the greatest number of miles in a year. It takes the form of a loving cup, bearing on the front an etched bicycle, artistically wrought, with the inscription, "The President's Cup." Above it on the reverse the tricycle is represented, and to make it still further distinctively a wheelman's prize the handles are made to represent the backbone of a machine.

THE Nashville young ladies have been at work for the cyclers, and on the occasion of the recent home-trainer race the prizes were fine specimens of embroidery, including outline designs of cycle subjects, initials of the club, etc.

THE official handicapper, Dr. N. P. Tyler, has located at New Rochelle, N. Y.

HENRY SANDHAM, the artist, has painted a group of wheelmen on the road, for Mr. Prang, and it will soon appear in the form of a chromo.

MR. BUTCHER, of the Butcher Cyclometer Company, has made a cyclometer for the use of record breakers. It registers revolutions, and it can be locked on the wheel. It will be let to record breakers at a moderate fee.

SIX members of the New Orleans Bicycle Club have agreed to attend the Boston Meet, and ride the whole distance on their wheels. They are A. M. Hill, E. W. Hunter, W. L. Hughes, H. W. Fairfax, C. M. Fairchild, S. M. Patton.

A. M. HILL, of New Orleans, has offered a gold medal to the New Orleans Club to be awarded to the winner of a series of fifty-mile contests in 1886. The club has also offered two medals, — one to the rider making the best road record, and the other for the best mileage for the year.

WILBUR F, KNAPP starts for the East next week, and will train for the season's races at Lynn or Springfield.

WE understand that J. A. R. Underwood has sold out his drug business, and will locate in Boston proper for the sale of cycles.

MR. E. R. BENSON, treasurer of the Massachusetts Club, was married on Wednesday last. His associate clerks at the Pope Manufacturing Company's office presented him with a Bible and a dictionary. With the latter in hand we suppose he will be able to find words to express his thanks.

THE hearing in the case of Pope v. Overman, called for Monday last, was postponed till Monday next, at the request of the latter. The hearing is before Commissioner Hallett, and is held for the qualification of bondsmen, who are to go upon the bond for $73,000, to raise the attachment now upon the goods of the Overman Wheel Company.

A COLUMBIA racer was shipped to Tom Eck, last week. There is nothing particularly strange in that item, but behind it is the fact that it was paid for.

WE have received a copy of the catalogue of Messrs. Stoddard, Lovering & Co., which is just issued. The outside cover shows a group of wheelmen on the road, while around and about in the corners and in the centre are cuts of the Rudge machines. The Rudge is a very popular wheel in Boston, and the 1886 catalogue has been waited for with impatience by those who wish to see all the wheels before buying.

"SACRED to the deathless memory of Ensign Stebbins.—the man who was 'in favor of the law, but agin' the enforcement of it.'" This famous monument is just now being glorified anew by the abundant wreaths and immortelles which "the amateurs" and their friends are industriously heaping around it; but when a thorough-going professional like myself gazes at the amusing spectacle, it seems as if the whole broad surface of Washington Square smiled back responsive to my grin. [The foregoing is a permitted extract from the private letter of a certain "free advertiser" not altogether unknown in the cycling world by the initials "K. K."— ED.]

THE Southern Cycler takes strong ground in favor of the Racing Board in its action against the makers' amateurs. The back country is being heard from, and she's all right.

AN easy method of ascertaining approximately how fast a bicycle is being propelled, is to count the number of revolutions of the pedals during one minute, then multiply this number by the size of the driving wheel and divide by three hundred and thirty-six; the result will be the number of miles per hour.

A FRIEND called on us the other day and assured us that the Pope Manufacturing Company had introduced a new tandem. He was certain of it, because he had seen one on the Milldam. We knew at once what he had seen, for we saw the machine at Stall's the day before. Stall has rigged one of his Adjuncts to a Columbia two-track tricycle, and in this way has made a very effective and a moderate priced tandem.

THE World may boast of the beautiful view from its office windows, and under this boasting we are squelched; but we are willing to give up the pretty for the useful, and we can talk back to them by pointing out the advantages to be had from a good view of the storm signals and the time ball, to say nothing of the advantage to be gained from hearing the fire-alarm bell. When views are in question, we go in for the utilitarian.

THE Belgium authorities have passed a decree abolishing duty on bicycles. Tourists have now but to show their C. T. C. ticket, or otherwise convince the customhouse officers that they do not intend to remain in the country, and they will be freed from all restrictions. The same laws prevail in Holland.

"THE Warren," in Roxbury, has made especial provision for the storage of cycles by the tenants.

THE Beverly strikes have thrown a large number of the wheelmen of that place out of employment.

THERE will be an international exhibition of cycles held at Vienna, Austria, during the months of May and June.

THE dates for the English championships, are out. The races are distributed freely through the country, and not confined to London, as was the case until the last few years. The five-mile tricycle takes place first, on 22 May, at Glasgow. This is the first time that one of the championships is to be run in Scotland. The date might have been more suitable, as the international meeting at Alexandra Park takes place on 21 and 22 May. The one-mile tricycle and twenty-five-mile bicycle races come off at Weston-Super-Mare, on 4 June. The famous Farrow track will be the scene of the one-mile bicycle on 26 June, and on 24 July the five-mile bicycle will be run on the new ground at Long Eaton, near Derby. The twenty-five-mile tricycle and fifty-mile bicycle will be run at the Crystal Palace, London, on 14 July and 14 August, respectively.

WE are obliged to confess that there is little that is exciting in a home-trainer race against time. We can look calmly on at the young man as he kicks circles in the air, and the blood does not flow faster in our veins, nor does our heart palpitate with ex-

citement at the spectacle. When we chop wood, we want to see the chips fly.

L. D. MUNGER, of Detroit, made fifty miles, using a 57-inch bicycle on an asphalt road, in 3.27.34, at New Orleans, 2 April.

GEORGE HUTCHINSON, the fancy bicycle rider, has entered the employ of the Pope Manufacturing Company as rink instructor.

LEAGUE CONSUL A. L. ATKINS's road book of Boston for 1886, enlarged and improved, is in the printer's hands.

A SMALL camera has been sent to Thomas Stevens at Calcutta, to allow him to take a few views along his route. Stevens has been giving us his views on various questions connected with travelling awheel, and it now appears that more picturesque views are wanted.

MR. S. A. MERRILL has accepted the chairmanship of the L. A. W. finance committee. His address is, "Bank of Mutual Redemption, Boston," and it will greatly convenience him if contributors will send their checks without giving him the trouble to call on them.

Is a maker's amateur's lot a happy one? Yes, as long as he remains in form; but once let him show any falling off, and, Othello-like, he will find his occupation gone. We could mention more than one instance where men have given up good situations to take service with makers, and after a bad season have found themselves unemployed. It is very pleasant having one's expenses paid and allowed to lead the life of a gentleman, if it would only last. Those who have good situations ought to pause before they throw them up to become a maker's employee, unless they wish to have to start in life again at the end of twelve months or so. — *Turf.*

IRELAND puts in a claim for a visit from touring wheelmen. Speaking of the proposed League tour to England, an Irish paper says: "Why is Ireland left out of the programme, we wonder? Surely a run through it would prove as interesting as one through Scotland. The party could land at Queenstown, visit the Lakes of Killarney, ride to Belfast, and cross to Scotland. We need hardly say the party would get a very warm and hospitable reception in Ireland."

THE Racing Board has sent out its second instalment of certificates, and suspended the following riders: L. J. Martel, Chicopee; C. P. Adams, Springfield; H. E. Bidwell, East Hartford; F. R. Brown, Springfield; L. A. Miller, Meriden; W. F. Knapp, Denver; A. B. Rich, New York; C. F. Haven, Boston. The last two are suspended under Rule H, all the others under the amateur law.

THE CYCLE has struck 'popular favor. Subscriptions are coming in very fast, but there is always room for more. Our trial trip of a month for ten cents is being taken advantage of by hundreds. If any one doubts this, let him come and look at our stamp drawer. Send one-cent trips, friends.

STODDARD, LOVERING & CO. expect a shipment of the new Rudge bicycles to arrive next week.

WE can see no advantage left for League clubs over non-league clubs, save the privilege of position in the League parade, and the right ro run League championships.

WE are sorry to lose the proxy votes, for we wanted to see everybody represented in the annual meeting. Claifornia can now have no voice, nor can any of the distant States.

MASSACHUSETTS has been called a hot-bed of makers' amateurism. If there is any truth in this, the amateur rule may have to go, for Massachusetts will have a large vote at the meeting.

ST. LOUIS papers are giving us rare specimens of Western journalism in commenting upon the action of the Racing Board The *Wheelman* has little in its columns outside of denunciations of the course pursued, and with rare inconsistency it booms Kirkpatrick for president of the League. There is an old saw about consistency and precious stones. We have forgotten it.

CHELSEA is going to have a club. We wonder if they will follow the example of the Newton Club, and have a dinner at every meeting. Would n't that make them a stuffed club?

L. H. JOHNSON, ESQ., of New Jersey, was in town this week. He tells us that Orange will send a large delegation to the Meet in May. Mr Johnson will handle the Columbia bicycles the coming season.

THE CLUB.

[WITH a view to obtaining a complete list of clubs with the officers elect, we will ask the secretary of each and every club in America to send us on a postal card a list of the principal officers after the following formula :—
BOSTON, MASS. Massachusetts Club. Officers elected 1 January, 1886: President, Col. T. W. Higginson ; captain, A. D. Peck, Jr.; secretary, F. Alcott Pratt, 1 Somerset street ;treasurer, E. R. Benson, 597 Washington street.]

EAST CAMBRIDGE, MASS. — East Cambridge Club; organized 2 April, 1886. President, Henry Lienhard; captain, C. N. Singleton; lieutenant, F. E. Lunt. A committee was appointed to draw up a constitution and by-laws, and was instructed to report as early as possible. Arrangements were also made for the initial club run, to take place on Fast day,

SOUTH BOSTON, MASS., 29 March. — Reorganization of the Suffolk Wheel Club. Officers elected : President, J. F. Charnock; vice-president, C. S. Willis; captain, Gid. Haynes, Jr.; secretary, D. G. Priest; treasurer, Geo. P. Osborn; first lieutenant, A. G. Collins; second lieutenant, H. A. Thayer. Bugler and color bearer not yet elected. The club received six new members at the meeting, adopted a uniform, and an active and progressive programme was outlined for the coming season.

CUMMINSVILLE, O. — Northside Wheelmen. Officers: President, George A. Blinn; captain, George H. Williamson; secretary and treasurer, W. H. McGarry. A club-house has been secured on the Hamilton pike, just a nice run from Cumminsville.

TERRE HAUTE, IND. — Terre Haute Club: President, F. Probst; captain, C. Bauer; secretary, A. Hulman; treasurer, F. Fisbeck.

WOODSTOCK, CAN. — Woodstock Club: President, A. M. Scott; captain, W. A. Karn; secretary and treasurer, S. Woodroofe.

THE gymnasium of the Massachusetts Bicycle Club is neatly fitted up, and classes meet Monday, Wednesday and Friday evenings under the direction of John T. Williams and N. Ethier. The club has received an invitation to visit the Turnverein gymnasium Tuesday evening, 13 April, when the first class will give an exhibition.

THE Gloucester Club will reorganize this spring, and don a uniform of dark green.

THE Lowell Bicycle Club held its annual meeting Thursday evening. It now numbers forty members, and will have its first club run on Fast day.

THE Massachusetts and other clubs have called moonlight runs to attend the Waltham Club's entertainment and dance 15 April.

THE Cambridge club-house scheme seems to have come to a stand-still. Nine members have pledged an aggregate of $1,800, but the line is apparently drawn at that sum.

UPWARDS of $800 has already been raised towards the erection of a dwelling for the Clinton Wheel Club of Northampton.

THE Harlem Wheelmen's Club has been incorporated. The managers are : William H. De Graaf, William Dutcher, Edwin C. Parker, George S. Curtis, Clinton H. Leggett, and F. A. Ryer.

THE regular monthly meeting of the Massachusetts Bicycle Club was held Tuesday evening at the clubhouse. There was a large attendance, and owing to the sickness of the president, Col. T. W. Higginson, vice-president Albert A. Parsons presided. Seventeen new names were added to the membership rolls. At the last meeting of the club, it was voted to establish the offices of captain and lieutenant of tricyclists; and John T. Williams was elected to the captaincy and W. W. Palen lieutenant. The election for librarian resulted in the choice of Mr. Colbath.

THE PATH.

JOHN S. PRINCE is to engage with Woodside and Eck in a series of races at the Washington rink, Minneapolis, Minn., ten miles, 10 April; twenty-five miles, 14 April; fifty miles, 17 April.

THE first race in the Prince-Neilson contest will take place on the Lynn track on 31 May, and the second will occur one week later.

THE Lynn Cycle Track Association has been incorporated, and starts off with a capital of $3,500. Contractor Tuttle, who took the job of building the track at $1,280, began work last week, and it will be finished without doubt for the races which are to take place 31 May. The association has invited the Essex County league to hold its regular meet in Lynn, 31 May, which they probably will, and on that occasion some very exciting races will take place. Neilson and Prince are also expected to be present.

THE BUTCHER CYCLOMETER COMPANY has decided to make the Kangaroo cyclometer the leading one for 1886. This has but three figures to count, and consequently measures but 999 miles, but it saves a few wheels, is lighter and has proved to be the best working instrument the company has put out. They are now filling orders.

W. W. STALL has just added twelve new 1886 Experts, 50 to 54-inch, to his letting department. These have ball pedals, cowhorn bars, Kirkpatrick saddle, and are finished in nickel and enamel. He will also have a number of new tricycles and tandems on hire.

STALL'S PONY CRIPPER is approaching completion. It will be a little beauty. It has 36-inch wheels with tangent spokes, and will weigh less than fifty pounds. We shall envy Mrs. Stall so light and pretty a mount.

W. B. EVERETT & Co. are letting a good many machines these warm days. Mr. Gilligan is in charge of this department, and is located on Berkeley street, directly opposite the main warerooms. The Apollo bicycle is winning a name for itself, and many of our leading wheelmen are adopting it for their season's mount.

A. P. MERRILL & Co. have a good thing in their bicycle lock. It is light and easily adjusted. Carried in the tool bag, it is easily taken out and does not get entangled with the tools.

THE KEYSTONE SADDLE has an inviting look. It is made by C. M. Clarke, of Pittsburgh, Penn., an old rider who knows what a good saddle is. Mr. L. D. Munger pronounces the saddle the best he ever rode upon, and his evidence is worth a good deal.

WM. READ & SON have issued their new catalogue. It comes from the press of the Springfield Printing Company, and has an ornamental cover. The new tricycle has not yet arrived, but is expected daily.

S. T. CLARK & Co. have issued a very neat circular describing the Rapid bicycle, and enclosing a fine engraving of the machine on heavy paper.

The first edition of 5,000 copies of the Agents Guide or How to sell the Rudge Bicycles and Tricycles, has become exhausted.

Another edition is in press.

MISCELLANEOUS

Advertisements will be inserted in this column for one cent a word, including heading and address; but no advertisement will be taken for less than twenty-five cents.

BICYCLES AND TRICYCLES. — 125 shop-worn and second-hand wheels now on exhibition. Stock constantly changing; no price list; correspondence and inspection invited; open Saturday evenings. BUTMAN & CO., Scollay Square, Oriental Building.

BICYCLES AND TRICYCLES. — Bargains fo cash; wheels not sold on instalments nor rented BUTMAN & CO., 89 Court Street.

BICYCLES AND TRICYCLES. — Specialty in furnishing new wheels for exchange. BUTMAN & CO., Scollay Square, Oriental Building.

BICYCLES. — Fair prices and spot cash paid for desirable second-hand wheels. BUTMAN & CO., 89 Court Street.

BICYCLES AND TRICYCLES received on consignment; no charges made when goods are furnished in exchange. BUTMAN & CO., Oriental Building, 89 Court Street.

THE AMERICAN CHAMPION, CHALLENGE, SAFETY AND IDEAL.

COLUMBIA SPECIALTIES

THE COLUMBIA DOUBLE-GRIP BALL-PEDAL.

All Bearing Parts Drop-Forged and Case-Hardened.

Interchangeable in Every Part.

Light and Easy Running.

The BEST PEDAL Ever Offered Wheelmen.

Balls Gauged $\frac{1}{1000}$ of an Inch.

Non-Slipping Elastic Double-Grip Rubbers.

Strong Tapered Shaft.

PRICE, NICKELLED, $10.00.

The BEST PEDAL Ever Offered Wheelmen.

THE KIRKPATRICK SADDLE.

IMPROVED IN LEATHER AND IN FRONT SPRING.   ADJUSTABLE FORE-AND-AFT.   FIT ANY STYLE OF BICYCLE.

PRICE, $6.00.

THE COLUMBIA SWING SPRING. | THE KNOUS ADJUSTABLE SADDLE.

Relieves both Fore-and-Aft and Vertical Vibration, while giving a Perfectly Steady Seat.

PRICE, NICKELLED, $5.00.

Has Elastic Spring Frame, Highest Grade Leather, and Adjustable Clip, allowing either end of the Saddle to be elevated; Adjustable at the Rear without removing from the Machine.

PRICE, $4.00.

CATALOGUE SENT FREE.

THE POPE MFG. CO.

597 WASHINGTON STREET, BOSTON.

Branch Houses: 12 Warren Street, New York; 115 Wabash Avenue, Chicago.

The Cycle.

VOL. I., No. 3. BOSTON, MASS., 16 APRIL, 1886. FIVE CENTS.

The Coventry Machinists' Co.'s New Tricycle for 1886.

THE MARLBORO' CLUB—Automatic Steerer.
ADMIRABLY ADAPTED FOR LADIES.
SEND FOR CATALOGUE TO 289 COLUMBUS AVENUE, BOSTON.

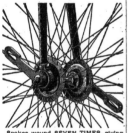

THE CYCLE

PUBLISHED EVERY FRIDAY BY ABBOT BASSETT, 22 SCHOOL ST., ROOM 19.

VOL. I.   BOSTON, MASS., 16 APRIL, 1886.   No. 3.

TERMS OF SUBSCRIPTION.

One Year, by mail, post-paid.........................$1.50
Three Copies in one order.............................. 3.00
Club Subscriptions...................................... 1.00
Six Months.. .90
Single Copies... .05

Specimen Copies free.

ABBOT BASSETT   .   .   .   .   .   .   EDITOR
W. I. HARRIS   .   .   EDITORIAL CONTRIBUTOR

A. MUDGE & SON, PRINTERS, 24 FRANKLIN ST., BOSTON.

All communications should be sent in not later than
Tuesday, to insure insertion the same week.

Entered at the Post-office as second-class mail matter.

THE Racing Board has taken final action
in the case of several of the promateurs, and
in the current number of the *Bulletin* the
following riders are declared to be professionals, and are expelled from the League:
A. O. McGarrett, W. A. Rhodes, F. F.
Ives, E. P. Burnham, W. A. Rowe, George
M. Hendee, A. A. McCurdy, W. H. Huntley, F. W. Westervelt, William A. Taylor,
Asa S. Wendell. The following parties are
suspended from the track until 30 May for
violation of Rule H.: W. N. Winans, D.
Edgar Hunter, John Williams, L. D. Munger, John Illston, F. D. Palmer. The following have had their cases dismissed: C.
E. Kluge, Joe Powell, George E. Weber, C.
O. Danforth, and A. B. Rich.

THE Board has accepted, in good faith,
the statements that have come from the
makers and dealers, and will, at present, require no more evidece from the suspected
parties.

IT has been stated by the promoters of
several prospective racing events, that the
suspected parties will be allowed to enter
races, the action of the League notwithstanding. We do not doubt that many of the
suspends will enter and race, for they cannot free themselves from charges made by
the Racing Board, and it matters little to
them whether they are made professionals
now or at the end of their time limit, but it
will make a serious difference to any amateur who may compete against them.

WE do not know that it is worth our
while to remind wheelmen that the mile
ground is in danger of being invaded by the
cable railroad, nor to spur them forward to

active endeavor in opposition to the scheme.
A hearing will soon be had at the State
House, and we hope to see a good represen-
tation of wheelmen present to oppose it.

SOME friend of Thomas Stevens ought to
get hold of the new editor of *Outing* and
demonstrate to him that the round-the-
world bicycle journey began at Oakland,
Cal., *two* years ago (22 April, 1884). An
editorial note to the Stevens story in the
March *Outing* gave "April, 1885," as the
date; and now the April issue repeats the
blunder by presenting a picture labelled,
"The start around the world a year ago."

A CYCLING RETROSPECT.

BY JAM SATIS.

PART III.

BEFORE taking up the subject of tandems
and sociables, I want to say a few words
about some of the methods of driving and
steering which have been tried from time to
time on single tricycles.

The oldest method of driving was by
levers or treadles which were connected by
rods directly to a double-cranked axle. This
gave great power, but the motion was tiring
and monotonous, and was finally superseded
almost entirely by rotary motion. Rotary
motion requires no description, but there
were several ways of communicating it to
the wheels. Chains were the favorite and
are now universally used on all tricycles,
but the earlier patterns of chains were not
well adapted to their purpose, and gear-
wheels and coupling rods with universal
joints and three-throw cranks were all tried
in place of them. Chains were lighter and
more convenient and caused so much less
friction that they finally took the place of
all other means of communicating the driving power from the crank-shaft to the
wheels. The patterns of chain now in use
are fine pieces of workmanship, and cause
less friction than any belt or gearing that
has been tried.

There are, it is true, a few machines which
drive direct from the axle, the rider being
seated high to enable him to do this; and
there are a few others which, like the "Rob
Roy," have the crank geared directly to the
axle, without the use of a chain or intermediate gear, but these machines are not very
much used. The Otto is the only machine
which used bands instead of chains, and the
improved Otto has a chain.

The old machines of 1881 were mostly
single drivers and rear-steerers, but the
rear-steerers were found too unsteady in
their steering when going down hill, and
were liable to throw the rider out if stopped
suddenly, so they fell into disfavor, and
front-steerers gradually superseded them.

Single drivers had the disadvantage of
being hard to drive on rough or sticky
roads, and were liable to upset if there was
not a good deal of weight kept on the steering wheel; and an improvement was made
on rear-steerers of that pattern by using two
large wheels in front, each driven by a separate chain. This necessitated the use of
clutches to enable the outer wheel to run
faster than the inner on curves. There are,
to-day, some riders who prefer clutches to a
balance-gear, because the rider can use his
put them into the best position for power
when starting by a mere touch of his foot.
Against this there is the inability to back-
pedal, and what is more serious, the fact
that all the driving must be done by the
inner wheel on curves, which makes it difficult to start a machine on a curve.

These various drawbacks finally convinced makers and riders that a perfect tricycle must have a balance-gear, and must
be a front-steerer.

Starley's was the first, and remains one
of the best balance-gears in use to-day. Described briefly, it consists of a pair of bevel
gears placed facing each other, each being
attached firmly to the main axle of the machine. The axle is divided in the middle,
just between the two gears, and the chain
wheel is placed between them. To the
inside of the rim of the chain wheel is pivoted on a short stud a smaller bevel gear,
which exactly gears with the other two.
When the chain wheel is turned, the small
gear is carried with it, and if both driving-
wheels are free to turn, it drags them round
with it, not turning on its own axis at all.
If, on the other hand, one driving-wheel
runs slower than the other, its bevel gear
becomes a fulcrum against which the teeth
of the small gear press, and the small gear
is accordingly turned, on its axis and forces
round the freely moving wheel proportion-
ately faster. By this arrangement, the
outer wheel is always the driver on a curve,
and both wheels drive alike when running
straight, either backward or forward. There
are now many modifications of this gear, of
which Humber's and Pritchard's are, perhaps, the neatest.

The Sparkbrook, or, as it was originally
called, the National, accomplishes the same
result by using in the middle of the axle a
pair of pinions carried on short arms connected to the axle by universal joints. The
whole contrivance is enclosed in an elliptical box, and when the machine is running
straight, the box and its contents merely revolve with the axle, but when the machine
is going round a curve, the pinions roll
round each other, the arms which carry
them turning on bearings in the box. This
was the first and, for several years, the only
balance-gear placed exactly in the middle of
the axle, whereby each wheel got an equal
share of the driving power.

There have been various attempts to use

clutches on the axle, which would be thrown out of gear automatically when the steering handle was turned; also a balance-gear has been made by means of an endless screw and a worm wheel, the screw being attached to the axle and the worm wheel to the hub, if I remember right; but the fault of all such contrivances is that they either cause too much friction, or do not work promptly enough, or get out of order too easily. I do not see how anything can be simpler and more effective than the gears now used, as it is not possible to use less than three pinions, or else two pinions and two universal joints, as in the Sparkbrook gear.

There is another method of driving tricycles, which does not seem to me to have received all the attention it deserves, and that is lever motion without the use of cranks, as in the "Star" bicycle and the original "Victor" tricycle.

This method has one advantage over any rotary motion, and that is the easy change from speed to power, and then there is also the ability to take any length of stroke without loss of power, as there are no "dead centres."

The chief objection that I can see to this form of lever driving, is that on a machine as heavy as an average tricycle, more exertion is required on the rider's part than on a "Facile" or "Star" bicycle, and where much force has to be exerted, an up-and-down movement is more fatiguing than a rotary motion, whereby all the muscles of the leg are used instead of merely one set.

About steering, there is not much to say. A few of the earlier machines were steered like a "bath chair," with a long rod fastened to the top of the steering wheel and ending in a cross handle held by the rider; to turn, it was only necessary to swing the handle to one side or the other, and the machine turned accordingly. This was clumsy and unsteady, and was entirely superseded—except on children's machines and on a few eccentric contrivances—by the "rack and pinion," which is the commonest form of steering to-day. Of bicycle steerers, the "Leicester Safety" was the forerunner, but the "Cripper" and "Ranelagh Club" were the first successful ones of the usual pattern. The Humber was, I believe, the first that had a handle-bar, but steering with both front wheels, it stands in a class by itself. Also, the Coventry Rotary stands alone in being the only successful single-driving tricycle now on the market. On smooth, hard roads, the Coventry is one of the fastest machines, and its fore-and-aft steering—the two small wheels being about five feet apart—makes it one of the steadiest steerers, having none of the tendency to spin round on one wheel that most single drivers manifest.

The "Humber" and "Cripper" share between them the distinction of being the most extensively copied machines in the world.

In my next, I want to give a very short sketch of sociables and tandems

FROM A FEMININE POINT OF VIEW.

ONE who signs herself "Polly" has sent me a sample of the light-weight ladies' cloth which the League of wheelmen has adopted, and with it comes a letter for the CYCLE, giving particulars regarding the goods. I am more than well pleased with the cloth, for I believe it will prove durable, and it will make up well. The color is dark enough to make grease spots inconspicuous, and it is withal a desirable thing.

NEVERTHELESS, I doubt if it will be generally adopted, for there are many lady riders who have to consider the cost of a riding suit, and these will be able to find something less expensive. I got material for a suit a few days ago, which, though it is not so good as the League cloth, is good enough, and it cost much less. For fifty cents a yard I purchased a light gray home-spun goods that will last me through two seasons at least. I do not wish it understood that I consider the price asked for the League cloth to be exorbitant, for I do not. It is well worth the money, and those who can afford to have what they want, will find the purchase of it an economical one.

I GOT six yards and a half, and this will make me a skirt with full back breadths, no drapery, foot trimming, a basque having somewhat the effect of a jacket, and helmet hat.

I CAN'T say that I like the idea of a uniform for the ladies, nor do I believe that one will be adopted with any considerable degree of unanimity. Ladies aim at more individuality in their dress than men do. They have to. A style of garment that would be becoming to one figure would look very badly on another. They have to suit their clothes to circumstances, and no established form would satisfy all. I can't believe that the uniform idea will be a popular one.

MRS. STALL is to be congratulated on the possession of a machine that weighs no more than fifty pounds, and a handle-bar steerer at that. We have heard that forty inches is the smallest practical wheel for a tricycle, and yet I can believe that she will show as good results from a thirty-six inch wheel. Why, they tell me that the races at Springfield last year were run on tricycles with thirty-six inch wheels, and surely if men can ride such wheels on the track, the ladies can ride them on the good roads around Boston.

MRS. STALL'S machine has another good thing, and that is a pedal that is not adjustable. It is fixed to the crank, and there is no such thing as a loose pedal possible. I think I have had more trouble with loose pedals than with everything else on the machine put together. I remember one ride that I had last fall when I was put to no little annoyance by a loose pedal. I was many miles from home when the thing happened, and a mile at least from any house. Searching my tool-bag, I found it to be wrenchless and I was forced to use my fingers to turn the nut up. But fingers are not the best wrench, and an application of them carried me not more than a thousand feet. I came at last to where some men were digging a well in a field, and I called upon them for assistance. They had no wrench, but one of them offered to go to a farmhouse a quarter of a mile off and borrow one. This I would not at first hear to, but with great gallantry he insisted and started on his errand. The others, considering no doubt that they had a guest, stopped all work and gathered around to inspect the tricycle, and I was deluged with questions, which I answered to the best of my ability. After a time came back the wrench-bearer with one at least a yard long over his shoulder, and in his hand a can of milk. "I told them," said he, "that I wanted a wrench to fix a lady's bicycle, and they told me here was the wrench and here was some milk, because them bicycle men always want a drink." It is needless to say that the great wrench tightened the nut, and that I enjoyed the milk; and with many thanks to my wayside benefactors, I rode off under a storm of good wishes and three cheers given with a will.

SOMEWHERE on the water, on the wharf, or in a warehouse is a machine that I shall ride the coming season. I think it will be a good one, and I feel that it will suit me, for I was consulted, and some of my ideas were adopted by the designers. It is to be made by the makers of the Invincible machines, and I am told that they stand in the front rank of manufacturers. I hope to be able to speak a good word for it later.

DAISIE.

W. A. ROWE, the amateur champion, accepted an invitation from the Lynn club for a road ride last week. As Rowe had done no road riding for nearly a year, the Lynn cracks thought that they would make it hot for Billy. Accordingly they set out a great pace, and for the first ten miles went faster than many of them had ever gone before. Rowe said nothing, but managed to push along in the rear. As soon as they started on the return, however, he woke up, and with scarcely an effort flew by the line and took the lead just as some of them were beginning to congratulate themselves on the neat way they had "done up" the champion. Such a pace as he set going home they never knew before, and never again do they want such a "scorch." — Globe.

THE Iowa Division L. A. W. held a meeting at Ottumwa, 27 March. It was decided to hold the fall meeting at Spirit Lake at the conclusion of the annual tour, which starts from Des Moines, 9 August. The tour will give the members one hundred and eighty-four miles of wheel riding, and twenty-seven miles will be on the train. On Sunday afternoon, at the Baker House, the Ottumwa Club banqueted the visiting wheelmen in a magnificent manner, the Rev. A. C. Stilson, of the Episcopal Church, presiding at one end of the long, well laden table, and Chief Consul Charles D. Howell at the other, the latter's right and left bowers being two of Ottumwa's most charming young ladies, Misses Vic. Palister and Edith Turner.

CYCLING is enjoying a large boom in Pittsburg, Penn., this spring. The Keystones participated in the first club run last week, accompanied by the Messrs. Bidwell on a tandem, who made the pace so hot for the rest of the riders, and left them so far behind, that they have not put in their appearance at the clubhouse since.

THE SEASON'S MOUNT.

EARLY in the springtime,
    While the March winds blow,
Cyclers' thoughts are wandering
    Sadly to and fro;
And he ever sitteth,
    Studying in zeal,
On one question ever, —
    "What 's this season's wheel? "

" Shall it be a Victor,
    Elegant of mold,
Or shall others test it,
    Till a season old?
Will a Rudge best suit me?
    Popular and light ;
It has proved its virtue,
    Winning in the fight.

" Winner of great races
    Is the Royal Mail;
With strong feet on pedals,
    Likely to prevail.
Elegant in contour
    Is the Sanspareil,
Run by a good cycler,
    Surely will do well."

" Not so light as these are;
    Others are as good
On the common roadway,
    By the hill and wood;
Stanch and very faithful
    Are Expert and Club,
Challenge, too, and Harvard,
    Vie in many a rub."

" Wheels that cost less money
    Than the ten I name,
Do their duty truly,
    Winning less of fame ;
And a host called Safety
    (Strange and wondrous thing)
To the halting cycler
    Many choices bring."

" Kangaroo, not pretty,
    In design or name,
Rudge, and Club, and Challenge,
    Likewise seeking fame.
Is the best the Facile?
    Or the pony Star?
I am wholly non-plussed,
    When I seek so far."   L. H. P.

THE CHOICE.

Sequel to " The Season's Mount."

IN the early springtime,
    While 't was bleak and cold,
Cyclers' thoughts were turning
    To a subject old.
Then they did consider,
    With increasing zeal,
Which held most of merit
    For one's private wheel.

Since the early springtime,
    Months have flown away ;
Crowded with their pleasures,
    Seeming scarce a day.
Wonderful proceedings
    Now are in the past ;
But the records 'established
    Destined are to last.

Through the dale and valley,
    By the travelled road,
Tourists gay have eased them
    Of care's weary load.
Joy and strength and gladness
    To the riders bring,
Their fair steeds of metal,
    Fleet as feathered wing.

Nearer no solution
    Is the question old :
Which wheel is the best one
    For the rider bold?
But methinks the finest
    For good men to budge
Is the stanch and graceful
    Wheel, " Light Roadster Rudge."

All makes have their uses ;
    Each as best they claim ;
But for good, strong riders,
    None like that I name.
I would not decry one ;
    Many makes are fine ;
But for speed and pleasure
    None surpasses mine.

" Give me back my old wheel;
    It is strong and true :
It has failed me never,
    And I love it too!
I will never sell it,
    While it 's firm and strong ;
More than friend, 't is faithful;
    I will keep it long ! "   L. H. P.

THE LADIES' COLUMBIA TWO-TRACK TRICYCLE.

THE Pope Manufacturing Co. announces a new triangle for ladies' use, which is many pounds lighter than the two-track machine of 1885, though it follows the same lines. The machine is described in brief as follows: Two 44-inch driving-wheels, and one 20-inch front steering-wheel, ⅞-inch tires, crescent felloes, 56 and 24 full-tangent spokes, No. 14 steel wire; tubular steel frame; dwarf steering head; Columbia lock steering; adjustable spade handles; cradle-spring; Columbia " double-grip " rubber ball-pedals; central crank and chain-driving gear; bicycle adjustable cranks; Columbia double-band brake; wire dress-guard. Width of track, 31 inches; total width, 36 inches. Finish, enamel and nickel tips. Weight, 70 pounds. Price, $175; or, with parallel pedals, $170. The tubing is much lighter than that of the ordinary two-track, and considerable weight has been saved in reducing the driving-wheels. The steering mechanism is new and is thus described: The rod running from the steering-head bracket-arm connects at its upper arm by a ball-and-socket joint with the long arm of a lever pivoted at its angle to the frame. The short arm of the lever is linked to a nut running on a quick thread upon the steering-handle upright, and receives its motion up or down by the turning of the handle to the right or left. While the action is positive and quick, without being over-sensitive, the steering-wheel cannot be deflected from its course, even when the hand is removed. The joints being adjustable for wear, all rattling is obviated. The Ewart chain is used in the machine. The company has the sole right to use this chain on cycles when made of drop-forgings. This chain can be taken apart link by link by simply turning them back at right angles. The machine will soon be on view, when we hope to have more to say about it.

THE COLUMBIA SAFETY.

ANOTHER new machine is the Columbia Safety. It is built on the well-known Kangaroo lines, and has 42-inch and 20-inch wheels geared to 52¼ inches. The cut gives a good idea of the machine and shows its lines. The rubbers are large, being 1 and ⅛ inch. The bracket carrying the lower sprocket-wheel and crank moves readily up and down on the fork-extension when its binding bolt is loosened, and a perfect adjustment is rendered especially easy by the use of the improved Ewart detachable-link chain. The machine has ball bearings all around, and sells for $140, or $135 with parallel pedals. This machine has not yet been placed on the floor, but it is daily expected, and orders are now being booked.

CHICAGO CHATTERINGS.

YOUR bright-looking, newsy new-comer is beginning to attract attention out here, and before long you will have strong supporters in the great West. Thinking a few random notes may be of some interest, I let fly my pencil to let you understand that, although in a new field of labor, you are not forgotten. Everybody admires courage and conviction in man, especially when he has the courage to carry out his convictions. Such a man I take the editor of the CYCLE to be, and therefore we expect to see it, as per your inaugural address, on top.

J. O. Blake sends greeting, and says he intends to boom things this coming season. Mark my word, also: J. O. will be our next State consul, as the riders want no other. Mr. Blake is not a politician in any sense of the word, and makes no efforts, pulls no wires, but will " get there all the same."

Major Wm. Durell, the manager of the elegant Columbia warerooms, is getting to be much liked in Chicago. He is affable and courteous, two very necessary attributes for a successful agent.

Dropping in yesterday to see Van Sicklen, our crack amateur Racing Board man, captain of the Chicago Club, president of the Bicycle Track Association, and the Lord knows what else. I found Van seated on a huge pile of best Scotch tweeds. As the gentleman had not been seen around the cycling haunts for several weeks (except his club, of course), I commenced to probe for his remarkable quietude. Says Van, " No, you will not catch me away from my business again, until the latter part of July, when my vacation time arrives. Then you can expect to find me hard at work training, for a few weeks, and I will go to Springfield to prepare for some races in the annual tourney." Van Sicklen does private work at his home in Englewood each evening, which accounts for his non-appearance.

We are expecting to have a Star boom here this season. Maynard, the local agent, is well liked, and is a worker from away back.

The affairs of the Bicycle Track Association are in a very unsettled state, and there seems to be no Moses at present to lead the way out of the difficulty. The track is made, and will be a good one, when the corners are raised a little, but is not as yet paid for; but what matters that, as A. G. Spalding is wealthy, and can afford to wait for the cash. There is some talk of professional races with pool selling on the grounds this summer.

Sam Miles, editor of the *Sporting Journal*, of this city, is an enthusiastic bicyclist, and proposes to get a tandem for his seven-teen-year-old wife and himself. Mr. Miles is an able writer on cycling events, and greets your paper heartily.

I was in St. Louis (Mo.) the other day, and saw Whittaker, or " Whit," as the boys call him; also saw Percy Stone, Hal Greenwood, Ladish, editor *American Wheelman*, Louis Leeders, and, in fact, all of them. They are a lot of hustlers in the "future great," and are very enthusiastic over their great fifty-mile road race.   SPOKES.

SINGER'S ✛ STRAIGHT ✛ STEERER.

Corey's Hill climbed by E. P. BURNHAM and Mr. Crocker each on first trial, on an S. S. S., geared to 52. The highest gear that ever reached the summit.

40-inch Drivers, 22-inch Steerer, easy running, light and rigid.

The fastest coaster and best hill climber yet built.

Illustrated Catalogue Free.

Send for Second-Hand List.

SINGER'S PATENT AXLE.

FIRST 1886 RECORDS,

APOLLO,

25 Miles by L. D. MUNGER at New Orleans, on March 27, in 1h. 24m. 46⅘s.

50 Miles on April 2, in 3h. 2m. 34s.

THE LATTER A WORLD'S RECORD.

W. B. EVERETT & CO., Sole U. S. Agt's, 6 and 8 Berkeley St., BOSTON.

STODDARD, LOVERING & CO.

AMONG the bicycle houses in this country there is probably not one better known than the house of Messrs. Stoddard, Lovering & Co., of 152 Congress street, Boston, Mass.

Their first connection with the bicycle business was in 1878, in the importation of various makes of cycles for other firms, but, recognizing the great future of the wheel business for this country, they subsequently secured the sole agency for the United States of Messrs. Singer & Co., of Coventry, England. Their chief importations for some time were from this firm, and later on they took up the sale of machines made by Messrs. Rudge & Co. Feeling, however, that they could not serve two·makers and give satisfaction to both, they decided to retain the agency of Messrs. Rudge & Co., and relinquish that of Messrs. Singer & Co. At that date their warehouse was at No. 10 Milk street, Boston, which soon became one of the centres of the bicycle industry. As their business increased rapidly, they were forced to remove to more commodious quarters, Nos. 152 to 158 Congress street, a glance at which is sufficient to show that they have taken up the bicycle business in earnest, fully believing in the great future of the wheel.

It has been the aim and intention of Messrs. Stoddard, Lovering & Co. to place on the market machines that will stand and make a name for themselves, and while several makers have copied a number of its principal features, the Rudge still maintains its enviable reputation, and its agents are to be congratulated on its increasing popularity. — *Wheelmen's Gazette.*

CONNECTICUT WHEEL NOTES.

THE CYCLE came, and is liked, and we hope to see the new paper soon preside up there where there is always room.

GLAD to see one lady, at least, enlisted with us, wheeling away for that upper district, and that she will post us on the points of that new tricycle, and the ladies' league suits.

WE shall put forth strenuous efforts to see Boston in May, and Daisie on her Tri.

ABOUT all the rain must be down, for it has poured here for the last two days, more or less, and The Solitary Club's Facile is about the only wheel seen on the streets.

THE Club has ridden on all but fourteen days of the past winter, on the regular trip between studio and residence, two miles, besides taking frequent runs on business to Greenwich and Mianus, five and three miles away.

THE Star fever has broken out among members of the Stamford (Ct.) Wheel Club, and more of a variety in wheels will be shown this season.

PRESIDENT MICHAELLS, of the latter club, has been very sick, but is out again.

RACING and the coming Meet are much discussed subjects during the floody weather that has prevailed hereabouts recently, and the verdict in regard to the Meet is, there will be some energetic pushing of pedals eastward toward the last of May.

HAS any one a cycling map of Boston, and the various routes to points of interest near by? How convenient a good map of the kind would be to us Nutmegers, and many others who have never yet seen "the city of the sinuous streets."

OUR neighbor, Greenwich, has recently organized a "Leisure Hour Wheel Club," with about a dozen members. They are in a hilly section, and Put's Hill, alone, will be good coasting, if they will risk the ·hard heads, which have been the cause of many a hard head-er, and will shake up a beginner at a lively rate.

AWAITING the advent of good wheeling and the next copy of the CYCLE, we are, fraternally,   STAMFORD.

THE CAPITAL CLUB'S HOUSE.

THE plans for the clubhouse of the Capital Club, of Washington, D. C., are now completed. The house will be three stories in height, and the main entrance will be through an archway that extends the whole width of the structure. A visitor will find himself, after passing under the arch, in a tiled vestibule seventeen feet wide and five feet deep. At his left, forming that side of the vestibule, he will discover the main entrance to the house, or the door into the hall. In front he will find the double sliding doors making a passageway six feet wide into the wheelroom. Entering the house by this. the visitor is in the main wheelroom, wherein bicycles and tricycles, temporarily housed, will be accommodated. This room is nineteen feet wide by twenty-eight feet long, and will accommodate in racks between thirty and forty bicycles, besides tricycles, sociables, and tandems. In cases of emergency, many_more machines may be received. By a simple, yet ingenious device, the racks to contain the wheels are flush with the floor and wainscoting, yet they hold the machines more firmly than any other arrangement now in use. The floor of this room, as indeed the entire first floor, will be concreted. At the rear of the wheelroom proper, approached through a passageway nine by nine feet, on the right of which is a room containing the heating

apparatus, and on the left steps leading to a landing on the main stairway of the house, the visitor will enter the machine room, nineteen feet four inches wide and twenty feet long, wherein will be stored such cycles as are left in the house for long periods, and where will be found a work bench and tools for such repairs as the owners are able to make on their machines. This room will be amply lighted by three windows. The rear of the first floor will be occupied by a locker room, with capacity for sixty lockers, and a bath-room, with all the approved ablutionary facilities.

The hall referred to above is five feet wide and twenty-four feet long, extending along the north side of the wheelroom, from which it will be separated by an ornamental partition, half wainscoting and half lattice work. At its foot rise five steps of the stairway to a landing, from which a large east window satisfactorily lights both stairs and hall. The stairway thence proceeds, with a turn to the right, to the second floor. Ascending, the visitor is received into what is the unique feature of the house's interior, and which dominates the plan of every floor, — a central hallway extending across the house from north to south, and nine and one half feet wide. Its north end is occupied by the stairway just ascended, which, with one more turn around an ornamental newel, mounts to the third floor. Its south end is graced by a mantel and grate surmounted by a mirror and flanked by divans. Sliding doors ten feet wide open on either side, one pair into the drawing-room in front, the other into the meeting-room behind. The drawing-room is twenty-four and one half feet wide by thirty feet long, with a twelve-foot ceiling. Its north side contains an open grate and mantel-piece, and it is lighted by the bay window, seventeen feet long, containing six windows. The bay window will contain upholstered window seats. The meeting-room, in the rear of the central hall, is nineteen feet four inches ·wide and twenty-four feet six inches long, lighted by three windows on the north. The remaining room on the second floor is the library·and committee room, ten feet by nineteen feet four inches, extending across the east end of the building and lighted from the east and north. The third floor is divided into a billiard room in front, whose dimensions are twenty-four feet and a half, by thirty feet and a half, with an eleven-foot ceiling, and well lighted by four large windows ; a card and committee room twelve by fifteen feet, and two rooms, each eleven by fifteen feet, to be rented to club members. The spacious attic will be fitted up for the accommodation of the janitor and for storage.

The wood work of the interior will be of white pine and cypress, with hard oil finish. The wheelrooms, meeting and committee rooms, billiard room, halls, stairways, and closets will be wainscoted. All the plumbing and sewerage will be contained in a detached wing in the rear of the main building, easily accessible from every floor, and the house will be heated by steam, and provided with electric bells. It is boasted by the club that this will be the most convenient bicycle clubhouse in the country. Three members of the building committee have visited and carefully examined the two leading clubhouses, that of the Massachusetts Club, at

Boston, and the Maryland Club's house, at Baltimore, and an attempt is made to avoid the errors in building into which those clubs are believed to have fallen. The stone for the first story of the new clubhouse is now being cut.

CONTRIBUTORS' CLUB

GEARING UP.

Editor of the Cycle : — I 've done it! Geared up! after due consideration and advice from various correspondents and — experts. Something I was bound to change or smash things. So I hied me to S-tall, and found that champion with what seemed a cross between an elevator shaft and an organ pipe sticking out of his coat pocket. O, yes, he could fix it! and down he squatted to examine and figure. It took a deal, for I wanted the thing to run easier as well as swifter.

And, lo! behold my 40-inch trike geared to forty-eight; my four and a half crank lengthened to six ; my round-shouldered handles raised with adjustable telescopic shafts, and the whole transformed from a pewter-hued nickel to a blackness that Ethiop would envy. And thus equipped, gayly I sailed away homeward in the teeth of the gale and dust most smothering. Easy? Well, not exactly! Swift? Well, not quite! Paint in the joints is the rheumatism of triking, and overmuch paint had I. The hills seemed steep as ever, and Harrison avenue quite as sad a thoroughfare. Sadder, since then 't was paved with good, but now with bad intentions, and the homeward way was not a joy forever. Behold my wheel to-day! It rains, and the wind is never weary ; mud lines the streets, but in my hall a four-year-old doth play, and finds the wheels of a tricycle on a jack to be a most noble whirligig. So he twirls away, and it serves a double purpose, in that the joints will limber up before roads harden, and it keeps him out of mischief. Am I not fortunate? Still, I see possibilities. I have my expectations. And when the streets are ridable again, you 'll hear from me, and I yet think in plans of thanksgiving.

　　　　　　　　　J. PARKE STREET.

P. S. — Lest S-tall should tell of it, I 'll here confess that in our figuring I innocently asked should I not change cyclometers for a geared wheel, and great was the laugh on me.

LEAGUE CLOTH.

Editor of the Cycle : — In your issue of last week, I notice an inquiry from your well-known contributor, "Daisie," concerning the ladies' L. A. W. cloth, and enclose a sample of the same for her inspection. Your lady readers may be interested to know what it is precisely the same in appearance as the regular League cloth ; only about one third as heavy, being a dark, mixed brown ladies' cloth, very firmly and closely woven; it is a yard and a half wide, and sells for $1.00 per yard. My sample was furnished by Messrs. Browning, King & Co., of 406 Broome street, New York City, who state that it is very extensively used by the lady members of the League, of whom, I understand, there are a hundred or so.

As to its wearing qualities, I am unable to state from personal experience, but feel quite sure it must wear very well indeed, as it is much firmer in texture than my present suit, which has gone through one season of hard wear, and evidently intends to last through another.

I also wish that some of the ladies would give us an idea of the cut of the L. A. W. uniform, if there is a prescribed uniform for the ladies.　　　　　　　POLLY.

CYCLETS

THE CYCLER'S LOVE.

To look at my love is a treat, sir,
Her figure is awfully neat, sir,
Like me, she is somewhat " *petite,*" sir,
But she 'll never become Mrs. Y.

In style she eclipses the Graces,
She has travelled and seen many places,
But I will not deny it, — she laces,
And she 'll never become Mrs. Y.

She is always, you 'll find, on the " go," sir,
She was never inclined to be slow, sir,
And I do n't think that she would say " no, sir,"
If I asked her to be Mrs. Y.

I have fallen in love with this rover,
When near her, I think I 'm in clover,
We do n't fight, but she oft " throws me over,"
And she 'll never become Mrs. Y.

Who my love is, perhaps you can guess, sir,
'T is my wheel, I will have to confess, sir,
And as she won't say " no, sir," nor " yes, sir,"
She 'll never become Mrs. Y.
　　　　　　　　　ARTHUR YOUNG.
　　　　　　　　　— *Spectator.*

THE Canadian Wheelman's Association has adopted a uniform of Halifax tweed. It is a very strong and durable cloth of a yellowish-brown color, and a whole suit will cost but $8.00.

THE Boston Club wants more room, and a larger house is among the probabilities of the future.

ELMER WHITNEY's tour to northern Maine will send twenty-five men into the wilds of that State which lie north of Bangor, the starting-point:

CHARLES E. PRATT, ESQ., was in New York, Monday, counting the ballots for League officers.

A HARTFORD young man named Thayer has started for San Francisco on a bicycle. The great advantage of the vehicle for such a journey is that it never fails. When it cannot be ridden it can be pushed. — *Record.*

THIS is what some members of Parliament were doing on the day of Gladstone's great speech : " At 2 P. M., a number of members who had hatted their seats, were promenading on the private terrace on the river side of the palace to pass away the time. Three of them were riding on a tricycle at a rapid rate, when suddenly it collapsed, throwing the occupants violently to the ground, and hurting them all more or less. J. P. O'Brien, Nationalist member from North Tipperary, was quite seriously injured, but he stoutly maintained his determination to be present if he had to wait till daylight and be carried into the lobby on a stretcher."

IT was wheelman's day at the Boscobel last Sunday. There sat down to dinner generous delegations from the following clubs : Allston, Brookline, Cambridge, Charlestown, Chelsea, Everett, Gloucester, Massachusetts, Maverick, Medford, Salem, and Somerville. It was nothing less than a monster reunion of bicyclists. Nothing of the kind was anticipated. The first of the spring Sunday runs was voted a grand success. Lynn bicyclers also took a run out of town, and found the roads in excellent condition.

THE Massachusetts Club, at their last meeting, created a new office, that of librarian, and intend forming a cycle library. Mr. D. W. Colbath was unanimously chosen for the office, and the club is fortunate in securing a gentleman who possesses so many qualifications for the success of the undertaking. Mr. Colbath has been with Cupples, Upham & Co. for many years at the old corner.

MR. ATKINS will soon issue the 1886 edition of his handy little road book.

THE new year book of the Massachusetts Bicycle Club will be ready in a few days.

THE professionals are going to make one more effort to organize. They expect to meet in St. Louis or Chicago shortly, when they will form an association and adopt rules. The rules of the National Trotting Association will be adopted, and these include the flying start.

THE young men of Montreal are to form a club to be called the " Victoria." The limit of age in the present club is eighteen years, and there are many young men who are below this in years and yet active riders.

FRANK P. PRIALL, who was editor of the *Wheel* under Jenkins. has again joined the forces of that paper.

MR. D. M. KURTZ has left the *Cyclist and Athlete*, and J. W. Barnes will in future wield the editorial pen.

A CERTIFICATE of incorporation of the *Cyclist* Printing Company was filed in the N. Y. County Clerk's office, 3 April. The capital stock is $5,000, of which one fifth is paid up. The incorporators are Charles H. Townsend, Theodore Hamson, Edwin R. Collins, and James W. Barnes.

THE District of Columbia Division League of American Wheelmen, at a meeting in Washington last week, elected A. P. Crenshaw, Jr., vice-president, and George M. Myers, secretary and treasurer. A committee of three was appointed to place the League stencil markings at all necessary places throughout the district.

THE Suffolk Club, South Boston, is arranging for a three days' tour along the north shore. It proposes to reach Salem 5 July, in order to witness the celebration. Already there are numerous inquiries regarding it, and it will undoubtedly prove a success. Captain Haynes will have charge of the arrangements.

BOSTON men will be glad to hear that extensive repairs are being made on Washington street, Dorchester, from Bowdoin street to Norfolk street.

W. C. STAHL, of the Massachusetts Bicycle Club, who went South on account of

Adjustment in Height in Front.   Adjustment in Length.   A Comfortable Coasting Plate.
Adjustment in Height in Rear.   Adjustment in Width.   A Bifurcated Seat.

THE LILLIBRIDGE SADDLE

Is the only one having any of these Points; is the only one that can be changed in Shape or Position at all; is the BEST and
CHEAPEST; is adapted to all makes of Bicycles. Special Styles for the Safeties and Star.

Price, Nickelled, $5.00. Price of Coiled Spring, with Straps, etc., for Old Saddles, 75 Cts.

FREEMAN LILLIBRIDGE, Rockford, Ill.

THE BOSTON BICYCLE SHOE.

The Perfect Shoe for Cycling.

Hand-sewed, hand-made, first-quality stock and warranted in every respect. Every pair of our No. 1 Boston Sporting Shoes is marked inside, "Boston: Strickland & Pierce, Hand-Sewed," and is stamped "Patent" on the bottom. None others are Genuine. Bicycle, Base Ball, Sprint Running, Pedestrian, Gymnasium, La Crosse and other shoes. Prices and rules for self-measurement sent on application.

STRICKLAND & PIERCE,

156 and 156½ Summer Street,

BOSTON.

STAR BICYCLES.

SAFE, PRACTICAL and FAST.

NO HEADERS OR DANGEROUS FALLS.

Best Road Record for 50 and 100 Miles.
World's Safety Records from 1 to 20 Miles.
First American Machine to make more than 20 Miles
within the Hour.
Three L. A. W. Championships for 1885.
Won all Hill Climbing Contests, both as to Speed
and Grade.
Won all the First Premiums, when in Competition,
since 1881.

NEW CATALOGUE READY.

H. B. SMITH MACHINE CO·

Smithville, Bur. Co., N. J.

RAILROAD STRIKES

don't affect the man who owns an **INVINCIBLE** wheel. *He* can ride where others walk. Light, strong, rigid, fitted with patent Double-Section Hollow Rims and full inch rubbers. They are the perfection of wheel manufacture. Send for catalogue or description of the Bicycle, Safety Bicycle, Single Tricycle (two or three track, or automatic), and tandem. New front-steering tandem has 42-inch drivers, 26-inch front wheel, and either rider can steer. Imported only by

GEO. D. GIDEON,

No. 6 South Broad Street, Philadelphia, Pa.

ill health, feels much improved, having added about ten pounds to his weight.

STEWART C. MILLER, of the Massachusetts Club, has left for a several months' trip through the Southern States.

ONE of the new traveller tandem tricycles is on exhibition at the salesrooms of W. B. Everett & Co.

A RUN of the Boston Club members who ride tricycles, will be made to the Faneuil House next Saturday evening. The start will be made at five o'clock, and supper will be served at six. The tricycle division of the club will be reorganized and new officers elected.

THE Columbia prize cup will probably make its last appearance in public at the Lynn races. Under the terms of competition for it, the cup will become the property of the rider who makes twenty miles in the hour, and that is not a difficult task for some of the men who will enter for it.

CAPTAIN PECK and Messrs. Atkins and Abl, of the Massachusetts Club, are arranging for a hare and hounds run, to occur some time in May.

THE dramatic association of the Massachusetts Bicycle Club contemplates giving a sketch from "The Jilt" at the clubhouse very soon.

THERE will be a series of great international races in Berlin during the month of August, on the occasion of the third annual congress of the German Cyclists' Union. The chief events will be a great ten-kilometres contest for the amateur championship of Europe. A challenge cup, value £25, is presented by the proprietor of Der Radfahrer. A similar contest, but over five kilometres, will also be held for tricyclists, the winner to take the tricycle championship of Europe. Entries close four weeks before the races, and an entrance fee of ten cents is required.

THE Essex County wheelmen will unite with the Lynn cyclists in the race meeting of 31 May.

THE road houses were well patronized on Sunday, and they do say that there was a good demand for hamamelis to cure the aching joints of the riders that were out for the first time.

ON Saturday night the Massachusetts club will ride to the Cambridge gymnasium, there to witness an athletic exhibition. Next week there will be a number of moonlight runs. On the evening of 18 April they will ride to Newton, where they will be met by the Nonantum Cycling Club, and escorted to its rooms, where a musical entertainment will be provided. The next night there will be a moonlight run about Chestnut Hill Reservoir. Many other runs are also being planned, and it is likely that one of several days' duration will be held later.

THE Somerville Cycle Club has arranged for the following runs: 11 April, Lynn; 18 April, through the Newtons, dining at the Faneuil House, Brighton; 25 April, Salem; 2 May, South Natick; 9 May, Lowell; 16 May, Brockton; 23 May, Lynn via Wakefield.

PRESIDENT H. S. KENDALL, of the Dorchester Club, has resigned the presidency of the club, as he leaves for the West in a

short time. He was made an honorary member of the club at the last meeting. George L. Haynes has been elected president in his stead.

THE show of bicycles which is to be given at the Meet, under the auspices of the Boston Club, is bound to be a success. Space is being taken up rapidly. Beside the exhibition of cycles, there will be a display of sporting goods of all kinds. The exhibition will open on Thursday, the 27th, the first day of the Meet, at twelve o'clock, and remain open until ten o'clock that night. The hours on the other days will be the same. Arrangements have been made for issuing season tickets admitting wheelmen in uniform for twenty-five cents. The regular price of season tickets will be fifty cents, and single admission twenty-five cents. Entertainments of some kind will be given on each evening of the exhibition.

MR. FRED B. CARPENTER, of Boston, formerly captain of the Crescent Club, was united in marriage last week to Miss Alice Beebe, of Wakefield. The ceremony was performed at the Beebe mansion on Main street, Wakefield, in the presence of a large circle of relatives and friends. A reception was subsequently held. The wedding gifts were very handsome.

CALIFORNIA wheelmen have been climbing Presidio Hill for a medal offered by Ingleside.

A NEW wheel club was so far organized in Chelsea last week as to get a committee at work on a constitution. Chelsea will be heard from.

A PRETTY maiden, pink and pert ;
A 'cyclist with a navy shirt ;
A wonder if the maid will flirt ;
A little exhibition spurt ! —
A sudden tumble in the dirt ! —
An angry maid with spattered skirt —
A shock that could n't help but hurt —
A 'cyclist with disaster girt !   — Tid Bits.

THE Iowa wheelmen held a banquet on Sunday afternoon, and had for a guest a prominent clergyman. The wheelmen might have done a worse thing. We have seen clubs at dinner when disorder and undue hilarity prevailed. We can believe that the Iowa banquet was carried out in an orderly manner.

CANADA wants a man. So says the Canadian Wheelman. They have yet developed no remarkably fast rider, and they find their association ignored by those who are proposing a world's championship. We hope the fast man will be forthcoming, and that he will give fame, not notoriety, to the land he hails from.

STROLLING into the Hollis-street theatre the other evening, we counted in the audience no less than ten well-known wheelmen. There are many pretty girls in the chorus of "Nanon."

H. S. TIBBS, ESQ., who has done so much for the cause of athletics in Montreal, and who has been particularly interested in bicycling, has resigned the position of secretary and treasurer of the National Athletic Association for a more lucrative one. On his retirement he was presented with an address and a purse of $250 by his fellow club members. He was the founder of the Montreal Bicycle Club, and one of the pioneer wheelmen of Canada. He is at present chief consul of the C. T. C. in Canada.

THE Troy Club has purchased the Coliseum in that city for $13,462.20, and they will at once set about converting the structure into a clubhouse.

THE Springfield Club has voted $100 towards the League Meet fund.

NEW YORK wheelmen have voted against the division organ scheme.

THE Sporting Life, of Philadelphia, one of the cleanest and best sporting papers on our list, comes to us this week in an enlarged form. It celebrates its fourth anniversary by enlarging, and a new Scott perfecting press has been added to its plant.

AT the last meeting of the Road Racing Association, Mr. Wetmore, who waxed eloquent, threw down a challenge on behalf of the Elizabeth Wheelmen for a team race of eight men to run fifty miles, open to any club. He hardly closed his mouth for the last time before Mr. Austin, on behalf of the King's County Wheelmen, took him up and accepted it. They now announce that their team will embrace A. B. Rich, Ed Pettus, H. J. Hall, Jr., E. W. Valentine, A. C. D. Loucks, M. L. Bridgeman, L. Weber, and an unknown. The date of the contest has not been set, but I presume it will be quite in the future, as the Elizabeth Wheelmen will require considerable training in order to get the better of such a team as above mentioned. — Jenkins, in Sporting Life.

A MEETING will be called shortly by the Inter-State Bicycle Association to make arrangements for the coming season to be held in Youngstown. The Association is now composed of Youngstown, Warren, Greenville, New Castle, and Sharon. The club at Beaver Falls has expressed a desire to join it, and it will probably be included in the membership at the next meeting. Pittsburg also wishes to get in, but members object, as it would make the circuit too large. Arrangements will be made for a meeting on 4 July, when it is expected every club will be admitted.

SPALDING'S New York house having taken the agency for the Star, it is now to be pushed vigorously in New York City, Jersey City, and Long Island. C. E. Kluge will be Spalding's salesman for the machine.

A TOURING committee has been appointed by the Missouri division to confer with the Illinois division about the compiling of a joint handbook for the two States, with maps.

THE Binghamton Club proposes to have at least one hundred and fifty visiting wheelmen there on 4 July next, the occasion of their annual parade and tournament.

THE Kenton Wheel Club, of Dayton, Ky., are arranging a tour through Ohio during July. Wheelmen in Kentucky, Ohio, and Indiana will be invited to join.

WORK on the new clubhouse of the Citizens' Club, N.Y., is rapidly progressing, and carpenters and masons are rapidly converting a dwelling-house into a comfortable clubhouse. It is expected that all the alterations will be completed about the 20th of this month, and the club will then take quiet possession, probably waiting until fall before formally celebrating their removal.

THE CLUB.

[WITH a view to obtaining a complete list of clubs with the officers elect, we will ask the secretary of each and every club in America to send us on a postal card a list of the principal officers after the following formula:—
Boston, Mass. Massachusetts Club. Officers elected 1 January, 1886: President, Col. T. W. Higginson; captain, A. D. Peck, Jr.; secretary, F. Alcott Pratt, 3 Somerset street; treasurer, E. R. Benson, 597 Washington street.]

LAWRENCE, MASS. — Lawrence Club annual meeting and election of officers, 5 April. President, Dr. Partridge; vice-president, E. A. Dean; secretary, William L. Reed; treasurer, Francis Cogswell; captain, Alonzo M. Tracy; first lieutenant, Frank W. Downing; second lieutenant, Harry Keep; club committee, Dr. Partridge, A. M. Tracy, William L. Reed, John F. Finn, Fred L. Leighton, J. Ed. Aldred.

MACON, GA. — Macon Club election. President, Dr. N. G. Gewiner; captain, John C. Flynn; secretary and treasurer, Chas. Guernsey.

CLEVELAND, OHIO. — Star Club. President, H. E. Chubb; secretary and treasurer, William Woodruff; captain, Walter S. Collins; first lieutenant, Robert Ruck; second lieutenant, Joseph Hatch.

ATLANTA, GA. — Atlanta Club. The officers are: President, J. P. Hodge; captain, R. L. Cooney; guide, Edward F. Chalfant; secretary and treasurer, F. Thatcher.

PHILIPSBURG, PENN. — Mountain Wheel Club: President, Neil Davis; captain, C. B. Holly; secretary and treasurer, T. J. Lee.

MONTREAL, CAN. — Annual meeting 8 April. Officers elected: President, J. D. Miller; captain, H. Joyce; secretary, R. F. Smith; treasurer, R. Lloyd. The secretary read an account of the year's doings, it being shown that there were seventy-eight riders; the largest distance ridden was one hundred and three miles. The number of rides compared most favorably with any previous year. The highest individual mileage was seven hundred and forty miles, the highest in the history of the club. The average attendance of riders was close to

the mark. The year's work was altogether most satisfactory. The retirement, through an accident, of Capt. McCaw was regretted. Up to that time he led the mileage, and had not missed a ride. The coming meeting of the C. W. A. in Montreal was referred to, and the hope expressed that the club would sufficiently recognize its importance.

WATERBURY, CONN. — Officers elected 5 March: President, Dr. Charles R. Upson; secretary and treasurer, N. C. Ovaitt; captain, L. A. White; lieutenant, R. R. Bird; bugler, W. D. Hall; standard bearer, S. J. Wells; club committee, Dr. Charles R. Upson, L. A. White, H. M. Acheson, L. S. White.

BROOKLYN, N. Y. The seventh annual meeting of the Brooklyn Club was held on Tuesday evening, 6th instant. Seven new members were admitted, thus swelling the list to fifty-one. The club, one of the oldest in the States, and the pioneer wheeling body of the City of Churches, is in a most prosperous condition, with a sound treasury and unbounded enthusiasm, which will show itself in the coming riding season. The following officers were elected for 1886–1887: President, Albert B. Barkman; vice-president, Isaac B. Potter; secretary, Hermann H. Koop, Jr.; treasurer, Howard E. Raymond; captain, Louis W. Slocum; first lieutenant, Frank B. Jones; second lieutenant, Howard Spelman; surgeon, Dr. A. C. Brush; color-bearer, William R. Snedeker; bugler, Benj. J. Kellum; trustees, F. B. Hawkins, W. W. Campbell, T. C. Snedeker, and Wm. I. Ticknor.

TROY, N. Y. — Trojan Wheelmen. Officers elected 7 April: President, C. E. Betts; vice-president, A. W. Ross; secretary, R. C. Marshall; treasurer, C. E. Wilson; captain, J. R. Torrance; first lieutenant, George S. Contie; second lieutenant, W. T. Lynd; bugler, F. E. Derrick; colors, T. T. Chase; surgeon, George E. Harder, M. D.

THE PATH.

MINNEAPOLIS, MINN., April 10. — The ten-mile bicycle race between W. M. Wood-

side and J. S. Prince, that occurred here to-night in the Washington rink, was one of the bicycle events of the season. Woodside has been considered almost invincible, and consequently betting was in his favor. Both were mounted on Columbia light roadsters. Prince's machine not having arrived, he was obliged to take one which was too small, and Woodside got the lead at the start and held it for five miles, when Prince took it away, leading for two miles. Woodside then made a beautiful spurt that placed him ahead. For the next mile the race was a hot one, both riding very fast. Two laps before the finish, Prince, who was riding close to Woodside's little wheel, made a grand effort, and, spurting past, closed the race with a lead of twenty feet. Woodside claimed a foul by Prince not giving him the pole when requested to do so, but the referee would not allow the claim, Prince stating that, probably owing to the noise occasioned by the great applause, he did not hear Woodside speak. The time for five miles was 15m. 21⅘s., and ten miles, 31m. 28½s.

MISS ELSA VON BLUMEN won the twenty-seven-hour race at the Fitzhugh rink, Rochester, last week. She rode 105 miles while Beldon traveled 102 miles.

AT the Eureka rink in Louisville, Ky., J. D. Macaulay won a two-mile race over John Adams, and Horace Beddo the slow race. Freidberg and Wells entertained the crowd with their inimitable trick riding.

THE TRADE.

· GEO. D. GIDEON, of Philadelphia, is pushing the Invincible machines to the front, a place they are well fitted to occupy. One of the Invincible tandems is now on view at the Pope Manufacturing Company's warerooms, and single tricycles will soon be seen in Boston. Mr. Smith, of the Surrey Machinists' Company, is one of the best designers in England, and anything that comes from his hands may be depended upon as first-class.

THE firm of Zacharias & Smith is dissolved, and Howard A. Smith & Co. succeed it. Mr. Smith has associated with

him Mr. A. M. Hall, a well-known wheelman of Newark. Mr. Zacharias will remain with the firm, and will have charge of the branch store at Orange.

THE largest bicycle establishment in Ohio, is that of A. W. Gump, at Dayton. Mr. Gump has worked up a very large business, and sends goods to every State in the Union. He has in rear of his store a complete repair shop, fitted up especially for bicycles, and gets work sent in as far West as Nebraska. His nickel-plating plant turns out work that is fully equal to that of any in the trade. To prepare for the coming season's business, he has removed to the double rooms directly over his present store. The second floor will be devoted to a show-room, where will be shown over a hundred new and second-hand bicycles, single and double tricycles, lamps, bells, and everything pertaining to the bicycle business. The third floor will be devoted to riding purposes, where different sizes of wheels will be kept and instructions will be given to learners. The two-story brick repair shops in the rear will be refitted with new machinery.

GEO. W. ROUSE & SON, of Peoria, Ill., are among the largest cycle dealers of the West, and they are distributing a large quantity of cycles in that region. They are an honorable and fair-dealing house, and can be depended upon for good bargains.

MISCELLANEOUS

The Cycle.

Vol. I., No. 4.　　　BOSTON, MASS., 23 APRIL, 1886.　　　Five Cents.

The Coventry Machinists' Co.'s New Tricycle for 1886.

THE MARLBORO' CIUB—Automatic Steerer.

ADMIRABLY ADAPTED FOR LADIES.

THE

"AMERICAN CHAMPION,"

POSITIVELY

THE GREATEST TRIUMPH OF CYCLING MANUFACTURE IN AMERICA.

ENTIRELY MANUFACTURED IN AMERICA, with our own plant and on our own premises, and with every care to suit the TASTE and NEEDS of an AMERICAN WHEELMAN.

☞ *The first CHAMPION shipped won the World's Long-Distance Record at Minneapolis recently, Albert Schock making 1,009 miles and three laps in six days of 12 hours each, defeating Woodside by nearly 100 miles.*

BE SURE AND SEE IT BEFORE YOU DECIDE UPON YOUR MOUNT FOR 1886.

BECAUSE

Only the best and most carefully selected Steel is used, and the distribution of the metal is so appropriate that it is the

Most Durable Machine Yet Devised.

With our patent G. & J. ball bearings all over (to pedals also), it is the EASIEST RUNNING. With hollow forks and backbone fitted and brased to the patent G. & J. head and neck, it is the STRONGEST AND MOST RIGID. With the direct acting and thick-ended spoke, it is the EASIEST TO REPAIR and LEAST LIABLE TO BUCKLE.

BECAUSE

It has the patent G. & J. "Solid Comfort Saddle," which fits close to the backbone and is the

Most Comfortable to Ride.

It has the patent G. & J. Adjustable and RUBBER CAPPED STEP. It has all the advantages both of a compressed and a contractile rubber tire made from the best RED PARA RUBBER. It is the most graceful in its lines of any known bicycle, combining EQUAL STRENGTH and RIGIDITY.

WITH THE G. & J. HOLLOW, DETACHABLE AND ONE-PIECE COW-HORN HANDLE-BAR, IT IS

The Easiest to Steer, and there is Little Danger of the Handle-Bar Breaking.

IT IS SOLD AT A REASONABLE PRICE.

50-inch, Standard Finish (Enamel and Nickel), $102.50.

And numerous other reasons which prove conclusively that it is the MOST SATISFACTORY BICYCLE on the Market, as can be determined by applying for our NEW AND HANDSOMELY ILLUSTRATED 48-PAGE CATALOGUE, Containing a minute description of this Machine, and an extended line of

BICYCLES, TRICYCLES AND SUNDRIES.

GORMULLY & JEFFERY,

222 and 224 No. Franklin St., Chicago, Ill.

N. B,—WE ARE MANUFACTURING A NEW LINE OF LAMPS AND BELLS.   MENTION THIS PAPER.

THE CYCLE

PUBLISHED EVERY FRIDAY BY ABBOT BASSETT, 22 SCHOOL ST., ROOM 19.

VOL. I. BOSTON, MASS., 23 APRIL, 1886. No. 4.

TERMS OF SUBSCRIPTION.

One Year, by mail, post-paid...........................$1.50
Three Copies in one order.............................. 3.00
Club Subscriptions...................................... 1.00
Six Months.. .90
Single Copies... .05

Specimen Copies free.

ABBOT BASSETT . . . . . Editor
W. I. HARRIS . . Editorial Contributor

A. Mudge & Son, Printers, 24 Franklin St., Boston.

All communications should be sent in not later than
Tuesday, to insure insertion the same week.

Entered at the Post-office as second-class mail matter.

EXERCISE.

"THE best thing a man whose occupation
is a sedentary one can do is to devote a certain length of time every day at certain
hours to vigorous exercise — say half an
hour in the morning and half an hour at
night. This exercise should be persistent,
not desultory." Thus spoke Dr. Charles F.
Page, a distinguished physician and athletic
expert of Boston, a few days ago, when addressed relative to physical exercise in general. The great question, "What can these
people do to so modify the conditions of their
existence as to secure for themselves as
good a chance of enjoying life as is possessed by those who live outdoors" was not
considered unanswerable by Dr. Page, although pronounced a difficult one." Physical exercise is all that these people need;
so let them take it. Of course they will
say: Our occupations are such that we have
no time for exercise ; but that is all nonsense.
They find time for eating and sleeping. The
trouble is that they do not realize that exercise is as much a necessity as food or repose.
Better would it be for them to borrow an
hour from sleep and devote it to the gymnasium, or better still to exercise in the open
air. That exercise is a necessity is declared
by nature. We are animals, with animal
appetites, and are rather inclined, most of
us, to eat more than we can digest. Now,
when we exercise our muscles a great deal,
we require more food to repair waste and to
supply fuel; but if we sit still all day long,
and do not exert our muscles, there is but little waste and the digestive capacity is les-
sened. The gastric juice which dissolves
the food in the stomach is secreted by the
glands of the stomach just in proportion to

the amount of exercise taken — so much
work, so much juice. A given amount of
juice will dissolve just so much food and no
more, and if there is not juice enough to
dissolve the food, the latter will remain undigested. This undigested food remaining
in the stomach, and rotting there, causes a
congestion of the blood vessels in the mu-
cous membrane which lines that organ, and
induces what I may call a dyspeptic languor.
If this sort of thing becomes habitual, the
entire system may be clogged with the
excess of nutritive elements — food products
which, in the case of a person who took
plenty of exercise, would be absorbed and
used. Vigorous bodily exercise has very
much the effect upon the human system as
that produced upon a sponge by squeezing
it, — a cleansing effect, in a word. The con-
traction of the muscles squeezes out all
waste matter, and the activity of the organs
of elimination is stimulated. But if the
muscles are not sufficiently used the tissues
become fatty and watery. The eliminating
organs fail to convey the waste matter out of
the body, and the machine becoming clogged
up ceases to work properly. The undigested
food ferments and becomes poisonous.

The tendency of our modern civilization is
to multiply employments which necessitate
sedentary habits. In the universal race for
wealth, mental and bodily health are overlooked, and physical exercise is regarded as
a luxury rather than as a necessity. A large
part of the population of a metropolis is composed of workers who are compelled, in order
to gain a livelihood, to habitually set at defiance the laws of health. A person who
suffers from chronic melancholy is usually
a victim of indigestion, and the most amiable people in the world are frequently
transformed into fiends by dyspepsia. But
these are only the mental troubles which result from indigestion caused by insufficient
exercise. You might say that pretty nearly
the whole list of physical ailments come
under the same head. Gone-fatty degeneration of the heart and rheumatism are but
phases of indigestion. Three fourths of all
the sore throats spring from the same cause,
through sympathy with the stomach. There
is no use in attempting to give a list of the
diseases, from biliousness to insanity, which
are caused by want of exercise. Physical
vigor is the basis of morals and the chief
condition of permanent health. At a very

early period the Greeks had recognized the
fact that, with the advance of civilization and
civilized modes of life, a regular system of
bodily training must be substituted for the
lost opportunities of physical exercise which
nature affords to her children in their wild
life. Solon, the most celebrated of the famous scientific men, said that "it was impossible to repress luxury by legislation, but
that its influence might be counteracted by
athletic games which invigorate the body."
Dr. Page's expression of views seem to be
at this season of the year especially timely
and worth the consideration of students and
men and women of sedentary life. No form
of exercise yet brought forward has the
pleasurable qualities that the cycle presents.

———

THE man who writes a letter to the cycling
press or to the *Bulletin* in advocacy of some
particular reform in the detail of League
work does a great deal, for he helps to form
public opinion, but he would do much
more if he would only take the trouble to
bring his case properly before those who
have votes to cast. To amend the constitution or the by-laws of the League it
is necessary that notice be given of the
intention so to do in the official organ. It
is not enough to write a letter for publication in order to bring about reform. The
letter must be followed up by a definite statement of what is wanted put in the proper
way. This is said for the benefit of those
who wish to bring anything before the meeting in Boston.

———

ONE question in particular has been
talked over informally for a year or more.
It relates to the restoration of the privilege
to elect the executive officers of the League,
to the members. It has been discussed pro
and con in the columns of the cycling press,
but it has never been before those who can by
vote make a change in the established order
of things. The request of those who ask
for a restoration of the privilege is not an
unreasonable one, and we hope to see it
receive proper consideration.

———

IT has been finally settled, we believe, to
engage a large hall for the banquet at the
League Meet. The experience of the past
should call for careful consideration of this
question. Pleasant surroundings give zest

to the appetite. At Buffalo the banquet was spread in an unfinished store, whose white and barren walls gave little pleasure to the eye.. At Washington the surroundings were well enough, but the dinner was not what should have been expected for the price paid. New York has scored the best on record so far, and Boston should do her prettiest to beat that record. It can do this only by employing the same or similar methods. Let the committee arrange to have the dinner at one of the big hotels. At Young's, Parker's, the Vendome, or the Revere, not less than two hundred and fifty guests could be accommodated in the large dining-halls, and as many more could find room in the smaller halls. Let the tickets be limited to the number of seats, and none sold after a certain fixed time. We doubt if all the tickets would find takers. After the repast, the men from all the small halls could be gathered in the large hall to assist in the post-prandial exercises. It is a dreary prospect when we contemplate going to a banquet in a large barn-like structure to eat, in a desert of ugliness, off pine-board tables.

CHARLES LEE MYERS, athletic editor of Outing, makes the following statement in Outing : —

"In the matter of fellowship, club membership, medals, championship honors, and other numerous advantages, not only this, but every amateur is aware that, once having lost his amateur standing, he cannot regain it, the National Association refusing to reinstate any amateur who violates the amateur law."

Mr. Myers is not well informed. We can give him the names of a number of men that have been reinstated by the National Association.

IT has come to be the proper thing at this time for the cycling press to nominate candidates for the presidency of the League. We have no candidate to nominate. We have considered for a long while that Chief Consul Kirkpatrick was to be the man, and our opinion is endorsed by the hearty reception that has been given to his candidature. Kirk will have a walk-over, and he will grace the office.

A CYCLING RETROSPECT.
BY JAM SATIS.
PART IV.

SOCIABLES are, perhaps, the most comfortable form of cycles, but have never had justice done them, because makers tried to make machines which would be equally good as singles or doubles, instead of devoting themselves to making a perfect double. A sociable has to be built very strongly because of the great width which is

required. On a tandem a short axle is used, so that it is not so liable to bend or twist as the axle of a sociable, which measures generally four feet between the wheel hubs, while a tandem axle is only two feet three inches.

In consequence of the weight of the frame and wheels, a sociable, when turned into a single, is heavier than most riders like. Another objection to a convertible sociable is that it is apt to be less rigid as a double if it is easily converted. If it has stay rods and braces to counteract the want of rigidity, it is a tedious piece of work to convert it into a single. The Coventry Convertible is an exception to this rule, being fully rigid as a double, readily convertible, and handy and fast as a single, but it is better as a single than as a sociable, because the wheels are driven independently, consequently they do not work together as they would if a continuous axle and a balance-gear were used, and in turning corners this is a disadvantage.

The early forms of sociable were merely single tricycles widened so to carry two riders side by side, and each rider drove a wheel with a separate crank and chain or gears.

The Salvo was, until 1882, the only sociable fitted with a balance-gear and driven by a single crank and chain. The crank was fitted with two pairs of pedals, and ran right across the front of the frame, having a bearing at each end, but none in the middle.

The advantage of a balance-gear was that each rider conveyed his power to both wheels instead of only to one ; so whether the riders were equally strong or not, the machine would run straight, and on curves it was not necessary for either rider to change his rate of pedalling, as it was when each drove a separate wheel.

There were many excellent sociables which were not convertible, but all were heavy, and their great width confined their use to highways, because in a narrow country road it would be sometimes difficult to pass a vehicle. The width also makes it hard to find a place to keep a sociable. It will not go through a door less than five feet wide unless it is lifted through sideways, and its weight makes this very difficult.

The tandem has practically taken the place of the sociable almost entirely. It is faster and lighter, is readily convertible into a single — in most patterns at least — and is no wider than a single, though it may be a good deal longer.

There are three leading patterns of tandems: the Centaur, a three-wheeled front-steerer; the Humber, a three-wheeled double front-steerer; and the Club, a four-wheeled front-steerer. The Invincible was the leading pattern of rear-steerer, but this year the company has brought out a front-steerer, apparently finding that riders were rather afraid of rear-steering. I might add to the above list several varieties of automatic-steering, three-wheeled tandems, but I do not know how well riders will appreciate that form of steering on a tandem. It is open to the objection that the rider who sits in front must steer, and so, if one rider is a lady, she has to steer or else ride behind — unless some special attachment is added, as in the Cunard Convertible.

As to the merits of these different types, there is much to be said for each kind. If possible, it is better to have an unconvertible tandem, as the machine will generally be more rigid and run better than any convertible.

A good tandem should carry nearly all the weight on the axle of the driving-wheel, only just enough being kept on the small wheel to prevent it from slipping sideways.

If a machine is properly balanced as a double, it does not run so well in single form, because too much weight is then put on the small wheel One maker of a front-steerer obviates this by sliding the whole frame back toward the axle when the rear seat is removed, and thereby making the balance of the machine exactly the same in the single as in the tandem form. The Humber type of tandem is one of the easiest running, but care must be taken in applying the brake, or the front rider will be thrown out. For safety on all sorts of roads and up and down hill, either the Club or the Centaur type are preferable to the Humber, as the brake can be put on as hard and as suddenly as may be necessary, without danger of a "spill."

The Club pattern has a steering wheel in front and a trailing wheel behind, and is very steady and easy running, though it is a few pounds heavier than the Humber. It is one of the easiest machines to convert into a single, and unlike most convertibles of other patterns, it runs equally well as a single, the balance not being affected by taking off the rear attachment, to any appreciable extent. Of course this type is open to the objection of having an extra wheel by which some slight drag is caused.

I have made no attempt in this article to give a history of tandems, because there were so many patterns brought out together, and each possessing so many points of convenience or otherwise, that it would be necessary to give an account of each pattern in order to give any idea of the subject. I preferred, therefore, to take the types which seemed to me to embody the most desirable features in tandems, and to give such a description of them as would enable the reader to learn what their special peculiarities were. In this connection I should have stated that the former pattern of Centaur front-steerer was practically non-convertible. It was possible to make it into a very heavy single, but there was too much taking out bolts, disconnecting braces, and removing various parts, to make it an attractive job. The new pattern, which is central geared, looks much lighter, and, though the riders seem to be as far apart as before, the rear attachment can be readily taken off, leaving a very satisfactory single. As I have only seen a picture of the machine, I have very likely overrated the ease of converting it into a single, but there seems no doubt that as a tandem it is a great improvement on the old pattern.

Rear-steering tandems have never become sufficiently popular to be called "leading types," so I have passed them over entirely.

THE PARABLE OF THE SHRIEKER. .

Now, it came to pass, in the days of cycling, that there dwelt in the Land of the East Wind, a certain man called Conscience,

THE RUDGE
GENUINE HUMBER TANDEM,
(CONVERTIBLE.)

SOLE UNITED STATES AGENTS,

STODDARD, LOVERING & CO.

152 to 158 Congress Street, Boston, Mass.

EXAMINE

OUR

New Specialties

RUDGE HUMBER TANDEM. STODDARD, LOVERING &CO   BOSTON, MASS.

SEND FOR

1886

CATALOGUE.

Size of Wheels, 42 inches. Width, 40 inches.

This Tricycle is introduced to meet the great want for a Double Tricycle that shall combine speed and good hill-mounting properties with a minimum of labor. The Rudge "Genuine Humber" Convertible, as a single machine, is the fastest and lightest in the market; in converting it into a double, we only add 20 lbs. Riders will readily understand the extra pace and speed that can be attained when the fact is realized that two riders carry only 20 lbs. extra weight. The first trial over rough roads convinced us that no single tricyclist will be able to maintain the pace obtainable by two moderate riders on the Rudge "Genuine Humber" Tandem. The splendid steering of the Rudge "Genuine Humber" in its single form is really improved when converted into a Tandem with two riders. It is suitable for a lady and gentleman, or for two gentlemen.

N. Y. Headquarters, GEO. R. BIDWELL, 284 E. 60th Street.

because of his still small voice, and he said unto himself: "Thus far my days have been as naught, and the labor of my hands bringeth not shekels in sufficient abundance; I will therefore make unto myself an instrument of torture, a screaming, shrieking horror, the sound thereof being mightier than a twofold steam Caliope, pitched without and within to the key of XX sharp; and behold, the people will stand amazed, and my fame will spread throughout the length and breadth of the land, and the multitude will cry, 'Great is he who bloweth his own horn.'"

Now, when he had gotten unto himself much cordwood and round holes; the length thereof which would reach from city to city, also a knife of the kind called *John*, he straightway fell to work, and from the rising of the sun even to the going down of the same he wrought with much strength of sinew; and when the even was come it was finished, even the instrument and the polish thereof was great, and he called it the "shrieker," and the cyclers were pleased, and all cried with a loud voice, "Gimmeone!"

Now, it came to pass on the morning of the next day, there arose a murmur among the people, and a man called "Hoppi," surnamed Longtogs, was among the first to speak. And he said, "What grudge hast thou, O Conscience, against mankind in general, and my family in particular, that thou shouldst have done this thing. My wife bewaileth the day of her birth and refuseth to be comforted. My children are nowhere to be found, and the hired girl, though deaf, uttereth direful threats, albeit I blew your lung-tester but once." And Conscience answered and said, "Go to "Hoppi'"; much blowing hath made thee mad," and he went. And among those who stood afar off, was one Gideon, and Conscience called to him and said, "What hast thou to say, O Tandemon, of the short legs and long breath?" and Gideon answered, "Thou hast made a great mistake, O Conscience. Our fellow-beings are but mortal." Then said Conscience, "Gideon, thou hast no music in thy soul; thine ear is bent."

And again, when the even was come, the people in the market place rested from their labors, and the dusty wheeler sought his own vine and fig tree, there arose a mighty desire in the heart of Conscience, even a longing for vengeance on a wicked and froward people, who turned their ears to nickel plated idols, yea, verily, to the whistle of the watchman at the gate of the city. And his soul was vexed within him, and thus did Conscience commune with himself, "I will make a trumpet fifteen cubits long, and forty camel power, and voiced with the power of seventy times seven beasts of burden, yea, even they of the long ears, and I will bring confusion unto mine enemies, and all, they that mock; all this and much more will I do." And he betook himself to the inner court yard, and with much labor and weariness of spirit he toiled two days and a night, and the vehemence of his language astonished all those round about the place, yea, even the case hardened.

When the hour of noon was well nigh come, he refreshed himself with sundry cakes, baked after the manner of the Athenian women, and he arose and went forth to a retired place called the "District of

Slaughter," and he filled himself with a mighty breath, moreover he humped himself, and blew, and there was heard a sound as of the voice of the beast of the seven heads and ten horns; and when the people round about the country heard the sound they were sore afraid, and said one to the other, "Lo! Our Horn, the city is in danger, even of fire," and they sent forth their young men in haste, and when they were come unto the place of the great noise, a deep wonderment fell upon them, for they found naught except the fragments of a curiously wrought instrument of wood, and a pair of drums; which were of the ears — burst asunder.　　　　　　　MERRIE WHEELER.

NOTES OF A CYCLIST.

THE advent of the "safety" and tandem, and the improvement of the tricycle, have in a measure drawn the attention of wheelmen away from the "ordinary." I have no doubt, however, that many will return to it after the novelty of the newer machines has worn off. In England, they have seen more of the novelties than we have, and a permanent basis will be sooner reached. I notice that over there the discussion of the new types occasionally provokes a letter from a believer in the ordinary, and one of these letters I want to quote from. The comparison drawn is of the ordinary and the tricycle; but it may be practically regarded as ordinary *v.* the field.

THE writer says that he is "an ancient cyclist of some fifteen years' standing, and . . . can say that in five years, pretty continuous riding — chiefly town roads to and from my office, and for three months one journey per day in the dark — I have not had a single accident." Still he admits that the tricycle has the advantages of being safer and faster in the dark and in crowded streets, and can better carry awkward baggage.

THE advantages of the ordinary he states to be: (1) the essence of simplicity, and therefore cheap and easy to keep in order; (2) can, at a weight of forty pounds, be made strong and comfortable enough for anything; (3) the fastest and easiest machine to ride, with a peculiar sweeping glide that you don't seem to get in any other machine; it seems part of yourself, and ready to leap forward or bend aside at a wish; (4) in touring, the best view is obtained from it, it is the easiest to transport, and allows picking the way on rough roads; (5) will carry sufficient clothing. In conclusion he says, "that for the active it is pretty clear that the ordinary is still the best *all-round* machine, and is possessed of advantages which have of late years been rather overlooked."

IT is worth remembering that an ordinary of the best light roadster type is the lightest, easiest-running, fastest, and most perfectly manageable wheel built. It can be controlled perfectly by a good rider with feet alone, so that the hands can be free at any moment; and when the hands are in use, they hold very lightly. With knack and experience, an ordinary becomes a part of the rider as

no other can. Of course it takes time, patience, and some tact to acquire all this; but even if I never acquire it, I want to ride a wheel that offers me the greatest possibilities, if I will but improve them.

WHILE talking wheel, I want to have my say about tricycles, even at the risk of a little repetition. I don't believe that the model machine has yet been built. But I do believe that the experiments of the present season are a long step forward. I am curious to see whether the so-called "automatic" steering, now so popular, will continue in favor. Personally, I doubt if it can without sundry modifications. I must confess that I am inclined to believe that a good handle-bar steerer, not "automatic," with an easily accessible saddle, and suitable for either sex, is what we need.

IN your first number, "Hudson" asked about the tandem. I should like to see answers to his questions from wheelmen who have ridden, and believe in, each one of the types in the market, viz: The front-steerer (three-wheeled); the front-steerer (four-wheeled); the side-steerers; the rear-steerers; and the Humber type.

HERE are at least five different classes of tandems — five radically different types. Each class is represented by several makes. There is undoubtedly great diversity of opinion concerning their merits. Let some advocates of each type set forth their merits, and let others, who have ridden several types, draw comparisons. Such experience will undoubtedly be profitable and entertaining.

MY own experience with tandems runs back about fifteen months. My first one was a single-driving, double side-steerer. It did fairly well, but the strain was too great for the single driving wheel. Its good points were great steadiness down hill, and a narrow track which was very convenient on side paths. Its bad points were too much strain on the driver; difficulty of propulsion on soft roads; and danger in turning rapidly with the driver on the inside. It was not up to my demand, so after a good test I sold it.

I THEN settled upon a Humber as containing the most good points and the fewest bad ones. After riding it nearly fifteen hundred miles, I can honestly say that I believe that I am as nearly satisfied with it as I could be with any machine. Its worst point is a deficiency in brake power, or what practically amounts to the same thing, an inability to apply the brake *suddenly* on a hill on account of the danger of a sudden tip forward. If all Humber-type tandems were fitted with the spring arrangement that has been patented in England, allowing the front guard-wheel to run on the ground when descending hills, I think the machine would be about perfect. Its advantages are bicycle steering; an unequalled bowling motion, ease of propulsion, great speed, light weight, perfect comfort, fine hill climbing and a sensitiveness in obeying every motion equalled only by the ordinary bicycle. It

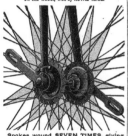

takes a little longer to get perfect control of a Humber than of a front-steerer; but as one approaches that condition of mastery, he delights the more in his mount. I suppose one can go on riding better with every trial, if one rides intelligently, and that to me is not a small attraction.   5678.

CONTRIBUTORS' CLUB

CYCLOS' COMMENTS.

Editor of the Cycle : — The first number of the CYCLE is at hand, and I hasten to extend a hearty welcome to the new-comer. I have not always agreed with you on cycling subjects, but I have always respected your honesty of purpose and your efforts to do what you believe to be justice, " even though the heavens should fall.'' And, by the way, in your late effort, as chairman of the Racing Board, to do justice to the dubious amateurs, you have stirred up the foundations of things so thoroughly that some of the brethren of weaker faith have been in a state of nervous dread lest the heavens were about to fall and crush you and the Racing Board and the L. A. W. generally. I don't see what grounds there are for abusing the Racing Board ; they have only done their plain duty under L. A. W. rules. Of course the L. A. W. rules, regulations, and definitions concerning amateurism and professionalism are antiquated, absurd, and unjust, but there they are, and as long as they are there, it is the plain duty of the Racing Board to enforce them. I notice that most of the kickers are the very ones who favored a stringent amateur rule They seem to be "in favor of the law, but *agin* its enforcement." Now *I* am " *agin* the law but in favor of its enforcement," till repealed or modified. But I don't believe in modifying it so as to let a lot of fellows pose as amateurs, and at the same time reap all the pecuniary advantages of professionalism. I don't see why a man that works for a bicycle dealer and teaches beginners to ride should not be an amateur just as well as his employer. I don't see why racing with or making pace for a professional *in public* should professionalize a cycler, when doing the same thing *in private* has no such effect ; and I don't see why a man who races for pay, or for a bicycle, or a big, fat prize, should *think* himself an amateur, or, if he is honest, be *willing* to be classed as one.

I am satisfied that outside of the great cities not one wheelman in ten cares a button about the refinements of the amateur rule, but would just as soon let into the League a man who had raced with a professional, or played polo with a professional, or raced for a five-dollar gold piece at the county fair, as they would the strictest amateur in the land. In fact, so long as it don't strike close home, they don't care enough about it to make their sentiments known, but simply regard it with tolerant contempt as a piece of dudery well enough for amateur athletes who travel on their shapes, and are therefore willing and even eager to appear in public, at race meetings, etc., in scanty tights, that seem as if they had been put on hot with a brush, so close do they fit, and so little do they comply with ordinary requirements of modesty,

not to say decency. On the other hand, there are honest fellows who hate sham, and their sympathies will be against any man who has been racing as an amateur while receiving pay for so doing. The rank and file will be down on these chaps, not because they have broken the amateur rule, but because they have, in effect, lied about and have been sailing under false colors. However, the recent action of the Racing Board has brought this question home to a good many who had before given it little thought, and the result will probably be a modification rather than an abrogation of the amateur rule.

I am sorry to see an organization formed for the promotion of road racing. If we desire to have *our* rights respected, we should be careful to respect the rights of others ; and I am satisfied that using the public highways as race tracks is not only unlawful but inequitable, and in the end can but work injury to the cause of cycling. I hope the League will put itself on record in this matter, and in favor of right and equity *by* cyclers as well as *for* cyclers.

I note that 5678 says : " It is a politic as well as a sensible and manly course to welcome ladies to club membership.'' Of course it is, and it may be added it is politic *because* it is sensible and manly.

There seems to be a strong sentiment developing in favor of electing some Western man president of the L. A. W. next time, and Kirkpatrick, of Ohio, seems to be a favorite. He is, perhaps, rather aggressive, but his management of the Ohio division has been practical and successful in a very marked degree, and he undoubtedly would make rights and privileges and touring the prominent features of his administration, and thereby greatly strengthen the League in numbers and influence. The question of who shall be our next president is an important one, and should be discussed fully and carefully in advance of election. To bring the matter before the League, I nominate Chief Consul Kirkpatrick, of Ohio. Will some brother please second the nomination ?   CYCLOS.

PUBLIC OPINION.

Editor of the Cycle: — Public opinion is a fickle jade, and he who reads her correctly is smart indeed. Until the action of the Racing Board was taken, I had supposed that there was a strong public sentiment in favor of the amateur law. Can it be that I am mistaken ? I look about me and I see the action of the Board condemned in the strongest terms by clubs, by individuals, and by the press. The cycling press seems to be divided. That part of it that backs up the Board does it in a feeble way ; the papers that condemn it are making a stir. From different parts of the country come reports that this or that club disapproves of the action of the Board. I have yet to see that one club has endorsed it. It has been said that the clubs of Philadelphia and Ohio and New York and Boston would endorse the action of the Board. I don't believe it. Not a word has been heard from them. If this was a popular movement, can it be supposed for a moment that such clubs as the Citizens', the Massachusetts, the Boston, the New York, or the Germantown would not

be heard ? Truth lies at the bottom of the well, but in this case it can be easily got at. There is no popular sentiment in favor of the amateur law, and those who were supposed to favor it are only looking on to see which side of the fence is the popular one before they jump.   E. M. G.

THE RULE WILL SATISFY.

Editor of the Cycle : — Being deeply interested in the cause of the makers' amateur, I have made it my business to get the opinion of several of them, and I have also talked with their friends about the rule which your correspondent " Barney '' proposes. I find that it will satisfy them, and that they will willingly stand in a class by themselves, as provided in the rule. Now, I hope to see the League members take a liberal view of this question, and give us some such rule as that proposed. If they ride a high horse and say "amateurs or professionals,'' there will be trouble, and an inevitable split in the League. The time has come for a compromise. No one wants to go back to the old order of things, and the suspended parties will not race as professionals.   LYNN.

A PROBLEM.

Editor of the Cycle: — Charlie Jones came into the club-room the other night, and gave us a problem which, though it appears plain enough on the surface, kept us in a discussion until the small hours. I want to give it to your readers and see what they say. Here it is : A sold a bicycle to B for $50 ; bought it back for $45, and again sold it for $65, how much did he gain by the transaction ? Will some expert bookkeeper give me the answer ?   CY.

TOUR OF THE SUFFOLK WHEEL CLUB.

THE Suffolk Wheel Club, of South Boston, is planning for a three days' tour along the North Shore for the coming summer, which promises to prove very enjoyable. The dates selected for the tour are 3, 4 and 5 July. The run will be under the command of Capt. Gideon Haynes, and the route, as laid out by him, is as follows : —

First Day. — Start from the corner of Berkeley street and Warren avenue at nine A. M. and ride *via* Beacon street to Alliston, to Cambridge, to Medford, to Malden, to Saugus, to Lynn, where a stop will be made and dinner served at the Boscobel Hotel at one o'clock. Distance for the first half day's riding, twenty-one miles. Starting again at 2.30 P. M., ride to Salem, Beverly, Beverly Farms, Manchester, and Magnolia to Gloucester, where the night will be passed at the Pavillion Hotel. Distance of day's riding, forty-two miles.

Second Day. — Leave hotel at nine A. M., for a ride around Cape Ann, visiting Rockport, Pigeon Cove, Bay View, and Annisquam, returning to hotel in time for dinner. Distance, sixteen miles. Starting again from the hotel, riding to Newburyport by way of Essex, Ipswich, and Rowley. The night will be passed at the Merrimac House. Distance about twenty miles, for the day thirty-six miles, or seventy-eight miles from Boston.

SINGER'S ✥ STRAIGHT ✥ STEERER.

Corey's Hill climbed by E. P. BURNHAM and Mr. Crocker each on first trial, on an S. S. S., geared to 52. The highest gear that ever reached the summit.

40-inch Drivers, 22-inch Steerer, easy running, light and rigid.

The fastest coaster and best hill climber yet built.

Illustrated Catalogue Free.

SINGER'S PATENT AXLE.

Send for Second-Hand List.

FIRST 1886 RECORDS,

APOLLO,

25 Miles by L. D. MUNGER, at New Orleans, on March 27, in 1h. 24m. 46⅘s.

50 Miles on April 2, in 3h. 2m. 34s.

THE LATTER A WORLD'S RECORD.

W. B. EVERETT & CO., Sole U. S. Agt's, 6 and 8 Berkeley St., BOSTON.

Third Day.— Returning, start from Newburyport at nine A. M., and ride through Newbury, Rowley, Ipswich, Hamilton, Wenham, Putnamvale, Danvers Plain, and Peabody to Salem, stopping at the Essex House for dinner. Distance, twenty-two miles. Starting at 2.30 P. M. for Boston, riding through Lynn, Saugus, Malden, Medford, Cambridge, Allston, and Beacon street to point of starting. Distance for the day, forty-five miles, or a total for the tour of one hundred and thirteen miles.

CHICAGO RECORDS.

THE following is the road riding as reported by the members of the Chicago Bicycle Club, for first three months of 1886: —

NAME.	JAN.	FEB.	MCH.	TOTAL.
Bishop	19	4	124	147
Conkling	15	90	—	105
Crennan	24	91	135	250
Ingalls	—	—	42½	42½
Kintz	50	76½	104	230½
Mehring	—	—	3	3
Miller	2	10	137	149
Ribolla, F. P.	15	—	99	114
Ribolla, S. A.	—	—	44	44
Ruhling, H. J.	—	—	70	70
Ruhling, A.	2	—	—	2
Shepherd	25	19	119	163
Stiles	10	—	—	10
Surbridge	75	110	108	293
Thorne, C. H.	20	5	114½	139½
Thorne, W. C.	20½	6	6½	90
Van Sicklen	129¼	17	36	152¼
	406¾	428½	1,169½	2,018¾

N. H. VAN SICKLEN, *Captain.*

THE FACILE.

THE Facile Company are experimentally making a few rear-driving geared machines of the Rover type in general, but having some distinctive features. The driving is by the usual Facile levers, working by a long connecting-rod, on a single chain wheel, placed not far beneath the top of the driving wheel. Four objects are thus effected: the chain-wheel is more out of reach of dust; the Facile short stroke is retained; foot-travel of thirty-two inches producing the same results as a travel of forty-four inches in a rotary path; the length of wheel-base is much reduced, lessening the clumsiness of the machine; and the saddle is only a little forward of the axle of the driver, this wheel also being much the larger of the two. The steering is similar to that of other machines of this class, but with a less rake in the front forks. "Automatic" steering is applied if wanted, and in this is part of the novelty. The crown or stem above the front fork slides vertically in a tube brazed to the head, and is surmounted by a spiral spring, also within the tube, this spring automatically adjusting itself to the rider's weight and reducing vibration. Next above the spring is a piston, and from the piston arms or pins project through slots in opposite sides of the tube. On each side of the neck is attached a "depressing fork" or cam, which passes outside the tube and rests in contact with the upper surface of the arms projecting from the piston as just described. When the steering-handles are turned to right or left, the head and tube move too, the projecting piston-arm is crowded upon the curved lower surface of one of the "depressing forks," the effect of this being to force the piston downward and compress the spring, which releases itself by throwing the wheel back to the straight line. This very effective arrangement was patented in England just before that of the Humber.

A new ball-bearing head for the steering of bicycles and tricycles has been produced by this company. Instead of ending in the usual spindle, the neck ends in a spindle of larger diameter, in which a hole is drilled completely through in a vertical direction; a recessed and hardened cup at top and bottom replaces the usual cones, and thus forms a bearing for the balls. Through this hole passes a pin with a fixed cone at one end and a movable one at the other, thus making an adjustable ball-bearing resembling those now used on back wheels and pedals. One of the cones on the pin is inserted in a socket at the bottom of the head, and fastened there against turning by a feather, a screw, or other suitable device; the other end of the pin is held in place, and the whole arrangement fastened in the fork by a recessed locking-nut turned down into the head from the top. The bearing may be adjusted while the neck is either in or out of its place in the fork; the neck may also be removed by taking out the fastening nut from the top without disturbing the balls. There is thus no danger of losing the latter out, and no difficulty in handling them.

A new mode of stringing wheels is also devised by this company. The hollow rim is preferably flat topped, something like an egg with a section cut off one end. The tire is either vulcanized on the rim or fixed on with a special chemical preparation; or the tire may be fastened on a thin metal band, which is itself pulled tight on the rim and its ends secured by screwing; the intent is that the tire be removable without disturbing the spokes. The flanges of the hub have a row of short projecting pegs; the inner side of the rims has also a flange. The spoke wire, which need not be larger than 22 or 20 BWG, is passed round a peg in the hub flange and returned to the rim at a tangent to the hub. Instead of attaching to the rim alternately on either side of a plane bisecting the rim in a vertical direction, the wires are in the same plane at the rim and are at its middle, this change removing the "rocking" tendency of laced spokes as heretofore. The ends of the spokes are attached to a screw, which passes transversely through the rim flange, and are tensioned by winding around this screw, the screw itself being turned and then fastened by a lock-nut. This method may be reversed and the tension be applied at the hub instead of the rim; or both ends of the wire may be fast at the rim, and tension may be applied by causing a roller to draw the looped end nearer to or farther from the centre of the wheel. One peg at the hub may carry four spokes. In lieu of lacing round the pegs, the spokes may be single, being attached by winding their ends around the pegs. This piano-like mode of stringing makes a true tangent wheel of great strength and marvellous lightness; a 54-inch wheel of this pattern has been exhibited, the spokes of which weigh only five ounces, or about *one sixteenth* as much as the spokes of a wheel as ordinarily constructed. Of course the same construction may be used with the solid rim.

CONNECTICUT WHEEL NOTES.

THE Stamford Wheel Club is admitting associate members, and its stock is away up and rising.

SEVERAL of our prominent business men are for the first time turning cyclers, and just now the Facile receives their attention.

THAT'S right, Miss Daisie, give us more of your experience on the roads, but do not forget your wrench and oil can. We tri-ed to think that front-page picture was of you, but that delayed trike item of yours puts us out again. "Boston in May, if it takes every spoke out of the hub!"

DELIGHTFUL moonlight runs home after the day's work fall to our lot lately, and are thoroughly enjoyed. Along much of the way we have charming views of Long Island Sound with its sail and steam craft, and the red, fiery eye of Stamford and other lights beyond that seem trying to outtwinkle and outshine the stars.

How refreshing again it is to inhale the salt-laden breeze as we speed away homeward on the regular evening run, after having wheeled down the railroad track, through the winter, because of bad roads.

They are good once more, and the old charm that is ever new, comes to us as in seasons past.

To-day, while gliding musingly along a country road, a great blue racer suddenly uncoiled himself by the roadside, and slid hurriedly away among some brush and through a hole in the stone wall. Our silent approach evidently surprised him, as it did a chattering red squirrel farther on, who stood head down, on a tree trunk, until we rode slowly past, as we listened to his animated discourse.

The birds favored us with their most cheery notes of welcome, and early as it is in the season, our outing was one of almost unmixed joy.

The Hartford to Denver, Col., tourist passed through here recently.

One vote by an old fogy here last fall prevented the graveling of a section of road that needs it very much. He will at least be bi-cotted, you can safely wager.

STAMFORD.

LEAGUE ENTERTAINMENT.

THE entertainment committee of the League has about perfected its programme, which is as follows: 27 May, a musical entertainment in Music Hall, by an orchestra of forty pieces. The musicians will be the best in the city, and the selections such as will meet popular favor. The music will be on the stage, and the floor will be occupied by tables and chairs. Light refreshments and cigars will be served. None but League members will be allowed on the floor, and they will be admitted free. 28 May, a minstrel entertainment in Music Hall, by the Jeffries and Oxford clubs with fifty men in the circle. In the second part of the entertainment, Prof. Eberhardt, of the German Turners' Association, will introduce a team from that association to give an exhibition on the horizontal bars, parallel

bars, and the Turners' horse. The Cadet Band Orchestra will appear this evening, also. Admission for League members, twenty-five cents ; reserved seats, fifty cents. All others will be charged twenty-five cents extra.

ST. LOUIS.

THE illuminated parade is already attracting the attention of the wheelmen, and already a number of designs for illuminating their cycles have been thought up by those who realize that they cannot begin work on the parade too soon. "The boys ought to appreciate the fine opportunity they have to distinguish themselves," said Mr. Jay L. Torrey, president of the Athletic Association. "The day we have set apart for them, 14 September, could not be better, I think. You see we intend to make that a great athletic week. The city will then be full of the arriving Knights Templar, and no better time could be selected to show the world the athletic associations of St. Louis. All the boating, turner, base-ball, gymnastic, and out-door sporting societies will be represented in a parade of some sort, and the wheelmen can readily see how well placed they are when they consider they have the honor of leading off with the first parade of the great carnival. They might also know that the carnival conference thought at first of joining them to another parade, until they learned of the magnitude of the cyclists' parade, and of how it was worth a night itself. The wheelmen can rest assured that they cannot be spared from athletic week, and that all who know their position in the cycling world are confident they will acquit themselves with honor to the sport they represent."

The schemes for making the parade the occasion for one of the greatest cycling events the United States have ever seen are multiplying, each one, too, being feasible. Those who have seen the celebrated "Demon Drill" by the expert squad of Cleveland, are urging that they be brought here to show their wonderful, weird evolutions with torches and lights at night It is also proposed to organize a similar company among the St. Louis wheelmen, and, if necessary, have a competitive drill on the Lucas market square on Twelfth Street. Still, again, the St. Louis members of the Cyclists' Touring Club want to see a convention of the club called to meet here at the same time. Now, considering it very likely that the Missouri division, L. A. W., will assemble at that time, what reason has any Western wheelman for not going into this parade with a hearty recognition of the opportunity of success thus offered ?

Any reference to the race meet of last May as a reason for one this spring will fail of its object, because it will simply call attention to the difference of the conditions then existing and now, — a difference so striking as to be more powerful and eloquent than any human voice. Then, cycling in St. Louis was still in its experimental stage, and had gained no special recognition from the public ; there was nothing else in view to engage the interest of the wheelmen ; the club proposing the tournament possessed a local champion whose development into a national champion they expected the races would bring about ; the club were certain of getting all the local glory out of the tournament. Now, cycling is a fixed fact, and the last race meet, last fall, was so grand an affair as to excite the wish that no ten-cent show or hippodrome may destroy its pleasant effect on the public ; with the fight by the usual agencies for the League meet next year there is enough to keep St. Louis bicyclers busy, without saying anything about probable team races between the clubs ; a great cycling light has been suddenly put out in a certain club, and local glory, a thing so precious in the past, is very, very far away. All these changes — some fortunate, some sad — ought to have great weight in shaping opinion before Monday night. — *Post Dispatch.*

CYCLETS.

ANENT THE L. A. W. PARADE.

DEFER !
Defer!
To the noble L. A. W.!
Defer!
Defer!
To this noble crowd,
To this noble crowd,
To the only L. A. W.!

Bow !   Bow ! Ye lower walking classes,
Bow ! Ye hoodlums,
Bow ! Ye masses !
As upon its lordly way,
This unique procession passes!
Tan, tan, tara, taing, BOOM !

And the brass will crash !
And the trumpets bray !
And they 'll cut a dash on their gala day.
They 'll wobble away,
As we 're afraid,
Like Peck & Co.'s Japanese parade !

PEDALS.

CHIEF CONSUL DUCKER has taken hold of the cash department of the League Meet. The Boston men seemed to be afraid of it, and as some one must do it, the Chief Consul came forward.

MR. DUCKER will be in Boston on Saturday and Sunday next. All who have business relating to the Meet should see him then

C. K. ALLEY, of the firm of Fleming, Brewster & Alley, has been awarded the contract to print the League programme. This firm publishes *Outing*, and two of the partners came from the establishment that printed the programme last year, and it was done under their especial supervision.

ASA DOLPH will have charge of the Cleveland athletic park this season.

A MEETING of the Missouri division L. A. W. will be held in St. Louis 15 May. A party will leave Chicago for a ride in St. Louis County the following day, 16th. Leave Chicago Saturday evening, getting back Monday morning.

FRED. WESTBROOK, of Canada, has gone to Philadelphia to join Forepaugh's circus.

GORMULLY AND JEFFERY are running to their full capacity. Last Monday night they added two hours to their regular day of ten and a half hours, so that their hands work an actual twelve hours per day. But they are paid for it.

PROF. STONE, and his promising son Percy, entertained me for some time at their Olive-street bicycle emporium, and the father of the lamented Cola confided to me the statement that it was his great wish to see Cola and Percy develop bicycling interests in his city. They were somewhat different in temperament. Cola was an excellent judge of a wheel and a thorough rider, and Percy was the careful, conservative business man, which would have made a good foundation for their success. "I have a son, however, the exact counterpart of poor Cola, whom I have great hopes for," added Prof. Stone, "and he will be a good man if I am not mistaken." Prof. Stone stated that wheel matters were commencing to boom. — *Cor. Chicago Journal.*

L. A. TRACY has been elected captain of the Hartford Wheel Club, vice A. P. Judson, resigned. A communication from the East Hartford Wheel Club was received. That club is to hold a race meeting next month, and will furnish a second prize and the use of the track if the Hartford club will furnish the first prize, and the race be open to members of both clubs. The offer was accepted.

GORMULLY AND JEFFERY are going to build a bicycle for a Tennessee man that stands seven feet eight inches in his stockings.

EDWIN OLIVER, at one time head of the firm of Oliver & Jenkins, is now in Chicago, and has lately joined the Dearborn Cycling Club.

ON the 28th of March the San Francisco bicycle club went on a run to Haywards, meeting the Oakland wheelmen on the other side of the bay by appointment. At the Haywards Hotel, after a very pleasant run down, about twenty-five wheelmen sat down to dinner.

A FACT — Mrs. B—loq to cycling friends : "Yes, and last week, finding the baby wheel of Mr. B——'s bicycle on the library table, where he 'd been cleaning the horrid greasy thing, I picked it up, — intending to give him a good scare by hiding it, — when a whole lot of little shot rolled out from somewhere inside and were lost. Mr. B—— wondered at dinner, this evening, 'how in the world (only I don't remember that he said "world") so much sand had gotten into his little wheel.' I 'm sure I don't know, for I bought some shot and put 'em in again as soon as I had lost the others, and it was good as new." — *Canadian Wheelman.*

MR. FRED G BOURNE, of the Citizens (N. Y.), is off to Europe on a pleasure trip. The "Cits" gave him a dinner before he left. Look out for him, you wheelmen on the other side, and if he goes out on a run with you, see that he doesn't leave you behind. That 's one of his old tricks.

THE entertainment committee of the League Meet has arranged for an athletic exhibition by the German Turners, and a minstrel show by the Jeffries and Oxford clubs.

BOSTON is working quietly in the interest of the League Meet. The boys are not

Adjustment in Height in Front. Adjustment in Length. A Comfortable Coasting Plate.
Adjustment in Height in Rear. Adjustment in Width.   A Bifurcated Seat.

THE LILLIBRIDGE SADDLE

Is the only one having any of these Points; is the only one that can be changed in Shape or Position at all; is the BEST and CHEAPEST; is adapted to all makes of Bicycles. Special Styles for the Safeties and Star.

Price, Nickelled, $5.00. Price of Coiled Spring, with Straps, etc., for Old Saddles, 75 Cts.

FREEMAN LILLIBRIDGE, Rockford, Ill.

THE BOSTON BICYCLE SHOE.

The Perfect Shoe for Cycling.

Hand-sewed, hand-made, first-quality stock and warranted in every respect. Every pair of our No. 1 Boston Sporting Shoes is marked inside, "**Boston: Strickland & Pierce, Hand-Sewed,**" and is stamped "Patent" on the bottom. None others are Genuine. Bicycle, Base Hall Sprint Running, Pedestrian, Gymnasium, La Crosse and other shoes. Prices and rules for self-measurement sent on application.

STRICKLAND & PIERCE,

156 and 156½ Summer Street,

BOSTON.

STAR BICYCLES.

SAFE, PRACTICAL AND FAST.

NO HEADERS OR DANGEROUS FALLS.

Best Road Record for 50 and 100 Miles.
World's Safety Records from 1 to 20 Miles.
First American Machine to make more than 20 Miles within the Hour.
Three L. A. W. Championships for 1885.
Won all Hill Climbing Contests, both as to Speed and Grade.
Won all the First Premiums, when in Competition, since 1881.
NEW CATALOGUE READY.

H. B. SMITH MACHINE CO.

Smithville, Bur. Co., N. J.

RAILROAD STRIKES

don't affect the man who owns an **INVINCIBLE** wheel. *He* can ride where others walk. Light, strong, rigid, fitted with patent Double-Section Hollow Rims and full inch rubbers. They are the perfection of wheel manufacture. Send for catalogue or description of the Bicycle, Safety Bicycle, Single Tricycle (two or three track, or automatic), and tandem. New front-steering tandem has 42-inch drivers, 26-inch front wheel, and either rider can steer. Imported only by

GEO. D. GIDEON,

No. 6 South Broad Street, Philadelphia, Pa.

talking much, but we shall give the visitors a good time.

THE late Dr. Chapin used to say that he lectured for F. A. M. E., — fifty and my expenses. Wheelmen seem to have the same idea of fame.

AT the request of the club to which he belongs, and many wheelmen of St. Louis beside, S. G. Whittaker has been allowed to enter the St. Louis road race, under protest. No decision has been arrived at in his case, and all prizes will be withheld pending the action of the Board.

THE total number of new members added to the L. A. W. rolls last week was one hundred and thirty-eight, of which Massachusetts contributed twenty-three.

THE Waltham Cycle Club came out $80 ahead on their entertainment. The club wishes to extend thanks to all visiting wheelmen on that occasion.

R. P. AHL, of the Massachusetts Club, will sail for England on Saturday. He will meet his brother, who is now abroad. They will return in about four months.

COL. ALBERT A. POPE and John Harrington, Esq., of England, attended the Citizens' Club dinner at New York, last week. Col. Pope was pleasantly introduced by the toastmaster as the George Washington of cycling.

TEN thousand copies of the official programme of the coming League Meet will be issued. It will be an elegant specimen of the printer's art. A copy will be mailed to every League member, and the balance reserved for use in Boston.

CHARLES B. THAYER started from Hartford last week to ride his bicycle to the Pacific slope. He will follow the Erie Canal tow-path to Buffalo, and will cross the Mississippi at Rock Island. Unlike most wheelmen, he carries his goods in a knapsack strapped to his back.

ON account of alleged ill treatment extended to D. H. Renton, of New York, by the officers of the L. A. W., the Richmond County Wheelmen's Club has resigned from the League.

ELSA VON BLUMEN, the female bicyclist, will shortly visit Boston for the purpose of trying to arrange a race with some of the unoccupied professionals hereabouts.

F. E. VAN MEERBEKE, who is riding an Expert bicycle from New York to San Francisco, via New Orleans, has reached Townville, South Carolina. He has experienced extremely hot weather.

ST. LOUIS wheelmen have been excluded from the fair grounds track. The wheelmen will retaliate by boycotting the fair grounds.

JOHN HARRINGTON, the English manufacturer of cradle springs, has presented Col. Pope with a three-seated settee, built on cradle springs.

MR. HENRY IRVING has presented the London Tricycle Club, of which he is president, with a tricycle to be raced for at the first meeting of the club.

THOMAS STEVENS writes from Teheran, 9 March, to say that he starts from that city, and rides via Meshed, Merve, Samarkand and southern Siberia. He is unable to say what postal facilities will be found along the route, but asks friends to write him so that he will find letters at Yokohama, Japan.

THE newspapers have been announcing a meeting of the Executive Committee of the League Meet, at the New Marlboro' about every Saturday evening, and those who have put in an appearance have gone away condemning the committee for not being on hand. Notices will be issued in due form when a meeting is to be held, and until such notices are received it is pretty safe to assume that no meeting will be held.

THE committee on Rights and Privileges had a hard task to count the vote. Their hours of labor extended from 10 A. M. to 12 P. M. on Sunday, and on Monday they were engaged from 9 A. M. to 4 A. M. of Tuesday. Some 5,000 ballots were cast.

THE tricycle division of the Boston Club was reorganized on Saturday evening last by the choice of the following officers: Captain, C. P. Donahoe; secretary, J. S. Dean; treasurer, W. G. Kendall. The Boston uniform was adopted, supplemented by a white cap, and black star for a badge.

THE Boston Athletic Association bids fair to grow out of the Boston Bicycle Club. The project has been discussed in the club, and has found general favor. Steps have been taken to clear off the indebtedness of the club by an assessment of $20 upon each member of record, 31 December.

A PARTY of riders halted at the Malden pump last Sunday, and while there a policeman put in an appearance and ordered them to take their wheels away from the sidewalk. Gideon Haynes, captain of the Suffolk Club, asked the policeman who he was in a very emphatic way, and was immediately arrested. In the Malden Police Court, on Monday, Haynes was arraigned on a charge of riding on the sidewalk. The charge was easily disproved, and Haynes was discharged.

THE Coventry Machinists' Company has just taken in the new Ranelagh Club for 1886. The machine has the automatic steering, small drivers, and a large steerer, and is withal as complete and comfortable a machine as there is in the market.

WM. READ & SONS have received a new Radial Steerer from the Royal Mail Works, and it has been tried by several well-known riders on the road. This firm promises us a good machine in the two-track form. It will have a number of improvements, and will be built with small drivers. A large number of wheelmen are waiting to see this machine.

IT is very probable that the League races will be run on the Union Grounds. A refusal of the track has been secured. If it is decided to run the races there, the track will be reconstructed.

ON the occasion of the visit of Boston wheelmen to the exhibition of the Waltham Club, 15 April, a party from the Boston Club was stoned by the hoodlums on the way out. While at Waltham, the riders resolved to make the return trip in a body, and to make aggressive warfare on any attacking party. No attack was made, however, and the cyclers reached Boston in safety.

CHELSEA is now fully equipped with a club. Stall's friend " James " has not yet joined.

THE keeper has departed from the office of the Overman Wheel Co. The attachment has been raised on the goods owned by the Overman Wheel Co., but it still holds on the Ames Manufacturing Co.'s goods. The goods now under attachment include all the 1886 machines which had not been delivered at the time it was put on.

NEW JERSEY is not a large State. It ranks the nineteenth in point of population; but in League membership it stands the fourth. This is owing to the liberal policy the State has pursued in distributing maps and road books to League members.

THE PATH.

MINNEAPOLIS, MINN., 17 April, 1886. — The fifty-mile bicycle race between John S. Prince and W. M. Woodside, which occurred at Washington rink, was the grandest ever run here. Prince got the lead and started out at a rapid pace. The men passed and repassed until the forty-seventh mile, when Woodside was a foot ahead, and it was hard to declare the winner. A boy ran across the track, — Woodside escaped him, but Prince took a severe header. He quickly got on his feet and was on the track again before Woodside had gained a lap. After riding four laps, however, Prince, who is thought to be injured internally, was obliged to leave the track. Woodside continued to ride, and finished the fifty miles in 2.46.3¾. Woodside had previously made several attempts to break this record, and on one occasion came to 2.55.38¾. At the close of the race, Prince's judge, Ed Moulton, the ex-sprint runner, made a claim of foul, which was allowed by the referee, it seeming, in his opinion, to be that Prince had an equal chance with Woodside to win, and that, under the circumstances, it was a put-up job to throw Prince. The decision was a draw, which was received with unanimous applause.

THE CLUB.

COLUMBUS, OHIO. — Buckeye Bicycle Club. Officers elected 3 Feb. 1886 : President, W. H. Miller ; vice-president, A. E. Pitt ; captain, F. W. Hughes ; secretary, Ward B. Perley, 25 S. Sixth street ; treasurer, Fred W. Flowers, 383 E. Oak street.

NEWTON, MASS. — Newton Club. Officers elected 24 April : J. S. Elms, president; J. H. Aubin, secretary ; H. Wilson, treasurer ; P. L. Aubin, captain ; E. H. Ellison, first lieutenant ; C. F. Haven, second lieutenant.

HAMILTON, CAN. — Hamilton Club. Officers : President, Chief Stewart ; vice-president, Chas. Tinling ; secretary-treasurer, J. Laidlaw ; captain, W. Rutherford ; first lieutenant, Charles Graham ; second lieutenant, R. A. Robertson.

MELROSE, MASS.—Melrose Bicycle Club. President, B. F. Eddy; captain, Dr. Charles Sprague; first lieutenant, Walter Stevens; bugler, A. Pemberton; secretary and treasurer, J. F. Cox; club committee, president and captain, Henry Johnson. The club has started with a membership of fifteen.

CANTON, OHIO. — Canton Bicycle Club. Officers elected 1 May, 1885: President, M. P. Fry; captain, Frank W. Jay; secretary-treasurer, Will G. Saxton, care First National Bank.

NEW YORK BICYCLE CLUB (organized 18 Dec. 1879). Officers elected 1 Feb. 1886: Captain (acts as president), Jas. B. Roy, 312 Produce exchange; treasurer, R. R. Haydock, 83 Chambers street; secretary, Edw. J. Shriver, 234 Pearl street; club address, 1770 Broadway.

CHICAGO, ILL. — Chicago Bicycle Club. Officers elected 12 Jan. 1886: President, T. S. Miller; vice-president, J. P. Maynard, captain, N. H. Van Sicklen; quartermaster, W. G. Wanzer; secretary-treasurer, W. C. Thorne, 189 Michigan avenue; librarian, S. B. Wright, 189 Michigan avenue; lieutenants, L. W. Conkling, W. G. E. Peirce, and A. G. Bennett; eighty members.

FLUSHING, L. I. — Mercury Wheelmen. President, Dr. A. Foster King; secretary and treasurer, Charles B. Turton; historian, L. A. Clarke; bugler, William E. Hicks; captain, A. Polhemus Cobb; lieutenants, Townsend Scudder and J. W. Whitson.

CHELSEA, MASS. — Chelsea Cycle Club. Officers elected 16 April: President, Abbot Bassett; vice-president, J. B. Seward, Jr.; secretary-treasurer, C. E. Walker; captain, L. H. Frost; first lieutenant, R. E. Burnett; second lieutenant, Walter Fracker.

ST. JOHN, B. B. — St. John Bicycle Club. Officers elected 7 April, 1886: President, G. F. Smith; captain, W. A. Maclachlan; secretary-treasurer, J. M. Barnes, 103 Mecklenburg Street; first lieutenant, C. Coster; second lieutenant, H. C. Page.

QUINCY, ILL. — Quincy Bicycle Club, organized 7 April, 1886. Officers: President, Thomas A. Burrows; captain, R. B. White; secretary-treasurer, T. C. White. Twelve members.

NORWALK, CONN. — Norwalk Wheel Club. Officers elected 29 March, 1886: President, Edw. M. Jackson; secretary, Chas. E. Miller; treasurer, Le Grand Raymond; captain, Wm. T. Olmstead.

ELMIRA, N. Y. — Elmira Club. President, Thomas K. Beecher, pastor Park Church and brother of Henry Ward Beecher; secretary and treasurer, Edward L. Adams, editor Advertiser; captain, H. C. Hersey, proprietor Mascot Academy; lieutenant, H. C. Spalding.

MT. VERNON, N. Y. — Mt. Vernon Club. Officers: President, A. E. Fauquier; secretary, F. W. Steinbrenner, Jr.; treasurer, F. W. White; captain, F. T. Davis; first lieutenant, E. M. Devoe; bugler, F. W. Steinbrenner.

ORANGE, N. J. — Orange Wanderers. Officers elected 17 Feb. 1886: President, L. H Porter; captain, W. A. Belcher; first lieutenant, Dr. R. M. Sanger; second lieutenant, C. Hening; secretary-treasurer, C. W. Baldwin. Membership, 40; ladies, 9; gentlemen, 31.

THE Massachusetts Club had a moonlight run, Monday evening, to the Nonantum Club rooms, at Newton, where a musical entertainment was held, and a spread of coffee and sandwiches was laid They were met at the Faneuil House and escorted to the club rooms. There were about sixty-five wheelmen in line. The entertainment was as follows: Song, by F. W. Perry, Massachusetts Club; banjo duet and songs, by Lowell and Fellows, Nonantum Club; recitation, by A. S. Bryant, Nonantum Club; cornet solo, by C. E. Lindell, Massachusetts Club; piano and cornet duet, Perry and Lindell; recitation, by Wm. Shakespeare, Waltham Club. The club reached the clubhouse on the return at 11.15. Last Thursday the club visited the German Turners' Gymnasium, where a fine exhibition was given for their benefit. Saturday night a moonlight run was taken to the new gymnasium in Cambridge, where another exhibition was given. To-night there will be a moonlight run to the Newtons.

THE TRADE.

GORMULLY & JEFFERY are having good success with their new Champion wheel. The following testimonials tell their own story:—

CHICAGO, 22 March, 1886.
MESSRS. GORMULLY & JEFFERY, CITY.

Dear Sir, — After giving the Champion several exhaustive trials on the road, I cannot refrain from saying that it is the most rigid, easy running and steering bicycle that I have ever ridden. Its high grade and very reasonable price will doubtless make a large sale for it the coming season. This is the first testimonial I have ever written.

Yours very truly,
JOHN O. BLAKE,
Chief Consul L. A. W. State of Illinois.

MINNEAPOLIS, MINN., 15 March, 1886.
MESSRS. GORMULLY & JEFFERY, Chicago, Ill.

Gentlemen, — We wish to congratulate you on the great success of your American Champion bicycle in its first race (the great six-day, twelve hours per day race just finished in this city). With Albert Schock its rider, it covered 1,009½ miles, winning the world's long-distance record. The machine came through in grand shape, not the slightest thing going wrong; requiring throughout the race but the care of an occasional oiling. One of the results of the contest is a lively demand for the new wheel in this city.

Yours very truly,
S. F. HEATH & CO.

MINNEAPOLIS, 16 March, 1886.
MESSRS. GORMULLY & JEFFERY, Chicago, Ill.

Permit me to express my appreciation of the Champion bicycle I used in my recent long-distance race at Minneapolis. The machine stood the 1,009½ miles without turning a screw, and the only tool used by my trainers was an oil can occasionally. The machine is exceedingly easy running and steering, and the most rigid of any I ever mounted and being very firm and solid, it did not tire me nearly as much as might have been expected. I understand it is a roadster, and such being the case, I shall be careful to ride a roadster in any races I may in future enter which requires endurance.

Yours sincerely,
ALBERT SCHOCK.

A REMARKABLE RECORD ON A REMARKABLE WHEEL.— Albert Schock, at Minneapolis, broke the world's long-dis-

tance record of 1,007 miles made by F. Lees, at Middleboro', England, in 1880, on an American Champion Roadster, making 1,009½ miles, and defeating the well-known Woodside on a racer, by nearly 100 miles. The Champion that Schock rode was the first one put together. The result is remarkable as well as significant.

MISCELLANEOUS

THIS SPACE RESERVED

──── FOR ────

JENS F. PEDERSEN,

MANUFACTURER OF

MEDALS,

1 1-2 Maiden Lane - - - NEW YORK.

The Cycle.

Vol. I., No. 5.   BOSTON, MASS., 30 APRIL, 1886.   Five Cents.

The Coventry Machinists' Co.'s New Tricycle for 1886.

THE MARLBORO' CLUB—Automatic Steerer.
ADMIRABLY ADAPTED FOR LADIES.
SEND FOR CATALOGUE TO 239 COLUMBUS AVENUE, BOSTON.

COLUMBIA SPECIALTIES.

THE COLUMBIA DOUBLE-GRIP BALL-PEDAL.

All Bearing Parts Drop-Forged and Case-Hardened.
Interchangeable in Every Part.
Light and Easy Running.

The BEST PEDAL Ever Offered Wheelmen.

Balls Gauged $\frac{1}{1000}$ of an Inch.
Non-Slipping Elastic Double-Grip Rubbers.
Strong Tapered Shaft.

PRICE, NICKELLED, $10.00.

The BEST PEDAL Ever Offered Wheelmen.

THE KIRKPATRICK SADDLE.

IMPROVED IN LEATHER AND IN FRONT SPRING.　ADJUSTABLE FORE-AND-AFT.　FIT ANY STYLE OF BICYCLE.

PRICE, $6.00.

THE COLUMBIA SWING SPRING.

Relieves both Fore-and-Aft and Vertical Vibration, while giving a Perfectly Steady Seat.

PRICE, NICKELLED, $5.00.

THE KNOUS ADJUSTABLE SADDLE.

Has Elastic Spring Frame Highest Grade Leather, and Adjustable Clip, allowing either end of the Saddle to be elevated; Adjustable at the Rear without removing from the Machine.

PRICE, $4.00.

CATALOGUE SENT FREE.

THE POPE MFG. CO.

597 WASHINGTON STREET, BOSTON.

Branch Houses: 12 Warren Street, New York; 115 Wabash Avenue, Chicago.

THE CYCLE

PUBLISHED EVERY FRIDAY BY ABBOT BASSETT, 22 SCHOOL ST., ROOM 19.

VOL. I.   BOSTON, MASS., 30 APRIL, 1886.   NO. 5.

TERMS OF SUBSCRIPTION.

One Year, by mail, post-paid...........................$1.50
Three Copies in one order............................ 3.00
Club Subscriptions.................................... 1.00
Six Months... .90
Single Copies... .05

Specimen Copies free.

Every bicycle dealer is agent for the CYCLE and authorized to receive subscriptions at regular rates. The paper can be found on sale at the following places: —
Boston, CUPPLES, UPHAM & Co., cor. Washington and School Streets. Tremont House news stand. At every cycle warehouse.
New York, ELLIOTT MASON, 12 Warren Street.
Philadelphia, H. B. HART, 811 Arch Street. GEORGE D. GIDEON, 6 South Broad Street.
Baltimore, S. T. CLARK & Co., 4 Hanover Street.
Chicago, JOHN WILKINSON & Co., 68 Wabash Avenue.
Washington, H. S. OWEN, Capital Cycle Co.
St. Louis, ST. LOUIS WHEEL Co., 1121 Olive Street.

ABBOT BASSETT . . . .   EDITOR
W. I. HARRIS   : .   EDITORIAL CONTRIBUTOR

A. MUDGE & SON, PRINTERS, 24 FRANKLIN ST., BOSTON.

All communications should be sent in not later than Tuesday, to ensure insertion the same week.

Entered at the Post-office as second-class mail matter.

A NEW CLASS.

THE proposition which has been made to form a new class of riders, who shall be neither amateurs nor professionals, is entitled to serious consideration. It will give us a class of riders who will always ride to win, who will ornament our record sheet with astonishing figures, and who will be above some of the practices of many professionals. But will it give us a state of things better than that which we have had? Let us see. The evil which we wish to correct is seen in the present use of amateur races to advertise machines. Now, there is nothing to be urged against a man who shows the capabilities of a machine, if he does it in a proper way; but when he announces himself as one who rides for honor only, when his leading motive is to advertise a machine, he is not acting an honest part. The League has gone too far to take any backward step. It must now adjust the racing interests so that there will be no temptation to prostitute the purposes of the amateur racing path. In fine, it must take the advertising value away from the amateurs. Will the proposed change do this? It is suggested that a class be formed of those who do not race for money prizes nor with professionals. This will not prevent makers or dealers paying large salaries to their employees and using them on the path. It will not prevent a man having pay enough to cover all his expenses, and leave a generous margin for his own profit. It will not prevent a cycle maker or dealer from racing on his own machine. It will not prevent a firm taking a good racing man into partnership, thus making him owner of his machine. It will not prevent a bicycle maker, and advertising his wares on the path. It will not, in fact, take the advertising value away from the amateur races. The weakness of the suggested reform is, that it does not go far enough. It might work to advantage, if at the same time a rule were made to exclude from amateur races all makers, dealers, employees of makers or dealers, and all persons whatsoever, who, either directly or indirectly, are interested in the sale of cycles or cycle accessories. We do not object to placing cycling journalists in this list. Some such rule as this was employed by the Tricycle Association of England. The weakness of that body failed to secure its enforcement. The underlying idea is a good one. Let the League put in force a rule of this kind, coupled with the suggestions for an intermediate class of riders, and we believe that the whole problem of racing will be solved. It may be urged that this step is too radical, and that the treatment of the subject is in the line of the heroic, but the time has come for some radical change, and while we are about it, let us do the work thoroughly.

THE Springfield Club protests. It says in effect: Do not employ the best method to right a wrong, but proceed in a manner that is impracticable, which will leave things uncorrected, and which will allow offenders to go scot free. The Racing Board has been trying to do for years just what the club thinks to be the best thing, and nothing has been accomplished. This is one of the cases where the ends justify the means.

THE LEAGUE MEET.

CHIEF CONSUL DUCKER came to Boston Saturday evening to perfect arrangements for the Meet of the L. A. W., 27, 28 and 29 May. The present indications are that it will be attended by no less than 5,000 wheelmen, representing every State in the Union, and a goodly delegation from Canada. The chief consul was in consultation all day with the chairmen of the various committees. Reports from all the committees save that on the banquet were received, and with the exception of a few minor details, all the plans have been arranged for. Reduced rates on most of the railroads running into Boston will be secured. Early next week, or as soon as possible, a pamphlet will be issued, giving in detail the programme of the Meet. Fifteen thousand copies of this are to be printed and sent to every member of the League. The chief consul has taken the matter of raising funds into his own hands. Among the contributions already received are the following : Massachusetts Division, L. A. W., $500 ; the Pope Manufacturing Company, $200 ; Fleming, Brewster & Alley, $200 ; Overman Wheel Company, $100 ; Stoddard, Lovering & Co., $50 ; H. B. Smith Machine Company, $100 ; Springfield Bicycle Club, $100 ; W. B. Everett & Co., $50 ; H. B. Hart, $25 ; Wheelmen's *Gazette*, $25.

RECEPTION.

Chairman Whitney reported upon the extensive arrangements which are being made to receive the visiting wheelmen. He is to be assisted by a committee of fifty prominent members of the various local clubs, several of whom will meet every incoming train at the depots and escort the wheelmen to the quarters assigned them. Barges for transporting wheels and baggage will also be in attendance. Mr. Whitney is to have charge of getting up the badges of the various committees. These are to be of a very tasteful design in metal, similar to the regulation League pin, pendent from which will be the ribbons of various colors.

THE RACES.

It was definitely decided to hold the races on the Union grounds, and work will be at once begun towards putting the track in condition. H. S. Tuttle, of Swampscott, who is constructing the Lynn track, will probably do the work, and the track will be ready for preparatory training at least a week before the races. The programme of events has been outlined as follows : —
One-mile bicycle, national championship.
One-mile tricycle, national championship.
One-mile bicycle, State championship.
One-mile bicycle, novices.
One-mile bicycle, handicap.
One-mile bicycle, invitation.
Three-mile bicycle, invitation.
Entries to the invitation races will be limited to those whom the committee invite to compete, and it is understood that the suspended parties will receive the invitations. Entries to the State championship will be limited to Massachusetts riders. The following will be officers of the day : Referee, Abbot Bassett ; judges, N. M. Beckwith, Stephen Terry, T. J. Kirkpatrick ; scorers, E. L. Miller, F. T. Sholes, N. H. Van Sick-

len; starter, H. E. Ducker; clerk, A. L. Atkins; umpires, C. S. Howard, W. G. Kendall, George H. Burt, Edward A. Sells; timers, E. E. Merrill, G. S. Lathrop, E. A. Church.

It was decided to hold a hill-climbing conquest on Corey hill, Brookline, at ten o'clock on the morning of the first day. Dr. W. G. Kendall will have charge of this event, and suitable prizes will be awarded. Early in the morning of the second day a tricycle road race will be run under the auspices of the Boston Bicycle Club. The course will probably be fifteen or twenty miles in length. It will be open to all amateurs, and gold and silver medals will be awarded the winners.

ENTERTAINMENT.

We published last week the details of the entertainment to be provided. A good programme has been arranged by Chairman Salkeld, and if the visitors attempt to take it all in, they will be kept on the jump from the time they arrive in town until they take the train for home. On Thursday evening a concert will be given at Music Hall, and on Friday evening a minstrel entertainment in the same hall by the Jefferies and Oxford Clubs.

HOTELS.

Chairman E. W. Pope has made special arrangements with the leading hotels of the city for accommodating the wheelmen. The Vendome will be the headquarters, and it will be from there that the parade will be started.

THE PARADE.

The chairman of the parade committee, A. V. Walburg, has laid out the route, which is as follows: Forming on both sides of Commonwealth avenue, with right of the line resting on Dartmouth street, proceeding down Commonwealth avenue to Arlington street, countermarching on the west side of Commonwealth avenue to West Chester park, Chester square to Harrison avenue, to Concord street, to James street, to Newton, to Columbus avenue, Dartmouth street and by Beacon street to Longwood, where the wheelmen will be photographed in a group on the bank of some grassy hillside. Returning, the parade will disband at the Mechanics building. The parade will move promptly at 10 A. M., and will be divided into four divisions, all under command of the chief marshal, Dr. N. M. Beckwith. For music, the Salem Cadet band of twenty pieces has been secured. The band will head the parade in a barge.

CONTRIBUTORS' CLUB

LADIES' UNIFORM.

Editor of the Cycle : — I like " Daisie's " idea regarding a uniform for ladies. It is very true that a style of garment that will become one lady will look badly on another. I myself am very short in stature, and the lady friend with whom I have ridden a great deal is very tall. I can wear a plain skirt; she cannot. On the machine, a plain skirt will not offend the eye in her case; but let her walk into a room or down a long dining-hall, and every eye will be centred on her. We cannot cut our garments in the same way.
MAUD.

THE BICYCLE PROBLEM.

Editor of the Cycle : — The problem is easy enough. A starts in business with a bicycle. He sells it for $50. He now re-purchases for $45. His capital is now a bicycle and $5. He re-sells for $65, making a profit on second transaction of $20, which, added to first profit of $5, makes the total profit $25.
S. M. F.

Editor of the Cycle : — Here is your solution in a nutshell. A has a bicycle worth $50 at the outset, and at the end has $70, but no bicycle. Deduct $50 from $70, and $20 (the profit) remains.
HOWE EASY.

Editor of the Cycle : — A has a bicycle which he sells for $50. Buying it back for $45, he certainly makes $5, and has his bicycle for a new sale. Now the problem stands: A has a bicycle which he sells for $65 ; how much does he make ? An absurd question and unanswerable. So that; taking the problem as it stands, I see no other profit than the $5.
H. S.

Editor of the Cycle : — I was in the club-room when " Cy." sprung his problem on us. Here is my solution : —

	A.		B.	
1		Bicycle.	1	Bicycle.
2	$50		2	$50
3	5	Bicycle.	3	45
4	65		4	Bicycle.
	$120		$95	

The above will enlist the eye in the work of convincing the brain.
BY.

YOUR problem in to-day's issue of CYCLE is so very simple that it makes me laugh ; and below you will find, I think, a correct solution : —

CR.

By sale of machine,	$50.00
" " "	65.00
	$115.00

DR.

To cost of machine,	$140.00
" Three suits : $8.00, $9.00, $13.00,	30.00
" Lamp, $5.00; gallon oil, $2.00,	7.00
" Chain and padlock,	1.20
" House of machine,	15.00
" Subscription to CYCLE,	1.50
" Meeting obstacles on road (twice), repairs,	38 70
" Express to and from shop,	4.80
" Surgeon (nine visits),	27.00
" Liniment and plasters,	6.20
" Second purchase of machine,	45.00
" Advertising in CYCLE three mos., "no offer refused,"	15.00
" Car fares for would-be purchasers,	.12
	$331.52
	115.00
Loss on transaction,	$216.52

ENTHUSIAST.

MASSACHUSETTS' VOTE.

BELOW we give the result of the election in Massachusetts. Many names for whom ballots were cast do not appear on the list. The committee threw out all Votes for ineligible candidates. The Boston Club sent in its applications for membership 22 February, and consequently the men were not members till after 1 March. This caused the rejection of all votes for C. S. Howard, Willis Farrington, T. H. Wakefield, and L. C. Southard. The committee also rejected all ballots cast for men than fourteen candidates, unless the voter specified that he wanted to Vote for fourteen men indicated, and for men if allowable. Springfield voted for seventeen men, and nearly all of this club's votes were thrown out. Names marked with a star were elected.

FOR CHIEF CONSUL.

*Henry E. Ducker, of Springfield	394 votes.
A. D. Peck, Jr., of Boston	18 "

FOR 14 REPRESENTATIVES.

*Sanford Lawton, of Springfield	257 Votes.
*F. P. Kendall, of Worcester	255 "
*F. E. Hawks, of Greenfield	254 "
*W. O. Greene, of Holyoke	253 "
*W. G. Kendall, of Boston	240 "
*George Chinn, of Marblehead	248 "
*Abbot Bassett, of Boston	248 "
*H. W. Hayes, of Cambridge	247 "
*Charles E. Pratt, of Boston	243 "
*A. S. Parsons, of Cambridgeport	198 "
*H. S. Wollison, of Pittsfield	190 "
*W. S. Slocum, of Newton	172 "
*W. I. Harris, of Boston	156 "
*J. S. Dean, of Boston	133 "
K. H. Foote, of Somerville	96 "
A. W. Dyer, of Lawrence	95 "
John Amee, of Cambridge	73 "
W. M. Pratt, of Brockton	12 "
Joseph L. Pindar, of Lowell	19 "
A. D. Claflin, of Cambridge	15 "
W. B. Everett, of Dorchester	11 "
A. D. Peck, Jr., of Boston	11 "
William Rowe, of Lynn	10 "
H. T. Conant	11 "
F. W. Archer, of Dorchester	8 "
Elmer Woods	7 "
F. E. Ripley, of Springfield	3 "
William C. Dillingham	2 "
E. K. Hill, of Worcester	1 "
F. K. Hollister, of Greenfield	1 "
William Marsh, of Springfield	1 "
C. A. Fisk, of Springfield	1 "

CHICAGO.

FINE weather and a great crowd of riders promenading the boulevards and avenues, have been the rule the past week. There is a great boom in bicycling in this, the greatest city of the world, at the present time, and the dealers and manufacturers are very busy keeping pace with their orders. In fact they are behind, as statements from the following will prove. Ed Oliver, representing Gormully & Jeffery, our Champion manufacturers, said in response to my query, " How is business ? " " Well, you can say it is great, and we are away behind on orders, notwithstanding the fact that our large force of men work early and late." Major Durell clasped his hands to his head, and said, "The fact is, I 'm pretty tired, and had to leave my correspondence a dozen times to-day, in order to assist my salesmen. Our business is the Columbia wheels, boats and engines is very large — the wheel business predominating." J. P. Maynard, the Star man, showed me a large assortment of the gay and festive Stars, and remarked that Smithfield was rather slow in sending on March orders. The Star has a formidable rider here, in the person of S. A. Rabolla, an athlete of exceptional brilliancy, and who would, if properly trained, make a hummer. J. O. Blake, with elegant silk tile and League costume, smoking a fragrant Havana, was leaning in his chair perusing the last *Bulletin*, when I dropped in on him. " Just back from the East," says J. O., "and was indeed glad to return. I think the West (the coming League Meet) will have a greater boom than the East, this year, by the present outlook.

I just received a telegram from the Overman Company, stating that our first instalment of Victors has been shipped, and we are getting them none too soon." Burley B. Ayers tackled me or my remarks ing in last letter, about "wire pulling." "'Ponmy soul, Burley, I don't understand what you mean."

Van Sicklen is greatly exercised over the makers' amateurs, and thinks they are bold, bad, wicked men; so don't I.

The Chicago Bicycle Track Association have squared their track indebtedness (so Mr. Maynard informs me to-day), and the prospects are now, will have some good races on the ball ground track this season. The Cheltenham Beach athletic scheme hangs fire, so we are not to expect much for a track in that direction. The six days' race is an assured fact; the dealers are taking hold, and we are booming it.

SPOKES.

A MODEL ROAD-BOOK.

WE have received a copy of the new road-book issued by the Penn., N. J., and Md. Divisions L. A. W., and compiled by H. S. Wood, assisted by E. M. Aaron, Dr. G. C. Brown, and W.S. Bayley. The book contains the principal through routes of New York, Connecticut, Massachusetts, Rhode Island, Delaware, and Virginia, and covers all the riding districts in the States of Pennsylvania, New Jersey, and Maryland. It has road maps of the riding districts of Philadelphia, Orange, New York City, New Jersey, Staten Island, Pennsylvania, and Maryland. It is a most complete work, and has been gotten out at the expense of months of patient labor and research. It describes 12,000 unrepeated miles, and has a total of 20,000 miles. There are two hundred pages in the book. When we add that this work is given away to members of the Divisions under whose auspices it is printed and sold for $1 to League members in other States, it will be seen what the workers in the League have done for that body. Until every State in the Union has such a road-book as this, there is a large scope for ambitious workers.

AUSTRALIAN RECORD.

MELBOURNE, 3 March. — Con Dwyer, the one-mile tricycle champion, of Victoria, made a run to beat the one-mile tricycle record, under the auspices of the Victorian Cyclists Union. We give his time, and also the English and American records.

		ENG.	AM.
$\frac{1}{4}$	45$\frac{3}{5}$	46	42
$\frac{1}{2}$	1.27$\frac{2}{5}$	1.29$\frac{1}{5}$	1.21$\frac{4}{5}$
$\frac{3}{4}$	2.13$\frac{1}{5}$	2.14$\frac{4}{5}$	2.10$\frac{2}{5}$
1	3.00	2.58$\frac{1}{5}$	2.53$\frac{4}{5}$

THE SPRINGFIELD CLUB'S PROTEST.

THE following is the substance of a formal letter of protest, sent by the Springfield Bicycle Club to President Beckwith, in relation to the L. A. W. Racing Board's suspension of the alleged "makers' amateurs": —

20 APRIL, 1886.

DR. N. M. BECKWITH, President L. A. W.

Dear Sir, — As Messrs. McGarrett, Hendee, and Westervelt have been expelled from the L. A. W. for failure to reply to certain charges against their amateur standing made to the Racing Board, we have this day suspended these men from active membership, pending investigation of the charges preferred by the Racing Board. It is our firm belief that our respected members have had no specific charges made against their amateur standing, and we deem the action of the Racing Board was unjust, inasmuch as the failure to answer certain questions does not carry with it the verdict of guilty.

We desire to endorse the L. A. W. and its policy as long as it appears to be wise and just, but we beg the privilege of protesting against any such method of proceeding as the Racing Board has adopted, — that of accusing a man of violation of certain rules, then requesting him to prove his innocence. We feel that a more just position to assume would be to prefer specific charges, with proof of same, and request the innocence then be proven.

We, therefore, Mr. President, respectfully request that we be furnished with a copy of such charges or protests as may have been lodged against Messrs. McGarrett, Hendee, and Westervelt, that we may act understandingly in the matter, and not expel, without good and sufficient reason for so doing, men whose membership we value.

SPRINGFIELD BICYCLE CLUB.

SANFORD LAWTON, *Secretary*.

FROM A FEMININE POINT OF VIEW.

"TELL us of your experiences on the road" is the request that comes to me from several quarters. I wish that I might be able to find more to talk about in this direction, but, truth to tell, striking incidents are like angels' visits; and although I take no ride that does not bring a rich experience, I fear me that there is little developed that can be placed on paper.

I WONDER if my readers would not be interested in a little episode that has just culminated in a sad conclusion, but which has had more or less connection with my cycling life? I will venture to jot it down.

IN a very quiet country village, not far removed from the city where I live, stands an old mansion-house, upon which the hand of Time has been writing characters for many decades. It is far removed from the village centre, and I first came upon it by accident, and stopped at the door to inquire my way and beg a glass of milk. A sweet-faced old lady answered my knock, and gave me a kindly welcome to the hospitalities of the homestead. The clock marked an hour upon the dial before I departed, and during that time I revelled in the delights of a by-gone day, sitting at the feet of one who might have stepped forth from some old family portrait.

THAT was my first visit to the place, and it was in the early days of my riding. Since that time I cannot tell how many times my wheel has stood before that door,— not always alone, for we girls found it an exceedingly attractive point of destination. Many an hour we have spent in sweet converse with the grand old lady, and our lives have been brightened by the attrition of communion. Here is her story as I have gathered it from time to time.

THE portrait which hangs upon the parlor wall tells a story of remarkable beauty. Hers was as fine a face as I have ever seen. The eyes were as black as sloes, and the cheeks like spice pinks. The family was "upper crust," and were paid homage by their neighbors which was without servility, and with great sincerity.

HER mother took Elizabeth to the sewing-bees and tea-assemblies of the countryside, but only the young men of certain families presumed to ask her hand in a dance. The family was not rich. It required a good deal of saving to buy and lay by the two dozen silver spoons of each kind which were to be a part of her wedding outfit, for, as was customary, as soon as the girl was born this outfit took its place in the family plans.

THE good mother put aside her lace cuffs and emeralds set in guinea gold, and as soon as Elizabeth was fifteen, being then a most expert needlewoman, webs of fine homespun linen were given her, which she embroidered and made up into underclothing for the time when she should be a bride. There were no balls, no lectures, no morning paper then, with its record of news and crime, to furnish her with thought; and when we remember how much of her life was spent in quiet sewing, and in pure, sweet, maidenly fancies of her life to come, it is not surprising that when marriage came at last she was a most true wife and tender mother.

SHE was just eighteen when Nathaniel —— asked her in marriage. The young people saw each other only in the presence of others. Their letters were studied and formal. The engagement was kept secret, as was the custom; but love was as strong and fiery then as now, and burned all the clearer because hidden under modest reserve. One can but envy them the delicious thrill of their sacred secret when their hands touched in the stately quadrille, or their eyes told the sweet, unspoken story. Nathaniel and Elizabeth were married in May of 1836.

NATHANIEL took his young bride home to the paternal roof, and there they spent their quiet and uneventful lives. Nathaniel lived long enough to grow cynical with a time which rewarded cheating and impudence rather than integrity and honor. His wife concerned herself very little with the times. She had a family of eleven children, and controlled a household of many servants. In it was carried on the business of a farm, weaving, dairy work, the making of clothes for the whole family. She personally superintended not only all these works, and the storing away of provisions, fruits, meats, herbs, but the teaching of her boys and girls came largely under her care.

MODERN instruction, she complained, was too wide and shallow. There was no thorough knowledge given of history, and accurate English was seldom heard. Nothing could be simpler or purer than her own use of language, in her letters or conversation. It strengthened the effect which her delicate face and always rich, dainty dress had, even upon strangers who did not know her. A curious part of that effect was that this woman did not belong to society nor to the world, but to her husband and friends and children. Her life was so filled with them, her great household controlled with such wisdom and order, her influence of strength and sweet humanity diffused subtly through so many hearts and lives, that they did not complain that there was no chance for her to become a public character.

HER sons have grown up honorable men; her daughters are faithful and happy wives. Her husband died the past winter, just as the sons and daughters began to lay plans for the celebration of the golden wedding in May. After his death she made no loud

SINGER'S ✦ STRAIGHT ✦ STEERER.

Corey's Hill climbed by E. P. BURNHAM and Mr. Crocker each on first trial, on an S. S. S., geared to 52. The highest gear that ever reached the summit.

40-inch Drivers, 22-inch Steerer, easy running, light and rigid.

The fastest coaster and best hill climber yet built.

Illustrated Catalogue Free.

SINGER'S PATENT AXLE.

Send for Second-Hand List.

FIRST 1886 RECORDS,

APOLLO,

25 Miles by L. D. MUNGER, at New Orleans, on March 27, in 1h. 24m. 46⅘s.

50 Miles on April 2, in 3h. 2m. 34s.

THE LATTER A WORLD'S RECORD.

W. B. EVERETT & CO., Sole U. S. Agt's, 6 and 8 Berkeley St., BOSTON.

outcry. The love of husband and wife had been sacred and wordless always; but the pink blush left the aged cheek, and she sat quiet and silent. Her friends knew that she felt that her work was done. When her sons, who loved her very dearly, found that the end was near, they hurried to the old homestead from their several homes, and like children, with their heads upon her knees, cried out that she must not leave them. "Your father wants me, boys," she said gently. "Nobody can take my place to him." And so it was that last week she left us and went back to the husband of her youth, and their golden wedding will be held in another land than ours.　　　　DAISIE.

A FEW RECORDS.

" THE Historian " of the *Record* has been turning his attention to wheelmen, and thus he discourseth:—

. They had just been introduced. She was a pretty country girl, and he a wheelman who was very vain of his personal appearance when clad in cycling costume.

He: I assure you there is scarcely a man who does not find the wheel suit most becoming.

She (doubtingly): Indeed!

He: As for myself, everybody insists that I look one hundred per cent better in bicycle costume than in an ordinary business suit.

She (innocently): Dear me! How *awfully* you must look in an ordinary business suit!

THIS also from the country, and he, too, a wheelman. He had called at a farmhouse for a glass of water, but the pretty farmer's daughter had offered him a glass of milk instead.

"Won't you have another glass?" she asked, as he drained the tumbler with a sigh, and appeared to be taking in emptiness with both eyes.

. "You are very good," he replied,."but I am afraid I shall rob you."

"Oh, no," with emphasis. "We have so much more than the family can use that we're feeding it to the calves all the time!"

"BOSTON wheelmen must have friends in the city government," said a Western cycler, on his first visit to the Hub.

"How so?" was asked.

"Because I notice that all the narrow, unridable streets, or those with ugly grades, and all the alleys that are strewn with old tin cans, or alive with goats and dogs, have signs up, "Dangerous Passing."

AN EPISODE OF THE NORTH SHORE.— *Bicycler to rural individual:* "How far is it to Blankville?"

"Wall! For a hoss'n kerridge it's a good three mile, but for one of them blamed things I guess it ain't much more'n a couple o' hundred rod. Fust road to th' left, mister; then keep straight ahead t'l ye get thare."

THE quick-wittedness of the Irishman was capitally illustrated the other day on the road between Lynn and Salem, where a gang of laborers were constructing a sidewalk.

"How soon will that be ready to ride on?", asked a passing wheelman . from Boston, pleasantly.

"Before you 're ready to pay the Lynn authorities for the privilege, begorra!"

And this on the heels of a big arrest in Malden for sidewalk riding.

NEW JERSEY NOTES.

THEY say down in Jersey:—

THAT they have about as good a League division as exists.

THAT they are going to make it the most efficient one, if work, growth, and enthusiasm will do it.

THAT last year they ranked fifth in point of membership.

THAT this year they rank fourth, having passed Ohio, and now lead her by seventy-five members.

THAT every member of the division will have a free copy, this spring, of the best road book ever issued.

THAT they have some of the best roads in the country, and lots of respectable road riders.

THAT they are going to have a half-mile track this spring, which, it is intended, shall be equal to the Springfield track.

THAT they have now hardly a road racer or a path racer, but don't feel very bad over it.

THAT cycling is growing there in a thoroughly healthy manner, having never been urged to an unhealthy development by any exciting cause.

THAT when they get the new race track, they expect to develop a few racers, and fairly start a boom in a new direction.

THAT stock in the race track association commands a premium.

THAT lots of wheelmen who refused to subscribe, now wish that they had.

THAT Jerseymen are not self-complacent, only confident.

THAT when Jersey is reviled, the hard things which are said are due to ignorance or envy, and we mind them not, for long experience has enabled us to rise superior to our detractors.　　　　N. J.

CONNECTICUT WHEEL NOTES.

MORE or less desperate hand-to-hand-*lebar* encounters are again in order with the wheelmen who have been out of practice all winter, and who seem to care little for that good advice we lately read in some wheel paper.anent " regular exercise," upon which too much stress cannot be laid. They are those upon whom the sun of the early spring days beats most severely, and they require frequent bracing up.

A CLUB officer, who is here nameless on account of modesty, says that he not only has wheeling on Good Fridays, but on nearly every other day of the year, good or bad. He is a little timid about giving the name, also of the wheel that makes possible such a maximum share of cycling joys in this our latitude of ice and snow, and is thankful that from present indications his King of year.'round roadsters is to be several times duplicated in this vicinity.

WE have discovered one reason why it is

difficult to get members of a club promptly on the spot for a start on a club run in early spring. Where they ride the ordinary, with the usual stiff-as-a-board spring, and hard-as-a-rock saddle, we pity more than blame them for being tardy, and only wonder that they ride at all; for with them comfort is quite out of the question on any but sand-papered roads.

ONE of our most entrancing short runs is along a fair road, that is closely skirted by a brook, that is in places noisily brawling as it breaks over the hard heads, foaming along in its impetuosity, only to cool off into tranquil, silent beauty farther on, reflecting in its dark depths the old wall, whose water-lined base it constantly laves, and repeating so perfectly the green of the grasses and willow branches that are daily growing stronger. Foam bubbles dance merrily along on the ripples, and play hide-and-seek in and out of hidden places; and we prolong our ride on this stretch, drinking in these good things as we never did so fully and delightedly in our pre-bicycle days, when our pedestrian strolls gave, as we then thought, such satisfaction. Then, the walking gave with the pleasure a certain amount of weariness; now, on the machine, spring, and saddle, we ride, we experience joy unbounded.　　　　STAMFORD.

THOMAS STEVENS IN CENTRAL ASIA.

THOMAS STEVENS the special correspondent of *Outing*, on a bicycle trip around the globe, writes as follows to a friend:

TEHERAN, March 9, 1886.— I start eastward to-morrow morning on the continuation of my journey around the world. General Melnikoff, the Russian minister at the Shah's court, promised me yesterday that he would telegraph to General Komaroff, at Asterabad, to remove all official obstacles from my route through Central Asia and Siberia. The Russian correspondent of the St. Petersburg *Nova Vremya*, who some time ago announced his intention of accompanying me on horseback, has either given it up or never seriously intended to carry out his proposition. I shall therefore again pull out alone, trusting to get through the Central Asian Khanates without a guard, as safely as I did through Koordistan and other places. My route then will be through Meshed, Merv, Bokhara, Samarkand, and Tashkend, and on into southern Siberia. In Siberia I shall probably touch at Tansk and Irkutsk. From Irkutsk I shall, if I find it even remotely practicable, strike south through Mongolia and endeavor to reach Pekin; if that course is found to be impossible, I shall reach the Pacific coast by way of the Amoor Valley. The distance from here to the north of the Amoor is not far from 6,000 miles, — a pretty long pull for a bicycle over the camel paths and desert wastes of Asia, and by a route where no extra tires or anything can reach me. But the distance is merely a question of time, health, and perseverance; and if my tire gets worn out, I can no doubt improvise makeshift tires from rawhide.

By the time this reaches you I shall probably have reached Merv or Bokhara. My bicycle is in excellent condition, my own health is splendid, and everything seems to

augur well for a successful termination of the journey around the world.

I beg leave to express my thanks for many letters and newspapers from wheelmen and others in various parts of the United States; they have been highly appreciated, and, whenever possible, replied to. Some will doubtless arrive here after my departure. They will be forwarded to Yokohama, Japan.

With the best of luck it will take me six months to reach that place by the route I intend taking.　　THOMAS STEVENS.

CYCLETS.

'T WAS A FUNNY THING.

'T was a funny thing that struck this town
Last night, just after the sun went down.
'T was made of silver and steel and wire,
And came on top of a ball of fire!

Dad was just coaxing the brindle cow,
When the terrible thing — don't know just how —
Came tearing along with a hop and a skip,
And took all the hair off the poor critter's hip.

It scared her outer a four months' growth,
And away she flew, while dad, with an oath,
Brought up the rear in hot pursuant,
And 't was lucky the pistol he had in his boot

Had n't been loaded since year before last,
Or that man on the "thing," or the cow, or me, —
One, or us all woulder had to passed
In their final checks, do yer see? ·

This morning I went to the old Red Inn,
And there in the yard, as sure as sin,
Was the fiery nightmare; Gollypywhop ! ·
With a real live man a'sitting on top!

He called it a gentle dismount that he took,
(He did n't take nothing at all !)
And he eyed the concern with a threatening look
And gave his short pants a long haul.

'T was a band of red rubber stretched over a wheel,
And the spokes was constructed of delikit steel, —
Just like our old rat cage, — the same size of wire,
An' inside of that was the "lantern" or fire.

We had just got our hands on the critter's backbone
And was wondering "where was its skin,"
And " why under heaVens it won't stand alone,"
And what does he carry it in ? "

When the man with a jerk, " took the saddle," so called,
(And I think in mid-air his breeches he hauled,)
GaVe a kick with his foot, waved his hand to the crowd,
(Oh, why should the spirit of mortal be proud !)

· When the animal quick, like our brindled cow, Beck,
Gave a twist of its tail and crawled up on his neck!

They took up a collection with a hay-cart, and after Dr.
Brows had glued him together, they covered him with a
postage stamp, and sent him home as third class matter.
　　　CLIF. S. WADY.

MAY Day impends.

DECORATE your wheels with roses and be off to the woods.

RIDERS have had to be in-dust-rious the past week.

AFTER a brush on the road has come a brush in the back porch.

THE ladies about Boston are all taking to tandems. It may be that in the future one who rides a single will be set down as one of the superfluous women.

THE Nemo Club seems to be in a minority so far as its opinion regarding doubles is concerned. And yet there is a deal of fun to be had on a sociable.

WE looked in at Murray's the other day, and saw some dozen Meteor sociables in parts and ready to be assembled. Here is a chance for the Nemos.

WE took a ride on a Quadrant tandem the other day, with " Jim " Underwood on the back seat. We did n't scorch much, but we had a delightful ride over River street to Mattapan and back. The machine carried the four hundred pounds of solid flesh speedily and safely, and there was an almost entire absence of vibration. Mr. Underwood has made several trips on the machine with his wife on the rear seat, and they have been able to climb some of the steepest hills.

THE *Clipper* is rather hard on the makers' amateurs. It says: " This is making a rather clean sweep of prominent propellers, some of whose names appear repeatedly on the record-slate, but as the avowed object — the purification of the amateur body — is dispensed with outside the ranks of the flat-footed professionals, to whom they should prove a strong acquisition, even though their presence may not tend to elevate the tone of that body."

NAPIER LOTHIAN, musical director of the Boston Theatre, is going to take a Quadrant tricycle to Saratoga with him this summer.

THE Boston Club has generally led the way into new paths which have been opened in the development of bicycling. They are all riding tricycles now. Can it be that this is what we are coming to? ·

HUMBER & Co. have been trying to restrain Humber, Marriott and Cooper from using the word " genuine " in describing their machines. The courts have decided that under the agreement made by the partners when the firm was dissolved, the Coventry firm has a perfect right to call their machines the genuine article.

ARDILL & CO. suggest that a dry day is better than a damp one to apply their enamel.

WHY is an eloping bank cashier's trotter like a bicycle ? Because it's a steed of steal.

IN a leading editorial in the " *Medical Record* " occurs these words by Mr. Holmes, in his address to students : " I do not want you to waste your time as students ; you have, in fact, not an hour to spare. But healthy recreation wastes no time. No one can study profitably without a large allowance of total rest, and in those happy hours it is well to mount your tricycle and drive it fearlessly along, forgetting that there is such a thing as anatomy or surgery. You will be none the worse anatomists and surgeons in the long run."

HENRY STURMEY has been trying the Fox " grip " rim on his tricycle. He says : " We have ridden it pretty frequently in town riding, and have taken it for several spins in the country, some fifty or one hundred miles in all, and the tires appear, if anything, more firmly seated than ever, and have shown no signs of loosening in riding, despite the fact that our last experiment with them was to run our steering wheel in the tram grooves and repeatedly twist it out again suddenly, a proof which satisfies us that, fairly used, the invention is a success." · ·

WE have received the League colors from the Tour-master. They constituted a part of the uniform of the touring department. Royal purple is the common color, and this is blended with other colors to denote the divisions. They are constituted of a narrow ribbon tied through the buttonhole of the jacket or attached to the badge. Each division will have a distinguishing color, to be worn with the purple, and consist of a similar ribbon, as follows : Eastern, red ; Middle, white ; Western, blue ; Southern, old gold. These colors touring members of the L. A. W. are recommended to wear on all appropriate occasions, whether on the annual tour or throughout the year.

AND now the New York Club wants a clubhouse. They now have forty-two members who have pledged $30,000, and when they get fifty members they will put their plans in operation.

P. HARVARD REILLY, of New York, has issued circulars relating to his proposed European tour.

FRED COOPER and W. Nicholson have made a tandem record on the Ripley road of 34.17 for ten miles. The American record is 39m.

GEO. M. HENDEE, A. O. McGarrett, and W. N. Winans have been suspended by the Springfield Club, pending the action of the League on the amateur question.

THE Springfield Club will hold its annual dinner 6 May at the Warwick. A large number of representative cyclers will be present.

THE Springfield Club will hold a minstrel entertainment 10 May, at the Opera House.

HAVE you seen Wood's road book ? Oh that Massachusetts had a Wood ! Perhaps Arbor Day will give us one.

KARL KRON now announces his book for the end of June. We can all stay at home on the 4th of July and read it.

AN English writer says of Furnivall : " Apparently, Furnivall will be as formidable as ever. He rides in the same ungainly style, leaning right over the handles, but retains his spurting powers. Asked as to his intentions, he means to ride hard this year, and will also make an effort with Gatehouse to get the tandem championships. His career has been a wonderful one. Last Whitmonday at Stortford he was almost unknown, except locally, and those who saw him never thought that in less than fourteen days he would be a celebrity at record breaking. Still less were his successes in America expected, and it was with no small interest his visit was looked forward to. During the winter he has been reading hard for his medical examination." He won his first race of the season 13 April, winning a two-mile handicap from Harvey (290 yards) and Talmage (410 yards).

W. W. STALL has issued his spring catalogue, which gives a list and full description, not only of the Star, but of the Columbia machines, the Sparkbrook tandem, and a number of others for which he is the agent.

WILBUR F. KNAPP, the fast man from Ohio, is in Boston, and will go into active training at once. He is one of the three flyers that will send the Columbia to the front this season, the others being Rowe and Hendee.

You do not often catch the Colonel asleep though he has taken a Knapp when looking for racing men.

DURING the month of March 1415 bicycles entered Fairmount Park, Philadelphia.

MR. DUCKER says the money is coming in, and we shall have enough to give the boys a good time.

IT is proposed to have a reunion of the "Big Four" tourists during the League Meet in Boston.

THE Pope Manufacturing Company has received an order for three Experts, for use in Germany.

BOSTON is going to give the visitors a chance to try a climb up Corey Hill. Now let us see if the men from the mountain districts can get up the hills any faster than we of the flat country.

A SPRINGFIELD young lady is the latest aspirant for Corey Hill honors. She thinks she can climb it.

THE Maverick Wheel Club, of East Boston, will give an entertainment at the Paris skating rink on the evening of 21 May.

WORKMEN will begin this week to put the Hampden Park track at Springfield in trim for cycling, and in a short time the racing men will put in an appearance and begin their spring training. It having been voted that "the League Racing Board will hereafter enter no record on its books that is not made in competition between men at an open race meeting, of which at least one week's notice has been given," all racing against time has thereby been prohibited. Should enough men go to Springfield, however, a series of Saturday afternoon races will be inaugurated and held regularly. It is thought probable that in a month or two enough flyers will be in town to warrant the venture, and if so, some lively sport may be expected.

THREE wheelmen started from New Orleans Sunday, with the intention of riding on their bicycles to Boston, for the purpose of attending the League Meet. Their names are Captain Charles Fairchild, H. W. Fairfax, and A. M. Hill. Each man will carry about ten pounds of baggage with him, and it is expected that they will arrive here about 25 May.

THE Pope Manufacturing Company has issued a neat little pamphlet, which carries out an original idea in a very ingenious way. It has the appearance of a manila scrapbook, in which are pasted a number of testimonials to the merits of the bicycle in general, and the Columbia in particular. A great many of these are reproduced from their block calendar. The outsides of the covers contain a reproduction of the first pages of thirty-seven newspapers and magazines.

BEACON PARK has been closed, and is in the market for a purchaser.

THE lease which the Boston Club had on its clubhouse expired 1 January, and the landlord immediately added $1,000 to the rent. The club is seeking other quarters where they will locate, pending action regarding the scheme for a large athletic club.

PHILADELPHIA wheelmen have taken a step worthy of imitation by the wheelmen of all other cities. Last week they held a meeting of cyclists and others in favor of improving the highways about the city. Eugene M. Aaron explained the object of the meeting, which is to bring every effort to bear upon the city government that may tend towards accomplishing the desired object. A constitution and by-laws were adopted. The title of the organization is "An Association for the Advancement of Cycling." The membership includes several classes, known as active, associate, and contributing members. The latter will consist of persons not wheelmen, but who are desirous of using their influence for the improvement of highways. The following officers were elected for the ensuing year: President, Eugene M. Aaron ; vice-president, Frank Read ; secretary, Charles M. Miller ; treasurer, H. B. Werrell.

IT is claimed that there are upwards of two hundred and fifty physicians in the United States who enjoy the delights of cycling.

A HANSOM cab driver in London was recently fined thirty shillings for driving into a cyclist while on the wrong side of the road.

A PARTY of Canadian wheelmen left Ottawa, Ont., 14 April, for England, where they propose to do some riding amid the green lanes.

DAN CANARY has been attracting crowded houses in Liverpool. He has excited no end of astonishment from those Englishmen who thought themselves clever riders.

RUDGE AND COMPANY have recently invented a combination tandem tricycle, or quadricycle for four riders. Roughly speaking, the machine consists of two tandems joined, a Humber pattern, and an automatic.

CHIEF CONSUL DUCKER has, in the name the Massachusetts Division of the League, instituted proceedings tending towards the conviction of certain roughs of Waltham, who, on the evening of 15 April, assaulted with stones a party of wheelmen. J. S. Dean has been retained as counsel.

MR. P. HARVARD RIELY, manager of the American Bicyclists' and Tourists' Association, with headquarters at the Grand Union Hotel, New York City, having made some very successful bicycle tours in this country and in Europe, will conduct a party to Europe, leaving New York about 1 July. The party will be absent about two months, and will visit parts of France, England, Ireland, and possibly Wales.

THE Boston Club is preparing for an all-night moonlight run to Gloucester.

NONE but words of praise are heard for Boston's new wheel paper, THE CYCLE. — Herald.

WE have it on good authority that some of the men who have been declared professionals are turning their prizes into cash. If they again become amateurs they will have a deal of cash instead of the prizes, and no one can question their right in selling them.

WESTFIELD, MASS., has an ordinance against sidewalk riding. In a town where there are such bad roads, the measure is so sweeping that it is practically inoperative save against one bicycle rider, who is a popular minister. He of course would not violate a rule adopted by the voters even if its legal enforcement is a question, and as a consequence his parochial calls are now made on foot instead of on his silent steed. But other riders use the sidewalks as freely as ever, and go so far in some instances as to intrude upon sidewalks they never presumed to use out of courtesy to the public until the prohibitory by-law was enacted.

"JENKINS" tells this yarn in Sporting Life : "The other evening, while a patrolman was pursuing his weary way along the sandy beaches of Long Island, near Moritus, he espied a nude figure astride of a Cripper tricycle, apparently enjoying a moonlight spin. He rubbed his eyes to make sure that he was not mistaken, and then started in pursuit. Just as he was about to over-take the venturesome being, it made a sharp turn and disappeared beneath the rolling surf with a happy chuckle. It seems that the inhabitants of the briny deep have recovered some of the consignment that was on the Oregon ; but the fun is likely to be stopped, as Anthony Comstock has decided that they must wear a League uniform and a nickeled badge."

THE patent war continues. On Saturday last the Ames Manufacturing Company furnished the bond required to dissolve the attachment on their works. This was between 11 and 12 in the forenoon. Immediate steps were taken to get the Victor machines out, and 192 of them were removed, when down comes the sheriff with another attachment, this time on behalf of John Harrington, of England, who sues for an infringement of the candle-spring patent. Mr. Harrington claims that the tricycle spring made in two parts by the Overman Wheel Company infringes his patent, and also that the Victor spring saddle infringes.

W. B. EVERETT & Co. took in a few Springfield tandems last week, but they were sold and taken away inside of two days. Mr. Charles Hopkins, of Wellington, took the only one that was built for two ladies, and he has been riding it with great satisfaction. He can hardly find words to express his satisfaction with a tandem that is light, easy running, and safe.

THE Massachusetts State Racing Board has established one and five mile State championships. The one-mile event will be run on the occasion of the League Meet, and the five-mile event will be located later in the season, at the discretion of the Board.

COL. POPE is getting into condition. He may be seen any morning at 5 o'clock scorching on the mill-dam with his son. They are about an even match. The hour chosen for practice precludes the idea that the Colonel rides to advertise his machine.

MR. JOHN R. HEARD, formerly captain of the Roxbury Club, has charge of the news stand at the Tremont House. All the papers, including the CYCLE, will be on sale at this place.

EDGAR L. DAVENPORT, brother of Miss Fanny Davenport, and a member of her company, has been playing at the Park Theatre the past week, and has taken the opportunity to look up his old wheeling acquaintances. Mr. Davenport has written not a little for the wheel press, and has won some distinction in the past as a racing man.

L. A. W. MEET.

SINCE the amalgamation of the Pennsylvania and Penn City clubs, this city can lay claim to possessing the largest and one of the most active clubs in the State. A contract has just been given out for the supplying of one hundred and fifty new uniforms for the members, and the gray suit, with keystone badge, will be a more prominent feature than ever on the riding road this season. Capt. Roberts is hard at work arranging a schedule of trips for the summer months, and it is expected that he will find himself at the head of a troop of about thirty wheelmen every time the bugle sounds for a start to Paoli or elsewhere. The new club house is being pushed forward, and will be a credit to the club when completed. — *Sporting Life.*

THE New Jersey Cycling and Athletic Association have secured a good plot of land for their new race track not very far from the Roseville station, just between Newark and East Orange. Two assessments of ten per cent on the stock ($10,000) have been made, and the track will be pushed through promptly.

PROF. J. W. VAN DE VENTER, of Sharon, Pa., sails for Europe 27 April, on a five months' Star bicycle tour.

EAST HARTFORD wheelmen talk of going to the League Meet in Boston, 27-29 May, by rail, and riding home on their cycles. A number of Hartford wheelmen would like to do the same thing, and there may be a large party on wheels going that way after the Meet.

ONE hundred and fifty new uniforms have been ordered for the Pennsylvania Bicycle Club, and a summer trip schedule is being arranged.

THE CLUB.

[WITH a view to obtaining a complete list of clubs with the officers elect, we will ask the secretary of each and every club in America to send us, on a postal card a list of the principal officers after the following formula :—
BOSTON, MASS.—Massachusetts Club. Officers elected 1 January, 1886: President, Col. T. W. Higginson; captain,

A. D. Peck, Jr.; secretary, F. Alcott Pratt, 3 Somerset street; treasurer, E. R. Benson, 597 Washington street.]

BAY CITY, MICH. — Bay City Club. President, D. C. Williamson; secretary, Will Walters; captain, Ed. Babcock.

BALTIMORE, MD. — Junior Wheelmen. President, W. Hills; secretary and treasurer, W. C. Crawford; captain, J. Hannay.

BROCKTON, MASS. — Brockton Club. President, W. M. Pratt; treasurer, H. A. Howland; secretary, O. P. Lovejoy; captain, D. C. Pierce.

BRATTLEBORO', VT. — Vermont Wheel Club. President, H. L. Emerson; secretary and treasurer, J. W. Drown; captain, F. T. Reed.

BROOKLYN, N. Y. — Long Island Wheelmen. President, W. W. Share; treasurer, S. W. Baldwin; secretary, J. D. Huggins; captain, Charles H. Luscomb.

CAMBRIDGE, MASS. — Cambridge Club. President, H. W. Hayes; secretary, E. B. Coleman; treasurer, A. L. Bowker; captain, C. L. Smith.

DETROIT, MICH. — Detroit Club. President, B. J. Holcombe; secretary and treasurer, A. F. Peck; captain, H. M. Snow.

DALLAS, TEX. — Dallas Club. President, C. J. Grant; secretary and treasurer, J. W. Cochran; captain, A. L. Knox.

EVERETT, MASS. — Everett Club. President and captain, W. C. Dillingham; secretary-treasurer, J. H. Larkin.

FLORENCE, MASS. — Florence Club. President, A. G. Hill; secretary and treasurer, W. H. Wyman; captain, A. E. Friedrich.

GREENFIELD, MASS. — Berkshire County Wheelmen. President, E. H. Kennedy; secretary, W. S. Kells; treasurer, H. G. West; captain, C. C. Kennedy.

HUMBOLDT, IA. — Humboldt Club. President, N. H. Knowles; secretary, O. A. Ward; treasurer, H. H. Perkins; captain, S. A. Taft.

HOOSICK FALLS. — Hoosac Wheelmen President, Danforth Geer; secretary and treasurer, Charles C. Gibson; captain, C. Jerome Stevens.

HUDSON, N. Y. — Hudson Club. President, H. J. Baringer, Jr.; secretary-treasurer, C. A. Van Deusen, Jr.; captain. H. R. Bryan.

JAMESTOWN, N. Y. — Jamestown Club. President, Robert Hazard; secretary, Ed. R. Dempsey; treasurer, Frank Reed; captain, Charles E. Gates.

LOUISVILLE, KY. — Louisville Club. President, J. D. Macaulay; secretary and treasurer, Harry Esterle; captain, C. F. Johnson.

MOLINE, ILL. — Moline Wheelmen. President, W. E. McClro; secretary and treasurer, E. H. Sleight; captain, G. D. Dunn.

MANCHESTER-BY-THE-SEA. MASS. — The Conomo Bicycle Club. President, C. A. Collins; secretary-treasurer, A. L. Churchill; captain, Louis Lations.

MANSFIELD, O. — Richland Ramblers. President, F. L. Casselberry; secretary, L. S. Hannan; treasurer, W. E. Sawin; captain, A. P. Seiler.

MINNEAPOLIS, MINN. — M. I. P. Club. Captain, Colie Bell; secretary and treasurer, Charles Miller.

NORTH ATTLEBORO', MASS. — Columbia Bicycle Club. President, O. W. Clifford; secretary, George L. Shepardson; treasurer, C. F. Kurtz; captain, F. I. Gordan.

PEORIA, ILL. — Peoria Club. President, Charles W. Freeman; treasurer, Fred. Wolcott; treasurer, George Bush, Jr.; captain, Charles F. Vail.

PITTSBURG, PA. — Keystone Club. President, C. M. Clarke; secretary and treasurer, F. C. Bidwell; captain, H. E. Bidwell.

POUGHKEEPSIE, N. Y. — Ariel Wheel Club. President, I. Reynolds Adriance;

secretary and treasurer, Charles F. Cossum; captain, Ed. A. King.

PHILADELPHIA, PA. — Philadelphia Club. President, Geo. E. Bartol; secretary-treasurer, H. A. Blakiston; captain, Ewing L. Miller.

PHILADELPHIA, PA. — Pennsylvania Club. President, Isaac Elwell; secretary, Samuel Chesney; treasurer, Fred A. Brown.

PEEKSKILL, N. Y. — Cortland Wheelmen. Captain, E. A. Hodgkins; secretary-treasurer, A. D. Dunbar.

PAWTUCKET, R. I. — Pawtucket Club. President, J. A. Chase; secretary-treasurer, Geo. C. Newell; captain, A. H. Littlefield, Jr.

READING, PA. — Reading Bicycle Club. President, W. I. Wilhelm; secretary and treasurer, J. L. Henritzy; captain, G. I. Betchel.

SYRACUSE, N. Y. — Empire Club. President, Fred. Brigham; secretary and treasurer, L. S. Wilson; captain, Edward Rice.

SAN FRANCISCO, CAL. — San Francisco Club. President, C. Waterhouse; secretary and treasurer, Geo. J. Hobe; captain, Harry L. Miller.

ST. LOUIS, MO. — Missouri Club. President, Louis Chauvenet; secretary, Edward A. Sells; treasurer, Geo. F. Baker; captain, W. M. Brewster.

SCRANTON, PA. — Scranton Club. President, George A. Jessup; secretary, John J. Van Nort; treasurer, Frank D. Watts; captain, A. J. Kolp.

WASHINGTON, D. C. — Capital Club. President, John M. Killitts; secretary, Thomas A. Berryhill; treasurer, Joseph E. Leaming; captain, Fred F. Church.

THE Suffolk Wheel Club rides to Downer Landing, Sunday, 2 May. The monthly meeting will be held Monday evening, 3 May, when ten new members will be balloted upon.

THE Brooklyn Bicycle Club offers medals to members of the club for the best road record made during the calendar year; the second best road record made during the calendar year; for the best twenty-four hour road record; for each century run; for each one thousand miles ridden, with an extra bar to attach for each additional thousand miles; to the member attending the most club runs. Members attempting twenty-four records, or century runs, must choose a course covering at least twenty-five unrepeated miles, and give previous notice to the captain that arrangements may be made for checking.

THE PATH.

THE ROAD RACE.

CLARKSVILLE, MO., 26 April. — The fifty-mile bicycle race was started promptly at ten o'clock this morning. A cool southwest wind, blowing briskly, made the climbing of the hills a fatiguing piece of work. The entire course around the belt road was lined with spectators. Weber and Whittaker were the favorites for the first and second places respectively. The following men started: George E. Weber, Smithville, N. J.; C. E. Kluge, Smithville, N. J.; R. T. Vanhorne, Denver, Col.; S. G. Whittaker, Percy Stone, R. C. C. Gordon, D. R. Davies, A. A. Hart, Henry Oellien, and H. H. Morris, St. Louis. As the distance around the belt road is but twenty and three fourth miles, the course had to be gone over twice. Before two miles, Whittaker had taken a good lead, but at that point he took a header, cutting open his hand. He remounted, and had nearly closed the gap when he fell again, badly bruising his shoulder, arm, and knees. He was compelled to give up. A short time after, R. C. Lee, who was passing Davies, took a terrific header, cutting open his face in several places.

Weber passed through Clarksville with a big lead, which he steadily increased to the finish. Percy Stone rode second till about ten miles from the finish, when Kluge, who had been fighting for second, passed Stone, and the two finished some distance apart. The rest of the racers straggled in. The time for the fifty miles was as follows: Weber, 3.7.42¼; Kluge, 3.22.34; Stone, 3.25.32¼. Munger's time at New Orleans was 3.2.34, and Traver's English record was 3.15.39.

MINNEAPOLIS, MINN., 25 April. 1886. — John S. Prince and William M. Woodside contested a fifty-mile bicycle race at the Washington Rink last night. The race grew out of the result of the one a week ago, in which Prince was thrown by what appeared to be an intentional foul on the forty-seventh mile, a boy running across the track, thereby giving him a "header." The decision then was a draw. To-night Prince had an apparently easy victory, and at the last six laps attempted to pass, calling "pole." Woodside refused to grant the request, keeping in the centre of the track, which was not wide enough to allow Prince to pass on either side. A claim of foul was made by Prince, which the referee refused to notice, giving the race to Woodside. The time was 2.44.37. Yesterday Prince covered Albert Schock's forfeit of $200 for a six-day, twelve hours per day, bicycle race; for $500 a side, with the privilege of increasing the stakes to $1,000 a side.

ON 5 July, the Binghamton (N. Y.) Club will hold their fourth annual race meet.

JUDGING from the improvements now going on at the Common, we shall see no race meeting there on the 5th of July. The old track is completely obliterated.

THE Ixions of New York will hold a road race on Decoration Day. It is proposed to run it over a sixteen-mile circuit in the Orange district where the roads are as good as many race tracks.

THE Hudson County wheelmen, of New Jersey, will hold a race 8 May, over the Inter-Club twenty-five mile course. The purpose of the race will be the selection of a team to represent the club in the coming team race, in which each club will have four men. Kluge has been selected on his merits, and the first three in this race will make up the club's quota.

A BICYCLE race will be held at the Madison Square Garden, New York, on 1, 8, and 15 May, on the occasion of the contests between W. C. George and L. E. Myers.

THE intercollegiate meeting is set down for 29 May. J. S. Kulp will represent Yale in the bicycle race, and D. H. Renton will represent Columbia.

THE New Castle (Pa.) will hold a race meeting 20 May on a four-lap track.

THE Alexandra Park track has been certified to be within three eighths of an inch of one third of a mile.

ALBERT SCHOCK and J. W. Snyder rode a twenty-mile race, at Fairbault, Minn., Saturday night, 17 April. The track was seventeen laps to the mile. There were over 300 people present, and the racing was very interesting, but on the last mile Snyder went to the front and beat Schock over half a lap. Time, 1.25.

C. W. RYDER, who refereed the fifty-mile race between Prince and Woodside, in his decision, stated that there was no positive evidence that the boy had been used as a tool to throw Prince, still as the men were so close together and near the finish, the circumstance of Woodside having escaped while Prince did not, together with the fact that Prince had at that time an equal chance to win the race, and that the boy had immediately after the foul escaped by running out doors, was at least suspicious, and in all fairness he should declare the race a draw and all bets off. This decision was hailed by an almost unanimous applause.

A SIX-DAY race, eight hours a day, will take place in Minneapolis next month. All the fliers will be there.

AN effort is being made by the Pottstown, Pa., Bicycle Club to arrange a twenty-five mile bicycle race on the track of the Montgomery, Berks, and Chester Agricultural and Horticultural Society of Pottstown. It is proposed to match Prof. High, of that club, against W. I. Wilhelm, of the Reading Bicycle Club, if the latter will agree to enter into the contest.

MISS ELSA VON BLUMEN was considerably injured by a collision with a contestant in a bicycle race at St. Catharine, Ont., 17 April, and is now at her home in Rochester. The plucky woman won the fifty-one hours' race by one mile and thirteen laps.

PRINCE, Woodside, and Eck will compete at Woodstock, Canada, 24 May.

THE TRADE.

Mr. H. W. FAIRFAX and Mr. C. M. Fairchild, who are touring from New Orleans to Boston to attend the League Meet, both ride Rudge Light Roadsters.

WM. READ & SON have cabled to England, and doubled their order for wheels. This tells the story of what they are doing.

S. T. CLARK & Co. report a good demand for the Rapid bicycles with the true tangent wheels. They will make an exhibit of wheels at the Boston show.

FOR several years subsequent to the manufacture of bicycles, paint, on account of its cheapness, and enamel, for its durability, were preferable finishes, for bicycles. The beauty of the nickel plate was acknowledged; but experience then showed it could not be depended upon for durability. There was a flaw somewhere in the method of applying it, and although every manufacturer strove to remedy it, none were wholly successful. A few years ago the Pope Manufacturing Company, of Boston, perfected a method of nickel-plating the Columbias, which has borne the test of four years without any complaint from riders save where the machines had been used near the salt water, against the influence of which no finish can wholly withstand. The fact that during one year, seventeen per cent of all experts sold were full nickelled, all of which were highly satisfactory to the riders, and that Thomas Stevens, now circumbicycling the globe, rides a full-nickelled export, thoroughly proves that nickel plate is the best finish for a machine away from the salt water. Its beauty and attractiveness, especially when the sun is glistening among the polished spokes, more than compensates for the little extra work in the care of the machine over the dull finish of paint or enamel.

W. B. EVERETT & Co. are having a great run on the "S. S. S." and the Traveller tandem.

THE Coventry Machinists' Company has in the Ranelagh Club one of the lightest and easiest running wheels on the market, and it avoids the vibration incident to many bar steerers.

MISCELLANEOUS

Advertisements will be inserted in this column for one cent a word, including heading and address; but no advertisement will be taken for less than twenty-five cents.

WANTED. — Bicycle repairer; one who understands trueing wheels; brazing and repairing. Address, A. W. GUMP, Dayton, Ohio.

OVERMAN WHISTLES with Chain, 25 cents. To advertise. LOWE BICYCLE CO., Fitchburg, Mass.

COW-HORN BARS, Nickelled and Complete, $5.00. LOWE BICYCLE CO., Fitchburg, Mass.

FOR SALE. — 54-inch Rudge Light Roadster, 1885 pattern, enamel finish, had careful use, *first-class condition*; too small for owner. "Z," care THE CYCLE.

BICYCLES AND TRICYCLES. — 125 shop-worn and second-hand wheels now on exhibition. Stock constantly changing; no price list; correspondence and inspection invited; open Saturday evenings. BUTMAN & CO., Scollay Square, Oriental Building.

BICYCLES AND TRICYCLES. — Bargains for cash; wheels not sold on instalments nor rented. BUTMAN & CO., 89 Court Street.

BICYCLES AND TRICYCLES. — Specialty in furnishing new wheels for exchange. BUTMAN & CO., Scollay Square, Oriental Building.

BICYCLES. — Fair prices and spot cash paid for desirable second-hand wheels. BUTMAN & CO., 89 Court Street.

BICYCLES AND TRICYCLES received on consignment; no charges made when goods are furnished in exchange. BUTMAN & CO., Oriental Building, 89 Court Street.

COLUMBIAS

A GENERAL REDUCTION IN PRICES AND MANY IMPROVEMENTS FOR THE

SEASON OF 1886.

Riders of Columbias HOLD MORE AND BETTER RECORDS than are held by riders of any other make of machine.

SEND FOR APRIL CATALOGUE, 51 Engravings.

EXPERT COLUMBIA $125
For a 50-inch, D or E Finish, with Ball Bearings all around, Columbia "Double-Grip" Ball Pedals, Kirkpatrick Saddle, and One-Piece Hollow Cow-Horn Handle-Bar, or with Columbia "Double-Grip" Parallel Pedals, $120.

COLUMBIA LIGHT ROADSTER $135
For a 51-inch, K Finish, with Ball Bearings all around, Columbia "Double-Grip" Ball Pedals, Kirkpatrick Saddle, and One-Piece Hollow Cow-Horn Handle-Bar, or with Columbia "Double-Grip" Parallel Pedals, $130.

STANDARD COLUMBIA $90
For a 50-inch, G Finish, with Ball Bearings to Front Wheel, or with Parallel Bearings to Front Wheel, $85.

COLUMBIA SAFETY $140
Ball Bearings all around, Columbia "Double-Grip" Ball Pedals, Kirkpatrick Saddle, and One-Piece Hollow Cow-Horn Handle-Bar, or with Columbia "Double-Grip" Parallel Pedals, $135.

COLUMBIA SEMI-ROADSTER $85
For a 46-inch, Finish D, with Cow-Horn Handle-Bars and Kirkpatrick Saddle.

COLUMBIA RACER $140
Weight of 55-inch, 22 1-2 pounds.

COLUMBIA TWO-TRACK TRICYCLE . . . $165
With "Double-Grip" Ball Pedals. With "Double-Grip" Parallel Pedals, $160.

LADIES' COLUMBIA TWO-TRACK TRICYCLE . $175
With "Double-Grip" Ball Pedals, or with "Double-Grip" Parallel Pedals, $170.

COLUMBIA RACING TRICYCLE $180
Weight, all on, 47 1-2 pounds.

COLUMBIA THREE-TRACK TRICYCLE . . . $160
With Power-Gear, $180.

THE POPE MANUFACTURING CO.

597 WASHINGTON STREET - - - BOSTON.

BRANCH HOUSES: 12 Warren Street, NEW YORK; 115 Wabash Avenue, CHICAGO.

The Cycle.

VOL. I., No. 6. BOSTON, MASS., 7 MAY, 1886. FIVE CENTS.

The Coventry Machinists' Co.'s New Tricycle for 1886.

1886 ROYAL MAIL.

EXTRAORDINARY DEMAND!!!   A PERFECT WHEEL APPRECIATED.   AGENTS WANTED EVERYWHERE!

5,056 MILES,
BEST ROAD RECORD OF 1885
On one Wheel, Won by ROYAL MAIL.

Six Improvements.

THE Wheel of the Year.

Spokes wound SEVEN TIMES, giving rigidity to whole wheel. No rattle. Note this tying.

Grip Fast Rim and Tire

NEEDS NO CEMENT.

Holds firmer than Cement; no thin edge of rim to dent; whole rim stronger; also seamless.

BALL BEARING HEAD.

No friction of cones, hence no loosening nor constant tightening up. Can be run six months with one adjustment and one oiling. All parts INTERCHANGEABLE in Royal Mails this year. Offered as the most perfect wheel yet shown,

DETACHABLE HANDLE BARS.

Merely unscrew nuts each side of head. Very simple and strong.

Before purchase, send Stamp for large Illustrated Circulars.

WM. READ & SONS, 107 Washington St., Boston,

SOLE AMERICAN AGENTS.

— READ THIS. —

EVer since the introduction of the India-rubber tire, it has proved itself, like many other things, not altogether an unmixed blessing, for the difficulty to keep it on has ever been a great one, and many and various have been the devices adopted by ingenious makers to make its fastening to the rim secure. A year ago at the Speedwell Exhibition a rim and tire had just been patented, and our opinion asked upon it. This rim was an ordinary crescent steel felloe, with the edges turned in so as to fit into a couple of longitudinal grooves cut in the rubber tire, and thus, without the aid of cement, holding the rubber firmly in its place. We at once spotted the idea as a good thing. As will be seen by the sketch, the tires are held firm in the rims without the use of cement, and are, therefore, cleaner in application than a cemented tire. Not caring to speak of such an important matter without testing the idea practically, we have ridden it in town riding, and, the tires appear, if anything, more firmly seated than ever, despite the fact that our last experiment with them was to run our steering wheel in the tram grooves, and repeatedly twist it out again suddenly, a proof which satisfies us that the invention is a success. As we have said, the tires have not yet come out with us. When they do, — IF they do, — we will let our readers know.

HENRY STURMEY, in the "Cyclist," April 14, 1886.

SPECIAL NOTICE!!!   SPECIAL NOTICE!!!

Owing to the now very common practice of prominent racing wheelmen, riding in the interest of certain makes and for their advertisement, we wish to announce BEFORE the racing season opens, that

The ROYAL MAIL has NO (nor will have any) SALARIED RIDERS IN ITS EMPLOY.

We believe wheelmen should not be and are not influenced, in selection of their mounts, by the fast riding or breaking of records by PAID riders on this or that wheel. We have in stock Royal Mail celebrated racers FOR SALE, and from their past reputation, offer them as the finest and most rigid racing wheel made. Our aim, to furnish a Perfect Roadster. We offer as such, the ROYAL MAIL.

WILLIAM READ & SONS, 107 Washington Street, Boston.

THE CYCLE

PUBLISHED EVERY FRIDAY BY ABBOT BASSETT, 22 SCHOOL ST., ROOM 19.

VOL. I.	BOSTON, MASS., 7 MAY, 1886.	No. 6.

TERMS OF SUBSCRIPTION.

One Year, by mail, post-paid..........................$1.50
Three Copies in one order.............................3.00
Club Subscriptions...................................1.00
Six Months..90
Single Copies...05

Specimen Copies free.

Every bicycle dealer is agent for the CYCLE and author-
ized to receive subscriptions at regular rates. The paper
can be found on sale at the following places: —
Boston, CUPPLES, UPHAM & Co., cor. Washington and
School Streets. Tremont House news stand. At every
cycle warehouse.
New York, ELLIOTT MASON, 12 Warren Street.
Philadelphia, H. B. HART, 811 Arch Street. GEORGE
D. GIDEON, 6 South Broad Street.
Baltimore, S. T. CLARK & Co., 4 Hanover Street.
Chicago, W. M. DURELL, 115 Wabash Avenue. JOHN
WILKINSON & Co., 77 State Street.
Washington, H. S. OWEN, Capital Cycle Co.
St. Louis, ST. LOUIS WHEEL Co., 1121 Olive Street.

| ABBOT BASSETT | . . . . . | EDITOR |
| W. I. HARRIS | . . | EDITORIAL CONTRIBUTOR |

A. MUDGE & SON, PRINTERS, 24 FRANKLIN ST., BOSTON.

All communications should be sent in not later than
Tuesday, to ensure insertion the same week.

Entered at the Post-office as second-class mail matter.

WE said a few words last week anent the
new class of riders which it is proposed to
form for the especial benefit of those who
cannot be amateurs, and do not wish to be
professionals. All propositions of this kind
look to the admission of this new class of
men to League membership. This portion of the proposition is now impossible
of solution at the League Meet in May.
The Constitution provides for its own
amendment, not at the annual meeting, but
at a constitutional convention which must
be called by the president at the date of the
annual meeting, and he must give at least
one month's notice of the convention. To
call such a convention for the 28 May is
now impossible, and any alteration of the
Constitution must be made by a mail vote.
It does not look as though we were to have
any but amateur wheelmen in the League at
present.

To bring about a change in the by-laws,
included among which is the amateur rule,
notice must be given of the proposed change
to every member of the board of officers.
The by-laws, it seems to us, are defective
in that they do not provide for amendment
by the general meeting ; but we believe the

general meeting is perfectly competent to
change the laws, always provided that notice
has been given. Those that have amendments to offer must publish them not later
than the 21 May issue of the *Bulletin.*

THE Springfield Club requests that specific charges be made in the cases of some of
its members who have been declared professionals by the Racing Board. The Board
having disposed of the cases refuses to furnish specific charges ; but it may be worth
the while to state that proceedings were instituted against two of these men on the basis
of a document furnished the Board, and
signed by the President of the Springfield
Club.

WE believe in the League of American
Wheelmen, its Racing Board, and all of its
rules, except Rule H. . . . . Was there ever
a more absurd rule adopted by a body of
men elected to serve their constituents'
interests ? — *Wheelmen's Gazette.*

Among the records of the Racing Board
is a vote on the Racing Rules taken in February last. The editor of the *Wheelmen's
Gazette* was a member of the Board at that
time, and his vote is recorded in favor of
Rule H.

WE have always contended that clubs
should be allowed to pay the expenses of a
favored member. — *Wheelmen's Gazette.*

Among those who have been suspended
for receiving expenses, there is not a case
where the proceedings were instituted because the man allowed his club to pay his
expenses.

CONTEMPTIBLE is the best word we can
find to express our idea of the flings which
our Tremont-street contemporary is making
at our lady correspondent. When gentlemen make war upon a lady, they merit the
contempt of all right-minded persons.

OWING to change of circumstance, Abbot
Bassett, of the *Cycle,* will run again next year
for the office of chairman of the Racing
Board. — *Globe.*

We have conferred with the gentleman referred to in the above, and he tells us that
he cannot well see how a man can run for
an office that comes within the appointing
power of the president of the League. Nor
can he see anything so attractive in the posi-

tion that a man would be tempted to run for
it. We do not believe our friend will run
very fast if he sees any one moving in the
direction of the office, nor will he try to head
any aspirant off. Moreover, in the present
aspect of things, it cannot well be told whether
there will be in the future such an office as
chairman of the Racing Board, whether the
present occupant would accept it again, or
whether the League would have him in the
position.

CONTRIBUTORS' CLUB

THAT BICYCLE PROBLEM.

[WE can't begin to publish all the answers
we have received to the problem. We give
a few more this week. — ED.]

Editor of the Cycle: Your correspondent
" Cy " proposes a problem, without stating
conditions. Supposing I said, " I sold my
bicycle for $100, how much did I make? "
You would immediately say, " There 's the
gate." If " Cy's " machine was an American Rudge, and cost $110, and *he had paid
for it,* I should say he lost $60 on his first
transaction, and made $20 on the second,
total net loss being $40. If he stole the
bicycle, I should say he made $50 on first
transaction and $20 on the second, or a net
gain of $70, with a good prospect of state
prison if he got caught. HERMES.

Editor of the Cycle: In that bicycle
problem, the question is not how much was
made on the wheel, but simply is, " What is
the gain on the two transactions?" The
reply is, $5 gained on the first, and $20 on
the second. We are to go no further. The
$45 which remains at the close represents
the bicycle (or the capital), and, as it was
unknown and not considered in the beginning, should also remain unknown and
ignored at the close of the transaction.
JOEY LADLE.

Editor of the Cycle: Let me put the bicycle problem in another way. A is a bicycle dealer. He has a second-hand wheel
which he took in trade for $50. It stands
him $50, and he hopes to get that for it. B
comes in and speaks for it. Does n't pay
for it, but deposits $5 to bind the bargain.
B never shows up again, and A scoops the
$5, which is all profit. C then comes in and
buys the bicycle for $65, and A has made
$15 on that trade, or $20 in all.

Editor of the Cycle: I send my clerk
to State street with a United States bond of
$50, with instructions to sell it. He sells it
at par, and brings back $50. The next day

I go away, leaving $50 in the drawer. The market is off that day, and my clerk goes down and buys the bond back again for $45; and the bond lies in the drawer with a $5 bill side of it. The next day the clerk sells the bond for $65, and when I come back he hands me $70, or $20 more than I left with him. If the profit is $25, as one of your correspondents says, where is the other $5?

BAN KERR.

Editor of the Cycle: The bicycle problem is too easy to waste time over. A is in business, and he determines to bank all his profits and live on faith. He sells a bicycle for $50. He has forgotten how much it cost him, and he does n't know whether he made a profit or not. A thing is worth what it will bring, and so it is fair to suppose at this point that the wheel was worth $50. B comes back again and wants to sell the wheel. A buys it and gives his check for $45. He now has a five-dollar bill and a bicycle for which he paid $45. He banks the $5. C comes along. By some circumlocution of trade he has come in possession of A's check. He gives to A the check for $45 (just the money A paid for the bicycle) and a twenty-dollar bill. Thus A has got what the bicycle cost him and $20 besides. He banks this $20 with the $5, and has in the bank profit amounting to $25.

H. T. R.

Editor of the Cycle: Here is the bicycle problem simplified: —

First cost to B, $50.

First loss to B . . . . . $ 5
Second cost to B 65
                          _____
                          $70
Deduct first cost to B . . . 50
                          _____
A's gain $20

TREASURER.

Editor of the Cycle: We had that problem up in our clubroom the other night, and after five scrimmages, six broken friendships, and no end of emphatic language, we resolved that we did n't care a continental malediction what the profit was on that bicycle. Forwarded by order of the club.

SEC.

CYCLOS' COMMENTS.

Editor of the Cycle: At last we have an official statement of the vote of the New York Division on the Division Organ question. For, 11; against, 216; rejected, 1; total, 228, out of a total membership of over one thousand. How does this chime with Secretary-Editor Aaron's claim concerning mail votes?

S. H. M., whose thrilling "Bermudian Rambles on a Tricycle" are chiefly noticeable for the extraordinary proportion of quotations and for the high culture displayed, reminding one at once of the *Waverley Magazine* and Bartlett's "Dictionary of Quotations," is much hurt by the requests made by some League members for permission to discuss wheels in the official organ of the League of American Wheelmen. This request is "a sporadic plaint of very wearisome nature." "The paucity of ideas manifested by this contingent of the League is phenomenal." "From the vantage-ground

of some quiet neighborhood, in which a cone-bearing Standard is still the marvel and village pride, . . . this minority attempts to prescribe for us in the *Bulletin* a diet of straw." The certainty and completeness of their judgment, and the profound self-assurance of their *ipse dixit* to the majority, indicate the characteristics of people who know next to nothing."

"I protest against the appearance in the *Bulletin* of any such sawdust dessert of inane correspondence as weights so heavily the quoted *C. T. C. Gazette.*"

Thus the refined and cultured "S. H. M." protests. At least he is consistent, for he has contrived to write, I know not how many pages, of "Bermudian Rambles on a Tricycle," with the very least possible amount of allusion to cycles or cycling, and a most remarkable display of quotation marks, gush and foreign phrases in italics. He "protests against the appearance in the *Bulletin* of any such" sawdust dessert of inane correspondence" as discussions of the merits and demerits of various forms of wheel construction, and gives us in place of it column upon column of "lovely" writing, of which the following choice bit is a fair sample: —

"There was another Gertrude, celebrated by Campbell in his tale of Wyoming, who was not a brighter fancy to the poet than this accomplished namesake in her jaunty Tam O'Shanter cap, who lingers in our memory with the notes of the grand Russian hymn. Near her then as always in Bermuda, was the graceful form of her Fidus Achates. This *petite* Missourian *ingenue* was as intrepid as she was charming. *A son excellent père qui est un invalide, cherche un autre climat plus deux pour sa sante,* she had come from the States alone, protected *en voyage* by only six devoted friends."

There, is n't that just too sweet for anything? Just think of a "petite Missourian *ingenue*" sufficiently intrepid to go around alone with "six devoted friends," and a "Fidus Achates," and in a warm climate, too. And, to think that there be those who, "from the vantage-ground of some quiet neighborhood," where a cone-bearing Standard is a marvel, and "French in Six Lessons" and "Bartlett's Quotations" are unknown, would ask the secretary-editor to consign S. H. M.'s commencement-day eloquence and French and Latin to the w. p. b. or the *Waverley Magazine*, and replace it alone with "six devoted friends," in plain English.

S. H. M. has something to say about "the visible tendency of the bucolic writers to affect a peculiar idiosyncrasy of style," and the charge *sounds* formidable; but it is to be hoped that few bucolic or other writers will "affect" the "peculiar idiosyncrasy of style" that leads S. H. M. to use a plural verb to express the action of a singular noun, and to interlard his "pieces" so freely with irrelevant quotations and foreign phrases Routes, meetings, tours, and even races have their places, and reports of them should have *their* places in the columns of the *Bulletin*; but to shut out a discussion of wheel construction from the columns of a paper professedly devoted to the interests and enlightenment of wheel users, is simply absurd.

We must and will discuss these things, if

not in the columns of the *Bulletin*, then elsewhere; and if we could be prevented from so doing, how is the resident of "some quiet neighborhood" ever to learn that there is something better than a cone-bearing Standard, and what that something is. It is through such discussion that improvement comes; and if I find my Columbia Light Roadster of to-day a lighter, stronger, swifter, and more delightful mount than my old cone-bearing Standard of five years ago, it is largely because discussions in the wheel papers have posted me on the advantages of hollow forks, hollow rims, ball-bearings, etc.

If any one should feel that I have been severe or unjust in my criticism of S. H. M.'s literary style, I beg of them to turn to page 287 of the L. A. W. *Bulletin* of March 2, 1886, and read, aloud, if possible, "Bermudian Rambles on a Tricycle, by S. H. M., XI.," and then say if I have not let the author off very easily?

In New York here we are looking forward to great things under the new administration. Our new chief consul, Mr. Bidwell, is one of the pioneers of cycling, has plenty of executive ability, believes in road riding and touring, and is deservedly popular. With such a chief consul we hope the New York Division L. A. W. will be as conspicuously at the head as it has heretofore been at the other end of the L. A. W. procession.

I hope nobody will charge my plain talk up against the editor. *I* am the responsible party, and my personality is hardly a secret, though in these columns I prefer to sign myself CYCLOS.

WHAT JAM SATIS DOESN'T KNOW.

Editor Bicycling World: Your correspondent, in the issue of 23 April, gives his opinion that, "rear-steering tandems have never become a leading type of the machine." In rebuttal kindly accept the enclosed clipping from about the best cycling authority in England.

The plurality of the gentleman's statement alone saves it from absolute inaccuracy. Rear-steering tandems, as a class, have really never been extremely popular, but the one type built and patented by the Surrey machinist Company, of London, has been a marked success and is exceedingly popular in England, being practically a class by itself. The Invincible is certainly safer than the Humber types, and easier handled, while a great many riders believe that, with equally powerful men on it, the Humber would not even have the advantage in speed.

The Surrey machine is safest because the weight of both riders is balanced on and back of the driving axle, so that to cause a spill the front rider must lift the entire weight of the rear man against a leverage of over two feet; and it is possible, without any remarkable exertion of agility or care, for the front rider to run the machine alone without any one on the back seat. There is, too, none of the sudden swerving when at speed characteristic of the Humber patterns, as the steering is controlled by a simple turn of the wrist, and an obstruction meeting one wheel, cannot swing the machine around against the rider's wish or will as it does with Humbers, where the leverage is bound to be against the steerer. The "peculiar bowling motion spoken of as characteristic of

the Humber is not wanting on the Invincible, whose broad strong hubs, hollow rims, tangent spokes, and large soft rubbers make it as nearly free from vibration as it is possible for any machine to be, and it is at the same time no heavier than the *genuine* Humber, to say nothing of the imitations. It is clear to my mind that James Satus has never mounted one of the machines in question.

"*The position held by the 'Invincible' machines is unique and second to none*, and as soon as the subsidized amateur is barred from the amateur racing path these machines will be as popular as any other make both on the road and the cinder path. The name 'Invincible' is singularly appropriate. The general plan of these machines is well known; plenty of rubber, few and thin spokes, hollow rims, and light frames, being especially identified with this type of machine. *The rear-steering Tandem so well known down the Ripley Road has proved to be a pronounced success, as it might well be, seeing that its designer puts it almost daily to a practical test.*

"The remarkably light frame, stayed scientifically up to a point of remarkable rigidity, the high-geared wheels, and the beautiful poise of the machine, *all go to make it noticeable among the tandems of the year.* A certain number of riders, however, yearn for a front-steerer, and their wishes in this direction will be gratified in 1886, as we were favored last week with a private view of the new F. S. 'Invincible' Tandem. This, as may be supposed, carries out, on the lines of a front-steering tandem, all the points to which we have referred above. The axle is light, but runs in *four* bearings, whilst a long 'bowsprit frame' runs out to a large front wheel, which, combined with the lengthened wheel-base, will prove very effective.

"The 'Invincible' Safety Bicycle will also be heard of. As to these small machines, the principles of 'Invincible' construction are applied with singular success, whilst of the merits of the full-sized racers and roadsters it is scarcely necessary to speak. *Where the sub-amateur does not exist, and all the racing men are amateurs with free choice in the matter of machines, the 'Invincible' racer is mounted by a majority of riders."* — *Bicycling News*, 12 Feb., 1886.

LORD DOLPHIN.

DISQUALIFIED BICYCLERS.

THE action of the League of American Wheelmen, in disqualifying so many of the leading riders of the day and forcing them into the professional ranks, should be the means of adding greatly to the interest taken in bicycling. The professionals sadly wanted an infusion of new blood, the performances of Prince and Woodside and their few assistants becoming very monotonous. With a score of fast riders now compelled to retire permanently or else ride in professionals there should be plenty of racing and matches during 1886. The cleansing of the amateur ranks in this manner, though it may be a damper to begin with, will undoubtedly be productive of good, as new men will be induced to race who previously had little encouragement to do so when such men as Hendee and Rowe were so much their superiors.

Now that makers' amateurs have been got rid of, the League managers must not relax their efforts, and by a little watchfulness the necessity for such a wholesale act of disqualification is not likely to arise again. —*Philadelphia Press, Sunday, 25 April, 1886.*

Editor of the Cycle: The above expresses very fully and emphatically the views of the majority of the riders of Philadelphia. I have noticed a remark that no club has yet "endorsed" the action of the Racing Board; doubtless from the fact that the said action is so evidently a good one that it requires no endorsement with thinking men. L. D.

PARADES.

Editor of the Cycle: A contemporary of yours is expending a great deal of force in trying to argue away the parade at the League Meet. I do not see that the talk has any effect. The wheelmen are coming to Boston not only as guests of the division, but indirectly as guests of the city. We owe the citizens of Boston a duty in so far that we should make an appearance before them in the capacity of wheelmen in a body.

The parade is an educator. It may be urged that Boston people do not want to be educated up to the advantages of cycling, but I believe the effect of a thousand men in line would be a good one. The wheelmen are not slow to ask the dealers to pay the bills of the Meet, and if they do away with the parade, what particular benefit will the dealers derive? I believe in the parade, and think it can be made one of the most effective features of the celebration.

DEALER.

NEBRASKA DIVISION.

ON 27 April, in response to a call for a meeting of bicyclists to form a state branch of the League of American Wheelmen, a number of young men met at the Millard Hotel. An organization was perfected, with the election of the following officers : Chief consul and State representative, W. S. Rogers; secretary and treasurer, B. F. Fell ; committee on constitution and by-laws, W. S. Rogers, B. F. Fell, Charles Woodman, Lucian Stephens, and Mr. Hughes; racing board, J. G. Hitchcock, Thomas Blackmore and O. H. Gordon. Much enthusiasm prevailed, and steps were taken to encourage wheeling in Nebraska. The meeting then adjourned, to meet 5 May at the same place, when the constitution will be submitted for approval.

We organize with an active force of fifty-two members, and expect to accomplish a great deal the coming season.

BENN F. FELL, *Secretary-Treasurer.*

SOUTHERN TOURISTS NORTHWARD BOUND.

IF all goes well they will probably reach Boston in time for the L. A. W. Meet. The Pioneer touring party of the South, consisting of Messrs. A. M. Hill, C. M. Fairchild and H. W. Fairfax, all members in good standing of the N. O. Bicycle Club and L. A. W. They left New Orleans early on the morning of the 25th inst. fully equipped and eager for the long, self-imposed journey of over 1500 miles.

At the present writing they are toiling along somewhere in the State of Alabama. The weather has not been all that could be desired ; the plucky trio having already received several thorough drenchings which have not, however, dampened their ardor in the least, as, when last heard from they were in good spirits and confident of success.

These three cyclists besides being enthusiastic on the subject of wheeling, are all first-rate riders, and gentlemen in every sense of the word, and we bespeak for them the kind attention and encouragement of the wheel world generally. The riders of the North and East can form but a faint idea of the interest that is centered in this trio of Southern wheelmen. Since their departure, the men, and cycling matters generally, have been discussed in places and at times where but the day before the subject would not have aroused the least interest, and we can safely say that the tour now in progress will do more to farther the cause of cycling in the South than all previous exploits combined.

The route chosen is as follows : New Orleans to Mobile, Ala., to Perdido, Sparta, Greenville, Union Springs. Ala.; to Columbus, Macon, Milledgeville, Warrenton, Ga.; to Hamburg, Columbia, Camden, Cheraw, S. C.; to Laurel Hill,Toomer, Raleigh, Weldon, N. C. ; to Sussex, Petersburg, Richmond, Fredericksburg, Washington to Baltimore,Philadelphia, New York, New Haven, Hartford to Boston. BI.

N. Y. AND N. J. T. R, R. ASSOCIATION.

Editor of the Cycle: The constitution of the above association provides that "there shall be regular race meets on Decoration Day and Election Day of each year." The location of the first race was left to the executive committee of the association.

The following statements as to the *time* and *place* of holding the first race have appeared in various papers : —

1. That they "may be prevailed upon to have their first race somewhere in the vicinity of Boston, on one of the dates set down for the League Meet."

2. That they have "decided to have the first race on Decoration Day over a course in Orange. It is an eight mile course."

3. At a meeting of the Association, "the sense . . . was to hold it on June 5, unless trial heats compelled its postponement to the 12th."

4. Over a course, "commonly known as the Milburn Course, extending from Irvington to and through Milburn, 12½ miles straight away."

5. "Beginning at the foot of the first hill below Irvington, thence down towards Milburn, and along the valley road towards Montclair, 12½ miles and return."

Most of these statements appear to have come from parties connected with the Association. The facts, however, seem to be : That it is to be in June, and somewhere in New Jersey.

That it can't be from Irvington "to and through Milburn " as no rideable race course

of anything like 12½ miles runs in that direction.

That neither can it be from Irvington "along the valley road toward Montclair 12½ miles " for, to ride so far straight away they would be compelled to leave the macadam for roads unfit for racing. The 12½ miles might, however, be completed by a detour through Orange.

If this last course is chosen, it will embrace a number of hills, one of them *long and steep*, a short stretch of dirt roads very muddy in wet weather over a mile of very narrow side path unfit for spurting, and a long stretch of worn macadam.

It is to be hoped that not over six teams will be allowed in the final. Even the twenty-four men that that would give would be more than ought to be racing on the road. It seems to me that it would be far better to hold trial heats in each of the three sections, and have each section send its champions to the final.　　　　　　　N. J.

THE ENGLISH CYCLING CHAMPIONSHIPS.

THE time standard of the English championships this year is as follows : —

The One Mile Bicycle. — Time standard, 2m. 48s. ; present holder, Sanders Sellers.

The Five Mile Bicycle. — Time standard, 15m. ; present holder, M. V. J. Webber.

The Twenty-Five Miles bicycle. — Time standard, 1h. 20m. ; present holder, R. H. English.

The Fifty Miles Bicycle. — Time standard, 2h. 40m. ; present holder, R. H. English.

The One Mile Tricycle. — Time standard, 3m. 5s. ; present holder, P. Furnival.

The Five Miles Tricycle. — Time standard, 17m. ; present holder, R. Cripps.

The Twenty-five Miles Tricycle. — Time standard, 1h. 30m., present holder, G. Gatehouse.

The following are the dates and places for this year's championship races : —

May 22 — Five miles tricycle championship, at Queen's Park Ground, Glasgow.

June 14 — One mile tricycle and twenty-five miles bicycle championship, at Weston-Super-Mare.

June 26 — One mile bicycle championship, at Jarrow, Newcastle-on-Tyne.

July 17 — Twenty-five miles tricycle championship, at Crystal Palace, London.

July 24 — Five miles bicycle championship, at Long Eaton.

Aug. 14 — Fifty miles bicycle championship, at Crystal Palace, London.

A WATERBURY young man is soon to wed a fair Naugatuck girl, and the romance of their courtship is as follows : The young man is an enthusiastic bicyclist, and careering along the road that leads by this fair girl's home one day, a year ago, he took a " header" directly in front of the house. The young woman happened to be seated by the window, and thinking the victim to be an acquaintance rushed to his relief. As he picked himself out of the dirt she saw her mistake. There was a charming, blushing confusion, an embarrassed young man, an invitation into the house to repair damages, an acquaintance, a courtship with objections from the girl's parents, an overcoming of all obstacles by the young people, and now there will be a marriage.

Geo.H.Benedlot Eng'r.,L.A.W. Tour Dep't.　　Map of the **L. A. W.** TRUNK LINES

TRANSPORTATION TO BOSTON MEET.

WHEELMEN attending the meet at Boston should, where possible, make their journey over the League trunk lines, as illustrated in map. These lines work very closely in the interest of wheelmen, and form the foundation of present facilities accorded the craft in the United States. The main Northern trunk line is the Michigan Central R. R. Through trains run from Chicago to Boston, with connections in Michigan, Canada, and Ohio. From St. Louis its through sleepers run over the Wabash, connecting with the Michigan Central at Detroit. Its connection from Cincinnati and Ohio points is the Cincinnati, Hamilton & Dayton R. R., also connecting with the Michigan Central train at Detroit.

Hence, by proper timing the entire West could be concentrated over the M.C.R.R. from Detroit East. From Cleveland and Eastern Ohio points the Lake Shore road runs through cars connecting with the N. Y.C. at Buffalo. The Baltimore and Ohio R.R. old and staunch League road, can take Southern members as shown in map, passing through Philadelphia and New York, and thence to Boston via the Fall River Line, steamer and rail through Newport, R.I. There is no League trunk road in New England save the Fitchburg. Wheelmen in the State of New York should take the West Shore road, which is the only line running through cars over the Fitchburg R.R. The Boston connection of the New York Central from Albany East, is a road that practically prohibits wheel travel over its lines during the year, but makes concessions to our parties when travelling over its lines in numbers. The Fitchburg is its competitor and accommodates wheelmen all the year around, when travelling alone as well as in parties.

From Eastern Pennsylvania and southern New York, the New York, Lake Erie and Western, and the Lehigh Valley roads afford every accommodation. From Portland down, the Eastern R. R. has worked closer with us than any other road. This whole map is a perfect general index of L. A. W. trunk lines. The regular printed transportation list will show all other lines. Arrangements for transportation can be made very conveniently by G. R. Bidwell, New York ; being in correspondence with all lines running from New York and Philadelphia to the East. W. S. Bull, Buffalo, can arrange matters with lines running from Buffalo and Canada to the East, while F. T. Sholes,

Cleveland ; H. S. Livingston, Cincinnati ; W. M. Brewster, St. Louis, and the undersigned at Chicago, place their services at disposal of the craft journeying from their respective section of country.

　　　　　B. B. AYERS, *Chairman.*

Chicago, April 21, 1886.

THE LEAGUE MEET.

Preparations for the League Meet are going actively forward.

ENTERTAINMENT.

The entertainment committee for the L. A. W. Meet met at the Massachusetts Club house Friday evening, to perfect arrangements and discuss matters. Capt. A. D. Peck, Jr., of the Massachusetts Club, was chosen chief usher, and will select ushers from the local wheel clubs. All will wear full dress. The tickets for the minstrel entertainment on 28 May, at Music Hall, are already selling rapidly. The price of admission was fixed at fifty cents, seventy-five cents for reserved seats. A discount of twenty-five cents on these prices will be made on presentation of L. A. W. ticket for one ticket only. Tickets can be obtained from the captains of the Massachusetts, Boston, Cambridge, and Dorchester Clubs, of A. D. Salkeld of the Massachusetts, and L. T. Field of the Boston Clubs. There will be fifty men in the acts of the first part of the minstrel show. The second part will consist of vocal and instrumental music, athletics, and local hits. The Cadet Band will furnish music.

RECEPTION.

Chairman Whitney of the reception committee reports upon the extensive arrangements which are being made to receive the visiting wheelmen. He is to be assisted by a committee of fifty prominent members of the various local clubs, several of whom will meet every incoming train at the depots and escort the wheelmen to the quarters assigned them. Barges for transporting wheels and baggage will also be in attendance. Mr. Whitney is to have charge of getting up the badges of the various committees. These are to be of a very tasteful design in metal, similar to the regulation league pin, pendent from which will be the ribbons of various colors. The chairman requests that all wheelmen from a distance advise him how and when they will arrive, so that some one may meet them. Address

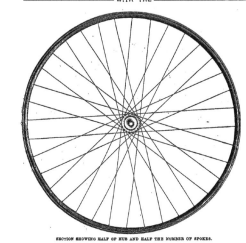

E. G. Whitney, chairman reception committee, Hotel Vendome, Boston.

TOURS AND RUNS.

The following is a corrected list of the tours and runs at the League Meet : —

THURSDAY, 27 MAY.

Morning Run. — Leave Mechanics Building at 9 A. M. sharp, for a run to Chestnut Hill reservoir over the mile ground through Brighton. Return by way of Beacon street to Corey Hill in time to take in the hill-climbing contest. The committee on tours and runs will be in charge.

Afternoon Run, No. 1. — Leave Copley square at 2.30 sharp. To the Reservoir and Great Sign Boards. Return through the Newtons over some of the finest roads, and still finer coasts. In charge of A. L. Atkins and F. Alcott Pratt.

Afternoon Run, No. 2. — Leave the Vendome at 2.30 sharp. Run to Cambridge, Arlington, Belmont, Watertown, Waltham. On this run visits will be made to Harvard College, the Hemenway Gymnasium, the Cambridge Club rooms, and also those of the Nonantum Club at Newtonville. Passing the Washington Elm, under which Washington took command of the army, Longfellow's late residence, the route of the troops to Lexington in 1775, the factory of the American Watch Company, and other places of note. In charge of Capt. A. D. Peck, Jr., and H. W. Hayes.

Afternoon Run, No. 3. — Leave Mechanics Building at 2.30 sharp. Run to Dorchester over Mt. Bowdoin, over River street (equal to any race track), to Mattapan and Dedham. This will take riders over the course of the road races run last fall in which many records were broken. In charge of Dr. W. G. Kendall and H. Robbins.

FRIDAY, 28 MAY.

This being the day of the business meeting, no runs have been called until late in the afternoon.

Afternoon Run. — Leave Mechanics Building at 4 P. M. sharp. Run to Echo Bridge. Here can be heard an echo that repeats itself fifteen times. In charge of A. D. Peck, Jr.

SATURDAY, 29 MAY.

Scorchers run out to and around the Reservoir. All those who like to ride with a fast party can join and return in time for the League parade. In charge of Dr. Wm. G. Kendall.

SUNDAY, 30 MAY.

All-day runs to various points, viz. Lynn Salem, Brockton, Lexington, South Natick, etc. These runs will be bulletined a day or to before the 30th.

MONDAY, 31 MAY.

All-day run to Lynn to attend the races that are to be held on that day.

The committee on tours and runs are A. D. Peck, Jr., F. A. Pratt, Henry Robbins, A. L. Atkins, H. W. Hayes, W. G. Kendall.

. THOMAS STEVENS.

MR. WILLIAM M. NORTH, the Agent of the British Telegraph Company at Teheran, Persia, sends the following in regard to Thomas Stevens, the intrepid wheelman, who is girdling the globe as special correspondent of *Outing.*

TEHERAN, April 5, 1886.

Mr. Thomas Stevens arrived at Meshed on the 29th of March, after the most severe journey he has yet experienced. He reports two feet of snow twenty miles from Meshed. He is not able to decide which way he will go, as he may not be allowed to pass through either Siberia or Afghanistan. It is to be hoped that he will not attempt the latter route, the natives being very treacherous and hostile to strangers. The weather throughout Persia unsettled, rain and snow alternating, with a bright day at intervals. Papers continue coming for the " Sahib who rides on a wheel." Shall inform you when Mr. Stevens starts, with further particulars.

Your obedient servant,

(Signed)   W. M. NORTH.

THE ENGLISH MAKERS' AMATEURS.

AT a meeting of the N. C. U., 13 April, several riders were suspended for having, as " makers' amateurs," broken the amateur laws of the Union. A full discussion took place as to the length of the period of disqualification necessary to be passed on each suspended rider in order to fulfil the object the Union has in view in endeavoring to purify the amateur ranks, and at the same time to avoid inflicting an injustice on members of a class of riders whose trespasses against the amateur laws were by no means equal in character. Ultimately, the following resolution was agreed to : " That the suspensions passed at this and previous meetings of the executive upon riders who have offended against the amateur law by riding as ' makers' amateurs,' be terminated one week from the present date, but that the attention of each suspendee be drawn to the fact that any further infraction by him of the Union rules will be carefully watched, and will entail permanent disqualification."

In answer to an inquiry as to the application of the rule limiting the value of a prize to £10 10s., the secretary was requested to state that the rule referred to open races only, and not to club races.

Mr. Todd has sent a circular to the press, in which he narrates the story of the makers' amateur business *ab initio.* He concludes as follows : " After a very careful and anxious consideration of the matter, the executive decided upon the following course of action : All riders who have been suspended are let off with the warning implied in their having been suspended for a short period. The executive now give notice that in the future they will investigate promptly and thoroughly every case which may come before them in which a rider is reasonably suspected of being paid by any manufacturer for riding his machine, and if the suspicion is not removed, they will, in the exercise of the power placed in their hands, effectually bar the riders from taking part in any contest held under N. C. U. rules. Whilst taking every care to avoid any injustice to individuals, the executive are determined that to the utmost of their power they will seek to put an end to an abuse which, if allowed to exist, can only render the name of amateur cyclist a laughing stock ; and they feel confident that in this endeavor they will receive the cordial support of the bodies which rule over kindred sports."

DISTANCE TABLE.

THE following table will be useful to those who wish to compare French racing records with those of America : —

200 metres, forty rods.		
800	"	half a mile.
1,000	"	200 rods.
1,200	"	three quarters of a mile.
1,600	"	one mile.
2,000	"	one mile and a quarter.
2,200	"	one mile, 120 rods.
2,400	"	one mile and a half.
3,000	"	one mile, 280 rods.
4,000	"	two miles and a half.

FROM A FEMININE POINT OF VIEW.

I HAVE to thank Mr. Ayers, of Chicago, for sending me a set of the colors which will be worn by League members while touring. Royal purple is selected as the common color to be worn by all, and this is combined with other colors to designate the particular division the wearer is connected with. I have one more cause to be thankful that I was born in the East, for that section is given red, which makes a remarkably pretty combination. The old gold and the white look well together, but I hesitate at the blue, and think this might be improved. The colors can be used in many ways to great advantage, for they can be worked into the suits of the ladies and the gentlemen in a way to relieve the sombreness always incident to clothing of uniform color throughout.

" MERRIE WHEELER " has been telling the story of the North-Shore trip of last fall, in which the ladies accompanied the gentlemen. She makes a very interesting story and places it before a class of readers outside the wheel world, through the columns of the *Phonographic Monthly.*

SHE advances one idea in harmony with my own thoughts, and I will reproduce it here : —

" Although fuss and feathers should have no part or lot in a lady's cycle suit, beauty should not be entirely sacrificed to utility, for with taste and ingenuity the two can be successfully combined. Now, an ordinary hat or bonnet is apt to give the wearer the look of a novice, sort of a trial trip as it were, while, on the other hand, a regulation jockey cap is too " horsey" ; but a cap of modified jockey shape, higher in the crown and broader visor, with a little feminine touch in the shape of a feather tip or bow, is both stylish and suitable for the purpose. A nicely fitting Jersey jacket and skirt, not too long or full, all to be of dark brown, navy blue, or gray, with gauntlet gloves, make a very becoming tricycle suit."

THE ladies will not and they should not make guys of themselves. Did you see the Mikado? and did you notice that the men were Japanese from the sole of their foot to the top of their head? Did you observe the ladies in the chorus ? If you did, you are probably aware that they were Japanese, all

Adjustment in Height in Front.   Adjustment in Length.   A Comfortable Coasting Plate.
Adjustment in Height in Rear.   Adjustment in Width.   A Bifurcated Seat.

THE LILLIBRIDGE SADDLE

Is the only one having any of these Points; is the only one that can be changed in Shape or Position at all; is the BEST and
CHEAPEST; is adapted to all makes of Bicycles. Special Styles for the Safeties and Star.

Price, Nickelled, $5.00.   Price of Coiled Spring, with Straps, etc; for Old Saddles, 75 Cts

FREEMAN LILLIBRIDGE, Rockford, Ill.

but their hair. A woman's hair is her crowning beauty. Change that and good-by to all beauty. The chorus girls drew the line at the hair, and contented themselves with inserting numberless fans in their coiffures. They looked very pretty but they were not Japanese above the eyebrows. I should not envy the manager who tried to make them dress their hair in regular Japanese. To look beautiful is a desire implanted in the female heart, and any pleasure that is purchased at the expense of beauty will be neglected by the ladies.

ANOTHER authority on dress I desire to quote at this time. It is "Violet Lorne." She says : "One wants something which looks as well out of the saddle as in, and is as graceful and elegant when one is dismounted as when one is riding. I have tried almost every variety of style, and find nothing so suitable and pretty as a tweed material for winter, and beige for warmer seasons ; dark gray, brown, or heather mixture in color, made with a deep kilt, well taped on the skirt, finished above with a sash drapery in front, and long, plain draping attached to the skirt at the back. The skirt must not be too full, and must be well tied back. No steels must be worn. The bodice should be a round one, the skirt buttoned to it, and finished with a neat belt. This transfers all weight to the shoulders, and insures great ease and comfort. The hat should be close-fitting and plain. Shoes must be worn, not boots."

A LADY writes from Newark : "Can Daisie give any information regarding the arrangements made for ladies at the coming League Meet?" I hardly comprehend the scope of her question. The lady riders of Boston will attend to the entertainment of the ladies who come to the Meet, and will make it pleasant for them. We shall have a short run the first day, in which it is hoped all will join and become acquainted. After that no formal plan will be arranged. We prefer to consult the wishes of our guests in regard to the runs of Friday and Saturday, and the longer tours of the succeeding week. We shall do what we can for the comfort and convenience of our guests, even to providing storage for their machines. All the details I will try to give in a future letter.

I WISH to hear from every lady who intends coming to Boston for the Meet. If each and every one of them will write me the time of her intended arrival, how long she will stay, what she will ride (single or double), whether she will have a gentleman escort or not, whether she would like to go on an extended run or a series of short ones, etc. etc., the Boston ladies will be materially assisted in preparing for the entertainment of their guests. We have in view a number of plans for the week succeeding the Meet, and would like to know how numerous a party we can depend upon.   DAISIE.

A LITTLE bottle of Ardill's Enamel will do as much for a bicycle as a little soap and water will do for the face. It will make a garden of delight out of a desert of ugliness. A little touch here and there will keep a machine looking at its best, and it takes less time to apply it than to rub up nickel plate.

THE AMERICAN RUDGE.

MANUFACTURED BY RUDGE & CO., COVENTRY, ENGLAND, AND IMPORTED BY STODDARD, LOVERING & CO., 152 TO 158 CONGRESS STREET, BOSTON, MASS.

THERE is a large class of wheelmen, and would-be cyclists, whose desires for a good wheel far exceed the capacity of their purses. Until within a couple of years very many have been compelled to put up with a poorly made machine, or, in their ignorance, have been led to buy some scond-hand and discarded rattletrap.

We are pleased to say that that day has gone by, for the machine which we have in mind, The American Rudge, is what has long been wanted for this market; viz., a machine which, while low in price, is handsome and well made, and just the thing for those who find it difficult to raise the cash to purchase a more expensive mount, and yet whose desire is to own a machine one need not be ashamed of.

The American Rudge is fitted with crescent steel rims, ⅞ and ¾ inch red rubber tires. The hubs are nickelled gun metal, well recessed and pierced with eighty and twenty No. 11 direct spokes, making the wheel immensely strong and rigid.

The backbone is a round, weldless steel tube, nicely tapered and curved, terminating in a nicely shaped rear fork. The head is of the Humber pattern, with long centres, similar to the well-known Andrews, and is protected by a neat dust shield.

The spring is plain, flat, and broad, and slides at the tail on a small steel plate attached to the backbone.

The handle-bar is solid, gracefully curved, and of good length, and to which is attached a stout double-lever spoon brake.

The front forks have received the makers' special attention, being hollow and elliptical, calculated to stand any strain that will be put upon them.

The bearings are the celebrated Rudge's "Unequalled" balls to both wheels. These bearings are so well known that comment is unnecessary. Plain parallel pedals are fitted, or ball pedals at a slight extra charge.

The machine has a leg guard and a saw step, and is fitted with either Lamplugh's and Brown's or Brook's long-distance saddles, and furnished with tools and oil can.

It is in a great many respects similar to

the Rudge Light Roadster, the only points of difference being the wheels where we have gun-metal hubs, direct spokes and crescent felloes instead of tangent spokes and hollow felloes. The handle bar being curved solid instead of hollow.

Having their house in Bradford, which brings them in direct communication with Messrs. Rudge & Co., its American agents are enabled to place large orders and handle this wheel on a very small margin, and it is especially intended to reach that large number of wheelmen who want a first-class article, but who cannot pay a high price.

The great popularity attendant on this wheel during the last three years, and the large number which Messrs. Stoddard, Lovering & Co, have sold, convinces them that the American Rudge has filled a want long felt by the large class of American riders ; viz., a first-class, thorough, reliable, easy running, and carefully built all-round roadster at a low price ; and it can unhesitatingly be said that there is no machine either on the English or American market that can compare with it, either in quality, workmanship, or finish.

In fact, many customers have sent unsolicited testimonials saying they prefer the American Rudge to other wheels costing from $20 to $25 more.

Before buying a second-hand wheel it would be well to consider whether it would not be better to add a few more dollars and order a new American Rudge. — *Adv.*

NOTES OF A CYCLIST.

SINCE my last notes were written I have had two struggles with the "Rover" Safety. The duration of the first struggle was, perhaps five minutes, and, I must admit it, the "Rover" won. Then I tried to balance on the step, I sailed along for a little distance quite gayly, but the moment I dropped into the saddle and caught the pedals I was ignominiously tumbled off. This sort of amusement is very good for the bystanders, but a little monotonous for the exhibitor. So I soon desisted.

A FEW days later I met my friend, the "Rover," again. Being naturally somewhat ashamed of my recent defeat, I embraced the opportunity for another trial. I mounted the machine, and was pleasantly surprised to find that I could ride it. I was not very graceful, it is true, but I could keep the saddle and go along, and could feel something of the qualities of the wheel. My ride was a short one, but I had conquered.

I DO not believe that anything less than a reasonably long experience with an object, or wide observation and comparison, can possibly entitle a man to an *opinion* which will carry any weight. On the contrary, an *impression* is usually formed almost at first sight, and possesses some interest, if little value.

I WILL confess that my impression of the "Rover" was more favorable than I had thought possible. I had so often said that so-called "safety" machines were not real safeties, and that they looked so absurd, that I was hardly prepared for a real safety that looked well, and had a pleasant motion.

THE advantages of this machine seem to be real safety, good appearance (as compared with ordinary dwarf "safeties"), and a smooth, pleasant motion. Its disadvantages seem to be its very sensitive steering which must always be more or less tiresome (though practice will largely change that), and the probability that it will not stand the wear and tear that the ordinary wheel will. Should I have further experience with the "Rover," I shall have something more to say on these points.

EVERY little while something creeps into the wheel papers about the length of handle bars for bicycles. The protests against the short bars of a few years back brought a beneficial change, but the matter has now been carried too far.

I AM free to assert that bars of thirty-inch and over are a cause of discomfort, and an injury, especially if curved down. Very few men indeed can stretch so far comfortably, and hardly one can do it without acquiring a wretched and ungainly stoop of the shoulders. The extreme distance on roadsters, should, I believe, be twenty-six, twenty-seven, or twenty-eight inches, according to the size of the wheel, and the rider's build. These lengths will give the best results for road riding. I have used various lengths up to thirty-one inches, and find on a 54-inch light roadster that those of about twenty-seven or twenty-eight inches are most comfortable. Other riders tell me of the same results.   5678.

CYCLETS.

. THE TEST.

In this fleeting world of ours,
  Memory holds most dear
Those in whom our lives are bound,
  Be they far or near

Fond associations dwell
  Where love sheds its light,
Where true friendship proves its worth,
  Ever strong and bright.

Ties of blood to many minds
  More than others bind;
What is blood, if hearts divide?
  Less than summer wind.

Often held by other ties,   •˙
  Friends prove true and strong;
Heart and deed are test of worth,
  Love, and service long.

That which true and perfect is
  Wins at last its way;
That on which we can rely
  Claims regard alway.

When the days and months and years
  Prove what we can trust;
Then we cherish for its worth,
  Then we love it most.

Sing I blithely of my steed,
  Always fresh and bright;
It has proved on many roads
  True and strong and light.

Ever fast and ever firm,
  'T is surpassed by none ;
For my wheel has never failed,
  Love and faith has won.   P.

MR. T. J. KIRKPATRICK declines to stand as candidate for president of the League. We are glad to know he has so much business on hand that he cannot attend to anything else, but we are sorry to hear that the League is to lose the benefit of his services as president.

DEALERS report that riders are selecting smaller wheels than usual. A 54-inch is a large wheel nowadays.

. THE cycler who races for gold,
      Tra-la-la,
  Has nothing to do with this race.
  Promateurs can't be enrolled,
      Tra-la-la,
  And so they have often been told,
      Tra-la-la,
  That is the state of the case.
  And that's what we mean when we say or we sing,
  They can't enter this race if they stay here all spring.
                        Spectator.

ARTHUR YOUNG, of St. Louis, defeated Weber, Kluge, Greenwood, Davies, Beckers, and a host of other experts in the hill-climbing contest at Clarksville, he being the only man who succeeded in climbing what is now known as "crank hill."

. ST. LOUIS and Chicago talk of a team race. The Spectator says : "In the team race between Chicago and St. Louis, the names already mentioned to represent St. Louis are : S. G. Whittaker, Percy Stone, R. C. Gordon, A. A. Hart, and one other yet to be chosen. The date should be settled upon when the Chicago boys are down here on the 15th. If they will not come and meet us on our hills, we will go to Chicago and meet them in a fifty-mile road race on their boulevards. May 31 would be a good date, as it will be celebrated as Decoration Day."

THERE seems to be a natural order of things when a Weber gets on a spider wheel.

ON Sunday, 18 April, Messrs. Thomas Barber and Eugene Crist broke the road record from Washington, D. C., to Cabin John's Bridge. At 2 P. M. they started from the cycle store of Crist & Higham on a Humber tandem for Cabin John's Bridge, the distance from the starting-point being about ten miles, and made it in fifty minutes.

WHILE the Boston Club is looking askance at the League parade, the Massachusetts Club is actively at work laying plans to take the record for numbers and appearance. We think they will do it· Seventy-eight is, we think, the largest number that any one club ever turned out in a parade, and it was n't a League club either.

/ W. M. WOODSIDE has a very pretty and wealthy lady admirer in Minneapolis. The lady's family, however, don't take kindly to the mode of life adopted by their prospective son-in-law, and have made vigorous "kicks" to no purpose. When all other plans failed to win their daughter from the six-foot record breaker, they sent her two hundred miles away, much to the young Irishman's sorrow. Four days later, however, when in the midst of a six-day race, the following telegram was handed to him on the track : —
"Keep up courage. Although far away, my heart is with you.   EMILY."

The spurt that followed surprised Schock, and the rafters of the rink re-echoed with applause from the admiring throng of spectators. Did they know the cause of the spurt? We guess not. — Sporting Journal.

BICYCLING on the asphalt was one of the

diversions of the Seventh Regiment of New York on its recent visit to Washington. A number of the Citizens Club, including the president of the League, were with the regiment.

THE cycling editor of the Herald has been astonishing the natives by tremendous spurts on the mill-dam. He is getting into condition for the scorcher's run during the League Meet.

MR. L. S. KING, of Belmont, has just finished a very unique bicycle picture which we have had the pleasure of inspecting. It is done with pen and ink in white holly, and consists of a number of spaces laid out to resemble cards overlapping one another, on which are sketches of incidents in the life of a bicycler. The sketches are well drawn and contain a good deal of humor and many fine points. The frame is also of holly, and is also decorated with sketches showing the "Seven Ages" of a cycler's life, his winter amusements, etc., etc. The whole is protected by a coating of shellac well polished. The picture goes to Philadelphia as a present.

DAN CANARY is just now the rage in Ireland. The Dublin papers devote columns to describing his wonderful performances. During the week of 11 April he was taken down to Ballsbridge and was shown the track. "Canary," says the Irish Sportsman, "was quite surprised with it ; he had no idea that we had anything like it in Ireland. He says that it is a perfect model, and is far superior to the majority of the tracks in England and America. We got him a machine, and he sprang into the saddle and rode a lap. He then stood in front of the stand and looked about him (here one of the ground men, who happened to be present, opened his mouth). He then rode down the straight backward, and returned on one wheel, wagging the hind one as a fish would his tail (ground man's mouth wider). He then stood upon the saddle, and guided the machine with one foot on the handle. He then dismounted, ran backward, and vaulted into the saddle with his face toward the hind wheel. The ground man now opened his mouth so much that all his other features disappeared. He could scarcely speak, but he managed to mutter that in his opinion Canary was a sanguinary smart chap."

⌐ THE New Orleans wheelmen who started for Boston last, are as follows: A. M. Hill, jeweller, 38 years old ; weight, 150 pounds ; height, 5 feet 7½ inches ; who will ride a 51-inch light roadster. Harry W. Fairfax, son of J. W. Fairfax, proprietor of the City Item, 5 feet 9½ inches high, 135 pounds, who will ride a 53-inch light roadster; and C. M. Fairchild, 23 years old, 5 feet 9 inches, 135 pounds, who will also ride a 53-inch Medinm. All three are well-known wheelmen, and Mr. Fairchild is the captain of the New Orleans Bicycling Club.

A. T. LANE, of Montreal, sends us his catalogue for 1886. It has an illuminated cover in black and gold, and contains a full list of cycles and accessories kept on hand by our enthusiastic Montreal friend.

IT has been proposed to erect a mural tablet to the late H. L. Cortis, in Ripley

Church. The Ripley Road is a favorite highway for London cyclists; and during the height of the season a short service is held at the church on Sunday afternoons, to which all cyclists are invited.

THE first organized tour ever held in California will take place under the direction of the Division Touring Board, starting from San Francisco 15 May and returning 22 May. An additional week's tour may afterwards be taken.

"So you call that well water?" remarked the stranger, spurting the offending liquid from his mouth. "Great Scott! how must it have tasted when it was ill!"

ANY amusement or pleasure in which woman can have no part or lot, is deservedly unpopular with them, and as a young wife remarked, when her husband rode the bicycle and would go off on long trips, she wished such a thing as a wheel had never been invented. Now, since the advent of the tricycle, and its adoption by herself and husband, she wished they had been invented a good deal sooner. — *Merrie Wheeler in Phonographic Monthly.*

THE annual "wheel around the Capitol," by the Capital Club, in celebration of Mr. H. S. Owen's birthday, will take place 7 May, at 4.30 P. M. from 409 15th Street. This is one of the peculiar institution's of Washington, and one which is always most heartily enjoyed.

THE Worcester Bicycle Club has offered three prizes to the members who shall cover the greatest number of miles from April 1 to December 1. The club will hold a race meeting some time this month.

S. G. SPIRE of New Lebanon, N.H., will start from Albany, N.Y., some time this month, with the intention of riding to San Francisco on a Columbia bicycle.

AN English cycle club will shortly hold a hill-climbing contest to decide whether an ordinary or safety is the better-climber.

JAMES P. BRUCE of Vicksburg, Miss., proposes to get up a grand cycling tournament in that city next September, especially in the interests of Louisville, New Orleans, Cincinnati, St. Louis and Memphis wheelmen. A daily paper will be issued during the meet.

THE California division touring board of the League of American Wheelmen has arranged the following tour: Leave San Francisco Saturday morning, 15 May, wheel to San Jose; spend forenoon of Sunday, 16, at San Jose and vicinity, wheeling to Gilroy after lunch. Monday, 17, Gilroy to Monterey *via* Pajaro. Tuesday, 18, spend day at Del Monte Hotel. Wednesday, 19, yacht excursion across Monterey bay to Santa Cruz. Thursday, 20, Santa Cruz and vicinity. Friday, 21, Santa Cruz to San Jose *via* Los Gatos. Saturday, 22, return to San Francisco on the Alameda side of the bay *via* Haywards and Oakland. After returning to San Francisco, if a sufficient number desire, an additional week's tour will be taken through Sonoma and Napa counties. A liberal estimate places the expense of the first week's tour at $15 per capita.

FRED E. VAN MEERBEKE, who started from New York, 1 March, arrived at Mobile, Ala., 27 April. He was on the road forty-six days, taking off twelve days, when he

stopped on account of heavy rains. Actual riding time: To Lynchburg, four hundred and thirty-five miles, in 133.11.; Lynchburg to Atlanta, four hundred and ninety-nine miles, 161. 5.; Atlanta to Montgomery, one hundred and seventy-five miles, 44h; Montgomery to Tensas bridge, one hundred and sixty-three miles, 57.20.; Tensas to Mobile by rail. Mr. Van Meerbeke started the same afternoon for New Orleans, where he expects to take a two weeks' rest before starting for San Francisco.

PRESIDENT DUCKER has received a letter from Christiana, Norway, asking advice as to the construction of a bicycle track; its shape, material to be used, etc. He has also had another letter from New Zealand, asking for full particulars in regard to the fall tournament.

THE Lynn Cycle Club will have a cottage at Nahant, this summer.

MR. GEORGE SINGER sailed from New York for England, Wednesday of last week.

THE first handicap bicycle race is said to have been ridden in 1869.

THE Springfield Club's banquet will be held this Friday evening.

THE demand for tandems for use by ladies and gentlemen during the League meet is brisk.

THE Massachusetts Club is contemplating giving a several days' tour soon after the League meet.

IT is estimated that there are upwards of 1,500 cyclists in Chicago, including fifty lady tricyclists. There are four leading clubs, as follows: The Chicago, with more than one hundred members, heads the list, and is the oldest cycling organization in the West. The Dearborn Cycling Club, in point of numbers, comes next, and is more of a social club than the former, with a number of lady cyclists in its ranks. The Owl Club is an organization of live and enthusiastic young men who have done much to popularize the sport. The Wanderers' Club is now in process of formation.

MR. EDWARD DUNTEN of Augusta, Me., has offered a gold medal as a reward to the local rider who shall cover the most miles on his cycle during the present season.

CHARLES S. FISKE and Martin B. Breck won the Springfield Club whist tournament. They won five games and lost one.

IT is becoming quite the thing with Boston wheelmen, who are fond of anything English, to turn the tops of their stockings down over the calves of their legs, fastening the stocking just below the knee with an elastic band. This method has at least the advantage of helping to conceal nature's shortcomings.—*Globe.*

THE wonderful performance of W. M. Woodside at Minneapolis, last Saturday, entitles him to the credit of having ridden fifty miles, at least a mile faster than any other man on earth. — *Sporting Journal.*

THE record was 2.44.37 on a board track. How about Keith-Falconer's out-door record of 2.43 58⅖, Mr. *Journal.*

MALTBY, the trick rider, is in California, and will go to Australia.

CHICAGO enthusiasts are claiming that their city will be the centre of cycling in five

years. And yet St. Louis is moving forward. We believe the latter city has the best racing records still, and she has what Chicago never yet could take, a Corey Hill record. Competition between the two great cities of the West is always interesting.

THE extensive buildings of the new bicycle factory at Rockaway, N. J., are completed, and most of the machinery in position to commence work. The entire plant is under the supervision of a machinist from England, who has occupied a position of prominence in the Coventry works. This company, it is said, intends to turn out a wheel somewhat after the pattern of the Royal Mail, but which will be a superior machine, and not so expensive. Operations will commence in about thirty days.

THE tricycle fever has struck Haverhill. J. Fred Adams has just purchased a Ranelagh Club, and is delighted with it.

A THIRD assessment of ten per cent on the capital stock of the New Jersey Cycling Association has just been called for by the directors. This will make $3,000 paid in.

STODDARD, LOVERING & CO. are pushing their sundries, of which they have a very large stock. Their leading goods are the Buffer saddle and the King of the Road lamp, which stand in the front rank in their respective lines.

MR. GASKELL tells us that he is going to have a full line of his wheels at the Boston show, and then we may see some of the new tandems made in Cripper lines from the Marlboro Club. The Coventry Machinists' Company still pin their faith on the Ranelagh Club, which avoids the jar of the Cripper form, though they make the latter. We are anxious to see the new Marlboro', which terminates its front wheel fork in a coil spring to avoid vibration.

W. C. MARVIN, the well-known bicyclist of Ovid, Mich., died Tuesday, the 13th inst. He held the 1¼-mile State championship medal for 1884. Mr. Marvin was the founder of the *Western Cyclist* and made it a very entertaining journal. He had push and enterprise enough to make the name of the little town of Ovid well-known in the wheel world, and to draw the attention of the country to the doings of himself and his club.

THE Massachusetts Club has voted $200 for the League Meet fund.

THE Wilmington (N. C.) Bi. Club has drawn up a petition to the turnpike company that forbids riding on its pike, and this has been signed by the entire club, by many leading citizens and by a large number of stockholders in the company. They submit a series of regulations that they agree to abide by if allowed on the road. It is thought that the petition will be granted, and the North Carolina case will thus be settled for the present.

THE Overman Wheel Co. has raised the bond required to dissolve the John Harrington attachment, and business is now running along smoothly with them.

THE Boston Cycle Show will be one of the most attractive features of the Meet. There will be shown not only the familiar mounts, but the importers are bringing over all the new goods.

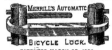

NOT many applications for championships were received up to the close of closing the list, 1 May. Cleveland wants one as usual, and so does Hartford. Three new applicants have entered the field, the Michigan Division and the Genessee Club of Rochester, New York, and also the California division.

THE PATH.

THE Spring races of the Hartford (Conn.) wheel club will be held on the afternoon of May 22, when the following events will be decided, and to the winners of each handsome prizes awarded : One-mile club championship; one-mile Hartford wheel club; one-mile club handicap for those who have not beaten 3.40; one-mile club, 3.10 class ; one-mile open, riders 18 years old or under ; one-mile club, 2.25 class ; two-mile open lap race ; three-mile open ten-minute class.

THE Yale Bicycle Club held a meeting last week, and appointed Messrs. Codding, '86, and Ivison, '87, as a committee to take charge of the spring races, which will probably be held on Friday and Saturday, June 11 and 12. The club has voted to change the style of its uniform.

An attractive programme of events has been arranged for the annual race meeting of the Woodstock Bicycle Club, which is to be held on May 24 and 25. Among the events is a mile sweepstake, professional race for the championship of Canada and a gold medal. Entries close May 18 with D. A. White, Woodstock, Can.

THE twenty-mile professional bicycle championship race, run at Leicester, Eng., 17 April, was won by the champion Howell in 1h. 9m. 46s. On the same day, the Surrey Bicycle Club had a race meeting at Kennington Oval. The event was the ten-mile scratch bicycle race, won by Speechly, after a terrific struggle with Furnivall. who was beaten by a yard in 41.44½.

THE CLUB.

NEWBURG, Y. Y. — Newburg Wheelmen : President, J. E. Wilson ; secretary-treasurer, L. W. Y. McCoskery ; captain, Frank Hollister.

AUGUSTA, ME. — Kennebec Wheelmen : President, G. E. Dunton ; secretary-treasurer, M. S. Campbell ; captain, H. L. Stone ; bugler, A. Pinkham ; 1st lieut., A. C. Walker ; 2d lieut., W. W. Ladd.

ELIZABETH, N. J. — Elizabeth Wheelmen. Officers elected Jan. 13, 1886 : President, Dr. G. Carleton Brown ; captain, George J. Martin ; secretary, George E. Pennell, 414 South Broad Street ; treasurer, Aug. S. Crane, Journal office.

ST. LOUIS, MO. — Star Club. Election of officers, 28 April ; President, F. W. Haid ; vice-president, Edward Lewis ; secretary-treasurer. W. W. Carpenter, Jr.; captain, Hal W. Greenwood ; 1st lieutenant, E. M. Beach ; 2d lieutenant, F. S. Carpenter.

WHEELING, W. VA. — Wheeling Wheelmen. Election of officers : President, Dr. Chas. E. Mason ; secretary-treasurer, A. Allen Wheat ; captain, Wilbur S. Wright ; lieutenant, Dr. R. H. Bullard ; color bearer, R. J. Smyth, Jr.; bugler, Dent A. Taylor.

CLEVELAND, OHIO. — Star Club : President, H. E. Chubb ; secretary-treasurer, W. Woodruff ; captain, Walter Collins.

THE Hoosac Wheelmen, a league club of Hoosac Falls, N. Y., have just moved into, and are fast furnishing in a most suitable manner. their new club rooms over the First National Bank. The rooms are pleasant, centrally located, and well adapted to meet the demands of a club. The organization is only of a few months' standing ; yet so en-

thusiastic are its members that already it is making a name for itself, and associate members are joining as fast as the club rules will permit. The roads in this vicinity are now at their best, and any time wheelmen may be seen in the new club uniform enjoying the pleasures of a spin. The entire club suit is of black; coat and knickerbockers, are made of a fine thibet cloth trimmed with black braid in clover leaf pattern, making the handsomest as well as the neatest bicycle suit we have ever seen. It does the tailor, Waddell, much credit. At the next monthly meeting, 3 May, will be held the election of officers for the ensuing year. It is intended to open the new rooms soon with a little reception to the ladies and friends of the club, and it is safe to predict that whatever the Hoosac wheelmen undertake they will push, as heretofore, to a successful issue. 8565.

CAPT. C. L. SMITH, of the Cambridge Bicycle Club has arranged the following races for the season: 2 May, Quincy, dining at the Robinson House; 9 May, Echo bridge, Newton; 16 May, Colt's Tavern, Sharon; 23 May; Belmont Spring; 31 May, Lynn, dining at the Boscobel and attending races in the afternoon. Moonlight runs will be held 14, 15, 17 May.

THE Owl Club, of St. Louis have shown a rare friendlessness towards Chicago by inviting the bicycle club of the latter city to visit them. The unaccustomed invitation has been accepted, and it is promised that twenty-five machines from the Lake City will roll down into St. Louis. The visit may result in perpetual peace between the two communities.

THE date of the Maverick Wheel Club's entertainment, which is to be given at the Paris Rink, East Boston, is Tuesday, 18 May, not 21 May, as has been stated.

SOUTH BOSTON.—The regular monthly meeting of the Suffolk Wheel Club was held on Monday evening, 3 May, President Charnock presiding. It was voted to hold semimonthly meetings in the future.

BLACK and gold were adopted as the club colors, and the S. W. C. will sail this season under a pirate's flag minus the skull and bones.

THE captain's dog was adopted as the club dog, and christened "Apollo" (of course).

THE membership was increased by eight members, and the club will this week move into larger and well appointed apartments.

THE TRADE.

MURRAY, at 100 Sudbury street, has taken in a lot of Gormully & Jeffery's Champion bicycles. This is the machine on which Schock made his wonderful record. It is sold at a very low price, and the makers are selling immense quantities of them. Call and look at the wheel and see what an American maker can do.

ARDILL'S Liquid Enamel has gained a most enviable reputation. It can be easily and quickly applied, giving a smooth jet black polished surface. Price seventy-five cents. Stoddard, Lovering & Co., are the sole United States Agents.

FOR neatness, durability, stock and workmanship, the King of the Road lamp stands unrivalled. Stoddard, Lovering & Co., 152 Congress street, Boston, the sole United States agents will be pleased to send you an illustrated catalogue.

IF you are in need of anything in the sundry line for your bicycle or tricycle you will do well to send to Stoddard,

Lovering & Co., 152 Congress street, Boston, and procure one of their large illustrated catalogues before ordering.

OUR compositor changed seventy to seventeen, last week, and made it appear that only seventeen per cent of the Experts sold were nickel plated, when in reality seventy per cent are finished in that way.

COMING EVENTS.

MISCELLANEOUS

Advertisements will be inserted in this column for one cent a word, including heading and address; but no advertisement will be taken for less than twenty-five cents.

The Cycle.

VOL. I., No. 7. BOSTON, MASS., 14 MAY, 1886. FIVE CENTS.

The Coventry Machinists' Co.'s New Tricycle for 1886.

COLUMBIAS

The Cycle.

VOL. I., No. 7.   BOSTON, MASS., 14 MAY, 1886.   FIVE CENTS.

The Coventry Machinists' Co.'s New Tricycle for 1886.

THE MARLBORO' CLUB—Automatic Steerer.
ADMIRABLY ADAPTED FOR LADIES.
SEND FOR CATALOGUE TO 239 COLUMBUS AVENUE, BOSTON.

Adjustment in Height in Front.
Adjustment in Height in Rear.

{Adjustment]in Length.
Adjustment in Width.

A Comfortable Coasting Plate.
A Bifurcated Seat.

THE LILLIBRIDGE SADDLE

Is the only one having any of these Points; is the only one that can be changed in Shape or Position at all; is the BEST and CHEAPEST; is adapted to all makes of Bicycles. Special Styles for the Safeties and Str.

Price, Nickelled, $5.00. Price of Coiled Spring, with Straps, etc., for Old Saddles, 75 Cts.

FREEMAN LILLIBRIDGE, Rockford, Ill.

THE CYCLE

PUBLISHED EVERY FRIDAY BY ABBOT BASSETT, 22 SCHOOL ST., ROOM 19.

VOL. I.   BOSTON, MASS., 14 MAY, 1886.   No. 7.

TERMS OF SUBSCRIPTION.

One Year, by mail, post-paid.........................$1.50
Three Copies in one order..........................3.00
Club Subscriptions.................................1.00
Six Months...90
Single Copies.......................................05

Specimen Copies free.

' Every bicycle dealer is agent for the CYCLE 'and authorised to receive subscriptions at regular rates. The paper can be found on sale at the following places:—
Boston, CUPPLES, UPHAM & CO., cor. Washington and School Streets. Tremont House news stand. At every cycle warehouse.
New York, ELLIOTT MASON, 12 Warren Street.
Philadelphia, H. B. HART, 811 Arch Street. GEORGE D. GIDEON, 6 South Broad Street.
Baltimore, S. T. CLARK & CO., 4 Hanover Street.
Chicago, W. M. DURELL, 115 Wabash Avenue. JOHN WILKINSON & CO., 77 State Street.
Washington, H. S. OWEN, Capital Cycle Co.
St. Louis, ST. LOUIS WHEEL CO., 1121 Olive Street.

ABBOT BASSETT   .   .   .   EDITOR
W. I. HARRIS   ,' . . EDITORIAL CONTRIBUTOR

A. MUDGE & SON, PRINTERS, 24 FRANKLIN ST., BOSTON.

All communications should be sent in not later than Tuesday, to ensure insertion the same week.

Entered at the Post-office as second-class mail matter.

THE N. C. U. of England has always been very free to say what it could do and what it would do, but it has seldom made good its boasts. It has played fast and loose with the makers' amateurs for several years, and has always been beaten in its attempts to check the evil. In the one case where America asked it to show its power, it proved itself singularly inefficient and powerless. It has talked about vigilance committees, has made rules to prevent men riding the machines of their employers, and in other ways it has tried to do something and done nothing. Its last venture is calculated to make the Union the jest and by-word of the makers' amateurs. It announced that certain men were under suspicion. It gave no names, and the only correspondence that leaked out showed that the suspects defied it. It tells us that it suspended certain racing men; but it does not appear that the suspension was regarded by the men, nor is it known who they are. After a long and very secret discussion of the subject, the executive now comes forward and removes the suspensions. All of this looks like child's play. If America can do no better than this in the enforcement of law, let us sweep the laws from the books. Better no law at all

than one that is held in contempt and cannot be enforced. We have said that this step will have no effect on the action of the League, and we thoroughly believe this. The action of the Racing Board was taken before and independent of that of the N. C. U. The Board came out openly, told what it was going to do, and has done it. We believe America will settle the vexed question; but England is as deep in the mire as ever it was, and the governing body has taken a course not likely to win the respect of the offending class.

OUR contemporary, the *Wheel*, says of the racing rules : "They are torturous, long-winded, meaningless "; and again : "They have been surrounded by an impenetrable halo of absurd sub-clauses, and these have been amended and tinkered with so often, that prominent League men will tell you they know no more about them than the babe unborn." We do not believe in generalities. If the editor will only point out some of the "absurd sub-clauses," and tell us just the things he fails to comprehend, we will try to enlighten him, difficult as the task will be. We don't know just who he means by "prominent League men," but we will give him the opinion of one man, who is not quite so thick-headed as our friend's friends seem to be. Dr. Beckwith said this in his annual address to the League last year at Buffalo : "In alluding to the events of the past year, I should be very remiss should I fail to mention in most commendatory terms the splendid work of the Racing Board. The complete remodelling of the racing rules has furnished the L. A. W. with what may safely be termed the *most complete and faultless set of rules* for the government of race meetings in the possession of any organization." It is now in order for the *Wheel* to bring forward its "prominent League man" with an opinion to offset that of our respected president.

THE Boston Club show of bicycles, tricycles, and accessories is to be held during the League Meet. Every large dealer has engaged space, and will make a good showing. We regard this exhibition as one of the best things for cycling that has been proposed, and the makers do right in supporting it. When the public see gathered together hundreds of wheels of different makes and patterns, and see many large and

wealthy firms and corporations represented, it will realize how great and diversified are the interests represented by cycling. The trade should do all it can to make this show a complete success, and should, in their general advertisements, invite the public to visit the Mechanics' Building and inspect their wares. For wheelmen generally the show will be extremely interesting. The wheelman who doesn't go to the show, will regret it, and the man who has anything to sell, and neglects to exhibit it, will be sorry.

CONTRIBUTORS' CLUB

SOCIABLE OR TANDEM?

Editor of the Cycle : Of the arguments of "Jack Easy" in the last two numbers of the *Bicycling World,* only one is of such a nature as to call for any reply. The public will hardly be misled by such singular claims as he makes for the superiority of the sociable. They "are simply rushing for tandems," and ' leaving the poor, old, heavy, slow, awkward, broad-guage sociable in the seclusion, to which the merits of its rival have consigned it.

It is not worth while to consider in detail what Mr. "Easy" says. The man who comes out in cold type, and tries to show that less weight, less width, less wind resistance, and greater speed are not advantages in a tandem *where ladies are concerned* (though he seems to admit that they are for gentlemen alone), takes a stand obviously opposed to common sense, and directly contrary to the experience of tandem riders. His reason for such a statement is his claim that these four great advantages produce "positive defects" instead of good results. This comes, he asserts, because the machine is light, and causes "greatly increased jar and vibration," and he adds "the vehicle in which violent jar and vibration are produced at comparatively low rates of speed, is, I urge, a very good and sufficient reason why, for healthful considerations alone, ladies should endeavor to resist its fascinations." He also prescribes for ladies the use of the tandem but twice a week, a speed of but six miles an hour, and only a five-mile ride at a time.

All this is arrant nonsense. There is neither rhyme nor reason in it. It is born of prejudice or ignorance. "Jack Easy" may be the oldest rider in the country, an expert with other wheels, a courteous and affable gentleman; but he knows absolutely nothing of tandem riding with a lady.

I have ridden two thousand miles on tandems with my wife. We have ridden almost daily. Our rides have been from five to twenty-five miles; our speed from seven to ten miles an hour. From a sick bed, she has grown vigorous and almost robust. She

never was so well before. A dozen lady friends with like experience.tell the same tale. All this would be impossible if the evils which "Jack Easy" fears were possible.

The great vibration he talks of does not exist. The front seat of a Humber tandem is the most comfortable and easy seat on any sort of cycle. Lightness does not make the tandem "erratic in its steering and to lack stability." Under careful hands the tandem is safe. It is easy and exhilirating; compared with it, the sociable is dead and dull.

In spite of "Jack Easy's" claim to have the welfare of the ladies at heart, his specious arguments belie him. On his theory, they would be forced to depend upon 160-pound sociables or 100-pound singles. The day for such folly is past.   TANDEM.

FEAR.

Editor of the Cycle: A certain manufacturer announces that a rival in business saw his machine in process of manufacture and put an attachment on the factory, because he was afraid the wheel would be so good that he could not compete with it. By the same process of reasoning, are we to infer that the American ball bearings are so good that the English makers fear their competition, and so bring suit to prevent more being made?   GANDER SAUCE.

ROAD BOOKS.

Editor of the Cycle: We have all of us made more or less fun of Karl and his road book, and yet the fact is he is going to give us a very good book for a dollar. But he does wrong to call it a road book. Of what possible use to a rider is a book which tells about a road three or four years ago. When we want a road book we should go to such works as the Penn. Book; but when we want entertainment let us read Karl Kron.   KRONIC.

THAT BICYCLE PROBLEM.

Editor of the Cycle: We beg to differ with "B_y" and "S. M. F." in regard to the B'cycle problem. It seems to us that they allowed the bicycle to depreciate $5.00 in value, and still solved the problem as if it was worth $50. When A buys the bicycle back for $45, he has either $5.00 and a bicycle worth $45, in which case he has made nothing, or he has $5.00 and a bicycle still worth $50, in which case he has made $5.00. Now, when he sells out for $55, he has gained in either case $20.

First case, $65 — $45 x c=$20.
Second " $65 — $50 x $5=$20.
        TWO TECHS.

AMATEUR PROFESSIONALS.

Editor of the Cycle: The greatest good of the greatest number is the principle which should govern League members in their treatment of the amateur question. It is best to have races in which none but pure amateurs may compete, let us vote for that plan. If it is best to have men masquerading as amateurs, when everybody knows that they are not, let us go in for that. If it is best to sweep the amateur law away, let it go. Personal feeling should not enter the discussions. Let us have the best thing, no matter who gets hurt.   H.

TWO SIDES.

Editor of the Cycle: Your bicycle problem reminds me of a little scene I witnessed at the last Mechanics' Fair in Boston. A man in charge of a bicycle exhibit had a wheel erected on a stand so that it would turn freely. A countryman would come along and get interested in the spinning of the wheel, and the exhibitor would proceed to tell him that the top of the wheel moved faster than the lower part. This fact he would demonstrate so clearly that the man would be convinced. Then the exhibitor would turn about and convince the man that all parts of the wheel moved at the same speed. This he would also prove, and the man would go away with his mental apparatus tied up in a knot. All of which was highly enjoyed by the exhibitor. If you asked the exhibitor which statement he really believed, he would say, "I believe the thing that you don't; do you want to argue the case?"   B. X. Y.

CLEAN HANDS.

Editor of the Cycle: One who undertakes to teach hand-washing may seem to be entering upon a work for which there is no call, but I believe that not everybody knows how to do this thing in the best way. A writer in an English paper, speaking of the wearing of gloves when on the wheel, complains that they make the hands too warm, but without them the hands get soiled. He prefers the soiled hands, and says that if the hands are first rubbed with glycerine, and afterwards washed in hot water with soap and "plenty of washing sand, well rubbed in with a nail-brush," there is no difficulty in removing every trace of dirt, etc. However serviceable this method may be, it is not, in my opinion, to be recommended. Mechanical cleaning will not compare with chemical cleaning, by which I mean dissolving the medium by which dirt is secured in crevices of the skin. By mechanical cleaning, dirt, skin surface and all is rubbed away, and a rough surface is left, to which dirt will more persistently adhere another time. The plan which I adopt—one well known to all chemists—is, first, to rub oil into the hands, a little vaseline or a teaspoonful of any oil will do, then to wash the hands in soft water containing a few drops of ammonia, using common soap. If the water is warm so much the better. The ammonia decomposes the grease, forming with it soap and glycerine in the crevices in the skin, while the skin itself is unaffected; so dirt of all kinds, having nothing to hold it, comes out, and the hands are left soft, clean and smooth. Washing in this way is a real luxury; I should recommend ladies to try it. Any one who has done so will cease to be duly horrified by the answer of the dirty boy who, when asked by a lady whether he ever washed his hands, is stated by *Punch* to have said, " No; I waits till they gets 'ard, and then I iles 'em."   S. C. D.

TEAM ROAD RACING AGAIN.

Editor of the Cycle: Just as your last issue arrived with my letter, noticing the contradictory statements that have been made concerning the first race of the N. Y. and N. J. Team Road Racing Association, I was

shown a notice sent out by the secretary of that association, dated 6 May.

This notice states that the race will be started at three o'clock, Saturday, 12 June. It also states that the course will be " from a short distance beyond Irvington, via Springfield Ave., to intersection of Valley Road, thence on Valley Road to or near Llewelyn Park Hotel, making 12½ miles from starting point, returning over same course."

The above description of a course is correct, but the distance is only *about* 8 miles instead of 12½ miles.

The WHEEL must be correct in stating that they are to ride to the hotel, back to Irvington, and then back to finish at the hotel. That would give the required 25 miles.

I am sorry to hear that *forty-four* men are to be in the race, for two reasons. I think it very bad policy for wheelmen to put such a number of racing men together on the road, where they will be sure from their number to interfere with vehicles and with one another. Second, the course is not adapted to any such crowd. I will describe it in detail:—

Three miles on Springfield avenue, good macadam, three or four moderate hills, and a long steep down grade, dangerous at full speed.

Quarter-mile on Valley road, slight up grade, no side path, decent only in dry weather.

One mile of *narrow* side path, with dips and twists, must be ridden with care.

Three quarter-mile macadam ending at a double curve on a short but very sharp decline.

Three and one third miles mostly poor macadam with ups and downs, to just beyond Llewelyn Park Hotel, where turn must be made at small triangle.

It is hardly to be supposed that this course was chosen without the advice of the New Jersey members of the executive committee, and if they recommended it, it looks very much as if they were not as familiar with it as they ought to be.

I believe in road racing, and want to see the new association successful; but as a New Jersey man, I protest against their putting *forty-four* racers (or half that number) on any of our roads, and I urge them to change that scheme before it is too late.

To overdo the matter in this extravagant fashion may quite possibly do wheelmen more harm in a day than they can ever gain good by road racing.   N. J.

TIRES.

I SEE "Daisie" has started the hat question. Will she listen for a space to a humble brother wheelman, and allow an ignorant but well-meaning individual to offer a suggestion. Some summers back a friend sat under a tree, trimming a summer hat. It was before the latter days of the Puritan church steeple variety, and she had a dark gray felt, what a man would call a wide-awake, or a slouch, according to the way he stuck it on; anyway it was *felt* and soft and "maltese gray." Well, she jammed it here and poked it there, and sighed over it with no distinguished success; finally I picked it up and pulled it into a low, broad slouch, with a gray ostrich feather running backward

along the side, after a fashion I recalled seeing in *Harper's Monthly* as a ladies' riding hat, many years ago. She oh-h'd ! and tried it on, and lo ! she was as pretty as a picture ; and adopted it ? Not at all. It was n't the fashion. And with a sigh she disregarded the fact that "the fashion" is just what any one chooses to make it, and thumped the felt hat into a something which might have been modelled from the coal scuttle of Father Noah, and in which style I never saw but one lady look other than a fright.

Now, I know from experience that for genuine comfort a stiff hat does n't begin to compare with a felt; and I know from experience also that "fashion," as a rule, is simply the mandate of one or two hat manufacturers, who strive after the new, not the beautiful.

In masculine dress we have gone back to our grandfathers' days, and have chosen perhaps the most graceful, certainly the most *fitting* costumes of past centuries. Now, "Daisie" won't you kindly consider the above and weigh it's merits ; if you cannot see it in your mind's eye from the above description — and it was long before your eyes saw light that it was dropped — just turn to a file of Harper's, and hunt backward a score of years.

This is a serious matter, really. It is one of the moments, few and far between, when one little pair of hands a new style rests .s fate. When by a wise decision the hideous, masculine survivor of the war, yclept a helmet, can be banished, and the eyes of all wheelmen be gladdened by the graceful lines of a hat which is in itself beautiful, and which does not murder the beauty of the face below it ; which neither makes the wearer "bold " in look, nor " fast," but heightens the feminine grace, which all true men love to look upon, and which in its adaptation to the shape. of the head, is, when ventilated, next to a straw in hygienic perfection.

All of which, Madame "Daisie," is respectfully submitted with a full knowledge as to my rashness in even venturing to *have* an opinion on such an occult subject; and if wrongly done, "deal gently with the erring ! "　　　J. PARKE STREET.

P. S. Another point ! *Gray* is dust color ; just remember that..

MASSACHUSETTS CLUB RUNS.

THE following runs have been called by Capt. Peck of the Massachusetts Club :

Thursday morning, May 13.— A breakfast run to Hotel Faneuil, Brighton, leaving club house at 6.30 a. m. and reaching the club house again about 8.15.

Saturday evening, May 15.— A moonlight run through Walnut Avenue, Jamaica Plain, Brookline, Longwood, etc., leaving club house at 7.30.

Monday evening, May 17. — A moonlight run to Chestnut Hill reservoir, and to Echo bridge, one of the wheelman's most favorite rides. Leave club house at 7.30, returning through Newton and Brighton.

Tuesday evening, May 18. — There is to be a special meeting of the club at the club house on matters pertaining to the League Meet, and as soon as the meeting is over there will be a run to Chestnut Hill reservoir and return.

Monday, May 31.— An all day run to Lynn

to attend the races to be given on the new track, taking dinner at the Boscobel Hotel. Leave club house at 9.45 sharp. All the visiting wheelmen are invited to join.

There are several runs called at the time of the League Meet, and the club members are earnestly requested to turn out then with the visiting wheelmen. The tricycle division, under the care of its captain, John Williams, will go on the above club runs, starting at the same time from the club house.

RACING BOARD DECLARATIONS.

THE Racing Board has declared the following wheelmen to be professionals, and they are expelled from the League : Reuben A. Punnett, Rochester, N. Y. ; Fred Russ Cook, San Francisco ; S. G. Whittaker, St. Louis ; L. J. Martel, Chicopee, Mass. ; C. P. Adams and F. R. Brown, Springfield; and W. F. Knapp, now of Lynn.

H. E. Bidwell, of Hartford, and C. F. Haven, of Boston, are suspended until 30 May. All charges against C. F. Cope, of Philadelphia, and L. A. Miller, of Meriden, are withdrawn.

IN FRUITFUL LANDS.

MISS MINNA CAROLINE SMITH has published a volume of poems, to which she gives the title, " In Fruitful Lands," taken from the first poem of the collection. Miss Smith is well known to wheelmen as a rider and as the author of a number of stories and poems published in *Outing*, over the signature of " Minimum," and they will accord a generous welcome to this new venture. We have read the poems with no small degree of pleasure. They have a fresh-air flavor, and breathe the spirit of pure poetry. They are twenty-five in number, and nearly all appear for the first time. The volume is bound in parchment, and dates from the Harvard Annex. Published by William B. Howland, and sold by Cupples, Upham & Co., Boston. Price, 60 cents.

ST. LOUIS IDEAS.

A ST. LOUIS wheelman writes to the chairman of the Racing Board : " I am coming to Boston loaded with proxies for Dr. Beckwith, who will positively accept the presidency once more. I should have voted for Kirkpatrick, in spite of his amateur proclivities, but he is out. I gather from Ducker's various articles that he proposes to make a lively attack on the Racing Board at the Meet. If he does, you can certainly count on the support of St. Louis as far as the endorsement of your action is concerned, but Rule H must go. My idea is to leave out the amateur rule as a qualification to League membership, and only retain it as a qualification for entering certain races; offer merely insignificant prizes for amateur races, relegating them to the duffers, and instead of offering merely money prizes to the professionals, offer valuable trophies in most of the races, as at present, in the prominent amateur events. This, in a short time, will drive the prominent amateurs into the professional ranks, while they will still retain their League membership. This will also actually result in the establishing of an unnamed third class, as the present professionals will race

only for gold. The Membership Committee will be able to prevent the admittance of disreputable professionals into the League, and they cannot use the League to bolster up their rink hippodromes. Thus the amateur idea which, as it now stands, is entirely foreign to the spirit of the age, will gradually be eliminated."

LEAGUELETS.

WE are cutting notches in the broom handle to mark off the days before the Meet. We have very little more to do in the way of knife work.

THE New Hampshire Division of the L. A. W. has a membership of one hundred and one. They will have the right of the line in the League parade, and ought to send fifty men, at least, to Boston.

THE League programme will have a good map of Boston, showing the hotels, club houses, stations, points of interest, etc.

THE committee in charge of the hill-climbing contest on Corey Hill consists of Dr. W. G. Kendall, chairman, Charles S. Howard, and H. W. Hayes. The committee will act as judges, and the following will serve as timers : N. Ethier, J. E. Savelle, D. N. C. Hyams, C. N. Reed, R. E. Bellows, Eugene Sanger.

THE New York clubs are going to turn out in force at the Boston League Meet. George R. Bidwell has charge of all arrangements, and it is probable that a large party will leave by the Fall River line on Wednesday evening, 26 May.

THE Boston Club will do its part in contributing for the entertainment of our guests at the Meet, by furnishing a large hall for the business meeting and a room for storage with attendants. It can be relied upon that these two items will be made satisfactory.

THE Racing Board reserves the right to reject any and all entries to the championships, and none but the purest of amateurs will go in unless the League upsets their action.

THE Citizens' Club, of New York, will have the freedom of the Massachusetts club house during the League meet.

JOHN T. WILLIAMS, of Boston, and C. H. Potter, of Cleveland, say they are going in for the tricycle championship. If Potter wins he will have to *urn* the medal.

THOSE who apply for admission to the League after this date cannot get their tickets for use at the Boston Meet, but secretary Aaron will furnish them with certificates of membership for use on that occasion.

GREAT inquiry has been made about hotel accommodations at the Meet. Boston can take care of all who come. It may be well to say to those who are coming, that Boston citizens retire between nine and ten, and they expect their guests to do the same. Our experience tells us that the wicked New York men have little use for beds.

How 's this ? Kirkpatrick not coming to the met ! Who will preside at the overflow meeting ? It will be tough meat without the Kirk juice.

DR. W. G. KENDALL has accepted the marshalship of the Eastern Division of the League Touring Board, and has already begun his arrangements for tours of the future. He proposes to have one on the Sunday following the League Meet. As now arranged the run will be to Nantasket Beach, starting at 7 A. M., and taking breakfast at Hingham. From there they will ride to Hotel Pemberton, on the beach. Dinner will be served at the Black Rock House, after a ride over the famed Jerusalem road.

A SERIES of home-trainer races will be run at the cycle show of the Boston Club, which is to be held in the Mechanics' building during the League Meet. It is probable that Herring and Harris, winners of the prizes in the late contest, will then meet, in which case the contest will be an interesting one.

THE League banquet will be held at the Vendome on the 29th instant. The guests will sit down at 7 P.M. A male quartette will furnish vocal music for the occasion, and the Salem cadet orchestra will attend to the instrumental music. The tickets will be limited to 300, and will cost $2.50. Applications for tickets should be made to H. W. Hayes, 91 State street, Boston.

MACHINES will be stored at the Meet on the check system. Men will not be allowed to take machines at their pleasure.

THE West is talking up Dr. Beckwith for president of the League.

WE suppose it is the proper thing to do, to invite the ladies to occupy the galleries at the Music Hall concert; but we do not know that the sight of the gentlemen on the floor below, drinking beer, smoking cigarettes and eating sandwiches, will be particularly agreeable to them. Smoke rises, you know. Moreover, we don't know that every man cares to have his wife looking down upon him when there are pretty waiter girls on duty.

PARTIES of fifteen and upward, from points fifty miles or more from Boston, will be entitled to reduced rates, provided they notify the general passenger agent of road they use, at least a week in advance, what train will be taken. Rates, two cents per mile for each person. Wheels carried free. Roads will not give this reduction, and many refuse carriage of wheels unless proper time and notice is given them to provide a special car for wheels.

Parties intending coming to Boston should unite and choose one of their number, preferably their local consul, to notify their passenger agent how many men will come and by what train.

These rates have been tendered by all the roads approaching Boston, and parties are advised to take the most direct route in every case.

HOW THEY GOT DOWN TO WEIGHT.

COLLEGE students enter into their athletic contests with an enthusiasm that is refreshing and "Featherweight," in the Boston Globe, tells an interesting story about the preparation of the technology students. At their games the juniors won the tug-of-war, and thereby hangs a tale. When the four men who were to represent the class of '87 began to pull together, it was found that they weighed

twenty-four pounds over the limit — 600 pounds. This, too, was when they were all supposed to be in the pink of condition; but they must take off those twenty-four pounds of extra weight, and every expedient known by the athlete to reduce weight was resorted to. In fact, they went through a course of training that would put to the blush a prizefighter preparing for a battle in the ring. Finally, on the night before the eventful day, they were again weighed, and, to their consternation, they were still too heavy by one and a half pounds. They were not going to give it up then, so they decided to refrain from any more food until they had been accepted by the officials on the following day. The time for the official weighing found each one fearfully hungry, but when they stepped on the scales and found that they weighed but 599 75-100 pounds and were eligible to pull, they thought no more of eating, but went to work on the cleats just a quarter of a pound under weight. When they had won their first heat they suddenly disappeared, but showed up in time for the last pull. The "sophs" were to be their opponents, and they demanded that the juniors be weighed over again, but the referee said no. The '87 men had been weighed and accepted once, and as they had pulled one heat they were eligible to pull again. Now, the juniors had precisely this view of the matter, and as they were decidedly hungry after winning once, they slipped out and broke their fasting. The sophomores discovered the clever trick of their elders, but the only satisfaction they could get out of it was that perhaps they could be as smart another year.

CYCLETS

THE header I took in the spring, tra la,
Was an act of marvellous grace.
I went thro' a highland fling, tra la,
And I cut quite a "pigeon wing," tra la,
Ere I measured the dust on my face.
And that's what I mean when I say or I sing,
Oh, bother the header I took in the spring.
Tra la, etc.   DARDALUS.

GASKELL is a disappointed man. Speechly has won the Surrey Cup three times, and it becomes his property. Gaskell had won it twice and wanted one more try for it, but it was not to be.

JAMES P. BRUCE, of Vicksburg, Miss., proposes to get up a grand cycling tournament in that city next September, especially in the interest of Louisville, New Orleans, Cincinnati, St. Louis, and Memphis wheelmen. A daily paper will be issued during the meet.

THE lantern parade at St. Louis has now been fixed for 29 September. It promises to be the grandest affair of the kind ever given in this country.

KAUFMAN and McAnney, the American fancy riders, now in England, have been engaged for the Edinburgh exhibition. Kaufman couldn't McAnney kind of a show without his partner. Canary one see that?

THE restaurant of the Boston Club House has been closed for the summer season, but it is understood that it will be reopened for the three days of the League Meet. During the warm months the club members prefer to dine at their out-of-town headquarters.

AT the last meeting of the Massachusetts Club, Col. Pope gave notice that he would, at the next meeting, move that the rules of the club be amended, limiting the membership to two hundred and fifty. The house is too small to accommodate a larger number.

A SECOND edition of the Pennsylvania Road Book is in press. The first edition of 2,000 would not go around. We like to call it the Penn. Road Book, for the title under which it is issued is altogether too long. Why not the "P. N. M. Book," Mr. Wood? Karl Kron has cut his title down to the smallest limits.

THE friends of Miss Minna Caroline Smith will be glad to know of her volume of poems, noticed elsewhere, and we believe she will find a good demand for it. Miss Smith will be at the Meet to assist in the entertainment of the ladies who come to Boston.

KLUGE's machine met with an accident in the Clarksville race, and he had to change his mount, thereby losing nine minutes. A friend of Weber's writes us: "When Whittaker took his first header, the riders were all close together, and Weber had to swerve from his course to pass him. In reference to the hill-climbing contest, it occurred a few hours after the fifty-mile race, and of course the boys were not fresh nor in condition to climb hills, nor does Weber claim to be a hill-climber, especially on high speed racing machines. Either of them could walk up almost any hill on a Pony Star. Young road a 46-inch vertical fork machine."

CHICAGO wheelmen will visit St. Louis in a body, 15 May, and the wheelmen of that city will entertain them. There will be some hard riding when the two parties get together.

BURLEY AYERS is so afraid of being called a maker's amateur, and of having it said that he advertises some particular manufacturer, that he has ordered a machine which will be a mixture of all known makes. — Mirror.

THE New York Club is not going to build a club house, and the $30,000 was never subscribed. New quarters have been taken at 302 West 58th street.

PRELIMINARY steps are being taken to form a bicycle club in the northern section of Philadelphia. The intention is to fit up a club house in the vicinity of Broad and Diamond streets, from which point easy access may be had to the Park over Diamond street with its asphalt pavement. Permanent organization will be effected this week, and at the same time a name will be chosen and a location decided upon.

A ROXBURY rider gives us a tip. He tells us to take ball-bearings to pieces and lubricate them with vaseline. Once treated in this way they will last a whole season without further need for lubrication.

THE advocates for plumbago as a lubricant seem to have abandoned their ideas.

BECAUSE wheelmen wear knee breeches they are called "dudes." If good fitting garments and a neat appearance make a man a dude, the wheelmen who gather at the reservoir on Sundays are not all entitled to this appellation. A wheelman in shirt sleeves, and long trousers, tied at the bottom with a

THE
AMERICAN RUDGE,

THE WHEEL FOR 1886.

IT HAS NO EQUAL AT THE PRICE.

SEND FOR 1886 CATALOGUE.

SEND FOR 1886 CATALOGUE.

AMERICAN RUDGE. PRICE, 50-INCH, $107.50.

READ WHAT THEY SAY OF IT.

"The American Rudge is a dandy; staunch and easy running."—H. C. OGDEN, Middletown, N. Y.

"For business purposes and general road riding it has no superior."—J. H. BROWN, Rochester, N. Y.

"Have ridden my 56 American Rudge 1,500 miles, and cheerfully recommend it."
C. W. SEAMAN, Lewisburg, Pa.

"It takes at sight. Those who intend getting a Bicycle should get an American Rudge."
E. E. CUMNER, Lewiston, Me.

A few Shopworn and Second-hand Machines in Stock at Low Prices. Send for list.

SOLE U. S. AGENTS,

STODDARD, LOVERING & CO.

Nos. 152 to 158 Congress Street, Boston, Mass.

New York Headquarters - - - - - GEO. R. BIDWELL - - - - 2 and 4 E. 60th St., N. Y.

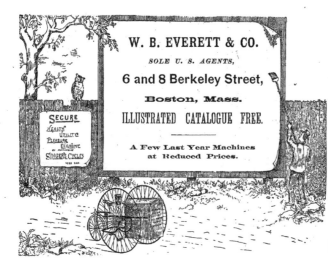

rope, is hardly the personification of dudeism.

IF our friend Stall doesn't send a check to the Massachusetts Club for their advertisement of his "Screamer," we shall have to say he is working the clubs.

THIS happened one evening, recently, not a thousand miles from Cambridge; Two tricyclers chanced to halt by the roadside for a brief rest, just as a group of Irish laborers were passing on their way home from work. Attracted by the bright new machines, two of the men paused a moment to look at them.

"If you only had a tricycle, Pat," said one of the cyclers to the nearer of the men, "you could ride to and from your employment."

"Ride to the divil!" said Pat, with a contemptuous look at the combination of man and wheels. "Do ye think I cam from the aould counthry to drive a donkey-caart, bedad, and be me own horrse?" — *Record.*

WM. READ & SON report a remarkable boom in bicycles the present year. The ball-bearing head of the Royal Mail and the grip-rim are giving great satisfaction.

CYCLING develops the lungs, improves the temper, and gives volume and sweetness to the voice. In proof of this I mention the fact that a well-known wheelman, who is connected with an evening paper, sat down one night to a piano, and accompanied himself to one of the popular songs of the day. This was at the club house, no one present. Meanwhile a brother member, intent on a game of euchre, softly entered. The music took possession of his soul, and gradually influenced by the purity of the tones and the pathos of the song, all evil inclinations left him, and he quietly retired. Oh, that we had more such warblers! — *Spectator.*

THE *American Wheelman* publishes a long account of its road race, with cuts of the start and finish, the winners and the prizes.

THE Rhode Island Division L. A. W., will hold a road race from Providence to Warren in June, a clam-bake in July, and an excursion in August.

THE clerical tour of 1886 will start from Central Park, New York, 3 August, and proceed northerly along the Hudson river to Albany, to Troy, to the Round Lake camp ground, to Sharon Springs, to Cobleskill and Howe's Cave. Rev. Sylvanus Stall will have charge of the party as before.

IN the home-trainer record-race, the prizes were awarded as follows: First prize, W. C. Herring, Ixion Club, New York City, 52⅘ seconds; second prize, P. M. Harris, of same club, 57⅘ seconds.

ONE who called himself Lieut.-Col. Paul Methuen, has victimized Burley B. Ayers, of Chicago, to the tune of $100. He presented a letter of introduction from a friend of Mr. Ayers' in Hamilton, Ont., and on the strength of this he was shown no little attention, and a draft for $100 was endorsed. The draft proved worthless.

GEORGE B. THAYER, who is wheeling across the continent, was last heard from in Buffalo. He expects to arrive in San Francisco in July.

THE wheelmen of Chicago were inexpressibly shocked and grieved by the death of one of their number, Mr. Felix Ribolla, as the result of a sad tragedy growing out of an altercation in which his only part was that of peacemaker. Mr. Ribola, the father of Felix, a man of considerable wealth, was afflicted with a violent temper, and on Sunday morning, 2 May, he became involved in a dispute with a neighbor's coachman about a trivial matter, and becoming enraged beyond control, procured a revolver and began firing at the coachman. Felix and Stephen Ribola hastened to the scene of the quarrel, and in the endeavor to quiet their father and induce him to give up the pistol, the weapon in the old man's hands was accidentally discharged, and Felix fell to the ground mortally wounded. His father, still further crazed by the awful result of his rage, rushed into the house near by and blew out his own brains. Felix lingered for two days, and expired Tuesday afternoon, 4 May. Mr. Ribolla was a member of the Chicago Club and of the Track Association. The clubs of Chicago have taken action, expressing their regrets at the loss of their fellow-member. — *Mirror.*

SANDERS SELLERS tore up his letter from the N. C. U., and returned the pieces to them.

WILLIS FARRINGTON, of the Boston club, has returned from his Bermuda trip.

THE Lynn Cycle Club promises to turn out a fine new crop of flyers this season.

THE Chicago strikes interfere considerably with the delivery of machines consigned to Western customers, and have delayed shipment of Gormully & Jefferey's goods to Eastern houses.

AN incident of the recent St. Louis road race, was the sudden bath taken by one of the contestants who rode too near the bank of a creek.

SOME genius out in Wisconsin has got up a four-wheeled affair, which he claims can clean out any tricycle ever invented. To prove the worth of his machine, he proposes a ride across the plains.

ROWE and Hendee are sleeping in the same bed, and sometimes Knapp crawls in. All of them are very fast riders when awake, and they are often fast asleep.

NEILSON is riding a Rudge machine that weighs but 304 ounces. This is one of the wheels that an English rider sent to the front at Springfield last year. We shall now see whether the pace is in the rider or the wheel.

THE initiation fee of the League has been raised to $1.00 The new rule will go into effect 15 May, and those who get their applications in before that date need send but $1.25, or fifty cents for initiation fee and seventy-five cents for dues.

SECRETARY AARON has been obliged to leave his post and seek health in the South. No one will begrudge him his leave of absence, and many good wishes will follow him. He has overworked himself.

WM. READ & SON have received the new pattern Royal Mail two-track, with small drivers and large steering wheel. It is a beautiful machine and sells very low.

MOSES SHERIFF, of Manchester, N. H., has ridden his 54-inch Rudge Light Roadster 5,000 miles from 1 March, 1884, to 1 May, 1886. He expects to roll up a greater record than ever this year.

V. C. PLACE, one of the fast men of 1881, will appear on the track this season mounted on Howell's 59-inch Rudge Racer, on which the latter rode the mile in 2.31 2-5.

WE have a supply of "Lyra Bicyclica: Sixty Poets on the Wheel," in flexible covers, at a very low price, for our L. A. W. period. This is the enlarged second edition, and is the most peculiar and thoroughbred of all cycling verse. The frenzied and rolling eye of the "Poemster," beholds cycling throughout the universe, from the Almighty on his starry orbits to the rotifer, or wheel-animalcule, under the microscope. Popular idols are undone and outdone by the flighty and superjuvenated bard, and true poetry and piety embodied in parodic guise.

THE tricycle division of the Boston Club will have an all-night moonlight run to Lynn, next Saturday. The course taken will be circuitous, through Newton and neighboring towns, and the pace an easy jog. The Boscobel will be the objective point for the night run, and the trip will be continued to Marblehead the next day.

DR. W. G. KENDALL, marshal of the Eastern Division of the touring department, will soon institute among other things a series of short Sunday runs to such points as Brockton, Scituate, Hough's Neck, and other of the many places where the doctor is well acquainted, and is sure of a good reception. Those who have been with him on trips in other seasons say, that there is no town within thirty miles of Boston in which he has not friends happy to entertain any party conducted by him.

H. O. DUNCAN left Montpellier, France, at 6.15 A. M., on Sunday, 4 April, and arrived in Paris, Friday, 9 April, at 7 P. M., a distance of about five hundred miles. Duncan missed the road several times, and was troubled with rain, head winds and hail, as well as mountainous roads made miserable by newly laid stones.

AT the annual meeting of the Iowa Division L. A. W. Rev. A. C. Stilson, an invited guest to their banquet, made a telling speech in marked terms of approval of the benefits and pleasures in the use of the wheel, which remarks took deep root in the minds of all present on that occasion. For the appreciation of the sentiments there expressed, the members of the Ottumwa Bicycle Club with stealth and kindly malice aforethought, secured by donation from the members of the club and friends, a sufficient amount of money to purchase an elegant Expert Columbia, 54-inch nickel plated and enamelled, 1886 finish, with all the modern improvements. This was presented to the reverend gentleman, the captain of the club making the presentation speech, to which an appropriate response was made.

SCENE, a wayside North Shore hotel; *dramatis personæ*, a party of wheelmen, several of whom had put up at this hostelry for the night a few weeks previous; time, morning, when about to settle bills.

Spokesman for party. — Why, how 's this? You have gone up thirty per cent on the prices you gave us when we stopped here before.

Hotel proprietor. — Yes, I know it. I had n't seen you feed then. — *Record.*

Before buying your new mount for the coming season, send for price list and description of the

"NEW RAPID" BICYCLES,

WITH THE

During 1885 not a single spoke broke or wheel buckled.

Universally acknowledged to be the strongest and most rigid wheel made.

SECTION SHOWING HALF OF HUB AND HALF THE NUMBER OF SPOKES.

TRUE TANGENT WHEEL.

At the Inventions Exhibition, London, 1885, the "New Rapid" was awarded *a Gold Medal*, the highest and only award for Bicycles.

PRESS OPINIONS.

"One of the best machines in the market."—The Cyclist.
"The best wheel ever built."—Bicycling News.

"The 'True Tangent' Wheel (New Rapid) is far and away the most perfect yet made."—Illustrated Sports.

SEND TEN CENTS FOR LARGE SIZE CABINET PHOTOS.

ENERGETIC AGENTS WANTED EVERYWHERE. *APPLY FOR TERMS.*	# S. T. CLARK & CO. ## IMPORTERS, BALTIMORE, MD.

FIRST GRAND OPENING TOURNAMENT

OF THE

Lynn Cycle Club Track Assoc'n,

Lynn, Mass., Memorial Day, May 31, 1886.

Although the centre of bicycling, Eastern Massachusetts has not heretofore possessed a complete and modern racing track. The necessity for such led to the formation of the Lynn Cycle Club Track Association, which, with commendable energy and dispatch, has evolved within the "City of Shoes" the finest bicycle racing track to be found in the world, being a dead level, three-lap track, of perfect design. The opening tournament will include the fastest men in America, and extraordinary time is expected. Visitors to the League Meet will regret much if they do not stop over and attend this grand event.

PROSPECTUS OF RACES.

FIRST RACE WILL BE CALLED PROMPTLY AT 2 P. M.

1. One-Mile Amateur Bicycle. — First prize, a fine gent's gold watch; second prize, pair elegant opera glasses.
2. Three-Mile Amateur Bicycle (9.45 class). — For League of Essex County wheelmen only. First prize, gold medal; second prize, silver medal.
3. Two-Mile Amateur Tricycle. — First prize, elegant hanging lamp; second prize, Smith & Wesson nickel-plated revolver.
4. One-Mile Amateur Bicycle (3.20 class). — First prize, gold-headed cane; second prize, base parlor lamp.
5. Three-Mile Amateur Bicycle Lap Race. — First prize, silver tilting water pitcher; second prize, elegant berry set.
6. First of a series for the professional championship of America. Five-Mile Professional Bicycle Race, between Robert A. Neilson and John S. Prince. — These two celebrated riders will meet to contest for a purse of $300 a side, and an additional purse of $500 offered by the Association, and the professional championship of America.
7. Twenty-Mile Amateur Bicycle Race, for the Columbia prize cup, valued at $1,500. — This cup shall become the personal property of the competitor who is first for three times winner in said races for it, or who, in winning one of said races, covers the twenty miles within one hour.

☞ Entries for all races to be made to E. M. BAILEY, secretary of Lynn Cycle Club Track Association, Lynn, Mass., accompanied by an entrance fee of $1.00 for each event, except the twenty-mile, entry which is $5.00, returnable to all who complete the distance.

☞ Entries close May 26. All entries will be received subject to the decision of the L. A. W.

☞ The Club reserves the right to reject any or all entries to the races.

ALBERT SCHOCK has replied to Phil Hammell's challenge, and refused to run except in a seventy-two hour race. Short distances he claims to have no claim upon.

IT is proposed to have a bicycle race on the Chicago track each day before the ball games.

THE Cyclist says Schock's record is not so good as Waller's. The track on which Schock ran was full length. Waller's track was about two feet short.

THE Maverick Wheel Club has called runs as follows: 16 May, Waltham; 23 May, Norwood; 30 May, South Natick; 31 May, Lynn.

To E. W. B. Daisie says she can hardly decide for you. "Our favorite runs are from six to fifteen miles over good roads, and a lady on a single would not be overtaxed. For the longer runs, which we hope to have the following week, a tandem would be better, for the riders will have to cover about thirty to forty miles a day. There is a good prospect that four out of five of the ladies in attendance at the Meet will ride tandems."

THE Cyclist does not believe in the International championship as proposed by the Springfield Club. Mr. Sturmey believes the associations of the two countries should run the championships if any are established.

MR. EVANS, of Cincinnati, who, by-the-by, had some strange champagne experiences with Madame Emma, at the Eden Theatre, Paris, left this country last month to return to his native land, with the intention, inter alia, of coming back and importing into England a young American lady, who, as a bicycle trick rider, can make Canary, Kaufman and McAnney "sit up." — Cyclist.

YOU, who have aching joints after long rides in this the early part of the season, anoint them with arnicated oil, and obtain relief.

THE Massachusetts Club photograph, by Notman, is now being mounted, and will be on exhibition soon. It is considered the best of the kind ever taken.

THE tricycle division officers of the Massachusetts Club have adopted the same badge on the sleeve as used by the regular officers, with a small gold tricycle in addition.

LAST week Bob Neilson, timed by three watches and paced by Harry Getchel, made a good record for "around the reservoir," doing it in 3.18. Burnham claims to have done it in 3.16.

THE Springfield Club has a committee to ascertain the desirability of keeping a record of the riding done by each member during the year.

PRESIDENT E. C. HODGES has been appointed a member of the Boston Club's Cycle Show Committee. Freelon Morris has resigned from that committee.

A NEW club is to be formed at Randolph this week. Mr. T. J. Strickland is prime mover in the affair. The club will probably start with twenty members.

THE dates of the next Springfield tournament will probably be 14, 15, 16 and 17 September.

ROWE and Hendee were weighed last week, and there was only an ounce of difference in their weight, both tipping the scales at about one hundred and seventy-five and a half pounds. That's where we are ahead of the champions.

THE PATH.

MINNEAPOLIS, MINN., 10 May. — The first day of the six-day, twelve-hour bicycle race, for $1,000 a side and the championship of America, between Albert Schock and John S. Prince, was started to-day by referee C. W. Ryder, sporting editor of the Minneapolis Tribune. In many cases Prince would pass Schock and gain one lap in five, the track being eight laps to the mile. Prince now holds all board-track records from 50 to 185 miles, having broken those made by Woodside in the other race. The score at the finish to-day was, Prince 185 miles one lap, and Schock 179 miles five laps. Woodside's record for the first day was 181 miles one lap. The betting is in favor of Prince.

NEW YORK, 29 April. — Sports of the college of the city of New York. One mile bicycle race. P. Slade (1), 3.43½; J. A. Constant (2).

MINNEAPOLIS. — Races were held at Minneapolis Fair Grounds, 4 May. After a scrub trotting race, T. W. Eck rode a quarter-mile heat race against an unknown 2.40 trotter. The horse won the first heat in 57¼s., and

Eck the second in 56⅓s. The third heat was not run, the track being too bad for the latter. The third race was for ten miles, between John S. Prince, America's champion cyclist, and Hank Seeley's gray horse "Crazy." The horse won in 38m. 37s. Prince stopped at nine and a half miles.

THE Lynn track will divide honors with Springfield.

THE annual tricycle race of the Boston Club will be held 28 May, and will be from Bailey's, at South Natick, to Boston, about twenty miles. Open to all. Two prizes. Entrance fee, $1.00, to R. J. Tombs, 87 Boylston street.

THE opening tournament of the Lynn Cycle Club Track Association will be held on Memorial day. The entries for the opening tournament will include the fastest racers in America, and quick time is expected. Many of the visitors to the L. A. W. Meet in Boston will attend the great event. On the same day the Essex County wheelmen will hold a business meeting; at one o'clock in the afternoon the Essex County parade will

take place, terminating at the track. Maitland's band, of Brockton, will furnish music during the races, and will probably take part in the parade. The official programme of the races, which will commence at 2 P. M., will be found in the advertisement elsewhere. THE officers of the Meet will be as follows: Referee, Abbot Bassett; judges, H. D. Corey, Frank S. Winship, John Wood, Jr.; scorers, William H. Pevear, George Chinn, A. D. Peck, Jr.; timers, George Butler, Eugene E. Merrill, O. S. Roberts; starter, Charles S. Howard; clerk, of course, W. W. Stall.

AT the international bicycle championship of the world recently held in England on Easter, the winners of the one, ten, twenty, and fifty-mile championships rode the Rudge Racer.

THE second annual fifteen-mile handicap road race of the Colorado Wheel Club will be held on the Littleton road, Sunday, 16 May, at ten A. M. The road over which the race will be run is a seven and a half mile course from the Exposition Building on

Broadway to Littleton and return. The best time ever made over the road is 1h. 4m., made by F. E. Kimball, of Denver, in the race last year. The handicaps will be sealed; all entries starting from scratch; handicaps being deducted from time made.

THE fifty-mile bicycle championship of England was contested at the Aylstone Park Grounds, Leicester, Eng., on the 25th ult. There was a large field of starters, including DeCivry of France and other fast riders. H. O. Duncan, an Anglo-French rider, was the winner, F. J. Lee was second and M. Dupois of France third. Duncan's was the third successive victory for the fifty-mile cup which has now become his property. The fifty-mile championship was first run in 1883, since which time the winners have been as follows: 1883, 24 March F. De-Civry, Paris, 3.13.14.; 3 August, F. Wood, Leicester, 2.48.10.; 1884, 17 April, T. Battersby, Newcastle, 3.3.26⅖.; 5 July, F. Wood, Leicester, 2.47.20.; 1885, H. O. Duncan, Montpelier, 3.17.14½; 1 August, H. O. Duncan, 3.5.42⅗.

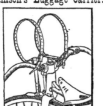

THE CLUB.

MASSACHUSETTS CLUB. — At the last monthly meeting of the Massachusetts Bicycle Club, three new members were admitted, Messrs. E. S. Beck, Edward Harrington and E. P. Faxon, making the total membership about two hundred and fifty, all active members. The club voted to contribute $200 toward the L. A. W. Meet, and will exert itself to the utmost to do its share of the work of entertaining the many wheelmen who will come to inspect our sandpapered roads. The second lieutenant of the club, Mr. R. P. Ahl, having resigned on account of absence in Europe, Mr. James M. Burr was chosen his successor. Mr. Burr is a popular member and will, without doubt, prove an efficient officer. The new "Year Book" of the Massachusetts Bicycle Club is nearly ready for the press, and Secretary Pratt, who has spent some time in its preparation, hopes that it will suit the members much better than last year's book. The following resolution was passed and the secretary was instructed to publish the same in THE CYCLE: *Resolved*, That the Massachusetts Bicycle club hereby expresses its disapproval of the article known and advertised as "Screamer," and that the captain is hereby requested not to allow the use of said article on any club run.

At the April meeting of the club, Mr. Daniel W. Colbath was chosen to fill the office of "librarian." Mr. Colbath has entered upon the duties with a spirit and enterprise that will soon place the library of that club on a firm basis, and give the club a collection of literature worthy of any organization of its standing and size. Mr. Colbath has issued a circular in which he says of the library, it is earnestly hoped to make it a retreat where members and friends can pass pleasantly a rainy afternoon, and use for reference at all times in making up runs and tours; in other words, a library of value to all wheelmen, and a credit to the Massachusetts Bicycle Club. We have little doubt but that there are in the homes of the members many books, pamphlets, etc., on cycling and kindred sports, which they would gladly donate to the club library. Several such gifts have already been received. Will you kindly look up what you may have and are willing to part with, and send the names, volumes, and condition of the same, with full address of giver, at your earliest convenience? This is in order to avoid possible duplicates. Subscriptions to the various periodicals, and donations of the "money of the realm" to be used for purchasing books, will also be in order, and we shall be pleased to hear from such members as can afford to respond. Such books and papers as are received and found worthy of it will be handsomely bound, and the donor's name suitably inscribed therein.

OMAHA, NEB. — Omaha Club: President, W. U. Rogers; secretary, C. M. Woodman; treasurer, Perry Badollett.

WHEELING, W. V. — Wheeling Wheelmen: President, Dr. Chas. E. Mason; secretary and treasurer, A. Allen Wheat; captain, Wilbur L. Wright.

CANTON, OHIO. — Canton Club: Presi-

MIDDLETOWN, CONN. — Middletown Club: President, E. G. Camp; secretary, E. L. Brockway; treasurer, D. D. Butler; captain, A. H. Rulty.

WILKESBARRE, PA. — Wilkesbarre Club: President, Robert L. Ayres; secretary, W. E. Shupp; treasurer, H. C. Robertson; captain, J. G. Carpenter.

ROCKINGHAM, N. H. — Rockingham Club: President, C. A. Hazlett; secretary and treasurer, W. C. Walton; captain, G. E. Philbrick.

HAVERILL, MASS. — Penctucket Club: President, C. P. Summer; secretary-treasurer, A. E. Leach; captain, C. E. Dale, 21 members.

PERTH AMBOY, N. Y. — Perth Amboy Cyclers: President, E. W. Barnes; secretary, F. W. Kitchell; treasurer, R. H. Barnes; captain, E. E. Hartshone.

BIDDEFORD, ME. — York County Wheelmen: President, R. A. Fairfield; secretary and treasurer, J. E. Etchells; captain, W. T. Bowers.

KANSAS CITY, MO. — Kansas City Wheelmen: President, T. Ellis, Jr.; secretary-treasurer, S. I. Platt; captain, Dr. G. L. Henderson.

EAST HARTFORD, CONN. — East Hartford Club: President, L. S. Forbes; secretary, W. L. Prior; treasurer, S. A. Pratt; captain, Geo. L. Forbes.

COMING EVENTS.

MAY.

8 Saturday. — Road races, Hudson County Wheelmen, New Jersey.
Bicycle race, Madison Square Garden, New York.

15 Saturday. — Bicycle race, Madison Square Garden, New York.

16 Sunday. — Road race of Colorado Wheel Club, Denver, Col.

20 Thursday. — Races at New Castle, Penn.

22 Saturday. — Races at Hartford, Conn., by Hartford Wheel Club.
Two-mile road race of Brooklyn (N. Y.) Club.

24 Monday. — First day of race meeting at Woodstock, Can.

25 Tuesday. — Second day of race meeting at Woodstock, Can.

27 Thursday. — First day of League Meet. Opening of Boston Club show. Ladies' run. Runs under auspices of tours and runs committee. Hill climbing contest at Corey Hill, at 10 A. M. Entertainment at Music Hall in the evening. Officer's meeting in the evening for election of president.

28 Friday. — Second day of League Meet. Annual business meeting. Entertainment at Music Hall in the evening. Afternoon run. Tricycle road race of Boston Club.

29 Saturday. — Scorcher's run in the morning. League parade in forenoon. Races in the afternoon at 3. Banquet in the evening.
Intercollegiate games at New York.

30 Sunday. — Informal runs under auspices of committee on tours and runs.

31 Monday. — Races at Lynn in the afternoon. Prince and Neilson championship race. Last day of Boston Cycle Show.
Two-mile race of the Brooklyn (N. Y.) Athletic Association games.
Essex County Wheelmen, annual meet at Lynn.
Fifty-mile road race of Ixion Bi. Club, of New York, at Orange, N. J.
Races at San Francisco, Cal., by Bay City Wheelmen.

JUNE.

11 Friday. — First day of race meeting at New Haven by Yale College Club.

12 Saturday. — Second day of race meeting at New Haven, by Yale College Club.
N. Y. and N. J. Road Race Association team race at Orange, N. J.

16 Wednesday. — Races of the Capital Club, at Washington, D. C.

19 Saturday. — Annual Championships of N. A. A. A. A. at New York.
Annual race meeting of K. C. W. at Brooklyn, N. Y.

JULY.

1 Thursday. — First day of annual meeting of C. W. A. at Montreal.

2 Friday. — Second day of annual meeting of C. W. A. at Montreal.

3 Saturday. — Third day of annual meeting of C. W. A. at Montreal.

5 Monday. — Race meeting at Binghampton, N. Y.

MISCELLANEOUS

The Road Book of Boston and Vicinity

The Cycle.

Vol. I., No. 8.   BOSTON, MASS., 21 MAY, 1886.   Five Cents.

The Coventry Machinists' Co.'s New Tricycle for 1886.

THE MARLBORO' CLUB—Automatic Steerer.

ADMIRABLY ADAPTED FOR LADIES.

SEND FOR CATALOGUE TO 239 COLUMBUS AVENUE, BOSTON.

Adjustment in Height in Front.   Adjustment in Length.   A Comfortable Coasting Plate.
Adjustment in Height in Rear.   Adjustment in Width.   A Bifurcated Seat.

THE LILLIBRIDGE SADDLE

Is the only one having any of these Points; is the only one that can be changed in Shape or Position at all; is the BEST and CHEAPEST; is adapted to all makes of Bicycles. Special Styles for the Safeties and Str.

Price, Nickelled, $5.00. Price of Coiled Spring, with Straps, etc., for Old Saddles, 75 Cts.

FREEMAN LILLIBRIDGE, Rockford, Ill.

THE CYCLE

PUBLISHED EVERY FRIDAY BY ABBOT BASSETT, 22 SCHOOL ST., ROOM 19.

VOL. I.   BOSTON, MASS., 21 MAY, 1886.   No. 8.

TERMS OF SUBSCRIPTION.

One Year, by mail, post-paid.........................$1.50
Three Copies in one order........................... 3.00
Club Subscriptions.................................. 1.00
Six Months.. .90
Single Copies....................................... .05

Specimen Copies free.

Every bicycle dealer is agent for the CYCLE and author-
ized to receive subscriptions at regular rates. The paper
can be found on sale at the following places : —
Boston, CUPPLES, UPHAM & CO., cor. Washington and
School Streets. Tremont House news stand. At every
cycle warehouse.
New York, ELLIOTT MASON, 12 Warren Street.
Philadelphia, H. B. HART, 811 Arch Street. GEORGE
D. GIDEON, 6 South Broad Street.
Baltimore, S. T. CLARK & Co., 4 Hanover Street.
Chicago, W. M. DURELL, 115 Wabash Avenue. JOHN
WILKINSON & CO., 77 State Street.
Washington, H. S. OWEN, Capital Cycle Co.
St. Louis, ST. LOUIS WHEEL CO., 1121 Olive Street.

ABBOT BASSETT . . . . . EDITOR
W. I. HARRIS . . EDITORIAL CONTRIBUTOR

A. MUDGE & SON, PRINTERS, 24 FRANKLIN ST., BOSTON.

All communications should be sent in not later than
Tuesday, to ensure insertion the same week.

Entered at the Post-office as second-class mail matter.

WHAT is left of the annual business
meeting of the League? Very little. The
deeper we go into the subject, the less we
can find that is left for the membership at
large to vote on. They cannot amend the
Constitution, and therefore the vexed question of admitting professionals to the League
cannot be decided. They cannot amend
the by-laws, and therefore they cannot touch
the amateur rule. The members can get
together in mass meeting and express their
ideas for and against certain measures.
They can instruct the officers to make certain rules, and they can order that the Racing Board be instructed to change its rules.
They can talk, they can resolve, they can
instruct, but they can do little else. Would
it not be a good idea for them to reclaim the
rights they have lost?

THE League will come to Boston on Anniversary week. This is a New England
institution that is fast dying out, but there is
enough life left in it to fill the city with clergymen from all parts of the country, and they
will be followed by their trains of laymen. It
always rains Anniversary Week. This is a
household word in Boston, and the natives
always put their umbrellas in order for that

occasion. Let us hope that the present year
will prove an exception. Rain has little
effect on the anniversaries; it would spoil
the Meet.

IT is very important that the committees
of the League organize quickly and get to
work; and we offer it as a suggestion to the
incoming president, that he make all of his
appointments during the Meet.

A VERY large and brilliant company
(we like that word "brilliant," it always
sounds well when we are talking about the
aristocracy) assembled on the Longwood
grounds last week to see R. D. Sears, the
amateur tennis champion, contest for the
championship of America with Thomas Pet-
titt, the professional champion. How different this would sound if we were to say
that Wm. A. Rowe competed with John S.
Prince with the same object in view. And
yet we cannot believe that any harm was
done in the tennis game.

IT is always interesting to know what papers think of their contemporaries. It is so
satisfying to know that the course of one
journal meets the approval of another. We
are glad to hear, for instance, that the
World thinks the *Herald* is "dry,
uninteresting, and rarely reliable," and that
the *Globe* is "bright, fresh, and *reasonably*
correct." We trust that the *Record* will
take into consideration the little slap the
same paper gave it, and deprive their readers of the bright little cycling stories they
have been publishing, if they think there is
a demand for their discontinuance outside
the office of the *World.* We are pained to
read also that our own paper comes under
their criticism, and that we do not manage
it according to their ideas of what is right.
We hope that the *Herald,* the *Record,* and
the CYCLE will reform, now that their shortcomings have been pointed out. But while
we are considering the opinions of papers
concerning their contemporaries, it may be
well to mention that we came across this
item in the last number of the *Star Advocate:* "The *Bicycling World* has more kicking and fault-finding to the square inch than
all the rest of the papers of cycledom put together — one continual growl and grumble."
And yet the *World* continues to be our esteemed contemporary.

WE have hesitated to nominate any man
for the president of the League, because we
don't know that it would do any good, and
because we think the League officers are able
to choose for themselves; but we want to
join in with several other papers, and cry,
"Down with the chairman of the Racing
Board!" We know him well, and we believe he ought not to be in the position he
holds. We think the place can be filled to
better advantage, and we shall withhold our
support from any man who does not depose
this officer. We like a quiet life, and we
are bound to have it; but the past has convinced us that we cannot get repose so long
as the present chairman of the Racing
Board holds his position. Down with him.

LEAGUELETS.

VERY little more in the preparatory line
remains to be done towards making the
coming League Meet the most successful on
record. The committees have all faithfully
discharged their duties, and are now resting
on their labors and hoping for favorable
weather. Reports from wheelmen all over
the country indicate that the attendance will
be far in excess of any previous year, and,
as there are far more wheelmen in Massachusetts than in any other State, it is not
improbable that upwards of ten thousand
wheelmen will be in Boston during the three
days of the Meet. From present indications there will be about fifteen hundred
wheelmen in line at the parade.

STORAGE.

Arrangements for storing wheels will be
superior to any ever offered before. The
lower dining hall of Mechanics' building
will be used for this purpose. The entrance
is at the rear of the building. There will be
sufficient accommodations provided for the
storage of several thousand wheels. The
machines will be handled with the greatest
care. The bicycles will be suspended by
their handle-bars from a framework above,
and each will be carefully checked. The
committee will be ready to receive machines
on Wednesday afternoon, 26 May, and will
store them until Tuesday, 2 June, when
they must be removed. During the three
days of the Meet and the two following
days, the storage room will be open from
7 A. M. until 10 P. M. Visiting wheelmen, who may wish to express their wheels,
are requested to tag them and deliver them
to the express company, with the understanding that they are to be retained
by the company until Wednesday afternoon, and then delivered at the Mechanics'
building. Those sending machines in this
way are requested to send notice of the fact
to the chairman of the Storage Committee,

Charles S. Howard, Boston *Daily Globe*. A corps of machinists, from the establishment of W. W. Stall, will be on hand to execute all needed repairs.

BAGGAGE TRANSPORTATION.

Arrangements have been perfected with the transfer companies for the transportation of baggage from depots to hotels, etc., within the city proper. Messengers will pass through trains, giving to wheelmen a numbered coupon corresponding to tag tied to each piece of baggage. On arrival at hotel, it may be secured by surrendering the coupon. For this service there will be no charge. The Armstrong Transfer Company will take baggage arriving at the Albany, Old Colony, New York and New England, Lowell, and Boston and Maine (both divisions) depots. Simonds' Transfer will take baggage from the Fitchburg, and Hadwen's from the Providence depots. This arrangement will allow every wheelman to look after his wheel, and avoid the risk of rough handling by inexperienced teamsters. Should, however, it be desired to send wheels by the transfer companies, they will be taken at a uniform price of fifty cents.

HOTEL LIST.

The following list of hotels has been prepared by the Hotel Committee. Where two rates are given, the second is for two persons together. Hotels marked with an asterisk are conducted on the European plan, and the price given includes rooms only. Distance from Mechanics' building, the place for storing wheels, given in each case: —

VENDOME, Commonwealth avenue, L. A. W. headquarters. First-class; $4 to $7. Can ride to door; ½ mile.

*ADAMS, 555 Washington street. First-class; $1.50. Near theatres and business centre. Can ride to within three blocks; 1¼ miles.

AMERICAN, 50 Hanover street. Very good; $3. Down town, near northern depots. Rideable within two blocks; 1⅞ miles.

BRUNSWICK, Boylston street. First-class; $4. Can ride to door; ½ mile.

COMMONWEALTH, 1697 Washington street. Very good; $3 to $5. Up town. Especially good rooms. Can ride to door; ½ mile.

*CRAWFORD, 88 Court street. Good; $1 to $1.50. Down town. Can ride to within one block; 1¾ miles.

CREIGHTON, 245 Tremont street. Good; $2.50 to $4.00. Near the centre. Can ride to within two blocks; 1¼ miles.

FANEUIL HOUSE, Brighton. Good; $2. Near the Reservoir. Can ride to door; 4 miles.

*INTERNATIONAL, 625 Washington street. Good; $1 to $1.50. Near theatres and business centre. Can ride within two blocks; 1¼ miles.

METROPOLITAN, 1166 Washington street. Good; $2 to $3. Up town. Can ride to within one block.

NEW MARLBORO', 736 Washington street. Good; $2. Near centre. Can ride to within three blocks; 1½ miles.

*PARKER HOUSE, School street. First-class; $1.50. Opposite City Hall. Can ride to within one block; 1¾ miles.

QUINCY HOUSE, Brattle street. First-class; $3 to $5. Down town. 1⅞ miles.

TREMONT HOUSE, Tremont street, corner Beacon. First-class; $3.50. Near City Hall and State House. Can ride to door; 1⅝ miles.

UNITED STATES HOTEL, Beach street. Very good; $2.50 to $4. Near Albany and Old Colony depots. Can ride to within six blocks.

*YOUNG'S HOTEL, Court avenue, off Washington street. First-class; $1.50. Down town. Can ride to within one block; 1¾ miles.

CONCERT PROGRAMME.

Mr. William Hayden has selected a fine orchestra of forty pieces for the promenade concert at Music Hall, on Thursday evening, 27 May: —

1. March, Wheelmen
2. Overture, L'Espoir De L'Alsace
3. Medley, Oh, How Delightful
4. Cornet Solo, by William Hill.
5. Concert Waltz, Autumn Flowers
6. Medley, Bric-a-Brac
7. Descriptive Piece, Forge in the Forest
8. Selections, Mikado
9. Piccolo Solo, by H. Roach.
10. Selections, Iolanthe
11. Descriptive Polka, Sleigh Ride
12. Selections, Martha
13. Spanish Fantasie.
14. Grafenberger Waltz.
15. Popular Airs.

The Entertainment Committee, in order to carry out their original intention of making this first night of the League Meet social and merry in its character, decided that a concert of popular music would be much more acceptable and would better further this end than something of a classical order. Refreshments in great variety will be served in first-class style, and will be in charge of Charles Rickenberg, well known to those who attended the popular concerts last summer. The public are invited to attend this concert, but will only be admitted to the galleries, and then by the payment of an entrance fee.

MINSTREL ENTERTAINMENT.

The musical entertainment on Friday evening, the 28th, at the same place, promises to be a grand success. The Jeffries men are making preparations to outdo themselves, and will be re-enforced in the chorus by some of the musical talent of the various bicycle clubs in and around Boston. The orchestra, led by Percy C. Hayden, will be A1; and the seating of the audience, in charge of Capt. Peck, will be carefully looked after. Tickets are selling rapidly, and those wishing to attend will do well to secure seats at once. A certain number of seats will be reserved for visiting wheelmen from a distance, which can be procured at the concert Thursday night. The programme is as follows: —

Opening Chorus, The Circle
Solo and Chorus,
"Magnolia of Old Tennessee"
S. G. Rollins, Jr.
End Song, "On the Levee"
J. B. Maccabe.
Tenor Solo,
"Annie, Dear, I'm Called Away"
Ed McClosky.
End Song, "Sitting on the Golden Fence"
E. H. Close.
Bass Solo.
End Song,
"We 'll Raise de Roof To-night"
T. E. Stutson.
Soprano Solo,
"Must We Meet then as Strangers"
L. D. Dunn.
Bass Solo, The Old Sexton
George M. Bacon.
End Song, "Ride on dat Golden Mule"
Clarence P. Lovell.
Orchestra, Mikado Gems
Lecture, "Freenology"
T. E. Stutson.
Gymnastics, Parellel Bars
German Turners.
Banjo Quartet.
Lansing, Grover, Paine, and Chase.
Gymnastics.

The German Turners in their complex and graceful movements on the German horse, to conclude with a series of pyramids.

TRICYCLE RACE.

The annual tricycle race of the Boston Club will be held in the early morning of the 28th. The route will be the same as last year, from Bailey's Hotel, South Natick, to a point on Beacon street, opposite the Public Garden. Two medals, first and second prizes, will be awarded. Entrance fee $1, to be made by mail or in person to R. J. Tombs, Boston Bicycle Club, 87 Boylston street, Boston, Mass.

LEAGUE RACES.

THE following riders have entered for the League races on Saturday, 29 May. Those marked with a star are received subject to the action of the League meeting: —

One-Mile Championship. — Charles E. Kluge, Jersey City, N. J.; J. R. Rheubottom, Weedsport, N. Y.; George E. Weber, Smithville, N. J.; *D. E. Hunter, Salem, Mass.; A. B. Rich, New York; Wm. E. Crist, Washington, D. C.; *George M. Hendee, Springfield, Mass.; Taylor Boggis, Cleveland, Ohio; Frank G. Gibbs, Cambridge, Mass.

One-Mile Tricycle Championship. — Charles E. Kluge, Jersey City, N. J.; A. B. Rich, New York: Wm. E. Crist, Washington, D. C.; *W. F. Knapp, Cleveland, Ohio; Thomas Fahy, New Britain, Conn.; C. O. Danforth, Cambridge; Charles H. Potter, Cleveland; J. T. Williams, Boston.

One-Mile Massachusetts Championship. — *D. Edgar Hunter, Salem, Mass.; *Wm. A. Rowe, Lynn, Mass.; Frank G. Gibbs, Cambridge, Mass.

One-Mile Novice. — D. G. Holbrook, Yonkers, N. Y.; Charles A. Stenken, Jersey City, N. J.; John A. Kennedy, Boston; M. F. Germond, New York; H. C. Getchell, Cambridge, Mass.; Harry L. Caldwell, Boston; E. A. Bailey, Somerville; Charles M. Phelps, New York.

One-Mile Handicap. — Willard P. Smith, Charles A. Stenken and Charles E. Kluge, all of Jersey City, N. J.; J. R. Rheubottom, Weedsport, N. Y.; George E. Weber, Smithville, N. J.; *D. E. Hunter, Salem, Mass.; A. B. Rich, New York; *W. F. Knapp, Cleveland, Ohio; John A. Kennedy, Boston; W. D. Edwards, New York; Taylor Boggis, Cleveland, Ohio; H. C. Getchell, Cambridge, Mass.; Frank G. Gibbs, Cambridge, Mass.; Charles M.

Phelps, New York; G. M. Worden, Fitchburg, Mass.; Eugene Valentine, New York. *One and Three Mile Invitation.*— Wm. A. Rowe, Lynn, Mass.; George M. Hendee, Springfield, Mass.; W. F. Knapp, Cleveland, Ohio; W. A. Rhodes, Dorchester, Mass. Entries for the two races are the same.

CONTRIBUTORS' CLUB

CHICAGO CRUMBS.

Editor of the Cycle: Leaving the city of riots and strikes, commonly called Chicago, last night, I arrived at Grand Rapids, Mich. this morning, 9 May, called by urgent telegram to meet a rival on the half-mile trotting track here, which report says is in good condition. The riots and strikes seemed to have claimed even the gay cyclers' attention in our "good city of Chicago," as Mayor Carter Harrison humorously puts it in his proclamation to his lively constituents. The fifty-mile road race, so successfully carried out by Editor Ladish, of the *American Wheelman,* at Clarksville, Mo., served to enthuse the Chicago roadsters, and now they are clamoring for a fifty-mile go at St. Louis. The , oposition is, as N. H. Van Sicklen puts it, as follows: Chicago will put five men against any five St. Louis can produce; and as St. Louis has been aching to do Chicago up for a long time, here 's the opportunity. One thing is certain, St. Louis has the most experienced and altogether the best men, when you look at them on public form. Whittaker, Stone, Rogers, Greenwood, Gordon, Lueders, Young, Davies, and Morris, could muster a strong five, and would be hard to beat. Chicago would probably select her five from the following: N. H Van Sicklen, Bennett, Pierce, Haywood, Surbridge, Miller, Hilton, Conkling, and Vowell. The race, if decided upon, and it most likely will be made, will take place on the Chicago smooth streets and boulevards, park drives, etc., and the mayor will be asked to give the right of way for about three hours and five minutes, as we expect one Chicago man to finish in that time.
The Owl Club is continually being chaffed over the gay colors they wear attached to every prominent portion of their bicycles. For instance, one of their wheels is decorated in this fashion: A broad piece of bright yellow ribbon is displayed prominently on the handle-bar, reaching nearly across; the cradle-spring decorated likewise; the hub and step also come in for the decorators' art; enough to make any sensible wheelman sick, and enough to bring public contempt on each and every cycler in Chicago. It makes one think of some lovesick swain, these loud-too-pretty-for-any-use patrons of the noble wheel. I like to see a man like Jack Rogers, of St. Louis, with a good cigar in his teeth and a pocket full of the latest cycle literature. It impresses the public that men and not effeminate youths are the representative cyclers.
The track at the World's Pastime Exposition, Cheltenham Beach, will be a reality, and will be a four-lap one of board, with well-raised corners. Manager Rickman, in conversation with your correspondent, stated it was his hearty wish to make the cycle

races and display one of the great features of the one hundred days of sport and pastime. Dealers and manufacturers should bear in mind that there is sufficient "space," and the exposition opens 3 July, to continue one hundred days. It will be a mammoth affair, such as characterizes all undertakings by Chicago. Let it be a mammoth exposition or riot, they are always of the first quality.
Poor Burley Ayers! He seemed to me, when I called on him last week, to be between laughing and crying over the loss of the hundred "cases" by swindle, and the consoling thought that Brewster, of St. Louis, and a Canadian chap got done too. He showed me the telegram from Brewster, asking if he (Ayers) had given a letter of introduction to one McVeigh to him (Brewster). Burley smiled and then looked sad, and said: "The rascal, after doing me for a hundred, has forged my good name." He walked of with tears in those "touring eyes."
The John Wilkinson company attract a large crowd to their "new old" State street store window, by T. M. Richardson's shrewd display of an old mildewed saddle and toolbag, relics of Tom Stevens' trip across the continent. Those relics spoke eloquently to me of the. now Asiatic wanderer, and while I looked at the emblems of civilization, words seemed to say, "you must win." On or about December, 1808, the first large gathering of Asiatic cyclers took place at ——, Asia. The meeting was called to order by the president, Stevens Pasha, who congratulated the secretary, Beckwith Pasha, on the largely increased membership of Asiatic cyclers. The touring manager, Ayers Pasha, stated the big four touring department had decided that the annual tour this year would be to Stamboul. After general routine business was disposed of, the meeting adjourned to partake of the annual banquet, consisting of green figs, frizzled eggs, coffee and cigarettes.
Major Wm. Durell, of the Chicago Columbia rooms, is getting no end of notoriety in the papers over his steam yacht and wheel business. He is selling the greatest number of Columbias ever sold at this time of the year.
J. P. Maynard, the Apollo and Star man is very busy. He takes off his kid gloves occasionally and puts in a spoke for a customer.
C. E. Kluge dropped in Chicago last week just long enough to say "How do," and skipped for the Quaker city, where he was to be fed. The *Inter-Ocean* had an interview with him all the same, and never saw him.
They say Harry Corey, with light brown mustache, light overcoat, and broad, new spring togs, passed through this city recently. If he had owed a large debt here, he could not have done it more quietly.
Sam Vowell has again been placed in command of the famous Rudge bicycles. By the way, Sam has taken to himself a brand new wife (that is not saying either have been married before), and will ride tandem on our boulevard. Vowell is a hard working, genial boy, and does a great business with the Caligraph, being Western agent. We will push the Rudge.
John C. Ellis, a member of the Chicago

Bicycle Club, has a family of five, and they will all ride some kind of cycle this summer.
"A large delegation of St. Louis bicyclists " was expected to be here last month, to take a run under the escort of the Chicago Bicycle Club. "The large delegation" comprised "Jack Rogers," John Rogers, and Mr. John Rogers, all in one. The others, "Jack" explained, were feeding Percy Stone, and pinning a medal on to his shirt (I beg pardon, his vest) In St. Louis; hence the small "delegation." About eighteen wheels were in line, and the "Owl" Club members had enough of flaring yellow ribbon on their handle-bars to start a millinery store. They should take a tumble to themselves.　　　　　SENATOR.

QUESTION.

Editor of the Cycle: Will some cycling M. D. rise and explain the following symptom: Triking in cold weather without gloves, my hands have at times concluded to cut a swell, particularly my right one; getting so fat *pro tem.* that I can hardly close it. It is not painful but uncomfortable, as my grasp on the spade handles is less firm. What is the cause and the remedy?
　　　　　　　　　　* * *

THE SUSPECTS.

Editor of the Cycle: What has not been said pro and con *re* the M. A. question, is hardly worth saying, but I propose to give my idea of the action of the Racing Board. The League of American Wheelmen is a national American organization, and is for the benefit of those who love the wheel for the recreation, health, exercise, and numerous other benefits to be derived from it. It has its constitution and by-laws, its definition of an amateur, its rule H, its racing board, and various other rules, etc. too numerous to mention, which are all very good in their various relative places. Among its members we find some who infringe on the amateur definition and rule H. They have been taken in hand by the Racing Board, whose duty it is "to make inquiries regarding any wheelman whose amateur status is questionable . . . shall immediately communicate with the party under suspicion, either in person or by registered letter, lay all charges before him, or set forth the circumstances which lead to a reasonable doubt," etc. Now, all this has been done; it was the duty of the board, and they did not shrink from it, well knowing that more or less blame and censure would be laid at their door; and one thing, I am glad to see is, that they do not weaken, as does a certain executive across the pond, and reinstate any of the suspects, but have expelled those who have not removed the "reasonable doubt." Those who are raising such a rumpus, as to the action of the board are, as a general thing, the semi-cycling papers, or him who has his own peculiar axe to grind; and it seems to me, and ought to every true amateur at heart, that we should have a distinction between the true amateur and the M. A. or pro-amateur. My plan would be to adopt a law that would place such men as the M. A.'s in a separate class. They are the fliers, and the race is always between them, for the reason that they are well matched, have trained, and are not racing for the glory of winning a race from their competitor, but that they are paid for

doing it, and if they don't they may "lose
their job." My only hope is that the meeting this month will adjust matters satisfactorily, and uphold the board in what they
have done.

Fraternally,
W. L. SURPRISE., L. A. W. 5633.
MEMPHIS, TENN., 12 May, 1886.

AUTOMATIC STEERING.

THE *Wheel World* for May has a description of John Harrington's appliance for
making the Humber form tricycles, and the
rack-and-pinion steering automatic. The
Cripper tricycles having set the fashion for
automatic, or fly-to-centre steering, appliances are multiplying for the adaptation of
this action to tricycles of other patterns; and
amongst the simplest and cheapest are those
patented by John Harrington, respectively
for Humber-pattern tricycles and for tricycles with rack-and-pinion steering. In both
cases the principle of the cradle spring
underlies the action; stout wire coils being
so arranged as to allow their ends to give to
pressure, but to spring back into their normal positions when that pressure is removed.
The spring for Humber tricycles is bolted
behind the steering-head, and its two extremities, which are furnished with smooth
grooved bushes to prevent friction against
the handle-bar, press on the bar equally each
side. For rack-and-pinion steering tricycles the automatic spring is fitted at the
junction of the long steering-rod with the
short arm on the steering-head; and one of
its ends being bolted to the long rod, the
other to the short arm, the tendency is to
keep the two at an exact right angle, or
such other angle as the shape of the long rod
may necessitate; and the spring allows this
angle to become acute or obtuse as the
steering movement demands, but always
presses it back to the normal position when
the pressure is removed. The latter of the
two appliances will, we consider, be very
largely adopted, because the chief objection
raised against rack-and-pinion steering is, that
the rider cannot remove his right hand from
the steering-handle; but with one of these
springs this objection is done away with, and
steady steering in a straight line is insured.
At the same time, it is well known that a
pinion, actuated by a spade handle, has such
a great leverage power over a rack, that the
extra force required to deflect the wheel
against the pressure of the spring will be
immaterial.

HE was an ardent cyclist, and had brought
his tricycle with him in hopes of an occasional ride. She was somewhat of an invalid, and did not cycle. It was a part of the
country rich in antiquities, and the stern
uncle encouraged archæological research in
the young. There was no carriage placed
at the disposal of the hapless pair, and the
distances were great; so every morning she
mounted the saddle of his tricycle, and
placed her feet upon the rests, and he, with
a devotion almost sublime in its character,
pushed her along the eight or nine miles of
road that severed them from ruined castle
or from Roman camp; returning in the same
manner, when the sinking sun warned them
to tear themselves from their antiquarian
studies. — *Violet Lorne in News.*

· CAPITAL CLUB HOUSE.

CAPITAL CLUB HOUSE.

THE above view of the new house of the
Capital Club, of Washington, D. C., is from
the architect's plan. In our issue of 16
April, we gave a description of the house.
Ground has been broken and work commenced. The house faces the grounds of
the White House, and the situation is one
of the finest in the city. The first contracts
are for $8,000, but the members expect to
pay $1,500 for the house in a completed
state. The land was purchased for $5,000,
and is now worth $6,000. The Washington
boys have done well.

A PARTY to accomodate wheelmen in New
York city and vicinity who wish to attend
the Boston Meet, will be formed by George
R. Bidwell, chairman of the League Transportation Committee, to leave on the Bristol
26 May, and return 31 May. If 150 join this
party, the fare for the round trip will be
$3.45.

NOTES FROM THE SOUTH.

THE cycling trade here is quite brisk, in
fact has never before been in a healthier
condition. Caused principally by the tour
now in progress.

THE tourists, Hill, Fairchild, and Fairfax
are now (14th) in Virginia. They are in
good health and spirits, and confident of
reaching the "Hub" on time.

THE N. O. B. C. annual races take place
on the 29th inst. The boys are getting in
trim, and good time is sure to be made.

THREE bicycle races are to be given at the
tournament here of the Young Men's Gymnastic Club, 24 and 25 May. The N. O.
Bicycle Club will be well represented there.

VAN MEERBEKE, the New York to San
Francisco tourist, who is stopping here on a
two weeks' rest, will leave in a day or two

ANNOUNCEMENT.

We have in stock a few

BRITISH CHALLENGES

left over from last season,

and in order to dispose of them quickly, we offer them at

━・$100・━

each, all sizes, nickelled or enamelled. Former price $136.50.

Send for list.   Correspondence solicited.   Don't fail to secure one of these machines.

STODDARD, LOVERING & CO.

Nos. 152 to 158 Congress Street, Boston, Mass.

New York Headquarters - - - - GEO. R. BIDWELL - - - - 313 W. 58th St., N. Y.

FIRST GRAND OPENING TOURNAMENT
— OF THE —
Lynn Cycle Club Track Assoc'n,
Lynn, Mass., Memorial Day, May 31, 1886.

Although the centre of bicycling, Eastern Massachusetts has not heretofore possessed a complete and modern racing track. The necessity for such led to the formation of the Lynn Cycle Club Track Association, which, with commendable energy and dispatch, has evolved within the "City of Shoes" the finest bicycle racing track to be found in the world, being a dead level, three-lap track, of perfect design. The opening tournament will include the fastest men in America, and extraordinary time is expected. Visitors to the League Meet will regret much if they do not stop over and attend this grand event.

PROSPECTUS OF RACES.

FIRST RACE WILL BE CALLED PROMPTLY AT 2 P. M.

1. One-Mile Amateur Bicycle. — First prize, a fine gent's gold watch; second prize, pair elegant opera glasses.
2. Three-Mile Amateur Bicycle (9.45 class). — For League of Essex County wheelmen only. First prize, gold medal; second prize, silver medal.
3. Two-Mile Amateur Tricycle. — First prize, elegant hanging lamp; second prize, Smith & Wesson nickel-plated revolver.
4. One-Mile Amateur Bicycle (3.20 class). — First prize, gold-headed cane; second prize, base parlor lamp.

5. Three-Mile Amateur Bicycle Lap Race. — First prize, silver tilting water pitcher; second prize, elegant berry set.
6. First of a series for the professional championship of America. Five-Mile Professional Bicycle Race, between Robert A. Neilson and John S. Prince. — These two celebrated riders will meet to contest for a purse of $300 a side, and an additional purse of $500 offered by the Association, and the professional championship of America.
7. Twenty-Mile Amateur Bicycle Race, for the Columbia prize cup, valued at $1,500. — This cup shall become the personal property of the competitor who is first for three times winner in said races for it, or who, in winning one of said races, covers the twenty miles within one hour.

☞ Entries for all races to be made to E. M. BAILEY, secretary of Lynn Cycle Club Track Association, Lynn, Mass., accompanied by an entrance fee of $1.00 for each event, except the twenty-mile, entry which is $5.00, returnable to all who complete the distance.

☞ Entries close May 26. All entries will be received subject to the decision of the L. A. W.

☞ The Club reserves the right to reject any or all entries to the races.

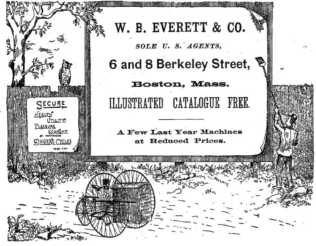

for his destination. He has kept himself in condition while here by taking daily spins on our six miles of asphalt.

THE subject of tours is receiving considerable attention from local wheelmen, and it is extremely probable that several tours of 400 or 500 miles will be made during the summer.　　　　　　　　　　BI.

N. O., 14 May, 1886.

FROM A FEMININE POINT OF VIEW.

"THE best laid plans," etc. This is running in my mind to-night as I think of my determination, made some weeks ago, to present, in this issue of the CYCLE, an elaborate plan of work laid out by those who are going to entertain our lady guests at the League Meet. But we have made no plans and we have laid out no work. A number of ladies have pledged themselves to do what they can to make the stay of our guests a continual delight, and we shall work in this direction to the utmost of our powers.

I AM very anxious that Boston should inaugurate the feature of a ladies' annex to the League meeting, and if we can make it pleasurable I do not doubt other places will follow our example. It can do no harm for the gentlemen to bring their wives and sweethearts with them to the annual meeting ; but from all that I can hear the previous gatherings have had little to interest the ladies. This because they have had no one to receive and entertain them. Boston ladies will try to do both.

THE plan for the ladies' run of the 27th is not yet perfected. We have made all arrangements for the start, but have not yet fixed upon the destination. We are debating between two well-known routes, but have as yet come to no determination. The rain which visited us early in the week prevented a run over the route, and it cannot well be laid out until later.

I FEEL, however, that this is a matter of trifling importance. We shall run out into the country over good roads, and shall proceed leisurely, so as to accommodate the slow riders, of whom there will be a great many. The entire run will not exceed 15 miles, and there will be a long rest.

THE start will be from the Vendome at 10 A. M. on Thursday. A committee of ladies will receive the guests in the ladies' parlor of the hotel, and the time between nine and ten o'clock will be occupied in an interchange of greetings. I have chosen this time because the gentlemen will be engaged at Corey Hill, and we can conduct our little run more quietly than we could if they were at leisure.

I AM sorry that the impression has gone abroad that this is to be a public affair. Nothing could be further from my intention. We shall try to avoid publicity, in every way possible, and go quietly on our way with as little demonstration as it is possible to make.

AFTER the first day no formal runs will take place. Our ladies have agreed to conduct small parties on quiet runs, or all can unite in a trip to some choice spot, if it is thought best.

OUR run is to be exclusively for ladies. Gentlemen will be welcome if they come as escorts to ladies, otherwise we prefer to conduct the affair and engage in it ourselves. Bicycles will not be forbidden, though tricycles will be more welcome.

I THINK that is all that it is necessary to say. Our friends will be welcomed at the Vendome on Thursday morning, at which time we hope to see many ladies from abroad, and we can assure them a cordial welcome from the Boston ladies.

MR. PARKE STREET suggests a hat for ladies' wear, and asks my opinion. I have crystallized my opinion by the purchase of a helmet, which I find to be comfortable to a very great degree. My criticism upon the hat which he proposes would be that anything with a wide brim takes the wind, and a fluttering feather is not to my taste.

　　　　　　　　　　　　DAISIE.

NEW CYCLING PATENTS.

R. Bean, Springfield, Ohio, bicycle saddle.
T. J. de Sabla, New York, velocipede.
E. G. Latta, Friendship, N. Y., velocipede.
B. S. Whitehead, Newark, N. J., bicycle.

1886 CHAMPIONSHIPS.

THE Racing Board L. A. W. has made the following assignment of championships for 1886:

¼ mile. To Genesee Club of Rochester, N. Y.

2 miles. To Cleveland (Ohio) Bicycle Club.

3 miles. To California Division L. A. W.

5 miles. To Connecticut Club of Hartford, Conn.

10 miles. To Michigan Division L. A. W. There is left only the twenty-mile bicycle and the five-mile tricycle championships, and these will be assigned later in the year.

NEW JERSEY NOTES.

IT is reported in Jersey : —

THAT five League clubs within twelve miles of New York contain two fifths of the L. A. W. membership of the State, which is now 750.

THAT these clubs average over fifty members each, the smallest of them now having, I am told, forty-two members.

THAT they are the Hudson County Wheelmen, New Jersey Wheelmen, Essex Bicycle Club, Orange Wanderers, and Elizabeth Wheelmen.

THAT the Hudson County Wheelmen ride well, drill well, have the new Chief Consul, the fastest rider in the State, and seem to be holding up their end generally.

THAT they will need to have more than one fast rider, if they hope to stand a chance for the Team Road-Racing Association cup.

THAT it is reported that the above mentioned fast rider (Kluge) will not ride in their team, in order to give others a show. •

THAT such magnanimity is uncalled for on the part of Mr. Kluge or his club.

THAT nobody will feel bad to see Kluge come in first, and nobody expects that that will give his club the race.

THAT the New Jersey Wheelmen are said to be a sort of Star-Columbia club, few of their members venturing to ride other wheels.

THAT their membership is large and enthusiastic.

THAT they are the principal promoters of the new race track, and expect to put some good men on it.

* THAT they are very well satisfied with themselves and their own achievements, though they don't say so much about them as some other clubs do.

THAT some of their members ought to be cautioned not to wear blue stockings with their green uniform.

THAT the Essex Bicycle Club is rather superior to racing matters.

THAT a large proportion of their members are no longer active wheelmen.

THAT their usual run is to Caldwell, and preferably by moonlight.

THAT ex-Capt. Mead is one of the best road riders in the country.

THAT with a new, light wheel he would be still better.

THAT he has taken to a Humber tandem this season.

THAT the Orange Wanderers have heretofore had the reputation of holding aloof from other clubs.

THAT increased membership, their Chinese lantern parade of last fall, and their rink tournament of this spring, seem to indicate a change of sentiment.

THAT they have discarded their gray homespun uniform, and adopted a dark blue one, made up in dressy style. .

THAT the Elizabeth Wheelmen ride, drill, play polo, and at least one of their members talks.

THAT they keep themselves in print through their "monthly records" in a very persistent manner. .

. THAT they straggle all over the road on club runs, with no semblance of order.

. THAT they doubtless simply meant to sacrifice appearance to utility.

THAT if they cared for the former they would adopt a new uniform.

. THAT they will probably fail to win their road race with the K. C. W., unless their Stars and familiarity with the ground saves them on the poor course chosen.

　　　　　　　　　　　　N. J.

Mr. POULTNEY Bigelow, editor of Outing, has received advices from Thomas Stevens, concerning his arrest in Russia, with full particulars, and in an interview disclosed the following : "Mr. Stevens, in the course of his bicycle tour around the world, had got as far as Meschid, on the Russian frontier, in Central Asia. He had permission and passports from the Russian authorities, and his money changed for the different countries on the route to Pekin. He was going via Merv, Tomsk and Irkutsk. Without warning he was ordered back. The last dispatches received related that he intended to get permission to go through Afghanistan under

THE "SPALDING."

Confidently presented to the Cycling Public as an embodiment of the highest state of perfection ever attained in Bicycle manufacture.

Light,

Graceful,

Strong,

Easy

Running,

Balls

All Around,

Including

Pedals.

Direct

Tangent

Spokes,

Warwick

Hollow

Rim,

Full Inch

Tire.

All Bright

Parts

Nickelled.

The American Premier,   The Humber Tandem,
The Kangaroo,   The Humber Cripper.

SEND FOR CATALOGUE.

A. G. SPALDING & BROS.

241 Broadway, New York.   *108 Madison St., Chicago, Ill.*

shelter of the British Boundary Commission. His arrest simply goes to show that he failed to get that permission, and chose to take his chances. He is very daring, and will, in my opinion, attempt to go through, whether he gets permission or not. His arrest only means a detention of a few days or weeks, and a definite decision as to whether he will be granted a passport."

MEMORIES OF '85.

WHILE wheeling serenely along a fine old clay road near Austinburg, between Saybrook and Andover, Ohio, one delightful July day. We "had evidence of the utter and unqualified badness of local cyclers of that vicinity, when a carriage load of young ladies driving down a cross road began a desperate and prolonged fluttering of parasols and fans."

This rather staggered the sedate Solitary Club, but on coming to, the club as one man raised helmets and urged the bugler to do his level best to wave the answer back, which he did with visible good will, and much noise.

Old Sol took blushing cognizance of all this, and his beams waxed warmer as we pushed on to Jefferson, where we halted a few minutes to look for a noted cycler, Ives, to write a line of greeting to wheelmen, in the Hotel register, and allow a smart eastern boy to try our new wheel, who succeeds in bending a handle bar.

Now we are speeding away past bountiful, growing crops of various kinds, many of which are unfenced, and come almost to the wheel tracks of the road; then again, there are pretty hedges like those seen in rural pictures of England.

By the way we see relics of the old plank road, in ends of the planks sticking up cracked and weatherworn by the sun and storms of years gone by, its mission having practically ended with the coming of the railroads.

Each house is the home of the dairyman, as is proven by the great milk cans on a platform at the gate. and the wheelman's favorite measure, and is easily paid for with answers to questions concerning the wheel of wheels. We have recollections of unridably rough stone pavements in many of Buffalo's business streets, in many of which were such holes that the great everywhere-present beer tracks were obliged to turn out for them as they bumped along. How the city dads ever allowed the League Meet men to ride on the walks, is enigmatical, but they were the only place one could ride much of the way.

The Stamford Wheel Club, and the Leisure Hour Wheel Club, of Greenwich, braced up to one another around the track at Woodside Park recently. The records for the various distances remain in *statu quo*.

Some one proposes that we skip building $20,000 race tracks, and put some money into macadamizing through routes in various directions, to benefit a few of the ninety-and-nine.   STAMFORD.

NOTMAN has finished a large picture of the Massachusetts Bicycle Club members.

There are one hundred and sixty-three represented, and the picture is in the form of a large wheel, the portraits of the officers forming the hub, and the men arranged in groups around the centre. It has been placed on view in the window of Cupples, Upham & Co. The picture will hang in the club parlor. Copies of reduced size may be had soon.

CYCLETS

THE L. A. W.

WHEREVER on wheel you may go,
From Boston to San Francisco,
You meet a rider you don't know,
Why show your badge, and just say so.

CHORUS.

If you 're a member of the Law,
You 're just the man we 're looking for, —
Fraternally to grasp your paw,
And shake you by the hand.

So brothers all, where 'er you be,
From pole to pole and sea to sea,
With perfect unanimity,
Go join in this fraternity.

CHORUS.

If you 're a member of the Law, etc.
A. S. HIBBARD.

THEY are coming.

THE wheelmen of America.

To Boston hearts, to Boston roads, and to Boston's pretty girls.

THEY will be made welcome by generous hosts.

BOSTON will put on her holiday attire in their honor.

WE shall do better than we did before, and make them want to come again.

THE man who takes in all that is provided will not live to tell the tale.

WE hope, however, that the attractions offered will not take away the interest in the business for which the wheelmen are gathered.

THE League must be wound up to run another year, and it is important that the job be done well.

WE are very near to 10,000, and shall pass it the coming year.

THE friends of Dr. Beckwith are rallying in his favor, and the friends of lawyer Terry are putting forth strenuous exertions in his behalf. Which will lead? as both men decline; but declinations don't count.

EVERY vote will count in the election for president, and no ballots will be thrown out.

THE members of the Board who will not be in Boston, should send their proxies to some one who will be on hand.

THOSE who have growls to growl will have a chance to be heard. There are sins of omission as well as commission; and he who says the League does nothing, should ask himself what he himself is doing for the general good.

THE League is a worthy institution, and it can be made a power for great good, if we will all take hold and work. The man who wants to draw at the spigot without putting anything in at the bung will go dry.

THE statue of Wm. Lloyd Garrison was placed on its pedestal last week. It is located in front of League headquarters, the Vendome.

WE are glad to know that we are to have the dinner at a hotel. We are confident that the men will not go away hungry. The tickets are limited, however, so be on hand.

THE Boston show will be a great centre of attraction. The dealers are bringing over the new wheels, and everything in the cycle line will be shown.

WE haven't heard that there are to be any League flags like those used at Buffalo. That was a very pretty idea, and one that should be repeated.

MR. LAMSON is making a very pretty pin for the badges at the League Meet. It is struck from a special die, and follows the design of the League badge.

THE Committee on Parade is preparing a diagram, showing the location in line of every club parading, so that there may be no confusion in the formation. The parade will be divided into four divisions. Two divisions will probably be required for the aecommodation of Massachusetts wheelmen. None but League members will be allowed to parade.

THE North Adams Bicycle Club is arranging for a tournament to occur 5 July, at which prizes to the value of $1,000 will be offered.

Unattached wheelmen should remember that unless they belong to the L. A. W., they will not be allowed to participate in the parade. The word "unattached" is not used to denote one who does not belong to the L. A. W., as an exchange of ours puts it, but refers to a man's connection with a club.

AND now comes Will Atwell, who has charge of Wm. Read & Sons' bicycle department, bearing in his hand a "Squawker." He tells us that fifty cents will take one, and he warrants them to make noise enough to suit the most noisy of wheelmen. We have tried it, and we are convinced. One squawk will last a life-time. We dare not contemplate the amount of stillness a small boy could conquer with one of these.

AT the last meeting of the Buffalo Club, Dr. Blackham, of Dunkirk, was elected an honorary member. The club passed a resolution urging the re-election of Dr. N. M. Beckwith, the present president of the League; also indorsing the recent action of the Racing Board, in expelling professionals who were trying to remain in the ranks as amateurs.

THE Mass. Club has passed resolutions disapproving the use of a band in the League parade.

SPALDING & Co., announce their specialty in our columns, this week. The Spalding is made by Hillman, Herbert & Cooper, and is in every way a first-class machine.

A FIRST-CLASS stocking supporter that will keep the stockings in place without bagginess, unpleasant tension or any discomfort, is needed by wheelmen and lawn tennis players. They have it in the Z & S. supporter, sold by Howard A. Smith & Co., Newark, N. J.

The *News* of 7 May has a cartoon showing Furnivall sitting in his room surrounded by his prizes. Some dozen or more clocks are shown and as many cruets and tea services. It is called "Too Much of a Good Thing."

W. B. EVERETT & Co. have on view a Courier Safety built on the lines of the Rover. It has 26 and 36-inch wheels, two chains running on sprocket wheels, and Bown's patent crank. It is built more compactly than either the Rover or the Bicyclette, the wheels being very near together. It is a fine machine, and, we doubt not, it is speedy.

PERCY FURNVIALL and Sanders Sellers have passed the first examination of the College of Physicians and Surgeons.

THE Newton and Nonantum Cycling Clubs will probably unite in a grand antique and horrible parade on wheels at Newton, 4 July. Wheelmen in general will be invited to fall in.

DON'T leave the Boston show till you have called at our stand. We want to shake hands with every wheelman in America. We will be glad to do it at the Boston show. If we're not at our stand we will shake hands by deputy. We shall have a good supply of bills to receipt.

G. C. DRESSER of Hartford Wheel Club has made a mile in 1m. 19 2-5s. on the home trainer. The quarter was made in 18 2-5s., half in 38s., three-quarters in 58 2-5s.

H. A. Ward of Richfield Springs, N. Y., writes that he and five other wheelmen will start in a few days for Boston to attend the League Meet. They will cycle to Albany, from where they will take the train to Springfield, and ride the rest of the distance to Boston on their wheels.

DEAN, Harvard '88, still labors at a disadvantage in having no one to train with for inter-collegiate sports. He can console himself, however, in having so fine a track to work upon.

How would it do for the three Columbia riders to wear Columbia's colors, — red, white, and blue? The red, white, and blue never runs, though. That's what we used to say in war times.

MR. BUTCHER finds it very easy to apply a spoke cyclometer to an Apollo tricycle. The little lug on the ball-bearing moves the finger of the instrument as it comes around, and it is so placed that it can be read from the saddle.

THE English *Bat* says: "It is pleasing to find that at last common sense is extending as far as prize giving, wherein for many years the most absolute imbecility has been shown. When I think of the useless volumes which I, or, to be accurate, my schoolfellows, used to take home before the holidays, of the senseless cups and pewters we vied for in later life, I gladly record that the Sheffield Brunswick Cycling Club, in their last half-mile race, awarded as a prize for him who did the slowest time, a box of liver pills."

"LYNN," says the *Item*, "is indifferent to base-ball, so far as local clubs are concerned; but the chances of her becoming a bicycling centre are good." What a rush there will

be to the single spot where the base-ball craze is in desuetude! — *Record.*

To dodge the racing laws we made
Some awfully clever arrangements.
In fact, of them we were n't afraid,
Because of these clever arrangements ;
But now they seem quite broad awake
(Though some still talk for talking's sake),
Our entries now they will not take, —
They 're going to make other arrangements.

They think they 'll keep the sport quite straight,
With these and other arrangements,
And that they still will draw a gate
In spite of the novel arrangements ;
But suppose that this they manage to do,
Without the men who records slew,
I 'll tell you what, you 'll find it 's true, —
We 're going to make other arrangements.
News.

A ST. LOUIS baker made a unique medal, to be given to the winner of the Clarksville race. A long Vienna loaf formed the bar, and a twelve-inch cake was the pendant. It went to Weber, who proved to be the "bread-winner."

THE annual meet of the Michigan division will be held 24 June, at Detroit. Races will be run on the new track of the Detroit Club.

OUR friend Weston has departed from the *World*, and the Sociable no longer has a defender. And yet there is a good deal of fun to be had on a Sociable.

MRS. STALL was out on her little tricycle last week, and found that it met all her expectations. It was just out of the shop and not finished. The hills were taken easily, and she got a deal of speed out of it. It will be at the Boston show.

To wear a uniform is the ambition of every male citizen in the United States. He feels that ambition when he draws on his first pair of pantaloons, and continues to feel it until he lies down to die. Since the war, the ambition to wear a uniform has become particularly noticeable. I am not sure but that it has led some individuals to break into the penitentiaries. — *Exchange.*

"WHERE ignorance," etc. One of the Southern racing men says: "Tracks must have a wooden curb at least 18 inches high." And this man claims to be an authority on records and racing in the South. — *Southern Cycler.*

JOHN F. MORGAN has made what he calls a bicycle leg. It is an attachment, capable of extension, for holding a bicycle erect when the rider dismounts, or when seated in the saddle at a stand-still. The holder or legs are firmly attached to the fork of the machine, within convenient reach, and are noiseless, serviceable, and of light weight.

THE Buffalo Club has a very fine club house which it is fitting up by degrees. When the house is fitted up, and it will be among the finest club houses in the city. The building is that known as the Clifton homestead, which has been leased for a period of three years. In addition to parlors, meeting and committee-rooms, there will be a billiard, pool and card-room, reception-rooms, and other extra apartments, to accommodate the ever-increasing membership of this popular wheeling organization.

J. LUMSDEN, the Scotch professional, had

his collar-bone broken by a fall during the fifty-mile race in Leicester, Eng., 24 April.

THE Yale Club has selected their new suits. They will be made of dark-blue cloth, and cut similar to the League uniform, but without plaits. They will be trimmed with black braid, with the letters "Y. Bi. C." on the collar in silver braid. The cap will be the same as heretofore, except the visor, which will be covered with cloth.

AT a recent meeting of the National Cyclists' Union, in England, it was decided "that no official timekeeper should be appointed unless he owns a chronograph watch reading minutes, and which shall have passed the Kew test." Whereupon *Pastime* remarks: "We think that the times would be more worthy of credence if the custom of our American cousins, who have three timekeepers at each meeting, were followed. The present grandmotherly legislation will make the Union a mere laughing stock."

THE riding record of the Elizabeth Wheelmen for the month of March, totals 2,536 miles. Twenty-nine men reported ; the highest record, 347 miles, being credited to D. B. Bonnett ; A. S. Roorback rode 205 miles.

IF Stevens goes through to Japan, he will establish a record for pluck and determination unequalled in this century. The bicycle goes with him, and it matters not if it goes on its rubbers or on his back.

THE Seaside Bicycle Club, of Norfolk, Va., has procured reduced rates on the steamer, and will attend the Meet almost to a man.

BERT OWEN's birthday run, which was to have taken place at Washington last week, was postponed on account of the inclemency of the weather. The programme for that occasion comprises an obstacle run about town, a polo game at the park, and a banquet to finish up with. Invitations are eagerly sought for, and wheelmen are expected from Baltimore to take part.

A CHIEF of the Sioux tribe of Indians is reported to be engaged in trying to learn to ride the bicycle. That settles it. The final extermination of the aboriginal race is now a question of a mere length of time, and it will not be necessary for the government to interfere with troops or ammunition. — *Ex.*

THERE will be no team race between the St. Louis and Chicago for some time, as the latter frankly admits that it has no team that could compete with St. Louis in a road race.

CONKLING, of Chicago, will be unable to ride a bicycle this year, owing to an injury his arm received last fall.

J. W. GIBSON, of the San Francisco Club, is projecting the monthly publication of a little pamphlet which will give full information concerning California roads and routes as fast as compiled by the Division Touring Board. It will be in addition a complete directory of division officers, local consuls, and League hotels, besides containing other information of interest and value to the wheelman. The work will fill a want long felt, and Mr. Gibson deserves every encouragement in his undertaking.

REPORTS from Secretary Aaron, who is at Luray, Va., say that he is improving in his general health.

Our exhibit at the "Cycleries" will contain a sample of our Custom Work, being a full seven-eighths inch tired Cripper Tricycle, suited for practical road work, weighing, with saddle and pedals complete, forty-nine and three-fourths pounds. We shall also show the Star Bicycle in perfected form, and think that the Hollow Frame Light Roadster will show up well in comparison with the best wheels in the show. Our Repair Department will be practically illustrated in the Storage Department, where we will "fix 'em up," *ad lib., gratis.* We have a large line of Second-Hand Wheels, which will be sold at low rates.

MR. HOWARD A. SMITH, of Newark, N. J., led Miss Lizzie Campbell, of the same place, to the altar last week. He has our congratulations.

WORK was commenced on the track at the Union grounds on Tuesday last, and it will be all ready to practise on by Tuesday of next week. It will cost $300, but when it is done there will be a good surface, and the curves will be improved.

IF any person wants to divert himself during the Meet, let him try to count the number of ways in which the name of the League headquarters is pronounced.

IF our visitors hear any one talking about "Trinity Square," and fail to find it in the directory, let them look for "Copley Square." No one outside of wheeling circles calls it Trinity Square. Before it was named, the wheelmen used to meet there and the rendezvous was at Trinity Church.

THE Connecticut Club has voted that it is the sentiment of the club that Rule H be essentially modified.

THE monthly riding record of the Chicago Club for April shows an adequate mileage of 2939½ miles. Surbridge leads with 197 miles, and the lowest score is 26 miles. Total since 1 January, 4934¼ miles.

THE CYCLE will have a stand at the Boston show.

WE don't like to brag about the success of our paper, nor to tell how fast the subscriptions are coming in. We have only one thing to fear, and that is a lack of paper to print on, if the boom continues. We have ordered two paper mills to work day and night, and we shall do our best to meet the demand.

CANARY was presented with an elegant gold medal at the close of the Leicester show, where he has been exhibiting. The presentation speech was made by the mayor, and Dan made a brief response.

THE makers are turning out a Kangaroo that weighs 20½ pounds, geared to 64. It is for use on the race track, but an English rider has been riding one on the road.

CANARY'S success in England has brought to the front a lot of imitators, and fancy riders are springing up all around in Albion. W. R. Thomas and J. W. Bayliss gave a fancy riding exhibition in Coventry lately.

THE international cycling tournament occurs at the Alexandria Park grounds, London, this week, Thursday and Friday. American crack riders will be conspicuous by their absence. There will be a five-mile bicycle scratch race for the international cycling shield, valued at fifty guineas, which must be won three times, not necessarily in succession, to become the property of the holder. When America gets to sending bicycles to England, we will see American racing men going across the pond to compete. Where there is no market for bicycles, our racing men do not go. But stranger things have happened than will occur when America supplies the world with wheels. English papers will please copy, and head, this paragraph, "A Specimen of Yankee Brag."

VISIT the CYCLE headquarters at the Boston show, and leave your little dollar and a half.

TALK about wheelmen at our road houses! What do you think of this: On Good Friday over four hundred wheelmen dined at the Anchor, at Ripley, England, and they ate a bullock, a calf, and a sheep, besides other things.

THERE are those who say that Rowe can beat Hendee, and there are others who say that George's rubber will strike the tape first. Those who have watched the two men at their training, tell us that the question cannot be decided till the two men meet.

THE Philadelphia Association for the Advancement of Cycling has already over two hundred members.

SINGER & Co. have fitted a crypto-gear to a small-wheeled, Extraordinary Bicycle. By a movement of the foot the machine can be geared up or down to suit the rider.

TEN members of the tricycle division of the Boston club participated in the all-night run to South Natick Saturday. The return to Boston was made Saturday afternoon. Capt. Donohoe was in charge.

MR. CLARK writes us from Baltimore that the new Rapid bicycle is taking well, and the best indication of its merit is the fact that the old riders are taking to it in large numbers. One noted wheelman of Philadelphia says it is the nearest approach to the perfect wheel he ever saw. Mr. Clark tells us that it "beats the Dutch on hills and coasts a quarter of a mile, ten seconds ahead of its shadow."

PALFREY street, on Locke's Hill, Watertown, is about a quarter of a mile long, and has a very steep grade. A crowd gathered Sunday afternoon to see a number of cyclers try to reach the top. At 2.30 o'clock P. M., Harry and Kirk Corey and E. P. Burnham essayed the hill. The elder Corey nearly reached the top, with his brother Kirk almost up to him. Burnham stopped nearly three quarters of the way up. After a few moments' rest, Harry Corey and Burnham started again. Corey started first. He forced his wheel around, and after a tremendous struggle reached the top in exactly 2 minutes 33 seconds. Burnham got about three quarters up, but was unable to go further.

THE winner of the Bull and Bowen home trainer contest was credited with a record of 52⅗ seconds for a mile. There must have been some mistake, or the mechanism of the trainer's register was out of order, for such a record is incredible. To cover the distance of one mile, it is necessary that the wheel be revolved about 354 times, and nothing short of steam could make that number of revolutions in 52 seconds. — *Globe.*

W. C. HERRING is willing to guarantee that he can cover the distance within 60 seconds at any time. His method of working the machine is a little peculiar. He lowers the saddle post until it is equal to a 40-inch wheel, and after shortening the cranks and pushing the saddle well back, straps his feet to the pedal and blazes away.

SECRETARY LOCKWOOD, of the Baltimore Cycle Club, writes that twenty-five members of his club will attend the League Meet.

KUM and C us at our stand. We shall be at the Boston show. We shan't have much to show, but come and see us all the same.

WE saw two wheelmen riding along the sidewalk of a principal street in a neighboring city last Sunday, and we wished a policeman might come around and arrest them. We have no sympathy with sidewalk riders, and we are glad to hear of their coming to grief. They discredit the sport, and we all have to suffer for their misdoings.

A ST. LOUIS paper says the sale of wheels in that city this year will run into the hundreds of thousands. A St. Louis "tough" wrote that.

THE Springfield Club is about ready to move into new quarters. 1 June is now set down as the auspicious day.

LAST Sunday was disappointing. The rains of the forenoon piled up mud in the streets, and those who ventured out in the afternoon had a sorry time of it.

ALL this talk about the West having the presidency is sheer nonsense. What matters it to us whether he comes from Maine or California? What we want is good highways, and privileges not more confined than are extended to the commonest cab; and it is the president's duty to shape the policy that will influence legislation, if need be, to secure that end. In the last national election, the vote of the New York division would have elected Mr. Blaine, if each member had worked for the Republican ticket. This is perhaps an extreme hypothesis, but not entirely unbelievable, and only goes to show what we can do if we are properly handled. We have spent a good long time in growing, and the time is pretty nearly ripe for us to be substantially felt. Don't you think so? — *Verax, in Sporting Life.*

HARTFORD men are looking with pride on their local racing man, John Illston, and they expect great things of him this season. They say he will not have to put on eyeglasses to see Rowe at the end of a race that they both start in. George Illston has returned to England.

ONE dollar is now the initiation fee of the L. A. W. Another quarter will be dropped from the fee after this month.

MUNGER was not allowed to race at Clarksville, but he made good use of his time and sold five machines for his employers, W. B. Everett & Co. The agent for the Star machine also kept out of the race and sold three wheels.

MR. LADISH, of the *American Wheelman*, is coming to Boston, and it remains to be seen if he will use as vigorous language at the business meeting as he does in his paper.

SOME Saturday afternoon handicaps, for the purpose of lowering records, are spoken of at Springfield.

20 JUNE has been spoken of as the probable date for a road race between St. Louis and Chicago.

THE fourth annual meet of the Canadian Wheelmen's Association at Montreal promises to be quite a treat for Canadian cyclists if reports are true. It will include three days' sport instead of one day, as has been hitherto. The Montreal club is one of the oldest in America, and correspondingly strong, and intends showing Canadians what annual meets should be. It will also be the first appearance of the C. W. A. uniform, which consists of a gray cloth somewhat

lighter than the L. A. W. uniform. The Montrealers have also laid down a new track which they claim to be very fast, and Canadians expect a "dark horse" to show enough speed to encourage a representative Canadian at Springfield this year.

GEORGE B. Thayer of Vernon, Ct., who is riding from Hartford to Omaha, writes from Cleveland, O., under date of 1 May, as follows: "Am getting along as you see. It is still early for good roads almost anywhere, but I have ridden 916 miles so far, the last 200 miles from Buffalo being made in less than three days; so you see the roads from Buffalo must have been pretty good. Expect to go south to Columbus, and then west to Indianapolis and Chicago."

THE PATH.

MINNEAPOLIS, MINN. — The six-day twelve hour per day race between John S. Prince and Al Schock closed last Saturday evening, 15 May. Six thousand spectators were present. Prince, in the whole seventy-two hours, was off the track but 9 minutes. Schock rode twelve hours each day until Saturday, when he rested for eight minutes, and that from necessity. Prince was held back for three days, and could easily have scored over 1,100 miles.

The score at the finish was: Prince, 1,042 miles one lap; Schock, 1,028 miles eight laps.

MINNEAPOLIS, 7 May. — John S. Prince made an attempt to lower the time accomplished by William M. Woodside in a fifty-mile race at the same place a short time ago. He had as pacemakers T. W. Eck, Frank Dingley, and Fred Shaw, and the score sheets before us state that he not only accomplished the task for which he set out, but lowered the previous best figures from the thirty-fifth to the fiftieth mile, inclusive, as follows: Thirty-five, $1.51.15\frac{1}{2}$; thirty-six, $1.54.20\frac{1}{2}$; thirty-seven, $1.57.27\frac{1}{2}$; thirty-eight, $2.34\frac{1}{2}$; thirty-nine, $2.3.46\frac{1}{2}$; forty, 2.7; forty-one, $2.10.9\frac{1}{2}$; forty-two, $2.13.21\frac{1}{2}$: forty-three, $2.16.31\frac{1}{2}$; forty-four, 2.19.43; forty-five, $2.23.\frac{1}{2}$; forty-six, $2.26.32\frac{1}{2}$; forty-seven, $2.29.32\frac{1}{2}$; forty-eight, $2.32.48\frac{1}{2}$; forty-nine, $2.35.51\frac{1}{2}$; fifty, $2.38.53\frac{1}{2}$.

WINONA, MINN. — Races under the auspices of the Winona Club, 6 May.

One-Mile Professional, two in three, — R. H. Spear (1), 3.28, 3.28, 3.27; Grant Bell (2) 3.31, 3.27, $3.27\frac{1}{4}$.

Half-Mile Amateur, two in three. — E. A. Savage (1), 1.47, 1.40; Ben Melvin won one heat, and was second in the final.

Five-Mile Professional. — W. M. Woodside (1); Grant Bell (2).

One-Mile Amateur. — E. A. Savage (1). J. R. Wilson (2).

DOLE won the two-mile race at the Amherst College spring meeting, 14 May. Time, $7.7\frac{1}{5}$.

THE bicycle tournament, under the auspices of the Brockton City Bicycle Club, is to be held 16 June. Extensive preparations are being made. The races will take place at the Fair Grounds, and a brass band will be in attendance to furnish music.

The following is a full list of races: —

First event. — Half-mile dash, open to the riders of Plymouth County. First prize, Hub lamp, value, $6.00; second prize, luggage carrier, value, $2.00.

Second event. — One mile, professionals of Plymouth County. First prize, $15; second, $10.

Third event. — Two miles, open to all amateurs. First prize, silver timer, value, $15; second prize, cyclometer, value, $10; third prize, cigars, value, $5.00.

Fourth event. — One mile, amateurs of 3.30 class, open to all. First prize, gold medal, value, $15; second, silver medal, $10.

Fifth event. — One mile handicap, open to Plymouth County riders. First prize, hand-bag, $10; second, Kirkpatrick saddle, $6.00; third, bicycle stand, $2.00.

Sixth event. — One mile, open to boys under fifteen years of age. First prize, gold medal, $10; second, bell, $2.00.

Seventh event. — Five miles, open to all amateurs. First prize, gold medal, $50; second, gold medal, $30; third, gold medal, $20.

Eighth event. — Two miles, professional, open to all; Prince and Neilson will surely ride. First prize, $35; second, $15.

Ninth event. — One mile, open to all amateurs. First prize, gold medal, $25; second, gold medal, $15; third, gold medal, $10.

Tenth event. — One mile tricycle race, open to all amateurs of Plymouth County. First prize, gold medal, $30; second, gold medal, $20.

Eleventh event. — One mile consolation race, open to all amateurs, First prize, Hub lamp, $6.00; second, cyclometer, $5.00; third, *Bicycling World*, one year, $2.00; fourth, bell, $2.00.

The entrance fee to each event will be $1.00, except in the boys' race, when it will be free. Entries are to be made with D. C. Pierce, Brockton.

THE annual meet of the Michigan Division L. A. W., will be held in Detroit, Thursday, 24 June. The one-half, one and five-mile division championship races will be run and also the ten-mile National Championship. The new one quarter-mile track of the Detroit Bicycle Club will be completed 1 June. Munger will train there this summer.

R. HOWELL won a one-mile championship at Wolverhampton, 28 April. Time, $2.52\frac{1}{5}$; H. O. Duncan (2); DeCivry (8.)

AT the Harvard spring meeting at Cambridge, last Saturday, Frank L. Dean rode a walk-over in the two-mile bicycle race. The wind evidently affected his work somewhat, as he rode in much poorer time than he has made in practice — $6.46\frac{2}{5}$.

IN the fifty-mile championship run at Leicester, 24 April, and won by H. O. Duncan, the following records were established by Fred Lees: Forty-one miles, 2.14.35; forty-two, 2.18.32; forty-three, 2.22.35; forty-four, 2.26.31; forty-six, 2.34.58; forty-seven, 2.38.32; forty-eight, 2.42.20; forty-nine, 2.46.13. Duncan's winning time was $2.49.35\frac{2}{5}$.

A RACE of five kilometres was run at Nymegen, 26 April, for the championship of Gelderland. A. R. W. Kerkhoven (1); C. W. Boer (2); W. Van Ittersum (3); P. H. Meyer Timmerman Thyssen (4). Time, 11.7.

PRINCE and Neilson will run the second of their series of races for the professional championship of America, on the Lynn track on the afternoon of 17 June, the distance to be ten miles. If a third race is necessary to decide the championship, that will also take place on the Lynn track. The Lynn Cycle Club will hold a series of races on that day, the contest between Prince and Neilson to be one of the attractions.

R. A. NEILSON, has left for Woodstock, Canada, where he will compete in the races to be held next Monday and Tuesday. On Monday there will be a mile sweepstake bicycle race for the championship of Canada, $50 and a gold medal added by the Woodstock Amateur Athletic Association, entrance, $10; a five-mile professional race, open, for $100, $40 and $20. On Tuesday there will be a two-mile sweepstakes; seventy-five per cent to first, twenty-five per cent to second, and $25 added by the association. Special arrangements will be made for the makers' amateurs.

THE CLUB.

GLOUCESTER, MASS. — Crescent Club: President, C. J. Gray; secretary and treasurer, J. C. Merchant; captain, D. T. McFee.

SEWICKLEY, PA. — Sewickley Club: President, F. L. Clark; treasurer, Hubert Nevin; secretary, Frank Richardson; captain, Robert Tate.

LE MARS, IOWA. — Le Mars Club: Captain, J. U. Sammis; secretary-treasurer, F. E. Davis.

BRATTLEBORO', VT. — Vermont Wheel Club: President, H. L. Emerson; secretary and treasurer, J. W. Drown; captain, F. F. Reid.

HARTFORD, CONN. — Connecticut Bicycle Club: President, Stephen Terry; secretary, J. G. Calhoun; treasurer, Charles A. Rogers; captain, Robert F. Way.

MACON, GA. — Macon Club: President, Dr. N. G. Gewiner; secretary and treasurer, Charles Guernsey; captain, John C. Flynn.

ST. PAUL, MINN. — Alert Club: President and captain, Charles Parker; secretary and treasurer, C. A. Johnson.

THE Brockton City Club will have a hare and hound's chase 22 May, starting at 7 A. M. The chase will cover a distance of about thirty miles.

THE Dorchester Club has announced the following social runs: 16 May, to Brockton, leaving club house at 10 A. M.; 23 May, to Waltham and the Newtons, leaving the club house at 9 A. M.

THE Lynn Club appointed the following additional officers for its race meeting on 31 May: Umpires, Dr. W. G. Kendall, Boston; L. S. Ladish, St. Louis; Gideon Haynes, Jr., Boston, W. S. Atwell, Boston.

THE Somerville Cycle Club will run to Gloucester, 30 May, and return, via Essex and Wenham, on Monday, 31 May. The start will be made from the club rooms, Broadway, corner of Marshall Street, at 9 A. M., and dinner will be served at the Essex House, Salem. Visiting wheelmen are especially invited to participate.

BOSTON BICYCLE CLUB SHOW.

THE FIRST EXHIBITION OF

BICYCLES, TRICYCLES and ACCESSORIES,

Under the auspices of the Boston Bicycle Club, will be held in Mechanics Hall, Huntington Ave., Boston, Mass.

MAY 27, 28, 29 and 31.

All dealers should apply for space immediately to J. S. Dean, 28 State Street, Boston. Special Wheelman's Season Ticket, admitting bearer at all times, when in uniform, can be obtained only of Theo. Rothe, 625 Washington Street, Boston. Price, Twenty-five Cents.

COMING EVENTS.

MAY.

22 Saturday. — Races at Hartford, Conn., by Hartford Wheel Club.
Two-mile road race of Brooklyn (N. Y.) Club.

24 Monday. — First day of race meeting at Woodstock, Canada.

25 Tuesday. — Second day of race meeting at Woodstock, Canada.

27 Thursday. — First day of League Meet.
Boston Club show opens at 10 A. M.
Run to Chestnut Hill Reservoir, from Mechanics' building, 9 A. M.
Hill-climbing contest, Corey Hill, 10 A. M.
Runs through the Newtons, from Copley square, 2.30 P. M.. A. L. Atkins in charge.
Run to Cambridge and Waltham, from the Vendome, 2.30 P. M.. Capt. A. D. Peck, Jr., in charge.
Run to Mattapan and Dedham, from Mechanics' building, at 3.30 P. M., over some of our road race courses. Dr. W. G. Kendall in charge.
Concert at Music Hall at 7.45.
Home trainer races, music and exhibition at Boston Club show, 8 P. M.
Ladies' run, starting from Vendome at 10 A. M.
Officers' meeting for election of president, at Mass. Club House at 7.30 P. M.

28 Friday. — Second day of League Meet.
Boston Club annual tricycle road race from Bailey's, finishing at a point opposite Public Garden at about 8 A. M.
Business meeting of the League. 10 A. M.
Run to Echo Bridge from Mechanics' building, 4 P. M.
Minstrel show at Music Hall at 7.45 P. M.
Home trainer races, music and exhibition, Boston Club show, 8 P. M.
Officers' meeting at close of general meeting.

29 Saturday. — Third day of League Meet.
Third day Boston Club show, opens 10 A. M.
Run for "scorchers," in charge of A. D. Peck, Jr., and Dr. W. G. Kendall, early morning.
League parade, 10 A. M. Cadet Band. Photograph of Meet.
League races at the Union grounds, 3 P. M.
Final heats for home trainer races at Boston Club show, 8 P. M. Music and exhibition.
Banquet in the evening at the Vendome.
Intercollegiate games at New York.

30 Sunday. — Informal runs under auspices of committee on tours and runs.
Eastern Division tour to Nantasket.

31 Monday. — Races at Lynn in the afternoon. Prince and Neilson championship race. Last day of Boston Cycle show.
Two-mile race of the Brooklyn (N. Y.) Athletic Association games.
Essex County Wheelmen, annual meet at Lynn.
Fifty-mile race of Ixion Bi. Club, of New York, at Orange, N. J.
Races at San Francisco, Cal., by Bay City Wheelmen.

JUNE.

5 Saturday. — Games of the Staten Island Athletic Club.
Spring games of Montreal A. A. A., three-mile bicycle race.

11 Friday. — First day of race meeting at New Haven, by Yale College Club.

12 Saturday. — Second day of race meeting at New Haven by Yale College Club.
N. Y. and N. J. Road Race Association team race, at Orange, N. J.

16 Wednesday. — Races of the Capital Club at Washington, D. C.

17 Thursday. — Second Prince-Neilson race at Lynn.

19 Saturday. — Annual Championship of N. A. A. A. A. at New York.
Annual race meeting of K. C. W. at Brooklyn, N. Y.

24 Monday. — Annual meet of the Michigan Div. L. A. W. at Detroit. Ten-mile National Championship.

JULY.

1 Thursday. — First day of annual meeting of C. W. A. at Montreal.

2 Friday. — Second day of annual meeting of C. W. A. at Montreal.

3 Saturday. — Third day of annual meeting of C. W. A. at Montreal.

5 Monday. — Race meeting at Binghamton, N. Y.

15 to 18, Tuesday to Friday. — Tournament at Columbus, Ga. State championships will be run.

MISCELLANEOUS

Advertisements will be inserted in this column for one cent a word, including heading and address; but no advertisement will be taken for less than twenty-five cents.

FOR SALE. — Beeston Humber Tandem; good condition; Lakin cyclometer, absolutely accurate; price reasonable. H. L., CYCLE Office.

FOR SALE. — 56-inch American Rudge, in first-class condition; Columbia ball-pedals, '86 pattern; six-inch cranks; long-distance saddle; enamelled and nickelled; for sale cheap. Address, J. M. TRYON, Toledo, Ohio.

FOR SALE. — 56-inch Rudge Light Roadster, in first-class condition. Address, Box 1593, Fitchburg, Mass.

BICYCLES AND TRICYCLES. — 125 shop-worn and second-hand wheels now on exhibition. Stock constantly changing; no price list; correspondence invited; open Saturday evenings. BUTMAN & CO., Scollay Square, Oriental Building.

The Cycle.

VOL. I., No. 9.   BOSTON, MASS., 28 MAY, 1886.   FIVE CENTS.

The Coventry Machinists' Co.'s New Tricycle for 1886.

THE MARLBORO' CLUB—Automatic Steerer.
ADMIRABLY ADAPTED FOR LADIES.
SEND FOR CATALOGUE TO 239 COLUMBUS AVENUE, BOSTON.

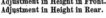

THE CYCLE

PUBLISHED EVERY FRIDAY BY ABBOT BASSETT, 22 SCHOOL ST., ROOM 19.

VOL. I.   BOSTON, MASS., 28 MAY, 1886.   No. 9.

TERMS OF SUBSCRIPTION.

One Year, by mail, post-paid...........................$1.50
Three Copies in one order............................. 3.00
Club Subscriptions.................................... 1.00
Six Months.. .90
Single Copies... .05

Specimen Copies free.

Every bicycle dealer is agent for the CYCLE and 'authorised to receive subscriptions at regular rates.' The paper can be found on sale at the following places : —

Boston, CUPPLES, UPHAM & CO., cor. Washington and School Streets. Tremont House news stand. At every cycle warehouse.

New York, ELLIOTT MASON, 12 Warren Street.

Philadelphia, H. B. HART, 811 Arch Street. GEORGE D. GIDEON, 6 South Broad Street.

Baltimore, S. T. CLARK & CO., 4 Hanover Street.

Chicago, W. M. DURRLL, 115 Wabash Avenue. JOHN WILKINSON & CO., 77 State Street.

Washington, H. S. OWEN, Capital Cycle Co.

St. Louis, ST. LOUIS WHEEL CO., 1121 Olive Street.

ABBOT BASSETT . . . . . EDITOR
W. I. HARRIS . . EDITORIAL CONTRIBUTOR

A. MUDGE & SON, PRINTERS, 24 FRANKLIN ST., BOSTON.

All communications should be sent in not later than Tuesday, to ensure insertion the same week.

Entered at the Post-office as second-class mail matter.

BOSTON puts on her holiday garb this week, and extends a kindly welcome to the League of American Wheelmen. She will do her best as a generous host to make the stay of her visitors pleasant and profitable, and from her bounteous store of good things she will give with unstinted hand.

OF first importance is the business meeting. Everything hinges on that. Let no wheelman fail to be present to cast his influence and his vote for those measures which he believes will tend to the good of the League. All else at the meeting is in the line of enjoyment, but pleasure should be sacrificed to business always.

"POLLY" advances some good ideas on adjustment of saddle. Not a few ladies who have had the disposition to ride have changed their ideas, after seeing the bad form of some lady who has had no good friend to fix her saddle at the right elevation. Little things like these go a great ways.

To be able to lubricate one's machine at the beginning of the season, and not do so

again during the year, is a thing to be desired. Our correspondent " Villsa " says that he has done this, and that it is practicable. We shall try vaseline by all means ; but if the facts are as put by our correspondent, why not persuade the makers to send out their wheels oiled for the season ?

THE advantages which the readers of the cycling press have over those who do not read this class of literature are many and varied. The reader keeps posted regarding the new wheels and coming events, he picks up here and there a few hints regarding riding, care of machines, etc., etc., and in numerous ways he is able to get more out of cycling than is possible for the non-reader. And for this the charge is only nominal. The price of a dinner at a first-class hotel, a much smaller sum than any club subscription, the price of a theatre ticket, will send you a paper for a year. Think of it, and send us a dollar and a half.

THE *Bicycle South* wants the League divided into four divisions, Eastern, Central, Western, and Southern, and suggests that annual meets be held by the riders in these divisions. What's the matter with our present plan? State divisions hold annual meetings, and in the back country it would not be a bad idea for one or two States to combine.

WE write this paragraph long before the meeting of the League, but it will not come to our readers until the meeting is well under way. It has been our policy to champion the cause of the Racing Board in its move against the suspects, but we have tried to deal fairly and give our opponents every opportunity to meet us on even terms ; but they have failed to take advantage of the League rules, and their hands are tied. We notified these men that no change in the rules could be made unless notice was given in the *Bulletin* of 21 May, but that paper has been issued and no notice has appeared. The rules will remain as they are.

MR. DUCKER is out with a long screed, in which he endeavors to show that the chairman of the Racing Board has exceeded his authority in his action against the makers' amateurs, and he seeks to bolster up his

side of the case by an attack on the method employed. We have no time to reply to the article. It is full of misstatements and wrong deductions. At the meeting of the League the chairman will substantiate every statement that he has made by the production of official documents, which will bear out what he says.

THE CYCLE will issue no special edition for the League Meet. We shall come out in our every-day clothes, and show you just what we are. It would be an easy matter for us to get out a great big number, and offer it to you as a sample of our regular work, but we should deceive you when we did it. We will not show you a fine baldwin as a specimen of our fruit, and fill your order with crab apples. The paper we give you this week is an ordinary edition, made as good as it was possible to make it under the pressure of League work incident to the Meet. We shall do better than this in future numbers, rest assured.

WE regret very much that our friend Aaron is not to be with us at the Meet. Ill-health produced by overwork has sent him to the South in search of health, and his physician bids him remain there. We shall miss the glint of those glasses very much.

"FAED" has some good ideas on the amateur question, and as they run in a similar channel to our own, we reproduce them : —

" I am aware that the tendency of thought at Springfield is against this process of purification in the amateur cycling ranks, but knowing your unvarying practice of supressing nothing that is written in good faith, I am emboldened to say that I consider the Springfield view to be a mistaken one. The foundation of amateurism is that " amateurs " in any sport are men who take part in that sport *for amusement in their leisure hours;* and it must be patent that such men as are represented by one of your American cracks, who admitted that he received very little money over and above his expenses (*i. e.,* that he made a livelihood and a little bit over) for riding a certain make of bicycle, is not an amateur, but one who rides *as a means of livelihood — ergo* a professional. The reason why it seems so distasteful to class such men as Rowe and Hendee with the recognized professional bicyclists is, that professionalism has been brought into such ill-odor by the hippodroming tactics of professionals as to make it unpleasant to regard these ex-amateur young gentlemen as on a

par with all other professionals ; but if we look at professional cycling from its best point, and also at professionalism in amusements of a non-athletic description, we can easily imagine that a strict drawing of the line between the two classes of riders will result in the elevation of the professional in the social scale. Music, for example, is the most universally pursued amateur recreation, and yet there is no social stigma attaching to the professional musician, but rather the contrary ; and when it comes to be understood that a professional cyclist can be a well-behaved and gentlemanly sportsman, subsidized amateurs need no longer dread riding openly as professionals in an honorable profession. Then just as people prefer to pay to hear good professional music to mediocre amateur music, so would good professional cycle-racing attract the paying public to witness it. And the makers would derive just as much benefit from openly subsidizing the professionals to ride their machines as they now do by secretly subsidizing amateurs to do so, records of fast speed being the only thing to be desired for advertising racing wheels."

CONTRIBUTORS' CLUB

LUBRICATION OF BEARINGS.

Editor of the Cycle : This much-worn subject has been discussed and re-discussed in the various cycling papers, but perhaps the readers of the CYCLE will bear a little more if it will benefit them.

This article will speak principally of vaseline, which has many advantages over thin oils, particularly for ball-bearings. The following experiments with a ball-bearing rear wheel will show the points of advantage.

After thoroughly cleaning the bearings, the wheel was dried perfectly dry, and would run 10 minutes and 56 seconds with one sharp turn. Of course it would never do to run the bearings dry, on account of heating. I next tried a little oil called " Black Oil " or " American Petroleum," and it would run 9 minutes and 48 seconds. After cleaning the bearings again, tried vaseline, and the wheel would run 9 minutes 38 seconds. The little difference shown is due, of course, to the thickness of the vaseline.

As to staying qualities, this wheel was run over all kinds of roads from 18 June to end of season a distance of 584 miles, without being again lubricated in any way. At that time it was taken apart to clean for the winter, and the vaseline was found nearly as good as new, and good for another 500 miles at least. The front wheel was run the same time under the same circumstances with like result. Vaseline will not gum, as will other articles used for this purpose. A machine left idle from 20 November to 1 March ran as easily as if just oiled, and the bearings, on being opened, showed no sign of being gummy or sticky.

Another point is cleanliness. You fill your bearings with vaseline, set the balls in and put the machine together. A little will run out ; wipe this off and your bearings are always clean on the outside, no oil running out to attract dust, and no gritting of the bearings. This method makes it necessary to take the machine entirely apart ; but as it will only have to be done, at most, twice a season, any cycler should be glad to do that,

and save continual oiling and dirty bearings. No oil of any kind should be put into bearings containing vaseline.

For ball pedals it makes them run a little slower when whirled with the hand, but is quite as good for them as for wheels.

The above will apply only to ball-bearings. For cone or parallel bearings the black oil mentioned above is excellent, if not the best oil obtainable, for the purpose. It is largely used for high speed machinery, and does not gum readily ; being quite thick it does not run out as much as thin oils. Most riders oil too much and too often. This does more harm than good, as the oil runs out and collects dust, which grinds and spoils the bearings and makes the machine run hard.
VILLSA.

POOR ADJUSTMENT.

Editor of the Cycle : I want to put in a plea in behalf of the amateur lady riders, — or rather the beginners, for I should be sorry indeed were there professionals among our sex.

My idea is this : Can't the people who rent tricycles be persuaded that it is for their best interest to take a little more pains to fit their machines, as nearly as possible, to the person hiring them ? All of us have seen ladies, evidently taking their initial ride, with machines on which the saddles were so low as to make the riders look as if literally working their passage, and with the handles so high or the saddle so far forward that their arms are spread akimbo, until it makes one fairly ache to look at them, they seem to be so uncomfortable. And then we tea, wonder expressed that ladies do not take more kindly to tricycling. . No wonder they don't. Probably few ladies take their first ride on a machine of their own adjusted to suit their particular needs, and consequently, unless they are fortunate enough to have a friend who knows something about the matter, they are so thoroughly uncomfortable that after riding a few squares they give it up in disgust, and assert that they don't see where the pleasure comes in ; and not only that, but if they hear any one of their friends talking of trying it, they immediately tell them, " Don't you do it ; I tried it, and it 's just horrid ; I never was so tired in my life " ; and we lose another possible rider.

Now, of course no one in this advanced (?) age would think of taking the trouble to fit machines out of pure love for the sport of cycling; but it does seem reasonable to argue that it would pay them well in the long run to do so ; for they would sell more machines if they took pains to make their customers as comfortable as possible on their mounts, and we all know how unhappy one can be on a " misfit machine."
POLLY.

ROUTE OF THE ROAD RACE.

Editor of the Cycle : After a careful re-examination of the course selected for N. Y. and N. J. Team Road Racing Association's initial race on 12 June, the executive committee find that Valley Road is not in as good condition as it was last season, owing partly to recent repairs, and think it best to modify the route by deciding on the following :—

The start to be on Clinton avenue, bout 1¼

miles east of Irvington (where the Elizabeth wheelmen will in a few days set up a signpost) ; thence via Clinton Avenue, to Irvington,and via Springfield avenue to the milldam and bridge just beyond Millburn, making 6¼ miles, which will be covered four times — twice each way — to complete stipulated distance of 25 miles, finishing at the starting point.

Detailed rules for the government of the race will be issued in a few days.
EDWARD J. SHRIVER,
President.

NEW YORK, 23 May, 1886.

TEAM ROAD RACING—LIGHTS AND BELLS FOR CYCLES.

AT the monthly meeting of the Orange Wanderers, on 19 May, they discussed the question of the first team road race of the new association. The last official notice received from the association described a course which they are well acquainted with, and do not consider suitable or safe. Nothing was said about preliminary heats, and it was at the same time stated in print that there would be none. Discussion of these facts led to the adoption of the following resolutions :—

Whereas, The Orange Wanderers joined the Team Road Racing Association on account of their interest in road racing ; and,

Whereas, It is evident that road racing should be conducted in such a manner as not to interfere with travel on the highways, or to violate in any degree the rights of others ; and,

Whereas, It is impossible for a large number of wheelmen to race together on the road without interfering with the public ;

Resolved, That the Orange Wanderers respectfully request the excutive committee of the N. Y. and N. J. Team Road Racing Association to order trial heats in each section, if more than one club from any such section enters for a race, so that in the final only one club from each of the three sections (New York City, Long Island and New Jersey) be represented. They also desire to call the committee's attention to the announced course, which they do not consider suitable or safe for the purpose, and suggest that it be changed.

Resolved, That these resolutions be forwarded at once to the executive committee of the Road Racing Association, with request for a reply, and published in the wheel papers.

The subject of compelling cycles to carry bells or whistles at all times, and lighted lanterns after sunset, was also discussed. The great increase in the number of cyclers throughout the Oranges has already brought this question to the attention of the authorities. It was the opinion of the club that prompt action on their part would aid in increasing the good feeling of the community toward them; consequently the following resolutions were adopted :—

Whereas, Cycling is becoming recognized as the most healthful, invigorating and pleasant of all recreations, the rapid increase in the number of cyclists in this vicinity being special cause for congratulation ; and,

Whereas, One of the objects of this organization is to promote the development of cycling and aid its healthful growth ;

Resolved, That the Orange Wanderers, being desirous of securing to all travellers on the public highways equal rights and justice, and recognizing the silence with which cycles move, do respectfully recommend to the Common Council of Orange and to the township committee of East Orange, South Orange, and West Orange, that they require all cycles to carry bells or whistles at all times, and a lighted lantern between sunset and sunrise.

Resolved, That the executive committee of the club are authorized to appoint a member, or members, to wait upon any of the above-named bodies, if they desire it, to furnish information concerning cycling, in order to secure justice to all in the proposed regulation, and that copies of these resolutions be sent to each of the above-named bodies, and published in the local papers.

THE PARADE.

THE details of the parade at the Meet Saturday next are as follows : Captains of clubs intending to parade will report at headquarters, Hotel Vendome, at 9 A. M. Friday, and state the number of men they expect to turn out, and no place will be given to those who fail to report before 10 A. M. Between 8 and 9 A. M. on Saturday, the captains of clubs to parade will report at headquarters, and receive instructions as to where they will form, after which they will get their men and proceed to the place designated for them to form in. The procession will form in four divisions, on the south side of Commonwealth avenue, the right resting in front of Hotel Vendome, and move at 9 A. M. over the following route : South side of Commonwealth avenue to Arlington street, countermarch on north side of Commonwealth avenue to Chester park, to Harrison avenue, to East Concord street to James street, to East Newton street, and proceeding by West Newton street to Columbus avenue, to Dartmouth street, to Beacon street to Longwood, where the picture is to be taken ; returning, Beacon street to Chester park, to Huntington avenue to Mechanics' building, where the parade will be dismissed. Each division will have a color : "A," purple ; " B," red ; " C," blue ; and " D," white.

THE RACING BOARD.

THE following letter from the secretary of the Executive Committee to the chairman of the Racing Board is printed to correct statements which are going about, to the effect that the chairman acted on his own responsibility in enforcing the laws : —

My Dear Mr. Bassett, — I notice that some parties are making a desperate effort to show that the action taken by the Racing Board recently, regarding makers' amateurs, was simply a personal matter with you ; that you are the only official who favored the steps taken.

Such persons have not the faintest conception of consistency. We had certain rules on our books which were not enforced, and which time and again parties said could not be enforced, and further dared the officials to enforce them. The action you have taken is no more nor less than enforcing the rules in their spirit and intent, and you deserve the thanks of all members for your courage and determination. The rules have been enforced ; if the results have been unsatisfactory, the remedy lies in changing the rules, if a majority can be persuaded so to do, and not in personal and childish attacks upon you. The fault, if fault it be, lies in the laws, not in the official who enforces them. I wish I could be at the meeting. You could depend on having my hearty support in your action. You did the right thing. I believe the rules should be radically changed ; but I honor you for your courage in enforcing the present rules — in short, for fearlessly doing your duty.

As for you being alone in the action you have taken, I have to say, as secretary of the Executive Board, that you submitted your action to the Board before beginning it, and that the Executive Committee, with the secretary-editor, pledged you their hearty and earnest support, and urged you to go ahead with the matter, believing that as our rules now stand, your course was the only clearly consistent one. All good government rests upon a strict enforcement of laws. If the laws are then unjust and unfair and burdensome, the laws must be changed. It is the duty of officials to see that the laws as made are enforced. This we considered was your duty and ours, and we have no reason to in any way withhold the support we pledged you.

T. J. KIRKPATRICK.

MAY 22, 1886.

FIVE-MILE HANDICAP.

THE Orange Wanderers run a five-mile club handicap road race in the spring and a ten-mile race in the fall.

The five-mile race was run last Saturday with the following starters : E. P. Baird, 54-inch Royal Mail, scratch ; L. H. Johnson and J. W. Smith, Humber tandem, scratch ; C. Hening, 54-inch Victor, 2.30 ; L. H. Porter, 54 Rudge, 2.30 ; C. S. French, 54 Victor, 3.00 ; A. E. Cowdrey, 52 Rudge, 3.15.

At two and a fourth miles the tandem struck a wagon, which turned in front of them, breaking several spokes, and detaining them probably a minute. Hening passed the two men in front of him at two and three fourths miles, and led to the finish. Baird rode a fine race, passing three men on the homestretch, and coming in only four seconds behind Hening. Had he begun his final spurt a little sooner, he would probably have won.

The positions at the finish were Hening, 20.29 ; Baird, 18.03 ; French, Cowdrey, Porter, tandem.

THOMAS STEVENS.

THE following letter has been addressed to the Secretary of State by the publishers of *Outing* : —

HON. THOMAS F. BAYARD :

Dear Sir, — A cable dispatch, dated 15 May, has been published in our papers announcing that Thomas Stevens, the special correspondent of *Outing*, has been arrested on the Afghan frontier. No further information in regard to his treatment by the 'authorities has as yet reached us, and as he may possibly have been deprived of his money, and unable to communicate with us or with the American Minister at Teheran or St. Petersburg, I venture to hope that a few words in regard to his journey may warrant the President in intervening in his behalf.

Thomas Stevens is an American citizen, who, after making the journey across this continent from San Francisco to New York on a bicycle, crossed the Atlantic a year ago, and in April of 1885 set out on a journey across the Continent of Europe, Turkey, Asia Minor and Persia, in the hope of reaching Pekin. His mission is solely as the special correspondent of *Outing*, an American Monthly Magazine devoted to out-door life and recreatory sports. He seeks to make this journey mainly for the purpose of displaying the powers of the modern bicycle, and his movements are watched with the keenest interest by at least half a million of wheelmen in this and other countries. Our last communication from him was dated Meshed, Persia, 31 March, 1886. It states that he had received from the Russian Minister, at Teheran, permission to go through Russian territory by way of Merve, Samarkand and Southern Siberia With this object in view he went to the expense of having sufficient money changed into the currency of the country to maintain him the whole distance. It now appears that in spite of this Russian protection, before he had gotten more than half way from Teheran to Meshed, he was arrested by Russian officials, and forbidden to enter Russian territory.

As Mr. Stevens has not cabled us, we are harassed by many painful uncertainties in regard to his situation. He may be in confinement, he may have been deprived of his funds and unable to incur the expense of a telegram, or he may have ignorantly rendered himself amenable to judicial penalties.

In view of these and other possible dangers to which he is exposed, I venture to suggest and request that our Minister at Teheran, and also our Minister at St. Petersburg, be instructed to inform themselves, as soon as practicable, of Mr. Stevens' situation, and to afford him such protection as an American, in the execution of a lawful calling in a foreign country, is entitled to.

Let me here add that Mr. Stevens is not open even to the suspicion of having any political errands or designs in his journeyings-but as I have already stated is simply anxious to make his journey across the solid portions of the Eastern and Western Continents on a bicycle, and through doing so to distribute as far as possible to the entertainment of the readers of *Outing*.

It can hardly be necessary for me to say that I shall be very grateful to you, sir, for any information which the State Department may receive, if it shall receive any which it is at liberty to communicate, about Mr. Stevens' arrest, his present situation, and what he lacks, if anything, for his present comfort and protection.

I am, sir, with great respect,
Your very obedient servant,
POULTNEY BIGELOW.

NEW YORK, 18 May, 1886.

THE CYCLE, Abbot Bassett's new paper, is about as well an edited wheel paper as any that find their way to this office. — *American Sportsman.*

FROM A FEMININE POINT OF VIEW.

BOSTON is in holiday attire this week. She has put on her best robes, and she extends a loving hand of welcome. With Coriolanus she bids her guests "one hundred thousand welcomes," and of her bounty she deals out an unstinted portion.

HER hotels will swarm with wheelmen, and the silent steed will throng her streets. Boston has two guests to welcome, the church and the wheel. The one ministers to the spiritual welfare, the other to the physical. It is a happy meeting and Modern Athens is to be congratulated

IT is a week of anniversaries. The wheelmen have been with us once before, the clergymen are yearly visitors. Can it be wondered at then if Boston should bestow a little more kindly welcome to the stranger guest? Will it be surprising if the grasped hand is more firmly pressed or longer retained? We trow not.

THE heart of Boston is large and generous, and both of her visitors will find it a very warm place for their nestling.

FROM a feminine point of view the present meeting means much. Never before have there been so many women a-wheel; never before have they enjoyed the anniversary as they will this.

IN the early days of bicycling the gentlemen used to tell us that there was no proselyting agent so potent as a League Meet. The sight of hundreds of riders on their glittering wheels implanted a feeling of desire among the onlookers that quickly gave place to a resolve.

THE gentlemen tell us that there is no longer need to proselyte, and that the army of cyclers is enjoying a healthy and a steady growth.

BUT how is it with us? We all know that we have to brave public opinion to a large extent when we take to the wheel, and we all know that many sensitive girls shrink from the ordeal. Can we not use the occasion as an educator, just as our brothers did years ago? And can we not show to the people of Boston that the wheel is doing a world of good for womankind, too few of whom appreciate its benefits?

WHEN this is read we shall be in the midst of our enjoyment. May that enjoyment be unchecked, and may we all look upon this occasion as a garden spot in our memories.

UNLIKE our brothers we are free from the cares of business, and no vexed questions of policy ruffle our feelings and mar our pleasure. Let us enjoy ourselves to the extent of our ability, throw care to the winds, and bid healthful pleasure be our constant guest.

A SHORT time since I suggested the idea of a riding school for ladies, and said it would not be a bad idea if some of the unused skating rinks were converted into riding schools. I have just come across this article in a paper, which tells what is being done by the ladies of Hartford, Conn.: "The rinking tricycle parties have been begun the past week, and have proved very attractive to a number of women. The plan is a private one, and thus far only the women friends of the man who got up the scheme have been invited. If the interest in the sport continues to increase, however, there will be an opportunity for somebody to make a regular business of what is now a courtesy. The women learn fast, and while they at first feel some awkwardness, they soon not only get used to the machines, but feel the big rink far too small and want to get out on the road. Already several of those who began riding in the rink are able to set a very good pace on the road, and seem to think nothing of a spin of five miles."

DAISIE.

ELECTRICAL TIMING.

E. H. FOOTE of the Massachusetts Bicycle Club has submitted to President Ducker a scheme for obtaining absolutely correct timing of races, and it is so practical and ingenious that the club will put it into practice. The details are as follows: —

Take a strip of rubber 2½ to three inches wide and one-sixteenth inch thick, long enough to cross the track. Sew or rivet on one side of this two strips of thin sheet brass or copper. Fold the two sides of the strips together, metal strips inside, and sew together. In use fasten one end to the ground on the opposite side of the track to the judges' stand, the other end to the ground on the side next the stand. This end to be attached to a block of wood or rubber having binding screws connected with the metal strips. These screws are also connected in circuit with a battery and a loud, single stroke bell. The strips are kept apart at the opposite end by a wooden plug if necessary. The riders to be started with their wheels just in contact with the strips. Whenever there is pressure enough put on the rubber to place the metal strips in contact, the bell will sound. The starting time to be taken at the first stroke of the bell when the first man crosses, as there would be a slight variation in the men getting away and the rear wheels would also cause a stroke. The time of finish to be also taken by a stroke of the bell. The time between the strokes of the bell would be absolutely correct, and could probably be taken more accurately than by the eye. This system could be extended by putting in the battery circuit a recording instrument which would automatically and accurately record on paper each and every time, how many men there might be in the race. This would necessitate quite an additional expense, as the recorder would have to be actuated by an accurate time piece. Mr. Foote is the inventor of the anti-header device, which may be seen at the cycleries.

ESSEX COUNTY PARADE.

THE fifth annual meet of the League of Essex County Wheelmen will be held at Lynn on Monday, 31 May, and promises to be one of the most successful in the history of this organization. The regular business meeting will be held in Mechanics' Hall, Market street, to o'clock. All members are requested to attend, for business of considerable importance will be transacted. Dinner will be served at 11.15 A. M., tickets for which may be obtained of W. G. Foster, E. L. Story and F. L. Tupper. The parade will be formed at 12 o'clock, and will proceed over an attractive route. At Highland square a photograph of the parade will be taken. Visiting wheelmen will be received at the Boscobel Hotel. From there all will ride to the Lynn Cycle Club's track at Glenmere, where races will be run at 2 o'clock. L. E. C. W. members will be admitted for thirty-five cents, others for fifty cents. In the evening the Lynn Club will give a dance at Exchange Hall, to which all are invited. E. L. Story will act as officer of the day, and club captains are requested to report to him on arrival.

THE MEET OF 1881.

A FEW facts about the former meet in Boston, 30 May, 1881.

THE Massachusetts Club had the largest number of men in line, 38. The Boston Club had 26 men. Chelsea Club, 33 men. Nearly 800 men in all.

Two tricycles were ridden. This machine is now only known as a relic of the sweet some-time-ago.

THE Commander was C. K. Munroe, New York; Division Commanders, E. C. Hodges, Boston; K. N. Putnam, New York; S. T. Clark, Baltimore. The membership was 1,700 at that time, and the treasury had a balance of $300.

AN exhibition was given at Music Hall. M. Chandler and G. E. Allen of Providence, Burt Pressey and Rex Smith gave some fancy riding; and the Hermes Club of Providence and the Crescents of Boston gave club drills. Prof. Rollinson gave his comic act, showing the experiences of a beginner on the wheel.

ON the Saturday before the meet (28th), races were given at Beacon Park. Woodside won the mile race in 3.36¾, and the two-mile race in 6.52½. Rollinson made a run against time to beat 3.25, and scored 3.37½.

THE business meeting heard reports and elected officers.

THE banquet was in Music Hall. Speeches were made by A. D. Chandler, Col. Henry Walker, Rev. F. B. Weston, Col. Jordan, Col. Pope, President Bates and others.

THE BLUE-NOSE TOUR.

THE pleasure derived from the "down East" tours of the past three years has caused a demand that a similar tour be planned for the present season. Acting on the suggestion of the New Brunswick members of last year's tour, we have decided to lay our course down the noble St. John River in that Province, from Grand Falls to the Bay of Fundy.

Below is the programme of the tour: —
16 July. — Night Pullman for Grand Falls, arriving there afternoon of 17th.
17 and 18 July. — At Grand Falls.
19 July. — Ride to Indian Rock. Canoe sail to Indian Rock.
20 July. — Ride to Florenceville, 24 miles.
21 July. — Ride to Woodstock, 25 miles.
22 July. — Ride to Half-way House; dinner at Eel River

FIRST GRAND OPENING TOURNAMENT

OF THE

Lynn Cycle Club Track Assoc'n,

Lynn, Mass., Memorial Day, May 31, 1886.

Although the centre of bicycling, Eastern Massachusetts has not heretofore possessed a complete and modern racing track. The necessity for such led to the formation of the Lynn Cycle Club Track Association, which, with commendable energy and dispatch, has evolved within the "City of Shoes" the finest bicycle racing track to be found in the world, being a dead level, three-lap track, of perfect design. The opening tournament will include the fastest men in America, and extraordinary time is expected. Visitors to the League Meet will regret much if they do not stop over and attend this grand event.

PROSPECTUS OF RACES.

FIRST RACE WILL BE CALLED PROMPTLY AT 2 P. M.

1. One-Mile Amateur Bicycle. — First prize, a fine gent's gold watch; second prize, pair elegant opera glasses.
2. Three-Mile Amateur Bicycle (9.45 class). — For League of Essex County wheelmen only. First prize, gold medal; second prize, silver medal.
3. Two-Mile Amateur Tricycle. — First prize, elegant hanging lamp; second prize, Smith & Wesson nickel-plated revolver.
4. One-Mile Amateur Bicycle (3.20 class). — First prize, gold-headed cane; second prize, base parlor lamp.
5. Three-Mile Amateur Bicycle Lap Race. — First prize, silver tilting water pitcher; second prize, elegant berry set.
6. First of a series for the professional championship of America. Five-Mile Professional Bicycle Race, between Robert A. Neilson and John S. Prince. — These two celebrated riders will meet to contest for a purse of $300 a side, and an additional purse of $500 offered by the Association, and the professional championship of America.
7. Five-Mile Amateur Bicycle. — First prize, diamond stud; second prize, gold handle silk umbrella.
8. Three-Mile Amateur Bicycle (handicap). — First prize, French marble clock; second prize, group Rogers statuary; third prize, gents' fine seal ring.

☞ Entries for all races to be made to E. M. BAILEY, secretary of Lynn Cycle Club Track Association, Lynn, Mass., accompanied by an entrance fee of $1.00 for each event, except the twenty-mile, entry which is $5.00, returnable to all who complete the distance.

☞ Entries close May 26. All entries will be received subject to the decision of the L. A. W.

☞ The Club reserves the right to reject any or all entries to the races.

RECORDS FOR THE APOLLO.

John S. Prince at Minneapolis, May 7, 1886, made World's Records from 35 to 50 Miles.

50 MILES IN 2 h. 38 m. 53½ s.

In the 72-Hour Race, PRINCE v. SCHOCK, May 10 to 15, inclusive,

PRINCE MADE 1,042 MILES, 220 YARDS,

Beating the Former Champion, SCHOCK, by 14 Miles, and making World's Records from 100 to 1,042 Miles.

— ALL THESE RECORDS WERE MADE ON AN —

APOLLO SEMI-RACER, WEIGHING 32½ LBS.

WITH DOUBLE BALL BEARINGS AND BALL HEAD.

W. B. EVERETT & CO., 6 and 8 Berkeley St., Boston, Mass.

SOLE UNITED STATES AGENTS,

23 July. — Ride to Fredericton ; dinner half way.

24 and 25 July.

26 July. — Take steamer for a delightful sail down the St. John to Westfield, at which place we disembark and ride to the city of St. John, a distance of 16 miles.

27 July. — At the city of St. John. Run over the Marsh road in the morning ; races on the Athletic grounds in the afternoon.

28 July. — Take "Flying Yankee" for Boston, arriving at 7 P. M.

The cost of the entire tour of 12 days, reckoning from and to Boston, will be $38.00. This includes berth in Pullman and extra freight car for wheels. Railroad tickets for the round trip ($12.50) will be on sale at the Eastern Railroad office on day of starting; the remaining $25.50 will be paid to treasurer of party on board train, who will pay all travelling expenses for the next twelve days. The distance covered by rail, wheel and steamer will be over 1,200 miles. The American party will be limited to 30, as this number, added to the New Brunswick contingent, under command of Capt. W. A. Maclauchlan, of the St. John Bicycle Club, will be as many as can be comfortably provided for at the hotels.

So many of the participants in previous "down East" tours are already booked, that not many vacancies are left; and all who have the tour under consideration are urged to decide as quickly as possible, that they may secure a place before the polls are closed.

CLOTHING. — From experience we recommend that jersey tights be worn when on the wheel, with change of regular bicycle suit in case of raw or rainy weather. One good bicycle suit should be taken along to put on at the end of the day's run. Of course the jerseys are optional, but, at all events, a riding and a fatigue bicycle suit should be taken. A flannel shirt and knee pants make a good working rig. These, with change of underclothing, should be put in hand valise. Baggage will be sent ahead each day by train, and will be found waiting on arrival.

Address all communications to Frank A. Elwell, Portland, Maine.

CHICAGO IN ST. LOUIS.

A CHICAGO rider sends to the *Journal* a sketch of the trip of Chicago wheelmen to St. Louis :—

"We arrived at our destination safely, and then came a great breakfast. Among the first on the spot were Whittaker and Munger. I have seen mischievous devils in my time, but none to compare with these. Their great pleasure seemed to be in finding some incline Chicago could not mount, or decline we could n't coast. To tell the truth they succeeded, but not without a gallant struggle. Nigger Hill was mastered all right, but Son-of-a-gun was too much, Van Sicklen, the only man in the hunt, breaking a pedal when near the top. This was followed by a more serious accident, for on coasting the other side on a borrowed machine, he found the brake would not work, and therefore threw himself forward, alighting on his feet. In doing so he sprained his ankle so badly that it is now in a very painful condition. Van was driven to town in a buggy.

"During the day we visited Baldwin's, and ate a hearty dinner. A portion of the crowd were genuine St. Louis pie-eaters, however, and when the supply was exhausted they visited the kitchen in a body, and nearly scared the innocent German baker out of his wits by howling in chorus, "We-want-some-more-pie." They got it. It is said that eighty gallons of milk were disposed of but I doubt it.

"We wound up one of the finest trips it has ever been my pleasure to participate in at Delmonico's, where another bounteous spread revived our somewhat lagging spirits. There is no knowing how mean a cycler may feel with an empty stomach, or how good with a full one We slept on the way home, for you can bet we needed it. At 7.30 we pulled up at Chicago, being unanimous in the opinion that St. Louisans are jolly good fellows, even if we can't mount Son-of-a-gun."

CYCLETS.

A HANDICAP RACE.

(28 AUG. 1885.)

ONCE a cyclen in the morning, time and distance calmly scorning, and indifferent to the warning that the pace would be severe,

Had the "gall" quite fabulistic, to race antagonistic with that speedy club, the "Mystic," though he 'd hardly learned to steer.

But he thought he pedalled so well, he could beat the champion Howell, and that he could race to Lowell that club of scorchers gay.

Said that he, "would gamble money, that for all they were so funny, he could down the whole gang, sonny, and would prove it any day."

Well, he started out, persistent, but he found the hills resistant, and every single instant saw him further in the rear.

Once or twice they stopped and waited, and then up he 'd come, elated, — then their speed accelerated, and he 'd promptly disappear.

Sometimes later, when they 're in a good hotel discussing dinner, enters in this poor beginner, an hour late, they say.

Orders dinner with decision, takes a lot of sly derision, and explains that a " collision " was the cause of his delay.

And loquacious and profuse is, in the matter of excuses, and swears the very deuce is in the luck, if he

Does n't make a better showing, when 'on the way home . going, and remarks in manner knowing, " They will see."

But they are men discerning, and with scorn that 's almost burning, they offer him, returning, a *twenty-minute start*.

He says they much mistake him, if they think to overtake him, and then laughter seems to shake him till the time comes to depart.

He mounts his cycle mighty with- the grace of Aphrodite, and until he 's out of sight he rides with sturdiness.

But his secret destination is the nearest railway station, and with greatest exultation he *boards the fast express*.

. . . .

Twenty minutes have departed, and the club has promptly started, and through the streets have darted in hot and vigorous chase.

Past swiftest trotters flashing, up hill and down hill dashing, no stop even for mashing in this terrific pace.

They have panted, and they 've spurted, and the sweat has fairly squirted, and they 're somewhat disconcerted at his unexpected power.

They may ride till the excess strain every muscle in the beet trained, but they can't catch an express train at forty miles an hour.

When they 've almost done the long road, one, who with the speedy throng rode, said, " I guess he took the wrong road, or has hidden as we passed."

And they jump at this conclusion, reach the club house in confusion, laughing at the man's delusion in thinking he was fast.

Imagine their amazement, disappointment and debasement, when a head 's thrust thro' the casement o'er that group of scorchers smart.

And a voice sings out with power, " Well, of racers you 're the flower ; I have beat you by an hour, on a twenty-minute start.

And one makes the meek inquiry, " Well, — how in — something fiery — did you beat us home, you flyer ? " He turns away his head.

And a burst of mirth restraining, as at something entertaining, he swears 't was *careful* TRAINING that brought him in ahead.   " CAP."

WELCOME !

CAED Mille Faethe !

WHEN the paper sees the light they will be here.

THE League of American Wheelmen, and every one of them a prince among good fellows.

WE are writing this in our attic office, and there will be a long hiatus between our scrawl and the type impressions.

NEVERTHELESS, we are glad to see you all, and here 's our hand on it. Shake.

IF it does n't rain, we 'll show you how to have a good time ; and if it does, we 'll attend to business.

THE Bostonese always distrust the weather on anniversary week, and they have to mount their umbrellas with the best of ball-bearings.

DON'T go away without doing the town. Take it all in, and then go home and rest.

BUT don't stay out late at night. Boston policemen are unused to seeing men on the streets after midnight, and you might be taken for a burglar.

ASK any Boston man if there is any work about a League Meet, and hear him proclaim ; and yet we 've done it twice.

THE amateur law is on the rack. Will it die ? Wait till our next issue and see.

MEANTIME, come and see us at the cycle show. We shall be ready to take subscriptions to any number.

IT is stated that the first high-class-ball bearing, hollow-fork bicycles in this country were made in 1878, by Thos. B. Jeffery ; and about the same time he made the first tricycle for A. H. Overman.

IT appears from a recent book on sea legends, that there are many ways to raise the wind. You may suspend a he-goat skin at the mast-head ; you may flog a boy at the mast ; you may burn a broom, and let the handle turn toward the desired quarter ; you may blow out to sea the dust from the chapel floor ; you may stick a knife in the mizzenmast, or scratch the foremast with a nail ; and so on. This will be interesting to all those who are too poor to buy a wheel.

THE "SPALDING."

Confidently presented to the Cycling Public as an embodiment of the highest state of perfection ever attained in Bicycle manufacture.

Light,		Direct

Light,
Graceful,
Strong,
Easy
Running,
Balls
All Around,
Including
Pedals.

Direct
Tangent
Spokes,
Warwick
Hollow
Rim,
Full Inch
Tire.
All Bright
Parts
Nickelled.

The American Premier,   The Humber Tandem,
The Kangaroo,   The Humber Cripper.

SEND FOR CATALOGUE.

A. G. SPALDING & BROS.

241 Broadway, New York.   *108 Madison St., Chicago, Ill.*

MR. EDWIN OLIVER, who looks after the correspondence and advertising of Gormully & Jeffery, will be at the L. A. W. Meet in the interest of the firm. Headquarters at the Vendome.

IT is suggested the wheelmen do not want a guide-book, for they are guyed enough by the hoodlums.

CINCINNATI wheelmen will attend the Boston Meet. See that the beans are kept brown; and say, while you are about it, don't forget the pork — plenty of pork and beans, our dear Bosting brothers.—*Cincinnati Sportsman.*

THE idea of pig city wheelmen coming to Boston for pork. Well, we'll show them what good country pork is.

STRANGE are the humors of fashion, and remarkable are the changes of opinion wrought by experience. The racing bicycles of the Surrey Machinists' Company are this year to have *very few spokes*, with a view to reducing the wind resistance ; yet it is only a few years since this firm made bicycles with *two hundred* spokes in a driving-wheel!

A PROMINENT furniture dealer is an enthusiastic tricycler. He has recently purchased a new Tandem, the praise of which he sings in no minor key. While enumerating its good points to a friend who called upon him at the store recently, the conversation was interrupted by the entrance of a customer looking for refrigerators, several of which stood near.

"Here's the very latest thing out," said the dealer, dropping his hand upon one of the articles in question, while his gaze wandered vacantly through the open doorway and across the street ; "the very best thing in the market to-day, — bar steerer, central gear, ball bearings all round, and good for 12 miles an hour on any fair road. In fact you can't buy — "

THE look of blank amazement on the face of the customer suddenly called the tricycler down from his hobby, and he proceeded to business.—*Record.*

PRESIDENT DUCKER of Springfield has received information that H. O. Duncan, the crack French long-distance rider, will appear in the Springfield tournament. He holds the 50-mile championship.

A LETTER has been received by the secretary of the Massachusetts Bicycle Club from the headquarters of the L. A. W., stating that the Massachusetts Bicycle Club is still the banner club of the League, having more than twice the membership in the league of any club in America.

J. KEMP BARTLETT is the worthy successor of James Thompson as Chief Consul for Maryland of the L. A. W. The bicyclers' "Mikado" at the Academy a short time since proved a brilliant financial success, netting a handsome sum for the Maryland club. Probably every wheelman in the city was present.

THE rapid growth of bicycling in New Orleans is shown by the attention it has received at the hands of the city council. Two recent ordinances relate entirely to this sport, the one requiring the use of bells and lamps, the other prohibiting riding on the sidewalks of the city. Glad indeed would the cyclists be if this was enforced upon vehicles (*i. e.,* that they should carry lamps), which have

led to more than one serious accident to cyclists.

GORMULLY & JEFFERY are getting out a show card made by the photo-graveure process. It will have views of the factory and the various departments, and also pictures of their wheels.

HERE's a "how d'ye do," every time two wheelmen meet.

A SURPRISE was in store for J. O. Blake when he arrived at his office on Monday, for there lay a letter from a man supposed to have been buried over a month ago. Fred. S. Rollinson, who is well known to nearly all old-time riders, showed plainly that he is still with us by writing for particulars concerning the six-day race which was talked of here. The strange part of the affair is that he appears to know nothing of the reports which have been circulated. He declares his intention of taking an active part in bicycling this summer. At present he is located on a ranch in California, doing good healthy work, and weighing ten pounds more than ever before, thus proving himself a particularly healthy corpse. He can be addressed in care of T. McConnell, Elk Grove, Sacramento County, California. — *Sporting Journal.*

WE have received from the Notman Photographic Company the latest production in the line of artistic photography. It is a group picture of the Massachusetts Bicycle Club, containing one hundred members. The portraits are in a large circle. In the centre are Col. Higginson, Col. Pope, A. S. Parsons, Henry W. Williams, Capt. Peck, Lieut. Sabin, Secretary, F. A. Pratt and Treasurer Benson, while around the outside and within the large circle are the members. In the corners are pictures of the interior and exterior of the club house, suggestions of the carnival, etc., The original will hang in the club parlor, and is now on view at Cupples, Upham & Co.'s. Small copies with key will be on sale.

THE League received three hundred and eighty-eight accessions last week. Best on record.

No changes can be made in the rules of the League.

WHITE jersey shirts, warranted not to shrink, are remarkable bargains. You use them as shirts one summer and as neckties the next.

MISS MINNA CAROLINE SMITH has chosen one of the new Royal Mail two-track tricycles for her mount the coming season.

ELWELL is going to have a "blue-nose tour." That's better than a red-nose one, everybody knows. But they are seizing our maritime visitors down in that country now-a-days, and who can tell but that they will pull in the bikes.

A PHOTOGRAPH got up in the style of that lately made of the Massachusetts Club, and containing the officials of the League and some of the noted wheelmen, would sell like the traditional hot cakes. When we hear about our officers we like to know what kind of looking men they are.

A NUMBER of racing men failed to get into the League races, because they did not read the cycling papers and find out when

the entries closed. Those who do not read the wheel papers are continually getting left.

THE Providence Club will hold a club run to Boston, Friday, 28 May, starting at 12 o'clock sharp from the First Baptist Meeting House, Benefit Street, and will remain over night in Boston. The club will return on the 6.30 train, Saturday, 29 May. A club run will also be held Monday, 31 May, Memorial Day, at Newport. The club will embark on the morning boat at 9.30, and return at 4.30.

THE Boston Club will have as its special guests during the League Meet the Albany, Montreal and Capital Bicycle Clubs.

ON the last day of the Meet the Boston Club will have an early morning run to some point half a score of miles from Boston, returning in time for the League parade.

THE Connecticut road-book will soon be issued. In addition to the tabular descriptions of roads, the book will be provided with maps and other matter in the way of general cycling information.

THE Chicago wheelmen do not sympathize with the anarchists, though they are revolutionists on the road.

NOTHING has been heard from Karl Kron. He is not one of us, but he is generally with us on these occasions.

* A WASHINGTON letter to the *Christian Union* says: "The rage for bicycles among men has grown into a tricycle craze with ladies. It was not so long ago that Belva Lockwood on her tricycle was an object of curiosity, but now you cannot walk anywhere in town without meeting ladies on their wheels. Early in the evening is the favorite time, for then they are accompanied by gentlemen. Tricycles, used in Washington for couples, either have the seats side by side or one behind the other. The former are certainly preferable so far as looks are concerned. Sometimes, at dusk, you meet a party with a dozen tricycles, moving along noiselessly on the asphalt pavement, or "coasting" at breakneck speed down the hilly streets. And this spring I notice many tricycles for a single rider, and ladies using them in the daytime to shop in and go to market. They are the coming vehicle in Washington, while as to bicycles, almost every clerk and boy in the schools who can get money enough to buy one exults in the possession of a wheel, and for nine months in the year is independent of the magnificent distances for which the city is famous."

THE fourth annual race meeting of the Kings County Wheelmen, of Brooklyn, N. Y. will take place at the Brooklyn athletic grounds on Saturday, 19 June. A full programme of the events will be found in our advertising columns. This popular club is noted for its successful race meetings, and they will keep good their record on this occasion.

THE Pope Manufacturing Company has turned out an Expert machine rigged with the Yost and McCune patent ratchet gear. The forks have a six-inch rake, and the rear wheel is twenty inches ; but otherwise the parts are those of the Expert. The gear works on the ratchet principle, and their action is very similar to that of the Star. The Pope Company has purchased the right to make high grade machines under this patent.

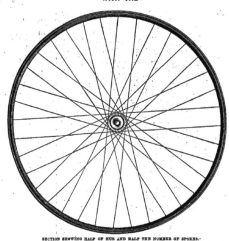

A DREAM OF CAPE ANN.

Now the drear spring days are over,
And the fields grow lush in clover.

Droop in tender green the willows;
Roll in blue the distant billows.

Apple blossoms, everywhere,
With their fragrance fill the air.

Songs of birds and wild bee's humming,
Tell the summer days are coming.

LoVed Magnolia, fairest vision!
Rest, my wheel, in fields elysian.

CHARLES RICHARDS DODGE.

THE New Orleans party arrived in Boston hale and hearty, having ridden the entire distance on their wheels.

THE band will not lead the parade after all. It will stand on the street and play as the procession moves along.

Go to the races and see the champions run.

JOHN S. PRINCE and his trainer, T. W. Eck, promise to follow the parade on a tandem.

ALL reports to the contrary, notwithstanding, the Pope Manufacturing Company did not ask for a postponement of the suit against them for infringement of the Bown patent, set down for 20 May.

THE topic of the time here, as in America, is the suspension of the makers' amateurs, and the prevailing feeling is decidedly one of admiration for the business-like boldness and straightforward action characterizing the L. A. W., as contrasted to the vacillating and timid half-heartedness of our N. C. U. Executive. Whatever may be one's opinion as to the point at issue, nothing but derision can be helped when the absurd dallying of the N. C. U. officials is considered. Why, even now, when the press in both countries has made the suspensions public, the officials of the Union maintain an absurd and unnecessary attitude of secrecy and caution, and are so grotesquely afraid of libel actions that, in replying to the inquiry of the secretary of a club about to promote a race-meeting, the N. C. U. secretary states that he appended a list of the suspended riders strictly in confidence and as writing to a member of the Union. — *Faed in Wheelmen's Gazette.*

THE bounds of a bicycle are unpleasant to the man who rides with a stiff spring, but its meets are very pleasant. Witness the present one.

RECENTLY Rev. O. D. Thomas, of Brockton, was arrested for riding a bicycle on the sidewalk. The case was placed on file by the payment of costs, but Judge Sumner said that hereafter the law would be enforced to its fullest extent, and a penalty would be imposed sufficient to prevent it. Judge Sumner said that while he did not doubt that the reverend gentleman used discretion, this was not provided for in the ordinance. "There are parties, however," said the judge, "who are careless in riding, and it was to prohibit all riding on the sidewalk that the ordinance was passed." Cyclists ought to take warning from this case, and have due regard for the law, which is no respecter of persons.

YOUNG, the professional, has gone into training for the season. He will enter events in the vicinity, and will show up at Brockton 16 June. He intends to go in for six-day events, and says that he will be ready in the fall to meet Woodside at any distance.

JUNE events follow each other in rapid succession with Yale, 11, 12 June; Brockton, 16 June; Lynn, 17 June.

At the request of the Brooklyn wheelmen themselves, the park commissioners have issued an order that the bicyclers and tricyclers riding in the park secure a badge, so that the officers shall be aware that the riders know how to manage the machines.

NORTH ADAMS' club men are working actively towards making a success of their tournament on 4 July. Upwards of $500 has already been subscribed for premiums.

THE 'Marlboro' Club tricycle won the tricycle championship at Vienna, and the second man also rode one of these machines.

JUST before Lent, a fond mother addressed her hopeful of ten, and reminded him that the solemn season of Lent was approaching, and asked what sacrifice he was prepared to make in order to show his reverence for the church. "Would it make you very happy, mamma, if I gave up something?". "Yes, my child." "Then, mamma dear, I'll give up going to church on foot, and go on my bicycle!"

BOSTON wheelmen have not put a directory of the churches in the League programme. It is thought that the wheelmen will have no trouble in hunting them out.

THE difference between a tailor and a header is this: the one puts the stuffin' in all around you, and the other knocks it out of you.

A CANADIAN paper says: "How are men who are working for their living, paying their own expenses, and only training after their day's work is done, to compete with men who do nothing else but ride and train all day, who are paid a salary and expenses to do so? It is impossible, and would speedily run every poor amateur off the racing track. In fact; it has almost done so to-day in the States. Fortunately we have not reached such a crisis in Canada, and it is to be hoped we never will."

WE have noticed that the very light racing machines are also very dark.

THOSE who ride to Lynn for the races should go via Saugus. The Lynn turnpike is closed to travel.

TOURING MARSHAL DR. W. G. KENDALL has arranged to have the Gloucester run of the Somerville and Dorchester Clubs take place under the auspices of the eastern division of the touring department L. A. W.; and visiting wheelmen are cordially invited to join this party for a Sunday and Monday run under charge of Capt. Sanger of the Somerville Club, or the one-day run, Sunday, to Nantasket, under Dr. Kendall's personal supervision.

THE Gloucester party will leave early Sunday morning, take dinner at the Essex House, Salem, pass the night at Gloucester, and return in time to witness the Lynn races or Monday. The Nantasket party will start from Mechanics' building at 7 A. M. Sunday, take breakfast at Hingham, dinner at the

Black Rock House, and return to Boston by boat in the evening, — a pleasant wheel of about twenty miles.

THE Hyde Park Ramblers intend to enter the L. A. W. parade, and wheel from the city to Salem, stopping over night, going from there to different places along the seashore, returning to Salem on Sunday the 30th, going from Salem the next morning in time to take in the races, returning home Monday night by moonlight.

JONES says that he feels like a bicycle when he comes to an article on the amateur question. "So awfully tired, you know."

A BICYCLER riding in the dark came suddenly upon two Irishmen, who were not a little startled. "What's that?" said one of them. "Oh, it's one o' thim bloody disciples!" replied the other.

SPEAKING of the Rapid bicycle, the *Cyclist* says: "We went over the works recently, and Mr. Palmer showed us the special tools used to make it thoroughly interchangeable throughout, and we also inspected the parts in all stages of completion, with the result that we cannot see where it can be improved in any practical and important point. The steering centres — spherical — are flint hard, the wheel strong as a horse, and we should say next to impossible to buckle, the axle strengthened for 1886, and generally as thorough a roadster as one could wish to see."

"IT is n't natural," said a friend who was looking at the portrait of a well-known wheelman in our collections the other day. "There 's too much repose about the mouth."

BURNHAM has tried in vain to climb Corey's and Locke's hill on a bicycle, but he has been up both on a tricycle. It was an S. S. S., and he found it easy to send it Surely Scudding Skywards.

"SHORT, sharp, and snappy" is what they denominate the races for Saturday afternoon. They are short enough, but there will be no room for sharp tricks and no soft snaps.

CHIEF CONSUL KIRKPATRICK has sent us the hand-book of the Ohio Division. It is a very creditable production, and contains a large amount of matter of value to wheelmen. It has a list of the officers L. A. W., the constitution and by-laws, racing rules, records, list of railroads, officers and constitution of the division, road reports from every town and city in the State, and also a list of consuls and hotels. Accompanying the book is a large map of the State made by a photographic process from a much larger one. The book is sold for $1.00, and is well worth the price. Surely every Ohio man should have one.

EVEN Bermuda is to be represented at the Meet. Mr. F. L. Godet, of Hamilton, will be here. He made many friends among the tourists who journeyed to that beautiful island, and they will be glad to welcome him.

SPECIAL. — A dispatch from the United States Minister at Persia, F. H. Winston, to Secretary Bayard, dated 24 May, announces that Thomas Stevens was turned back on the frontiers of Afghanistan, and has been forced to retrace his steps to Constantinople. From here he will seek to work his way through India.

ONE YEAR'S SUBSCRIPTION
TO
"CYCLE."

See how insignificant a dollar and a half looks beside a year's subscription to the CYCLE. You will know the truth of this if you will only take steps to make the comparison.

BICYCLING IN WESTFIELD, MASS.

The *Republican* correspondent tells of the recent action of the town meeting : —

The local cyclists are pained that Chief Consul Ducker of your city did not know more about the action of Thursday's town meeting in rescinding the recently adopted by-law prohibiting the riding of bicycles on all sidewalks. His approval was not asked by either our voters or wheelmen, neither was his condemnation. Mr. Ducker barks up the wrong tree in supposing that by the town vote authority is given to ride bicycles and tricycles on the sidewalks of all streets, save the three or four excepted by name. Nothing of the sort has been done.

The action taken simply put the matter on like footing with most other towns. Riding of this sort of vehicles on sidewalks is not authorized by Thursday's vote on any street. The whole matter is now under direction of the selectmen, in accordance with section 16, chapter 53, of the Public Statutes, and they may make such restrictions as in their judgment seem desirable. It was for this purpose the effort was made to rescind the by-law, which could not be easily enforced, if indeed enforced at all. Under it, violations could only be punished by a civil action of tort, and to recover the $2 penalty would entail large expense to the one bringing suit. This made it quite as inoperative as ever was a prohibitory liquor law.

But under the general law a violation of sidewalk rules, passed by the selectmen, becomes a criminal offence, and the officers may take an offender in the act of violating without a warrant. The bicyclists and their friends desired some privileges, but at the same time were anxious that the general public should not be incommoded. This was

accomplished by the wiping out of the greater part of the new by-law, and there is little danger that in future any cause for complaint can be reasonably made against riders of the silent steed.

It has been determined by the thirty "active" members of the wheelmen's organization, who will be given in the movement the cordial support of their seventy "honorary" associates, to prohibit at once any member riding on certain specified sidewalks on penalty of expulsion ; and also to do all in their power to have non-members owning bicycles observe like rules. In addition to the sidewalks named by the town the club will probably prohibit riding on these streets. School, east side of Broad, north side of Court to Day Avenue, east side of Day Avenue and south side of King; also the entire public square. President Herrick and Captain Goodnow are anxious that the slightest discourtesy or carelessness shown by riders toward pedestrians should be brought to their knowledge, and promise that in such cases expulsion from the club shall follow if the rider be a member; and if not a member, that riding will be made so uncomfortable for him that he will be glad to abandon it.

ST. LOUIS HILLS.

THIS is what is said of the St. Louis hills by Chicago wheelmen, who have been fraternizing with their neighbors. These hills have been famed in story and song as the nearest approach to paradise at their summits, while the swift rush down their sides is equalled only by an elevator in a hurry. Withal, easy to climb and easier to descend, because of the perfect quality of the roadbed, which everywhere stretches out like

long narrow ribbons of fine macadam over and around the great green agricultural billows, affectionately termed by the natives, grades. Strangers in Chicago have always expressed surprise at our barren levels, without a rise from the monotonous mid-ocean-like flatness for miles around; but a visit to St. Louis will show where the hills have escaped to. A most wonderful piece of road-making is demonstrated in the famous stretch called the De Soto road. It strikes a beeline out of the city and makes for destination fifty miles away, without turning to the right or left, apparently. When the steeps come in its path, it crosses, like Mark Twain's ant, right over the top and down the other side. Even that greatest roadster the world has seen, so far as record bears out, Cola Stone, was wont to walk these hills, and where Cola walked, locomotive dare not climb. George Hendee journeyed from the East to try his prowess on the heights, and last fall made some wonderful dashes that surprised the natives and himself as well ; yet Cola's records remain untouched. This is not the road the ambling tourist takes when out for a quiet stroll. Although, like an Atlantic voyage, the journey is continually up and down, the Manchester road is more fitted to Chicago's size. On this road is that famous coasting gem, Solomon Hill. From its summit the whole country spreads out, like McCormick's advertisement of the battle of Gettysburg ; but as the gradual descent begins, with the mountain growing higher on the right and the abyss on the near left, interest of the novice centres in number one. Presently the road sweeps almost at right angle around the mountain, and reveals a longer and steeper slide in the distance and usually a team across the road,

which sometimes has to be climbed over at full speed, or else dexterously avoided by hurling over the cliff. The Chicago man must see that his brake is in good shape. The next hill on this road is beyond Manchester, where it gradually rises nearly two miles, affording a splendid slide on the back-stretch. Just off the Manchester road are the two famous hills, the Undertaker and the Son of a Gun. These terrors of the West are not climbed as a regular thing; but on state occasions there are but few men in St. Louis, it is said, who fail to ascend their rugged heights. There was somewhere around a dozen ascents last year, for a prize.

THE PATH.

WOODSTOCK, ONT., 24 May, 1886. — A strong breeze was blowing while the bicycle contests of the Woodstock Amateur Athlet c Association were in progress here to-day. The mile professional championship of Canada was won by R. A. Neilson of Boston, with W. M. Woodside of Minneapolis, second; time, 2m. 52 3-5s. The five-mile amateur race, open to all, was won by George E. Weber of Smithville, N. J., with H. W. Cook, of Woodstock second; time, 17m. 5s. The half-mile race, without using the hands, was won by Williams of Woodstock, with Weber of Smithville, N. J., second; time, 1m. 36 4-5s.

In the five-mile professional race, Woodside was winner, and Neilson of Boston second; time, 15m. 23 1-5s.

In the one-mile amateur race, Weber was first and Clarke second; time, 2m. 56 3-5s.

W. M. WOODSIDE defeated a pacing horse in a five-mile race at Winona, Minn., on 10 May. The horse was withdrawn at the end of the fourth mile. Woodside's time for the full distance was 16m. 21s.

SINCE the programme of the Lynn races was printed, the Columbia prize cup has been withdrawn, and the two following races substituted: Five-mile bicycle — first prize, diamond stud; second prize, gold handle silk umbrella. Three-mile bicycle (handicap) — first prize, French marble clock; second prize, group Rogers' statuary; third prize, gent's fine seal ring.

CHARLES M. ANDERSON, the long-distance rider, has made arrangements for a six-days' contest, which is to be decided at Madison Square Garden, 31 May to 5 June. It is to be a half-hour bicycle against horse race. Anderson will ride twenty horses and change at will, in his competition against the combined efforts of America's two greatest long-distance bicyclists, William M. Woodside, of New York, and John Brooks, the champion bicyclist, of Pennsylvania, who will ride alternately each hour.

NEW CASTLE, PA. — A tournament of the New Castle Bicycle Club was held 20 May. Results were as follows: W. H. Barber, of Rochester, N. Y., 1-mile unicycle race, time 4.01 Elder Morehead, of Beaver Falls, Pa., won the 1-mile race for novices; W. J. Wilhelm, of Reading, Pa., the mile race for the 3.18 class; Charles M. Browne, of Greenville, Pa., the 1-mile special; Elder Morehead, the ½ mile for boys under 16 years; Fred P. Root, of Cleveland, O., the ½ mile, open, with W. J. Bailey, of Philadelphia, Pa., second; W. J. Wilhelm, the ½ mile, open; C. M. Browne, of Greenville, Pa., the 5-mile race; W. L. Horner, of New Castle, the ½ mile club race.

THE third annual tournament of the Yale Bicycle Club will be held at Hamilton Park, New Haven, Friday and Saturday, 11 and 12 June, 1886. Fifteen hundred dollars in prizes will be given and sixteen races will be run, including a five-mile record, three-mile record (ten-minute class), one-mile open, two-mile handicap, one-mile tandem, two miles without hands, one-mile tricycle, one-mile ride and run, etc. The track is one of the best in the country, and it is proposed to spare no expense in making the tournament a success.

NEW YORK, 14 May. Sports of the Berkeley Athletic Association. *Two-mile bicycle race.*—F. S. Miller (1), 8.13.

BETHLEHEM, PA. Sports at Lehigh University. *Two-mile bicycle race.* —R. P. Barnard (1) 8.10½.

TORONTO, CANADA. Sports of Upper Canada College. *Half-mile bicycle race.* — A. A. Macdonald (1); P. Burnam (2).

NEW YORK, 15 May. Columbia College Games. *Two-mile bicycle race.*— D. H. Renton (w. o.), 6.59¼.

BROOKLYN, N. Y., 15 May. Nassau A. C. Games. *Two-mile bicycle race.* — J. W. Bowers, Jr., 100 yards (1), 7.36¼; F. L. Ray, 75 yards (2).

THE races at New Orleans will not take place till June or July, date not fixed.

THE CLUB.

JAMESTOWN, N. Y. — Chautauqua Wheelmen. Officers: President, R. P. Hazzard; captain, Chas. E. Gates; secretary-treasurer, F. A. Clapsadel; 1st lieutenant, R. P. Hazzard; 2d lieutenant, E. R. Dempsey.

THE Berkshire County Wheelmen of Pittsfield have changed their constitution, so that election of officers now occurs semi-annually, in January and July. The club has weekly runs, and is discussing the question of new uniforms.

AT the regular monthly meeting of the Chelsea Cycle Club, Thursday evening, three new members were elected. The captain has called the following runs: Saturday, 29 May, breakfast run to Faneuil House, Brighton, returning to Boston in time to participate in the League parade; Sunday, 30 May, Chestnut Hill reservoir; 3 May, Lynn races.

THE Meriden Wheel Club has voted to have the word "Meriden" on the club cap, instead of the present monogram "M. W. C." The club will send ten or a dozen riders to the League Meet at Boston, and it is expected they will unite with Hartford wheelman, and that a special car will be secured to transport the wheels of the party. Dr. Rust, L. A. Miller, F. F. Ives and Wm. McMaster have been chosen as special delegates to represent Meriden at Boston.

COMING EVENTS.

MAY.

27 Thursday. — First day of League Meet.
Boston Club show opens at 10 A. M.
Run to Chestnut Hill Reservoir, from Mechanics' building, 9 A. M.
Hill-climbing contest, Corey Hill, 10 A. M.
Runs through the Newtons, from Copley square, 2.30 P. M. A. L. Atkins in charge.
Run to Cambridge and Waltham, from the Vendome, 2 30 P. M. Capt. A. D. Peck, Jr., in charge.
Run to Mattapan and Dedham, from Mechanics' building, at 2.30 P. M., over some of our road race courses. Dr. W. G. Kendall in charge.
Concert at Music Hall at 7.45.
Home trainer races, music and exhibition at Boston Club show, 8 P. M.
Ladies' run, starting from Vendome at 10 A. M.
Officers' meeting for election of president, at Mass. Club House at 7.30 P. M.

28 Friday. — Second day of League Meet.
Boston Club annual tricycle road race from Bailey's, finishing at a point opposite Public Garden at about 8 A. M.
Business meeting of the League, 10 A. M.
Run to Echo Bridge from Mechanics' building, 4 P. M.
Minstrel show at Music Hall at 7.45 P. M.
Home trainer races, music and exhibition, Boston Club show, 8 P. M.
Officers' meeting at close of general meeting.

29 Saturday. — Third day of League Meet.
Third day Boston Club show, opens 10 A. M.
Run for "scorchers," in charge of A. D. Peck, Jr., and Dr. W. G. Kendall, early morning.
League parade, 10 A. M. Cadet Band. Photograph of Meet.
League races at the Union grounds, 3 P. M.
Final heats for home trainer races at Boston Club show, 8 P. M. Music and exhibition.
Banquet in the evening at the Vendome.
Intercollegiate games at New York.

30 Sunday. — Informal runs under auspices of committee on tours and runs.
Eastern Division tour to Nantasket.

31 Monday. — Races at Lynn in the afternoon. Prince and Neilson championship race. Last day of Boston Cycle show.
Two-mile race of the Brooklyn (N. Y.) Athletic Association games.
Essex County Wheelmen, annual meet at Lynn.
Fifty-mile road race of Ixion Bi. Club, of New York, at Orange, N. J.
Races at San Francisco, Cal., by Bay City Wheelmen.

JUNE.

5 Saturday. — Games of the Staten Island Athletic Club.
Spring games of Montreal A. A. A., three-mile bicycle race.

11 Friday. — First day of race meeting at New Haven, by Yale College Club.

12 Saturday. — Second day of race meeting at New Haven by Yale College Club.
N. Y. and N. J. Road Race Association team race, at Orange, N. J.

17 Thursday. — Second Prince-Neilson race at Lynn.

19 Saturday. — Annual Championships of N. A. A. A. A. at New York.
Annual race meeting of K. C. W. at Brooklyn, N. Y.

24 Thursday. — Annual meet of the Michigan Div. L. A. W. at Detroit. Ten-mile National Championship.

JULY.

1 Thursday. — First day of annual meeting of C. W. A. at Montreal.

2 Friday. — Second day of annual meeting of C. W. A. at Montreal.

3 Saturday. — Third day of annual meeting of C. W. A. at Montreal.
Suffolk Wheel Clubs' three days' tour begins.

5 Monday. — Race meeting at Binghamton, N. Y.

15 to 18, Tuesday to Friday. — Tournament at Columbus, Ga. State championships will be run.

MISCELLANEOUS

BOSTON BICYCLE CLUB SHOW.

THE FIRST EXHIBITION OF

BICYCLES, TRICYCLES and ACCESSORIES,

Under the auspices of the Boston Bicycle Club, will be held in Mechanics Hall, Huntington Ave., Boston, Mass.

MAY 27, 28, 29 and 31.

All dealers should apply for space immediately to J. S. Dean, 28 State Street, Boston. Special Wheelman's Season Ticket, admitting bearer at all times, when in uniform, can be obtained only of Theo. Rothe, 625 Washington Street, Boston. Price, Twenty-five Cents.

LEAGUE RACES.

The following races will be held under the auspices of the L. A. W. at

Boston, 29 May, 1886,

AT 3 P. M., ON THE

Union Grounds, Dartmouth Street.

EVENTS.

1 Mile Amateur Bicycle. — League National Championship.
1 Mile Amateur Tricycle. — League National Championship.
(The Racing Board L. A. W. reserves the right to reject any or all entries to the above races.)
1 Mile Amateur Bicycle. — Mass. State Championship. (Entries limited to Massachusetts Riders.)
1 Mile Amateur Bicycle. — Novice.
1 Mile Amateur Bicycle. — Handicap.
1 Mile Bicycle. — Invitation Race.
3 Mile Bicycle. — Invitation Race.
Entries made to Abbot Bassett, 22 School Street, Boston. Entrance fee, $1.00. No fee for invitation races. Entries close 17 May.

Admission to the Races, 50 cents.
Grand Stand, 75 cents.

Lamson's Luggage Carrier.

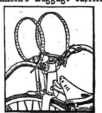

The most useful of all attachments for bicycles. Manufactured and for sale by *C. H. LAMSON, Portland, Me.* For sale by all dealers. Latest Detachable Form, price, $1.00.

TESTIMONIAL.— "I never tire of advising tourists to get your Carrier, as by far the best thing of the sort ever devised." — *Karl Kron.*

Used by Thomas Stevens in his tour around the World.

The Cycle.

Vol. I., No. 10. BOSTON, MASS., 4 JUNE, 1886. Five Cents.

The Coventry Machinists' Co.'s New Tricycle for 1886.

THE MARLBORO' CLUB—Automatic Steerer.

ADMIRABLY ADAPTED FOR LADIES.

SEND FOR CATALOGUE TO 269 COLUMBUS AVENUE, BOSTON.

ROYAL MAIL

SECOND ANNOUNCEMENT.

We first announced, at the beginning of the year, the important improvements added to this Favorite Wheel for 1886, from which time the demand has been EXTRAORDINARY and INCREASING. From all parts of the country orders have poured in upon us, far exceeding our expectations, and taxing our ability to fill. We have been obliged to cable for a large increase of the year's complement. Such shows the appreciation of these Common Sense Improvements and the Great Popularity of the Wheel. Wheelmen can understand the increased strength of the New Rim, which having thick double edge (which in other rims is the weak point), cannot buckle and cannot become dented or put out of true. Especially adapted to rough American roads. The Ball Head has universal praise. No other Bicycle has the Grip Fast Rim or Triggwell Ball Head. A Perfect Roadster. We have got THE Wheel.

DON'T

PURCHASE A MOUNT

Till after Examining a

ROYAL MAIL.

Just received from steamer, a lot of the Royal Mail Celebrated Two-Track Tricycles, small drivers and large front wheel, and convertible Tandems. Superb Machines. See them. In the Royal Mail Tandem, the lady sits behind allowing the gentleman to command the machine. Also appears better. The Handsomest Tandem in the Market.

WM. READ & SONS,
107 Washington St., Boston.

The First Hollow-Forked, Ball-Bearing Bicycles manufactured in this country
were made in 1878, by Thos. B. Jeffery, who superintends
the mechanical department of the firm of

GORMULLY & JEFFERY,

CHICAGO, ILL.,

MAKERS OF THE

AMERICAN CYCLES

Mr. Jeffery also made the first tricycle at about the same period,
and has been making Cycles ever since. If experience
is the best teacher, surely the American Cycles,
which to-day combine his long experience and many inventions,
are the best.

PRETTIEST CATALOG IN THE TRADE FREE.

THE CYCLE

PUBLISHED EVERY FRIDAY BY ABBOT BASSETT, 22 SCHOOL ST., ROOM 19.

VOL. I.   BOSTON, MASS., 4 JUNE, 1886.   No. 10.

TERMS OF SUBSCRIPTION.

One Year, by mail, post-paid...........................$1.50
Three Copies in one order...........................3.00
Club Subscriptions...........................1.00
Six Months...........................90
Single Copies...........................05

Specimen Copies free.

Every bicycle dealer is agent for the CYCLE and author-
ized to receive subscriptions at regular rates. The paper
can be found on sale at the following places: —
 Boston, CUPPLES, UPHAM & Co., cor. Washington and
School Streets. Tremont House news stand. At every
cycle warehouse.
 New York, ELLIOTT MASON, 12 Warren Street.
 Philadelphia, H. B. HART, 811 Arch Street. GEORGE
D. GIDEON, 6 South Broad Street.
 Baltimore, S. T. CLARK & Co., 4 Hanover Street.
 Chicago, W. M. DURELL, 115 Wabash Avenue. JOHN
WILKINSON & Co., 77 State Street.
 Washington, H. S. OWEN, Capital Cycle Co.
 St. Louis, ST. LOUIS WHEEL Co., 1121 Olive Street.

ABBOT BASSETT   . . . .   EDITOR
W. I. HARRIS   . .   EDITORIAL CONTRIBUTOR

A. MUDGE & SON, PRINTERS, 24 FRANKLIN ST., BOSTON.

All communications should be sent in not later than
Tuesday, to ensure insertion the same week.

Entered at the Post-office as second-class mail matter.

THIS issue of the CYCLE is full of Meet.
We intend to make every issue full of meat,
but in this case there is *a* difference.

IN our last issue we welcomed the coming
and now we speed the parting guests. They
have been among us and they have gone,
giving us the assurance that they have had
a good time.

BOSTON has done her best, and we think
there is general satisfaction. The boys have
had a good time. They have neglected
business, the parade, and the races, and they
have been out upon the roads enjoying
themselves. The hotel corridors have not
been thronged as they have been in other
Meet cities, and it has been very hard to
find the boys.

THE business meeting was not altogether
successful. There was a small attendance
and little enthusiasm. It put into the hands
of those who desire to see it given up a very
powerful argument.

THE amateur question was met and settled. There was no uncertain sound in the
decision. We think the members must

have been readers of the CYCLE, for they
acted and voted in accordance with our
preaching, which was radically different
from that of nearly every contemporary we
have.

WHERE were the friends of the racing
man? and where were these men who were
going to down the Racing Board? They
were very conspicuous by their absence.
There has been a deal of talk and no end
of clamor, and the final result is that the
Racing Board has been unanimously indorsed. The friends of the racing men were
invited to meet the Racing Board in this
arena. They were given every chance to
be heard. The chairman was prepared to
act speedily in accordance with the instructions of that meeting, but the suspends appeared to have no friends, and there was no
battle. The vote was unanimous.

AND now there is more talk and more
clamor. The opposition declined battle
after all their talk, and now they want to
talk some more. Was there ever a more
absurd situation of affairs?

A NEW society has been formed. For
what? To control racing and to antagonize
the League. The members say they do not
intend to antagonize the League, but no
other construction can be put upon their
course. The new Union is doomed to a
speedy death. It is in the hands of the
same parties that conducted the campaign
against the Racing Board. We have seen
how they succeeded in the one case. The
result will be same in the other. The Union
not only antagonizes the League, but it antagonizes every cycling and athletic association in America and England.

UNDER the rules of the Racing Board, a
man renders himself liable to suspension if
he competes at a tournament not governed
by League rules. The Racing Board will
not fail to enforce its rules after the indorsement they have had.

THE parade was not altogether a success.
It was expected that the number scored in
the parade of 1881 would be doubled. It
was not reached. And yet there were more
wheelmen at the parade than at the business
meeting, the races, or the banquet.

A DECIDEDLY novel and pleasant feature
of the Meet was the ladies' programme.
On Thursday some thirty ladies and half as
many gentlemen enjoyed a short run, and
on Friday a more extended run was taken.
The Boston ladies exerted themselves to
make the stay of their guests pleasant, and
from every indication we think they succeeded.

THE Meet was a grand success. We can
only say this or that thing was not as it
should be ; but, taken as a whole, no greater
success has been secured by the association.

"ARE you coming down?" has been the
question asked of us again and again the
past week, in view of the action of our contemporary, the *World,* whose price has
been made one dollar. We have invariably
answered, "No." This action on the part
of our contemporary only goes to show that
the CYCLE has been giving it a very hard
rub. We do not believe in cheapening our
wares. We propose to make the CYCLE
worth a dollar and a half, and we have thus
far had no trouble in getting that sum from
our readers. The *World* has always stood
by its colors and refused to come down in
price, even though every other cycling
paper was put upon the market at a less
sum. It did not strike its colors until the
CYCLE appeared. The meaning is easily
guessed. We have got them on the run.
We shall give you in the CYCLE the full
value of what we ask in return, and we
shall not go down to a dollar, for we think
our readers want the best and are willing to
pay for it.

THE LEAGUE MEET OF 1886.

THEY have been with us and they have
departed. Boston has put one more Meet
upon her record books, and we can well believe the visitors will pronounce the affair a
grand success. On Wednesday they began
to come, and Monday saw the lingering
remnant at the Lynn races. The entertainments have been many and varied, and all
have been well patronized. The wheelmen
have not been content to remain in Boston
proper, but have been out and about upon
the roads of the suburbs. The hotels have
been deserted during the daytime, and we
fear that many have forgotten the business
matters which were so important a part of
this occasion.

The runs projected and carried out by the
Tours and Runs Committee were very successful, and were attended by large num-

bers. They were wholly informal. In several of these runs there were very near to two hundred participants.

COREY HILL.

The first formal affair was the hill contest at Corey Hill. This was arranged to allow the visiting wheelmen to try their powers.

Several thousand people were assembled to witness the contest. The field officers for this contest were: Judges, Dr. W. G. Kendall (chairman), C. S. Howard, H. W. Hayes; starter, E. S. Wheeler; timers, N. Ethier, J. E. Savelle, R. E. Bellows, G. L. Haynes, D. C. Pierce, W. M. Rogers. The first event did not occur for nearly an hour after the time set (ten o'clock), the rider being C. E. Kluge, of Jersey City, N. J., mounted on a Star bicycle. He got a good send off, and pushing steadily reached the summit with apparent ease. He was followed a few minutes later by William Haradon, of Springfield, who won third position in the contest last year, and he had no difficulty in mounting the hill on this occasion. He road a Royal Mail bicycle. The third starter was C. A. Crosby, of Bangor, riding an American Club bicycle; but he was not so fortunate as the others, being dismounted about half way up the course. Horace Crocker, of Newton, was the next, and easily reached the top on a Singer straight-steering tricycle. George Weber, of Smithville, N. J., on a Star followed, and easily mounted the hill with a steady and rapid motion. He started without premeditation, and without his racing rig or usual machine. This ended the contest; but Williams, the colored rider, took the hill against time, reaching the top easily. The time was as follows:—

| | Half Way. | | Finish. | |
	M. S.		M. S.	
George E. Weber	1	30	3	16¼
William Haradon	2	45	3	42
C. E. Kluge	1	00	4	13½
C. H. Crosby	....		....	
Horace Crocker, tricycle	2	00	4	14¼
John Williams, tricycle	1	45	4	2½

For the bicycle contest three prizes of gold and silver medals were awarded, and in the tricycle event gold medal to Crocker.

THE LADIES' RUNS.

Not to be behind their brothers in the practice of every courtesy and hospitality toward their guests, the lady tricyclists arranged a few runs for the entertainment of the visiting ladies. The run of the first day was called for 10 o'clock A. M. The guests were received in the parlors of the Hotel Vendome, and a happy hour was spent in the interchange of greetings and in anticipating the pleasures of the proposed journey. At 10.30 everything was in readiness for the start. The ladies took their places in line, and away the procession went, led by a couple on a Sociable, who were selected as pacemakers. It was a pretty sight as the procession moved around toward Longwood, and every window along the route was thronged with spectators. The majority of the machines were Tandem Sociables, carrying a lady and gentleman; while a number of the ladies, preferring to go it alone, moved along on single tricycles, and found genial company in the gentlemen, who in similar numbers were carried by bicycles and single tricycles.

Along the shady highways of Longwood, and through the beautiful town of Brookline to Chestnut Hill reservoir, rode the party, and thence to the Faneuil House, Brighton. Some thirty ladies were in the party, and including gentlemen forty-five sat at table for dinner. A number of the weaker riders left the party at Corey Hill, and made direct for the Faneuil House. It was intended to go to Newton after dinner, but rain came on, and it was thought best to return to the city at once. The ladies voted the affair a grand success.

The second day a trip was proposed with Harvard College as the destination, Miss Minna Caroline Smith having invited the party to visit her at the University. Some twenty ladies engaged in this trip. After visiting Harvard a run was made to Watertown and Newtonville, where a visit was made to the Nonantum Club Rooms. The ladies made about twenty-five miles on this run.

THE PROMENADE CONCERT.

The promenade concert at Music Hall was a grand success. The wheelmen were present in large numbers, and an interested crowd watched them from the galleries, the ladies being well represented. The music of the National Guard Band, William Hill, director, found the greatest favor, and the selections, which were of the popular order and well chosen, received many encores. The cyclists went to enjoy themselves, and they were not long in making themselves thoroughly at home. They sung, told stories, cheered prominent wheelmen and clubs and, as a matter of course, the ladies. Light refreshments were served, and as smoking on the floor was allowed, the sociability of the occasion was increased.

PRELIMINARY MEETING.

A preliminary meeting was held at the Massachusetts Club House on Thursday evening. Abbot Bassett was invited to preside, and John C. Gulick, of New York, was made secretary. There was an attendance of about forty members of the Board of Officers. After a general discussion on various matters, Mr. Parsons asked what the meeting was called for. President Beckwith stated that it was an informal caucus preparatory to the meeting to be held next day. A long discussion followed this, and some one raised the question whether or not the office of League secretary was vacant. At the meeting the Board held in New York last February, it was voted that the office be retained during the occupant's good behavior. The question raised was whether that rule went in force until another election had occurred.

Dr. G. Carlton Brown moved that it be the sense of the meeting that the office of secretary is not now vacant. On this being put to vote the motion was carried, 11 to 8. The New York delegation did not vote. Mr. Harris moved that the meeting proceed to nominate a list of officers. The sentiment of the meeting, however, seemed little in favor of this, and finding this to be so Mr. Harris moved that the meeting adjourn, and upon this motion the vote was unanimously in the affirmative.

This ended the programme for the first day.

SECOND DAY.

The second day was eminently a business day, and nothing was put upon the programme of events which would in any way interfere with the business meetings.

THE TRICYCLE RACE.

The third annual tricycle road race of the Boston Bicycle Club was run early in the morning from Bailey's Hotel at South Natick to Boston, finishing at a point on Beacon street not far from Charles street. The course was the most direct one, through Wellesley and Newton Lower Falls to the great sign-boards, and thence on Beacon street to finish, and was about sixteen and one-half miles in length. The contestants were C. O. Danforth, of Cambridge, and John T. Williams, of the Massachusetts Club. The two named were started from the hotel at just 6 o'clock, and E. P. Burnham was sent away three minutes later, on a run against time to beat his own record. The riders found the roads quite muddy from Thursday's showers, and were also bothered by a head wind; but in spite of these drawbacks they set out at a rattling pace and kept it up to the finish. Burnham made a most determined push for the lead from the start. At Wellesley he came in sight of the riders ahead of him, and at Newton Lower Falls, just before reaching the great sign-boards, caught up with them and passed them. From there on he gradually drew away from them, and was about ten minutes ahead at the finish. From the great sign-boards Mr. Burnham was assisted by Mr. Crocker as pacemaker, while W. A. Rhodes acted in the same capacity for the others throughout the course. Burnham's time was 1 h. 4 m., beating all records over the same course, the best time previously made being 1 h. 10 m. 40 s., in the race two years ago. The two contestants finished as they had run the race — close together — with Danforth a few seconds ahead. Owing to the early hour at which the race was run, but few of the wheelmen had gathered at the finish.

The judge at the finish was Mr. R. J. Tombs; the starter, Mr. C. P. Donahoe; and the timers at the finish, Messrs. E. C. Hodges, F. M. Robinson and H. A. Baker.

OFFICERS' MEETING.

The annual business meeting of the League's board of officers was held in the gymnasium of the Massachusetts Club House.

It was 9.45 o'clock when the meeting was called to order by President Beckwith, who stated that there was a meeting of the old board, and that it was in order to adjourn without further proceedings; and on motion this was done, and the new board at once convened. Burley B. Ayres of Chicago was unanimously chosen temporary chairman, and John A. Wells of Philadelphia temporary secretary. At the conclusion of the reading of the list of proxies represented, the election of officers was proceeded with.

J. C. Gulick of New York nominated, on the part of the New York delegation, Dr. N. M. Beckwith, the present incumbent.

Dr. G. C. Brown of New Jersey, and A. S. Parsons of Boston, seconded the nomination, and, on motion of W. I. Harris, the secretary was instructed to cast one ballot for the office.

.The president was escorted to the chair, and when the applause with which he was received had subsided, he made a brief address, thanking the members for their kindness in electing him for the fourth time to such an important office.

The election for vice-president resulted in the choice of T. J. Kirkpatrick of Springfield, O.

Sanford Lawton of Springfield, Mass., was unanimously elected treasurer; and to fill the office of third member of the executive board, John C. Gulick of New York was elected.

Chief Consul Ducker of Massachusetts inquired if it was not necessary to elect a secretary, and the chairman replied that according to his construction of the rules he did not consider the office vacant, and that he had carefully looked into the matter.

On motion, the reading of the various reports, with the exception of that of the secretary and treasurer, was postponed until the general business meeting, to be held after the adjournment of the board.

In the absence of Secretary Aaron, who is sick and on a vacation down South, the secretary's report was read by John A. Wells, the substance of which was as follows: —

The total number of former members who renewed their membership for the current year is 4,379. The new members who have entered the League, to and including the list of applications 28 May, is 4,084, making a total of 8,643; and in addition fifty names have been presented during the present week for membership in the L. A. W. Compared with the membership of 1885, the present number is an increase of nearly 64 per cent. The total of 8,463 members down to May 22 is apportioned among the different State divisions as follows: New Hampshire, 138; Massachusetts, 1,341; New York, 1,432; New Jersey, 831; Michigan, 188; Pennsylvania, 1,218; Ohio, 734; Minnesota, 93; Indiana, 129; Connecticut, 518; Illinois, 374; Iowa, 97; Maryland, 165; Vermont, 58; District of Columbia, 53; Kentucky, 68; Louisiana, 45. And the following new divisions in the order of their formation: Rhode Island, 108; Tennessee, 51; Colorado, 42; California, 124; Nebraska, 50; Maine, 77.

The number of new division members is 330, of which the following States and Territories have the largest quota: Virginia, 49; Wyoming, 43; West Virginia, 32; Kansas, 31; Wisconsin, 22; Delaware, 20; Alabama, 12; Georgia and Texas, 11 each. The first four have each more than sufficient to organize a division, and in most of the cases steps toward that end have been taken.

At the conclusion of the secretary's report Mr. Wells read a report prepared by himself, in which he traced the success of the *Official Bulletin*, and told how the weekly circulation at the present time is nearly 9,000, and constantly increasing. The cost of publishing the *Bulletin* this year was less than one half what it cost last year, and he thought before another year the *Bulletin* would be self-sustaining. He concluded with some highly complimentary remarks regarding the work done by Mr. Aaron. Following this he read the secretary's report of the balance of money due the various divisions.

Mr. Harris thought that this report was not sufficiently in detail, and said that he wanted a general statement of the financial condition, which he did not think the report already read covered. After considerable more discussion, the acting secretary stated that the expenses of conducting the *Bulletin* had been during the last year, $7,365.65; the advertising receipts, $6,120.13; total expense over receipts, $1,245.52, which is a gain of $2,500 over previous years.

Mr. Harris again was not satisfied, and said that he did not think that any gentleman present could learn of the financial condition of the League by what had been read. The lengthy discussion which followed was ended by a motion to lay the secretary's report on the table until the treasurer's report had been read.

Treasurer F. P. Kendall was absent, and his report was read by Mr. Lawton.

President Beckwith stated that he had been assured by the secretary of the executive committee of a report from that committee, but it had not arrived.

On motion of Mr. Dean this report was ordered to be printed in the *Bulletin*.

Mr. Luscomb announced that he would at the business meeting, move the adoption of certain amendments to the Constitution, to wit : In Article IV., Section 1, add "and each such blank shall designate the number of representatives for whom the member is entitled to vote." Section 2, in fifth line, after words " entitled to," strike out " under these rules " and insert " on March 1st."

Section 2. Before commencement of sixth line insert, " except in divisions of 500 members or over, where special regulations governing the ballot have been adopted."

Insert after Section 2 : —

Section 3. Each State division comprising a membership of 500, and such divisions as they hereafter reach such limit, may make such rules and regulations not inconsistent with the Constitution of the League, regarding the method of apportioning, casting and counting the vote for chief consul and representatives, as its officers may adopt, providing only that the number of representatives so chosen shall be indicated by the membership of the division on March 1.

After considerable more discussion the board took a recess until 2.30 o'clock, and at once proceeded to the Mechanics' building, where the annual meeting of the general membership was to be held.

BUSINESS MEETING.

Immediately after the adjournment of the officers' meeting, the general meeting of the League was convened in the Mechanics' building, the small hall being used for the purpose. The hall was finely and profusely decorated with festoons of evergreen, enlivened by colored papers in Japanese designs. The attendance at this meeting was comparatively small, as might have been expected. President Beckwith called the meeting to order shortly after 11 o'clock. He explained the reasons for the small attendance, which he said was due to the attractions which the beautiful weather and inducements for a ruve offered.

President Beckwith then read his report, while A. S. Parsons took the chair.

" To enter into a detailed statement of the accounts," said Dr. Beckwith, will be an un-

dertaking too arduous to receive consideration, so it shall be omitted.

" The magnificent growth of this organization has been unprecedented in any country, and the evidences now tend to show that the cycling public is gradually conceiving the necessity and benefits which will accrue to a national assembly. There may be, perhaps, no publication which has done more to assist the L. A. W. in its successful work than the publication which has received the indorsement of the cycling world, the *Bulletin;* and while here let me say a word of respect and admiration for the secretary-editor of that sheet, to whom much of our present excellent standing is due. A year ago I took great pleasure in commending the splendid work of the Racing Board, and I called attention to the fine code of laws they had given us. They have been before us very conspicuously during the past months, and have won our thanks for their bold stand and its successful issue. The touring interests of the country have been taken under our fostering care, and that we may meet with success in the future, which the past has obtained for us, is almost certain. To-day brings us to the end of the old bicycling year and the beginning of the new, and indications to-day point to a continuance of the pleasures and success of what is now a national sport."

On motion of Mr. Jones the report was accepted and ordered printed.

The report of the Racing Board was then called for, and Chairman Abbot Bassett submitted the result of the work of that committee. The report was a complete review of the work of the board for the year, and especial prominence was given to their action in the case of the makers' amateurs. The report was too long for our columns. It will be published in the *Bulletin*, and we commend it to the attention of our readers. It contained appendixes giving lists of the suspended men, cycle records accepted by the board, League champions and championships for 1885-6, and resolutions passed by the Racing Board endorsing the action of their chairman.

Mr. Dean moved to accept the report, and also moved to have it printed in the *Bulletin*.

It was asked whether or no an acceptance of the report carried with it an adoption of the recommendations.

It was decided that to accept it merely took it from the committee. The motion of Mr. Dean prevailed.

The questions brought forward in the report were then taken up, and the first item was the action taken by the board declaring certain riders to be professionals.

Chief Council Bidwell, of New York, spoke for that State, and said it was unanimous in favor of sustaining the action of the Racing Board.

Mr. C. S. Butler, of Buffalo, said he represented a club of ninety-eight members, and by a unanimous vote they had instructed him to vote to sustain the Racing Board.

Chief Consul Ducker moved that the names of all the men on the suspended list be dropped, save William Brooks and E. E. Phillips, and the motion brought up considerable discussion.

Dr. Butler thought the action of the Racing Board should be sustained through-

out the entire list, to the exclusion of none.

Mr. Carroll, of Indiana, stated that the Indiana division had voted to uphold the action of the Racing Board, and hoped for his part that such action would be taken.

Mr. Harris favored sustaining the Racing Board, as did Mr. Cooley, of Plainfield.

Consul Ducker explained that the reason for the motion was to prevent the punishment of innocent men for the guilty; and, moreover, he added, that there were men on that suspended list who would be willing to make affidavit that they were innocent of charges preferred.

Mr. Jones asked if these men were innocent, why they had not proven so when the opportunity was given, and no satisfactory answer was given.

Consul Ducker's motion was acted upon, but the meeting almost unanimously refused to accept it; and the motion of Dr. Butler, to support the Racing Board in its action, was unanimously carried.

It was then voted unanimously that the suspension of certain members until 30 May for violation of Rule H, as ordered by the Racing Board, be approved.

The report on Rules and Regulations was then called for, and Mr. Harris announced that the committee at the present time had no report to make, as the rules were deemed sufficiently good as they now existed. The report of the Transportation Committee was then read as follows and accepted : " Our president, in his report, has referred to the number of railways over the country granting accommodations to wheelmen, but your committee would rather say that every road west of Buffalo and Pittsburg is free, and nearly east of that point as well; while others charge reasonable tariff. But one railroad in the country, which has stood out against us, withdrew from its position. Yesterday the Fitchburg road issued orders making wheels free. There is every indication that the question in New England will be speedily settled, and that bicycles be placed on the same basis as theatrical troupes." (*Laughter and much applause.*)

The Touring Board's report was also presented by Mr. Ayers, who stated that the board had completed its organization, and touring marshals had been appointed, as previously published. He also gave a brief sketch of the proposed tour next fall through the Shenandoah Valley, and briefly made some statements regarding the proposed European tour next year, and told of the elaborate preparations being made for entertainment by the Englishmen.

The report of the bookmaker showed that in Massachusetts much good work had been done by A. L. Atkins, Boston L. A. W. Consul. In Connecticut there was 6,000 copies of the road-book published, and could be obtained at reasonable sums. Satisfactory reports came from New York, Buffalo, Pennsylvania and other States. Ohio was the most important State in cycling literature this year, and her division book will prove most valuable. One thousand one hundred dollars has been spent in publications, and to meet this expense a nominal charge is made for copies. Success had rewarded the efforts of the L. A. W. men in Illinois and Minnesota, and their road-book promises to be most interesting. Indica-

tions at present point to a most successful year, and a continuance of the bureau of information.

Mr. Bassett here arose and stated that the L. A. W. ought to go on record once more; and, in order to get a definite expression on the subject, moved that it be the sense of the meeting that professional wheelmen be admitted to membership in the League.

Mr. Harris moved that the motion be laid on the table.

Mr. Bassett hoped the motion would not be disposed of in so summary a manner. He had introduced it in a spirit of fair play towards the racing men. They had repeatedly asked for some such change in the laws, and he had supposed they would be on hand to represent their side of the case at this meeting. He wanted to hear their plea.

Mr. Ducker said that the League would lose many clubs and several divisions would secede, if they could not keep these men in their ranks in some way.

Chief Consul Rogers, of Illinois, said that his State was in favor of such change as that proposed, but if it did not prevail they would stay in the League and remain loyal to it.

Mr. Harris thought the League could afford to lose any division or club that was not in sympathy with it on the amateur question. The motion to admit professionals was lost.

E. J. Shriver, of New York, moved that in order that the general body have more representation in the management of the League, that the board of officers be instructed to so amend the rules that the president and vice-president be elected by the membership at large. The motion was carried.

Rev. Mr. Gregson said that the League had voted to sustain the Racing Board, but he thought it should go farther ; and in view of the attacks that had been made on the board, he moved that a vote of thanks be given it for its faithful work. Carried.

Votes were passed thanking the Boston Club for the use of the hall, and thanking the Massachusetts and other clubs and the division for courtesies extended. Adjourned.

OFFICERS' MEETING.

In the afternoon the board of officers held its adjourned meeting at the Massachusetts Club House, with President Beckwith in the chair. The following appointments were announced and confirmed : For Representatives, New Hampshire, W. E. Stone of Concord; New York, A. B. Barkman and William W. Share of Brooklyn; Indiana, W. C. Edgerton of Fort Wayne; Massachusetts, Charles S. Howard of Boston ; Ohio, Frank S. Casselbury of Mansfield and Frank H. Chapman of Toledo; Pennsylvania, George A. Wells of Philadelphia; Missouri, Arthur Young of St. Louis ; Nebraska, Warren M. Rogers. A. A. Hathaway was confirmed as chief consul for Wisconsin. C. H. Luscomb of New York here presented the amendments which at the morning session he gave notice of, and asked that the board take action upon their adoption. W. S. Slocum of Boston rose to a point of order, stating that inasmuch as the Constitution demanded certain notice to be given of changes therein, and the required notification had not been given, the meeting had no power to act upon the amendments at that time. President Beckwith sustained the objection.

Mr. Luscomb appealed from the decision of the chair, and Mr. Dean, while admitting the appeal, thought the decision of the chair but right, and hoped that it would be sustained. The yeas and nays were called on the question, and the ballot showed that 59 had voted in favor of the chair and 9 in opposition, and the amendments were withdrawn.

On motion of Dr. Butler, the secretary's report was taken from the table and accepted. On motion of Mr. Luscomb it was voted that the necessary notification be given to the board of officers of the L. A. W. of the proposed amendments to the By-Laws ; and on motion of Mr. A. S. Parsons it was voted that the committee on rules and regulations be instructed to define the duties of chief consul. The same committee will also on motion of Mr. Bassett fully define the meaning of a League club, since the equivocal definition thereof has caused no little trouble among men and clubs. The same committee will add such articles to the present rules as will allow each small division 75 per cent of all dues, instead of the proportion of which heretofore they have been in receipt.

It was voted that consul blanks be furnished by the secretary of the L. A. W. to such chief consuls as may demand them.

The question of the election of officers was again discussed, and it was moved that the recommendation of the general meeting regulating such elections as made at the morning session be referred to the Committee on Rules and Regulations, and in supporting this action instances were cited in which, should the power of elections be taken from the board of officers and placed in the hands of the general membership, the result would be detrimental to the L. A. W.

The board, so Mr. J. S. Dean claimed, was able to give much better satisfaction than could the local ones, and the wire-pulling which must follow in the latter case, and which would hamper perhaps the election of good candidates, would be avoided.

Mr. John S. Rogers of St. Louis stated that his city would like to have the Meet next year, and that while he was not in a position to make a positive offer to that end he would make the suggestion, in the hopes that the attention of the board would be directed thereto, promising a royal good time to all who would attend. After the thanks of the board had been tendered to the Massachusetts Bicycle Club for courtesies extended, the meeting adjourned.

FRIDAY'S RUNS.

In the afternoon 150 bicyclists, in charge of Capt. Peck, of the Massachusetts Club, had a very enjoyable run to Echo Bridge. The party returned about 6 o'clock. They were delighted with the roads and the scenery. The members of the Citizens' Club, of New York, with an escort of Massachusetts men, went out to the reservoir and Newton Centre, and had a delightful time.

THE MINSTREL ENTERTAINMENT.

The amateur minstrel entertainment at Music Hall, last evening, under the auspices of the Massachusetts Division L. A. W., was a decided success. The Jeffries Club, of East Boston, constituted the talent, music being furnished by the Boston Cadet Band Orchestra, Percy C. Hayden, leader. There were fifty men in the circle, and the singing

THOMAS STEVENS writes of some of his hindrances on the road; "After the Russian minister at Teheran speaking to me so fair, after going to considerable expense and trouble to provide myself with Russian money sufficient to carry me clear through to Japan, via Merv, Samarcand and Southern Siberia, I received notice when half way to Meshed, that I would not be allowed to go through. Here, also, with 'Holy Russia' blocking my road on the one hand, I am assured on the other that I shall also be turned back at the Afghan frontier; that the Afghan government, unable to guarantee my safety, will simply turn me back. This is comforting, to say the least. I am here the guest of Mr. Gray, an English telegrapher, connected with the Afghan Boundary Commission. Knowing before the news reached me on the road that the Russians had refused to give me the road, he kindly sent a letter by the Boundary Commission courier explaining the difficulty to Col. Sir West Ridgway, and asking him to try and obtain permission for me to go through Afghanistan. The return courier with an answer is expected every day. The commission camp is some five hundred miles east of Meshed, and if no insurmountable obstacles present, I shall probably reach India, via their camp, Cabul and Peshawer. Great crowds are at this moment vociferously howling, 'Tomasha! tomasha! asp-i-awhen' (Let us see the iron horse!) on the street outside. Armed guards have just been stationed at our door by the authorities to keep off the mobs.

ST. LOUIS has commenced thus early to angle for the Meet. They may have it.

LADY cyclers will do well to examine the Jersey fitting garments advertised in another column.

THE Missouri Club opened its new house 2 June.

PITMAN was in the parade with all his medals in front. We have heard that the dazzling sight completely overcame two young ladies.

THE wheelmen were given a special invitation to attend church on Sunday by the First Baptist society.

THE Boston Club attended the Lynn races in a body, and there was a good deal of spirit manifested.

THE League is organized to protect amateur wheelmen, and it cannot countenance the action of any association that opens amateur events to professionals.

THE new Union says that it is organized merely to get the League to take a mail vote, but it declares war on the League by its every action at the outset.

WE shall have no good racing until time standards are established. Make a man run his distance within a certain time, or give no prizes.

THE Lynn track is found to be a formidable rival to Springfield, but we regret that the proprietors have taken a course to ruin its prospects.

OUR congratulations to the Presidential couple. The single tricycle must now be laid aside, and a tandem secured.

IT may not be out of place to say that the bride has had no end of Folsom praise.

was very fine. The tambos were C. P. Lovell, E. H. Close; interlocutor, Benjamin S. Palmer; bones, J. B. McCabe, T. E. Stutson; musical director, Charles C. Roby. Applause and encores were frequent. The gem of the evening was the bass solo of Mr. T. F. Murphy, "A Hundred Fathoms Deep." The lecture of Prof. P. J. B. Stutson on "Zoölogy" was simply side-splitting, and took the audience by storm. The lecturer had "lifelike" representations of animals on a chair before him, and his elucidations were thereby emphasized, enabling his hearers more readily to grasp the points presented. The jokes of the end men were well received. The banjo · quartette, — Messrs. Lansing, Grover, Paine and Chase, — were encored for their fine rendition. The German Turners gave their exhibition of complex movements on the German horse in their usual graceful and polished style, and were deservedly applauded. Their exhibition closed with a series of pyramids. The audience was large and enthusiastic.

EVENING AT THE CYCLERIES.

In the evening many of the visitors attended the exhibition in the Mechanics' building. The Salem Cadet Band furnished excellent music, and George Hutchinson gave exhibitions of his skill as a trick rider. There were two interesting races on the home trainers for a gold and silver medal. Spencer and Dresser, of the Hartford Club, and a young fellow named Alexander participated. In the first heat Dresser made the mile in 1.38, Spencer in 1.38¼, and Alexander in 1.42. In the second heat Dresser reduced his time to 1.35. Spencer made exactly the time he did in the first heat, and Alexander was three seconds slower than he was before. Mr. Dresser was awarded the gold and Spencer the silver medal.

THIRD DAY.

THE long-looked-forward-to run of the "scorchers" was started at an early hour Saturday from the Vendome Hotel. This was a run of those wheelmen who delight to rush over the roads at a break-neck pace, and some of the local flyers had announced their intention of breaking up the visitors who dared to start. Those who started were F. A. Lane and F. N. Perry of the Massachusetts Club; W. L. Orsman of the Morris Wanderers; W. T. Williams, Yantic; A. T. Lane and A. Bennet, on a tandem tricycle; W. S. Doan and W. A. Rhodes of the Dorchester Club; F. H. Keller of Richfield Springs; H. S. Wolliston and C. H. Parker of the Berkshire County Wheelmen. Away they went at a terrific pace along Commonwealth avenue and then out over the Milldam to Brighton, and thence around Chestnut Hill reservoir back to the starting point, a distance of about twelve miles. Rhodes arrived first in 44½ minutes, and Doane second, 25 seconds later.

The rest came straggling in at various distances in the rear, many sadly broken up and so tired that they could scarcely sit upon their wheels. There was only one accident on the run, but this was most unfortunate. Perry of the Massachusetts Club, while speeding through Brighton, collided with a dog who attempted to jump through the wheel, causing the rider to fall heavily

to the ground. He fell on his side and dislocated his right arm. A physician who was near by attended him, and so fixed his arm up in a sling that he was enabled to ride home on his wheel.

THE PARADE.

EARLY on the morning of Saturday the wheelmen began to assemble in numbers, and the vicinity of the Vendome was filled with people. The wheels were stacked in groups on the park and Commonwealth avenue, and Chief Marshal Beckwith and his able adjutant, George R. Bidwell, had their hands full in arranging matters. At 10.40 the line began to move.

The procession was formed according to priority of the League divisions, and the New Hampshire division, having been formed 18 Sept. 1882, was first. Following is a full list of the clubs and riders participating : —

Mounted police.
Pacemakers — C. P. White, C. A. Martin.
Chief Marshal — Dr. N. Malon Beckwith, New York.
Staff — Col. A. A. Pope, Boston ; Charles E. Pratt, Boston ; B. B. Ayres, Chicago ; Stephen Terry, Hartford ; W. I. Harris, E. G. Whitney, W. S. Slocum, Boston ; H. W. Hayes, Cambridge ; Dr. C. S. Butler, Buffalo.
Adjutant — George R. Bidwell, New York.

FIRST DIVISION.

Commander — Henry E. Ducker, of Springfield.
Aids — Dr. T. S. Rust, Meriden ; A. V. Walburg, Dorchester ; S. Rogers, St. Louis ; Dr. W. G. Kendall, Boston.

NEW HAMPSHIRE CLUBS.

Chief Consul — H. M. Bennett.
Aid — C. A. Hazlett.
Rockingham Bicycle Club, Portsmouth, 25 men, Capt. G. E. Philbrick.
Manchester Bicycle Club, 20 men, Capt. Moses Sherif.
Crescent Bicycle Club, Great Falls, 9 men, Capt. G. H. Hanson.
State Capital Wheelmen, Concord, 10 men, Capt. J. C. Estes.

MASSACHUSETTS CLUBS.

374 men. Chief Consul — Henry E. Ducker, Springfield.
Massachusetts Bicycle Club, 87 men, Capt. A. D. Peck, Jr.; 1st Lieut. H. M. Saben ; 2d Lieut. J. M. Burr. Tricycle division, Capt. J. T. Williams; 1st Lieut. W. W. Palen. Ten tricycles, four tandems. Two ladies on tricycles and three on tandems.
Springfield Bicycle Club, 22 men, Capt. A. O. McGarrett ; 1st Lieut. E. F. Leonard ; 2d Lieut. C. L. Bartlett.
Holyoke Bicycle Club, 10 men, Capt. C. Clark.
Dorchester Bicycle Club, 25 men, Capt. A. V. Walburg ; 1st Lieut. W. S. Doane ; 2d Lieut. R. E. Bellows.
Cambridge Bicyele Club, 20 men, Capt. C. L. Smith ; 1st Lieut. J. H. Grimes ; 2d Lieut. C. O. Danforth.
Knockabout Bicycle Club, Gardner, 8 men, Capt. A. F. Knowlton.
Worcester Bicycle Club, 25 men, Capt. E. F. Tolman ; 1st Lieut. G. D. Putnam ; 2d Lieut. C. Bruso.

Somerville Cycle Club, 25 men, Capt. Eugene Sanger ; 1st Lieut. George Beals ; 2d Lieut. F. A. Hobart. Three tricycles.
Columbia Bicycle Club, North Attleboro, 10 men. Capt. Fred Gorton.
Hyde Park Ramblers' Bicycle Club, 10 men, Capt. H. S. Peare.
Northampton Bicycle Club, 3 men, Capt. H. S. Campbell.
Everett Bicycle Club, 3 men, 1st Lieut. J. H. Larkin.
Chelsea Bicycle Club, 14 men, Capt. L. H. Frost ; 1st Lieut. R. E. Burnett ; 2d Lieut. W. Fracker.
Nonantum Cycling Club, Newtonville, 12 men, Capt. G. F. Williams.
Puritan Bicycle Club, Salem, 10 men, Capt. E. N. Bassett.
Brockton City Club, 6 men, Capt. D. C. Pierce.
Crescent Bicycle Club, Gloucester, 9 men, Capt. D. S. McPhee.

SECOND DIVISION.

Commander, George R. Bidwell.
Aids, Gerry Jones, Binghampton, N. Y.; W. S. Bull, Buffalo, N. Y.

NEW YORK CLUBS — 135 MEN.

George R. Bidwell, New York, Chief Consul.
Brooklyn Bicycle Club, 15 men, Capt. L. W. Slocum.
Ixion Bicycle Club, New York, 7 men, Capt. M. G. Peoli.
Long Island Wheelmen, Brooklyn, 15 men, Capt. C. H. Luscomb.
King's County Wheelmen, Brooklyn, 15 men, 1st Lieut. M. L. Bridgman.
Harlem Wheelmen, New York, 15 men, 2d Lieut. C. M. Phelps.
Mercury Wheel Club, Flushing, 4 men, Capt. A. P. Cobb.
Citizens' Bicycle Club, New York, 51 men, 1st Lieut. T. C. Smith, ten tricycles.
Syracuse Bicycle Club, 6 men, 1st Lieut. J. P. Becker.
Albany Wheelmen, 4 men, Pres. W. C. Hickox.
Yonkers Bicycle Club, 6 men, Capt. F. H. Keeler.
Troy Bicycle Club, 4 men, Raymond Coon commanding.

NEW JERSEY CLUBS — 42 MEN.

Dr. E. W. Johnson, Chief Consul, Jersey City.
Hudson County Wheelmen, Jersey City, 15 men, Capt. E. W. Johnson.
Trenton Bicycle Club, 3 men, Capt. F. N. Robinson.
Plainfield Bicycle Club, 4 men, Pres. J. H. Cooley.
East Orange Wanderers, 4 men, Capt. G. K. Wallace.
Morris Wanderers, 5 men, 1st Lieut. A. B. Osmun.
Elizabeth Wheelmen, 4 men, Capt. L. K. Hazard.

PENNSYLVANIA CLUBS — 25 MEN.

Philadelphia Bicycle Club, 8 men, Capt. J. E. Bartol.
Pennsylvania Bicycle Club, 9 men, Capt. J. A. Wells.
Williamsport Bicycle Club, 8 men, 1st Lieut. I. A. Dayton.
Wellsboro' Wheelmen, 7 men, Capt. Frank A. Davis.

CONNECTICUT CLUBS.

Waterbury Wheel Club, 8 men, Capt. L. A. White, one lady.
Hartford Wheel Club, 22 men, Capt. L. A. Tracy; 1st Lieut. E. N. Way. Three Stars and two tricycles.
Connecticut Bicycle Club, Hartford, 12 men, Capt. F. R. Way.
Pequannock Bicycle Club, Bridgeport, 16 men, Capt. F. A. Smith.
New London County Wheelmen, 5 men, Capt. Fred Williams.
Meriden Wheel Club, 7 men, 1st Lieut, J. F. Ives.
New Haven Bicycle Club, 7 men, Capt. W. H. Hale.
Elm City Wheel Club, New Haven, 2 men, Capt. S. C. Sperry.

RHODE ISLAND CLUBS — 24 MEN.

Bristol County Wheelmen, Bristol, 10 men, Capt. A. B. Staples.
Providence Bicycle Club, 14 men, Capt. O. M. Mitchell.

OTHER CLUBS.

New Orleans Bicycle Club, 4 men, Capt. C. M. Fairchild.
Baltimore Cycle Club, 4 men, Capt. J. F. Baetjir.

THIRD DIVISION.

Commander, Will R. Pitman, of New York.
Aids, A. B. Barker, East Bridgewater; F. O. Swallow, Westboro'.
Portland Wheel Club, Portland, Me., 20 men, Capt. H. S. Higgins; 1st Lieut. W. W. Beckett.
Maynard (Mass.) Bicycle Club, 6 men, Capt. J. E. Denniston.
Pawtucket Wheel Club, Haverhill, 3 men, 1st Lieut. Guptil.
East Bridgewater Wheelmen, 3 men, Pres. A. B. Parker.
Florence Bicycle Club, 7 men, Pres. A. G. Hill.
Representatives of the Indianapolis, East Cambridge, Bangor, Augusta, Mt. Kilburn, Wilkesbarre, Pa., Walton, N. Y., Fort Wayne, Ind., South Framingham, Racine, Wis., and other clubs.

The route over which the wheelmen passed was a long one. It would be impossible to estimate the total number of people who viewed the parade. It is safe to say that there were at least 20,000 in the throng.

Passing down Chester Park to Harrison avenue, the route then lay over the following streets: Through East Concord to James, thence through West Newton to Columbus avenue. No better position could be found from which to view the parade than here, and hundreds availed themselves of the opportunity. The sidewalks were packed by enthusiastic crowds, and the applause was long and frequent.

The parade proceeded up Columbus avenue as far as Dartmouth street, where they crossed over to Beacon, and proceeded as far as the Perkins on Brighton avenue, where hundreds of cyclists wheeled into the beautiful grounds and dismounted preparatory to the taking of a photograph.

The photographic ordeal having been safely passed, the cyclists gave a lusty shout and scampered up the hill, where a collation had been prepared for them.

The number of machines in the parade, as shown by the checking of three cyclists, which is as nearly exact as could be practically made under the circumstances, was 711, fifty of that number being tricycles.

THE RACES.

THE races were not altogether satisfactory. There was a feeling among the members of the Racing Board that since Boston had no good track it would be folly to give a race meeting, but there was a demand for this kind of entertainment, and they determined to do the best they could under the circumstances. Three hundred dollars was spent to put the track in order, and then it was very far from satisfactory. The results of the races were: —

One-Mile Novice. — Chas. A. Stenken (1), 3.17¼; Harry S. Caldwell (2), 3.18.

One-Mile L. A. W. Championship. — A. B. Rich (1), 3.26; Taylor Boggis (2), 3.27¼; J. R. Rheubottom (3). C. E. Kluge and Geo. E. Weber were entered for this race, but their entries were rejected by the Racing Board. This was the first time the new rule was enforced. The board reserves the right to reject any or all entries to its championships without giving a reason to the public for so doing. When the entries for this and the tricycle championship came before the board, they scratched the names of these two men for reasons discussed among themselves, but which will not be made public.

One-Mile Tricycle L. A. W. Championship. — A. B. Rich (1), 4.6; T. Fahy (2), 4.13⅓.

This race was run in three heats. The first heat was contested by T. Fahy, New Britain, Conn., Charles H. Potter, Cleveland, and John T. Williams, Boston. The heat was a procession for three laps, when the men bunched, and in trying to spurt to the lead Williams lost his steering and ran into the fence, throwing him from his machine. The other two continued on, followed by Williams, who had pluckily remounted and was speeding on a hopeless chase. Fahy won. Williams entered a protest of foul against the other two men, and it was allowed so far as to permit him to ride in the final heat, but this he did not care to do.

The second heat was between A. B. Rich, of Brooklyn, and C. O. Danforth, of Cambridge. The latter spurted on the second lap, and won handily in 1.42½; Danforth, 2.45⅗. Rich and Fahy were the competitors in the final heat.

One-Mile Handicap. — H. C. Getchell (1), 3.1¼; G. E. Weber, scratch (2), 3.7½.

One-Mile Mass. Championship. — H. C. Getchell (1), 3.19; F. G. Gibbs (2), 3.22½.

There were on the programme two invitation races. The committee put these on out of compliment to the suspended riders, and they were invited to compete. Rowe, Hendee, Knapp and Rhodes entered, but only the latter appeared. He was allowed to run a mile for each event, and took the two prizes in 3.17¾ and 3.20½. The officers of the meeting were: —

Referee. — N. M. Beckwith.
Judges. — A. D. Peck, Jr., Massachusetts Club; Stephen Terry, Hartford; George D. Gideon, Philadelphia.
Starter. — H. E. Ducker, Springfield.
Scorer. — C. E. Bassett, Chelsea.
Clerk. — A. L. Atkins.
Assistant Clerk. — H. L. Hiscock.
Umpires. — C. S. Howard, W. G. Kendall, E. W. Hodgkins, H. W. Hayes.
Timers. — E. E. Merrill, J. E. Savelle, George E. Butler.

THE BANQUET.

ONE hundred and fifty wheelmen sat down to the annual banquet of the L. A. W. at eight o'clock Saturday evening in the grand banquet hall of the Hotel Vendome. An excellent repast, which included Boston baked beans, was thoroughly enjoyed, and when the smoke began to curl upwards, President Beckwith rapped the wheelmen to order, and introduced Mr. Charles E. Pratt, of Boston, as toastmaster. Mr. Pratt said this was his fifth term in that position. After a short speech on the progress of wheeling, he announced the first toast: "The United States, a country slow to adopt, but foremost to carry on the interest of the favorite recreation." The orchestra and guests responded with "America." "The Commonwealth and Boston" was responded to very ably by Mr. W. S. Slocum, of the Massachusetts Club. He said he hoped the time would come when the State would make each town in it liable for accidents to wheelmen who got "headers" on account of bad roads. He referred to the wonderful progress made in getting wheelmen right of way on the thoroughfares of the State, and gave Mr. Pratt much of the credit for it. He told an amusing story of an early tour into New Hampshire. He came to a toll-bridge, and the tollman had never seen a bicycle before. The rider asked the rate of toll, and after looking bewildered for some time, he finally exclaimed: "By gosh, I hain't got you on the list." A Cambridge quartet sang "The Welcome Guest" very sweetly. Its members were G. Frank Monroe, W. L. McDonald, B. F. Gilbert, and F. L. Pratt. President Beckwith then made a speech, giving a history of the League and a eulogy of the handsome appearance of its members. Mr. C. K. Munro, the first commander of the League, responded to the toast to the past officers in a happy speech, and Mr. Abbot Bassett spoke for the Racing Board. Col. Pope gave his views on the makers' amateur question; and Mr. Stephen Terry, of Hartford, told the company that he could not run for president because he was not big enough to ride a 62-inch wheel. Mr. George T. Wilson, of the Citizens' Club, of New York, responded to the toast to the ladies in an address that enlivened the proceedings very much. He quoted freely from Shakespeare and Pope's calendar, and did his subjects full justice. Mr. McDonald, of Cambridge, sang a Scotch song, and there was more instrumental music by Mr. Yungeling, of the Citizens' Club, which did a great deal toward making the evening pass pleasantly. The party broke up a little before midnight, having enjoyed a delightful entertainment. On behalf of the League, Mr. Beckwith extended thanks to the hospitable entertainers belonging to local clubs.

THE CYCLERIES.

ONE of the very attractive features of the Meet was the "Cycleries," an exhibition of cycles made under the auspices of the

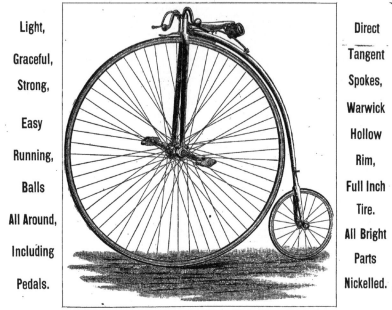

Boston Club at the Mechanics' building. The display was a remarkable one, considering the present condition of cycle manufacturing in this country and the small number of American manufacturers; for it evinces not only the rapid growth of the trade here, but also the marked improvement in styles and methods, and promptness and enterprise on the part of our makers in meeting the demands of experienced riders for first-class machines. A few years since no home manufacturer could be so bold as to claim equality for his machines with the best of foreign importations; but now, although English cycles are much improved and still improving over those of three years since, connoisseurs find it hard to determine in what they are superior over those of native manufacture, so perfect in all points have the latter become.

The hall, especially in the evening, presented a most picturesque appearance under the glare of the electric light, and the bright nickel-plated trimmings of the hundreds of machines sparkled like diamonds. Around the hall underneath the galleries were arranged show-cases filled with lawn tennis outfits, bicycle accoutrements, amateur photographers' outfits, and everything that a lover of the phantom steed could possibly connect with his riding trips into the country. From gallery to gallery across the hall were stretched signs bearing the names of the different exhibitors; while around the sides of the galleries were hung painted banners, cards, etc, bearing the legends "Star," "Rudge," "Humber," and a variety of colored cards got up in beautiful arabesque designs announcing the name of this or that machine.

The ladies present were especially interested in the tricycles, and asked as many questions and displayed as much business tact in their inquiries as did the old veterans of the wheel.

On entering the hall, the first exhibit encountered was that of the Pope Manufacturing Company, in charge of Mr. A. L. Atkins. A full line of the company's various styles of Columbia machines were shown,— bicycles of every style, the lightest of which weighing twenty-two and a half pounds, while the heaviest tips the scales at forty-nine pounds, and several makes of tricycles weighing from forty-seven to ninety pounds. First to catch our eye was the new Ladies' Columbia two-track tricycle, which was shown for the first time. This has been described at length in our columns. It is fitted with a new steering device which is operated by a screw, prompt to act and noiseless. The machine scales 68½ lbs. Then there was the new 1886 Racer bicycle, weighing but 22½ lbs., built for W. A. Rowe, the world's record holder, and having tangent spokes and cow-horn handle-bar. The Columbia safety, a new pattern of the Kangaroo, was also here. It has 42-inch wheels, and its special feature is, that it can be readily adjusted to fit any person by a simple method of detaching or adding a section of the gear chain. This particular machine was built for George M. Hendee. The Columbia racer that Rowe made his remarkable records on last year was also on exhibition here, and the company intend keeping it as a souvenir of those events. Then there was, besides, the new semi-

roadster bicycle, a fine style of wheel; a racing tricycle for Hendee, together with a full line of 1885 experts, as well as the light roadster of this year, direct-spoke roadsters, and several styles of Standard Columbias, and the regular three-track tricycle. An Expert fitted with Yost & McCune's clutch drew considerable notice from riders.

An interesting feature was the display of separate parts of the cycles in their rough and finished form. The number of parts in a single machine is shown to be about 184.

Gormully & Jeffery's exhibit was in charge of Edwin Oliver. They showed an assortment of their wheels, including the Champion, the Challenge, the Ideal and the American Safety. The machines for this exhibit were taken from the stocks of dealers in town, and the firm tried to do no more than show a line of their regular goods.

The Coventry Machinists' Company, H. W. Gaskell, agent, showed a fine lot of various styles and grades of the famous Club machines, among which may be mentioned, of tricycles, the convertible tandem, the ladies' tandem, the ordinary Club tandem, fitted with automatic steering, the Marlboro' tandem, a fine double, with the bicycle automatic steering, and weighing but 111 lbs., the Imperial central-gear club for ladies, a beautiful mount, with 42-inch wheels, the celebrated Ranelagh club, a favorite machine this year, and weighing but 68 lbs., the Marlboro' racer and roadster, the Sandringham and others.

During the progress of the show, Mr. Gaskell received a new Marlboro' Club tricycle that bids fair to be a very popular lady's machine. It is built on the Cripper lines, but avoids two faults of that machine. A spring at the bottom of the forks absorbs vibration from the front wheel; and then, by pressing a lever the inclined steering-bar can be pulled to an upright position, which allows plenty of room for the lady to mount from the front. When the bar is upright the brake is on, and the machine is held firmly in place. A very large number of orders were taken for this wheel. This exhibit was the most attractive at the cycleries, for the wheels were on a slightly elevated platform which was covered with red cambric, against which the machines showed to great advantage. A number of plants in pots set off the exhibit and made it especially attractive.

The Overman Wheel Company made an excellent exhibit of its bicycle, but had no tricycles on view. The new lantern made by the company was also shown, and also Foote's Anti-Header. C. R. Overman was in charge.

Wm. B. Everett & Co. showed some of the finest wheels ever manufactured, both in quality and finish, from the ordinary roadsters to the lightest and most graceful light roadsters, both bicycles and tricycles.

The Apollo ordinary bicycle, a standard mount and a great favorite, is this year fitted with cow-horn handle-bars bent backwards, so as to enable the rider to get a powerful strain on hill or rough road work. There were several handsome racers of this pattern in the exhibit; and here also was the machine John S. Prince made his Minneapolis record on, the tire showing the effects of his work on a board track. The Xtraordinary Safety was also seen, and

one of these is soon to be fitted with the Cripto two-speed gear. Of tricycles, Mr. Everett shows the Traveller Tandem, the Singer Straight Steerer, with four bearings on the axle, and weighing but seventy-five pounds, the same machine Crocker won the race at Corey Hill with, the Carrier tricycle, and several other notable mounts. He also shows a new Singer Challenge of a cheaper grade than the ordinary, but fitted with all the improvements of the first-class machine,— a fine wheel. This exhibit was in charge of Gideon Haynes.

William Read & Sons, agents for the Royal Mail bicycles and tricycles, showed a good variety of that excellent make of machine. A racing two-track tricycle, weighing only forty-eight pounds, with hollow rims and tangent spokes, was much admired by the fast riders, and we also saw the two-track double-steering Royal Mail Tandem. This machine is fitted with adjustable saddles, especially adapted for two ladies, and the double steering is operated in a similar manner to the well-known Coventry Rotary; except that the steering wheels are on opposite lines. The original Kangaroo Safety was shown here, also, with a full line of racers and roadsters. W. S. Atwell had charge of this display.

Stoddard, Lovering & Co., one of the earliest and still the largest cycle importing house in the country, and the agents for the Rudge machines, gave a showing that in quality was second to none in the exhibition, although not so numerically large as it was complete. They also showed a good line of tricycles, both two and three track, and the Humber tandem.

One other large manufacturing concern was represented here by W. W. Stall, with a fine exhibit, namely, the H. B. Smith Machine Company, makers of the American Star. Star bicycles of all sizes and qualities, were presented here, and their excellent finish and fine mechanical construction were as attractive to the uninitiated as to the bicyclers themselves. Here was also shown the pretty little Cripper that Mr. Stall has just built for his wife. This machine weighs but fifty pounds, has many novel features designed and applied by Mr. Garrood, and it is the object of much favorable comment.

S. T. Clark & Co., of Baltimore, showed the New Rapid. This machine was admired by good judges, and none but favorable comment was heard. It has the true tangent spokes, and no stronger wheel of the same weight can be found.

McCoy & Williams, of Newark, N. J., agents for the Sparkbrook Manufacturing Company, and Wright, Ditson & Co., of Boston, had a good show of various athletic goods.

Fred Jenkins, of New York, had a stand to show the Excelsior cyclometer, a good and standard record keeper.

A. G. Spalding & Co. had a full line of the popular Beeston Humbers, and also showed the Spalding.

J. A. R. Underwood made an exhibit of the Quadrant and the Rover Safety.

E. P. Howe, of Northboro, had his new lever tricycle on view, and the American tricycle, made with a clutch, was also shown.

Messrs. Ducker & Goodman had on sale a neat little book, gotten up especially for wheelmen. It contains a collection of

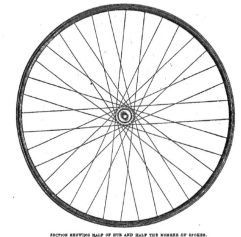

forty-nine fine lithograph portraits of the leading lights in the bicycle fraternity, a history of the L. A. W., hints on training, touring, racing, and a thousand other bits of information invaluable to all lovers of the wheel.

A unique and attractive feature of the show was a collection of old-style cycles and velocipedes which the Boston Club had got together, and gave a deal of amusement to the riders of the modern wheel.

Here was the original Lallement velocipede, which is always an interesting object. A tricycle of 1861, a quaint old vehicle, with wheels like those of a road wagon, made by Mr. Boynton, of Hartford, Ct., was put on exhibition by the Overman Wheel Company. Another machine, made by the same gentleman in 1868, showed that he had progressed somewhat as an inventor. A machine with two wheels, made in 1868 by the Ames Plow Company, came a little nearer to the modern machine; and one imported from Paris in 1869, at a cost of $165, was only superior to it in point of finish. Mr. E. R. Frost loaned the foreign article to the exhibition. Then there was an old tricycle that was propelled by rowing machine motions, and next to it one of the first Standard Columbias, which had been sold twelve times for an aggregate of $532.50. An Expert Columbia, ridden 6,756 miles by Mr. Hugh J. High, was an object of much curiosity, as were also the machines ridden recently to Boston from New Orleans.

The cycling papers had stands, and the *World*, the *Wheel*, the *Cyclist and Athlete*, the *Star Advocate* and the CYCLE had representatives.

The display of cycling accessories was very large, and nearly every saddle, bell, whistle or lamp known to the trade was shown.

FROM A FEMININE POINT OF VIEW.

MY dear friend "Minimum" was with us on our delightful run held on the first day of the Meet, and this is the way she writes of it in the journal with which she is connected :—

"Of the twenty-seven women who met at the Hotel Vendome on Thursday morning for the tricycle ride to the Chestnut Hill reservoir, nearly all were fairly strong riders, all were enthusiastic, and three were beautiful. It was an interesting sight to a spectator in a Commonwealth avenue window as the procession rode away. There were thirteen men in the party, and the riders went in single file until they got out of town; but as soon as they broke up into little groups of twos and threes, and rode at a leisurely pace for three or four miles, when six of the forty riders left the rest and rode across to wait at the Faneuil House, while the others went on to ride around the Chestnut Hill reservoir, before coming down to dine at the hotel. It threatened rain after the two o'clock dinner, and the riders dispersed, going to Boston, Cambridge and Newton."

WE had a very delightful run, albeit we had to make long halts for the weaker riders to catch up. Some of the party fretted at this delay, for they wanted to "scorch," as the men call it; but for myself I find more pleasure in the society of my friends than in hard riding, and I hope I shall never be

guilty of running away from a friend let her ride never so slow.

WE were not a little disappointed to think that several ladies who wanted to go could not do so for want of machines. Many of the visitors did not receive their wheels from the depot till the afternoon, and they were forced to stay at home.

THE second day we went to Cambridge to see "Minimum" at the Harvard Annex. We were late at the rendezvous under the Washington Elm, and lost not a little time in hunting up our friends who were to meet us. After looking about a little at Harvard we bade adieu to those of our party who were content with the run to Cambridge, and we wheeled over to Watertown and Newtonville. At the latter place we were entertained at the rooms of the Nonantum Club, and our photographer took a picture of us. Some twenty ladies were with us the second day, and of these many were new friends made since the day before.

THIS in brief is the story of the ladies' gathering. It is not much when held up to the light of day, but behind it there is much that the public has no interest in. On my list of friends there are many new names which I value highly, and in my memory there dwells the recollection of many golden hours of enjoyment spent with these new people to whom I have been drawn by a common interest in the wheel. New Jersey sent us a large contingent, and from Philadelphia came the champion and his lovely wife. We were all drawn to the bright-faced little lady from Portland, and the brother and sister from Connecticut excited our admiration as specimens of physical grace and beauty.

I ALWAYS enjoy a good thing, even if it is at my own expense; and I want to assure my friends that I had several quiet laughs when I found myself upon a tandem for these occasions. I have said not a little anent the sociable and the tandem in the past, and have been set down as an enemy to the latter; but now that I am riding one perhaps the impression will be removed. Mr. Tandemon did not join us, and therefore could not laugh at me as he surely would had he been there.

I CAN well believe that our visitors enjoyed their visit. Surely we enjoyed them. And I hope that future meetings of this kind will see the ladies in greater force and in the enjoyment of greater pleasure even than Boston gave to them.

DAISIE.

THE AMERICAN CYCLISTS' UNION.

THE outgrowth of the vexed amateur question is the American Cyclists' Union. As a result of the feeling against the action of the League at the annual meeting, a meeting of nineteen members of the Springfield, Lynn, and Nonantum cycling clubs was held at the Hotel Vendome Saturday morning. Chief Consul Ducker of Springfield presided, and Capt. A. O. McGarrett of the Springfield Club was chosen temporary secretary. It was voted to form an association to protect the racing men and promote the interests of cycling. The name American Cyclists' Union was adopted. The fol

lowing definition of an amateur was adopted : "An amateur is any person who has never raced or exhibited his skill for public or private stake or for a purse or gate money, or contested under a false name, or has backed or allowed himself to be backed in a public race." A committee of four, consisting of E. G. Gordon, Lynn; J. H. Lewis, Newtonville; H. E. Ducker and A. O. McGarrett, Springfield, was appointed to draft a constitution and by-laws. The meeting adjourned, subject to the call of the chairman.

Chief Consul Ducker says : "You know how affairs stand at the present time. The L. A. W. has sustained the action of the Racing Board, and a large number of the best racers are debarred from the track. Many of us think that so important a question should be decided by a mail vote, and with that end in view thirty of us have signed a petition by which the president is obliged so to put it. The members are given thirty days to vote, and it will be nearly if not quite two months before the result is known. Meanwhile racing for this season at least will be killed. With the idea of averting this we have formed what is to be known as the American Cyclists' Union. This organization is at present only temporary in its features, but it will be placed on such a firm basis that should the mail vote sustain the annual meeting it can easily be made permanent. If the suspended and expelled men are received back, our object of formation is at an end. If, on the other hand, they fail of readmission, we propose to furnish them an opportunity to race. The purpose of the new organization is the fostering of racing.

We propose to recognize only two classes —amateurs and professionals ; there can be no intermediate class. Our division will be as strict as that of the League, only we intend every man shall have a fair trial and hearing. The rules under which we shall act will be those of the N. C. U. of England. These are virtually those of the L. A. W., except Rule 8, which will define as an amateur any man who has not raced for a purse or gate money, or set pace for a professional, or raced in the interest of bookmakers ; but in all probability we shall allow him to receive reasonable expenses. Our means of testing a man's strength will be by his record; and class races will be the standard, a record made at any time barring a party forever from competing in a class below it. The new association starts off very auspiciously, and the clubs which have already joined include the Springfield, Hartford, Meriden, Lynn, and Nonantum. We do not consider that we are in the least conflicting with the League, except on this one question of racing, and as we are perfectly free to join any association that we desire, our present relations and standing in the League will not in any way be jeopardized.

CYCLETS.

1886.

BOSTON.

LEAGUE of American Wheelmen.

WOUND up for another year.

THE amateur rule stays just where it is.

AND the professionals stay just where they are.

THEY had no friends to speak for them.

WHERE was the Down-with-the-Racing-Board party?

IT was a one-sided fight, and there was not enough talk to make things lively.

WE would like to have some of our contemporaries read over their files, and ask themselves what impression they have made on voters. Not a single vote against the board.

STALL had a bicycle circus on view. A horizontal bar was rigged between two Star bicycles, and on this a clown performed antics in the parade and about the streets.

NEW HAMPSHIRE turned out well. She sent a large delegation to represent her at the right of the line.

COL. POPE received the Citizens' Club of New York at his residence on Commonwealth avenue on Thursday evening.

"TOM OF GARVEY'S" the cycling instructor and trainer, is now at Bidwell's, N. Y. City.

PATENTS.

LIST of cycle patents granted this week: A. W. McClure, Chicago Ill., velocipede; C. T. Ryland Jr., San José, Cal, velocipede; H. G. Sellman, South Lyons, Mich., wrench.

L. E. C. W.

THE annual meet of the L. E. C. W. was held at Lynn, on Monday, 31 May. The business meeting was held in Mechanics' Hall at 10 o'clock.

The president laid before the wheelmen the treasurer's report, which showed that $48 had come in from new members; and after $71 had been expended, over $70 remained in the treasury. These gentlemen were elected by acclamation to office for the ensuing league year: President, E. G. Gordon of Lynn; vice-president, T. S. Webb of Lawrence; corresponding secretary, Arthur W. Webb of Salem; recording secretary, Gardner Hathaway of Marblehead; treasurer, G. Chinn of Marblehead. It was decided to reduce the quorum from 50 to 30, and thanks were extended to retiring officers. Then the whole body went over to Monroe street and sat down to a repast. When the tables were cleared they gave three cheers for the caterer, and went back to Market street to form the county parade. This was soon done, for the effort to get all the wheelmen into line was abandoned. Mr. E. L. Story of the Lynn Club was officer of the day, and had as aids W. G. Foster, Frank West, F. L. Tupper and Frank Winship. The Lynn Club, 20 strong, in charge of Captain George E. Butler, led the line, and the Boscobel Club of Lynn, 35 strong, under Captain Robert Herron, rode next, looking very trim in their neat fitting suits of blue. Fourteen men of Capt. Williams' Beverly Club, twenty from Capt. D. E. Hunter's Salem Club, twelve from Capt. Lloyd's Peabody Club, two from Melrose and eight from Capt. Dole's Haverhill Club, six from Capt. Knight's Amesbury Club, six from Capt. A. M. Tracy's Lawrence Club, six from Capt. Sherman's Lowell Club, nine from Capt. Shirley's Marblehead Club and twenty unattached wheelmen completed the column. They rode through the principal streets under the gaze of many admiring eyes, and got through in time to prepare for the races, which were the event of the day.

[OFFICIAL NOTICE.]

OFFICE OF THE RACING BOARD,
BOSTON, 31 May, 1886.

FOR competing with professionals for a prize in a public race at Lynn, Mass., this day, the following wheelmen are hereby declared to be professionals:—

Charles E. Kluge, New York.
George E. Weber, Smithville, N. J.
Charles E. Whitten, Lynn, Mass.

Amateur wheelmen are warned against competing with these parties. This notice carries with it expulsion from the League, if the parties be members. Mr. Kluge placed his resignation in the hands of the chairman of this board before he lost his status, and although it should have gone elsewhere to comply with our rules, the board recognizes the action as evidence of good faith, and they will recommend to the proper officials that he be entered on the books as having resigned.

ABBOT BASSETT, *Chairman.*

OFFICE OF THE RACING BOARD,
BOSTON, 31 May, 1886.

FOR competing in races held under rules other than those of the L. A. W. at Lynn, 31 May, 1886, the following parties are suspended from the race track for thirty days from date:—

Geo. W. Porter, Lynn, Mass.
F. B. Kimball, West Somerville, Mass.
Chas. E. Tracy, Waltham, Mass.
A. E. Jacobs, Boston, Mass.
Chas. A. Stenken, Jersey City, N. J.
A. D. Grover, East Boston, Mass.
F. B. Brigham, North Attleboro', Mass.
H. C. Getchell, Cambridge, Mass.

Wheelmen are warned not to compete with these parties, under penalty of suspension from the track, for such a time as the Racing Board thinks adequate to the offence.

ABBOT BASSETT,
Chairman.

OFFICE OF THE RACING BOARD,
BOSTON, 31 May, 1886.

THE board desires to call special attention to the following rule made by the board for the protection of amateur wheelmen:—

A. Any amateur wilfully competing at races not stated to be held and actually held under the rules of the board, or rules approved by the board, shall be liable to suspension from the race track for such a time as the Racing Board may determine; and amateurs are notified that to compete against any rider who has been suspended will render them liable to the same penalty.

The board has had little occasion to enforce this in the past, for all promoters of race meetings have adopted its rules; but, now that another society has been formed, it has become necessary to protect amateur wheelmen, and we issue this as a note of warning to wheelmen, to clubs, and to race committees. Wheelmen are cautioned not to enter races unless it is clearly stated that they are held under League rules; and promoters of race meetings are notified that unless they state clearly that their races are to be held under League rules, the board will consider that they are held under other rules and act accordingly.

ABBOT BASSETT,
Chairman.

THE American Rudge has not lost its great prestige, as is easily proven by the number Stoddard, Lovering & Co. are daily shipping to all parts of the United States.

THOSE who predicted that the Safety was a thing of the past, would be surprised at the way the Rudge Safety is holding its own with both old and new riders.

EVERY one should have their machine in the best possible condition. This can be done by using a bottle of Ardill's Liquid Enamel; price, seventy-five cents. Stoddard, Lovering & Co., Agents, 152–158 Congress street, Boston.

THE PATH.

LYNN, MASS., 31 May. — The new track at Lynn was inaugurated to-day, and a large crowd of interested spectators was present. The association announced that its races would be run under the rules of the American Cyclists' Union, and many entrants refused to compete. The track was in fine condition, and justified all the praises that have been bestowed upon it. Many of the officers of the day refused to serve when it was announced that other than League rules would be used, and it was very difficult to find out the names of those on duty. The races resulted as follows:—

One-Mile Professional. — Wm. A. Rowe (1), $3.18\frac{3}{5}$; Chas. E. Kluge (2), $3.18\frac{4}{5}$; E. P. Burnham (3), Geo. E. Weber. This was announced as an amateur race, but the names of both amateurs and professionals appeared in the list of entrants. There were twelve entries, and four men only appeared at the scratch. Kluge and Weber lost their status in this race.

Three-Mile 9.45 *Class.* — L. E. C. W. Chas. E. Whitten (1), $9.43\frac{3}{5}$; G. W. Porter (2), $9.47\frac{3}{5}$. Five entries and two starters.

Two-Mile Tricycle, Professional. — E. P. Burnham (1), $7.42\frac{1}{5}$; Geo. M. Hendee (2). Hendee's tricycle became disarranged in the steering gear, and he ran off the embankment on the last lap. Eight entries and two starters.

One-Mile 3.20 *Class.* — Charles E. Whitten (1), $2.51\frac{4}{5}$; H. C. Getchell (2), $2.52\frac{1}{2}$; Chas. A. Stenken (3); Chas. E. Tracy (4); F. B. Kimball (5); A. D. Grover (6); A. E. Jacobs (7); F. B. Brigham (0). Seventeen entries and eight starters. A very close race between Whitten and Getchell.

Three-Mile Lap Race, Professional. — G. E. Weber (1), 14 points; W. F. Knapp (2), 13 points. No time was announced. There were ten entries and two starters.

Five-Mile Professional. — Geo. M. Hendee (1), $18.37\frac{2}{5}$; Chas. E. Kluge (2), $18.39\frac{3}{5}$. There were eight entries and two starters. The men ran a lap over the distance owing to an error in scoring.

Five-Mile Professional. — John S. Prince (1), $19.29\frac{4}{5}$; R. A. Neilson (2), 19.30. This was the first race in the series of three for the professional championship of America. It was the slowest kind of a waiting race, and the crowd was incensed at the riders. It was announced after the race that the ten mile race, which is to run 17 June, would have as a condition, that the distance must be run in 32 minutes. Time, by miles, scored by Prince — 4.11, 7.57, 12.2, 16.3, $19.29\frac{4}{5}$.

Three-Mile Handicap. — Charles E.

Whitten, four hundred and fifty yards (1), 9.40⅘; E. P. Burnham, scratch (2); C. E. Kluge, scratch (3).

On the fourth lap they turned into the homestretch about together. Kluge, when spurting, has a tendency to wild steering, and just at this point he made an effort to get a lead. He was in the inside position, and his wheel caught Rowe's, throwing both riders. In falling they also brought down Knapp and Burnham. The men and machines were piled up together on the track, and in an instant the spectators had closed in on them like an excited mob. Kluge got his machine out, and walked with it down the track past the judges. Burnham seized Rowe's machine and rode off on it. Rowe was badly shaken up, and was n't fit to resume, even if he had been able to find a machine to carry him, which he was n't. By this time Whitten had got a full lap in advance of Burnham, and when the latter had made another lap, Kluge remounted and resumed the race. Knapp was carried off the field. He thought he was dangerously injured, but soon recovered sufficiently to start for the city. Rowe, Kluge and Burnham were all badly scratched and bruised.

A Mr. Marshall, of Beverly, gave a very good exhibition of fancy riding, and rode on a unicycle to beat the record of four minutes. His time was 4.51.

Among the entrants for the races were Charles H. Potter and Taylor Boggis, of Cleveland. They entered with the understanding that all entries would be received, subject to the decision of the L. A. W. When the Lynn Association determined to disregard that decision, they immediately entered suit, and the box receipts were attached on Monday for $500 in behalf of Mr. Potter, and $300 in behalf of Mr. Boggis. The treasurer met the attachments by depositing the amount with the officer.

COMING EVENTS.

June.

5 Saturday. — Games of the Staten Island Athletic Club. Spring games of Montreal A. A., three-mile bicycle race.
11 Friday. — First day of race meeting at New Haven, by Yale College Club.

12 Saturday. — Second day of race meeting at New Haven by Yale College Club.
N. Y. and N. J. Road Race Association team race, at Orange, N. J.
17 Thursday. — Second Prince-Neilson race at Lynn.
19 Saturday. — Annual Championships of N. A. A. A. A. at New York.
Annual race meeting of K. C. W. at Brooklyn, N. Y.
24 Thursday. — Annual meet of the Michigan Div. L. A. W. at Detroit. Ten-mile National Championship.

July.

1 Thursday. — First day of annual meeting of C. W. A. at Montreal.
2 Friday. — Second day of annual meeting of C. W. A. at Montreal.
3 Saturday. — Third day of annual meeting of C. W. A. at Montreal.
Suffolk Wheel Clubs' three days' tour begins.
5 Monday. — Race meeting at Binghamton, N. Y.
15 to 18, Tuesday to Friday. — Tournament at Columbus, Ga. State championships will be run.

MISCELLANEOUS

The Cycle.

VOL. I, No. 11.   BOSTON, MASS., 11 JUNE, 1886.   FIVE CENTS.

The Coventry Machinists' Co.'s New Tricycle for 1886.

The First Hollow-Forked, Ball-Bearing Bicycles manufactured in this country
were made in 1878, by Thos. B. Jeffery, who superintends
the mechanical department of the firm of

GORMULLY & JEFFERY,

CHICAGO, ILL.,

MAKERS OF THE

AMERICAN CYCLES

Mr. Jeffery also made the first tricycle at about the same period,
and has been making Cycles ever since. If experience
is the best teacher, surely the American Cycles,
which to-day combine his long experience and many inventions,
are the best.

PRETTIEST CATALOG IN THE TRADE FREE.

THE CYCLE

PUBLISHED EVERY FRIDAY BY ABBOT BASSETT, 22 SCHOOL ST., ROOM 19.

VOL. I.　　　　　　BOSTON, MASS., 11 JUNE, 1886.　　　　　　NO. 11.

TERMS OF SUBSCRIPTION.

One Year, by mail, post-paid..........................$1.50
Three Copies in one order.............................3.00
Club Subscriptions....................................1.00
Six Months..90
Single Copies...05

Specimen Copies free.

Every bicycle dealer is agent for the CYCLE and authorized to receive subscriptions at regular rates. The paper can be found on sale at the following places: —

Boston, CUPPLES, UPHAM & Co., cor. Washington and School Streets. Tremont House news stand. At every cycle warehouse.

New York, ELLIOTT MASON, 12 Warren Street.

Philadelphia, H. B. HART, 811 Arch Street. GEORGE D. GIDEON, 6 South Broad Street.

Baltimore, S. T. CLARK & Co., 4 Hanover Street.

Chicago, W. M. DURELL, 115 Wabash Avenue. JOHN WILKINSON & Co., 77 State Street.

Washington, H. S. OWEN, Capital Cycle Co.

St. Louis, ST. LOUIS WHEEL Co., 1121 Olive Street.

ABBOT BASSETT ． ． ． ． EDITOR

A. MUDGE & SON, PRINTERS, 24 FRANKLIN ST., BOSTON.

All communications should be sent in not later than Tuesday, to ensure insertion the same week.

Entered at the Post-office as second-class mail matter.

THE A. C. U.

HENRY E. DUCKER, of Springfield, has forwarded the following communication for publication, addressed to the wheelmen of America: —

Whereas, the arbitrary action of the Racing Board, L. A. W., in expelling certain wheelmen from League membership has been deemed as unjust and unwise, a new organization was formed at Boston, on Saturday, 29 May, called "The American Cyclists' Union," whose object is to promote the sport of cycling, and to secure for wheelmen the rights of the path, to protect and defend our racing men from impositions, and, for the public, to add new charms for what is to-day the leading sport of the world.

The A. C. U. appeals to wheelmen, clubs, track associations, manufacturers and all others interested in cycling to support us in a laudable endeavor to encourage and foster the true spirit of amateur races, viz., the desire to win ; and, furthermore, to keep our noble sport free from the abuses of gambling and jockeying which have ruined many a sport that has preceded cycling. Our rules are just, our motto, " Jamais Arriere," with a friendly feeling for all.

CAUTION. — The underhanded methods now being pursued by the chairman of the Racing Board, L. A. W., should not be countenanced by any fair-minded wheelman. The attempts to stab the A. C. U. out of existence before it has fairly begun life is fully characteristic of the proceedings of the L. A. W. chairman, but we feel our cause is a just one, and we are proud of the hearty support now accorded us. To the racing men : We offer a protection such as is not within the province of the League to offer you. We have declared no war on the L. A. W., but shall protect our rights and those of our number against their arbitrary actions ; and if necessary shall buckle on the armor and fight to the bitter end. "We court peace and the good-will of all." At the same time we shall maintain our rights at all hazards.

Remember, the A. C. U. is not an organization of to-day, but one for all time. Copies of our rules and regulations may be obtained of A. Q. McGarrett, secretary, Springfield, Mass. Clubs and associations are cordially invited to hold their meetings under our rules, and to avail themselves of the protection afforded by the aegis of cycling organizations, the American Cyclists' Union.

Respectfully yours,

HENRY E. DUCKER,

President A. C. U.

We are glad to see something official from the new League, even if it is glittering with assumptions and false ideas. The Union has been formed simply because the League insists that professionals shall not race as amateurs. Mr. Ducker says the Union is formed to defend our racing men from impositions. At every meeting held under A. C. U. rules, both amateurs and professionals alike have been admitted to amateur races, and the League has had to step in and warn wheelmen against these impositions.

The Yale Club managers announced certain races for amateurs, and amateurs entered them in good faith. After the entries were closed, it was found that professionals had been admitted to these races, and those amateurs who had entered were forced to stay out or lose their status, and their entrance fees were forfeited. This is defending our racing men from impositions with a vengeance.

Mr. Ducker says his League desires to encourage and foster the true spirit of amateur races. Mr. Ducker has very strange ideas in view of the amateur rule adopted by the Union and the public acts of its members. When Mr. Ducker talks about "underhanded acts," we recognize it as one of his peculiar methods of conducting a campaign; for personal abuse was a marked feature of his campaign against the Racing Board, and it resulted in the unanimous indorsement of the board, and a vote of thanks to them for what they had done. The A. C. U. is formed in order to allow Messrs. Rowe, Hendee and Knapp to enter amateur races. This is the thing in a nutshell.

THE Racing Board has recalled its order of suspension against the men who competed in the Lynn races, so far as H. C. Getchell, Chas. A. Stenken, A. D. Grover and F. B. Brigham are concerned. Said parties have shown to the board that it was clearly understood by them that the races were under League rules, and the officials certify to this effect. The positions taken by the Board is this : It was publicly announced that the races were to be run under A. C. U. rules, and no change was made in the determination until it was found at the last moment that the men would run under none but League rules. Many riders kept away from the tournament when they found that the A. C. U. rules would be used, and in justice to them the League cannot countenance the action of the Lynn officials. This is the first case, however, and the Racing Board is disposed to deal leniently with all who are loyal to the League. It should be clearly understood, however, that mixed meetings will not be countenanced. The A. C. U. advertises amateur races and admits professionals to them. It imperils the status of every amateur rider who enters its races, and in the interest of the amateurs, the League must step in. The League hopes to have the support of all members who have any regard for the amateur rule, and loyalty to the institution will forbid them to serve in any capacity at race meetings held under any rules but those of the L. A. W.

THE League Meet at Boston was not the success that it should have been. We do not doubt the boys had a good time, and measured in this way, it was an unqualified success ; but the business meeting was not a success, and it did much to injure the institution. We had a right to expect a larger attendance and more enthusiasm. Failing to get it, the world will say that wheelmen take little interest in League affairs, and they may well predict a rapid decay for the association. We do not consider the parade a success. We had a right to expect twice as many wheelmen in line. The races were not a success. But then we do not remember a more successful meeting at any League Meet.

We do not regard the general apathy that prevailed in Boston towards everything of a formal character to be in any way an index to the feeling of League members towards that body, but we are obliged to confess that the effect of the Meet upon the outside world was not such as we would liked to have seen.

MR. STEPHEN TERRY of Hartford has made a suggestion to the Racing Board that will in all probability be adopted. He proposes that the League furnish a medal or badge of small intrinsic value to each member who in any race under L. A. W. rules and sanction shall run a mile in three minutes or less from scratch, with a bar giving the year it was done, and an additional bar each year he repeats it. This is like the plan for marksmen's badges in the National Guard ; and one or two entries made for this special purpose in any race will be apt to make the fast men go. All

over the country will be found fast riders who would like to win such a badge, and that will add interest to races; in fact many riders would value the badge above the regular race prize.

SPEAKING of the new association, the A. C. U., Mr. Ducker says the rules are modelled after the N. C. U. We are glad to know this, because the N. C. U. has a much stricter amateur rule than the L. A. W. has. Under the N. C. U. rules a man who accepts his expenses from a cycle dealer becomes a professional; under the L. A. W. rules he is suspended from the track for a short time. Under the N. C. U. rules any bicycle agent who teaches a man to ride as part of the agreement in the sale of a machine, becomes a professional; under the L. A. W. rules this is allowed without affecting a man's status. The N. C. U. never reinstates a professional. The L. A. W. does not regard professionalism as an unpardonable sin.

MR. DUCKER says that the new organization is formed in order to get the League to change Rule H. There is not a man in the country whose standing is affected by this rule. Strike out the rule and there would be no change in the condition of the men in whose interest the new association is formed. The new association is formed in order to break down the amateur rule. Nothing more, nothing less. It is a shield which the organizers are putting up to allow professionals to hide their true status and appear to be amateurs.

IT is very pleasant to have one's motives impugned, and the following from our Tremont street contemporary makes us sit up and cry "shame!"

"Then a long discussion ensued as to the question whether or not there was a vacancy in the office of secretary-editor. Mr. Bassett, who was said to be anxious to obtain the position of secretary-editor, vainly tried to have a vacancy declared; but the board would have none of it, and voted that it was the sense of the meeting that no such vacancy existed."

Mr. Bassett had refused to be considered a candidate for the office, and he made no attempt whatever to have the office declared vacant. The whole statement is as false as it is ungenerous.

THE *Bicycling News* cuts things very fine. It tries to show that when a race committee returns entry fees to starters who finish the race, it makes them ride for money. Speaking of the Pope cup race, in which the entry fee is returned, it says: —

"To suppose an instance which will put the matter clearly. If a man, after riding nineteen miles, found himself entirely outpaced and made a show of when racing began, he would probably retire were the rule in question non-existent. But as the case stands he would very possibly keep on his machine and literally ride the last mile for $5. The line must be drawn somewhere, and if men who ride a certain distance are to be paid back a certain entrance fee, what is to prevent a number of men making a race for sweepstakes of entry fees for the man who stops on his machine longest, or rides a given distance in the shortest time, and still remaining amateurs? It is indeed only necessary to imagine a man in the particular race now referred to, thoroughly pumped out at fifteen miles, retiring, and subsequently, when laps behind, getting on to ride the remaining distance at a dollar a mile, to appreciate properly the amateurism of the men who ride in a race under such conditions."

We can imagine no such condition of things. The referee has the right to call a man off the track at any time, and when he is thus called off he loses none of his rights. It is the same as though he had finished the race. This is one of the unwritten laws, and it is often used to good effect to spare the auditors. It does look as though the *News* was splitting hairs.

THE INTERNATIONAL TOURNAMENT.

THE great international tournament, projected and carried out by Mr. Cathcart, came off as per announcement at the Alexandra Palace, on the evenings of Thursday and Friday 20 and 21 May, and the afternoon and evening of Saturday, 22 May. All the fliers were on hand and a number of records went by the board. W. A. Illston won the half-mile handicap from scratch, making the distance in 1.16. and beating the English record of $1.19\frac{3}{5}$., though it is behind Rowe's, $1.12\frac{2}{5}$. Illston reduced the record twice in this event, for in the second round he made $1.16\frac{1}{5}$.

In the five-mile tandem tricycle race Mr. E. Kiderlen and E. de Benkelaer of Holland were too much for the Englishmen, and won in $16.5\frac{3}{5}$. This beats the American record of $16.49\frac{4}{5}$, but is behind the English record, $14.22\frac{3}{5}$. The final in the one-mile tricycle handicap was won by F. S. Buckingham from the 75-yards mark, in $3.0\frac{1}{5}$. The English record was $2.58\frac{1}{5}$. In the heats R. J. Mecredy of Dublin, the Irish champion, covered the mile in 2.58 from scratch, and A. E. Langley lowered the record another peg by scoring $2.55\frac{1}{5}$.

In the three-mile scratch our old friend Furnivall came in ahead, with Illston and Speechly close behind. The time was 9.25. Furnivall did the last lap in $49\frac{4}{5}$.

The two-mile tricycle race was taken by J. Lee in $6.54\frac{3}{5}$. In the first heat Kiderlen, of Holland, was pitted against Mecredy the Irish champion, and defeated the man from Dublin in $6.15\frac{4}{5}$, beating the English record of 6.17. The American record is $6.03\frac{2}{5}$.

The one-mile handicap was taken by Illston in $2.45\frac{4}{5}$. Illston tried for some records in this, but failed to secure them.

The great event of all was the five-mile international bicycle race for the Challenge Shield, valued at fifty guineas. One of the conditions of this race was that each country should have not more than four representatives. There was an English, Scotch, Irish and Dutch team; and Belgium was represented by E. de Benkelaer, the amateur champion. The first heat was won by Furnivall in $16.11\frac{1}{5}$; the second by D. W. Laing, of Scotland, in $16.52\frac{3}{5}$; the third by H. A. Speechly, who had a walk-over; and the final by Furnivall in $16.1\frac{2}{5}$.

The tournament resulted in new records as follows: —

TRICYCLE.

$\frac{1}{4}$ mile,	$41\frac{1}{5}$.	H. C. Sharp.
$\frac{1}{2}$ mile,	$1.27\frac{4}{5}$.	J. M. Inglis.
$\frac{3}{4}$ mile,	$2.13\frac{1}{5}$.	A. E. Langley.
1 mile,	$2.55\frac{1}{5}$.	A. E. Langley.
2 mile,	$6.15\frac{4}{5}$.	E. Kiderlen.

BICYCLE.

$\frac{1}{2}$ mile,	$1.16\frac{1}{5}$.	W. A. Illston.

GERMAN RECORDS.

RECORD breaking on the continent has been on the bills of late, and several cases have occurred. At Frankfort, 15 May, a special race of thirty kilometers took place between H. O. Duncan and F. De Civry. Duncan was winner in 1.2.12, beating the record of 1.5.44.

At Munich, Bavaria, 16 May, a race meeting was held in which M. V. J. Webber, of England, was a participant, and took the ten kilometre record in 18.54 and the five kilometre record in $9.14\frac{2}{5}$. Duncan and De Civry were also present at this meeting and broke the record for ten kilometres.

AT Munich, 18 May, De Civry ran against time to beat the one kilometre record of $1.46\frac{4}{5}$, made by Pundt at Berlin last year. He scored 1.41. Duncan rode to beat the German mile record of $2.55\frac{2}{5}$, and made 2.43. Dubois then rode to beat Webber's time of $9.14\frac{2}{5}$, and made $8.55\frac{3}{5}$.

FROM A FEMININE POINT OF VIEW.

THERE is a very old lady who gives one a great deal of trouble. In fact she has been a source of trouble to a great many people in this world, and yet she lives on and her *ipse dixit* is law to thousands.

SHE is not an amiable old lady, and even those who are guided by what she says, have no great love for her. I confess that I do not like her. Her influence is baneful and she does little good work in the world.

YOU all know her? It is Mrs. Grundy. That same old Mrs. Grundy that has stood in the way of our pleasure time and again. That same Mrs. Grundy who turns up her nose at a deal of innocent fun and bids the world to put on a sober face.

I REMEMBER very well when we were school girls that we used to regard her mandates when we were in the city, but when we got out into the country among the trees and in the green fields, we let nature assert itself and went in for a jolly good time.

MRS. GRUNDY did not allow us to romp and run when we were in her dominions,

and if we told her we were going to dig worms and go fishing she would have been horrified, and we would have staid at home. Thank goodness she did n't go into the country with us.

AND now Mrs. Grundy is doing what she can to keep women off the wheel. Mrs. Grundy says it is not ladylike, and she does n't approve of it. I know that this is so, for I have it on the best authority. Not a few young ladies have told me they would like to ride, but they were afraid of Mrs. Grundy. I am very sorry, for this means that the missionary work of the leaders is not yet done. A class of women have taken to tricycling who are above listening to Mrs. Grundy. They see in the sport a healthful and joy-giving exercise, and they are independent of the old lady.

I CAN well believe that the Boston Meet did a great deal to confound Mrs. Grundy. There is a force in numbers, and the gatherings of the ladies must have made an impression. I happen to know of several who have become imbued with the wheel fever from what they saw at the Meet, and as every lady who goes into the sport is sure to bring others along, we may be sure that we are progressing in point of numbers.

I WISH that I had the pen of an Edward Everett Hale, that I might put into the choicest of fiction the story of a young woman, a sister of Harry Wadsworth, perhaps, who should take to the wheel and lead ten others to join her. These ten would each in turn bring ten more into the fold, and so continuing, after a while the whole world would be a-wheel. What better field for the employment of the " Ten Times One " idea could be found ?

HAVE you read Minna Smith's charming little book of poems called, " In Fruitful Lands "? No? Well, then, get a copy and read it. It is a dainty little volume, in parchment covers, and it sells for sixty cents. The poems are readable and meritorious to a great degree. True, they are not on cycling topics, but we can imagine that the wheel inspired a great many of them.

OUR enthusiastic friends of Wellington have been travelling on a tandem to Worcester, and I can well believe they are full of their adventures. I wonder if they climbed all the hills, and whether or not the rough country roads did not make them sigh for Eastern Massachusetts ?

DAISIE.

GLEANINGS FROM GOTHAM.

WELL the wrecks have returned from the Hub, and the tale of the pilgrimage and the conquests made will fill many a wintry hour when the blaze of the log fire lights up the cosey club parlor, and the crackle of the chestnuts enlivens the dull monotony. We did have a really good time, better than at any other meet, and the Bostonians can swell themselves with pride for many a day to come. Only in some respects was there

any disappointment. We fully expected to see the portly chairman of the Racing Board toasted by the fiery chieftain of the wilds of Springfield. He did not toast worth a cent, and the meeting was as quiet as a Sunday-school picnic, as some one very justly observed. Well perhaps it is as well that no disturbance was made, as the policy of peace and good-will to men is the better in the long run.

I WONDER what the American Cyclists' Union will-accomplish ? If the races at Lynn are a sample of the work we are to expect, I am disappointed. From all accounts the races were not a very great success. In fact I am told that the audience hissed them roundly on several occasions. Now if the A. C. U. expects to amount to anything it should try to correct the supposed evils of the League rules. As I understand it there is not so much difference between the rules of the two organizations as the principle of the amateur rule. The League requires the racing men to pay their own expenses, and the A. C. U. allows them to be paid by any one. This latter course may have a broader end in view, but its effect will be to confine racing to the few favored ones in the employ of manufacturers and dealers ; and as the dealers are smart enough to put a fresh man in every race, the chances of the *bona fide* racing amateur are seen through the wrong end of the spy-glass.

BUT simmer it down in all its phases, it narrows down to the State of Massachusetts. We have few racing interests here, and have been in a position of spectators to the controversy that has taken in my mind almost too much space. It is the question of a handful of men against thousands. I like racing and think I have attended as many race meetings in an official capacity as the next man, but I think that if the League cannot handle it successfully it ought to be dropped and delegated to some one else. Racing and racing interests have caused more trouble than any other branch of the sport. The line between the amateur and professional has become so finely drawn that it does not exist in many minds. For my part I do not see why Rowe and the rest of them do not come out flat-footed and be professionals. There is no disgrace attached to it. If the ways of the professional are unworthy of the newly acquired batch, let them organize among themselves and bring the sport up to its proper level. The word professional does not carry any odium. I would rather pose as a professional journalist than an amateur. If a man can do anything well enough to receive remuneration, I fail to see the point of trying to hide one's light under a bushel, and making people think that you are doing it for the fun of the thing.

THINGS are quite dead in the way of news. We are just at that point where quiet runs, that interest the few who enjoy them, need no chronicling by the cycling scribe, and we have to discuss men and things in general. I often wonder how the vast membership of the League like the way things turn out at the election of officers. We meet pretty much the same faces at the meetings year

after year and of course know their feelings; but one should remember that somewhere there are hundreds and hundreds of members that evince their interest year after year by renewing their membership, but do not put in appearance at the meetings, and are rarely heard of unless it be upon a mail vote. This must be pretty conclusive evidence that the policy of the League is established on the right basis, or else we would not have the vast number of renewals that pour in to us year after year. The remarkable increase in the number of applications shows that good missionary work is being done in many directions. The day seems to be past when it becomes necessary to select men for the chief offices to satisfy certain localities. I was much interested in hearing Mr. Kirk Munroe tell of the old days of the League, when we had the president in Boston, the vice-president in Chicago, the secretary in New York, and the treasurer in Saratoga. Now they seem to place them where the men who are willing to do the work are to be found. The old feeling of sectional jealousy is dead, and I think that the general membership are content to have all the chief officers in one city if they are able men.

WE had a six days' race at the Madison Square Garden last week, with Brooks and Woodside on bicycles, and Anderson on horses. From what I can learn it was not a financial success, mostly owing to lack of the proper advertising. The management told the press early in the week to go to thunder; and so the boys staid away and so did the crowd. The bicyclers won by a few miles, Brooks doing the greatest amount of work. It was a bad season for the affair anyway, as the out-door racing is in full blast and the weather too warm for any one to patronize an in-door wheel contest.

THE arrangements for the twenty-five mile race of the New York and New Jersey Team Road Racing Association, for next Saturday, are nearly all completed, and considerable attention is being taken in this event. The Brooklyn Club will not compete, but there will be about eight teams in the race, and with thirty-two men on the road it will be very lively. I trust that no accidents will occur, but as road-racing as a rule ends somewhat seriously, I am afraid some will feel sore before the event is over.

THE Kings County Wheelmen are to have a race meeting on 19 June, at the Brooklyn Athletic Club ground, under the rules of the League of American Wheelmen. A number of club championships will be run off, together with a State championship. The complete programme is as follows : One-mile novices, one-mile tricycle, two and three mile handicap, and the five-mile State championship ; all open events. The club championships are for the Brooklyn, Ilderan, and Bedford Cycling Clubs, and there will also be a novices' race for the members of the Kings County Wheelmen. The entries close 12 June, and should be sent to Chas. Schwalbach, 124 Penn street, Brooklyn, N. Y.   JENKINS.

PENCILLED PARAGRAPHS BY ARTY.

ONE looks in vain among the Hartford tournament winners for Jack Illeston's name.

———

C. E. WHITTEN is now the darling of the Lynn men, who think he will make another Rowe ; Whittier's best mile in practice is 2.49

———

THE Massachusetts Club will help the Charlestown boys celebrate in the early morning of the 17th, and will run to Glenmere Park in the afternoon to attend the races.

———

BURNHAM'S resolution made at Lynn, to never race on a bicycle again, is gradually oozing away as his wounds grow better.

———

ROWE'S left arm is still very stiff from his fall, so much so that he is not able to get down to his old spurt yet.

———

WHEN Knapp and Rowe bit the dust in the handicap last week, the feminine hearts in the grand stand fluttered high with fear for a moment.

———

BURNHAM is the coolest-headed racer in America, as proved by his doings at Lynn.

———

IT is one of the unwritten rules of the track, that in a smash-up the riders can seize the best machine handy to finish on.

———

ABOUT twenty Massachusetts men dined at Nantasket, Sunday, with Capt. Peck at the head of the table.

———

THE butterfly Reservoir riders have transferred their affections to the Hotel Faneuil, and can be found any Sunday lounging in the smoking-room, or spoiling the piano in the reception-room.

———

DR. KENDALL has some very interesting photos taken by himself during the Meet, including views of the Massachusetts Club in the parade ; the finishes of Weber and Haradon at Corey's ; the start of the first heat in the tricycle championship, and also of the Prince-Neilson race at Lynn ; and a group picture of the L. A. W. race officials.

———

RIDERS who ride in tights should remember that however appropriate they may seem on the wheel, they are out of place in a public dining-room.

———

KIRK COREY climbed Corey Hill, Friday night, on a bicyclette.

———

THE captain of a local club, in calling a run to a celebrated hill in this vicinity, recently announced that " the second lieutenant would climb the hill " ; and now there is a coolness between the officers of that club, caused by the failure of the lieutenant to complete his portion of the announced programme.

———

CYCLISTS with the photographic craze should turn down Crystal avenue on Beacon street, beyond Newton Centre, and try a few plates on the picturesque little lake lying in the hollow.

———

ROWE makes an emphatic denial to the statement that he contemplates a match with Neilson or any other professional.

———

DR. KENDALL took a number of views of Chestnut Hill and the assembled wheelmen on Sunday.

———

THE amateur photo fever has broken out quite violently. Consul Saville, of Roxbury, and his friends fear, from the acute symptoms shown, that he cannot recover. The usual symptom in cases of this kind is an inordinate desire to shoot at the crowd every time they stop for a drink at the wayside pump.

———

TWO new tricycles appeared at the Reservoir Sunday. The machines were of the handle-bar steering pattern, weighing 55 pounds, and fitted with wooden wheels and steel frames, running by a lever and clutchgear, which could be, by a mere turn of the bar, geared anywhere from 38 inches to 63 inches. The machines looked clumsy, but embodied many new and good ideas.

———

EX-PRESIDENT MILLER of Columbus has the most complete amateur collection of stereopticon views in the country, and takes great delight in amusing his cycle friends with private entertainments and lectures with the same.

———

CAPT. PECK will call a run for the Massachusetts Club to Brockton on the 16th to attend the races.

———

THE Back Bay religious societies are flooding the Massachusetts Club House with circulars, inviting the members to their Sunday services.

———

LEFEVRE, of the Massachusetts Club, now carries a broken arm caused by a fall.

———

REGESTEIN, of the same club, is out at Hotel Faneuil, entertaining himself with an attack of rheumatism.

———

IT seems that Lock's Hill is climbed on the asphalt walk, not the road, as at Corey's.

———

THE Meet photograph is very fine, showing each face perfectly and bringing out with perfect distinctness the gentlemen solacing themselves with the bottle at the rear.

———

A. W. GUMP has on exhibition at the Pope Mfg. Co.'s a bicycle stand, which can be reversed and made into a comfortable stool.

———

THE Wheelman's Reference Book credits Hendee with the quarter-mile tricycle record in 42 seconds, instead of 40 seconds, and gives the quarter-mile bicycle as a tie at 36½ to both Rowe and Hendee, instead of 35½ by Rowe ; and yet at least one of the editors saw both these records made.

———

THE A. C. U. Executive, so-called, have a meeting on the 13th.

———

MR. A. F. STURTEVANT, of Concord, N. H., ascended Corey Hill last week on a 50-inch Expert Columbia.

———

MAJOR C. L. HOVEY, of the Massachusetts Club, is located at the camp in Framingham for a week.

A NEW WRENCH.

J. H. LESTER, of Philadelphia, has sent us a beautiful silver-plated wrench with trimmings gold plated and inscribed with our name. It is modelled after a full-sized wrench made by the Read Railroad Wrench Manufacturing Company of Philadelphia, which is used extensively on railroads. By pressing the thumb against a dog the movable jaw is released and can be pushed along to any position, and one does not have to go through the tedious process of moving the jaw slowly along by turning a screw. It is proposed to make a small wrench for bicycle use, and as the movement of the jaw is instantaneous the wrench is bound to be a popular one.

PATENTS.

LIST of cycling patents granted this week : C. S. Leddell, Morristown N. J., velocipede ; Jno. Payne, San Francisco, Cal., bicycle saddle ; T. N. Petersen, Boston, Mass., velocipede ; D. H. Rice, Brookline, Mass., bicycle ; J. H. Schulz, Berlin, Germany, velocipede ; C. C. Shelby, Paterson, N. J., stocking supporter.

———

As predicted early in the season, the Buffer Saddle has had a most flattering run, and it well deserves it. Stoddard, Lovering & Co., sole U. S. agents, 152-158 Congress street, Boston.

———

THE greatest safety for night riding is a thoroughly *reliable* lamp. The celebrated " King of the Road " has the above quality in a very marked degree. Stoddard, Lovering & Co , 152-158 Congress street, Boston.

NOTES FROM THE SOUTH.

OF course, all attention for the past few days has been directed towards Boston and the Meet, all news therefrom being eagerly sought after. The information received so far is very meagre and unsatisfactory, and full particulars are anxiously awaited.

So far as heard from all appear satisfied with the result of the election, and believe that the gentlemen selected are as " good as the best."

THE action of the League in sustaining the recent move of the Racing Board against the makers' amateurs is the subject of much comment, some taking sides with the board, others against it. There is, however, a vague report of a " split " in the League, which, however, lacks confirmation ; but until reliable information is received, further comment on this subject is reserved.

29 and 30 May the Young Men's Gymnastic Club of this city gave their annual tournament, at which three bicycle races were run, with the following result :

First race ; 1 mile ; 4 entries. Won by W. L. Hughes in 4 03½.　E. E. Marks second.

Second race ; ½ mile ; 5 entries. First, W. L. Hughes ; second, G. McD. Nathan. Winner's time, 1.51.

Third race ; 1 mile ; 2 starters. Also won by Mr. Hughes in 3.51¼. E. E. Marks second.

The contestants were all of the N. O. B. C. The time made is fair, considering the extremely poor track on which the races were run.

THERE is now on exhibition a very handsome jewelled medal, offered by Mr. A. M. Hill of the N. O. B. C. for a fifty-mile race between the members of the club. The race will probably occur sometime during the present month, and will very likely be run over the same course on which Munger recently broke the 25 and 50 miles record.

Hill is about the best rider here for the distance, but he may have to do some fast pedalling to win his trophy.

THE first Champion seen in these parts was received here a day or two since. It has been examined and pronounced a daisy in every respect, appearance, make and finish.

BI.

NEW ORLEANS, 1 June, 1886.

THE MISSOURI BICYCLE CLUB RECEIVES ITS FRIENDS.

ON 26 July, 1881; six gentlemen, who were imbued with the idea that the bicycle would eventually become a leading factor in daily locomotion, met at what was then known as the Catalpa Swimming School, on Ninth near Gratiot street. They organized what they called the Missouri Bicycle Club. Members in considerable numbers flocked to its standard, and with the newly-acquired members came lethargy and inaction in equal proportions, and the club, after enjoying an existence of three years, on 4 May, 1884, gave up the ghost. It had died of inanition. The more active members, however, not to be deterred in the least, on the very next day met at the Southern Hotel and drew up articles of incorporation which called into life the present Missouri Bicycle Club. Infused with the vigor, energy and determination which is born of youth, it succeeded almost in spite of itself, until, at the present time, it enjoys a membership of 175.

On Wednesday, 2 June, it threw open to its friends the monument of its success, its new club house. It is a three-story brick and brown-stone structure, situated on the west side of Cardinal avenue, between Pine and Olive streets, and is truly a model of completeness in detail and appointment.— In these regards ranking higher than any bicycle club house in the United States. Entering an arched entrance, the visitor finds himself in an ante-room, to the north of which is an elegantly furnished parlor. From the ante-room, a flight of broad stairs take one to the floor above. A hall leading westwardly passes between the concrete-floored wheel-room and well-furnished bath-room and terminates in a gymnasium, which is simply perfect in its equipment. Passing to the second floor, the two rooms facing on Cardinal avenue are the lounging-room, which is carpeted, furnished with willow furniture for those of the members who are the disciples of Euterpe, while the other room is supplied with the appurtenances which go to make the heart of the billiard and pool player. To the west of these rooms is the card-room and what is known as the " locker " room. If it be borne in mind that it cost $2,700 to

furnish the rooms mentioned, their elegance will become more apparent.

The 175 members of the club were out this night in full numbers. They were accompanied by their own female relatives, and in many cases with ladies who were relatives of somebody else. Shoen's orchestra enlivened the occasion with " heavenly strains," to which the majority of those present danced. At 10 o'clock a light lunch, supplied by Spilker, was served, and by 11 most of those present turned their faces homeward, but only after wishing the Missouri Bicycle Club much luck and joy in their palatial new quarters.

The ladies who graced the occasion with their presence were Mmes. Frank E. Richey, A. Moore Berry, E. S. Jeffrey, Schuyler, Cavier, Farris, Carpenter, Charles M. Skinner, A. S. Barnes, W. M, Brewster, George F. Baker and Misses Sadie Culcord, Oeter, Woestman, Mary and Sadie Sells, Morrison, Emma Moore, Annie Webb, Waldron, Bushman, Peters, Carton, Bartlage, Brant, Carpenter and Hilda Clements.

REMEMBER that by using a bottle of Ardill's Liquid Enamel you can make your machine look like new in a few minutes. Price 75c. Stoddard, Lovering & Co., 152-158 Congress street, Boston.

WM. READ & SONS request us to state that there were seventy-five Royal Mail bicycles in the late L. A. W. parade, instead of thirty-six, as elsewhere reported, besides many of their tricycles.

CYCLETS.

A boon
In June
Is breezy,
Sneezy
Weather,
Whether
By the sea
Or in the city
Or on the lea.
But what a pity;
Yes, 'tis a pity
That on the lea
Or in the city
Or by the sea,
Whether
Weather
Be sneezy
Or breezy
In June,
'T is a boon.

He sat on a bicycle as straight as an icicle, and rode on a tri-
    cycle rode by his side.
He talked like a jolly fop, and naught could his folly stop,
    with all kinds of lollipop enlivening the ride.
At last, incidentally, more instinctive than mentally, he
    grew sentimentally sochärtpe sweet;
And he told with intensity of love's strong propensity,
    its force and immensity, its fervof and heat.
Just then o'er some hummocks he sprawled on her-flum-
    muxee,
And she thought what a lummux to tumble just then !
But he climbed to his station, while she said with elation,
" Renew your salutation ; say it over again."
                                    Tid Bits.

Now we have the perfect days. June gives us the longest days in the year.

OUR readers will have to excuse us if we have to talk amateur rule too much. Our opponents force it upon us. They gave us talk, talk, talk before the Meet, and they got beaten ; and then, being beaten, they want to talk some more.

A CHICAGO preacher who rides a bicycle has been asked to resign. His parishioners think that a man addicted to the bicycle habit is very likely to fall.— Ex.

THE Highland Park Wheelmen will this summer introduce a novel watermelon

race. It is purely a Highland Park wheelman's idea. The race will be open to all L. A. W. bicyclers. Each rider will be required to ride the Alvarado bridge within a given time, and carry under one arm a watermelon. All those who accomplish this feat without breaking the melon will be invited to a banquet. So look out for a future announcement of the watermelon race. — Ingleside.

" IF our men are declared professionals we cannot be a League club," said a club man to us the other day. Why not? There is no such thing as a League club known to the L. A. W. There used to be a provision that allowed those clubs whose entire active membership belonged to the League to send proxies to the annual meeting ; but that is gone, and so is all mention of a League club. If in the future the old definition should be restored, the professionals could join clubs as associate members.

ST. LOUIS was regarded as an enemy to the Racing Board, and her representatives were depended upon to help " down " it ; and yet the only word from the great city of the West was that which came from Chief Consul Rogers, who replied to Mr. Ducker's assertion that clubs and divisions would leave the League, with the statement that Missouri would be loyal to the League, no matter which way the vote went. Missouri is all right.

HAL GREENWOOD may now be considered the champion hill climber of America, if not of the world. Last Sunday, in the presence of the entire touring party, he climbed Son-of-a-Gun hill six times without a dismount. The only watch held on him showed that the time he consumed was only nineteen minutes. This hill is the steep rough one to the left of Manchester going out, and last year was deemed such an unclimbable ascent that the Rambler's Club offered a medal to any one climbing it during the season. Now that Greenwood has climbed it half a dozen times without a rest its old sublimity has gone, but Hal's unapproachableness has increased correspondingly. He went up the first of the six times as fast as the hill was ever climbed. To-night he goes to Clarksville, and intends to go up " Crank " hill twice in succession before coming back. — Post Dispatch.

" WHEN the League admits professionals, or when it weakens on the amateur rule, you will see the whole New York Division go out of it," said a prominent New York wheelman the other day. Boston and its immediate vicinity is a hot-bed of makers' amateurism, and outside of a line two hundred miles from the Hub the amateur sentiment is very strong.

WHEN America finds out which is the best tandem and the best tricycle, they will come into the field. Meantime the importers are finding a good market for these wheels.

A MODEST old maid met a Cincinnati wheelman on the Lebanon road last Sunday, and the festive cyclone attempted to mesmerize her with his childlike smile. She gave him a look that froze the smile and bent his backbone, and hiding her face behind a Yum-Yum fan, she screeched out : —

"O Lor', boy! go hum and dress yourself!"

Moral: Never mash anything that would stop a clock. — *Sportsman.*

THERE is a little war in the camp of the ladies. One of the Boston dailies, referring to those who took part in the run of the first days, said "three of them were beautiful," and now the ladies want to know, — which three?

GORMULLY & JEFFERY have just shipped a large lot of American Ideals to Guatemala.

SPEAKING of tricycles, so many changes have been rung upon the tendency of the bicycle to stand on its head upon occasion, that some innocent people hold the idea that even riders of the tricycle now and then indulge in the luxury of a "header." While one may be thrown from the three-wheeler through carelessness or recklessness, just as the same person might be thrown from a carriage under similar circumstances, the fact remains that tricycle accidents are of very rare occurrence. One of these rare occurrences was noted not very long ago in Maplewood, at a point on Salem street where there is quite a down grade. The machine was a "tandem," and the riders, a gentleman and his wife, were full of inexperience with the machine. The tricycle had become unmanageable, and, running at the very side of the road, where the bed was somewhat loose, met its fate, rolling over in the most approved form, after dashing its occupants to the ground. Beyond receiving a good dusting, the riders were not hurt in the least, though the machine looked as though it had been struck by a cyclone.

There was nothing particularly funny about this experience, — on the contrary it was too serious a matter, to those concerned, to be joked about. As a remarkable coincidence, however, it may be stated that at the precise spot where the riders struck *terra firma* the water main sprung a leak, shortly after, which required the services of four brawny men the best part of half a day to repair. — *Record.*

MR. A. L. ATKINS has issued the second edition of his "Road Book of Boston and Vicinity." It contains fifty-five routes, many of which are newly prepared for this edition; and all those that appeared in the first edition have been corrected where they were faulty, and in many ways improved. The little volume is a very handy companion, and no Boston wheelman should be without it. The distances have been measured carefully, and are to be depended upon. Get it of Mr. Atkins at the rooms of the Pope Manufacturing Company, 597 Washington street.

MUCH has been said for and against tricycling for women. People who disapprove of it say that it is bold and unfeminine, just as cavillers used to condemn skating when girls just began going on the ice in this part of the world twenty-five years ago. People who like the three-wheel seem to be certain that it is just as rational for a woman to ride a machine as to ride a pony, and it is certain that there is a charm and fascination in the self-propulsion which is comparable to no other form of exercise. A woman who rides is often asked if it is not hard work.

Yes, at first ; but those who persist in regular practice gain strength and courage, and there is at least one Boston woman who can do fifty miles a day with the same ease with which an ordinary rider can do fifteen or twenty. She came to the Meet on a tandem with her husband, and with her five-year old boy towed behind, riding in a little cart made purposely for an annex to the machine that the parents ride. — *Record.*

THE Rev. Mr. Scott, pastor of the First Congregational Church, of Evanston, Ill., has been asked to resign. This he declines to do until there has been an investigation of the charges against him. The specific offences against Mr. Scott appear to be cigar smoking in public and riding a bicycle. Nothing involving his moral conduct is charged.

"ANNIVERSARY week — anniversary week. Let me see, what is anniversary week? " said a young suburban wife to her husband the other day. "Seems to me I 've heard of it before, but I never knew what it meant."

"Why, don't you know? It's the regular annual convention of the bicyclers and tricyclers of the whole country. City 's beginning to be full of them, and they 're going to have a grand parade Thursday." — *Exchange.*

MR. H. H. GRIFFIN has resigned from the executive of the N. C. U., because of the leniency shown to the makers' amateurs. Griffin is a thorough amateur, and is against anything approaching professionalism. He is thoroughly mixed up in cycling, being handicapper to the N. C. U., and one of the editors of *Bicycling News.*

A GOOD tandem, that can be ridden by two ladies, seems to be in demand, and those who have them find it difficult to get enough of them.

CHOIRMASTER, in search of a tenor to supply the place of one who has been taken ill, comes upon a friend who is a cyclist. "I want a singer; where shall I go?" Cyclist: "Go? Why go to Everett's in Berkley square." Choirmaster goes as directed, but when he asks Gid Haynes for a tenor it throws him off his base.

THE races at Lynn on Monday were races by makers' amateurs. They were a failure, and a class of them in a tournament would be a failure as an event. The value of the makers' amateur to the race, as well as to his employer, lies in the fact that his character and relationship are unknown to the lay public. To stamp him, to get up a class between the agents of the different companies, to label them the "Victor" rider, the "Columbia" rider, the "Star," etc., etc., would make them as flatly ineffective as related to the rest of the tournament as is the gaudy advertising wagon that usually trails after the military procession or the circus. — *Providence Journal.*

PRESIDENT BECKWITH has the power to restore harmony all around without much exertion on his part. The Racing Board is "a law unto itself," makes its own rules and is governed by its own rules and no other. The president appoints the Racing Board and its chairman. If he so desires, he can appoint a board, every member of which would be favorable to the M. A.'s, and this board could make such rules and regulations as it pleased, or, in other words, could revise

the rule defining amateurs and make it conform with that adopted by the A. C. U. It is doubted if President Beckwith will take the responsibility of such a step. — *Springfield Union.*

COPIES of the League Meet group photograph may be obtained upon application to W. B. Everett, Odd Fellows' building.

IT is stated that Pitman, the New York medal phenomenon, came all the way to Boston solely to attend the parade, don his glittering breastplate of trophies, and return home immediately after the parade.

WHEEL ethics, as put forward by the *Globe* : —

What little betting there is in the next race between Prince and Neilson seems to be largely in favor of the latter. As the races are to be best two in three, it seems nothing more than fair that Neilson should win at least one of them.

SINGER & Co. are fitting rubber cushions to the front forks of their straight steerers. This will do away with much of the vibration.

DR. W. G. KENDALL succeeded in getting a very good view of the officials at the League races. It comes out clear and sharp, and is in every way a success.

WHILE out on a run the other day, we came to a drawbridge, and a sign bearing these words confronted us : "No person allowed on this draw while in motion." We could n't well see how we could go across unless we were in motion, and so we disregarded the law, and moved across, breathing a sigh for the culture of Boston, within whose classic precincts the sign was allowed to stand.

E. P. BAIRD, of New York, rode one hundred and twenty-six miles on Decoration Day, and took one of the medals offered by the Orange Wanderers.

THE American Cyclists' Union is the new creation. Its objects are to foster racing. It admits clubs and individuals, and started in to run the Lynn races. Its racing rules in a measure are similar to those of the League, but its amateur definition is of course different. It divides professionals from amateurs, but allows the latter to receive their expenses from any source — dealer or otherwise. Well, it ran the Lynn races, and what was the result? The contests were narrowed down to two makers. If two "amateurs," friends of a certain dealer came to the scratch, one was sent back, and the other competed. This disgusted the crowd, who went to see Hendee and Rowe race together, and were disappointed. But Rowe raced Weber, and Hendee was reserved for Kluge, and the result was a certain crank machine carried off the prizes. Now this is not strictly amateur sport, and one can hardly blame the League for refusing to receive these men back and to sanction the races. But I fail to see why these gentlemen do not come out flat-footed and become professionals. I see no harm in it. It does not change their character, and the public will think just as much of them as if they were in the ranks and masking as amateurs. Take the case of L. Myers, the runner, who turned professional in order to defeat his old rival, George. He lost none of his standing by the act, and has, indeed, made new friends by his behavior. — *Jenkins in Sporting Life.*

GORMULLY & JEFFERY did not send any wheels to the L. A. W. Meet, preferring to satisfy the urgent demands of the dealers who had unfilled orders placed with them of long standing. They were able, however, to pick up about thirty wheels in Boston, and showed a full line of American Ideals and Safeties, about half a dozen Challenges, and three Champions. The American Ideal was the only youth's machine on exhibition at the Cycleries. The Safety attracted a good deal of attention, and was tried by nearly every expert who visited the show; while the Champion was critically examined by all the makers and importers, none of whom were disposed to find any fault with it. Their exhibit was in charge of J. S. Murray, their Boston agent.

IN our report of the Cycleries last week we made no mention of the exhibit made by Julius Wilcox of New York, in which a number of the new Faciles were shown. We regret that our reporter failed to see the old reliable safety machine, for it is deserving of especial mention. Mr. Wilcox has established a Boston agency at 23 Water street, and the machine can be seen there. As a safety it has earned a good reputation for speed, as well as comfort, and the record of the world for a long distance run is held by it. We are glad to know that it has come to Boston.

POPE'S "Calendar" is responsible for a great many paragraphs in the wheel and non-wheel press.

THE Wakefield Club will hold its annual 25-mile road race for the club championship next Saturday, 12 June, at four o'clock. There will probably be some eight or ten starters, among whom are J. C. Clark, G. E. Coombs, F. C. Patch, L. M. Beebe, E. A. Wilkins, C. E. Nott and H. R. Emerson. Clark is looked upon as a probable winner, and so the club has decided to offer a second prize to make it more interesting and to keep the men in the race to the finish.

AT the Yale bicycle races next Saturday there will be a balloon ascension by Prof. S. M. Brooks of Collinsville, who has made 160 ascents. There will be exhibitions of fancy riding by T. R. Finley, and many noted riders will be entered in the races.

THE effect of the Meet and parade as a practical illustration of the worth of the wheel is already shown in the increase of the number of wheels on the road. Among noticeable additions to the ranks are Mr. John Orth, the musician. and Master A. I. Fiske of the Boston Latin School, both of whom find delightful recreation on a tricycle.

FRED E. VAN MEERBEKE, who is riding a Columbia bicycle from New York to San Francisco, via New Orleans, arrived at Houston, Tex., on the 29th ult. He reports that the weather has been intensely hot, 96° in the shade, allowing riding only in the early morning and evening. For four days he rode over the more or less unbroken prairies.

JOHN N. McCLINTOCK, A. M., the editor of the *Massachusetts Magazine*, has written a sketch of Col. Albert A. Pope, which occupies several pages in the June number. A frontispiece portrait of the colonel accompanies the article.

THE Point of Pines Association intends to have a race track on its grounds, and will offer inducements to clubs holding races there.

GEORGE E. BUTLER, captain, and William Bond, of the Lynn Cycle Club, start for Portland, Me., Sunday, and go from there to Rangeley lakes on a short vacation.

WHEN Bangs wrote a sonnet to his lady-love, who rides a tricycle, he addressed it to "A fair rider of the wheel," and he wondered why she was not pleased. She told him he was depreciating her ability, and that she claimed to be more than a fair rider, — she was a good rider. They paid a visit to the dictionary in company.

How many wheelmen can claim a record of attendance at every League Meet? Such a record will soon be worth boasting of.

THE Chelsea Club has made " Daisie " an honorary member, the only one they have.

R. E. BURNETT, of Chelsea, climbed Locke's Hill at Watertown on Sunday.

THE Englishmen are putting their names on the German record tables just as they did on ours. The Germans must develop a Rowe to wipe them off.

AMERICA had no representative at the international tournament.

A WAGER was made about six weeks ago between F. H. Burrill and C. E. Nott, of the Wakefield Bicycle Club, that Nott could not climb Cowdrey's Hill (the Corey Hill of Wakefield). On Saturday last Nott tried and failed to mount it. When within about twenty-five feet of the summit he slipped his pedal and had to give up that trial. He tried four more times, but did not either time succeed in going as far as the first time. The consequence of Nott's failure is that he has to pay for the suppers for eight at Young's Hotel.

RACE committees are still advertising "record" races. There is no such race down in the rules, and in every case a definition of the race and the conditions should appear on the programme. Race officials should have some authority to stand upon, and if committees insist upon putting unknown races on the list, they should define them in a way to permit of no misunderstanding.

A BOSTON man was out on a run with a New York party during the Meet. He took a header, and in reply to a question as to whether he was hurt, he said : " I really believe I have fractured the extensor ossis metacarpi pollicis manus." The New York party rushed in pursuit of a dictionary, and found that he thought he had broken his thumb.

THE much debated question of the proper dress for the tricycle is before dozens of cyclionnes this week, and each one proves her good taste by wearing just what she pleases. A uniform will do very well for a man's club, but it would spoil the picturesqueness of a group of gowns to have them all alike. Besides, the same thing will not suit all sorts and conditions of femininity. A pretty young girl looks very suitably dressed in a brighter gown and a jauntier cap than an elder and plainer woman could think of donning. One thing is certain, full-gown skirts and pleatings of all sorts are a

nuisance and a trial on the three-wheel.— *Record.*

GORMULLY and Jeffery have one of the most complete cycle factories in the country. Every part of the machine except the rubber tire, the rubber handles and the leather on the saddles is made at their works.

AND it is a fact that the modern Athens, which begins to be as fond of hearing or seeing some new thing as the ancient Athens was, is too all agog over the wheelmen and women, to whom the rest of this week belongs. We shall hear more of evangelizing agencies, and a good deal more of the proper sort of skirts to wear on a tricycle than of the work of women in the Sunday schools. The " True Sphere of Women " was talked about at an anniversary meeting last night, but the chances are that most people who saw the title of that lecture in the papers this morning thought that it referred in some way to the Columbia tricycle.— *Record.*

SHE wanted a tandem : —

Miss Dash (residing on Back Bay) : How very fashionable tricycles are becoming ! I am seriously thinking of asking pa to buy me one.

Miss Blank : Yes, I know : they are quite the rage this spring ; but what kind would you buy ?

Miss Dash : Oh, one of those with the seat behind for the coachman, of course ; they are so much easier to run, you know !— *Record.*

ABBOT BASSETT then trotted out his hobby, viz., the admission of professionals to the League and *the abolishment of all distinction, by moving the abolishment of the amateur rule.* W. I. Harris immediately moved to lay it on the table, but on Mr. Bassett's urgent request, he withdrew this motion, that the idea might be discussed. A dead silence prevailed, but Mr. B. called upon the friends of the racing men, pointing out that by this means they could reinstate the expelled racing men. Mr. Ducker caught at it as a drowning man clutches a straw, and he rose and declared himself in favor of such a move. But when the question was put, the motion was killed by a large majority, and Mr. Bassett stored this dead issue in his mental refrigerator, whence he will withdraw it next year, to expose it to another discharge of buck-shot. It is claimed, and, in the light of the facts, with very good foundation, that all Mr. Bassett's actions for the past two months *have been but stepping-stones to his attempted abolishment of the amateur law;* and looked at in this light, it is something to be thankful for that he received such a set-back. — *Wheel.*

The above is too silly to call for a reply.

Overheard at afternoon tea. He and she in a distant corner, conversing earnestly under shadow of a Syrian curtain, and cover of a subdued clatter of tea-cups and tea-spoons. She : " So you 're getting a new tricycle ? " " Yes, a central driver ; best thing out ; told me so at the Show," etc., etc. She : " Oh, *how* I should like to try it." He : " Would you, really ? Bring it round any time you 'll say." She : " But can I ride it ? Has it a dress guard ? " He (recklessly) : " No but I 'll have one put on at once." She (pretending to deprecate his intention) : " Oh, pray no ! It would be

THE "SPALDING."

Confidently presented to the Cycling Public as an embodiment of the highest state of perfection ever attained in Bicycle manufacture.

Light,

Graceful,

Strong,

Easy

Running,

Balls

All Around,

Including

Pedals.

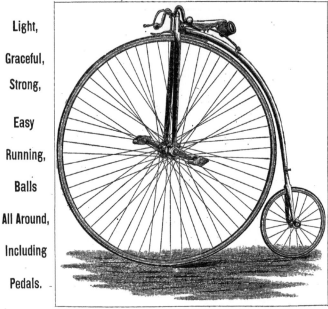

Direct

Tangent

Spokes,

Warwick

Hollow

Rim,

Full Inch

Tire.

All Bright

Parts

Nickelled.

The American Premier,   The Humber Tandem,
The Kangaroo,   The Humber Cripper.

SEND FOR CATALOGUE.

A. G. SPALDING & BROS.

241 Broadway, New York.   *108 Madison St., Chicago, Ill.*

no use for you, and it would n't be worth while for just once." He (with dark duplicity): "Oh, yes it would. In fact, it 's an investment; only costs half a sovereign, and doubles its value when one comes to sell. I 'll get it done at once." Cynical man by piano: "Jones, did n't I hear you say you were looking out for a 'Singer'? Better get the first refusal of Smith's; he 'll be wanting a tandem." — *News.*

MR. KLUGE is not a little troubled that upon his shoulders has been put the accident at Lynn. The immediate cause of the accident was the touching of Kluge's wheel by Rowe, who in turn, it is thought, was forced inward by other riders, all without intention. It was an accident for which no one can be blamed more than another. Up to the time of writing, Kluge is confined to his bed.

MR. LAMSON, of Portland, has a new wrench for wheelmen, which he calls a vice grip. A butterfly sleeve-nut moves the jaw, and there is a generous spread to this nut which allows one to tighten the wrench securely on to a nut.

BURGLARS recently made an entrance into the warerooms of the Pope Manufacturing Company, and captured a lot of League medals and a sum of money belonging to the Massachusetts Club.

THE prizes to be offered in the proposed one-mile international championship race at the fall tournament of the Springfield Club will be a gold watch, valued at $425, to the winner, and also to the man who shall make the fastest heat. No one will be allowed to compete in this race who has not made a record of 2.45 or under.

THE Boston Club will, next Sunday, have a run to Hough's Neck, Quincy (ten miles), starting from the club house at 10 o'clock A. M. Fish dinner at Taber's. Ample opportunity will be afforded for boating, fishing and bathing. A photograph will be taken of those present.

DURING a practice spin at Lynn the other day, Hendee ran five miles in 14.27, and Rowe made a mile in 2.48. In coming down the home-stretch to finish the mile, Rowe could not make the turn and ran over the embankment, falling heavily among the stones. He was taken up insensible and remained so a long while.

CHELSEA will have races as usual on 5 July. The programme calls for a novice, a lap, a championship, and a run and ride race.

BOSTON wheelmen say they had a good time, but they are very tired.

OWEN'S BIRTHDAY RUN.

MR. H. S. OWEN, one of the charter members of the Capital Bicycle Club of Washington D. C., has for many years been in the habit of celebrating his birthday by giving a run on wheels to his brother members of the Capital Club; but the celebration this year surpassed all others in ingenious eccentricities. The rules of the run, which occurred on Friday, 21 May, were that each man should be given a numbered badge before the start, and should take his place in line accordingly. In case of a fall or a dismount he should relinquish it and fall back to the end of the line. The position of each man at the finish when compared with the number on his badge would show his record. The riders met at 4.30 o'clock at 409 15th street, the location of the new club house of the Capital Club, and before starting witnessed the setting of the keystone of the arch of the club house. Messrs. P. T. Dodge, F. H. Noyes and Max Hansmann of the Capital Club, were present with their cameras and took several photographs of the assembled wheelmen and the embryo building. Mr. B. W. Hanna, the club bugler, then gave the signal to mount, and the hundred odd wheelmen filed silently up 15th street. The route this year, always a very difficult one, was made more so by the recent heavy rains. Upon reaching Q street the line filed westward and took to the commons and gutters, when the real riding of the day commenced. Nearly half an hour was consumed in riding the most difficult gullies in the vicinity of the P street bridge. One of the severest tests was a deep and narrow ravine opening from the hills to the north upon P street near the bridge, christened "Header Gulch." In attempting to ride the narrow, stony and slippery gully, many a good rider bit the mud. Many spectators gathered on P street and with great interest watched the wheelmen slowly pick their way down the gully, only to be pitched headlong in the mud or bushes upon meeting a particularly difficult rut. Rex Smith, Crist and S. E. Lewis on upright machines, Max Hansmann on the Little Rover, dubbed "the Skate," and J. Q. Rice, E. P. Hanna, Will Robertson and Jannus on Stars, were successful and were loudly applauded. Messrs. Dodge and Noyes succeeded in ge ng several instantaneous photograghs of men shooting over the heads of their bicycles. From here the route continued down around the observatory, where many difficult feats were accomplished; thence to the vicinity of the flats, Washington monument, bureau of engraving and printing, Smithsonian institution, Capitol hill and Kendall Green, the customary highways being studiously avoided. At Kendall Green the riders were refreshed with a copious supply of iced lemonade. From here they proceeded to the bicycle park on New York avenue, the end of the ride. Notwithstanding the difficult places ridden and attempted, no rider was at all injured and no bicycles were seriously damaged. At the close of the run a long table loaded with a substantial lunch awaited them. The park was brilliantly illuminated with electric lights and Chinese lanterns. After refreshments the evening's sport began. A game of polo between Rex Smith and Will Robertson was won by the latter after an half-hour's stubborn contest. A game of tag on wheels by half a dozen of the most expert wheelmen excited a good deal of interest. In the obstacle riding over rolling logs, bicycle crates, benches, etc., Rex Smith excelled, while Knoerr surprised everybody by the recklessness with which he followed Smith. Rex Smith, S. E. Lewis and Max Hansmann, were the only men who succeeded in riding all the knolls and gulches in the neighborhood of the Observatory as well as "Header Gulch," and were announced as the champions of the day. It was a late hour when the crowd dispersed, all vowing to be present again next spring.

THE new Royal Mail tricycle is certainly very fine, being light and snug, and the new brake very ingenious. Royal Mail is alive this year in both bicycles and tricycles.

THE PATH.

CAMDEN, N. J., 22 May. — Races under the auspices of the Camden Wheelmen, at the Merchantville Driving Park. *One half-mile run.* — F. Collingsby (1), 2.4½; W. H. Duckett (2); C. Atkinson (3). *Half-mile heat race. club.* — W. M. Justice (1) 2.3½; 1.58½; C. P. Chew (2). *One-mile race, club cup.* — H. Weaver (1), 3 54; W. J. Atkinson (2). *One mile, President's Cup.* L. A. W. members. — J. Powell, Smithville, N. J. (1), 3.46½; L. Hill, Philadelphia (2), 3.55; W. J. Atkinson (3). *Two-mile race.* — H. Weaver (1), 9 3⅘; B. O. Miller (0).

PRINCETON, N. J., 20 May. — Races under the auspices of the Princeton College A. A. *Two-mile amateur.* — L. Stearns, '87 (1), 7.11; Segur, '89 (2); Adams, '88 (3).

NEW HAVEN, Conn., 22 May. — Races under the auspices of the Yale Athletic Association. *Two-mile amateur.* — J. S. Kulp, '87 (1), 7.0⅕; S. Carlton, '87 (2).

NEW YORK, 29 May. — Races under the auspices of the Inter-collegiate Athletic Association. *Two-mile.* First heat: S. A. Maguire, '89, Columbia (1), 6.43⅖; F. L. Dean, '88, Harvard (2), 6.44⅕, W. B. Segur, '89, Princeton (3). Second heat: J. C. Kulp, '87, Yale (1), 6.54; D. H. Renton, '86, Columbia (2), by two feet. Third heat: C. B. Keen, '89, University of Pennsylvania, and L. Stearns, '87, Princeton, rode over. Final heat: Keen (1), 6.39; Kulp (2), by 40 yards.

BROOKLYN, N. Y., 31 May. — Races run under the auspices of the Brooklyn Athletic Association. *Two-mile handicap.* — Fred Ray, 50 yards (1), 6.22½; J. S. Kulp, 75 yards (2), by ten yards; E. J. Halstead, Harlem, W., 100 yards (3).

CONCORD, N. H., 26 May. — Races run under auspices of the St. Paul's School. *One-mile amateur.* — J Armstrong (1), 3 48; P. P. Wilcox (2), 3.52.

CHESTER, PA., 29 May. — Races run under auspices of the Chester City Cricket Club. *One-mile novice.* — Lewis A. Hill (1), 3.35; E. S. Worrell (2). *One-mile amateur.* — L. A. Hill (1), 3.26; A. Rice, Chester (2).

EAST HARTFORD, 5 June. — The bicycle races of the East Hartford Wheel Club, on their quarter-mile track this afternoon, proved very interesting and attracted a crowd of about fifteen hundred. The track is necessarily a slow one, but there was some fine speeding. The one-mile club championship was won by H. E. Bidwell in 3m. 14s. The race of the Hartford Wheel Club was one of the most interesting. In it John Illston, with a record of 2m. 45s., was beaten by E. A. DeBlois in 3m. 12s. J. A. Lounsbury, of Hartford, who led at the three-quarters, thought the race finished and slowed up, and lost too much ground to regain the first place. The one-mile club handicap was won by S. H. Tyrrell, of East Hartford, in 3m. 19s.; one-mile club, by E. S. Horton, in 3m. 18s.; one-mile open for boys eighteen years old or less, by H. H. Stockder, of Meriden, in 3m. 19⅜s.; one-

Before buying your new mount for the coming season, send for price list and description of the

"NEW RAPID" BICYCLES,

———————————— WITH THE ————————————

During 1885 not a single spoke broke or wheel buckled.

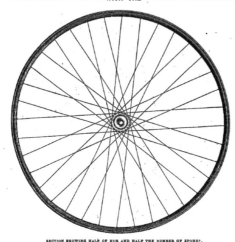

Universally acknowledged to be the strongest and most rigid wheel made.

SECTION SHOWING HALF OF HUB AND HALF THE NUMBER OF SPOKES.

TRUE TANGENT WHEEL.

At the Inventions Exhibition, London, 1885, the "New Rapid" was awarded *a Gold Medal,* the highest and only award for Bicycles.

PRESS OPINIONS.

"One of the best machines in the market."—The Cyclist. | "The 'True Tangent' Wheel (New Rapid) is far and away the most
"The best wheel ever built."—Bicycling News. | perfect yet made."—Illustrated Sports.

SEND TEN CENTS FOR LARGE SIZE CABINET PHOTOS.

ENERGETIC AGENTS WANTED
EVERYWHERE.
APPLY FOR TERMS.

S. T. CLARK & CO.
IMPORTERS,
BALTIMORE, MD.

mile open, by E. S. Horton, of Glastonbury, in 3m. 16s.; half-mile for boys, by W. M. Haradon, of Springfield, in 1m. $47\frac{1}{5}$s.; one-mile club, 3.25 class, by E. E. Arnold, in 3m. 39s.; quarter-mile in heats, by H. E. Bidwell, of East Hartford, in $46\frac{4}{5}$s. and $45\frac{4}{5}$s.; three-mile open in 11m. $19\frac{3}{5}$s., by E. A. DeBlois, of the Hartford Wheel Club.

BROOKLYN, N. Y. — The initial race of a series of three for the championship of the Brooklyn Bicycle Club, two miles, took place on the Boulevard, leading to Coney Island, 22 May. Three started, and T. B. Hawkins, taking the lead from L. W. Slocum a half mile from home, won by a yard; W. Vail third, by a foot. Time, $6.19\frac{3}{4}$.

PITTSBURG, PA. — A race up Ice-House Hill, 22 May, was witnessed by over three hundred persons, and was won by W. D. Banker, Pittsburg, in 2.30 (distance, 2,000 feet, all up-hill); W. I. Wilhelm, Reading, second, by a yard; C. M. Clarke, Pittsburg, third, by a like distance; F. A. Minnemyer, Pittsburg, fourth.

AT the Pottstown, Pa., fair, 3 and 4 June, a one-mile race was won by Wilhelm, of Reading, in 3.25. Wilhelm also beat Hugh J. High, of Pottstown, in a 25-mile race by about fifty feet, in 1.35.3. H. B. Swartz, of Reading, beat three competitors in a two-mile race, in $7.24\frac{1}{2}$.

IN the race of bicyclists against horses, at Madison Square Garden, New York, last week, the wheelmen won. Anderson, the horseman, stopped Saturday forenoon with a score of 953 miles. Woodside made 473 miles and Brooks 484, or a total of 957 miles.

THE two-mile L. A. W. championship, located with the Cleveland Club, will be run 5 July, at Athletic Park. The club races of the same club occur to-morrow, 12 June, and the August Meet is down for the 26th, 27th and 28th of that month.

THE ten-mile championship will be run 24 June at Detroit, Mich.

THE Trojan Wheelmen will hold their third annual race meeting at Rensselaer Park, Troy, N. Y., 23 June. The following events will be on the programme: —

One-mile novice, three-mile Rensselaer County championship, three-mile club championship (one medal), one-mile open, two-mile open, five-mile open record (?), one-mile club, two-mile team, Troy and Albany, consolation race, fancy riding.

OFFICE OF THE RACING BOARD,
BOSTON, 9 June, 1886.

THE Racing Board is informed that the races of the Yale Bicycle Club will be run under A. C. U. rules. The club has put forth its advertisments announcing amateur races and accepted entries from amateurs, taking their entrance fees. It has come to the knowledge of the board, officially that professionals will be allowed to race in the events for which amateurs have entered, and this is to warn all amateurs against competing in the tournament. The Racing Board will promptly declare to be professionals all who contest against professionals, and it will suspend from the track all amateurs who compete at meetings not held under League rules.

ABBOT BASSETT,
Chairman Racing Board.

THE CLUB.

JAMESTOWN, N. Y. — The new officers of the Chautauqua Wheelmen are: President, R. P. Hazzard; captain, Charles E. Gates; secretary-treasurer, F. A. Clapsadel; first lieutenant, R. P. Hazzard; second lieutenant, E. R. Demps.

ATLANTA, GA. — The Atlanta Bicycle Club was organized 28 May with the following officers: C. H. Smith, president; M. Thatcher, secretary and treasurer; E. P. Chalfant, captain; J. Rapp, color bearer. Committees on constitution and for the selection of a club house were appointed.

COMING EVENTS.

JUNE.

12 Saturday. — Second day of race meeting at New Haven by Yale College Club.
N. Y. and N. J. Road Race Association team race, at Orange, N. J.
Races at Cleveland, Ohio.

17 Thursday. — Second Prince-Neilson race at Lynn.

19 Saturday. — Annual Championships of N. A. A. A. at New York.
Annual race meeting of K. C. W. at Brooklyn, N. Y.

23 Wednesday. — Races of Trojan Wheelmen, at Troy, N. Y.

24 Thursday. — Annual meet of the Michigan Div. L. A. W. at Detroit. Ten-mile National Championship.

JULY.

1 Thursday. — First day of annual meeting of C. W. A. at Montreal.

2 Friday. — Second day of annual meeting of C. W. A. at Montreal.

3 Saturday. — Third day of annual meeting of C. W. A. at Montreal.
Suffolk Wheel Clubs' three days' tour begins.

5 Monday. — Race meeting at Binghamton, N. Y.
Race meeting at Cleveland, Ohio, two miles, L. A. W. championship.
Races at Chelsea, Mass.

15 to 18, Tuesday to Friday. — Tournament at Columbus, Ga. State championships will be run.

4th Annual Race Meeting

KINGS COUNTY WHEELMEN,

AT

BROOKLYN ATHLETIC GROUNDS,

Saturday, June 19,

AT 3 P. M.

HANDSOME AND VALUABLE MEDALS.

EVENTS.

1 Mile Novice, K. C. W.
1 " " open to all Amateurs.
1 " Tricycle, " " "
2 " Handicap, " " "
3 " " " " "
5 " N. Y. State Championship, N. Y. Members L. A. W.
1 " Brooklyn Bicycle Club Championship
1 " Ilderan " " "
2 " Bedford Cycling Club "
1 " Consolation Race "

Entrance fee to all open events, 50 cents, and close with Chas. Schwalbach, 124 Penn Street, Brooklyn, June 12.

FOR SALE. — One 54-inch, '86 pattern, Rudge Light Roadster, run ten miles, $120; guaranteed in perfect condition. Address Box 2571, Boston.

FOR SALE. — Beeston Humber Tandem; good condition; Lakin cyclometer, absolutely accurate; price reasonable. H. L., CYCLE Office.

BICYCLES AND TRICYCLES. — 125 shop-worn and second-hand wheels now on exhibition. Stock constantly changing; no price list; correspondence and inspection invited; open Saturday evenings. BUTMAN & CO., Scollay Square, Oriental Building.

BICYCLES AND TRICYCLES. — Bargains for cash; wheels not sold on instalments nor rented. BUTMAN & CO., 89 Court Street.

BICYCLES AND TRICYCLES. — Specialty in furnishing new wheels for exchange. BUTMAN & CO., Scollay Square, Oriental Building.

BICYCLES. — Fair prices and spot cash paid for desirable second-hand wheels. BUTMAN & CO., 89 Court Street.

BICYCLES AND TRICYCLES received on consignment; no charges made when goods are furnished in exchange. BUTMAN & CO., Oriental Building, 89 Court Street.

TO LADY CYCLE RIDERS.

The Jersey Fitting Underwear Co.

MANUFACTURE A

JERSEY FITTING

UNION UNDER GARMENT,

Specially adapted for wear on the

TRICYCLE.

Patented April 7, 1885.

Ladies should examine these garments at

T. D. Whitney's, 145 Tremont Street, C. F. Hovey & Co.'s, Summer St., Boston, and A. A. Smith's, 1029 Walnut St., Philadelphia.

We also make the

Only Perfect Fitting Full-Fashioned

Bicycle & Lawn Tennis Jersey

IN THE MARKET.

TRADE MARK.

Full Tights, Knee Tights, Rowing Suits and Trunks.

These garments all bear our TRADE-MARK, and parties buying would do well to look at these goods before buying any other. We send Sample to any Club in the country.

HOLMES & CO.

17 Kingston Street - - - BOSTON, MASS.

Before you buy a BICYCLE, send to H. B. HART, 811 Arch St., Philadelphia, for illustrated 60 page catalogue (free), and price list of second-hand Machines. DIFFICULT REPAIRING A SPECIALTY.

LYRA BICYCLICA:

SIXTY POETS ON THE WHEEL.

By J. G. DALTON.

Much enlarged second edition. One hundred and sixty filled pages, elegantly bound. In boards, 75 cents; flexible, 40 cents; sent post-paid. This is the standard and only book of thorough-going cycling verse, and comparable in art to none but the first-rate poets. No reading cyclist should overlook it. Old edition, 20 cents. For sale at CYCLE office.

·THE·

❦ COLUMBIAS ❦

FOR 1886

ARE CONFIDENTLY PRESENTED AS THE

STAUNCHEST, MOST RELIABLE, AND EASIEST-RUNNING MACHINES MANUFACTURED.

⁂

The COLUMBIAS have been continually ridden by almost every trick and fancy bicyclist, and have withstood this most severe test for several years.

⁂

THE COLUMBIAS ARE THE HIGHEST GRADE OF MACHINES MADE.

⁂

They have Stood the Test of the Roads **for Eight Years,** and so far as known there is not a COLUMBIA which by wear or breakage is unfit for use.

⁂

·THE RIDERS OF COLUMBIAS
HOLD
THE BEST RECORDS OF THE WORLD.

⁂

The COLUMBIAS are·Ridden by the Majority of Wheelmen at Every League Meet, and are almost invariably chosen by the **Long-Distance Wheelmen.**

⁂

EVERY PART IS INTERCHANGEABLE,
AND CAN BE OBTAINED AT OUR BRANCH HOUSES, OR AGENCIES AT EVERY IMPORTANT CENTER.

EXPERT COLUMBIA.

A Scientifically-Constructed, High-Grade Roadster.

COLUMBIA LIGHT ROADSTER.

A Genuine Light-Weight Bicycle.

COLUMBIA SEMI-ROADSTER.

A High-Grade, Moderate-Priced Bicycle for the use of boys and light men of small stature.

COLUMBIA RACER.

Upon this Racer were made the World's Records for ¼ and ½ mile, and from 2 to 38 miles (inclusive); the World's Amateur Records for ¾ and 1 mile; the World's Professional Records for 4 to 10 and 21 to 43 miles (inclusive); the Greatest Distance Ever Made Inside the Hour (20¼ miles, 396 feet).

STANDARD COLUMBIA.

This "Old Reliable" Wheel has Gone Into the Largest Use of Any Bicycle in This Country. A Thoroughly First-Class Machine at About the Price Charged for Second-Grade Bicycles. For the Money it is the Best Bicycle Manufactured.

COLUMBIA TWO-TRACK TRICYCLE.

Strong, Staunch, Rigid, Light, and Easy-Running. The Simplest and Most Scientifically Constructed Tricycle in the Market.

COLUMBIA RACING TRICYCLE.

Weight, all on, 47½ pounds. Remarkably Strong, considering its weight.

COLUMBIA SAFETY.

Strong, Light, Simple, Easy-Running.

LADIES' COLUMBIA TWO-TRACK TRICYCLE.

A Light and Elegant Machine for Ladies, and Men weighing up to 130 pounds.

CATALOGUE SENT FREE.

THE POPE MFG. CO.

597 WASHINGTON STREET, - BOSTON.

12 Warren Street, NEW YORK. ——— BRANCH HOUSES ——— 115 Wabash Avenue, CHICAGO.

The Cycle.

VOL. I., No. 12.　　　BOSTON, MASS., 18 JUNE, 1886.　　　FIVE CENTS.

The Coventry Machinists' Co.'s New Tricycle for 1886.

Adjustment in Height in Front.　　　Adjustment in Length.　　　A Comfortable Coasting Plate.
Adjustment in Height in Rear.　　　Adjustment in Width.　　　A Bifurcated Seat.

THE LILLIBRIDGE SADDLE

Is the only one having any of these Points; is the only one that can be changed in Shape or Position at all; is the BEST and
CHEAPEST; is adapted to all makes of Bicycles. Special Styles for the Safeties and Star.

Price, Nickelled, $5.00. Price of Coiled Spring, with Straps, etc., for Old Saddles, 75 Cts.

FREEMAN LILLIBRIDGE, Rockford, Ill.

THE BOSTON BICYCLE SHOE.

The Perfect Shoe for Cycling.

Hand-sewed, hand-made, first-quality stock and warranted
in every respect. Every pair of our No. 1 Boston Sporting
Shoes is marked inside, "Boston: Strickland &
Pierce, Hand-Sewed," and is stamped "Patent" on
the bottom. None others are Genuine. Bicycle, Base
Ball Sprint Running, Pedestrian, Gymnasium, La Crosse
and other shoes. Prices and rules for self-measurement
sent on application.

STRICKLAND & PIERCE,

156 and 156½ Summer Street,

BOSTON.

STAR BICYCLES.

SAFE, PRACTICAL and FAST.

NO HEADERS OR DANGEROUS FALLS.

Best Road Record for 50 and 100 Miles.
World's Safety Records from 1 to 20 Miles.
First American Machine to make more than 20 Miles
within the Hour.
Three L. A. W. Championships for 1885.
Won all Hill Climbing Contests, both as to Speed
and Grade.
Won all the First Premiums, when in Competition,
since 1881.
NEW CATALOGUE READY.

H. B. SMITH MACHINE CO.

Smithville, Bur. Co., N. J.

THE AMERICAN CHAMPION, CHALLENGE, SAFETY AND IDEAL.

The above Machines have been awarded First Prize at the New Orleans Exposition, and the Champion holds the World's Long Distance Record. They Run Easy; Sell Easy; Repair
Easy; and the Prices are Easy. They are the best. These are the only Machines of high grade sold at a medium price. It will pay you to examine them, or send two-cent
stamp for Catalogue and Prices. We also have a large stock of Children's Machines at very low prices. First-class Repairing and parts for repairing. All
kinds of Machines constantly on hand; also Sundries. Discount to the Trade. Call or write to the New England Headquarters.

MURRAY'S - - - - 100 Sudbury Street - - - - BOSTON, MASS.

THE Z. & S. STOCKING SUPPORTER.

Every wheelman should have them in his wardrobe or on his back. They are unquestionably the best yet produced. It is made so as to be worn beneath the flannel
shirt, passes over the shoulders and down each leg. It has a sliding buckle, which
allows for tension, and which can be unfastened by a spring in an instant without
inconvenience.

Price Per Pair, 65 Cents.

☞ Send stamp for new Illustrated Catalogue, now ready, of our Cycling Goods.

HOWARD A. SMITH & CO., successors to ZACHARIAS & SMITH, Oraton Hall, Newark, N. J. Branch Store, Orange, N. J.

BEFORE YOU BUY A BICYCLE

A. W. GUMP,

Of any kind, send stamp to

DAYTON, OHIO,

For large Illustrated Price List of New and Second-hand
Machines.
Second-hand Bicycles taken in exchange. Bicycles repaired and nickel-plated. Cash paid for Second-hand Bicycles. Largest stock of second-hand Wheels in America.

BARGAINS THIS WEEK:

52-inch PREMIER, new tires, ball bearings	$50 00
54-inch ENGLISH, new tires, ball bearings	55 00
SOCIABLE TRICYCLE, for two riders	80 00
VICTOR TRICYCLE, late pattern, just like new	100 00
VICTOR TRICYCLE, good running order	75 00
50-inch EXPERT, No. 1 order	75 00

Mention THE CYCLE when you write.

THE CYCLE

PUBLISHED EVERY FRIDAY BY ABBOT BASSETT, 22 SCHOOL ST., ROOM 19.

VOL. I. BOSTON, MASS., 18 JUNE, 1886. NO. 12.

TERMS OF SUBSCRIPTION.

One Year, by mail, post-paid...........................$1.50
Three Copies in one order............................ 3.00
Club Subscriptions................................... 1.00
Six Months... .90
Single Copies.. .05

Specimen Copies free.

Every bicycle dealer is agent for the CYCLE and author-
ized to receive subscriptions at regular rates. The paper
can be found on sale at the following places : —
  Boston, CUPPLES, UPHAM & Co., cor. Washington and
School Streets. Tremont House news stand. At every
cycle warehouse.
  New York, ELLIOTT MASON, 12 Warren Street.
  Philadelphia, H. B. HART, 811 Arch Street. GEORGE
D. GIDEON, 6 South Broad Street.
  Baltimore, S. T. CLARK & Co., 4 Hanover Street.
  Chicago, W. M. DURELL, 115 Wabash Avenue. JOHN
WILKINSON & Co., 77 State Street.
  Washington, H. S. OWEN, Capital Cycle Co.
  St. Louis, ST. LOUIS WHEEL Co., 1121 Olive Street.

ABBOT BASSETT . . . . . EDITOR

A. MUDGE & SON, PRINTERS, 24 FRANKLIN ST., BOSTON.

All communications should be sent in not later than
Tuesday, to ensure insertion the same week.

Entered at the Post-office as second-class mail matter.

IF the boom in wheels this year does not
convince American capital that there is
money in manufacturing cycles, then capital
is very blind.

OF all the cycling papers, there is not one
that has come out boldly in favor of the
amateur rule, save alone the CYCLE. We
do not hesitate to state just where we stand,
and no motives of self-interest will induce
us to adopt another platform. The oldest
cycling paper should be heard from. It has
taken no position except that of opposition
to the chairman of the Racing Board in all
his acts, and that opposition has led it to
hide its true opinion. The *Wheel* is run by
one who never gets on the right side of a
statement, except by accident; and the *Cyclist
and Athlete* is fast coming around from an
active opponent of the Racing Board to a
firm supporter of it. The CYCLE is young
yet, and it has taken a big fight on its
shoulders; but it proposes to stand by its
guns and fight the good fight to the end.

"THE League should give up racing," is
now the cry of many. Granted, when a
worthy successor is found. The A. C. U.
wants to take it under its protecting wing.
What good will come from the change?

The A. C. U. has taken the racing rules of
the League, and it makes but one change :
It will let men race in amateur events who
are hired to ride the wheels of certain
makers. Who will say that the League
should give over its work to an association
that can present no better claim than this?

———

"THE League should give up racing and
attend to touring," comes from Massachusetts. Granted; let then Massachusetts
set the example. The chief consuls of
Pennsylvania, Maryland and New Jersey
point with pride to a road book that is freely
distributed among the members of those
divisions. The chief consul of Massachusetts organizes an association antagonistic to
the League, and attacks the corner-stone on
which it is founded. Nothing that the
League has done for racing has deterred
these officials from attending to a very important part of League' work. Let New
England officials go to work and show us
good road books, and if they find that the
racing department of the League interferes
with their work, let us throw it overboard.

CONTRIBUTORS' CLUB

AN EPISODE.

Editor of the Cycle : I want to tell you of
a very funny experience a friend of mine
had the other day on the road. I will not tell
you his name, but you know him well as an
enthusiastic tandem rider. He started out
one day last week with his Springfield tandem, accompanied by his wife, in anticipa-
tion of a pleasant trip to a friend's. The
weather was beautiful, the roads were in
perfect condition, and nothing was wanting
to make the day's ride one of the most
pleasant in his experience.
  They rode merrily along, and all went
merry as a marriage bell. After riding
about five miles they came to a hill and
started to coast, but suddenly their ears
were assailed by an ominous "click, click,"
which startled our friend so much that,
knowing as he did that that noise meant a
disarrangement of the gearing and the
quicker he stopped the better, he applied the
brake and they came to a stand-still.
  Fearing to turn the wheels, he sought the
assistance of a man in front of whose house
he had stopped, and the machine was lifted
up carefully from the road and deposited on
the lawn in the gentleman's front yard.
They were very careful not to turn the
wheels, for he knew when the gearing was
out of order to turn the wheels would be
fatal to the machinery. He then, with the
assistance of his newly-acquired friend, set

to work philosophically to repair the damage. You must know that the Springfield
is central geared, and consequently the machine had to be taken all to pieces to get at
the trouble.
  After two hours' hard work the machine
was taken all apart and spread out on the
lawn, but everything seemed all right to
the practical eye of our friend, and the gearing was in perfect condition. There was
nothing to do but put the machine together
again, which was done after considerable
time and trouble, and then our friend, lifting
the machine up by the axle, told the gentleman
who had been so kind to assist him to turn
the wheel. He did so, and the noise had
stopped. They then triumphantly mounted
the machine again and started, but oh, horror! the same " click, click " came forth.
  Almost discouraged, my friend, suddenly
looking down at the front wheel, saw that
the mud-guard had become displaced, and as
the wheel moved the spokes came in contact with the guard and made the noise
which had caused them so much trouble.
With a sigh of relief he remedied the difficulty, and looked back with disgust on his
three hours' lost time. The trip had to be
abandoned, and he started for home a sadder
but wiser man.   HAWKSHAW.

STAND TO YOUR COLORS.

Editor of the Cycle : I have just received
and refused a position as official at a race
meeting advertised to be held under A. C.
U. rules. It seems to me quite the time for
men to show their colors and stand by our
grand old institution. Any association that
lets professionals race as amateurs will be
short-lived, and that's just what the A. C. U.
is doing. The success of that union will do
more to kill out the amateur idea than we
can think. It must be nipped in the bud.
                                      CAPTAIN.

FROM A FEMININE POINT OF VIEW.

I HAVE just received a letter from a lady
who has heard of the tricycle but has never
seen one. She lives in a part of the country
where the roads are sandy and the hills are
high, and she wants to know if it will be
possible for her to get any pleasure out of
the machine.

I AM constrained to answer her nay, and
assure her that there will be more hard work
than pleasure for her on roads such as she
describes. American roads, except in a
few localities, such as the vicinity of Boston, Orange, N. J., Buffalo, Chicago, and
the city streets of Washington, are not yet
perfect, and perfection of roads must precede
perfection of riding.

AMERICA is a very large country, and
when I contemplate the very, very few
places where it is possible for a lady to use
the wheel, I have to look very far ahead to

see a condition of things such as our English sisters enjoy.

I CANNOT envy the lady who attempts to ride along the country road that poets like to celebrate and lovers like to haunt. A sandy road, deep rutted and strewn with decayed branches, looks very well in a picture, but the beauty vanishes to her who would ride a tricycle over it.

I WISH it were otherwise, for what more charming field of delight can we find than is laid out for us in the forests? What pleasure-ground more fruitful in resources to charm the eye and divert the mind? And yet it is forbidden ground to us, and we must content ourselves with runs through town centres, along well-travelled highways, and about the edges only of nature's great treasure-house.

IT is little satisfaction to one who wants to go into the woods to be obliged to leave his vehicle at the threshold and walk. Will the time ever come when the wheel will not succumb to soft and uneven surfaces?

.. I KNOW that many will say that the end and aim of tricycling is to ride, ride, ride,— to go as far and as fast as one can within a given period, and to do nothing but ride. I don't quite agree with this, for I believe we should ride with a purpose. I do not sympathize with those who go nowhere and see nothing, and whose minds are always on the cyclometer and the watch. Let us go somewhere, and let us do something.

I THINK we all keep to the good roads too much. We don't strike out into new territory, explore new fields of observation, try unfamiliar paths. I seldom go upon the road that I do not seek to find some new way to reach this or that point, and I have to thank this disposition for much that is rich in my experience.

MY friend Maud had a very funny experience the other day which I cannot refrain from telling about. She was riding a strange machine loaned her by a dealer who was putting her own in order, and it had been sent to her without a dress-guard. She was out on the road and came to a hill, down which she started to coast. Her progress was good at first, but when she was half way down the machine stopped short, and she would have been thrown out had she not been securely held to the saddle by the winding of her dress about the toothed wheel that carries the chain. Here was a pretty state of things. She found herself unable to move hardly, and to extricate herself from the dilemma was simply impossible in the absence of shears.

SHE could not get off the machine, she could not propel it, and she was on a lonely road far from human habitation with night coming on. There is nothing to be told of her experience for the next half hour. It was monotonous and wholly devoid of interest to the outside world. She did nothing; she thought volumes. A farmer's wagon came along at the expiration of the thirty minutes, and two strong men succeeded in

divorcing skirt and wheel. Maud pedalled home a sadder and a wiser girl, and now she is burning midnight oil in her hurry to get a new riding costume. Do you say that you will not ride the wheel if such things are likely to happen? It does not discourage Maud, in fact she tells about it as though it was a delightful experience.

DAISIE.

OFFICIAL NOTICE.

OFFICE OF THE RACING BOARD,
BOSTON, 13 June, 1886.

FOR competing with professionals for a prize in a public race at New Haven, Conn., John Illston, of Hartford, Conn., is declared to be a professional wheelman, and expelled from the League of American Wheelmen.

ABBOT BASSETT,
Chairman Racing Board.

OFFICE OF THE RACING BOARD,
BOSTON, 13 June, 1886.

For competing in races held under rules other than those of the L. A. W., at New Haven, Conn., 11 and 12 June, the following parties are suspended from the race track for thirty days from date : —

A. W. Ives, New Haven, Conn.
G. G. Knapp, Auburn, N. Y.
A. N. Welton, New Haven, Conn.
W. M. Frisbie, New Haven, Conn.
E. A. DeBlois, Hartford, Conn.
A. B. Rich, New York.
G. B. Buxton, Meriden, Conn.
L. A. Miller, Meriden, Conn.
H. H. Stockder, Meriden, Conn.
F. G. Warner, Hartford, Conn.
J. A. Hubbard, Meriden, Conn.
S. Carlton, New Haven, Conn.
E. S. Horton, East Hartford, Conn.
J. A Kulp, New Haven, Conn.
E. B. Patterson, New Haven, Conn.

Wheelmen are warned not to compete with these parties, under penalty of suspension from the track, for such a time as the Racing Board thinks adequate to the offence.

ABBOT BASSETT,
Chairman.

GLEANINGS FROM GOTHAM.

THE last number of the CYCLE contains the startling information that during the League Meet a Boston man took a header, and in answer to inquiries as to whether he was hurt, replied by saying that he had fractured the *extensor ossis metacarpi pollicis manus.* The *Bicycling World*, of the same date, says that the fellow was a girl. The CYCLE still further tells us that the New York party rushed in pursuit of a dictionary, and from it interpreted the remark that the fallen party had broken his or her thumb. Now we do not doubt that the Boston man took the header, and though he imagined he had hurt his thumb, we don't for a minute doubt that he made the reply stated, which, however, is grossly inaccurate; and we marvel much at the combined wisdom of the editors of the journals quoted, for falling into the pit laid for them. We doubt that any New Yorker had to consult a dictionary; and if he was obliged to, we know he would not have found the solution to the very simple problem therein ; for as any school-boy knows, what the Boston man really said while laboring to give a mystical and high-sounding expression for a small hurt, was

that he had fractured (?) an extensor (that is, a muscle), that moves not the thumb but the metacarpal bone of the thumb. This will be plainly seen is widely different from the metacarpal phalanx of the thumb. While it is generally conceded that Bostonians yearn after culture, New York is satisfied to deal with facts ; and the attempt of the CYCLE to represent the New Yorker as being ignorant of the elementary terms used at the very threshold of anatomical study, evinces a spirit which, to say the least, is decidedly ungenerous.

* * *

* THE first great road race has passed into history, and the New York and New Jersey Team Road Racing Association can congratulate itself upon a decided success. Last Saturday was a fine day for wheeling, a trifle warm, but the fine condition of the roads made up for any deficiency that was experienced in other details. The starting point of the road race was some two or three miles from the Newark cycling headquarters, and my good friend Smith having placed a Cripper tricycle at my disposal, I started to follow a party of Hudson County Wheelmen to the course. It was a stern chase and a long one, and the trip was the longest three miles I had wheeled over for many a day. I had the honor of being born in Jersey, but I left at a tender age and before the League was organized, and my knowledge of the country has been confined to a study of the road books. I trusted to the leader of the party, however, but next time I take a trip to Irvington by the way of Orange and Milburn, I will take the horse cars before I trust a resident of Jersey. I only regret that I was unable to keep my appointment as timer, as the race was started before I was able to reach the starting point.

The arrangements for checking and handling the men were perfect, and the course was kept comparatively clear of teams. Upwards of five thousand people were scattered along the six and a quarter miles of highway, and groups of ladies wearing the club colors enlivened the scene as they wildly cheered their favorites. It was a hot race from start to finish, and the winners never faltered. To write the history would take many a column, but I will confine myself to the brief facts. Six clubs put in appearance. The Kings County Wheelmen were represented by E. Pettus, E. M. Valentine, H. L. Bridgman and L. P. Weber. The Ilderan Club had W. Richardson, H. H. Farr, H. Greenman and W. J. Savoy. Elizabeth put in the field, A. S. Bellinger, A. S. Roorbach, L. B. Bonnett and H. Caldwell. Harlem wheelmen quartette consisted of E. I. Halsted, M. F. Germond, A. T. Steiner and C. Pearse. The Rutherford team consisted of E. W. Dean, Jr., F. T. Doolittle, A. P. Jackson and H. R. Jackson; while Hudson County was represented by Charles A. Stenken, Ed. F. Baggot, L. Allen and Chas. Leé Myers. The contestants, as a rule, were dressed as if for the track, and at the start were ranged in rows of four, with about twenty-four feet between each row. Over three hundred people witnessed the start, and manifested considerable interest throughout the contest. The course led over hill and dale,—a gentle, rolling country, with several steep rises. The road was uniformly in good condition, except in a few

spots where repairs were being made. There were fewer accidents than was to be expected under the circumstances, and the association is to be congratulated. The start was not made until after half past four, but when the men got under way they made up for lost time. C. Lee-Myers led the van at the commencement of the first round, with the others bunched close behind. The pace proved too much for him, and at the end of the third mile Stenken, of Jersey City, went to the front, followed by Valentine, Halsted, Caldwell and Bridgman. This order was maintained throughout the first round, Stenken being the first to finish the twelve and a half miles, his time being 48m. 12⅘s. Before the hotel at Irvington was reached on the second round, Valentine passed him and took the leading position, which he held to the finish, winning the race and the gold medal in 1h. 4¼m. 5s. The second man, Stenken, receives a silver medal, and the Kings County Wheelmen hold the cup until next fall, when it will have to be run for again.

The K. C. W. scored first, fourth, fifth and seventh place, making a total of 83 points. The Elizabeth Club took third, sixth, ninth, and eleventh, making 71 points in all. The Harlem Wheelmen came next with 54 points, having taken eighth, tenth, twelfth, and sixteenth places. Halsted, of this club, who was riding a good second at the first turn, took a bad header, but pluckily kept through and finished sixteenth. The Ilderan team scored 33 points, winning thirteenth, fourteenth and fifteenth places, their other man, Farr, taking a bad header. The Hudson County wheelmen only had one man in at the finish, Steuken; the-others dropping out from disability, headers, etc. The riding of Pettus, of the Kings County Wheelmen, was noticeable for grit. He was eleventh man at the end of the first round, but managed to pull up into fifth place at the finish, although he had not especially trained, and did not expect to start. The following table of the order of finish has been prepared and forwarded through the courtesy of Mr. E. K. Austin, of the Kings County Wheelmen :—

1	E. M. Valentine, K. C. W.,	1.41.05
2	C. A. Stenken, H. C. W.,	1.42.40
3	Ed. Caldwell, Elizabeth W.,	1.48.14
4	M. L. Bridgman, K. C. W.,	1.50.24
5	Ed. Pettus, K. C. W.,	1.50.45
6	L. B. Bonnett, Elizabeth W.,	1.52.45
7	L. P. Webe⸗, K. C. W.,	1.52 45
8	C. Pearse, Harlem W.,	1.56.3
9	A. S. Roorbach, Elizabeth W.,	1.56.17
10	M. F. Germond, Harlem W.,	1.56.40
11	A. S. Bellinger, Elizabeth W.,	1.56.41
12	A. T. Steiner, Harlem W.,	1.58.40
13	W. J. Savoy, Ilderan B. C.,	1.59.35
14	H. Greenman, Ilderan B. C.,	2.00.15
15	W. Richardson, Ilderan B. C.,	2.01.18
16	E. I. Halsted, Harlem W.	2.02.20

The remainder straggled in at all hours, and no official recognition was taken of their performance. The best of feeling prevailed throughout, and the close finish proves that the competition will be very keen next fall, after a season's riding has toughened the muscles of the racers. The Kings County and Elizabeth Wheelmen race for teams of eight men will take place on 3 July. The officers of the race were : Referee, A. Fauquier ; judges, W. W. Share, T. C. Smith,

and W. C. Smith ; timers, E. H. Douglass, W. H. DeGraff, and W. H. H. Warner. The scorers places were ably filled by E. K. Austin, W. Adams, J. C. Willever, and C. C. Pennell ; while Elliott Mason acted as starter. Mr. T. C. Crichton fulfilled the onerous position of clerk of the course.

JENKINS.

NEW AMATEUR RULE.

AT a meeting of the American Cyclists' Union at the Commonwealth Hotel, Monday, the racing rules were overhauled and the following, defining amateurs and professionals, were adopted :

An amateur wheelman is any person who has never, either in public or in private, raced or exhibited his skill for a public or for a private stake, or for a purse, or for gate money, and who has never competed under a false name, and who has never backed, or allowed himself to be backed, either in a public or private race.

A professional wheelman is one who, at any time, in any degree, has violated his amateur standing as defined above.

The temporary officers chosen at the time of the League Meet were formally placed in nomination. After the election the committee will be appointed, and the membership committee will act on the many applications already received.

THE C. T. C. SPEAKS.

To avoid possible misconception, the members of the American Division are warned, that while they are not denied full liberty of membership in any other organization, the definition of an amateur as established by the N.C.U. of Great Britain, and the L.A.W. of the United States, has not been changed, and must continue, unless altered, to control the conduct and actions of those members of the C. T. C. who may appear upon the racing track as contestants. As every member of the C. T. C. in this country has, with his application for membership, signed an agreement to observe the above, intended violations should always in honor be preceded by resignation from club membership. Violations not so preceded must necessarily be dealt with as provided in rules 51, 53, and 54. (See hand-book.)

FRANK W. WESTON,
United States Chief Consul.
SAVIN HILL, BOSTON, MASS., 1 June, 1886.

A REFORMED MAN.

ONE of the " suspends " writes thus to the chairman of the Racing Board : —

" I wish to say my little say in regard to the position you have taken. When I first received your notice telling me of the action of your board in regard to the ' makers' amateurs ' and expelling me from the path, I was inclined to consider the whole thing decidedly ' fresh ' and a matter not worthy my attention. I was not aware, at that time, that your rules were the recognized racing rules of America, and were backed by the N. A. A. A. and N. C. U.

" I now see my folly, and must frankly admit that you were perfectly right in doing what you did, and must say that I admire your pluck. I was as sour as any one on the action of the League, *at first;* but what's the use beating round the bush, now that the thing is as plain as the nose on your face.

" The boys had a chance to defend themselves, and they didn't improve it ; what's the use of kicking now ?

" Why do they object to a ' third class ' ? It is known that they are paid for racing, and why are they not willing to go by themselves ?

" I think that this ' third class ' system an excellent one, and hope to see it carried out. I would, however, like to see ' Rule H ' done away with, and a new rule inserted which would allow men their *actual travelling* expenses, but which would *not* allow them to be paid for their *time* or *riding*. There are many good men who could take the time to race, but who would not ' stand the pressure ' ; and if a friend, no matter whether he is a ' cycle dealer ' or not, is willing to pay the cost of the trips, I don't think that the riders should be obliged to refuse the offer.

" Another rule I would like to see on your books is in regard to the return of entry fees. I don't think that a man should pay for giving an entertainment.

" The racing men certainly are the attraction at a race meeting, and I think they should have their fees returned *after finishing* their races."

THE NEW ORLEANS TO BOSTON TOURISTS AT HOME.

ON Wednesday evening, 9 June, a number of the members of the League of American Wheelmen, Louisiana Division, and the New Orleans Bicycle Club, gathered at Asiredo's, West End, for the purpose of giving a hearty welcome home to the Boston tourists.

Capt. A. M. Hill and Capt. C. M. Fairchild, of the tourists, were present, wearing their L. A. W. uniforms. Harry Fairfax remained in the North, seeing the sights, and therefore missed the reception, although toasts were given to him and a medal forwarded.

The reception was hearty and delightful. The tourists occupied the seats of honor at each end of the table, and the chairman, Chief Consul Ed. A. Shields, of the L. A. W., was all around the table.

After a fine dinner Mr. Shields arose and made the speech of welcome, dilated on the achievement of the three representatives of Southern pluck, endurance, and cycling skill, and then on behalf of those present and others, presented the tourists with handsome gold medals. The medals are an elaboration of the idea of the League badges, and each bears the name of the recipient, the year, and "From Boston to New Orleans in thirty days." Messrs. Hill and Fairchild made replies acknowledging the compliment.

After once starting the speech-making, the wine was so good and the eloquence so far above the average, that the cyclists were not satisfied until every member at the festive board had expressed his sentiments, praising the exploits of the tourists. The club, the League, the new members, the various wheels, the guests from other cities, the press, the caterer, and numerous other persons and things were brought to memory by a bumper, and it was a late hour when the jolly meeting adjourned. Fortunately the last train had not yet departed, and the tourists were not compelled to add to their walking record.

THE AGE OF FABLE.

SCENE at the Cycleries. The Proprietor of a low-priced newspaper is talking with a Gigantic Monopolist. He says : "I am going to crush out the CYCLE." G. M. : "What for? Have you got a patent on newspapers that is being infringed?" P. of L. P. N. : "No, but they have forced me to put down my price, and I shall kill the paper." G. M, : "You are the man that has always called me a monopolist, and now you want to be one yourself. You haven't got a patent on a newspaper, and you can't show any title to a right to publish one that others don't enjoy as well as yourself. Go to; you are not worthy to be a monopolist!"

The moral of this is, that the first sign given by a newspaper to show that it is being crushed is a reduction of its subscription price.

A DIRTY little Ragamuffin was once seen throwing Mud at a Passer-By, but the Mud did not Stick to the Passer-By. It fell around him in showers made up of Dollar Bills, and the hands of the Ragamuffin were soiled and dirty.

The moral of this is, that when a merchant sells flour for one dollar a barrel, it shows that the great public will pay no more for it.

AN African went out to fight an Enemy, and he took a Boomerang to chuck at him ; but when he chucked it the weapon flew back and he was slain himself.

The moral of this is, that it does n't pay to notice insults from those who know no better than to sow them broadcast.

A NAUGHTY little Boy took for his motto : "I will jump on Everything." He lived up to his Motto, and one day he jumped on a Ball. The Ball rolled from under him and he broke his Toe.

The moral of this is, that it is a good plan to cry down all monopolies till we can get hold of one for ourselves.

A WHEELMAN met a tramp on the Common the other day. "Can you tell me," said he, "where I can find the Cycleries?" The tramp eyed the wheelman with a look of disgust, and blurted out : "There ain't no cycleries no more, but if you want the Kickeries go to 179 Tremont street.

A MAN once invited his Uncle to see his new House. He showed him around the Building and pointed out the good points. "It is n't much of a House" said the Uncle, "but as a shanty it will do." "But," said the man, "I built every mite of it myself." "That does n't keep it from being a Blooming Shanty," said the Uncle.

The moral of this is, that a pair of sharp shears in the hand of an artist is better than a dull pen in the hand of a tramp.

NEW MACHINES.

SPRINGFIELD is to give the world two new machines. The *Union* thus describes them :

A Steam Tricycle. — J. H. Bullard, of the Bullard Arms Company of this city, has for several months past been at work on a tricycle for which steam shall furnish the motive power. The experiment has so far succeeded that recently several trial trips have been made with such satisfaction as to already cause two manufacturers to apply for the

right manufacture. Several details are yet to be perfected, and when the machine is entirely to the satisfaction of its inventor a public exhibition will be given. A minute description is not possible at present, as the inventor wishes to secure his patent rights before making public the details of his invention. It is proposed, however, to have the machine so constructed as to be easily controlled by a lady or child. The power of locomotion will be automatic, so that all the rider will need to do is to get seated on the machine, take hold of the steering apparatus, and then devote one's self to the pleasures of a trip over hill and country with a steed that requires neither food nor grooming, and if so desired that can compete with the lightning railroad train. It is the inventor's intention, however, to regulate the speed to eight miles an hour, as the roads to be found in this country would not make a higher rate of speed enjoyable. But 20 miles an hour will be guaranteed possible. This machine will be a "hill climber," and warranted to overcome anything in that line without exertion or fatigue. It will be so arranged that light baggage can be fastened on, and the appliance will be adapted to either the single or sociable form of tricycle. It is thought the sociable will prove the more popular form of the two, and the manufacturers will be able to cater to either taste of a purchaser. The weight of a machine will be increased comparatively little as the appliance will be very compactly arranged. The water supply will be capable of five to seven hours' use before needing renewal. Kerosene oil will be the fuel. It is claimed that the invention can be applied with equal success to a four-wheeled carriage. As stated above, several trial trips have recently been made, and those who have been fortunate spectators speak enthusiastically of the entire success and practicability of the invention. Patents will be applied for in France, Belgium and Germany and other portions of the continent as well as in this country.

A Safety Bicycle. — A unique safety bicycle has been completed and just tested on our streets. It has many new features, is constructed so entirely upon new principles that it has none of the features of other bicycles now covered by patents. It is a lever machine, giving a constant application of power, so appreciated on muddy or sandy roads, or in hill climbing. The inventor, Rev. Homer A. King of Clinton street, this city, has been inventing and securing patents for three years, making new application for a patent nearly every four or five months. Having discovered the motor, he has continued on a new line of cycle invention suited to the motor, bringing out the new adjustable anti-friction bearings,which have less friction, as they cannot roll together, than ball bearings ; being more durable and capable of supporting great weight, are applicable to other kinds of machinery. The new hollow felly rim is more ridged than any other. Several can be made at not more than the cost of one of any other hollow felly rim. The new gearing, without cogwork or changing the point of the flexible connection to the levers, enables the rider without dismounting to set a 50-inch wheel to the speed of a 40, 50, 60 or 70-inch crank bicycle with very little added friction, and absolutely none when set for power for sandy or muddy roads

or hill climbing. The new silent ratchet is appreciated, especially in coasting, and is so simple that any person can take it apart and put it together. The steering with the small wheel in the rear, by the depression of either end of the bent handle bar and the position of the hands, is most natural and effective, and enables the rider to increase the advantages of the new motor. This enables him to bear his whole weight upon the pedals, thus utilizing his weight as well as his muscle ; and as the depression of one lever, without a spring, automatically raises the other foot and lever, much fatigue is avoided. Many other points might be mentioned or summed up in ease, speed and especially safety. As the pedals are in the rear of the hub, and the fulcra in front of the hub, the downward pressure upon the pedals produces an uplifting at the fulcra, enabling the rider to pass safely down a steep hill, through a rut, or over a large obstruction, with no danger of taking a header. While Mr. King was in the pastorate of the First Baptist Church of Mystic, Ct., which he resigned to engage again in evangelistic work, he felt the need of pastors and all who would avoid the risk, care and expense of keeping a horse, and now offers them a beautiful, safe, fleet horse, which eats nothing and may stand in the hallway always saddled and bridled ready for recreation or business. For the last nine months Mr. King has only preached each Lord's day, spending five days of each week at his cycles, but he intends soon to return either to the pastorate or evangelistic work, as a company is forming for the manufacture and sale of the King bicycles, tricycles and quadricycles. His brother in New York will probably be the general agent, but the manufacturing may continue to be done here or somewhere this side of New York. Mr. King favors the idea of setting apart a large share of the company's stock to be used as part pay to skilled labor, and as most of the parts of the vehicle can be made by machinery, this arrangement would enable the company to soon pay large dividends, and between the two extremes settle for themselves in the golden mean the vexed labor problem.

AN OUTSIDE VIEW.

THIS action of the Racing Board was ratified by the League at its recent meeting in Boston, and the result was the immediate withdrawal of the disaffected men and the formation of a rival association, to be known as the American Cyclists' Union. Personal ambitions and jealousies have doubtless had much to do with this consummation, as well as the local prejudices and ambitions of the clubs to which the deposed men belong, or which are accustomed to fill their treasuries by the holding of periodical race-gatherings of greater or less magnitude. But whatever the merits of the controversy may be as between individuals, or as regards methods of procedure, the significant fact to the country at large is that an influential portion of the Wheelman's League has stood ready to defend or to ignore serious violations of the laws that are intended to keep a great and steadily growing pastime wholesome and enjoyable. For of the truth of the charges against the expelled members there is practically no moral doubt, even among those who have demanded their reinstatement.

The injurious effect which this defection must for a time, at least, have upon the League is evident, since it leaves upon its list of eligible contestants scarcely one of the men best known upon the track capable of noteworthy achievement. Still more serious, however, is the injury which bicyclists have inflicted upon their own sport. So far as the mass of the public is concerned, it matters little whether the rider does his best to show the excellencies of the machine he rides or to gratify a personal ambition, so long as he does his best. It is of importance to the bicyclists, however, and of consequence to the public, that the conditions of bicycle racing shall be above the suspicion of double dealing in rider or association. To this belief, that bicycle racers are fired by no other desire than the desire to win, the sport owes its great popularity more than to any other cause. If that belief is shaken or gives way to any serious suspicion, even, this new sport will quickly fall into the disrepute which has more or less fully overtaken almost every other form of out-door pastime. This is the danger which is threatened by the formation of the new union. It insures fine races the coming summer, no doubt, and perhaps that is all some of the promoters of the secession care for. But it is an association based upon the assumption that vital laws may be broken ; and the evil is no less real because the assumption may be unconscious. Further than this it brings the dangerous money element into a sport whose charm is that it has been free from that taint, and it is a question if it does not operate to the injury of young riders who, relying upon their own resources, cannot successfully compete with men who, though amateurs in name, are still in a sense professionals, and can certainly afford to devote much more time to a special training. In a word the tendency of the revolt is towards a semi-professionalism, which, while it may not introduce any element of dishonesty, is still calculated to confine the reward of racing to a privileged few, to build up a class against the interest of the many and against the best interests of the sport at large. — *Providence Journal.*

An actual count of the bicycles used by the members of the Massachusetts Bicycle Club, of Boston, which is the largest club in this country, shows that there are more Rudges used than any other make. This speaks well for this popular machine.

While in Boston, both Capt. W. M. Brewster, of the Missouri Bicycle Club, of St. Louis, Mo., and Sanford Lawton, of the Springfield Club, of Springfield, Mo., were smitten with the appearance of the Rudge Light Roadster, and each of these gentlemen took one home with him when he left.

NOTHING NEW UNDER THE SUN.

It has been said that "there's nothing new under the sun." We were almost confirmed in this belief while looking over Low's "Almanac," published in the year 1820. Heading one of the pages of miscellaneous matter we noticed a rough cut of a "velocipede, or walking machine," as it is termed. The vehicle in appearance is similar to our modern bicycle, with the exception that the wheels are of uniform height and the rider's feet touch the ground, by this means accel-erating his speed. Following is a brief description of this wonderful "machine," as printed under the cut : —

Mr. Charles Davis was the inventor of this machine, which, though not yet introduced into practical use in this country, is calculated to be an important discovery, because it is applicable to the movement of armies, and will render rapidly practicable marches far more distant than have ever yet been undertaken. The principle is taken from skating. — *Salem Telegram.*

CYCLETS.

Those who think the English riders will come over this fall and race under A. C. U. rules, at the risk of their amateur status, will find themselves mistaken. The N. C. U. and the L. A. W. are in harmony, and the man that is declared a professional by the L. A. W. will be so looked upon by the N. C. U.

The Massachusetts Division and the League shared the profits of the races as follows : Massachusetts Division, $22.90 ; League, $11.45.

The California Division has got the three-mile championship of the League, and they hope to make it the central feature of a large race meeting.

"The boom has not yet stopped," said a dealer to us the other day ; "the orders are still pouring in, and we are getting out of the best sizes." This we found to be the case everywhere.

The new Royal Mail tricycle has a ratchet brake, has small drivers and large steerers. It has, moreover, the best foot-rest for coasting that we have seen on a two-tracker.

Chelsea parties are talking of a repetition of the combined tour of horseback riders and bicyclers made in 1881 to the White Mountains.

A tandem that two ladies can ride seems to be in demand. The Royal Mail gave us the first of this kind, and then followed Singer & Co. The Coventry Machinists' Company showed a new pattern of the Club tandem at the cycleries, and took orders for all that they could get. More are coming, though.

Letters of machines say that it doesn't pay very well to let tandems. The riders scorch all the time and get careless, hence accidents and repairs. Livery men never let out trotters.

The C. T. C. comes out boldly and stands shoulder to shoulder with the L. A. W. on the amateur question.

The man who likes public office has a queer view of the pleasures of this life. To work like a dog and get only kicks in return, is not the kind of fun we delight in. And yet we should all be willing to share the burdens, and not stand outside always and do the kicking.

The decision on the Bown ball-bearing case is not yet announced. It is held in reserve. Great things depend upon that decision.

Ripley and Hersey, the two famous run-and-ride men, will meet at Binghamton in a race of that kind on 5 July.

It is rumored that the Independence Day races in Boston will be held on the Union Grounds. A poor track is better than an improvised one from the Common paths.

You can always tell a Columbia racer on the track, because the spokes are nickelled from the hub to the lacings. This idea has been adopted by the makers, and now let some one else give us a distinguishing mark as plain as this.

Last week Morgan lost his pocket-book, containing all his funds and a ticket from Boston to Chicago. He will hereafter travel with less than a thousand dollars in his pocket, having decided that it is n't safe to carry so much.

Thirty-three members of the Missouri Club reported over 8,500 miles in the aggregate for the May riding. There were ten men with over 400 miles apiece to their credit. The leaders were Ab. Lewis, with 666 miles ; Alex. Lewis, 613 ; E. F. Woestman, 532 ; Percy Walden, 521 ; W. M. Brewster, 411½.

It is difficult for one man to give another a piece of his mind without destroying the peace of both their minds.

Chicago is talking over a new bicycle track. A party of wheelmen, including J. O. Blake and Major W. M. Durell, visited Cheltenham Beach last week to look over the ground whereon the new bicycle track is to be laid. The ground affords ample room for a much larger track than it is intended to lay, but the gentlemen in charge of the work have decided that a quarter of a mile will be the most convenient size. The track is to be of 2 x 6 matched boards, eighteen feet in width on the straights, and twenty-five feet on the ends. It will be raised two feet on the outside, so that riders may take the corners at full speed, without fear of accident. Inside the bicycle track there will be a cinder path for foot racing, and outside a half-mile track for horses. It is doubtful whether a more suitable piece of ground for the purpose could be found anywhere, as the shade-trees afford excellent shelter for the spectators without in the least obstructing the view.

One of our local clubs has in view a basket picnic to the woods. The ladies will attend, some on tricycles and some in a barge. Would it not be a good idea for other clubs to fall in line with this idea ? It gets monotonous when we always go to an hotel.

What a boon to cycling editors this A. C. U. business has proved.

The Missouris had an informal opening of their club house last Wednesday, and a very good joke was played on Capt. Brewster. Mr. A. Moore Berry made a speech complimenting him for his many virtues and alluded to a present. Brewster cocked up his ears and said to himself : "A watch, I hope, or a new bike would go." Then the door was opened and a horrible boneshaker was rolled in. It was constructed by a Kansas jay-hawker of the roughest kind of lumber. The backbone was of six-inch stuff, and the pedals were wood throughout. Brewster was put on in a sort of dazed state and ridden around the asphalt amid the plaudits of the crowd. The machine was then labelled ".Capt. Brewster's latest mount," and prominently placed in the club house. — *Journal.*

WAS there ever a horse *v.* bicycle race that was not a hippodrome and a failure? We trow not.

THE tricycling parties at the rink seem constantly to gain in favor with the ladies, and about twenty-five are present each morning. Several ladies have purchased machines and are doing road riding, and there is talk of forming a club. — *Hartford Courant.*

"WHAT is that Bicycle Man doing, father? See! he has Jumped Forward from his Wheel and is putting his Face to the Earth. Is he Kissing it?" "No, my son; the Man has his Ear to the Earth. He is Listening. He thought he heard Something Drop."— *Burlington Free Press.*

"SONNY, you need n't do that any more, I 'm satisfied ; here 's a dime."
"What 's the dime for?"
"Why, to pay fer the exhibishun ; don't you generally take up a collection?"
Now, there is nothing in the above to make a wheelman mad, yet the bicyclist who was practising the pedal mount in a little town, in Kentucky last Sunday, became almost dangerously violent, simply because the honest old countryman offered him a dime for witnessing his contortion acts. — *Ex.*

A UNIQUE vacation by a clergyman will be taken by Rev. Mr. Utter, of the First Unitarian Church of Chicago. He proposes to make a bicycle tour through portions of England, Germany, and France.

THE new $250 tandem tricycle that Dr. Rust brought from Boston yesterday, came to grief early. He and Will Collins had ridden it a number of times up and down Colony street in the afternoon, followed always by the admiring glances of all spectators. Later the Miller brothers started out to ride the four-wheeler. Up Colony street they had the hard luck to run foul of the curbstone, and one of the large wheels of the machine was considerably damaged and the machine injured so that it will cost something for repairs. — *Meriden Journal.*

AT races on the Crystal Palace track, London, 29 May, P. T. Letchford made a half mile against time in 1.26⅘, and H. A. Speechly made a quarter mile in 38⅘, both times beating the English record.

THE *Bulletin* of 11 June is a star number. It gives a report of the League Meet in full, and a very large quantity of interesting matter.

MR. H. S. WOOD resigns as bookmaster. This is a great loss to the League. Mr. Wood is conspicuously able in the direction of the work allotted to his office, and it will be no easy task to fill his place.

FROM advice received at New Orleans, it is learned that Fred Van Meerbeke, the New York to San Francisco tourist, arrived at San Antonio, Texas, late in the evening of 5th inst., having been 20 days out from New Orleans, which city he left on 17 May, after a two weeks' rest. He is in good health and spirits, and three days ahead of time.

THE members of the Toronto Bicycle Club, who are now touring in France, were last heard from at St. Gervais, a small town between Rouen and Paris. They are very much pleased with the French roads.

WILMOT and Sewell, the well-known Boston fancy riders, have been with Barnum's show four weeks this season, and three weeks in New York, at Miner's Bowery Theatre, the London, and Miner's Eighth Avenue Theatre.

J. G. HITCHCOCK, the Omaha racer, arrived here Thursday. He visited the Yale College races at New Haven. He will be domiciled at Hotel Faneuil for the summer.

IN point of active membership in the League, the Massachusetts Club ranks first; the Pennsylvania Club second, and the Chicago Club a close third, with 89 riding members.

THE St. Louis Ramblers have issued a very neat schedule of runs for the season of 1886, extending from 2 May to 31 October. The shortest run is 26 miles, and the longest about 200. The member who attends every one of these runs will have covered 1,274 miles during the season.

BURNHAM has broken or sprained his arms six times, as a result of bicycle racing; and for the sixth time he recently made the resolution to never again race on a bicycle, being firmly determined to devote all his efforts in the racing line to tricycles.

THE Melrose Bicycle Club will give a series of races on the road 4 July. The programme will probably include a slow race, a race with hands off, and a ride-and-run race.

HARRY COREY has been riding up the Brighton side of Corey Hill. This is a much more difficult feat than that of riding up from Beacon street, and it has been accomplished by very few. Arthur Young, of St. Louis, rode it several times last fall; and these two are the only ones that we know of who have got to the top.

HILLIER'S German records were knocked out by Webber at Munich, the stout-hearted Islesman winning both his races after a terrible fall the day before. He writes us: "I don't expect I shall be able to race any more this year. No matter! I 'll smoke my rides out this season and go for 'em next year." We wish him a speedy recovery and a return to the path at an earlier date than now seems possible to him. — *London Wheeling.*

THE annual meet of the New Hampshire division will occur at Portsmouth, 5 July.

WHEN M. V. J. Webber left for England last September, he left his 56-inch Rudge Humber Racer with Mr. H. D. Corey. This is the machine on which he rode during the famous race of twenty miles within the hour, and was only used at Springfield. Mr. Corey offers the same for sale and invites correspondence. Address, 152 Congress street, Boston, Mass.

NOW is the time to secure anything in the cycle sundry line which you may need. Call or send to Stoddard, Lovering & Co., 152-158 Congress street, Boston.

HOWELL says he will ride a tricycle twenty miles in the hour the coming season. We hope he will do it.

SINGER & Co. have increased their plant by buying up the establishment of Settle & Co.

THE English papers are not taking kindly to the proposed international tournament.

THE *Mirror of American Sports* will make changes, and, pending these, the paper will discontinue publication. The new paper will appear 3 July.

THE *American Wheelman* has three different accounts of the League Meet. There is something in the lot to suit all parties.

KAUFMAN has been having a try at the one-mile unicycle record held by himself. He made the run at Aston Lower Grounds, and scored 4.7⅜. His Rochester record is 4 minutes.

W. K. MENNS, of Everett, is making an illuminating oil for cyclists' use. He warrants it not to gum nor to crust over, and the vibration of the wheel will not put out the light.

MISS KIRKWOOD, of Maplewood, has been made an honorary member of the Everett Wheel Club.

" By telegraph " and " special " and other terms are familiar in the daily papers as showing how the news comes. " By bicycle" appeared, probably, for the first time in the world in a daily paper, in Monday's St. Louis *Post-Dispatch.* About 10.30 Monday morning, the *Post* was advised by telegraph of a murder at Kirkwood, fourteen miles distant. Quicker work was required than could be got out of a horse and buggy. Reporter Hicks, one of the best in the city, is an expert wheelman. Accompanied by Al. Stewart as pace-maker, he made the fourteen miles to Kirkwood (road in bad condition) in an hour and twenty minutes. The return was by train, and the *Post* had two-thirds of a column covering the essential points in the case.

THE agents of the Buffer saddle have been taxed to their utmost to make the supply equal the demand, but are now pleased to say that their stock is complete. Stoddard, Lovering & Co., 152-158 Congress street, Boston.

" KING of the Road " lamps, of all sizes, prices, finishes, and patterns, can be found at Stoddard, Lovering & Co.'s, 152-158 Congress street, Boston.

BAYLISS, THOMAS & Co. have turned out a racing tricycle, with 7¼ inch cranks, which scales 33¾ pounds.

JAMES LENNOX was to start on the 7th inst on a record-breaking trip to John O'Groats.

AT a Muswell Hill contest held lately in England, the winning rider had his machine built with the forks racing forward and the handles bent half way down the forks, and the English wheelmen say that all contests of the kind in future must include a ride down the hill as well as up it.

" ARRAGIT," as we heard a person call it last Sunday (the Harrogate of ordinary mortals), is destined this season to be a big thing in camps, and already claims a record as the first camp lit with the " electric light "; whilst the programme is a most full one, Saturday, Monday and Tuesday being all occupied with races. The campers' sports on Tuesday will include some novel features, amongst them being ring tilting on bicycles, tug-of-war, bicyclists *vs.* tricyclists ; a prize will also be given to the losing team. Trick-riding. Bath chair race; one man to pull, one to push, and one to ride ; *competitors to hire their own chairs.* Hopping contest, 150 yards. Wheelbarrow

race (handicap); one lap ; one man to ride and one to push ; wheelbarrows will be supplied. Pig-a-back race (handicap), 200 yards ; one man to carry another. — *News.*

ONLY six teams started in the Team Road Race, though eight were down on the official programme. The Kings County Wheelmen were the favorites, and were the winners. The Harlem Wheelmen were looked upon for second place, but only took third. The Elizabeth Wheelmen took second place. The fact that the first and second clubs are the ones that already have a race arranged between themselves will add largely to its interest. As the teams in the coming race will be composed of eight men, a close contest may be anticipated.

THE New Jersey Cycling Association called for the fourth payment of ten per cent on 1 June. They have also sent out letters inviting the smaller subscribers to pay up in full, both as a matter of convenience and because they expect to need money faster than it will come in at the rate of one call a month. Work on the track has been begun, and its opening is announced for 5 July. It hardly seems possible from present appearances that it can be in good shape then.

MR. DUCKER says the desire to win is the true amateur idea. That's where Mr. Ducker is at war with the dictionary.

THE BATTLE IN BICYCLE LANE.

A SOBER young man in knee breeches,
    Trundled into our gossipy town ;
In his heart had been numerous breaches —
    'T is a paradise here for the gown.

The June air was cooling and bracing,
    The gleam of his shimmering wheel
Mysterious flashes kept tracing
    In air like a phantom of steel.

His head was well balanced and steady,
    Was level, and clear was his brain,
But a sorrow had crossed it already,
    With wrinkles of grief in its train.

In his call was a quiver of anguish,
    In his eye lurked the demon of wrath ;
His thoughts took a turn of the languish
    As he crossed a macadamised path.

" Tooth-inserter," sweet angel of healing,
    A bulldog of cannibal mien,
Had claimed his acquaintance with feeling ;
    And the size of his grip could be seen

Marked in red on the young athlete's stocking,
    As the hero, with never a word,
But with thoughts that were perfectly shocking,
    Sped on like a shot-peppered bird.

Straight on, neither right nor left turning,
    He hied to an armorer's shop,
And his bosom with vengeance was burning
    As he entered that door with a hop —

And closed it. What further, I knew not.
    Three hours in the den did he plot;
Then emerging, to right or left threw not
    A glance (on his cheek was a blot!)

    .   .   .   .   .   .

" Tooth-inserter " sat up in the twilight
    As a bicycle swept into sight.
He smiled, with a yawn like a skylight,
    And murmured, " I like that taste, quite ! "

He rose and walked slowly to meet him :
    The wheelman had turned rather white.
With fear ? ah never r-r! to greet him
    His vengeance arose in its might.

From his shoulder (just where the crusader
Once wore his dread weapon of woe)
He unclasped a non-patent persuader,
And grimly confronted his foe.

'T was a foil. Three feet was its measure,
On the point was a round ball of steel,
Like a two-per-cent apple — a treasure
To all devotees of the wheel.

" Ho ! ho ! " grinned the demon, approaching ;
" Ha ! ha ! " hissed the bicycler low ;
And stealing his soul 'gainst reproaching,
He dealt him one lightning-like blow.

With a yell of wild maniac cadence,
He dashed down the shadowy lane,
As the farmer came out with a rail fence,
And walked o'er the face of the slain.

Up and down that broad turnpike we wheelmen
Oft whirl on our jubilant way.
" Tooth-inserter " lies buried ! we feel men
Set free from demoniac sway.

LEAGUE TOUR.

TOURMASTER BURLEY B. AYERS, of the L.-A. W., has decided upon the following route for the annual tour of the League : The start is to be made from Canandaigua, N.Y., on Monday, 6 September, and the tourists will ride to Geneva for dinner ; then by steamer down Seneca Lake to Watkins' Glen, where there will be a hop in the evening, and the night will be passed at the leading hotel : —

Tuesday, 7 September. — Leave Watkins' Glen at 2 P. M., and ride to Havana, thence to Elmira, where the night will be passed. The late start is to give the. tourists time to recover from the effects' of the festivities of the previous night.

Wednesday, 8 September. — Start from Elmira at 9 A. M., wheel to Chemung, Waverly to Oswego, where the party will take special Pullman car for Port Jervis.

Thursday, 9 September. — Start from Port Jervis at usual hour, which is 9 A. M., and·ride to Milford, Penn., Duigmaus, Bushkill, Delaware Gap and Portland, a distance of forty-four miles ; but as the wheelmen will by this stage of the trip become very well hardened, they will not mind the extra miles.

Friday, 10 September. — Leave Portland for Columbia, ·N. J., Knowlton, Hope, Budd's Lake, and Flander's ; distance for day, thirty-one miles. .

Saturday, 11 September. — Ride to Ironia, Morristown,· Summit, Milburn, South Orange, Newark, Jersey City, · New York City, making headquarters at the Grand Union Hotel. This will complete the northern division of the tour, and the following day and a half of rest will be appreciated.

Monday, 13 September. — Leave New York at 3 P. M. on one of the Old Dominion steamers for Old Point Comfort, Va.

Tuesday, 14 September. — Arrive in evening at Old Point Comfort, .where headquarters will be established at the Hygeria Hotel. A complimentary hop will be given in the evening, and the wheelmen will be in fine condition after their long rest to enjoy the fun.

Wednesday, 15 September. — Spend day about Norfolk and vicinity, and in the evening leave by Pullman car for Staunton, Va.

Thursday, 16 September. — Start on a four days' trip down the Shenandoah Valley, winding up at Harper's Ferry. Here the

tour will end, but it is likely that individual tourists will continue on in smaller parties.

CONVERTIBLE CLOTHING.

· As a general rule, it may be said· that the garments worn for cycling should be essentially cycling clothes, and not be used for any other purpose ; but there are occasions in some riders' experiences when it is highly desirable to temporarily doff the close-fitting nether garments for the orthodox trousers of every-day life ; and it has been the custom for such cyclists as use their wheels in business to wear ordinary trousers, and to pin them closely round the ankles when necessary for riding. Such an arrangement is not at all neat, but confers an awkward and inelegant appearance upon the rider ; and to provide against this inconvenience the firm of Goy seems to have tackled the matter very thoroughly, with the result that a complete suit of convertible clothing is invented which· meets, in its component parts, the above-mentioned and other requirements. The trousers are arranged with cunningly concealed hooks and eyes, so carefully placed in position as to convert the trousers into very neatly-fitting knickerbockers and close leggins, complete for riding, without any difficulty or need for removal, the appearance in the first case being that of ordinary tailor-made trousers, and in the other case of a well-fitting garment free from the ungainly bagging and creasing induced by pinning trousers around the ankles. For the rider's trunk, a jacket is made with the front of a waistcoat attached inside it, so that the wearer can either ride with·the double protection across his chest, or with·the jacket opened, and in the latter event it is impossible for the sides of the jacket to fly wide open even when going against the wind, as the·buttoned vest underneath prevents the jacket-flaps opening to more than a graceful extent. For the head, a cricket-cap is made with a second flap behind, which can either be folded inside the lining, or opened out·to convert the cap into a neat two-peaked soft helmet. — *Wheel World.*

UNITED STATES ·CIRCUIT COURT, NORTHERN DISTRICT OF ILLINOIS.

THE POPE MANUFACTURING COMPANY }
　　　　　　　vs.　　　　　　　　　　} Bill.
HARRY B. OWSLEY, HEATON OWSLEY }
　　and GEORGE S. MARBLE.　　　　}

HARRY B. OWSLEY, HEATON OWSLEY }
　　and GEORGE S. MARBLE　　　　　} Cross-Bill.
　　　　　　　vs.　　　　　　　　　　}
THE POPE MANUFACTURING COMPANY· }

This cause coming on to be heard upon the bill of complaint filed herein, the answer thereto and the replication of the complainant, the cross-bill of said defendants, the answer thereto, the replication to said answer, the proofs taken in· said cause, and arguments of counsel ; and the Court, being fully advised in the premises, doth find :

· That the equities of this cause are with the complainant in the original bill.

. That the defendants entered into the agreements with the complainant in the original bill, as stated in the bill of complaint in this cause, whereby the defendants became licensees of the complainant, under certain

Letters Patent specified in said agreements, and that said agreements were in force at the hearing of this cause, excepting the agreements marked "Exhibit A" and " I " in the original bill of complaint.

That the defendants have violated the said licenses and agreements entered into with the complainant, by refusing to make monthly reports or returns in writing to the complainant, on or before the tenth day of each calendar month in each year, of machines manufactured by the defendants during the month preceding ; that said defendants have refused to make such reports, or to pay the royalties or license fees due the complainant for such manufacture from February, 1883, except as ordered by the Court, since this suit was commenced. That since that period said defendants have continued to manufacture machines and other articles which they were licensed to manufacture under said licenses, and have neglected to make returns and pay royalties thereon, except as ordered by the Court ; and have sold different machines manufactured under the patents referred to in said licenses, and containing the devices patented in said Letters Patent, without affixing or stamping on such articles the word "Patented," in accordance with the terms of said licenses, and without attaching thereto a printed list of patents under which the said machines were made, in accordance with the conditions of said licenses.

The Court further finds that the defendants, under the order of the Court, have reported a number of machines that they had manufactured under said licenses, and that the amount due under said license agreements on said machines, so reported by the defendants, is seven thousand, five hundred and forty-eight dollars and ninety cents ($7,548.90) ; and that there was due the complainant, at the time of hearing this cause, said sum, with interest thereon from the date. when said license fees or royalties became due and payable, to March 29, 1886, amounting in all to the sum of one thousand, one hundred and fifty-nine dollars and one cent ($1,159 01), making a total of eight thousand, seven hundred and seven dollars and ninety-one cents ($8,707·91), which said sum was then due the complainant from the defendants for royalties on machines reported by the defendants, and the interest thereon.

It is therefore ordered, adjudged and decreed by the Court that the said defendants pay the complainant the said sum of $8,707·91 for said royalties and interest due up to the twenty-ninth day of March, 1886, and that a judgment for that amount be had against the defendants, and the surety signing the bond, which was given by the defendants under the order of this Court to secure the payment to the complainant of such sum as might be found by the. Court to be due the complainant.

It is further ordered that there be a reference to E. B. Sherman, one of the masters of this court, to ascertain and report to this Court what machines the defendants have made· and sold in violation of their agreements, and which are covered by complainant's patents, other than and besides those reported by the defendants as aforesaid as having been made under said. license agreements herein ; and the master is directed

to take proofs and report the same with his conclusions thereon. And he is hereby authorized to summon the defendants, their agents and employés before him and examine them on oath, and require said defendants or their employés to produce their books of account touching the matters hereby referred.

It is further ordered, adjudged and decreed by the Court that the defendants shall perform each and every obligation in said licenses contained which are obligatory upon the defendants to perform, and that the defendants shall make returns and pay royalties in accordance with the terms of the said licenses.

It is further ordered, adjudged and decreed by the Court that the defendants, and each of them, their and each of their servants, agents and employés be, and they hereby are, enjoined from manufacturing or selling any velocipedes, bicycles or baby carriage wheels specified in said several licenses, without affixing or stamping thereon the word "Patented," in accordance with the terms of said licenses, or without attaching thereto a printed list of the patents under which said several machines may be made, in accordance with the conditions of said licenses. That the defendants and each of them, their servants, agents and employés be, and they hereby are, restrained and enjoined from manufacturing or selling any velocipedes, bicycles or tricycles other than or different from what they are allowed to make in and by their aforesaid licenses, or in violation of the conditions in said licenses contained, so long as the patents or any of them mentioned in said license shall remain in force. The said defendants, and each of them, are hereby enjoined from in any manner, directly or indirectly, violating any of the provisions in the said several licenses mentioned in said bill of complaint.

It is further ordered, adjudged and decreed that the cross-bill of the defendants herein be dismissed, for want of equity, at the cost of said defendants, Harry B. Owsley, Heaton Owsley and George B. Marble.

THE PATH.

RACES OF YALE BICYCLE CLUB.

FRIDAY, 11 JUNE, 1886.

ABOUT five hundred persons were present at 2.30 P. M., the first day, when the one-mile open race was called. G. Weber, Smithville, C. P. Adams, Springfield, Mass., W. A. Rowe, and C. E. Whitten, Lynn, Mass., started. Rowe won in 3.0⅘; Weber a very close second, 3.22; Whitten third.

A. W. Ives and G. G. Knapp won the one-mile tandem race in 3.51⅗.

The one-mile handicap race had ten starters, and was won by F. G. Warner, of Hartford, who had a twelve seconds start, in 2.36. L. A. Miller, Meriden, scratch, second, 2.56⅖; A. W. Ives, third. Just at the finish, as Ives and Warner were tied for first place, Ives slipped a pedal and was thrown over the tape. No bones broken.

The three-mile open record race was contested by George Weber, C. P. Adams and George M. Hendee. Hendee took the lead and made the one half mile in 1.20. The pace was too hot for Adams, and he dropped out. Hendee kept up the same pace for the three miles, winning in 8.52; Weber second, in 9.31⅗. Hendee's time is the fastest ever made on this track.

Thomas R. Finley then rode his Star for the gratification of the spectators and a money consideration.

G. B. Buxton, Meriden, F. G. Warner, Hartford, and S. Carleton, Yale College, contested in a two-mile novices' race. Warner won in 6.43⅗; Buxton second.

W. F. Knapp, C. P. Adams, and C. E. Whitten rode the two-mile handicap, open race. On the beginning of the last half mile, C. L. Hyde, starter, stepped on the track in front of Adams and Whitten, and both men were thrown. Adams mounted again and finished second, but Whitten had to be carried from the track. He was not hurt, but stunned. Knapp's time was 6.29.

J. Illston, A. B. Rich, were the only entered men who started on the twenty-mile Pope Cup Race. F. G. Warner rode, however, under protest. Rich won the race in 1.10.30⅗, Illston second, and Warner over a mile behind.

SATURDAY, 12 JUNE, 1886.

First race, one mile, 3.05 class, had E. S. Horton, E. Hartford, G. B. Buxton, Meriden, H. H. Stockder, Meriden, F. G. Warner, Hartford, E. A. DeBlois, Weathersfield, and S. Carleton, Yale College, as starters. DeBlois won in 2.55⅗; Horton second; Stockder third.

George Weber, J. Illston, and George M. Hendee rode in the five-mile open record race, Hendee winning in 15.23; Weber second.

F. A. Clark, Plantsville, Wm. F. Graham, W. Randall Seymour, were the starters in the one half mile boys' race. Randall finished first, with Clark second; but he fouled both Clark and Graham, so they were given first and second places.

T. R. Finley once more rode the Star. J. S. Kulpp, S. Carleton, and E. B. Patterson then rode a mile for the club championship, which Carleton took, with Kulp second.

The three-mile open race with G. Weber, W. A. Rowe, and W. F. Knapp as starters, was the only race of the day. Knapp took the lead, and held it most of the time. On the last one-half mile Rowe took the lead, and for the distance round the track into the home stretch Weber was trying to pass him, but Rowe won in 8.37, with Knapp second.

Mr. J. Brooks then made his one hundred and sixty-eighth balloon ascension.

The last race, a three-mile handicap, had five starters, with L. A. Miller as scratch man. E. A. DeBlois won in 8.53⅘ (twenty seconds); J. S. Kulp, second, 9.13 (twenty seconds); H. H. Stockder, third 9.20 (ten seconds).

JEWETT.

HAMILTON PARK, New Haven, Conn., 11 and 12 June, 1886.

LAWRENCE, MASS., 5 June. — Races under auspices of Lawrence Cricket Club. *Two-mile amateur.* — M. Fuller (1), 7.25; S. Smith (2); A. M. Tracy (3).

BOSTON, 2 June. — Races under the auspices of the Roxbury Latin School. *One-mile amateur.* — G. L. Batcheller (1), 3.48.

MONTREAL, 5 June. — Races run under the auspices of the Montreal Amateur Athletic Association. *Three mile handicap.* — J. H. Robertson, scratch (1), 11.14; H. M. Ramsay, 10 seconds (2), 11.21½; F. W. S. Crispo, 10 seconds (0).

PHILADELPHIA, PA., 5 June. — Races run under auspices of the Schuylkill Navy Athletic Club. *One-mile amateur.* — M. J. Bailey (1), 3.9; S. H. Crawford (2). *Two-mile amateur.* — C. B. Keen (1), 6.1⅘; S. H. Crawford (2); M. J. Bailey (3).

W. NEW BRIGHTON, L. I., 5 June. — Races under auspices of Staten Island A. C. *One-mile amateur.* — First heat: A. B. Rich (1), 3.42⅖; E. Valentine (2), by five yards; E. C. Parker (3), by ten yards. Second heat: Rich (1), 3.50¼; Valentine (2), eight yards; Parker (3), fifteen yards. *Three-mile handicap.* — F. S. Ray, 75 yards (1), 10.45⅘; E. Valentine, 150 yards (2), two yards; T. H. Burnett, 250 yards (3), seven yards; E. C. Parker 225 yards (4), two feet; A. B. Rich, scratch (0).

ST. PAUL, MINN., 31 May. — Races under the auspices of the University. *Half-mile amateur.* — Pillsbury (1), 1.37½.

CLEVELAND, O., 12 June. — The regular spring race meeting of the Cleveland Bicycle Club was held at Athletic Park, this day: —

Five-Mile Club Championship (bicycle). — Prize, the Wade gold medal: G. T. Snyder, 1; George Collister, 2. Time, 2.59½, 6.05, 9.21½, 12.55, 16.20.

Quarter-Mile Open Heat Race (bicycles). — Prizes, silver cup and gold scarfpin: Taylor Boggis (Cleveland Club), 1, 1; George Valliant (Cleveland Club), 2, 2; W. N. Eyster (Canton, O.), 3, 3. Time, 40 sec., 41 sec.

One-Mile Open Handicap (tricycles). — Prizes, gold and antique bronze medals: George Collister (Cleveland Club), 20 sec., 1; Clarence Howard (Akron, O.), scratch, 2. Time, 3.34⅘.

Two-Mile Open Handicap (bicycles). — Prizes, diamond scarfpin and gold scarfring: W. P. Sargent (Cleveland Club), 30 sec., 1; F. P. Root (Cleveland Club), 10 sec., 2; Taylor Boggis (Cleveland Club), scratch, 3; C. E. Farnsworth (Cleveland Club), 20 sec., 4. Time, 3.09, 16.30½.

Half-Mile Open Race. — For 1.30 class riders, bicycles. Prizes, pair of tennis racquet and silver-headed cane: F. P. Root, (Cleveland Club) 1; George W. Valliant, (Cleveland Club), 2; W. N. Eyster (Canton, O.), 3. Time, 1.27½.

One-Mile Time Race. — Bicycles: Prizes, gold and antique bronze medals. J. T. Huntington (Cleveland Club), 3.24⅗; W. P. Sargent (Cleveland Club), 3.34¼; George Collister (Cleveland Club), 3.34⅕.

One-Mile Open Race. — For riders of the 3.10 class (bicycles). Prize, gold cuff buttons. F. P. Root (Cleveland Club), 1; Lucien Davis (Cleveland Club), 3. Time, 3.13.

ST. LOUIS, MO., 30 May. — Races under the auspices of the Missouri A. A. Club. *Two-mile handicap.* — S. G. Whittaker, scratch (1), 5.57; A. A. Hart, 170 yards (2); H. Morris, 260 yards (3).

ALMEDA, CAL., 31 May. — Races run under the auspices of the Albion Athletic Club and Bay City Wheelmen. *One-mile novice.* — R. W. Turner (1), 3.27; A. S. Ireland (2); F. James (3). *Half-mile amateur.* — F. D. Elwell (1), 1.33; H. G. Kennedy (2). *One-mile State championship.*

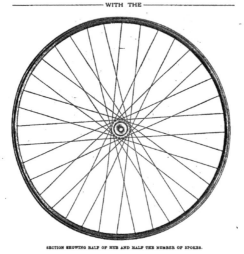

W. G. Davis (1), 3 10½; F. D. Elwell (2). *Two-mile handicap.* — F. D. Elwell, scratch (1), 6.56½; H. D. Kennedy, scratch (2); H. S. Blood, 50 yards (3); C. A. Biedeman, 60 yards (4). *Five-mile handicap.* — H. G. Kennedy, scratch (1), 19.4¼; H. J. Blood, 150 yards (2); H. B. Churchill, 175 yards (3).

·THE order of races in Boston, 5 July, will be as follows : One-mile amateur, three-mile promateur, two-mile amateur, one-mile tricycle, three-mile amateur. Makers' amateur races will not be accepted for amateur races. The medals, as usual, of gold and silver, will be of the highest order of workmanship. The rules will be similar to those of last year, though there will be no restriction in the winning of prizes, and there must be no loafing. Mr. Charles H. Orr will referee the races, and Messrs. ·McEttrick and Sullivan will be the judges.

THE programme of the North Adams Wheel Club's tournament, at Hoosac Valley Park, will include the following races: Mile, novice, three prizes; three-mile county championship, one prize; one mile, boys, 17 years, two prizes; one mile, open, two prizes; three miles, open, two prizes; five miles, open record, three prizes; half-mile dash, two prizes; one mile, 3m. 20s., two prizes; consolation race. There will also be a foot race and a military drill. The skating rink will be open in the evening, and there will be racing and dancing.

ARRANGEMENTS are in progress for a 20-mile road race by members of the Springfield Club, on the morning of 5 July. The race will probably be started at 6 A. M., and the course will be from the west end of the North End Bridge to the Suffield House, via Agawam Bridge and the brewery, and return. Suitable prizes will be given to the winners, and Westervelt, Whipple and Eldred will be handicapped according to their records for road riding.

C. B. KEEN, of the University of Pennsylvania, lowered the intercollegiate two-mile record, 5 June, at Philadelphia, covering the distance in 6m. 1⅘s.

THE track of the New Jersey Cycling and Athletic Association will be opened 5 July.

A 20-MILE championship club road race, open to all clubs in Connecticut, will be will be given 26 June, under the auspices of the Meriden Wheel Club, over the well-known course from Meriden to New Britain and return. Each club to enter a team of three men, the position at the finish to count as in tug-of-war races. The race will be ridden under L. A. W. rules, and none but those strictly amateur will be allowed to compete. The prize for the winning team consists of a real bronze figure of Mercury, in bas-relief, framed in plush, with easel, value $30; and individual prizes for the first three men, as follows: First, gold championship medal, value $25 ; second, lamp, value, $15; third, Smith & Wesson revolver, value, $8. An entrance fee of $3 per team will be charged, returnable to those who finish the race. The start will be made between three and four o'clock P. M. Entries close 22 June.

THE third annual tournament of the Connecticut Bicycle Club will be held on · Charter Oak Park, 8 and 9 September.

THE CLUB.

ROXBURY. — The Roxbury Club was organized Friday evening, with headquarters at 1177 Tremont street. The club starts with a membership of eighteen, and has elected the following officers: President, W. H. Emery, M. D. ; captain, John S. Lowell ; secretary, B. W. Potts ; treasurer. W. T. Johnson.

OWING to absence in Europe, Mr. Charles F. Cossum has resigned the position of secretary and treasurer of the Ariel Wheel Club, Poughkeepsie, N. Y. At the regular meeting of the club, held Tuesday evening, 8 June, Mr. Frank J. Schwartz was unanimously elected to fill the vacancy.

HARTFORD, CONN. — The South End Girls' Tricycle Club met on the Capitol Grounds last Saturday morning, and elected the following officers: President, Kate Deming; vice-president, Pauline Mayer ; secretary, Callie Belden ; treasurer, Lizzie Belden. The club will meet Saturdays on the Capitol grounds, and later in the season contest for prizes. — *Hartford Censor.*

MERIDEN, CONN. — At the annual meeting of the Meriden Wheel Club, held 9 June, the following officers were elected: President, T. S. Rust ; captain, Wm. Collins ; secretary, H. G. Miller ; treasurer, J. E. Brainard ; first lieutenant, L. A. Miller ; second lieutenant, F. A. Stevens.

COMING EVENTS.

JUNE.

12 Saturday. — Second day of race meeting at New Haven by Yale College Club.
N. Y. and N. J. Road Race Association team race, at Orange, N. J.
Races at Cleveland, Ohio.

17 Thursday. — Second Prince-Neilson race at Lynn.

19 Saturday. — Annual Championships of N. A. A. A. A. at New York.
Annual race meeting of K. C. W. at Brooklyn, N. Y.

23 Wednesday. — Races of Trojan Wheelmen, at Troy, N. Y.

24 Thursday. — Annual meet of the Michigan Div. L. A. W. at Detroit. Ten-mile National Championship.

JULY.

1 Thursday. — First day of annual meeting of C. W. A. at Montreal.

2 Friday. — Second day of annual meeting of C. W. A. at Montreal.

3 Saturday. — Third day of annual meeting of C. W. A. at Montreal.
Suffolk Wheel Clubs' three days' tour begins.

5 Monday. — Race meeting at Binghamton, N. Y.
Race meeting at Cleveland, Ohio, two miles, L. A. W. championship.
Races at Chelsea, Mass.
Races at Boston, Mass.
Races at East Saginan, Mich.

15 to 18, Tuesday to Friday. — Tournament at Columbus, Ga. State championships will be run.

THE CYCLE

PUBLISHED EVERY FRIDAY BY ABBOT BASSETT, 22 SCHOOL ST., ROOM 19.

VOL. I. BOSTON, MASS., 25 JUNE, 1886. No. 13.

TERMS OF SUBSCRIPTION.

One Year, by mail, post-paid..........................$1.50
Three Copies in one order.............................3.00
Club Subscriptions...................................1.00
Six Months..90
Single Copies...05

Specimen Copies free.

Every bicycle dealer is agent for the CYCLE and authorized to receive subscriptions at regular rates. The paper can be found on sale at the following places: —

Boston, CUPPLES, UPHAM & Co., cor. Washington and School Streets. Tremont House news stand. At every cycle warehouse.
New York, ELLIOTT MASON, 12 Warren Street.
Philadelphia, H. B. HART, 811 Arch Street. GEORGE D. GIDEON, 6 South Broad Street.
Baltimore, S. T. CLARK & Co., 4 Hanover Street.
Chicago, W. M. DURELL, 115 Wabash Avenue. JOHN WILKINSON & Co., 77 State Street.
Washington, H. S. OWEN, Capital Cycle Co.
St. Louis, ST. LOUIS WHEEL Co., 1121 Olive Street.

ABBOT BASSETT . . . . . EDITOR

A. MUDGE & SON, PRINTERS, 24 FRANKLIN ST., BOSTON.

All communications should be sent in not later than Tuesday, to ensure insertion the same week.

Entered at the Post-office as second-class mail matter.

THE A. C. U. will never succeed upon its present basis. The great and mighty public to whom it looks for support will not brook deceit, and the man who races for money, and pretends that he does it for the love of the sport, practises a deception.

An amateur is one who enters into a sport for the love of it. He who draws a salary cannot claim that love alone inspires him. And yet we believe there is room for an association that will do in a straightforward way what the A. C. U. proposes to do in a questionable way. There is great need for a society that shall step in to regulate professional racing and road racing. Let the A. C. U. take these under its wing and then establish three classes of riders as follows : —

Class A. — Those who are pure amateurs under the definition of the L. A. W. and the N. C. U.

Class B. — Those who have never raced for a money prize in any form, nor with a professional.

Class C. — Those who have raced for a money prize in any form.

Note. — A rider who competes in races under Class B forfeits his right to enter races under Class C. A rider who competes in races under Class C forfeits his right to enter races under Class B.

It is not possible for the League to establish a system as this, but it is practicable for such an association as the A. C. U., and they would make a strong bid for favor should they do it. Under this system there would be no dishonesty. A rider would come upon the path in his true colors and pretend to be nothing more than he is. We believe that in time, if the new association proved itself worthy, the League would hand over to it all jurisdiction over racing. We believe the riders in Class B would be sought as the drawing cards in all tournaments. We believe the fast men would gravitate to that class, and the amateur races would be left to those who ride for love of the sport, who are, and must be, in the nature of things of the "Duffer" class.

We believe the new society should admit professionals and formulate rules with a system of fines for professional races. For such a society as this, we can see a brilliant future, and with a programme like this there would be no conflict with the League. But the A. C. U. has done nothing of this kind. They have struck at the League in its most sensitive part, and they have set against themselves every man who likes to see true honor in sport.

———

To the above plan there is just one drawback. How shall we adjust the relations between the Class B men and the League? The League only knows two classes, and all who are not amateurs must be professionals. We do not doubt the makers' amateurs would go into Class B if the League would recognize them in that class and allow them membership; but just so long as they are to be called professionals they will actively protest. The desire to form a class more elevated in its tone than the professional, and at the same time to respect the amateur rule, is certainly a most worthy one, and the League would do well to encourage those who hold it; but such a radical change as the one we have proposed takes time to bring about, and meantime it behooves the A. C. U. to take measures to win the confidence of the rank and file of the League by showing itself worthy the important trust it asks to have handed over to it.

———

A CORRESPONDENT writing in good faith asks us if Rule A is not too arbitrary, and suggests that the League allow wheelmen to exercise their own sweet will about entering races. We will try to answer him. Here is Rule A : —

Any amateur wilfully competing at races not stated to be held and actually held under the rules of the board, or rules approved by the board, shall be liable to suspension from the race track for such a time as the racing board may determine; and amateurs are notified that to compete against any rider who has been suspended will render their labors the same penalty.

The rule was made for a special purpose which it admirably served. It was the practice of agricultural societies to offer money prizes in bicycle races held at their fairs, and in many instances cities and towns gave purses for Fourth of July races. A great many amateurs were led to engage in these contests and serious complications arose. In order to break up this practice, Rule A was put upon the books and League officials were asked to see that League rules were adopted in all races in their respective districts. The evil was corrected in a very short time, and up to the date of the Lynn races on Decoration Day, League rules were in universal use throughout America. With the League rules in force, an amateur wheelman was in no danger of losing his status, and he was given a protection of no little value to him. If the League has done nothing else, it has done this. It is the duty of the League to give protection to amateurs. This they have done and this they will do. A new association has arisen that advertises amateur races and allows professionals to enter. A rider who goes to a tournament under A. C. U. rules hazards his status. The existence of the A. C. U. fills his path with snares and pitfalls. In the interest of the racing men, the L. A. W. must hold a firm position and secure the purity of the path. The League is working for the benefit of amateur racing men, and, strange as it may seem, the very men it seeks to protect are the ones that are making the most complaint.

THE HERALD'S IDEA.

THE idea of the American Cyclists' Union attempting to have such riders as Hendee, Rowe, Knapp, and Weber parade before the public as amateurs is simply preposterous. If such men are amateurs, better at once abolish the distinction between the amateur and the professional. It may be that these men prefer to pose as amateurs, because there is more money in it than in the professional arena. Does any sensible person suppose that Weber travels from Smithville all over the country at his own expense; that Rowe can spend several weeks at

Springfield, and break records simply for the glory accredited an amateur wheelman; that George M. Hendee can spend months in training on the Lynn track simply for love of the sport and the honor therein contained? Yet this is only a part of what might be alleged. These men are in the hands of the most experienced and competent trainers. Who pays for them? Their wheels are the best that skill can make and money procure. Who furnishes them? And yet the American Cyclists' Union tries to wink at this farce, as the League of American Wheelmen did for a long time, and as the National Cyclists' Union of Great Britain confessedly has for a still longer term. The Springfield and Lynn clubs have made a great mistake in their attitude. They cannot expect to be the gainers by it. Undoubtedly the racing interests have been injured by the present state of affairs. But if either the amateur interest or the racing interest has to go, let the latter go by all means. It will have ample time to recover from the shock. The English "amateurs" won't come here and defy the L. A. W. They do not care to lose their own caste. Where anything has been said in favor of the A. C. U., it has been said simply from motives of self-interest, not unselfishly and independently. Many will ask, what other course was open to the A. C. U.? The answer is very simple. There is every reason to believe that an amicable compromise of some nature could have been effected between the supporters and opponents of the makers' amateurs. This would probably have resulted in the establishment of a third class, midway between the amateur and the professional. The prizes in the new class would be very valuable, and on this account would doubtless continually draw from the first men in the amateur ranks. This would have made the races in three classes interesting and exciting. The outcome will be watched with the greatest interest by all interested in wheeling. — *Herald.*

PATENTS.

LIST of cycling patents issued this week: D. G. Biggs, Louisville Ky., velocipede, F. F. Foster, Mount Pleasant, Mich., velocipede sleigh; J. A. Lamplugh, Birmingham, Eng., luggage carrier; E. G. Latta, Friendship, N. Y., velocipede; A. H. Overman, Chicopee, Mass., velocipede saddle; T. J. Strickland, Randolph Mass., bicycle shoe; W. L. Fay, Elyria, O., tricycle; C. H. Ross, Albany, N. Y., luggage carrier.

281 9-10 MILES IN TWENTY-FOUR HOURS.

THE Boston *Herald* has the following dispatch from Indianapolis, 19 June. The record is a remarkable one, if it can be proved; but it must be remembered that every care was taken to secure the record as it now stands, and unless the new claimant can show as satisfactory proof as that on which Munger's record rests, no record can be given.

S. P. Hollingsworth, of Russiaville, Ind., was wonderfully successful in his attempt to beat the long distance amateur bicycle record of this country and Great Britain. He completed his task at Greenfield, 19 June, at four o'clock, and in the twenty-four hours scored a total of $281\frac{9}{10}$ miles. His actual riding time was twenty-one hours and twenty-three minutes, two hours and thirty-seven minutes being lost in eating and in being rubbed down. Heretofore the best American record was $259\frac{13}{16}$ miles, made by Munger, of Detroit, at Boston, while the English record is $266\frac{1}{4}$. The best race track record is 276. Hollingsworth's course ranged along the National road, from the Gayman House, Greenfield, to the toll gate immediately east of Cumberland, the round trip covering $17\frac{3}{4}$ miles, cyclometer measure, and $17\frac{4}{10}$ miles by more careful survey. The track was an average piece of road lying nearly straight. Early in the day, Hollingsworth broke a spoke in his bicycle, and, while having it repaired, he rode a strange machine, and by this means received a "header," which severely injured one knee. But for this accident he is none the worse for his exertion to-day. His "running" weight is one hundred and fifty pounds, and he lost six pounds in the race. His age is twenty-five years, and he is purely an amateur rider, having never engaged in a professional contest. The result of the race, fortified by affidavit, will be immediately forwarded to the American Association (?), and his claim as champion will be recorded. The race created great interest in Greenfield and the country generally.

SUFFOLK WHEEL CLUB'S TOUR.

THE Suffolk Wheel Club of South Boston has perfected its arrangements for a three-days' tour along the North Shore, and there is every prospect that the tour will prove a delightful one. It will be run under the auspices of the eastern division of the League Touring Board, and all wheelmen of the State are cordially invited to participate. By special arrangements with the various hotels, the price of tickets for the entire tour have been placed at the low figure of $5. All intending to participate are requested to obtain tickets at once, so that proper arrangements may be made with the hotels. First Lieutenant A. G. Collins will be in command, and J. A. Channock will act as quartermaster.

The programme has been changed materially since first announced, and as now arranged is as follows: —

SATURDAY, 3 JULY.

3 P. M. — Start from corner Berkeley street and Warren avenue for Salem. Supper, lodging, and breakfast at Essex House. First day's ride, 25 miles.

SUNDAY, 4 JULY.

9 A. M. — Start for Gloucester. Dinner at Bass Rock House. 3 P. M. — Start on the famous "ride around the Cape," distance 16 miles. Supper, lodging, and breakfast at the Bass Rock House. Second day's ride, 32 miles; from Boston, 57 miles.

MONDAY, 5 JULY.

8 A. M. — Start for Essex House, Salem, for dinner.

2.30 P. M. — Start for Boston, arriving at starting-point about 6 P. M., where the tour ends. Third day's ride, 41 miles. Total for tour, 98 miles.

ROAD RACE, 5 JULY.

The road race will be started from the Bass Rock House at 11 A. M., allowing the tourists a view of the finish at the Essex House, Salem. First prize, gold medal; second prize, silver medal. Entries free to tourists; $2 fee to all others. Entries close to Mr. J. J. Gilligan, 6 and 8 Berkeley street, Boston, 2 July.

A large number of wheelmen have already signified their intention of participating, and it is expected that the party will be one of the largest which has ever enjoyed a tour of this kind. The road race will be particularly interesting, and as several very fast men are to enter, some lively time may be expected.

NOTES OF A CYCLIST.

THE *Bulletin* has contained two surprises lately. The issue of 4 June reprinted a paragraph from the *Bicycling News*, which was a good take-off of the rules regarding the character of the matter allowed in the official organ. Perhaps the editor was not back in time to prevent the perpetration of the joke. The issue of 11 June contained some verses in praise of a particular machine. The editor had certainly returned before this number appeared, for it contains one of his characteristic editorials. Perhaps these verses were not in "the columns devoted to reading matter." If they were in them, however, it is fair to presume that they constituted an advertisement; but on that theory they should have been followed by the usual "adv.," which was absent. What, then, can such extravagant praise of a machine mean in the columns of our organ?

I THINK the membership at large will heartily approve of Mr. Harris's demand, at the meeting of the board of officers, for a full report of the financial condition of the League. It looks very much now as if the treasurer was a sort of figure-head, and the secretary-treasurer an overburdened officer. Either the treasurer ought to have more of a treasurer's usual duties, or the work of the secretary-editor's office ought to be better systematized, and enough help secured to keep it in the best of running order. If League work is killing the secretary, he ought to have more help. If he is not able to keep the work up promptly, the remedy rests with the officers of the League.

THERE seems room for improvement in some directions. The *Bulletin* rarely, if ever, reaches the vicinity of New York before Monday afternoon, and for several months now it has not arrived until Tuesday afternoon. Its publication day is supposed to be Friday. Why should it take till Tuesday to travel a hundred miles? The CYCLE is also published on Friday, and it arrives on Friday night from double the distance.

UNDER the existing circumstances, it is charitable to charge to ill health this and other shortcomings that could be mentioned. I am glad to hear that the secretary is better, but I think he ought to have had a longer rest.

5678

W. B. PAGE, of the University of Pennsylvania, the American champion high-jumper, is also a devotee of cycling. He intends taking a 1,500-mile tour on the wheel through the White Mountains and Canada this summer.

CYCLETS

THE RUDGE.

[I WAS asked if I wrote "The Humber," in the *Bulletin* of 11 June. I did not write it, as my sentiments are those given below.] L. H. P.

Was there ever wheelman
With a heart so cold,
But he loved the cycle
Upon which he bowled?

Was there ever cycler,
Callous to all worth,
But he thought his own wheel
Best of all the earth?

I have rarely met one,
So devoid of zeal,
But he sang the praises
Of some maker's wheel.

Nor am I exception
To the mighty throng,
Neither when I praise one,
Do I others wrong.

All makes have their lovers,
Each as best they claim,
But the wheel most perfect
Is the one I name.

Of all, 't is most graceful;
Yields in speed to none;
Faster than its compeers,
Records best has won.

Lighter than all others,
As "light roadster" claimed;
Stronger than the strongest
Which "light" wheels are named.

Firm, and very rigid;
True beyond compare;
On the coast the fastest,
Like a bird of air.

Smoothest in its motion,
Fastest up the hill;
Like a sentient being
Yielding to the will.

More than any other,
Life endowed it moves;
Its surpassing virtues
Always fresh it proves.

Ask you what the wheel is,
Chiefest known to fame?
Need I but pronounce it,
Light Rudge is its name!

THIS is the month of perfect days. Did n't June O it?

LAST Monday was the longest one we shall have this year.

NOW the sweet girl graduate talks about climbing the hill of learning.

NOW the bull-frog pipeth in the marsh.

NOW the wheelman wonders if he had better not lay off till September.

BUT the sun does not shine by night, and illuminating oil is not expensive.

WE have had more fun riding at midnight than we ever enjoyed at mid-day.

NED OLIVER has been tendered and will probably accept the secretaryship of the touring department of the L. A. W.

WHEN the Pope Manufacturing Company swoops down upon a tournament with its team, all the others have to stand aside. Witness Lynn and New Haven.

ON the fifth of July Rowe will be at Lynn, Hendee will go to Springfield, and Knapp will appear at North Adams.

THERE will be a lengthy parade of bicycles at Hagerstown, Md., 4 July. A large number of Baltimore riders will take part in the affair.

THE Capital Bicycle Club has made arrangements for a very interesting five-day bicycle run of two hundred miles, from 13 to 18 June, through Maryland. The first day they will travel $36\frac{1}{4}$ miles; the second, 38; third, 42; fourth, 49; and fifth, 32. The run will be made under the guidance of Capt. Elsen Bolds.

MR. CHARLES E. GATES, of Jamestown, N. Y., will start about 1 July, for a ride to Lake Minnetonka, Minnesota. A 48-inch Star Light Roadster, weighing forty-five pounds, will be the machine used. The route will be *via* the Ridge Road along Lake Erie from near Dunkirk (forty miles south of Buffalo), N. Y., Erie (Pa.), Painesville, Cleveland, and Toledo, Ohio, then by way of Jackson, Mich., to Chicago, and from there to St. Paul, Minn., Minneapolis, and after a stay of over a month at Lake Minnetonka with relatives, and a short tour to the northern part of the State, the tour will be continued to lower Iowa, where another stop will be make with relatives. From Iowa the return trip will be made by the way of St. Louis, Indianapolis, and possibly through Cincinnati to Western New York again, taking in the fall tournaments *en route.*

CAPTAIN COFFIN'S series of articles on yachting, now running in *Outing*, will, when completed, be published in book form. They will make the first comprehensive history of American yachting ever published, and will be elaborately illustrated by the celebrated marine artist Cozzens.

CAPTAIN AUBIN has sent the following circular letter to the clubs about Boston: —

The Newton Bicycle and Nonantum Cycling clubs will give an antique and horrible parade on Monday morning, 5 July. You and the members of your club are most cordially invited to aid us, with your presence, in making this affair a success. The start will be made from Cycle Hall, Newtonville, at 6 A. M. The route of the parade will be over eight miles in all of Newton's "sand-papered" roads, and returning to Newtonville, where a breakfast will be served to those participating. Wheelmen are expected to appear in fancy dress, and it is particularly requested that nothing will be worn that may in any way unpleasantly impress the spectators.

Costumes may be forwarded in care of the Nonantum Cycling Club, Newtonville, *via* Boston and Albany Railroad, or by Hunting's, Parker's, Patch's, or Thomson's expresses, prepaid, prior to 5 July, plainly marked with owner's name, and the same will be cared for by the committee.

THE Boston club is planning for a repetition of its cycle picnic in the woods, which proved so successful last year.

BOB ENGLISH is not yet able to go upon the path, and his friends say that it is extremely doubtful if he was in any of the championships. America did not agree with Bob, and it looks as though he would remain at home this year.

HOWELL has done the mile in 2m. $39\frac{3}{5}$s. at Leicester, *starting from a stool*, a performance equal to about 2m. 36s. with a push off. Howell also did the half mile in 1m. 17s., both of which performances are English professional record.

ARRANGEMENTS are being made with the Fitchburg, Troy and Boston and other railroads, for reduced rates on their lines, between all principal points, for the bicycle races at Northampton, 5 July.

THE Worcester Bicycle Club will hold a field day, Saturday, 26 June, at Lake Quinsigamond.

THE Wakefield Bicycle Club has been offered the management of the 5th of July antique and horrible parade in that town, but has not yet decided whether or not to accept. The club will, at all events, contribute a feature in the parade, and will hold races in the afternoon.

SAYS the Springfield *Union:* The way the Westfield boys do it is to tackle a sort of "square" over there, the distance around which is about two miles, and keep pegging away at it for a number of hours. Goodman, so it is said, used to leave the bank about 4 o'clock and ride into the night, and sometimes, on moonlight nights, he would ride all night. They have a good hard sidewalk, and the road is thus an easy one to travel.

MR. W. T. WILLIAMS, of Yantic, Conn., wheeled to Boston and returned to the L. A. W. Meet. The first day he ran from Yantic to Putnam, a distance of $41\frac{1}{2}$ miles, in $8\frac{3}{4}$ hours. The second day he made $30\frac{1}{2}$ miles, reaching Milford at 5.15 P. M. He was on the road $9\frac{3}{4}$ hours, but had to stop frequently to escape hard showers. On the third day he made 34 miles in $3\frac{3}{4}$ hours, reaching Boston at 12.15. Returning, he made 68 miles the first day in $12\frac{1}{4}$ hours, and the second day he made 54 miles in $10\frac{1}{2}$ hours. He made a total distance of 228 miles over country roads, with one day of foul weather, in five days, which is good travelling.

MR. PARKER, of the Manchester, N. H., club, was in Boston last week, hunting for a bicycle that had been stolen from him. A young man called at his store and hired a bicycle for an afternoon, promising to return the machine the next morning; but instead he took the first train for Boston, and that is the last Mr. Parker has heard of his bicycle. The young man claimed to live in Brockton, and he is now being hunted for in that locality.

GASKELL has gone West to look up his agents. The Club people are having a big run on tricycles, and are meeting a demand for new goods better than any other house in the city.

TWO decisions of interest to bicyclists have recently been made in the Newton court, as follows: Commonwealth *v.* Carr, Commonwealth *v.* Green. The former case was one in which a bicyclist was assaulted by one Carr, who threw stones at the rider while riding in a public street. None of the stones struck the rider, but, upon complaint being entered, the defendant was convicted of assault and fined with costs. The latter case was one where one of two boys concerned in the first mentioned case, brought an action, alleging assault and battery against one Green, the victim of the assault, who had taken him without a warrant, and by force had carried him to the station-house. The defendant was discharged, the court ruling that the circumstances warranted the act, as any delay to obtain an officer would have endangered the probability of an arrest, and that the force used was only such as was necessary in order to hand the offender to the proper officers.

GORMULLY & JEFFERY have recently received a very handsome bronze medal from the New Orleans Exposition Company, as a souvenir of the fact that their wheels took the first award at the New Orleans Exposition. On one side of the medal is an allegorical design of "The Three Americas," similar to that on the Prince Albert Memorial in London; and on the other is a suitable inscription.

THE *Sporting Journal* has been made the official organ of the Illinois division.

SHE was a dainty little miss, and he was a most enthusiastic cyclist. He was explaining to her the wonders of his new wheel — 1886 pattern. "And wha̧t are these?" she asked. "Those? those are the pedals which I put my feet on in riding," he gallantly replied. "Oh, I see," she exclaimed, "and now I know why men's feet are called pedal extremities." He wiped his foamy brow with his tool bag, and endeavored to end his existence in the next road race. — *Cyclist and Athlete.*

MR. T. R. FINLEY, denies that he competed at Yale College races for a money consideration.

MR. A. W. FISHER, of Boston, was riding in Malden last week, when he was attacked by a savage dog. Mr. Fisher, who is quite a scorcher, by the way, tried to run away from the beast, but was not fast enough, and left the whole of his boot heel and a small amount of flesh in the mouth of the canine.

KLUGH has returned home, much the worse for the header indulged in at the Lynn races. It is feared that he will not be able to race again this season. We met him the other day, and found that he was unable to straighten his left leg. He was on crutches, and in the best of spirits, despite his misfortune.

THESE gentlemen will constitute the executive board, and any one can see that it has a decidedly Eastern flavor. I doubt that any other States will be affected by the Union. We will have our races served up with League sauce, and although we do not expect to break many records, we can at least have the enjoyment of knowing that the winners are *bona fide* amateurs, and that they race for their own enjoyment, besides defraying their own expenses. The League certainly has more to offer than the new organization, and if it is left as a matter of choice between the riders, I think that very few will care to throw away their League membership for the privilege of competing at the tournaments of the Springfield and Lynn clubs. It might pay the class of men that are centred around the vicinity of Boston, but there the benefit will cease, and an attempt to make the Union provide for the whole country will result in a miserable failure. — *Jenkins in Sporting Life.*

THE Institute Building is in ruins. It will live in history as the scene of the International races between John Keen and John S. Prince and C. D. Vesey and L. T. Frye. On its track the record for a mile first fell below three minutes, and within its walls were witnessed many a notable event in cycling history.

AN excellent crayon portrait of Cola E. Stone, by his mother, is at Glover & Finkenaur's. It is quite large, and represents Cola sitting on the pedal of his "bike." He has just climbed Son-of-a-Gun Hill, the first time it was ever climbed on a wheel. He is near the small tree towards the top, with his back to it, and the deeper shadows of the wood across the road on his left. He sits facing you, and looks squarely into your eyes, as you have seen him look when he was interested in something you were saying. The expression is better, more like Cola, than that of any picture of him I have seen, either in photograph or drawing. The attitude is as easy and confident as the rather difficult seat on the pedal admits, a great deal easier than you or I could assume, much less feel; but Cola was at home in all things difficult on the wheel. His arms are folded naturally, his shoulders fall forward a little as they used to when under no special excitement; the expression is that of the big, good-natured, confident repose so familiar to every one who knew him, but out of his eyes and around the mouth there is an unmistakable suggestion of the grim determination and personal force that never faltered at an obstacle, nor stopped to measure the size or strength of an opponent. The portrait conveys an excellent impression of the personality of Cola Stone, and before this achievement the petty technical defects, which a critic might pick out fall into matters of the smallest importance. The portrait is to be given to the Ramblers Bicycle Club, of which Cola was the pride and ornament. — *Spectator.*

BROOKLINE will celebrate the 5th by a parade of antiques and horribles on bicycles in the morning and bicycle races in the afternoon.

THE professionals are about to start off on another tour. Mr. Morgan claims for them no more than they are entitled to, for from their Southern and Western trips came good results to the wheelmen thereabouts.

COL. POPE goes to England next month.

THE board of officers of the New York State Division will hold their spring meeting at the Grand Union Hotel on 29 June, and a large attendance has been promised. Considerable business will come before the meeting, and plans will be perfected for the publishing of a road book, and arranging for the annual meet of the division some time in the fall. I understand that the Buffalo Club will make a bid for the event, and think that they will have no difficulty in securing the prize. The talk of a State camp grows beautifully less as the time approaches, and will, I think, be dropped altogether. In fact, there are so many meets and races going on all the time that they wear upon one's pocketbook, besides taking valuable time. One cannot attend everything, and the fact that the numbers at the last meet were less than the event held in the same place four years ago, when cycling was in its infancy, prove that the word "meet" no longer provokes the enthusiasm of bygone days. — *Jenkins in Sporting Life.*

SEVERAL appeals have been made at the Boston police headquarters within a few days by bicycle dealers who have had valuable machines stolen from them by persons to whom they had been let. Six bicycles have been stolen within a few days in this way. Persons who steal machines from doorways have also been doing a good business of late. An Apollo, valued at $150, was stolen from a door on Columbus avenue Saturday evening. None of the men at police headquarters knew enough about bicycles to readily recognize machines of which they have descriptions, so there is a poor chance of the offenders being caught.

HE who says a bike is not made for two knows not whereof he speaks. Klipstein and Harry Gordon were mounted on a wheel the other evening, Harry being seated on Klip's shoulder. At Sixteenth and Locust, Klip's getting off place, Harry stood on to the handle-bar and gradually slid down on to the saddle, while Klip went *via* the backbone to the ground. — *Sunday Sayings.*

MESSRS STODDARD, LOVERING & CO. wish to state that they are now prepared to fill orders for the American Rudge. They report the demand for this machine has been something extraordinary, and they have been taxed to their utmost to keep up with sales. The American riders are beginning to appreciate that they can get a first-class machine for, in the vicinity of $110.

A GOOD RECORD.

ON 20 June, a tandem record for twenty hours, for a lady and gentleman, was established by Mr. and Mrs. L. H. Johnson, of the Orange Wanderers. They began their ride at midnight, when their Lakin cyclometer was checked by Captain Belcher, of the Wanderers. They rode steadily until 10.20 at night, when they had completed 150⅝ miles. During their ride they were accompanied by different members of the club.

NEW ORLEANS.

WELL, the particulars of the late Meet are all in, and we breathe easy once more. Of course there are to be found some who still denounce the Racing Board for its recent action, but that was expected, so not much is thought of it, and it is your humble servant's opinion that ere many months have fled, that the M. A.'s and their friends will have become reconciled to their fate, and gradually cease their idle talk and threats. So far as the A. C. U. is concerned, it is apparent that it can hope for but little aid from the South; for, notwithstanding the difference of opinions regarding the Racing Board's action, one and all still swear by the League. I fear if Mr. Ducker was to see the lukewarmness with which his pet hobby is received down this way, that he would grow "faint-hearted," and give up the ghost at once.

THERE is before our State Legislature, now in session, a bill to require the paving of this entire city. It is needless to say with what favor it is received by the cycling community. Should it pass, good-by to frequent dismounts and trundling of wheels.

THE St. John's, Sporting Club, of this city, give their annual tournament on the 24th inst. Among their sports is a one-mile bicycle race, to which there are already some eight or ten entries, with a prospect of several more. Hill and Hughes, two of our fast men, will come together for the first time in this race, and there is some little speculation as to who will prove the speedier man.

THE race for the Hill medal has been fixed for 15 July, the course to be selected later. Mr. Hill, being the donator of the medal, will not run in this race, which will make it all the more interesting, as he being conceded the palm for the distance (fifty miles), there is a doubt as to who will prove the second-best man.

THE election of the secretary-treasurer of this division, as well as officers of the N. O. B. C., will occur on the 23d inst.

FROM what your correspondent can learn, the meet of Southern wheelmen at Columbus, Ga., 15 to 18 July, promises to be the biggest thing in the wheel line that has yet occurred in the South. A splendid programme has been arranged, including tours, road races, hill-climbing contest, etc. They have a splendid track (probably the best in the South), and with fair weather, some new Southern records are sure to be made. BI.

NEW ORLEANS, 18 June, 1886.

LEAGUE COMMITTEES.

PRESIDENT BECKWITH of the L. A. W. has announced the following appointments (those in italics are new): —

Membership committee L. A. W. — Edward F. Hill, chairman; Dr. G. Carlton Brown, 16 Broad street, Elizabeth, N. J.; J. R. Dunn, Massillon, Ohio.

Racing Board — Abbot Bassett, chairman, 22 School street, Boston; Ewing L. Miller, 134 South Front street, Philadelphia, Pa.; N. H. Van Sicklen, 2 Adams street, Chicago, Ill.; *Charles H. Potter*, Cleveland, Ohio; *Gerry Jones*, Binghamton, N. Y.

Rules and regulations — W. I. Harris, chairman, box 5132, Boston, Mass.; *Dr. C. S. Butler*, 263 Main street, Buffalo, N.Y.; *Knight L. Clapp*, 328 West Sixtieth street, New York.

Rights and privileges — Charles E. Pratt, 597 Washington street, Boston, Mass.; John C. Gulick, 132 Nassau street, New York; *A. S. Parsons*, Cambridge, Mass.

Transportation committee — Burley B. Ayers, chairman, 152 South Hoyne avenue, Chicago, Ill.; George R. Bidwell, 2 East Sixtieth street, New York; W. S. Bull, 587 Main street, Buffalo, N. Y.; J. H. Livingston, editor the *Reformer*, Bennington, Vt.; Fred T. Sholes, Marsh-Harwood Company, Cleveland, Ohio; Frank Read, Equitable Life Assurance Society, Philadelphia; Frank A. Elwell, *Transcript* office, Portland, Me.; Columbus Waterhouse, San Francisco, Cal.; Frank X. Mudd, A. & W. P. R. R., Montgomery, Alabama; W. M. Brewster, Vandalia line, St. Louis, Mo.; M. E. Graves (at large) Minneapolis, Minn.

THE N. A. A. A. A.

AT a meeting of the Executive Committee, N. A. A. A. A., held 17 June, the following resolution was passed: —

Resolved, That whenever our definition of an amateur is identical with that of the League of American Wheelmen, and the League in any such instance finds that a person has violated the said definition and declares him a professional, that this committee will not investigate the matter further, but will concur with the decision of the League.

GLEANINGS FROM GOTHAM.

WELL, the League drove a nail in the coffin of the A. C. U. last Saturday by demonstrating that successful races, and a paying meeting could be held without the presence of the M. A.'s. League rules, league men, and amateurs predominated at the fourth annual race meeting of the King's County wheelmen, at the grounds of the Brooklyn Athletic Association Grounds. A lovely day, little wind, and a good track combined to make the occasion memorable, and the crowds of Brooklyn's fairest representatives applauded vociferously as the doughty knights of the wheel spun around on their shining steeds of glittering steel. (Mem. This is cribbed from a daily paper.) The racing was all that could be desired, and it was a pleasure to welcome many new faces on the track. It seems that we can have *bona fide* amateur races; and although the time was not so fast as at Springfield, otherwise the contests were close and interesting.

THE novices had the first innings, and there were so many of them that they had to be divided into heats, the first, second, and third to compete in the final. As usual, there was the spurter on the first lap, but E. I. Halsted got to the tape first in 3.14, H. F. Hornbostel and F. B. Jones getting second and third. The second heat, was taken by T. H. Burnet in $3.19\frac{1}{5}$, with E. B. Moore and E. R. Lamson coming in in time for a slice of the final cake. This was quite a pretty brush between the six, and resulted in favor of Halsted, who finished first in $3.12\frac{2}{5}$, with Burnet second.

The King's County wheelmen members, who have never won a prize in a bicycle race, then struggled for a mile, and T. C. Crichton delighted himself and his wide circle of friends by winning handily in $3.18\frac{2}{5}$. R. J. Knox was so delighted at finishing second that he nearly took a header, C. R. Neville securing third. A two-mile handicap had so many entries that two heats were necessary. A. B. Rich made his first appearance in this race, and was cheered as he rode slowly to the starting-point. There was a little flurry as to whether he would be allowed to compete, but a telegram from Chairman Bassett set matters straight, and he was obliged to ride under protest, all prizes being withheld pending the investigation as to whether Rich had violated the rules of the League. It was a very pretty brush throughout. Rich made the first mile in $3\frac{1}{5}$, the fastest time for the day, and captured the heat from Kavanaugh of Cohoes by two feet. Time for the total distance, 6.15. In the second heat, Powers and Wilhelm of Reading, Pa. had a lively tussle for the lead, but the former was not in good condition, having just recovered from malarial fever. He made a good race and secured a place in the final. The final heat was interesting, Rich and Kavanaugh having a lively struggle throughout, the former crossing the line after a lively brush on the homestretch, taking 6.7 to cover distance.

A job lot of club championships followed, interesting to the contestants, and keeping the audience awake. The Brooklyn Club medal was captured by Wm. Meeteer in 3.25. The Ilderans ran a little faster, W. M. Richardson winning in $3.19\frac{4}{5}$. The Bedford Cycling Club spread theirs out two miles, and C. F. Pray captured the race in $7.14\frac{2}{5}$. The band then cleared the deck for action, and the best contest of the day, the five-mile championship for the State of New York, was announced. This brought out a fine field of starters. A. B. Rich, E. Valentine, T. W. Roberts, W. S. Gilson, P. M. Harris and E. C. Parker faced the handsome starter, Mr. Edward Pettus (this means a good cigar). Kavanaugh was in the swim and kept dangerously near the front. Long-legged Gilson, who is the best road rider Gotham has produced, made his second appearance on the track, and proved that with a little training he would be a dangerous man. He rides a 59-inch wheel, and the way he negotiated the turns takes one back to the days when Louis Hamilton charmed us on the old Manhattan track in a fifty-mile race. He started out at the crack of the gun, and led a very lively bunch of animated legs for four laps. Harris spurted across the tape and took the first mile in $3.16\frac{2}{5}$, but afterwards dropped back to second place. Valentine bobbed along serenely, keeping a sharp lookout for the leaders, but not lagging too far behind. Roberts and Parker struggled for the honors of last man with varying success. Harris rode well; in fact, never better, considering he had not been on a wheel for a week. He needs a little training. There were a few changes on the next mile, but Gilson humped over the line in $6\ 34\frac{1}{5}$. Harris popped up to the front at the commencement of the third and fourth miles, and as the time came for the final rush, every one jumped to their feet in excitement. Round they came, with Gilson leading, and at the bell Rich made a break for the lead, and got it amid tremendous excitement. Kavanaugh followed, but suddenly Valentine rushed into second place, and in that order they finished. Gilson secured fourth and Harris fifth. The time of the winner was $16.17\frac{1}{5}$., and last lap 33 seconds.

Between dr——, the races I mean, a three-mile handicap was run off, and was neatly captured by Rich, with Kavanaugh second by about ten; yards time, $9.31\frac{1}{5}$. Rich and Valentine had a tumbling match on tricycles, but Valentine did all the tumbling, and Rich won easily in $4.48\frac{2}{5}$. These two events came before the championship, and then came the final event, a consolation race, which brought out lots of good men that were not quite as good as the men who had won the previous events. The doughty Wilhelm plowed his Star to the front, after a hot run with Honson, of Troy, Bridgeman, Harris, and several others. His time was $3.7\frac{2}{5}$. This closed the tournament, and all departed well satisfied with the result of the day's sport.

I dropped into the Ixion Club after the races, and saw Mr. Herring do a quarter of a mile in $14\frac{1}{5}$ on a home trainer. The machine was not in perfect order, and he was unable to finish the mile, but I think he can come close to a minute on ordinary occasions, and there is no doubt in my mind but that the fifty-two odd seconds was correct. There is as much of a knack about pedaling on a home trainer as anything else, and while many may be able to pass the gentleman on the track or road, it seems reasonably fair to credit the performance, especially as it was certified to that the timing was correct, and the maker has given a clean bill of health as to the accuracy of the instrument used. JENKINS.

THE COLUMBIA IN THE WEST.

THE RECORD BROKEN.

Splendid Performance of S. P. Hollinsworth, Greenfield, Ind.

[Special Dispatch to the Sunday Herald.]

INDIANAPOLIS, IND., June 19, 1886. S. P. Hollinsworth, of Russiaville, was wonderfully successful in his attempt to beat the long distance amateur bicycle record of this country and Great Britain. He completed his task at Greenfield this morning at 4 o'clock, and in the 24 hours scored a total of 285 9-10 miles. His actual riding time was 21 hours and 23 minutes, 2 hours and 37 minutes being lost in eating and in being rubbed down. Heretofore the best American record was 259 1-3 miles, made by Munger of Detroit, at Boston, while the English record is 266. The best track record is 276.

This record was made on a 55-inch wheel, COLUMBIA LIGHT ROADSTER. — *Indianapolis Times.*

THE COLUMBIAS AT LYNN.

June 17, 1886.

1-MILE NOVICE.
1st, S. L. TRUESDALE.
2d, HENRY McBRIEN.

1-MILE OPEN.
1st, W. A. ROWE.
Time, 2.37 2-5.

2-MILE LAP.
1st, G. M. HENDEE.

2-MILE HANDICAP.
1st, F. S. HITCHCOCK.

1-4-MILE PROFESSIONAL TRICYCLE, WORLD'S RECORD.
T. W. ECK.
Time, 42 2-5.

THE COLUMBIAS IN NEW JERSEY.

25-MILE INTER-CLUB ROAD RACE, (NEW JERSEY.)

JUNE 19, 1886.

1st, E. H. VALENTINE.
3d, H. CALDWELL.
(On Columbia Light Roadsters.)

THE COLUMBIAS IN BROOKLYN.

June 19, 1886.

The following Events were won on Columbias.

1-MILE NOVICE,
3-MILE HANDICAP,
3-MILE HANDICAP,
2-MILE BEDFORD,
C. C. CHAMPIONSHIP,
5-MILE N. Y. STATE CHAMPIONSHIP.

THE POPE MFG. CO.

597 Washington St., Boston, Mass.

| 12 Warren St., New York. | Branch Houses, | 115 Wabash Ave., Chicago. |

THE State division of Rhode Island has in immediate prospect a hill-climbing contest in July, and excursion to and ten-mile run at Newport, and will conduct the tournament at the State Fair in September, inaugurated last year by the Providence Club, under its auspices.

PENCILLED PARAGRAPHS.

THERE is a scheme on foot to put Rowe in a ten-mile race against the three best men of Essex County, — the "three best" to relieve each other every mile.

EUGENE M. AARON, the secretary-editor L. A. W., has applied for admission to the A. C. U.

THE A. C. U. should at once appoint an official handicapper, or some scratch man will slay the Lynn officers in cold blood after being defeated by some 560-yards man.

THE old illustrations of "sitting on the ragged edge," so much used in the Greeley presidential campaign, could be worked in with good effect to show the standing of some of our pure amateurs.

STRICKLAND & PIERCE will soon close their Boston office and move to the factory at Randolph. They have outgrown their present location.

THE Rev. David Utter of Chicago was spent several days among our dealers preparing for an extended continental cycle tour.

WOODSIDE will give Eck 200 yards in the mile race at Lynn on the 26th. Eck evidently is more modest about his abilities as a racer than as a trainer.

A. E. PATTISON, of the Pope Manufacturing Company, is sick with pneumonia.

PERRY, of the Massachusetts Bicycle Club, is doing private detective work in the interest of the riders who have lost machines lately. The Coventry people are the gainers by his services so far.

DR. COOKE, of the Massachusetts Bicycle Club, leaves for a fishing trip in Maine this week. If he reports favorably on the fishing outlook for the section of Maine he intends to visit, several more of the Massachusetts men will follow him.

A NEW book will soon be put upon the market, entitled "The Earth and how I run It," by T. W. Eck.

LEONARD AHL, of the Massachusetts Bicycle Club, has returned from Europe, and reports that his brother Ralph will bring back with him from England a semi-racing tandem that will set all the Massachusetts tandemons wild with envy. It may not be out of place to say that when he gets into a race with his club members, he will *tan dem all.*

KLUGE is still unable to ride his knee, and will, as soon as he can travel, retire to New York, and endeavor to get well before the fall meets.

IF handicaps show anything, the Lynn men evidently intend that Rowe shall break all the short records on their track in an open meeting.

HOSMER'S rowing machine appeared on the Lynn track, and was the source of much amusement to the men training on the track,

who succeeded in about equalling three minutes in three circuits of the track. The machine has a terrific pull when the whole force of the body is put into the stroke.

A. A. GLINES has been appointed consul for the Newtons.

THE Caledonian games at Springfield on the 5th will include three handicap races. "Our George" will be scratch in the mile.

THE Springfield Club has ordered one watch to cost over $1,000 for the first prize in the mile, open for its next tournament, and two more of high value as the second and third prizes.

THE Boston tailor who will buy League cloth by the piece and make the uniform at the regular L. A. W. prices, will make money. It has been tried successfully in other cities.

MR. C. E. WHITTEN is still confined to his house from the effects of his fall at New Haven.

COREY HILL climbing is now considered a sign of effeminacy among our local cracks.

THE corners of the Lynn track will be raised twenty-two inches after 5 July.

THE Springfield club has vacated its old rooms for more commodious quarters nearer the track.

THE best cycle racing reporter in the State is Merrill of the *Springfield Union.* Nothing escapes his eye, and he gives you the position of each man during the entire race, so that in perusing his accounts you can see the faster riders gradually drawing up and away from their slower brethren.

E. P. BURNHAM has located at Watertown a branch store for the letting and sale of cycles. His arm is much improved, and Burnham now longs for a brush with his old opponents.

PAPA WESTON has suddenly revived sufficiently to issue a manifesto against the A. C. U., and has had a bad relapse into his old comatose state. What is the reason Acting Chief Consul Potter did not issue the warning over his own name?

UBIQUITOUS.

THE PATH.

BROCKTON, 16 June. — The Brockton races were eminently successful. There was no very fast time made, but the races were closely contested and interesting. The track was in excellent condition, and as the turns are good every opportunity was given for good racing. The races were under the auspices of the City Bicycle Club of Brockton, and much credit is due it for the success of the meeting. The parade in the morning was participated in by about seventy-five wheelmen, who, headed by the band, marched through the following streets : East Elm, Montello, Elliott, Main, West Elm, Warren avenue, South, Main to East Elm, where the procession was dismissed. H. A. Churchill acted as chief marshal, with Walter Brown, George Pinckney, and F. G. Parker as aids.

The races were as follows : —

Half-Mile, Plymouth County Wheelmen. — Ed. Séverance (1), 1.30½ ; Walter Brown (2) ; Wm. Randall (3) ; S. A. Little (4).

Two-Mile Professional, County. — A. P. Holmes (1), 6.35$\frac{3}{5}$; Will Mason (2).

One-Mile 3.30 Class. — D. C. Pierce (1), 3.13$\frac{1}{5}$; W. S. Doane (2); Walter Brown (3).

One-Mile Handicap. — A. E. Randall, scratch (1), 2.57$\frac{4}{5}$; Ed. Severance, 40 yards (2); W. Randall, 60 yards (4); Walter Brown, 50 yards (4).

One-Mile, Boys. — A. W. Porter (1); White (2).

Five-Mile Handicap. — This was between John S. Prince and T. W. Eck. The only feature was the time of the first mile, 2.51. Prince conceded 400 yards start to his opponent and had his man caught at 3$\frac{1}{4}$ miles, but managed to keep behind until the finish, when Prince spurted and won by a few lengths. Time — one mile, 2.51; 2 miles, 6 02$\frac{1}{2}$; three miles, 9.18$\frac{3}{5}$; four miles, 12.42; five miles, 16.02.

Five-Mile. — D. E. Hunter (1), 16.57$\frac{1}{5}$; H. C. Getchell (2); D. C. Pierce (3); Eugene Sanger (4).

One-Mile against Time. — R. A. Neilson endeavored to break the record of 2.51, made by Prince on the same day. He made a good effort, but failed by two seconds. Time — quarter, 41$\frac{1}{5}$; half, 1.23; three quarters, 2.13$\frac{3}{5}$; mile, 2.53.

One-Mile. — H. C. Getchell (1), 2.53; Frank Gibbs (2); A. E. Randall (3). Getchell did splendid work and succeeded in equalling Neilson's time of 2.53. He made the quarter in 48$\frac{2}{5}$; half, in 1.27$\frac{1}{5}$; and three quarters, in 2.11$\frac{4}{5}$. He was deservedly applauded for this splendid performance.

One-Mile Tricycle, County. — A. E. Randall (1), 3.50; D. C. Pierce (2).

The officials were as follows: Referee, A. D. Peck, Jr., of Boston; judges, J. S. Dean of Boston, L. C. Southard of North Easton, G. C. Holmes of Brockton; timers, J. G. Hitchcock of Omaha, J. E. Savell of Dorchester; scorers, R. E. Bellows of Dorchester, W. B. Briggs of Brockton; umpires, W. S. Atwell of Charlestown, J. J. Gilligan of Boston; starter, W. M. Pratt of Brockton; clerk, A. E. Brayton of Brockton.

LYNN, 17 June. — Races under the auspices of the Lynn Cycle Track Association. A good meeting. The track was in fine condition and there was little loafing. The races were run under the rules of the A. C. U., and a new crop of professional racing men was added to the already large list. The races were as follows:

One-Mile, Novice. — S. L. Truesdale (1), 3.5$\frac{4}{5}$; H. McBrion (2), 3.12$\frac{2}{5}$; J. L. Lang (3); Fred Woodbury (4).

One-Mile, 2.50 Limit. — W. A. Rowe (1), 2.37$\frac{2}{5}$; Geo. E. Weber (2), 2.43; W. F. Knapp (3).

The start was very bad, and several seconds were stolen on the pistol. It is doubtful if the record will be allowed by any good authority. It was announced on the track that this was the best record ever made in an actual race; but we have in mind the record of Fred Wood, 2.35$\frac{4}{5}$, made in a race at Springfield.

Quarter-Mile Tricycle, against Time. — This brought out T. W. Eck, in an attempt to beat the record. He was off before the word and got the advantage of the pistol. He made the distance in 42$\frac{2}{5}$, but the record will not stand.

Three-Mile Lap Race. — Geo. M. Hendee (1), 27 points; Geo. E. Weber (2); A. A. McCurdy (3). All but Hendee were mounted on Stars. Hendee won every lap. Weber made a very game race, but McCurdy fell out at the end of the first lap. The times were as follows: Mile, 2.53$\frac{2}{5}$; two miles, 5.57$\frac{1}{5}$; three miles, 8.41$\frac{4}{5}$.

Ten-Mile Professional. — The entries and starters were John S. Prince and R. A. Neilson of Boston, and W. M. Woodside of Chicago. The race was exceedingly interesting throughout.

Leader.	Time.
One mile, Woodside	2.50
Two miles, Woodside	5.47$\frac{2}{5}$
Three miles, Prince	8.50
Four miles, Woodside	11.44$\frac{3}{5}$
Five miles, Woodside	14.49
Six miles, Prince	17.55
Seven miles, Prince	20.58
Eight miles, Woodside	23.41$\frac{1}{5}$
Nine miles, Neilson	27.07$\frac{1}{5}$
Ten miles, Prince	30.08$\frac{1}{5}$

R. A. Neilson (2), 30.8$\frac{3}{5}$; W. M. Woodside (3).

Two-Mile Handicap. — F. S. Hitchcock, 560 yards (1), 5.19$\frac{2}{5}$; A. A. McCurdy, 350 yards (2); W. A. Rowe, scratch (3), 5.29. Rowe's mile time, 2.40.

CLEVELAND, O., 31 May. — Races run under the auspices of the Cleveland A. C. *One-Hundred Yard*, two in three. — F. P. Root, first and third heat and dead heat for second, 11$\frac{2}{5}$, 11$\frac{3}{5}$, and 11$\frac{1}{5}$; W. S. Upson (2); G. Valiant (3). *One-Mile Amateur.* — G. Valiant (1), 3.1$\frac{2}{5}$; J. Huntington (2); F. P. Root (3).

HARTFORD, 19 June. The 20-mile road race of the Hartford Wheel Club was run this day. The start was from Thompson's corner in West Hartford, over a carefully measured 20-mile course which led to New Britain and returned through Newington and Elmwood. There were 11 starters, but of these only seven finished, the rest dropping out when they felt sure of getting no place in the race. The start was made at 6 A. M. to ensure clear roads, and the first man in was William Harding, who came through Capitol avenue and up Main street to the club room at great speed with F. G. Warner as pacemaker. Only two minutes behind, however, was A. F. Judson, who had started ninth, four minutes behind Harding. He also came in at a great pace, dropping one pacemaker who met him two miles out, picking up another whom he met in the city and dropping him also, and finishing in the remarkable time of 1.29.16. Harding's time was 1.31.14. Howard Wilcox finished in 1.41.20, and the other men in the following order: C. H. Way, 1.47.15; E. N. Way, 1.49.10; H. Starkweather, 1.53.05; Frederick King, 1.55.17. Wilcox took the wrong one of two parallel roads, but it was the worst of the two, and his claim to third place was not probably be contested. Judson, Harding, and Wilcox will be the club's team in the State road race of the Meriden Club 26 June. The best record over this course previous to to-day was 1.28 for 18 miles, made by F. F. Ives, of Meriden.

NEW YORK, 19 June. Games of Manhattan Athletic Club. — *Two Mile Bicycle Race.* — C. M. Phelps (1), 6.33$\frac{1}{2}$; L. S. Squire (2).

PRINCETON, N. J., 18 June. Games of Princeton College. — *Two Mile Bicycle Race.* — Stearns (1), 6.55$\frac{1}{4}$.

NEW ORLEANS, LA., 29 May. — Races run under the auspices of the Young Men's Gymnastic Club. *One Mile Handicap,* — for members of the New Orleans Bicycle Club, — W. L. Hughes (1), 4.3$\frac{1}{4}$; E. E. Marks (2), 4.5; G. McD. Nathan (3), 5. 30 May. *One Mile Amateur.* — W. L. Hughes (1), 3.51$\frac{1}{2}$; E. E. Marks (2), several lengths.

MOTT HAVEN, N. Y., 12 June. — Races run under auspices New York Athletic Club. *Three Mile Handicap,* — S. Gilson, ninety yards (1), 18$\frac{1}{5}$; F. Thayer, one hundred yards (2).

THE twenty-five-mile road race of the Wakefield, Mass., Bicycle Club took place 12 June, and resulted as follows: First prize, J. C. Clark, time, 1.4?.5; second, H. R. Emerson, 1.48.13; third prize, J. F. Coombs, 1.57; fourth prize, a silver cup, F. C. Patch, in 1.58.20.

IN a practice spin Saturday, on the Lynn bicycle track, George M. Hendee made five miles in 14.4$\frac{2}{5}$, beating Rowe's world record of 14.7$\frac{2}{5}$ by 3 seconds. Rowe wheeled ten miles in 29.18$\frac{2}{5}$, that being only 6 seconds slower than the professional record. Knapp was the first man to go ten miles inside of 30 minutes on this track, making the distance in 29.58.

THE Meriden Wheel Club has now on hand \$750 of the \$1,500 necessary to construct a third of a mile track at the trotting park. Of this sum the wheelmen subscribed \$400, N. L. Bradley \$100, and Mayor Doolittle and H. Wales Lines raised \$135 among their friends. The track will be ready for use in six weeks. It will be twenty feet wide.

THE next race between Prince and Neilson will be run at Lynn, 26 June. No other races will be run at that time. It is understood that the men will then try to break the ten-mile record.

THE Rhode Island Division of the L. A. W. will hold a twenty-five-mile road race on Saturday, 26 June, 1886, which will be open to all members of the Rhode Island Division of the L. A. W. The course will be as follows: From a point just beyond the Red Bridge in East Providence, taking the Warren road straight down twelve miles, and return by the same road. On returning to the starting-point, the race will be made one half mile along the Pawtucket road and back, that completing the twenty-five miles. It will be seen that under this arrangement spectators may view the race three times at the starting-point, and have a splendid opportunity to see the mile race with turn at the finish. Start will be made promptly at 3 P. M. The prizes will consist of gold medal to first, and silver medals as second and third prizes. If the entries are seven or more, a fourth prize may be added.

THE Inter-State Meet will be held at Youngstown, O., 15 July. The programme for the day is: One mile novice race; half mile open, two heats in three; one mile open; five miles open, lap race; two miles open; hundred and fifty yards foot race; half mile Inte.-State championship; one mile Inter-State championship; two mile Inter-State championship; two mile consolation.

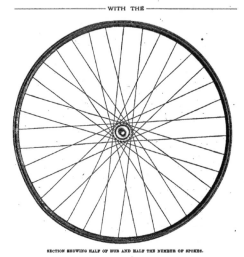

THE following is the programme of races at the Illinois Division L. A. W. Meet, to be held at Cheltenham Beach, on 5 July : No. 1, 3 P. M., one mile, novice, bicycle ; No. 2, 3.10, one mile, Chicago and St. Louis, bicycle ; No. 3, 3.20, two mile, handicap, bicycle ; No. 4, 3.35, two mile, 7.15 time race, bicycle ; No. 5, 3.45, one mile, State championship, tricycle ; No. 6, 3.55, one mile, 3.15 class race, bicycle ; No. 7, 4.00, one mile, State championship, bicycle ; No. 8, 4 05, three miles, open to all amateurs, bicycle ; No. 9, 4.20, five miles, State championship, bicycle ; No. 10, 4.40, one mile, handicap, bicycle ; No. 11, 4.50, one mile, open to all amateurs, bicycle ; No. 12, 5.00, one mile, consolation, bicycle. No. 3 is not a team race, but is arranged for the benefit of the best of St. Louis' and Chicago's men.

THE tournament of the Binghamton Bicycle Club bids fair to be an event of no little importance in cycling circles. The club will accept entries only from pure amateurs, and the races will be run under League rules. President Beckwith and Chief Consul Bidwell will be among the officers of the day. There will be a parade at 11 A. M., and an entertainment in the evening.

AN open ten-mile road race will be held by the Orange Wanderers on 10 July. The course will be two laps over good macadam roads, the finish being a straight half-mile stretch with a very slight down grade. The course is a fast one. Three medals will be given. Full particulars may be had from E. P. Baird, Brick Church, N. J.

THE CLUB.

THE Rover Bicycle Club is a newly formed organization of the wheelmen residing in Brighton and Allston. The club begins life under very favorable circumstances, and, considering the very large number of wheelmen in that district, the club should soon be on a strong and prosperous foundation. The present officers are : President, H. A. Fuller ; secretary and treasury, C. G, Brazier ; captain, H. J. Taylor. A meeting of the club will be held next Tuesday evening at the residence of President Fuller, 15 Sparrowhawk street, Brighton, and all wheelmen of the district are cordially invited to attend.

THE Winona (Minn.) Club held a largely attended meeting, 7 June, at the Merchants Bank. The election of officers for the ensuing year resulted as follows ; President, C. H. Porter ; vice-president and captain, W. H. Elmer ; secretary, A. W. Laird ; treasurer, John I. Wilson ; first lieutenant, H. S. Bolcom ; second lieutenant, J. R. Marfield ; executive committee, L. W. Worthington, R. E. Tearse, H. H. Norton. Work is in progress on the bicycle track at the lacrosse grounds, and the track ranks as one of the very best in the State.

THE Capital Bicycle Club's election, 12 June, for the term ending 31 Dec. 1886, resulted as follows ; John M. Killits, president ; Rudolph Kauffmann, vice-president ; Charles A. Burnett, recording secretary ; James Q. Rice, corresponding secretary ; Joseph E. Leaming, treasurer ; Edson B. Olds, captain ; D. E. Sharretts, sub-captain ; William M. Dougal, junior sub-captain ; executive committee, the officers ex-officio ;

and J. West Wagner, P. T. Dodge, William B. Hibbs, J. McK. Borden.

THE Florence (Mass.) Cycle Club, at its last regular meeting, voted to offer prizes to members attending most club runs, also for riding largest number miles during the season. This step was taken to renew the interest of the members and sustain the reputation of being a live, active organization. The captain was also instructed to call a run every Sunday, and also one during the week in addition.

COMING EVENTS.

JULY.

1 Thursday. — First day of annual meeting of C. W. A. at Montreal.

2 Friday. — Second day of annual meeting of C. W. A. at Montreal.

3 Saturday. — Third day of annual meeting of C. W. A. at Montreal.
Suffolk Wheel Clubs' three days' tour begins.

5 Monday. — Race meeting at Binghamton, N. Y.
Race meeting at Cleveland, Ohio, two miles, L. A. W. championship.
Races at Chelsea, Mass.
Races at Boston, Mass.
Races at East Saginaw, Mich.
Races at Brookline, Mass.
Races at No. Adams, Mass.
Races at Springfield, Mass.
Races at Lynn, Mass.

10 Thursday.— Road Race of Orange (N. J.) Wanderers.

15 to 18, Tuesday to Friday. — Tournament at Columbus, Ga. State championships will be run.

FOURTH

ANNUAL RACE MEETING

OF THE BINGHAMTON

BICYCLE CLUB

Monday, 5 July, 1886.

GOLD MEDALS GIVEN IN ALL EVENTS.

One-Mile Novice Race, Open.
Two-Mile Dash, Open.
Three-Mile, 9.45 Class, Open.
One-Mile New York State Championship.
One-Mile Ride and Run. Open.
Three-Mile Handicap, Open.
One-Mile B. B. Club Handicap.
One-Mile Consolation.
One-Mile Team Race, three men from each club, Open.

L. A. W. RULES TO GOVERN. ENTRANCE FEE, 50 CENTS FOR EACH EVENT.

Entries close July 1, to

Chas. E. TITCHENER

BINGHAMTON, N. Y.

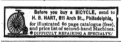

The Cycle.

VOL. I., No. 14.   BOSTON, MASS., 2 JULY, 1886.   FIVE CENTS.

The Coventry Machinists' Co.'s New Tricycle for 1886.

THE MARLBORO' CLUB—Automatic Steerer,
ADMIRABLY ADAPTED FOR LADIES.
SEND FOR CATALOGUE TO 239 COLUMBUS AVENUE, BOSTON.

Adjustment in Height in Front.
Adjustment in Height in Rear.

Adjustment in Length.
Adjustment in Width.

A Comfortable Coasting Plate.
A Bifurcated Seat.

THE LILLIBRIDGE SADDLE

Is the only one having any of these Points; is the only one that can be changed in Shape or Position at all; is the BEST and CHEAPEST; is adapted to all makes of Bicycles. Special Styles for the Safeties and Star.

Price, Nickelled, $5.00. Price of oiled Spring, with Straps, etc., for Old Saddles, 75 Cts.

FREEMAN LILLIBRIDGE, Rockford, Ill.

THE BOSTON BICYCLE SHOE.

The Perfect Shoe for Cycling.

Hand-sewed, hand-made, first-quality stock and warranted in every respect. Every pair of our No. 1 Boston Sporting Shoes is marked inside. "Boston: Strickland & Pierce, Hand-Sewed," and is stamped "Patent" on the bottom. None others are Genuine. Bicycle, Blue Ball Sprint Running, Pedestrian, Gymnasium, La Crosse and other shoes. Prices and rules for self-measurement sent on application.

STRICKLAND & PIERCE,

156 and 156½ Summer Street,

BOSTON.

SAFE, PRACTICAL and FAST.

NO HEADERS OR DANGEROUS FALLS.

Best Road Record for 50 and 100 Miles.
World's Safety Records from 1 to 20 Miles.
First American Machine to make more than 20 Miles within the Hour.
Three L. A. W. Championships for 1885.
Won all Hill Climbing Contests, both as to Speed and Grade.
Won all the First Premiums, when in Competition, since 1881.
NEW CATALOGUE READY.

H. B. SMITH MACHINE CO.

Smithville, Bur. Co., N. J.

THE AMERICAN CHAMPION, CHALLENGE, SAFETY AND IDEAL.

The above Machines have been awarded First Prize at the New Orleans Exposition, and the Champion holds the World's Long Distance Record. They Run Easy; Sell Easy; Repair Easy; and the Prices are Easy. They are the best. These are the only Machines of high grade sold at a medium price. It will pay you to examine them, or send two-cent stamp for Catalogue and Prices. We also have a large stock of Children's Machines at very low prices. First-class Repairing and parts for repairing. All kinds of Machines constantly on hand; also Sundries. Discount to the Trade. Call or write to the New England Headquarters.

MURRAY'S - - - - 100 Sudbury Street - - - - BOSTON, MASS.

THE Z. & S. STOCKING SUPPORTER.

Every wheelman should have them in his wardrobe or on his back. They are unquestionably the best yet produced. It is made so as to be worn beneath the flannel shirt, passes over the shoulders and down each leg. It has a sliding buckle, which allows for tension, and which can be unfastened by a spring in an instant without inconvenience.

Price Per Pair, 65 Cents.

☞ Send stamp for new Illustrated Catalogue, now ready, of our Cycling Goods.

HOWARD A. SMITH & CO., successors to ZACHARIAS & SMITH, Oraton Hall, Newark, N. J. Branch Store, Orange, N. J.

BEFORE YOU BUY A BICYCLE

Of any kind, send stamp to

A. W. GUMP,

DAYTON, OHIO,

For large Illustrated Price List of New and Second-hand Machines.

Second-hand Bicycles taken in exchange. Bicycles repaired and nickel-plated. Cash paid for Second-hand Bicycles. Largest stock of second-hand Wheels in America.

BARGAINS THIS WEEK:

52-inch PREMIER, new tires, ball bearings	$50
54-inch ENGLISH, new tires, ball bearings	55
SOCIABLE TRICYCLE, for two riders	80
VICTOR TRICYCLE, late pattern, just like new	100
VICTOR TRICYCLE, good running order	75
50-inch EXPERT, No. 1 order	75

Mention THE CYCLE when you write.

THE CYCLE

PUBLISHED EVERY FRIDAY BY ABBOT BASSETT, 22 SCHOOL ST., ROOM 19.

VOL. I. BOSTON, MASS., 2 JULY, 1886. No. 14.

TERMS OF SUBSCRIPTION.

One Year, by mail, post-paid..........................$1.50
Three Copies in one order..........................3.00
Club Subscriptions..........................1.00
Six Months..........................:..........................90
Single Copies..........................:..........................05

Specimen Copies free.

Every bicycle dealer is agent for the CYCLE and authorized to receive subscriptions at regular rates. The paper can be found on sale at the following places: —

Boston, CUPPLES, UPHAM & CO., cor. Washington and School Streets. Tremont House news stand. At every cycle warehouse.

New York, ELLIOTT MASON, 12 Warren Street.

Philadelphia, H. B. HART, 811 Arch Street. GEORGE D. GIDEON, 6 South Broad Street.

Baltimore, S. T. CLARK & CO., 4 Hanover Street.

Chicago, W. M. DURELL, 115 Wabash Avenue. JOHN WILKINSON & CO., 77 State Street.

Washington, H. S. OWEN, Capital Cycle Co.

St. Louis, ST. LOUIS WHEEL CO., 1121 Olive Street.

ABBOT BASSETT . . . . EDITOR

A. MUDGE & SON, PRINTERS, 24 FRANKLIN ST., BOSTON.

All communications should be sent in not later than Tuesday, to ensure insertion the same week.

Entered at the Post-office as second-class mail matter.

THE personal war that is being waged in the columns of the cycling press is very much to be regretted. It is doing an incalculable injury to our sport. We have endeavored in all that we have said anent the A. C. U. to confine ourselves to the acts of that body, and have never allowed ourselves to attack its exponents beyond controverting what they have said. *Per contra,* our opponents have showered unstinted abuse on us, and have left no chance escape them to attack us personally. We have no room to reply to personal attacks, but we wish to correct several errors that have crept into the statements of those who profess to speak for the A. C. U.

It often happens, through an oversight, our great and only Barnum does not possess all of the leading curiosities, and we have in mind two great inconsistencies that would prove a valuable addition to the great moral show. For one, we refer to the action of Mr. Bassett, as chairman of the L. A. W. Racing Board at the Lynn races. It was announced that these races would be run under the A. C. U. rules, and the A. C. U., pending the report of the committee, adopted as theirs the racing rules of the N. C. U. of England. This body and its rules are recognized by the L. A. W., yet the chairman, in his endeavor to strangle the new-born infant, repudiated the very rules he has for the past year endorsed. Perhaps it is as well, seeing that the N. C. U. has failed to recognize the L. A. W. Truly, consistency is a jewel. — *Wheelmen's Gazette.*

We venture to say that not two men at the Lynn races knew the rules of the N. C. U., which are in many cases radically different from those of the L. A. W. Under those rules a man who accepts expenses from a cycle manufacturer becomes a professional. Will any man who was at Lynn say that none of the men who contested in the so-called amateur races were in receipt of their expenses from cycle manufacturers? Under the rules of the N. C. U. there is no referee but a judge, who has all the powers of our referee and judges. At Lynn there was a referee and three judges. These are but two instances. We should show several more to prove that the Lynn races were not run under N. C. U. rules. Where, for instance, is there a provision for a lap race in the N. C. U. rules?

The second is the action of Charley H. Potter, of Cleveland, who has sued the Lynn Association for running the races under the very rules for which Mr. Potter is the chief consulate (sic) of America. Rather an awkward position to say the least, and we wait to see how this gentleman will extricate himself from the very embarrassing position he is now in.

Mr. Potter is acting chief consul of the C. T. C., a body that has no racing rules.

Mr. Bassett expelled the English riders who visited us last fall, and the N. C. U. has paid no attention whatever to it. To-day the men are all in good amateur standing in the N. C. U. — *Mr. Ducker in the World.*

The English riders have never been declared professionals, nor expelled by Mr. Bassett, nor any one else. The Racing Board will accept their status as it is declared by the N. C. U., until they violate the amateur law in the territory under the jurisdiction of the L. A. W. If the English riders come to America the coming fall with certificates from the N. C. U., asserting their amateur status under N. C. U. rules, and this precludes their accepting expenses from manufacturers, they will be accepted as amateurs by the L. A. W., and allowed to compete in amateur events; but if they compete with our professionals, they will lose their status, and our word for it, any action in this direction by the L. A. W. will be sustained by the N. C. U.

THE *World* tries to convict us of a falsehood by exposing a correspondence written on the 14th of June (Monday), and stating that it was written on the 16th (Wednesday). It is a question of dates. A messenger came to the CYCLE office on Monday, and we gave him a note to the effect that we were waiting information. That information came to us Tuesday afternoon. And now the *World* would have wheelmen believe that the messenger came to us on Wednesday. We have been charged with every crime in the calendar since we started the CYCLE, but we don't believe wheelmen think we are a liar or a murderer. On Wednesday, 16 June, the day when the *World* says a messenger was sent, it would have been impossible to reach us in the forenoon, and the editor of the *World* was in Brockton in the afternoon. It is not to the point that the official letter of the Board was dated 13 June, for letters of this kind are not always given the date of writing. Our contemporary has given us the lie in this matter. It remains to be seen whether it will retract what it has said.

THE Chief Consulship of Massachusetts has been declared vacant by President Beckwith. Mr. Ducker, the incumbent, says he will not retire without a struggle. Of the motive which prompted this action on the part of the president, we are not fully informed, but we have faith in him, and we can well believe that he considered that the best interests of the League demanded the step. That Mr. Ducker will declare war we do not doubt, but we believe he will find the great majority of wheelmen with the president.

THE following circulars have been sent out: —

To whom it may concern:

Dear Sir, — A number of prominent wheelmen wish to have a mail vote on the inclosed proposition. As our rules require a certain number of names to insure a mail vote, I inclose a form for you to sign, hoping thus to insure the settlement of this vexed question beyond dispute. I would be glad to receive your signature by return mail. Send same to

HENRY E. DUCKER,
Springfield, Mass.

DR. N. M. BECKWITH, *President L. A. W.*:

Dear Sir, — Believing that the interests of the League can be best served by disposing of what has been the bone of contention for the past few years, we, the undersigned, desire a mail vote upon the following, as per Article II., Section 5: —

Resolved, That the League of American Wheelmen strike from its by-laws all matters pertaining to racing, and confine itself to touring and legislative work, and such other matters as are deemed for the best interests of the wheelmen of America.

Sections to be struck out in by-laws : Article II., Section 3, entire section. Article III., Section 1, strike out "Committee on Racing (to be called the Racing Board)"; (b) "except Racing Board." Section 6, strike out entire section.

I hereby join in the desire for a mail vote on the above proposition.

In brief, this is a call upon the League to give up the racing interests. To whom? It is a very important trust, and before the League parts with it the members should know into whose hands it is to be placed. The request comes from the President of the A. C. U., and it is fair to infer that the new association desires to have charge of racing. It will not do. The record of the A. C. U. has not been a good one. At all races held under its rules, well-known professionals have been allowed to enter amateur races. The A. C. U. is not in harmony on the amateur question with any athletic association, or with any cycling body in this country or in England. Its own members are not in sympathy with its ideas. We have talked with prominent members of the A. C. U., and with a number of its officials, and we have yet to find one of them who will say that he thinks Rowe and Hendee and Knapp should be allowed to enter amateur contests. It may be that the A. C. U. will change its tactics and give protection to amateur wheelmen on the path, but until that time comes the League must continue to supervise the racing of America. The A. C. U. must prove itself worthy before it can be trusted.

PENCILLED PARAGRAPHS.

PENCILLED paragraphs are not written with vinegar, nor yet with gall. Your paragrapher is modest to a fault, and brimfull of the milk of human kindness. Plumbago pushing is my profession, and I scorn to be an amateur. I write for lucre, and when the lucre comes not I do not write. I commend myself to your favor, for when I lose that away goes my salary, and I take my place with duffers. So read me patiently, and I am your slave forever.

PRINCE stated to me that as the Lynn Track Association took no interest in his race, did not properly advertise the same, and secured practically no audience, he considered he was justified in refusing to race. Jack always takes the Princess to his races.

THE Prince-Neilson race will probably be run off on the new Newark track. The management has offered to put up $200 in addition to the regular stakes.

TRICYCLE Capt. Williams, of the Massachusetts Bicycle Club, trains all alone at Lynn every night at six o'clock, and has got his mile down to 3.48 already.

COREY and Omaha Hitchcock are after the twenty-four hour Tandem record. It is needless to say that McCurdy will not act as pacemaker *this* time.

CROCKER, of Newton, will make himself remembered on the Common on the 5th, and will push his self well up to the front on the road and track before this fall.

THE new Roxbury Club was out in full uniform, and the usual accompaniment of scroll badges on Sunday, and took in a quiet clam-bake before returning.

THE manager of one of the teams of makers' amateurs says he wishes race committees would not hold meetings for two weeks, after 5 July. He wants to go on a vacation.

D. EDGAR thinks the Racing Board will have to Hunter long while to get evidence against him.

SUCH jokes as that are hard to get. The reporter of the *Globe* will tell you Howard they are.

IT is said that the races at Chelsea will be nipped by a Frost. It's a cold day when Frost gets left on the path, you know.

SAVILLE, Hunniman, and Wiggin of the Roxbury riders will form the Dudley Wheel Club this week. The club will start with about thirteen members, and membership will be limited to members of the Dudley Associates, whose rooms will be the meeting place of the new club. The new club will not have Sunday runs, so that the usual Sunday trip of the Roxbury wheelmen will not be broken up.

SOME members of the Massachusetts Club are looking with envious eyes on the twenty-four hour record of 125 miles. made by Lang and Ladd last week.

IT is not safe to state in the press that any one rider is riding especially fast on the road, for all the scorchers at once proceed to hunt the wheelman up and run him to death on the road, simply to show him he is not what he thinks he is. A Massachusetts man is the next one marked for the slaughter, and the Suffolk Club Tour will be the scene of his execution.

FREQUENTERS of Hough's Neck, Quincy, should remember that the Boston Club considers that it holds the first mortgage on the entire place, and visitors will please conduct themselves accordingly.

HUNTER and Getchell will compete at the Montreal races. It is said that they have an Aunt who is Everett-y to pay the expenses of a little trip like this.

ANY pure amateur looking for what the English call a " quiet corner" on the 5th, will find them at Melrose, Chelsea, Boston Common, Salem and Brookline. A " quiet corner" is defined as a race meeting where the bulk of the first prizes can be scooped by some flyer, by a practical walk over in each event.

THE A. C. U. will probably divide the country up into districts and appoint a handicapper for each.

HUNTER throws down the gauntlet to his enemies, and defies them to show a blot on his amateur standing. Verily, the decision

of the Racing Board is like charity, it covereth a multitude of sins.

SEVERAL of the officers of the A. C. U. met at the Commonwealth Hotel on Sunday, and some important business was transacted.

PIERRE LALLEMENT, the original inventor, etc., is circulating among his friends photographs of himself and his original velocipede, with another view showing him on his new Expert Columbia.

WILL A. ILLSTON made 2.43 on the Aston Lower Grounds Track in a race lately, and considered the time something great. Some one ought to import Willie and take him to Lynn some day to see 2.37 run off.

SOME of the amateurs who have trained on the Glenmere track, but have declined to compete in the races, have found the atmosphere of the track so chilly since their last declension that they will find it necessary to remove their training quarters elsewhere. They made tracks, so to speak.

A PARTY of five Highland riders start on the 11th for a fortnight's tour through Southern New Hampshire. They are off to the highlands.

CONSUL SAVILLE of Roxbury is about to issue a second edition of his work, " Timing the Flyers ; or, Eleven Years' Experience on the Race Track." Watch for it.

LINEMEN are now daily engaged in removing the accumulation of taffy from the telephone wires connecting Overman's office with Pope's.

THE Massachusetts Division will hold a meeting the last of next week, and some lively tilts will take place.

THE Nonantum Cycle Club will run a series of road races, including a club championship, a boys' race, and probably an open event, with cycling sundries as prizes. The races will be under the A. C. U. rules, and under the new ruling of the board no one who competes will be disqualified.

THE third prize in the handicap at Lynn now ornaments the club room piano. Rowe scorned to accept it when it was tendered him.

ROWE made five miles in practice on Monday in 14.1¼ exactly, 5⅜ seconds ahead of world's record. In the afternoon he ran alone for the mile (in practice), and made it in 2.35½, ¼ seconds ahead of his own record.

THE East Cambridge Cycling Club runs to Salisbury Beach for its 4 July tour, and returns on Monday.

THE A. C. U. one-mile championship has been assigned to the Connecticut Club for its fall meet.

MASSACHUSETTS CHIEF CONSUL.

THE following notice has been issued : —

To the Members in Massachusetts:

There being a vacancy in the office of Chief Consul, L. A. W., for Massachusetts Division, I take this opportunity of acquainting the membership of my desire to make such appointment to fill the vacancy created by the retirement of Mr. Ducker, as shall meet the approbation of the greatest number of members of the division, and solicit such action on their part as shall bring about this end.   Fraternally,
N. MALON BECKWITH, *President.*

JENKINS ON THE A. C. U.

FRED JENKINS thus discusses the A. C. U. in *Sporting Life :* —

If I am correctly informed, there are a number of the prominent men in the A. C. U. who have come to the conclusion that the course they have thus far been pursuing is not a wise one, and counsel an immediate change ; but in an organization of this kind, they naturally meet with no end of opposition when they try to do anything sensible. Among the first reforms advocated by these sensible members is the cessation of all personal abuse towards the chairman of the Racing Board, and changing the definition of an amateur, whereby such men as Rowe and Hendee will be thrown in a class distinct from the amateurs. They have come to appreciate the fact that it is the height of absurdity to try and palm off these men as straight amateurs. The American public is famous for its gullibility, but it cannot swallow the makers' amateur for the genuine article. At the last meeting of the Union, which was held in Boston, one of the members advocated this change, but he received little support, for most of those present were of the unreasonable element, which having got an idea into its head that it wants something, is bound to have it in spite of everything. These men started the Union with the idea of forcing the League to reinstate the expelled makers' amateurs, and at the time of its birth they really had little idea of making it into an association which should have the entire control of the racing interests of America. But those of a more sensible character who have since joined aim at a higher future for the Union than a temporary organization for intimidation purposes. They rightfully consider that a large portion of the League membership cares absolutely nothing for racing, and would be well pleased if the League withdrew entirely from all connection with it. This being the case an organization having for its sole object the promotion of racing would have a prosperous future before it, because the League could be easily induced to retire in its favor. They are, however, sensible enough to appreciate the fact that the League never will surrender its racing interests to an organization which has so little regard for the protection of its much-prized amateur rule as to place no mark of distinction upon the dealers' pets. Accordingly, they are now hard at work trying to induce the Union to adopt a third class. When this is done it is quite probable that the League will be willing to make some concessions. There will, no doubt, be some who may consider these concessions as a sign of defeat on the part of the League, but this will be in no sense true ; rather, on the contrary, the League having forced the new organization to adopt its definition of an amateur before making any concession. As for the League withdrawing from the management of races, that would certainly be for its best interests, and that it should do this when a worthy organization appeared upon the field is certainly no sign of defeat.

PHILADELPHIA CLUB HOUSE.

THE corner-stone of the new club house of the Philadelphia Bicycle Club, at Twenty-sixth and Perot streets, was laid Thursday afternoon, 24 June. President George E. Bartol deposited the tin box, in which were all of the Philadelphia daily papers, the names of the officers and members of the club, a notice of the corner-stone laying, a copy of the rules and regulations of the club, together with the rules of the Park Commissioners governing bicycling in the Park, and items of interest in reference to the club. The president also made an address. The new building will have a frontage of twenty-six feet on Twenty-sixth street, and a depth of eighty feet on Perot street. It will be of stone to the height of the basement, and will have three stories above that, made of black certar brick. The basement will be used for storing machines, and will have an entrance on Twenty-sixth street, leading from the Park drive. The first floor will contain a parlor, billiard room, and ladies' dressing room ; the second floor, a gentleman's dressing apartment ; and the third floor, a gymnasium twenty-four and one half by seventy-eight feet. The building will cost $18,000, and is expected to be finished by 15 September. The officers of the club are : President, George E. Bartol ; secretary and treasurer, H. A. Blakiston ; captain, Ewing L. Miller ; lieutenant, E. W. Burt ; chairman of building committee, H. R. Lewis ; and chairman of house committee, G. N. Osborne. The club was organized 22 May, 1879, and incorporated 19 December, 1885. The present headquarters are in the Park Club rooms, at Belmont and Elm avenues, West Philadelphia.

FROM A FEMININE POINT OF VIEW.

I AM going to let you look over my shoulder this week, and you shall read with me a letter that I have just received from an enthusiastic young lady who rides the wheel. Like all enthusiasts, she has entered into the sport with her whole soul, and she feels it to be a sort of religious duty to do everything commonly considered to be within the line of a cyclist's obligation to the craft. Here is her letter : —

Dear Friend, — I want to ask you a lot of questions, and ↳ want you to give me a little bit of your time and answer them. I have come to consider you a sort of female Gamaliel (was n't he the man who used to have men sit at his feet and ask questions?) and so I hope you will do the best you can to relieve me from certain difficulties that I have got into. We have formed a club. That 's the plain English of it, and from that statement you can probably conjure up the situation of affairs. We did the deed at the suggestion of some gentlemen friends who told us that we must have club ties or we should never half enjoy cycling. We tried to get some ideas out of them, but they told us we must organize under our own ideas or we should never be successful. They said that it would n't do to follow in the same line with the men's clubs, for what was a man's meat was a woman's poison. We had a very strong suspicion that they were making game of us, but we determined to get it them, and so we called a meeting for Saturday last. We met in G——'s wood a favorite rendezvous of ours under a big tree in the "clearing," as it is called. We all rode to the spot, and there were seven of us, "one for each day in the week," as the club jester put it. We prevailed upon A—— to preside, for she is our leader in everything, and then we set to work to talk over the objects of the club and what we were expected to do. A—— said we must have a constitution, and when G—— asked her, "What for?" she replied, "We must have a constitution in order to have something to talk about at the meeting. My friend R—— tells me that his club spends most of its time at the meetings talking over the constitution, and he assures me that they have the most exciting discussions over it." But G—— said she did n't quite see the force of this, for ours was a girls' club, and "if you once get the girls together they will find plenty enough to talk about without having a constitution which none of them will understand." We decided, however, to have a constitution, and A—— produced a copy of that in use by a club of gentlemen of which her friend was a member. Our first difficulty was over the question of membership. Our model limited it to "amateurs," but what is an "amateur"? S—— said an amateur was one who was just learning to ride and that all others were professionals, but G—— told us that this was not quite correct, for professionals were the more expert of wheelmen and amateurs do not race. One young lady asked what class the girls who could ride well belonged to, but no one could answer her, for we would not confess that we were just learning to ride, and modesty forbade us claiming to be experts. We left the question unsettled. We finally concluded to adopt the gentlemen's constitution just as it stood. G—— said that in all human probability we should never use it, and if we did, and at any time "ran against a snag," we could easily change it. That was the easiest way out of the difficulty, and so we took it. We elected officers and there was one for each of us. Every member is an officer, and every officer is distinguished by a bow of a particular color worn on the left side. After we had got this thing off our minds, we sat down and had a real good talk and formed our plans for the future. We are going to have a run every Saturday afternoon, and we all promised to go as often as possible. I think those who knew what was in the constitution have forgotten it by this time, and I don't believe more than three can tell what office they hold ; but we have got our club, and now we are looking for the advantages to be derived from club life.

. . . .

I WILL omit the questions put by my little friend, but I have tried to answer them

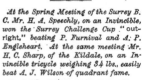

and put her right on the amateur question and several others. I am glad to note the enthusiasm of the writer and her friends, and I heartily wish success to the club.

DAISIE.

HOLLINGSWORTH'S RIDE.

FURTHER particulars are given concerning the ride of S. P. Hollingsworth, 19 June. Hollingsworth's course ranged along the National road from the Guyman House, Greenfield, to the toll-gate immediately east of Cumberland, the round trip covering 17¾ miles, cyclometer measure, and 17₁₀⁴₆ miles by more careful survey. His fastest round trip was made in 1h. 3m., and the slowest in 1h. 35m. The race was made under the auspices of the Indianapolis Club. The track was an average piece of road, lying nearly straight. Early in the day Hollingsworth, broke a spoke in his bicycle, and while having the same repaired he rode a strange machine, and by this means received a "header," which severely injured one knee. Following is the official score :—

Trip.	Start.	Return.	Time.	Rest.
1	4.00 A.M.	5.11 A.M.	1.10	10 M.
2	5.21 A.M.	6.26 A.M.	1.05	3 M.
3	6.29 A.M.	7.32 A.M.	1.03	14 M.
4	7.46 A.M.	8.59 A.M.	1.13	12 M.
5	9.11 A.M.	10.25 A.M.	1.14	5 M.
6	10.30 A.M.	11.43 A.M.	1.13	17 M.
7	12 00 M.	1.22 P.M.	1.22	6 M.
8	1.28 P.M.	2.44 P.M.	1.16	20 M.
9	3.04 P.M.	4.31 P.M.	1.27	6 M.
10	4.37 P.M.	6.04 P.M.	1.27	15 M.
11	6.19 P.M.	7.30 P.M.	1.11	10 M.
12	7.40 P.M.	9.14 P.M.	1.34	22 M.
13	9.36 P.M.	11.05 P.M.	1.29	5 M.
14	11.10 P.M.	12.32 A.M.	1.22	13 M.
15	12.45 A.M.	2.10 A.M.	1.25	0 M.
16	2.10 A.M.	3.35 A.M.	1.25	1 M.

At the end of the sixteenth trip the distance covered was 278 miles. After a rest of one minute, during which a cyclometer was attached to his machine, Hollingsworth rode around the principal streets of Greenfield, covering a distance of three and four-tenths miles, completing this at 3.57 A.M., making a total distance travelled in twenty-four hours of 281₄⁷₆ miles, with three minutes to spare.

The officers who supervised the performance are : Referee, M. F. Robinson, of Indianapolis; Judges, M. A. Hughes, of Greenfield; W. F. Furnas, of Indianapolis; scorers, C. F. Smith, Indianapolis; O. F. Jamison, of East Germantown ; checkers, Messrs. Foley, of Charlottesville, Ind. ; Stutaman, of Gem, Ind. ; Baldwin, of Greenfield, and the tollgate-keeper at turning point.

This record was made on a 55-inch wheel, Columbia light roadster. Hollingsworth is a member of the Indianapolis Bicycle Club. His riding weight is 150 pounds, and he lost six pounds in the race, but when not in condition he weighs about 175 pounds. His age is 25 years.

EVERY one should have his machines in the best possible condition. This can be done by using a bottle of Ardill's Liquid Enamel, price 75 c. Stoddard, Lovering & Co., agents, 152–158 Congress street, Boston. MESSRS. STODDARD, LOVERING &Co., have just received a supply of light Crippers for the use of light-weight gentlemen or ladies. These are of the latest pattern, and are very suitable for both sexes.

PATENTS.

LIST of cycling patents issued 22 June, 1886: A. J. Barnes, Detroit, Mich., wrench ; H. S. Brownson, Portland, Me., screwdriver ; L. E. H. Spree, New York, one-wheeled velocipede.

CALIFORNIA DIVISION.

AT a meeting of the California Division, held 17 June, it was resolved to accept the assignment of the three mile national championship. It will be competed for on 9 September, which is admission day, and a legal holiday, and will be run at Alameda Park.

By a vote of the meeting, the action of the League and the Racing Board in the matter of the Makers' Amateurs was indorsed.

N. H. DIV. L. A. W. MEET.

THE Rockingham Bicycle Club of Portsmouth have for the fourth time extended to New Hampshire wheelmen, whether members of clubs or not, an invitation to attend the Annual Meet of the New Hampshire Division of the League of American Wheelmen, to be held in Portsmouth on 5 July. It is expected that over one hundred and twenty-five wheelmen will be present. The programme consists of a short parade, a steamboat ride down the Piscataqua River to the ocean, a dinner at the Wentworth, a concert by an orchestra of twenty-two pieces, and a run of about a dozen miles, which includes a fast wheel trip to Gravelly Ridge. Reduced rates have been secured on the Concord Railroad and at the League hotel. A circular with full details may be had by addressing H. M. Bennett, Manchester, N. H. and dinner tickets, which must be secured in advance, from C. A. Hazlett, Portsmouth, N. H.

THE TANDEM RECORD.

WE have further particulars of the Orange tandem record as follows :—

The Orange Wanders having offered the club medal for seventy-five miles in the day by a lady and gentleman on a tandem, Mr. and Mrs. L. H. Johnson started at midnight on the 19th inst. to place a record on the club's books, choosing a comparatively level circuit of thirteen miles, embracing Doddtown, Watsessing, Bloomfield, Newark, and the Oranges, and checked at the start by Capt. W. A. Belcher and Dr. T. N. Gray, the run was commenced. Riding a steady nine-and-a-half-mile pace, fifty miles was completed at 5.20 A. M. A passing milk-man hailed, and under the stimulus of a quart of good milk, another ten miles was added to the score, and a stop made for breakfast at 6.25. In the saddles again at 8.05, with Mr. H. C. Douglas, of the Wanderers, on a cripper, as pace-maker, forty and three-quarter miles were completed at 12.40, the total distance ridden being one hundred and three-quarters miles ; riding time, ten hours and forty minutes. After a hearty dinner and a nap, with Mr. and Mrs. J. W. Smith on a Humber tandem and Miss A. H. Johnson on a cripper, the afternoon run of thirty miles was commenced at 3.05 and finished at 6.35, both riders dismounting in good condition. Supper was dispatched with a relish, lamps lit at 8 o'clock, and ac-

companied by Capt. Belcher on a Royal Mail bicycle and Mr. A. Walcott on a cripper, one hundred and fifty and one-half miles were completed at 10.27 P. M., the actual riding time being sixteen hours and thirty-seven minutes. Mr. and Mrs. Johnson rode the Beeston Humber tandem on which they made an English tour of eight hundred and fifty-eight miles last October. The machine was geared to fifty-nine inches.

JOHN-O'-GROATS.

JAMES LENNOX, of Dumfries, has beaten the John-o'-Groats record. He started from Land's End on a bicycle 7 June, at midnight, and reached John-o'-Groats in 6 days, 8½ hours. The distance is 885 miles. Previous records : Bicycle, 6 days, 16 hours, 7 minutes, by Lennox, 29 June. 1885. Tricycle, 6 days, 15 hours, 22 minutes, by Marriott, 27 September, 1885. The *Cyclist* has this account of the ride: "James Lennox, Dumfries, left Land's End on Monday. 7 June, at midnight, and reached Bodmin at 6 A. M. and Okehampton at 3 P. M. On leaving this town a thunderstorm burst. Exeter, distance, 160 miles. Second day : Leaving Gloucester at 2 A. M., road heavy with second thunderstorm, Wellington was reached at 12 noon ; distance, 140 miles. Third day: Leaving at 6 A. M., Whitchurch was reached at 8 A. M., Faversham at 2 P. M., over roads heavy with night's rain. At Standish heavy thunderstorm burst. After sheltering an hour and half, and finding no clearing, faced weather to Preston (8 A. M.), Garstang, over slimy roads (11 A. M.) ; distance, 105 miles. Fourth day : Starting — the road deep with sticky mud — for Kendal (6 A. M.), Carlisle (1 P. M.) in time to shelter from very severe thunderstorm, which made road soaking for rest of day. Near Findleton another storm burst, and Selkirk was reached *via* Hawick at 11 P.M.; distance, 144 miles. Fifth day : Started at 3 A. M. in drenching rain, reaching Edinburgh at 8 A. M., Grandton (9.40 A. M.), Perth (2 P. M.), Blair Athole (8 P. M.), into Dalwhinnie ; distance, 138 miles. Sixth day : Started at 3.40 A. M., Carrsbridge (7 A. M.), rain falling, streets and roads heavy in extreme. Ploughed into Inverness' 10.30 A. M., crossed Ferry, Dingwall, 2 P. M., over heavy road, Clashmore 7 P. M., Helmsdale 11.30 P. M., Wick 6 A. M., John-o'-Groat's 8.25 A. M., distance, 198 miles ; total distance, 885 miles ; total riding time, 6 days 8½ hours, beating best previous record by seven hours.

THE Boston Club has removed from its quarters at 87 Boylston street to 26 St. James street. The new quarters are very desirable, but it is expected that before many months the club will proceed with plans now under consideration for the erection of a club house at an expense of several hundred thousand dollars. The club has occupied the house 87 Boylston street for three years.

THE Wheeling, W. V., wheelmen have set the dates for their first annual road race and hill climbing contest for 13 and 14 July. The road racing will be in fifteen and thirty mile runs. The hill-climbing contest is to be held on Frelton Hill, which is a twin to "Corey" in grade and length.

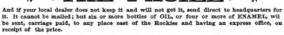

COLONEL ALBERT A. POPE, of Commonwealth avenue, the president of the Pope Manufacturing Company, in company with Mr. George H. Day, the manager of the factory, will sail on the North German Lloyd steamship "Aller," from New York, next Saturday, for a two months' business and pleasure trip abroad.

MUCH interest is manifested in the proposed road race of the Suffolk Wheel Club during its tour along the north shore. The race will end at the Salem Common, instead of at the Essex House, as previously announced. The course of the race is a fine one, and some excellent time is expected. The medals are now being made by E. E. Merrill, and are of very handsome design. A list of officials has been appointed, who will manage the race, and checkers will be stationed at various points along the route to guide the men on their course.

HUNTER wants an explanation. He has been barred from the races for the Pope cup, and he would like to know the reason why.

CONTRIBUTORS' CLUB

WANTED A MUD GUARD.

Editor of the Cycle: Having had rather a rainy spell in this region of late, I have become convinced that some cheap contrivance to prevent the mud from being spattered all over one's back and head while riding just after a shower, would meet with a ready sale among cyclists, as well as being of vast benefit to them in the way of saving clothes, etc.

I have ridden on an asphalt drive after a rain, and had the back of my coat so spattered with dirt as to render the color of the goods doubtful, to say nothing of the sand, etc., lodged in my hair.

It seems to me that some inventive genius could construct a small, movable guard to prevent this at a very slight expense. Please urge it.　　　　　　B. CYCLE.

J. P. S. TRIES HIS HAND AT MOTORS.

Editor of the Cycle — Question : who wants to travel at no matter what speed if they must have the perfume of a kerosene lamp with them ? What lover of his fellow-girls would dare to invite his lady to a ride when it would necessitate her sending her garments next day to a bleachery? Away with new-fangled trikes that run by steam, and listen to one who has not been there, and is consequently fully competent to judge accurately of everything he don't know. Away — and listen to my plan !

Let every trike be compelled by law to carry a condensed-air motor and tank. Have air reservoirs established throughout the country, supplied by force-pumps run automatically by windmills warranted to shut off connection at a certain pressure ; and there you have the great to-be-desired. No weight of water or of fuel to be carried. Fresh supplies on tap at every hostelry. A hose adjusted, a fizz, and a day's power stored under your axletree in no time, and your home reservoir filled as the wind blows, without concern or care of yours. There 's millions in it !

　　　　　　J. PARKE STREET.

TOUR OF CHAMPIONS.

Editor Cycle: Having made arrangements with the bicycle and tricycle champions, John S. Prince and T. W. Eck, to arrange contests between themselves and fast trotting horses in various parts of the country, I beg leave to make a few statements regarding the probable good result to cycling which must surely follow in the wake of such a trip. This is not the first undertaking of the kind, for our Southern and Californian trips must surely be fresh in the minds of those who read and retain in mind cycling history. Who but professionals would have the nerve to tackle such a trip as the one undertaken by Prince, Eck, Higham, and Rollinson, to California in '84 ? No one, I say, but the most crazy enthusiast. Yet the above quartet bravely tackled the trip to the Golden Gate, and came back thoroughly satisfied after losing over $2,000. Not much, you say. No, not much, truly; but when I tell you it was the earnings of a year, and the greater part of it came from the hard work of a six-day race, you will say with me it was much.

Again, in the winter of '85, Prince, Eck, Woodside, and myself tackled the barren South (I say barren, because in many places a 'bicycle was a curiosity), and Memphis, New Orleans, Texas, and the South generally, to-day, show the golden fruit the seed to produce which was sown by the toiling professionals. Mobile, Pensacola, Montgomery, Macon, Augusta, Charlotte, N. C., Columbia, S. C., can all lift up their hands and say aye, when called upon to testify to the good results of the work done by Mr. Prince. The first cycler in Mobile, Mr. J. T. Thorpe, was taught by me, and to-day Mobile boasts of a club. Many other instances could be related, but the above goes to prove my assertion, that professionals are the greatest help possible to spread cycling. Still, the makers and dealers show more favor to a class by courtesy called promateurs, or in another polite term, "makers' amateurs." No, the efforts of the professionals have not been rightly recognized, and they are a wronged class of athletes. The newspapers have done much for professionals and have used them kindly, for which my brother pros feel devoutly thankful, and such contests as Messrs. Prince and Eck will engage in will command much attention from our friends the newspapers. There is an idea which should die an early death, that all contests between professionals on a trip of the kind now under way, must necessarily smack of that much abused and meaningless word "hippodrome." The races (handicaps) between Messrs. Prince and Eck and between the champions and the equines will be on the square, and the best will win.

　　　　　　W. J. MORGAN.
NEW YORK, June 20, 1886.

A WARNING.

Editor of the Cycle : — Should the tricycle of any lady tourist chance to misbehave in the vicinity of Beverly, and should she, guided by Mr. Atkin's road book, hie to the repair shop of John Wood for aid, let her be warned by another's experience, and make her bargain before hand, or, at least, insist upon being told the price per hour of work there.

For, behold, the undersigned, appearing at aforesaid establishment with a tricycle containing a mysterious squeak, which copious applications of oil seemed powerless to alleviate, was most politely attended to, her pedals overhauled, the squeak annihilated, her tool-bag supplied with a much needed handful of cotton waste, and then she herself, overwhelmed with confusion (as she reflected upon the various things she had coolly ordered done' by a complete and absolute refusal on the art of father and son to take any pay but th' 's for services and time.　　　　　　D. Q.

CONNECTICUT DIVISION.

THE Connecticut Division, L. A. W., held its annual meeting on Tuesday, delegates being present from all sections of the State. Chief Consul Huntington reported five hundred and fifty members, against three hundred and seven a year ago. He sharply criticised the action of the Racing Board of the L. A. W., claiming that makers' amateurs should not be classed with professionals. He closed by advising the Connecticut Division to suggest to the L. A. W. to adopt rules similar to those lately introduced by the American Cyclists' Union.

At the officers' meeting the question of publishing a State road book was discussed. The book will cover about 3,000 miles of road, and be published next fall. Changes in the racing rules were discussed, but no action was taken. It was voted to formally demand of E. M. Aaron, the secretary-editor, the sum due the division. A motion to ask a mail vote on declaring the office of secretary-editor vacant was lost.

At the general meeting, D. J. Post was elected secretary-treasurer of the division, and the report of the chief consul, C. G. Huntington, was read. The part of this report specially interesting refers to the racing interests of the division. The chief consul says : " I beg to here state that I consider the course now being taken by the National Racing Board most unwise and unreasonable. The effect of its recent action, if consummated, would cripple the tournaments, without gaining any offsetting advantage.''

A discussion ensued in relation to the racing rules of the L. A. W., after which the following was unanimously adopted :—

Whereas, The present attitude of the L. A. W. towards bicycle racing has created much desertion in its ranks, and its frequent suspensions and expulsions under the ruling of the Racing Board have led to the formation of a rival organization, and have aroused wide discontent among all its followers.

Resolved, That fairness towards those clubs who desire to continue in the future the attractive and expensive race meetings of the past, and justice in treating with those riders who have so advanced the cause of wheeling by lowering records upon the track in the honest exhibitions of speed and skill, demands a change in the treatment of this subject by the officers of the League, and we request the president of the L. A. W. and the chairman of the Racing Board to devise some means by which to avert the unfortunate results that seem certain to follow.

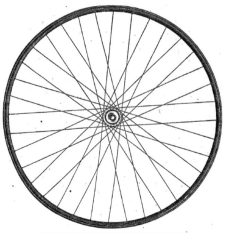

CYCLETS

In order to supply the demand for a narrow tricycle that can be taken through the ordinary door, the Coventry Machinists' Company has built a Marlboro' Club thirty inches wide over all.

Henry Sturmey met with an accident in a race 12 June, and broke his collar-bone. The tire of his tricycle came off, and he was thrown.

Hillman, Herbert & Cooper have built a racing tricycle for F. S. Buckingham, with 34-inch wheels and 30-inch steerer, and with all on it weighs 30½ lbs.

The route of the annual London-to-Bath 100-mile road race was changed this year and a much harder road taken. Macrae was the first man in. Time, 7.18.53.

The Chicago Club has secured a benefactor, and will have a new club house.

The Hampden Park track, Springfield, is now in good condition for training purposes, and local wheelmen have already begun practice there. It is in such conditton that it could be put in perfect shape for a race meeting on comparatively short notice. With the care that is bestowed on it daily, there is no reason why it should not be productive of more records at the meeting to be held there 5 July, in connection with the sports of the Caledonian Club.

Clams are now ripe, and the rubber-tired wheels are making tracks in the direction of the beaches.

The Toronto Bicycle Club is to give a reception to their members, Messrs. Webster and Eyrie, next week, who have been touring through England and France.

M. E. Santon and George F. Warren, of Worcester, recently made a trip to Boston and back, ninety-nine and one half miles, in 8h., 30m., the run down being made in the very good time of 3h. 30m. Messrs. Santon and Warren are both members of the Worcester Bicycle Club.

Two local wheelmen have records, respectively, of one thousand and nine hundred miles, made this season and on the road. They have not selected the easiest roads either, but have done good, honest road riding, taking anything that came, good, bad, or indifferent. — *Springfield Union.*

A very neat and ornamental A. C. U. pin has been designed. It consists of a wheel, with wings spreading from each side at the hub, and a bar surmounting the wheel has the letters " A. C. U." across its face. Capping all will be the stone, to suit the taste of the individual wearing the pin.

Speaking of the action of the Missouri A. A. C., which refused to recognize Whittaker as an amateur because the N. A. A. A. A. had not declared him a professional, the editor of the *Bulletin* says : "The L. A. W. and N. A. A. A. A. do not seem to work together, as we have been told they do." We desire to say to the editor that the officers of the M. A. A. C. have been notified by the Secretary of the N. A. A. A. A. that their position was wrong and not in accordance with the ideas of the National Association. To show that the L. A. W. and the N. A. A. A. A. are in harmony, it may be well to state that Rich was not allowed a place on the programme of the races on Saturday until the N. A. A. A. A. was assured by the Racing Board that his suspension was recalled.

The Racing Board is getting up a good reputation for path work. Van Sicklen has just won the ten-mile championship, and Potter has been having a try for the tricycle event.

The League has now very near to nine thousand members.

I received a letter from one of the leaders in the A. C. U. yesterday. It would surprise you to hear the way he gushes about the success of the affair, and how confident he is that the League will soon be on its knees, and Bassett, instead of meting out punishment to the unruly amateurs, will himself be begging for mercy. There are some things about the Union which I like, but I certainly disapprove, and fail to understand, their methods of personal abuse upon Mr. Bassett. Why, they don't comprehend that all Mr. Bassett has done is as an official of the League, and merely carrying out the rules of that association, I cannot understand. If they only went to work in a different way they would have a far larger field of friends. Such a lot of cheap talk cannot but do them much harm. — *Jenkins, in Sporting Life.*

The last number of the *Cyclist and Athlete* has been published. A new paper to be called *Recreation* will take its place. It will be published by the Cyclist Printing Company, and will take in cycling, tennis, cricket, lacrosse, archery, athletics, football, yachting, canoeing, and fishing. It will be published Saturdays, and the subscription price will be $1.50 a year.

The *Herald* says of Gerry Jones, who is newly appointed to the Racing Board : "Jones is said to be a man who does n't believe at all in bicycle racing, thinks it debasing and all that. Nobody is able to give the reason why he should be appointed on such a committee." Mr. Jones is chairman of the committee that is running the big bicycle tournament set down for 5 July at Binghamton, and he is working like a beaver to have a good meeting.

We came across a new term for the bicycle in a country newspaper the other day. It was called a "silent steed." We suppose it can be called silent, because the rubber tire makes little, if any, noise in contact with the ground. It struck us as a very happy expression.

It was a Boston girl who broke her thumb. That was a case where the anti-scissor organ used the shears, and we used the pen.

On 2 June, P. C. Darrow of this city started on a trip from Boston to Indianapolis on an Expert Columbia bicycle. He reached home after a tour of eighteen days. The route taken lay through Connecticut, along the Hudson River, across New York State, along the lakes, and reaching home by way of Fort Wayne and Peru. — *Indianapolis Times.*

* Albert Schock was arrested in Minneapolis, Minn., 17 June, upon a charge of having assaulted an employé in Brown Bros.'

restaurant, with a carving-fork. A dispute arose over the filling of an order, and resulted in the assault. Schock's examination was to have been held 19 June.

Reduced rates on the Concord Railroad have been secured for bicyclists attending the Meet of New Hampshire Wheelmen, at Portsmouth, on 5 July. Special rates will also be made at the local hotels.

Eugene M. Aaron has tendered his resignation as chief consul of Pennsylvania Division, owing to the poor state of his health.

The corner stone in the foundation for the new club house of the Philadelphia Bicycle Club, located at the northeast corner of Twenty-sixth and Perot streets, was laid with appropriate ceremony 24 June. The building will have a frontage of 26 feet on Twenty-sixth street, facing the Park, on the line of the Philadelphia and Reading Railroad, and a depth of 80 feet on Perot street. The structure will be built of stone to the height of the basement, and have three stories above that, of black mortar and brick.

The Meriden Wheel Club has now on hand $750 of the $1,500 necessary to construct a third-of-a-mile track at the trotting park. Of this sum the wheelmen subscribed $400, N. L. Bradley $100, and Mayor Doolittle and H. Wales Lines raised $135 among their friends. The track will be ready for use in six weeks. It will be 20 feet wide.

Members of the Maryland Club are arranging for a pleasure trip for the Fourth of July. They will leave on Saturday night, 3 July, on the Baltimore and Ohio Railroad for Harper's Ferry, where they will spend the night. In the morning they will run to Winchester on their machines, a distance of 30 miles. After dinner they will again mount and run to Martinsburg, a distance of 20 miles. On Monday morning the party will run to Hagerstown, where they will be the guests of the Hagerstown Bicycle Club. The Hagerstown wheelmen have arranged a parade and banquet, and the Baltimore cyclists will participate in both. Tuesday morning the party will split. Some will go to Frederick and return to Baltimore on Wednesday. Others will go from Hagerstown home. About thirty-five members are expected to go on the trip.

The championships seem to be going to the Rich this year. The Rich young man of New York has already taken three.

The American Rudge has not lost its great prestige, as is easily proven by the number Stoddard, Lovering & Co. are daily shipping to all parts of the United States.

Those who predicted that the Safety was a thing of the past would be surprised at the way the Rudge Safety is holding its own with both old and new riders.

THE PATH.

The fourth annual State Meet, together with the races of the Michigan Division, L. A. W., was given at Detroit, Thursday, 24 June. There was nearly two hundred wheelmen present, making it the most successful ever given in the State.

The business meeting was held in the morning, at which a new constitution and by-laws were adopted, and ordered printed.

The Cycle.

Vol. I., No. 15.   .   BOSTON, MASS., 19 JULY, 1886.   FIVE CENTS.

The Coventry Machinists' Co.'s New Tricycle for 1886.

THE MARLBORO' CLUB—Automatic Steerer,
ADMIRABLY ADAPTED FOR LADIES.
SEND FOR CATALOGUE TO 269 COLUMBUS AVENUE, BOSTON.

Adjustment in Height in Front.
Adjustment in Height in Rear.

Adjustment in Length.
Adjustment in Width.

A Comfortable Coasting Plate.
A Bifurcated Seat.

THE LILLIBRIDGE SADDLE

Is the only one having any of these Points; is the only one that can be changed in Shape or Position at all; is the BEST and CHEAPEST; is adapted to all makes of Bicycles. Special Styles for the Safeties and Star.

Price, Nickelled, $5.00.   Price of oiled Spring, with Straps, etc., for Old Saddles, 75 Cts.

FREEMAN LILLIBRIDGE, Rockford, Ill.

THE CYCLE

PUBLISHED EVERY FRIDAY BY ABBOT BASSETT, 22 SCHOOL ST., ROOM 19.

VOL. I.   BOSTON, MASS., 9 JULY, 1886.   No. 15.

TERMS OF SUBSCRIPTION.

One Year, by mail, post-paid.........................$1.50
Three Copies in one order...........................3.00
Club Subscriptions..................................1.00
Six Months..90
Single Copies.......................................05

Specimen Copies free.

Every bicycle dealer is agent for the CYCLE and authorised to receive subscriptions at regular rates. The paper
can be found on sale at the following places : —

Boston, CUPPLES, UPHAM & Co., cor. Washington and
School Streets. Tremont House news stand. At every
cycle warehouse.
New York, ELLIOTT MASON, 12 Warren Street.
Philadelphia, H. B. HART, 811 Arch Street. GEORGE
D. GIDEON, 6 South Broad Street.
Baltimore, S. T. CLARK & Co., 4 Hanover Street.
Chicago, W. M. DURELL, 115 Wabash Avenue. JOHN
WILKINSON & Co., 77 State Street.
Washington, H. S. OWEN, Capital Cycle Co.
St. Louis, ST. LOUIS WHEEL Co., 1121 Olive Street.

ABBOT BASSETT . . . . . EDITOR

A. MUDGE & SON, PRINTERS, 24 FRANKLIN ST., BOSTON.

All communications should be sent in not later than
Tuesday, to ensure insertion the same week.

Entered at the Post-office as second-class mail matter.

WE have always maintained that an organization like the League, which has for its
purpose the securing of rights to wheelmen
under the law, could not well assume jurisdiction over road racing, which is seldom pursued save in violation of law. It has been
urged against us that the N. C. U. regulated
this kind of racing, and therefore the League
should. It does not follow. A fifty-mile
road race was run in England last month,
and a notice of it is thus introduced by
Wheeling :—

"Owing to rumors of police interference,
the course for this race was kept as dark as
possible, but intending competitors were
given to understand that it would take place
somewhere in the neighborhood of Dan
Albone's comfortable little hostelry at Biggleswade."

We hope it will be a long day before the
League has to work in the dark for fear of
the authorities.

THE air is full of rumors of an agreement
between the A. C. U. and the L. A. W. It is
possible that the two associations will come to
some understanding at an early date ; but no
one man of either has the power to adjust
the differences that have arisen, nor will the
new order of things come about until the
pros and cons have been discussed.

THE fifth of July gave us a large crop of
records, and new difficulties have been placed
in the path of those who would like to lower
figures at Springfield.

VICTOR C. PLACE re-enters the racing
world and takes a championship in his first
race meeting. Pretty good for Victor. He
knows his Place.

OHIO AROUSED.

OHIO wheelmen have been up in arms in
consequence of the arrest of John A. Green
for riding a wheel at Cincinnati. An indignation meeting was held at the Gibson House,
and addresses were made by wheelmen, by
Chief Consul Kirkpatrick and others. Gov.
Foraker and the mayor addressed the meeting and assured the wheelmen that the chief
of police had made a mistake. The mayor
stated that the whole trouble arose from a
misconstruction of the order of the chief by
the officers. The order, he stated, was
simply intended to prevent the use of the
little strip of asphalt on Race street as a
race-course ; that if wheelmen would con-
gregate in large numbers on that little patch
of asphalt street, they would of course interfere with carriage travel. The mayor stated
(as every one knew) that he was a friend and
stanch advocate of the bicycle, and that he
was as anxious as any one that they have
their rights ; and as long as wheelmen com-
plied with the law regulating vehicles, they
would have no trouble.

Governor Foraker stated that he had
come all the way from Columbus to attend
this meeting, and wanted to say a word for
the bicycle. The statements of the mayor
and governor were received with hearty
rounds of applause and the customary wheelmen's chorus : "What 's the matter with
the mayor ?" "He 's all right."

Mr. Kirkpatrick, chief consul of Ohio, and
vice-president of the L. A. W., who came
down from Springfield to see that the
cyclists' rights were maintained, stated that
he was backed up by the League, and he
wanted the Cincinnati boys to feel that the
League was with them and would give them
its hearty support in protecting their rights.
He congratulated the wheelmen that the
victory had been so easily won. His remarks were heartily received and a number
of new converts added to the L. A. W.
thereby.

Upon motion, a committee was appointed
to secure the use of the city parks to wheel-
men, as follows: A. A. Bennet, Cincinnati
Club ; Kessler Smith, Brightons ; Charles
Stevens, Avondales ; Thomas Willison,
Kentons, and Mr. High, of the North Side
Wheelmen.

A vote of thanks was tendered Governor
Foraker and the mayor, also the proprietors
of the Gibson House for the use of their
rooms, after which the meeting adjourned,
subject to a call from the chairman.

PENCILLED PARAGRAPHS.

SOME tournament should appoint Dr.
Kendall official photographer, after the English style. The doctor has now the finest
collection of cycle and racing photos in the
East.

THE Bostons have now issued an official
straw hat, with a green ribbon attachment,
and it is now quite the thing to wear them
down town, you know.

GLENMERE TRACK is all choked up with
fragments of broken records, so much so
that the directors have closed the track for
two weeks, while the surface is undergoing
repairs.

MR. E. F. LANDY, the Cincinnati crack, is
rusticating in Boston this week. Mr. L.
has recently passed his examination at Yale,
and will for the next few years be located at
that college.

MR. "OMAHA" HITCHCOCK and Mr. A.
A. McCurdy are located at the Faneuil
House, Brighton, training for road and track
work.

THE maddest man in town was McCurdy
when he learned that to break Hollinsworth's
24-hour record made on a strip of road 17¼
miles long, he must not use a circuit of less
than 50 miles.

THE smile on Rowe's face during the bell-
lap of his ten-mile record, was a twin to the
one our genial editor habitually wears. Did
you not notice it?

WEBER has gone to Smithville to recu-
perate for a couple of weeks.

HENDEE is located at the New Marlboro',
and is tandeming with his lady friends
through the Newtons daily.

MR. CARL SCHUMACHER, of *Outing*, has
located at the Highlands for a rest from his
labors.

FEW would recognize in the name of G.
Haines, mentioned as being at Cleveland on
the fifth, the fiery young John L. Sullivan,
of Odd Fellows Hall.

NEILSON was a trifle discouraged over his
defeat on Monday, and will retire to the
country for a few weeks to recover some of
his exhausted energies.

THE Massachusetts Club has one application for its next meeting. The officers

are pluming themselves considerably on the fact that the raising of the dues did not diminish the membership more than two or three men.

SEVERAL of our local clubs, when stopping at the hotels along the Salem roads, seem to completely forget their early instruction in table etiquette, and are transformed into a mob of yelling hoodlums. A word to the wise is sufficient.

THE Amesbury wheelmen indulged in a very quiet but interesting parade during the celebration of the glorious Fourth.

THE heat and an attack of sickness must be the excuse for the poor notes of this week.   PEN SYL.

TWO HEART STRINGS AND A FIDDLE-STRING.

[*Times Annual.*]

"THERE!. I always thought Dummet Vyse was full of sentiment," said I.

"What 's he been doing now?" said my brother Fred, looking up from his book.

"He has sent in *such* a story! So highflown! By Jove, you would laugh if you read it," I answered.

Our club had started a magazine, of which I was editor. The first number had been a great success, and I was now hard at work upon the second, and spent many of my evenings in perusing manuscript sent by enthusiastic wheelmen.

"Read it to us," cried my sisters.

"All right. It is n't very long. Mind you attend, though, and, remember, there is to be no laughing until I have finished."

*   *   *   *

"Where on earth am I? I must have taken the wrong turn at the cross-roads, ten miles off," and the speaker, a young fellow on the top of an unusually high bicycle, cast anxious looks about him. "I ought to have reached Llanwchllyn a couple of hours ago."

It was about eight o'clock on a warm July evening, and the sun was already out of sight behind the golden-covered Welsh hills. The rider, Jack Medlicott, was progressing but slowly, owing to the roughness of the lane, which, like most Welsh by-ways, seemed to delight in throwing up sharp points of rock wherever a wheel most desired to turn itself. He jogged along, however, with much grumbling, and a feeling that he should not mind having his supper, in the hope of seeing round each corner he reached either a village in one of the numerous small valleys, or some native wandering homewards from his day's work in the hay-field. Presently he came to a sharp turn, and found himself dashing away down a steep incline. He endeavored to dismount, but in doing so rode over a huge stone, and, while he was regaining his balance; away rushed the bicycle twenty miles an hour down hill. There was no chance now of getting off; the only thing he could do was to throw his legs over the handles, and strive to avoid, as long as possible, as one does with all unpleasantness, the dreadful smash which he felt must take place before he reached the bottom.

He saw some one coming up towards him,

and shouted a warning, but before the words were well out of his mouth, there was an awful crash, and then — a blank for a short period. When he opened his eyes, which he did in a few moments, he found a young girl bending over him, with a face pale with fright. With her assistance he got up, for the purpose of ascertaining the extent of his injuries. A sprained wrist, a large bump on the back of his head, and a general accompaniment of scratches, and tears in his clothing, was all, however, and he rejoiced at his good luck in having escaped a fearful accident. But the poor bicycle lay silent, mangled and maimed. The backbone was snapped in two, and every part was broken or twisted out of all reasonable shape, while his *multum-in-parvo* had burst all its fastenings, leaving his little property, consisting principally of handkerchiefs and road-maps, to wander down the hill at its own sweet will.

"As you have so kindly come to my assistance," said Jack, while rescuing some collars which had perversely intermingled with the spokes, "perhaps you can direct me to the nearest village, or even cottage, where I can put up for the night, and generally patch myself and steed."

"Carndochan is only about a mile off," said the young lady, who was helping Jack collect the fragments of his belongings. "My father, my aunt, and I are stopping there. The inn is overflowing already, but there are several lodging-houses. Anyway, Mrs. Williams, the landlady, will have pity on you, for one night at least, in your present wounded condition, even if she has to turn out one of the numerous artists for a while."

The things were now all back in the bag, but so badly had it been treated that nothing would stop there.

"Have you a piece of string?" said he, after much fumbling in his pockets with his usable hand.

"No, I'm afraid— but stay— here 's the A string of my fiddle, that broke yesterday. Can you manage with that?"

The wounded *multum* was tied across the middle, and, although not presenting a prepossessing appearance, managed to keep its contents within reasonable bounds; and only feebly protested against such rough treatment by dropping a collar or toothbrush here and there on the way to the village. Jack, shouldering the backbone and hind wheel, pushed the front one before him; the young lady carried the smaller pieces, and they then slowly set out upon their journey.

It was almost dark when Jack, having somewhat got over his fall, though still aching much, had a good look at his companion. He saw only a slight girl, with a fair face crowned by a mass of golden hair, but by the time they had reached the narrow street of Carndochan, and when he had glanced aside at her many times, he began, instead of being thankful that he had narrowly escaped death, to rejoice that he had fallen headlong at the feet of such a wondrous maiden. As they neared the hotel door, an elderly, aristocratic-looking gentleman hurried towards them, followed by the landlady, and about a dozen other people.

"Where *have* you been, Lilith? I was getting terribly frightened about you. But who on earth have we got here?"

Explanations followed, and Jack became, for once in his life, a hero for a few hours. He was plastered and patched by the men, and then generally doctored by the ladies staying in the house. He went to bed that night, having made bosom friends of most of the artists, and though feeling much knocked about, fell asleep with a laugh on his lips as he thought of a certain head of golden hair which had suddenly, why he could not tell, become very dear to him.

Next morning he awoke late, and having managed to dress, with much groaning, for his wrist was very painful and his body bruised, made his way down stairs. Most of the visitors had gone to the shore, for breakfast was over, so he hobbled to the front door to have a look at Carndochan in the daylight. The street, if, it could be called such, was deserted; only a few children there, playing truant, and a couple of fat ducks that waddled slowly about, enjoying the sunshine on their blue-black heads; but soon he espied, coming round the bend, his preserver (as he called her) and her father.

"Who are they?" asked he of the landlady, nodding his head towards the approaching couple.

"Lord Heskington and his daughter, the Honorable Lilith," said Mrs. Williams, who had come out to ask after her guest's health, and gently hint that she had no room for him, if he intended making a long stay.

"And I 'm a music master," murmured Jack to himself, as, with the aid of a stick, he went to meet them.

(*To be continued.*)

CYCLING IN CENTRAL ASIA.

[THE earliest authentic report which has reached America concerning the return journey to Constantinople of Thomas Stevens (whom the Afghans refused passage through their country, and who will now seek a different eastward route "around the world on a bicycle"), is contained in the following itinerary, dated at Constantinople, 16 June, the day after his arrival there. It was addressed to Karl Kron, who received it 5 July, and at once forwarded to us for publication in the CYCLE.]

Have sent full account of past movements, future intentions, etc., for publication in *Outing*. Thought perhaps itinerary of route and distances, and nature of road on my route from Meshed into Afghanistan, and back to Caspian Sea, might interest you and cycling papers. Will not enter into details here, as you will learn everything through other sources. Hope you have met with every success with X M. Miles. Should be pleased to find letter and copy of book at Canton, China, care American Consul. Best regards to yourself and all cycling friends.

Sincerely,   T. STEVENS.

6 April.	Meshed.	
7 "	Sherifabad, hilly from Meshed.	
8 "	Wayside caravanseri, chiefly hilly; some excellent going, though.	
9 "	Torbet-i-Haiderie ; mountainous.	
10 "	Benighted on desert ; splendid wheeling from T. H.	
11 "	Kakh ; some sand ; some good gravel.	
12 "	Nukhab ; bad mountains from Kakh.	

13 April.	Small hamlet; average fair wheeling.
14 "	Beerjand; 300 miles from Meshed; good wheeling.
15 "	Ali-abad; Ameer of Seistan's guest.
16 "	Darmian; bad mountains from Ali-abad.
17 "	Tabbas; chiefly plain; fairly ridable.
18 "	Huts on edge of desert; mountainous from Tabbas.

AFGHANISTAN.

19 April.	Camp out on *Dasht-i-Naumid* (Desert of Despair).
20 "	Nomad camp; one half fair wheeling; much rough.
21 "	Village near Harood; some bad sand hills from Nomad camp.
22 "	Ghalakue; cultivation and irrigating ditches.
23 "	Nomad camp; gravel plain; good wheeling.
24 "	Furrah; a prisoner (about 200 miles from Beerjand).
25 "	Deh Baland? just across river from Furrah.
26 "	Nomad camp; much fair wheeling; flinty, though.
27 "	Subzowar; 80 miles from Furrah; wheeling decent most of way.
28 "	Nomad camp.
29 "	Camp in open plain.
30 "	Herat (suburban village).
	28, 29, and 30 April, self and bicycle carried on horses 80 miles from Subzowar to Herat.
10 May.	Village (name refused by Afghans); road one third ridable.
11 "	Water umbar; but little road for wheeling.
12 "	Camp in Heri Rud jungle; bad road for bicycle.

PERSIA.

13 May.	Karize, 100 miles from Herat; released by Afghans; fair riding from Heri Rood.
14 "	Nomad camp; very good wheeling.
15 "	Furriman; excellent road for Persia.
16 "	Meshed, 1 P. M.; 160 miles from Karize in 2½ days.
19 "	Wayside caravanseri.
20 "	Village near Nishapoor.
21 "	Lafaran.
22 "	Water umbar.
23 "	Mazinan.
24 "	Caravanserai (camped out near).
25 "	Camp out.
26 "	Shahrood, 300 miles from Meshed; no bad mountains, and road decent whole distance.
28 "	Camp out.
29 "	Asterabad.
	28, 29, and 30 May, Elbuz Mountains; fearful trail; carried bicycle on mule.
31 "	Bunder-Guz, port on Caspian Sea; embarked 4 June; 120 miles from Shahroon.
6 June.	Baku.
7 "	Tiflis.
8 "	Batoum.
15 "	Constantinople.

AN EARLY TWO-SPEED GEAR.

ACCORDING to the following letter, which appears in a contemporary called *Illustrated Bits*, two-speed gears for bicycles are very old ideas. The remarks made by the correspondent anent the modern cycle, with which he is evidently not practically acquainted, are at least amusing: "I see you give Mr. Galvin Dalzell as the first inventor of the bicycle. Now above forty years since, George Furniss, wheelwright, and William Farrer, blacksmith, both of Birstall,— the last one my godfather,—made one out of two old jenny wheels, the axle cut in two with hangers, 1½ in. square axletree, one axle fast in each wheel, so that one wheel could move without the other. To turn corners, the front wheel was about a yard in front, about 18 in., and one was guided with the knee, and either side of machine had two sets of three cog wheels, slow and fast, with a crank and handle, that both hands had to work to force it up a hill; no working with the feet. I could go up Hopper Hill faster than any one could walk; then we had to change cog wheels, throw them out of one gear into the other, to go on level or downhill. I could beat any one running on the level, and I am of opinion that they will come to the old way of forcing by the arms up a steep incline. I look at them, and I pity their poor feet. I have thought if a double one could be made, the first to work by the legs and the last one by the arms, the front one could go on level and downhill, but the last one would be a grand help going uphill; then throw this out of gear, and both go by the feet on level. The last one, with his strong arms, would be worth half-a-dozen legs up a long, stiff incline. I should like to see one worked in that way, or with chain motion."— *Wheel World.*

ENGLISH NOTES.

H. G. PRIEST rode a mile on a tricycle on the road at Biggleswade 19 June in 2.38. He was carefully timed.

ALFRED H. FLETCHER has taken the English twenty-four-hour tricycle record. On Monday, 21 June, he rode 253 miles.

THE Records Committee of the N. C. U. have passed the following claims to path records :—

Bicycle, one quarter mile.—H. A. Speechly, 38¼, at Crystal Palace, 29 May; one half mile, W. A. Illston, 1.16¼, Alexandra Palace, 21 May.

Tricycle, one half mile.—P. T. Letchford, 1.26½, at Crystal Palace, 29 May; threequarter mile, A. E. Langley, 2.13½, Alexandra Palace, 21 May; one mile, A. E. Langley, 2.55¾, Alexandra Palace, 21 May; two miles, E. Kiderlen, 6.15½, Alexandra Palace, 22 May.

The committee have considered the claim of Mr. H. C. Sharp to the quarter-mile tricycle record, but having regard to the gradient of the Alexandra Palace track, they have decided that this claim be not allowed.

THE N. C. U. has established an official organ, called the "N. C. U. Review and Official Record."

THE fifty-mile road record in England, called the North Road ride, was contested 19 June. S. Golder and F. S. Buckingham made the

run on a tandem in 3.0.25, but were disqualified for going off the course. C. E. Liles and A. J. Wilson finished on a tandem in 3.16.58. E. Hale finished on a safety in 3.29.55. O. G. Duncan rode the first bicycle to the winning mark in 3.31.22. C. W. Brown on a Phantom tricycle, 4 1.50.

THE *Cyclist* points out that while a starter for a bicycle must keep his feet beyond the mark, and cannot therefore take a step in pushing a tricycle with its little wheel on the mark, allows the starter to be a good distance behind, and he is able to take at least two steps without going over the mark. And yet we have noticed that when a starter gives more than a moderate push, his man goes over backwards. Experience in pushing may correct this, however.

THE fifty-mile amateur championship road race of Scotland was run on the 18 June, and won by J. H. A. Laing in 3.19½.

P. T. LETCHFORD made a run against time to beat the tricycle record at the sports of Cambridge University, 17 June. His time was taken as follows: Quarter mile, 46; half mile, *1.26; three-quarter mile, *2. 12; mile, 2.56; two miles, *5.58¾. Times marked with an asterisk take record.

THE *Cyclist* does not favor the push-off in starting tricycles. The editor admits that machines are often broken at the start, but he thinks machines should be made stronger, and be able to stand the jump at the start.

CONTRIBUTORS' CLUB

HE IS WRONG.

Editor of the Cycle: In reading an interview with the president of the A. C. U., published in a Boston daily, I came across this statement: "The A. C. U. will do in America just what the N. C. U. has done in England. When the C. T. C. showed itself incompetent to control racing, the N. C. U. came forward and took it away." I don't think this is exactly right: what do you say?
　　　　　　　　　　　　　　　　F. W. C.

[The N. C. U. was organized in January, 1878, and one of its objects at the start was the promotion of the racing interests. The C. T. C. was founded in August, 1878, and never had anything to do with racing.— ED.]

THE *Cyclist* reports that Howell completed a mile in 2.39¾ at Leicester starting from a stool, a performance equal to about 2.36 push-off. Howell also did a half mile in 1.17, both of which performances are English records. These are two more for the Rudge Racer.

W. W. BERRY, captain of the Pittston, Pa., Bicycle Club, writes: "I received my 58-inch Rudge Light Roadster last Thursday. It is the finest machine I ever saw. It runs so easy I don't know I am pedalling half the time."

NOTES FROM THE SOUTH.

THE date of the fifty-mile race for the Hill medal has been changed from the 15th to 10th of July, on account of the former date conflicting with that of the Columbus, Ga., races. The route has been selected and measured. It comprises stretches of asphalt, fairly good shell roads, and a few miles of *some-*

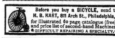

thing which, in days gone by, may have been a road, but which is now so plentifully interspersed with fine large holes and meekeyed bovines, quietly resting and disputing the passage, as to render the term road rather an exaggeration, and to preclude all possibility of good time being made. It will, however, insure a header or two to each contestant, and thus vary the monotony.

The race will be started about 4.30 A. M., so as to avoid the numerous vehicle - which, at a later hour, traverse a portion of the course.

———

The one-mile bicycle race held 24th inst., under the auspices of the St. John's Sporting Club of this city, resulted in a victory for W. L. Hughes (N. O. B. C), over six competitors. C. P. Guillotte (N. O. B. C.) second; Geo. E. Guedry (unattached), third. Time not caught.

This is Mr. Hughes' first season of racing, and so far he has won every event in which he has started, — four in number. He will represent New Orleans in the Columbus races next month, and will, doubtless, give a good account of himself, if one may judge by his recent exploits.

———

The first tandem ever ridden in the Southwest, or at least this portion of it, has made its appearance on our drives. It is the property of one of our rising young doctors and his wife. To say that they are the observed of all observers as they speed along, is drawing it mild. Many and varied are the comments, but methinks the doctor and his wife deserve much credit for the pluck exhibited in thus initiating a healthful and pleasant exercise into our midst ; and now that the crust is broken, it may lead to the use of more tandems and tricycles by our married population.

At the last meeting, Mr. Geo. Bacquie was elected secretary-treasurer of the La. Division for the ensuing year.

Chief Consul Shields has appointed Messrs. A. M. Hill, E. A. Tyler, C. M. Fairchild, W. L. Hughes, and E. E. Marks, of the N. O. Bicycle Club, as the Division Racing Board for the current year.

At the last meeting of the club, enough new members were elected to swell the roll to 51. This entitles the Division to another representative. A meeting will be held shortly, when some one will be elected and recommended to President Beckwith for the position.   Bi.

New Orleans, 28 June, 1886.

———

W. M. Allen, of New York, writes us : " I ride a Rudge Light Roadster and am proud of the machine. There is not another make of machine in the market that I would exchange for it."

The *Cyclist* reports that R. Howell will endeavor to ride twenty miles in an hour on 'a Rudge Crescent Tricycle, and states that he feels certain he can do it.

Mr. E. D. Woodman, of California, has, after a retirement for five years, emerged upon the track, using a 50-inch Rudge Light Roadster.

Trial trips are over, now respond.

NOTES OF A CYCLIST.

Were it possible to ascertain the real effect of advertising, it might appear that the plain, straightforward statements of a certain large manufacturer have had more to do with his success than most people imagine. Prospective purchasers want to get at facts. The man they believe can be depended upon to state them most literally, is the one the majority seek, and the one who succeeds.

———

It is a difficult question where and how to advertise. It is always possible to sell a certain amount of goods by advertising ; but it often happens that the advertising comes to a good deal more than the profit on the goods sold. Of course, such advertising does not pay. The end of successful advertising being to make the returns exceed the expenditures, the secret of success lies in choosing proper mediums, and in presenting the facts in the right way.

———

Competition leads to many expedients to attract attention and impress the buyer. Some of them are amusing, some interesting ; others absurd, and yet others reprehensible. Fictitious letters of a jovial nature show an advertiser's wit, and interest many of the public in him. Details of construction and testimonials, *based on experience,* are interesting. Claims of superiority for any given machine *in all points* are simply absurd. Misrepresentations of any nature or in any degree are reprehensible.

———

That advertisement is best which tells a man what he wants to know. It can't be done in a single advertisement, unless a complete catalogue is issued, for different men place different degrees of reliance on different points. It is foolish to try to crowd a quantity of matter into small type. It is better to vary the matter, style, and form. Details of construction require a few weeks, records a few more, and testimonials can be used as long as decent ones are at command.

———

The value of testimonials has been greatly decreased by the appearance of those written, to reciprocate favors extended to influential men, on the one hand, and by the use of those couched in terms of great praise, but written without regard to experience, on the other.

———

Then, too, the claims of universal superiority, which some put forth, are preposterous to the well informed. There are too many high-class cycles built to-day to make it possible for any one make to be in advance of its competitors in *all* respects. All the leading makes, undoubtedly, have certain points or combinations of points in which they excel. One make thus commends itself to one rider, and a different make to another. I believe that for me a certain make surpasses all others ; but I would not recommend it to everybody. I do not hesitate to declare my belief, but I see and admit good points in other machines.

———

The question of misrepresentation is delicate, and charges cannot be lightly made.

Perhaps the most common errors of this class concern the weight of machines. On this point few men are posted. Advertisements and descriptions make mistakes ; catalogues advance claims rarely substantiated by the scales. Wheelmen thus led astray make ludicrous blunders.

———

A general claim that a given machine is the best is always taken *cum grano salis.* But when one asserts that some specified detail in construction is the best, and that his machine is unquestionably the strongest, lightest, most rigid, easiest running, and fastest machine built, he not only exaggerates, but misrepresents, for it is simply impossible to combine in one and the same wheel all these points.

———

The lightest wheel cannot be the strongest; neither can the heaviest one be the fastest, other things being equal. Of course, the metal, the fitting, and the bearings used by different makers go a long way toward determining the character of a wheel, and a heavy one of one make may run more easily than a lighter one of another. It follows that what constitutes the "best" wheel for you or me depends upon how each of us rides, and what sort of use we are going to put it to, and it behooves the dealers to give such information as will enable each one to judge on these points.   5678.

CYCLETS

MIND AND MUSCLE.

Two thousand years and more ago,
    Men were wiser than to-day;
Then they sought to make the body
    Fit for mind's imperial sway.

All the heroes, born of fancy,
    All the gods whom men adored,
Held the homage of the people
    By the might of deed and word.

Mind gave dignity to muscle,
    Muscle stronger made the mind ;
As the great, Homeric heroes,
    Ever thus these powers combined.

But as ages followed ages,
    Bringing in the modern day ;
Grew apace men's busy striving,
    Commerce holding world-wide sway.

Lost, the wisdom of the ancients,
    Lost, and no man sought to find ;
None remembered that their glory
    Was sound body joined to mind.

When the tension, growing stronger,
    Proved that mind was not supreme,
If the body fell exhausted,
    Men awoke as from a dream, —

Sought once more the air and open,
    Sought brave sports like those of old ;
Revelled in the air and sunshine,
    On the river, field, and wold.

But of all the sports and pastimes,
    Rich in blessing, crowned with joy,
Ever stands the wheel supremely,
    Yielding good without alloy.   L. H. P.

Now rest. The hot season is upon us, and in it we must do little work.

The racing men are taking a rest from their training, and the tourists are waiting for cool weather.

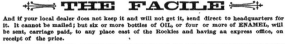

THE editor alone cannot rest. His work goes on forever, let it be hot or cold. It is generally hot where the editor is.

BICYCLES and tricycles are being used in England in the collection of the general election returns.

THE Colorado Wheel Club, of Denver, has challenged the St. Louis wheelmen to a fifty-mile team road race.

AND so fourth has gone. Now bring along the etc.

MR. GASKELL, of the C y Machinists' Co., has established a new agency in St. Louis, at 515 Pine street, under the management of some live business men,— Messrs. Watson, of the *Age of Steel*, H. A. Fisher, of Gillespie Coal Co., and Mr. Barnes. The agency is known as the Coventry Cycle Agency, and a full line of wheels will be carried.

J. S. ROGERS, chief consul L. A. W. for Missouri, has purchased T. J. Smith's interest in the *American Wheelman*, L. S. C. Ladish, the editor of that paper, still retaining his half interest.

GORMULLY & JEFFERY were first to use the word "American" for their machines, and obtained thereby a right to the title. A sense of justice should lead others to respect this right, and not take the name when there are so many in the English language that may be used. There are already too many wheels called "American."

BICYCLES and tricycles are in future to play their part in war. A stock of these vehicles has been dealt out to a German infantry regiment at present stationed at Frankfort, and the men are being exercised in riding them.

TWO local bicyclists wheeled it to Mt. Monadnock recently, stopping at the halfway house and returning the same day. It was a tough and plucky job.— *Athol Transcript.*

MUNGER met with an accident at Detroit, 24 June, that prevented him from participating in the races in that city.

OUR friend the *Wheel* does not seem to be aware that America has employed the push-off for tricycles for a year, and he was surprised to see the three-wheelers pushed at the League Meet. And yet all the large tournaments of last season used this plan.

"WORTH five times its cost when you are caught five miles from no place and your tire loose," is what a prominent wheelman says of Adhesive Tire Tape. It costs but twenty-five cents a package, and is for sale by Howard A. Smith & Co., Newark, N. J.

WE have received from W. B. Everett & Co. a photo of the League Meet taken by Notman. It is one of the most artistic pictures of the whole series of League Meet photos, the effect of the lake in front and the trees overhead being very beautiful. Every cycler whose portrait is in the group should have one of these views.

MR. A. H. OVERMAN sails for England on the 15 inst.

IN order to increase the interest and stimulate the ambition of the members, the Florence Cycle Club voted at the last meeting to offer prizes to members for attending club runs, and also for the number of miles ridden during the season. It was also voted to have an excursion to some point of interest every Sunday, and have at least one run additional every week.

THE grand fall tournament of the Lynn Cycle Club will be held at the track 23, 24, 25 September, immediately after the Springfield tournament.

THE North Shore hotels were well patronized Sunday.

P. HARVARD REILLY'S European party sailed from New York on Saturday in the City of Berlin. They will be absent about two months, and will make a tour through England, Ireland, and Scotland on bicycles. A run to Paris will be made as well.

A. E. PATTISON, of Boston, has been appointed representative for Massachusetts by President Beckwith.

EASTERN people are beginning to "catch on" to the Prince and Neilson "fake." These riders should go out West again, where such exhibitions are appreciated. Eastern people are too "well up" in good bicycle racing to patronize such alleged contests.— *Springfield Union.*

THERE is no reason to suppose the Prince-Neilson races were not to be run on their merits. Certainly the first one was as fairly run as the amateur events contested the same day. The professionals are entitled to justice.

A CYCLISTS' road book of Connecticut will be issued this fall. It will contain careful detailed description of about 3,000 miles of road in the State, with maps and distances. From the last report of Chief Consul Huntington, it is learned that the division has 550 members.

L. D. MUNGER has been looking over the course traversed by Hollingsworth in his recent ride of 281 miles in twenty-four hours, and writes that it is the finest stretch of road he ever saw, and that he considers himself competent to cover 300 miles under the same conditions. It is probable that he will shortly essay the feat.

IT is funny, though, to hear Tourmaster Ayers talk on the subject. Burley gets up in the morning and takes poached tour on toast for breakfast. He tops off his dinner with fromage de tour, and at supper he has it broiled over a gas stove. But it is always tour. His digestive capacity, both mental and physical, for the different varieties of tours, is something abnormal. And talk about the scientific aspect of touring! Why, Burley even goes into conditions of the atmosphere at certain hours of the day. He can tell you the temperature of Seneca Lake in places where it is four hundred feet deep, and they say at the Atchison, Topeka and Santa Fè office that he has looked holes into all the maps in the place. All joking aside, however, it is gratifying to see one department of the L. A. W. enthused over, and Burley is so full of it that every one who has anything to do with the department is bound to catch the same spirit. Just let Burley alone and give him plenty of rope, and the League will come pretty near fulfilling its obligations in this respect.— *Sporting Journal.*

BUFFALO is going in for a big fall tournament on a pure amateur basis.

THE PATH.

CONDENSATION must be the order of the day this week. The Fourth of July celebration always leads to a large number of races to report, and to get them all in we must make them short.

LYNN, 5 July. — Very successful meeting. Large crowd and much enthusiasm.

One-Mile, Novice. — H. N. Farnham (1), $3.4\frac{1}{5}$; F. M. Barnett (2), 3.05; E. A. Packard (3).

Two-Mile. — W. F. Knapp (1), 5.45; Geo. E. Weber (2), $5.45\frac{1}{5}$; E. P. Burnham (3).

One-Mile. — W. L. Lewis (1), $3.0\frac{4}{5}$; F. S. Hitchcock (2), $3.2\frac{3}{5}$; Geo. E. Porter (3); C. G. Whitney (4).

One-Mile, Boys. — W. H. Senter (1), $3.14\frac{3}{5}$; M. Porter (2), $3.15\frac{3}{5}$.

Three-Mile, Handicap. — W. A. Rhodes, 250 yards (1), 9.35; A. A. McCurdy, 350 yards (2), $9.35\frac{1}{2}$; F. S. Hitchcock, 450 yards (3).

One-Mile. — W. A. Rhodes (1), $2.51\frac{1}{5}$; S. L. Truesdale (2), $2.58\frac{4}{5}$; Geo. E. Porter (3).

Five-Mile, Professional. — W. M. Woodside (1), $15.0\frac{1}{5}$; R. A. Neilson (2), $15\ 0\frac{4}{5}$. Summary by miles below: —

		M.	S.
1.	Neilson	2	52
2.	Woodside	5	52
3.	Neilson	8	$54\frac{3}{5}$
4.	Woodside	12	02
5.	Woodside	15	$00\frac{1}{5}$

Ten Miles, for a Record. — The final event of the day was an attempt by W. A. Rowe to lower the ten-mile record of $28.37\frac{4}{5}$, made by himself at Springfield last fall. He did not try to make record below four miles, but including this distance up to ten miles he succeeded in beating his last year's time. Knapp, Weber, Burnham, and Rhodes made pace for him at different times. Below is a summary: —

New Record. M.	S.	*Miles.*	*Old Record.* M.	S.
2	44	1	2	$35\frac{3}{5}$
5	30	2	5	$21\frac{4}{5}$
8	18	3	8	$07\frac{4}{5}$
11	05	4	11	$11\frac{4}{5}$
13	$57\frac{3}{5}$	5	14	$07\frac{3}{5}$
16	47	6	16	$55\frac{3}{5}$
19	38	7	19	$47\frac{4}{5}$
22	$24\frac{3}{5}$	8	22	$41\frac{4}{5}$
25	$18\frac{4}{5}$	9	25	$41\frac{4}{5}$
28	$03\frac{3}{5}$	10	28	$37\frac{4}{5}$

BOSTON, MASS., 5 July. — Races under the auspices of the city of Boston, at Boston Common: —

One-Mile, Novice. — F. W. Perry (1), 3.26; W. W. East (2), 3.30.

Two-Mile, Amateur. — C. W. Ware (1), 6.55; F. G. Gibbs (2), 7.07.

One-Mile, Tricycle. — H. G. Crocker (1), 3.55; J. T. Williams (2), 3.57.

Two-Mile, Lap. — C. W. Ware (1), 6.55; F. W. Perry (2).

SPRINGFIELD, 5 July. — Caledonian sports at Hampden Park.

One-Mile, Handicap. — W. M. Haradon, 150 yards (1); Geo. M. Hendee, scratch (2), 2.34. Hendee made his quarters as follows: Quarter, $36\frac{3}{5}$; half, $1.13\frac{3}{5}$; three quarters, 1.52; mile, 2.34.

One-Mile, High School. — W. Haradon (1), $3.6\frac{3}{5}$; J. G. Norton (2).

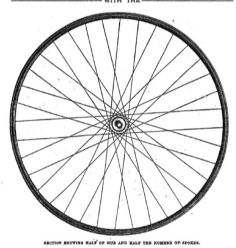

Half-Mile, against Time. — C. P. Adams, 1.21¾.

CLEVELAND, O., 5 July. — The Cleveland bicycle races, at the Athletic Park to-day, had about 600 people to see them..

One-Mile, Novice. — S. J. Herrick, Jr. (1), 3.11½; Lucien Davis (2).

Half-Mile, 1.30 *Class.* — V. C. Place, (1), 1.26; W. D. Banker (2).

One-Mile, Handicap. — J. T. Huntington (1), 2.59; V. C. Place, scratch (2).

One-Mile, Tandem. — G. Collister and C. Howland (1), 3.00; Fred Palmer and W. L. Martin (2).

Quarter-Mile, .50 *Class.* — Lucien Davis (1), 42½; H. Crumley (2).

Two-Mile, 6.30 *Class.* — F. P. Root (1). 6 26½; J. T Huntington (2).

Five-Mile, 17 *Class.* — J. T. Huntington (1), 17.11½; 'L. Davis (2).

One-Mile, Tricycle Handicap. — George Collister, scratch (1), 3.20⅘; G. C. McNeill (2).

Two-Mile, L. A. W. Championship. — V. C. Place (1), 6.15; F. P. Root (2).

Half-Mile, Handicap. — H. Crumley (1), 1.30¼; J. T. Huntington (2).

One-Mile, 3.00 *Class.* — J. T. Huntington (1), 2.56¾; V. C. Place (2), and W. D. Banker (3).

SPRINGFIELD, 5 July. — Road race of twenty miles, — F. A. Eldred, scratch (1), 1.19.50; C. P. Adams, two minutes (2), 1.25.17; H. B. Wadsworth, scratch (3), 1.29 29.

WALTHAM, 5 July. — *Half Mile*, — Alfred Hales (1); A. M. Haines (2).

Half-Mile, Safety. — G. W. Chamberlain (1); G. F. Walters (2).

BROOKLINE, 5 July. — *One Mile*, — W. K. Corey (1), 3.47. *Slow Race*, — H. B. Seamans (1).

NORTH ADAMS, MASS., 5 July. — *One-Mile Novice.* — H. Lee (1), 3.13. *Three-Mile County Championship.* — C. D. Heath (1), C. D. Heath (1) 10.15; *One-Mile Open.* — H. L. Burdick (1), 3.03; *One-Mile*, 3.20 *Class.* — Grant (1), 3.06; *Three-Mile Open.* — C. D. Heath (1), 10.13; *One-Mile Tricycle.* — Gardner (1), 4.8; *Five-Mile Record.* — Burdick (1), 17.10; *One-Mile Boys.* — Kiernan (1), 3.29; *Half-Mile Dash.* — H C. Getchell (1), 1.25; *One-Mile Consolation.* — Dewey (1), 3.19; *Five-Mile, Horse and Man.* — Horse (1), 1.7.37; W. J. Morgan (2).

NEWTON, 5 July. — *Ten Mile Road Race.* — H. C. Crocker (1), 40.46; C. W. Page (2), 41.12; G. F. Williams (3). *Ten-Mile Road Race. for Boys.* — A. E. Vose (1), 41.49; E. B. Bishop (2), 41.59.

WAKEFIELD, 5 July. — *Five Mile.* — J. Clark (1), 14.34; J. E. Coombs (2).

Three Mile Handicap. — J. Clark,· 13 29; H. R. Emerson (2).

Two Mile, Boys. — Eugene Cann (1), 10.6; R. J. Eaton (2).

CHELSEA, MASS., 5 July. — *One-Mile Novice.* — A. B. Stoddard (1), 3.00; A. D. Grover (2), 3.05.

One-Mile Championship of Chelsea. — L. H. Frost (1), 3.4½; F. A. Woodman (2).

Ride and Run. — A. D. Grover (1) 4.5½; G. H. Danforth (2).

One-Mile Lap. — First Heat. — F. A. Woodman (1); B. M. Thayer (2); second heat, A. B. Stoddard (1); G F. Field (2);

final heat, F. A. Woodman (1), 3 08; A. B. Stoddard (2).

BRUSHTON, PA., 26 June. — Races held under auspices of the Pittsburg Cricket Club : —

One-Mile Handicap. — W. D. Banker, scratch (1), 4.57; John E. Harris, 55 yards (2).

One-Half Mile Amateur. — W. D. Banker (1), 1.34½; J. W. McGrady (2).

OTTAWA, CAN., 26 June. — Races under auspices of the Amateur Athletic Association : —

One-Mile Handicap. — M. F. Johnston, scratch (1), 4.31; W. H. Sproule, 70 yards (2).

. IT has been decided to open the Orange Wanderers' ten-mile road race to resident members of the L. A. W. in Hudson County, as well as those in Essex and Lennox, and call the race a tri-county championship. Three prizes will be offered : the first, our champion medal, to be a solid gold wheel set with a diamond, and arranged to be worn, as a watch charm or pendant ; a gold medal will be given to second man, and a silver one to third. Tandem tricycles, as well as bicycles, may enter, each man being entitled to a medal if the machine is first or second at the finish, or to but one prize if third, — in either case the riders of the tandem to arrange between themselves the division of the prizes or take.

The race will take place Saturday, 10 July, at 4 P. M., and will be run over the Wanderers' five-mile course, starting from the corner of Central avenue and Grove street, west on Central avenue to Harrison street, to Centre street, to Highland avenue, to Essex avenue, to Central avenue, and finishing the first lap of nearly five miles, three sixteenths less, at Grove street : the second lap is a repetition of the first, the finish being three eighths of a mile east of Grove street. As three handsome prizes are offered, and the course, being hilly, favors strong road riders, we hope to receive a fine field of entries. Newark, Jersey City, Elizabeth, Westfield, Plainfield, and Orange have each several strong and fast road riders of whom they are justly proud, and it is our earnest wish to see at least three representative men from each club in the three counties come to the scratch on 10 July. Entries closed Wednesday, 7 July, and with $1.00 entrance fee, should be sent to W. A. Belcher, captain Orange Wanderers, East Orange, N. J.

The Cycle.

Vol. I., No. 16. BOSTON, MASS., 16 JULY, 1886. FIVE CENTS.

The Coventry Machinists' Co.'s New Tricycle for 1886.

THE CYCLE

PUBLISHED EVERY FRIDAY BY ABBOT BASSETT, 22 SCHOOL ST., ROOM 19.

VOL. I. BOSTON, MASS., 16 JULY, 1886. No. 16.

TERMS OF SUBSCRIPTION.

One Year, by mail, post-paid.............................$1.50
Three Copies in one order............................. 3.00
Club Subscriptions....................................... 1.00
Six Months.. .90
Single Copies... .05

Specimen Copies free.

Every bicycle dealer is agent for the Cycle and author-
ized to receive subscriptions at regular rates. The paper
can be found on sale at the following places: —
  Boston, Cupples, Upham & Co., cor. Washington and
School Streets. Tremont House news stand. At every
cycle warehouse.
  New York, Elliott Mason, 12 Warren Street.
  Philadelphia, H. B. Hart, 811 Arch Street. George
D. Gideon, 6 South Broad Street.
  Baltimore, S. T. Clark & Co., 4 Hanover Street.
  Chicago, W. M. Durell, 115 Wabash Avenue. John
Wilkinson & Co., 77 State Street.
  Washington, H. S. Owen, Capital Cycle Co.
  St. Louis, St. Louis Wheel Co., 1121 Olive Street.

ABBOT BASSETT . . . . . Editor

A. Mudge & Son, Printers, 24 Franklin St., Boston.

All communications should be sent in not later than
Tuesday, to ensure insertion the same week.

Entered at the Post-office as second-class mail matter.

The new rules of the A. C. U. have been
given to the public, and have been submitted to the Racing Board, L. A. W. for its
approval. Below, we give the amateur ru
and its explanations. This is somewhat different from the rule as it has been published
in a number of our exchanges, but it is from
official sources, and may be relied upon as
correct.

SEC. 3. The standing of a member in this association
shall be determined by the following rules: —
  SEC. 4. An amateur is any person who has never engaged in, nor assisted in, nor taught, any recognized athletic exercise for money, or who has never, either in public
or private, raced or exhibited his skill for a public, or for a
private stake, or other remuneration, or for a purse, or for
gate money, and never backed or allowed himself to be
backed either in a public or private race.
  SEC. 5. A promateur is one who at any time or in any
degree has violated his amateur standing, as defined above,
by receiving expenses or other remuneration for cycle riding,
or any other recognized athletic exercise.
  SEC. 6. A professional wheelman is one who at any
time and in any degree has violated his amateur or promateur standing as defined above.
  SEC. 7. To prevent any misunderstanding in interpret-
ing the above, the Union draws attention to the following
explanation: An amateur forfeits his right to compete as an
amateur, and thereby becomes a promateur, by,
  (A) Receiving expenses, or other remuneration for
riding the cycle, or for engaging in any other athletic exercise, or competing with, or pace making for, or having the
pace made by a promateur in public or private for a prize
or gate money.
  SEC. 8. An amateur or promateur forfeits his right to
compete as such, and thereby becomes a professional, by,
  (A) Riding the cycle or engaging in any other recognized athletic exercise for a money prize, or for gate
money.
  (B) Accepting payment for training or coaching others
for cycle riding, or any other athletic exercise.
  (C) Competing with, or pace making for, or having the
pace made by a professional in public or private event.
  (D) Selling, realizing upon, or otherwise turning into
cash any prize won by him.
  (E) The Union recognizes as athletic exercises all the

sports under the jurisdiction of the National Association of
Amateur Athletes of America, the L. A. W., and the
N. C. U., of England, viz.: Running, walking, jumping,
pole leaping, putting the shot, throwing the hammer,
throwing the weights, tug of war, and also rowing, boxing,
sparring, lacrosse, polo, roller and ice skating.
  SEC. 9. The Union wishes it understood that the above
rules apply to road-racing and hill-climbing contests, as well
as track racing.

The Union promises to enforce these
rules in their letter and in their spirit.
Given this, and the League can ask no more
of it. We think it very probable that the
Racing Board will approve the new rules,
and allow the Union to hold races unmo-
lested. The League has secured from the
A. C. U. all that it had a right to ask, —
protection for the amateur, — and now the officials should be content to sit quietly by and
watch the experiment the sister association
is about to make.

At this point it may be well to ask what
the racing men have gained. The League
has been called despotic, and its officials
have been styled autocrats, and charged
with high-handed proceedings. Its laws
have been said to be unfitted for democratic
America, and to the new Union the eyes of
certain racing men have been turned for relief from these so-called oppressive laws.
Does the A. C. U. afford this relief? No,
it is even more despotic than the League.
Not one of the men who were made professionals by the League can become amateurs
or promateurs under the rules of the A. C.
U. A great deal of fault has been found
because the League inflicted a mild penalty
when a man allowed a manufacturer to pay
his expenses. Under the A. C. U. such an
one cannot be even an amateur. This goes
farther than the League ever went. Hendee,
Rowe, Knapp, Burnham, and the rest must
be professionals under the A. C. U. rules.
In saying this we do not condemn the A. C.
U., we think they have done the right
thing; but we do maintain that the League,
having erred on the side of liberality, has a
right to due credit for that liberality, and we
believe that all who attempt to legislate for
the racing interests will find, as the A. C.
U. has found, that the lines have to be
drawn tightly.

The Racing Board, by a unanimous vote,
has disclaimed all jurisdiction over road-
racing. This seems to be the only consistent step for the League to take. Those
who claim the protection of the law should
respect it.

The *World* is of the opinion that the
League should give up racing and attend to
other things. We can see no good reason
why this department should be abandoned
by the League, especially at this time. Very
many places which lie beyond the domain
where the promateur flourishes desire to run
tournaments under the jurisdiction of the
League, and there is no good reason why
they should n't if they want to. What the
League has done for racing has in no way
interfered with the prosecution of other
work. Five men out of many thousands
have attended to the racing department, and
all that they have done, or may do, will not
tie the hands of those who desire to push
touring. The *World* would have us believe
that one man has run the racing interests.
Much as that man regards praise from our
esteemed contemporary, he informs us that
the compliment does great injustice to the
other members of the Racing Board, and he
will not have it.

Another paper complains that much of
the time of the business meetings of the
League is taken up with discussion of the
amateur question, and it thinks this to be a
good argument in favor of the abandonment
of racing by the League. We beg leave respectfully to draw the attention of this other
most esteemed contemporary to the fact
that all arguments upon the amateur question at League meetings have been directed
to a consideration of that question in its
bearings upon League membership, and so
long as the League confines its membership
to amateurs, these discussions will continue,
let the League abandon racing or retain it.

The promoters of the Binghamton and
Cleveland tournaments write us that they
did not suffer from the absence of the promateurs. They had good races, and the
amateurs were able to carry home all the
first prizes. How would it have been had
the League continued to recognize the
members of the Columbia team as amateurs? Mr. Atkins could have selected
either of these places, and swooped down
upon it with his team of racing men, and
carried off every first prize.

The Boston Club has voted to join the
A. C. U. The question came up and the
vote was a tie. The casting vote of the
President decided it.

TWO HEART STRINGS AND A FIDDLE-STRING.

[*Times Annual.*]

(Continued.)

THE boat was gliding swiftly through the water before a fresh sea-breeze. Jack Medlicott was managing the tiller, with Lilith by his side, while her aunt, Mrs. Deloraine, instead of fulfilling her duties as chaperon, was wrapped up in rugs amongst the fishing-lines and bait-cans, sleeping off the effects of a bad attack of sea-sickness. The old sailor, David Thomas, sat in the bows, silently smoking his pipe, and studiously keeping his eyes from the young couple.

It was three weeks after Jack's accident, and his wrist was perfectly well; his bicycle, too, had, with much trouble and no small use of bad language, been taken in a cart to the nearest station, and sent for repairs to the maker's. But he, poor fellow, was hopelessly in love, and could not tear himself away from Carndochan. He knew that if Lord Heskington should happen to learn his true feelings, he would be dismissed at once and with calm contempt; for the noble lord was proud of his blue blood, and at the same time exceedingly polite to those who were unfortunate enough not to possess that aristocratic commodity. In spite of this, Jack was determined to be madly happy for a few weeks, although it might make him miserable for years afterwards.

"My bicycle came yesterday. I shall have to be going back to work now, at once."

"Shall you?" with a little shiver.

"You are cold. Let me put this shawl around you."

"Thank you. So you are going, are you? Then we shall have no more sails together?"

"No, I shall go back to work, and you —" with a catch in his breath — "you will marry this lord whom your father has procured, and he would a new house, and whom we shall have the pleasure of seeing to-morrow. Are you sorry that I am going away, Lilith?"

"I am very much afraid I am."

"I know I have no right to speak to you, Lilith, you are so much above me, and will soon be married to another man; but I think there is little need of speaking, for you must know, by this time, how deeply I love you."

"Oh! Jack, Jack, *must* you go?" whispered Lilith, and straightway burst into tears.

When Mrs. Deloraine had been safely escorted to the hotel, and left to the tender mercies of Mrs. Williams, Jack entreated Lilith to come for a farewell ramble in their favorite wood at the back of the house. Hand in hand they wandered, silent, but determined to be happy for one short hour. A pretty picture, too, they made as, having come to the end of the glade, they leant against the low stone wall, looking over the blazing mass of gorse and heather, — a picture that would have pleased every one but the man who was lucky enough to see it; for that individual was Lord Heskington, who, while taking the air in his own starchy and peculiar manner, came upon them and close to them before they heard even a footfall. It would be impossible to describe his horror and indignation! Having hurriedly sent his daughter back to the inn, in spite of

tears and entreating, he turned upon Jack, and with a great show of politeness but hot rage at his heart he explained that, although the musical profession was a noble one, yet he must decline, with many thanks, a son-in-law who followed such a calling. In vain Jack begged to be allowed to say good-by — only good-by; it was of no avail, and after spending a most uncomfortable ten minutes, the noble lord requested him to promise, on his honor as a gentleman, to leave Carndochan the next morning, and poor Jack was obliged to make the promise, though he did so with a bad grace.

Two hours afterwards he met Lilith's maid in the street. She informed him that her mistress was to be kept in her own room until he was safely on his journey. Jack induced her, for she was good-natured, and rather in love with him herself, to take a message to Lilith to the effect that he would be under her window, at three o'clock the next morning, to say farewell. So, with a hastily-scrawled note on the leaf of a pocket-book, she turned towards the inn, while Jack, with a heavy heart, made preparations for departure.

At three o'clock, just as the day was beginning to think of getting up, he was under the window, and heard Lilith, who was dressed and waiting for him, softly whisper his name. The room was on the road-front, and the house, being old-fashioned, was very low, so that the window was only eight or nine feet from the ground. He searched about for something to stand upon, for he felt that he *must* look into her bright blue eyes once again before he left her forever; but in vain, for the benches used by the loungers in the daytime were too short, and there was nothing else. But at last a happy thought struck him, and, placing his bicycle against the wall, with a large stone against the front wheel to balance it aright and give a sense of security, he climbed, with some difficulty, into a standing position on the saddle, which he retained by grasping the window-sill with one hand, and placing one arm round the fair Lilith's waist.

"Oh, dearest," said he.

"Oh, Jack! Jack!" murmured Lilith, and bending down she put two soft arms round his neck, while her mass of hair, breaking loose, covered his head and shoulders with a golden glory.

For a time they were happy once again, but only for a few moments. A party of drunken villagers, returning from a harvest home, were heard coming down the road, bawling incoherent songs, and shrieking with laughter.

"We must n't be seen together, Lilith. Good-by, darling, good-by."

"Oh, Jack! Jack!" was all she could sob, as he jumped to the ground and was gone.

"Out of the way, you Welsh devils!" shouted he, as, mounted on his bicycle, with lamp lit, he dashed through the group of frightened countrymen. The laughter and jests died away upon their lips, and, holding to each others' coat-tails, they went home quietly and as straightly as they could under so great a stress of liquor, believing from that day that they had seen the Evil One. Lilith, with her head bowed down on her arms and her golden hair hanging all round her, never moved as they passed under her

window; so that each and all imagined her to be some angel, who had kept them safe from the awful apparition that had sailed past them in mid-air. So, with a half-roused sense of their depravity, and thoughts of what their wives would say on the morrow, they slunk away in the darkness, while Jack was riding up and down Welsh hills as he had never done before, in the vain endeavor to leave behind him the image of the blue-eyed maiden who was sobbing his name and wondering why the world was so cruel to her.

Two months afterwards Lilith was married to the noble lord; and Jack, although he vowed he never could, has survived it. He threw himself heart and soul into his profession; and now, when he is acknowledged to be one of the greatest violinists in the world, should any of his intimate friends joke with him about his remaining so long a bachelor, and ask him what he carries in the locket that always hangs from his chain, he opens it with a half-smile, and says, "Only a fiddle-string." But to one or two he has related the story of the blue-eyed maiden with the sunny hair, and these few men, who themselves have had their troubles, know, without —

"Oh! hang it all!" interrupted my brother, "shut up, for goodness' sake! We've had quite enough of that stuff. Dummet Vyse is a fool?"

"You might have allowed me to finish, for there were but a few lines more."

"I don't care. A few lines more would have finished me off. I don't want to seek the solitude of an early tomb."

"Well," said I, "shall I put it in?"

"No?" they all cried in one breath.

I did n't.

CONTRIBUTORS' CLUB.

ST. LOUIS IN CHICAGO.

Editor of the Cycle: I would like to use a little of your valuable space, in which to draw a few comparisons between two cities, St. Louis and Chicago. We are always on terms of friendly rivalry (and sometimes other than friendly), and always try to outdo one another; but when it comes to courtesy to visiting wheelmen, St. Louis is way ahead of anywhere, and Chicago as much behind the poorest cycling town in this country.

I was one of a party who, a little over a month ago, visited St. Louis. We were met at the train, escorted to breakfast (which they would not hear of our paying for), from whence we were shown around town, to the parks, and to Baldwin for dinner, where again they paid the bill. Wherever we stopped *en route* for beverages, such as cyclists are wont to imbibe, who paid for it? St. Louis, you bet. On the return, a very fine banquet was served at Delmonico's, which was again paid for by St. Louis. After spending a very pleasant day, we were escorted to the depot, put aboard the cars, and when the train pulled out, three rousing cheers were given for Chicago by St. Louis. Who on earth would entertain friends in this manner but St. Louis?

And now Chicago has had a chance to reciprocate. Did she do it? Not much!

St. Louis wheelmen arrived here, some on Saturday morning and more Sunday morning, to attend our State meet and races. On Saturday, one man met the train. He showed the way to the clubhouse and hotel ; let them go to breakfast alone ; let them pay their own bills ; left them to entertain themselves as best they could. On Sunday, no one met the second party at the train ; did not see any of them until the time set for a run, and then let them pay their own dinner bill at Pullman. Let them go off by themselves ; did not go back to the hotel with them Sunday evening ; and left them for the greater part to take care of themselves. On race day (Monday), after the races, at which St. Louis won every race she wanted, they were allowed to go home without escort, pay their own bills, etc. Verily, I do not believe that $5 oo was spent in three days by Chicago wheelmen in entertaining St. Louis in particular, and some one hundred visiting wheelmen altogether.

This is not the only time that this thing has occurred, but is almost invariably the case when we have visitors ; and the more liberal, enthusiastic members of the club are becoming very much disgusted at the acts of the majority, especially those who have, from time to time, been the guests of the St. Louis boys, and who never show up when they can do the same for our visitors. Here is a matter that should be taken in hand, and I do hope that the next time St. Louis wheelmen visit Chicago they will be treated like white men, as they certainly are.

NUMBER FIVE.

Chicago, 7 July, 1886.

ILLINOIS DIVISION.

THE Illinois Division held its annual meeting at Cheltenham Beach, 5 July. At the business meeting, reports were read from the various officers, showing the division to be in good condition, It has in the treasury $21.44, to be increased in a few days by the reception of $152.00 due the division from the League treasury. B. B. Ayers was elected Secretary-Treasurer and the *Sporting Journal* was made the Division organ. L. W. Conkling was made Chairman of the Racing Board with other members as follows : — Charles F. Vail, Peoria ; Freeman Lillibridge, Rockford ; E. H. Wilcox, Genoa ; and H. H. Munger, Chicago.

A "biquet" at the Pavilion, a ride to Pullman, and the races, concluded the meeting.

O. W. A.

THE annual business meeting of the Canadian Wheelmen's Association was held 1 July in the Montreal Amateur Athletic Association hall, the president, J. S. Brierley, of St. Thomas, Ont., in the chair, and a very large attendance of members being present.

The chairman addressed the meeting, and in a few well chosen words expressed the appreciation of the Western wheelmen of the efforts of the Montreal Bicycle Club in entertaining them.

The treasurer's statement showed receipts from all sources to be $819.21 and expenditures $499.42, leaving the handsome balance of $319.79 in the treasurer's hands. To this

should be added the amount of about $130, due from advertisement in the *Canadian Wheelman*.

The secretary's annual report is a very full and exhaustive one, and was unanimously adopted.

The selection of officers resulted in W. A. Karn, of Woodstock, Ont., as president, and J. D. Miller, of Montreal, as vice-president.

A motion was passed recommending the board of officers to take into their careful consideration the matter of a paid secretary-treasurer.

After a vote of thanks to the retiring officers, the meeting adjourned to attend the complimentary hop tendered the wheelmen by the management of the Windsor Hotel.

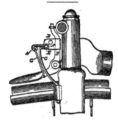

FOOTE'S ANTI-HEADER.

THERE have been many devices for removing the danger of headers on the ordinary bicycle, but most of them have been complicated and of little value. Mr. E. H. Foote's device is at once simple and effective, and has proven itself valuable by actual use on the road. It is not claimed that this device will entirely remove the danger of a forward fall on the bicycle, but it will reduce the danger to a minimum, for while it will not check a fall in which rider and machine are thrown over as one object, it will prevent the nasty little croppers that come upon a man unawares when he is off his guard for a moment. Two rubber rollers impinge against the fork and rim. These turn outward when the wheel goes forward, and it is free to move at will ; but let it try to go backwards, or let the fork come forward, and the rollers are jambed between fork and rim and stop wheel or fork at once. To run the machine backwards, a simple movement of the thumb throws the device out of place. The device renders the pedal mount very easy and in many ways improves the machine it is applied to. It is controlled by the Overman Wheel Company, 182 Columbus Avenue.

VERMONT DIVISION, L. A. W.

THE formal opening and business meeting of the Vermont Division, L. A. W., took place at Bellows Falls, 9 July. Chief Consul C. G. Ross, of Rutland, presided at the business meeting. Secretary and Treasurer F. E. DuBois, of West Randolph, was re-elected, and J. W. Drown elected as member of the finance committee. Resolutions

were adopted demanding the balance due from Secretary-Editor Aaron, and declaring the sense of the meeting to be in favor of each division managing its own elections. A committee was appointed to arrange for a road book, and the constitution of the State division was so amended as to conform to the League constitution.

At 4 P. M. the parade took place, followed by a hill-climbing contest for first and second prizes, both being silver cups. The distance was eight hundred feet. There were eight starters, and six reached the top ; H. L. Emerson, of Brattleboro', making the first in 48 seconds, and C. R. Crosby of the same place taking second place, three quarters of a second later.

At 6 P. M., the Mount Kilburn Club, of Bellows Falls, tendered the Division a banquet at the Commercial House. There were present during the day a number of prominent wheelmen from outside the State, including a large delegation from Keene, N. H.

THE CYCLIST ON THE A. C. U.

THE object of the new Union is to usurp the power of the League of American Wheelmen so far as the legislation of the path is concerned, for it is plain, although the promoters state that they are opposed to nobody, and are at antagonism with no one, there cannot be two associations governing the same persons in a different manner any more in America than has proved to be the case in England, whilst, despite the assertion that no antagonism is aimed at the League, the very first rule of the A. C. U. for the government of race meetings runs as follows ; "Any amateur wilfully competing at races not stated to be held, and actually held, under the rules of the Union, or rules approved by the Union, or to compete against any rider who has been expelled, will render them liable to the same penalty." From this it will be easy to see that the sole management of American legislation is claimed, and it is absurd for Mr. Ducker or any other man to talk about non-antagonism to the L. A. W.

We are not sufficiently intimately acquainted with the condition of racing in America to be able to see exactly in what circumstances — save the greater distances that places are one from another — racing differs in America from England, but unless the vast majority of riders in the States are makers' men, and want — and can get — their expenses paid, we have little reason to believe that the A. C. U. will obtain any permanent hold. The N. C. U., having recognized the L. A. W. as the governing body of the sport in America, cannot acknowledge its ruling, and one effect of the new Union will be to prevent finally the competition of any English amateurs at Springfield this year, and if Mr. Ducker takes our advice he will convert his monster meet of the present season into a gigantic professional gathering, for it is certain that until matters are definitely settled between the L. A. W. and the A. C. U., it will not be safe for English amateurs to compete in the States, and it will not be worth their while to do so except the suggested interna-

tional championship be arranged between the League and the National Cyclists' Union.

Bicycling World does n't quite seem to know what to do, whether to support the A. C. U. or oppose it, and it sort of halts between two opinions.

With reference to the L. A. W. *versus* A. C. U. dispute, the L. A. W. will do well to follow the lead of the Union in this country, and decree that meetings must be held under either one or the other rules, and not some races under one set of rules and some under another.

The members of the League of American Wheelmen have supported the Racing Board in their action with reference to the makers', amateur question, and H. E. Ducker, with three others, have formed an opposition body styled " The American Cyclists' Union." We note that the A. C. U. magnanimously decides to recognize the N. C. U. This does not, however, decide the question as to whether the N. C. U. will recognize it, which we rather think will not be the case.

PATENTS.

LIST of cycling patents granted this week : —

G. F. Atwood, Swanton, Vt., garment supporter.

E. E. Miller, Canton, Ohio, oil can.

G. A. Stiles, Newark, N. J., cyclometer.

R. S. Willard, St. Albans, Vt., stocking supporter.

FROM THE POEM MANUFACTURING COMPANY.

THE famous lines beginning, " Go call a coach," etc., in the burlesque play, Chron-onhotonthologos, suggested and assisted the following : —

WHEELS, YE GODS.

Go ride a wheel, and let a wheel be rode ;
And let the one who rideth be a rider ;
And for his riding let him rather ride
The wheel-wheel-wheel, over three.
Wheels, ye gods !   D.

CYCLETS.

AFTER LONGFELLOW TWO MILES.

Turn, turn, my wheel, the god of day
Bids us asleep no longer stay;
The morn is fair, the roads are dry,
Aurora's blushes tint the sky,
Come, let us greet her on the way.

The robin's whistle, clear and gay,
The bluebird's merry roundelay,
Like matin music sounds on high ;
Turn, turn, my wheel.

Through budding boughs soft breezes play,
And rain a fragrant, dewy spray
Upon our path where squirrels try
A losing race as we flash by.
Joy leads, we cannot go astray ;
Turn, turn, my wheel.

DUDLEY C. HASBROUCK.

THE Massachusetts Bicycle Club Year Book for 1886 is out.

THE Cyclists' Touring Club numbers over 21,000 members.

W. S. Bull, of the Buffalo Club has been appointed vice-consul of the New York State Division by Chief Consul Bidwell.

THE Springfield and Lynn Clubs have voted to forbid racing on their tracks on Sundays.

E. F. LANDY, Cincinnati, crack amateur, enters Yale College in the fall.

THE *Pastime Graphic* has succeeded the *Mirror of American Sports* at Chicago.

THE Chicago Club has accepted the challenge of the Owl Cycling Club for a team race for the State championship banner. Van Sicklen to be barred from the Chicago team.

LEVENS & SON, of Birmingham, have come out with a " Trouser Clip." It is to be used in holding the trouser reef. The trouser is folded over as usual when the clip is passed over the reef from the foot upwards as a clothes peg might be.

AN English bicycle lock is made with a long staple which grasps crank and fork, and prevents the former from moving.

W. B. EVERETT & Co., show the proof of a circular sent them by Singer & Co., which went down in the Oregon. It lay at the bottom of the ocean a number of months, and was recovered last week.

THE American *Bicycling World* used to be a respectable paper, quoting the source from whence it took its cuttings ; but in the latest issue we find a very glaring theft from Welford's " Photographic Notes," as well as an unacknowledged extract from the " *Wheel World* " concerning the size of wheels controversy. — *Bi. News*.

PERHAPS the most remarkable performance in the late fifty-mile ride of the North Road Club was that of Major Knox-Holmes, who with Marriott, on a tandem of the latter's make, covered the full distance in 4.17. The major, who is now close upon his eightieth year, was highly delighted with his ride, which, when we take into consideration the tremendous wind blowing, was truly wonderful. The joint ages of the pair amount to one hundred and fourteen years, and yet they finished in front of numerous bicycles and single tricyclists, and kept up a pace of about twelve miles an hour all through, The major finished strong and well, and put in another eleven miles to Hitchin in fifty-two minutes, to catch his train. — *Wheeling*.

REV. S. H. DAY, of the Massachusetts Club, pastor of the Methodist Church at East Greenwich, R. I., rode from his home to North Dighton, the 5th, on his bicycle, a distance of forty-two miles. He started to return *via* North Easton, where he stopped at night, making a trip of nearly sixty miles in one day.

MR. C. L. McDONALD, of the St Louis Ramblers, recently rode from St. Louis to Cincinnati on his wheel in five and a half days. It rained during most of the journey.

ELWELL'S Blue Nose tour will leave Bos-

ton for a twelve days' tour down the St. John river, from Grand Falls to St. John, Friday, of this week.

THE Springfield lithograph is out. It shows Uncle Sam on a wheel getting ahead of John Bull, while the crowd applauds. Around the outside are portraits of leading cyclists.

DUCKER & GOODMAN'S " Wheelmen's Reference Book " is just to hand. The book has been held back for the purpose of inserting a page of errata and omissions. The book contains a deal of interesting matter, including a number of descriptive articles on " Modern Mounts." a club directory, racing men's directory, biographical sketches of racing men and wheelmen, the best records, hints on training, and a list of dealers. A number of very good portraits are in the volume. The book retails for 50 cents, and can be had at any cycle dealer's.

LEAGUE cloth must now be purchased through Secretary Aaron.

ACTION on life memberships in the League has been postponed till the fall meeting of the Board.

THE Massachusetts Club has a run every Saturday afternoon, starting from the club house at three o'clock.

BURNHAM has joined the Columbia team, and has gone into active training. E. P. has shown us what he can do without training, and now we shall see the benefit he gets from it. If Burnham could show his little wheel to Rowe and Hendee, he would be a happy man. Stranger things have happened.

McCURDY is going to show us what the Star is capable of for a long distance. If he can beat the twenty-four record made by him on an ordinary, it will be a good card for the Star, for that machine has now no good long-distance record.

THE *World*, our esteemed contemporary, has given us the lie direct and by implication, and having been shown that itself was the falsifier, it refuses to retract. So much the worse for the *World*.

THE races of the C. W. A. were timed by electricity, but we do not get a description of the apparatus.

WE saw two or three wheels on the 4th inst. whose backbones were wound with ribbons of red, white, and blue.

W. W. CRANE has retired from the editorial chair of the *Bicycle South*.

WE have no trouble in getting $1.50 for the CYCLE. Subscriptions are coming to us very fast, but we are willing to have the record broken every day. By the way, do you subscribe ? Better send us a check ?

H. F. HORNBOSTEL and J. W. Schroeder on 28 June, rode on bicycles from Brooklyn to Islip, L. I., and return, about fifty miles, in 5.05.

THE Racing Board has reinstated Fred Russ Cook as an amateur wheelman.

DR. N. P. TYLER, of New Rochelle, N. Y., has been elected official handicapper for the League year 1886-7 by the Racing Board.

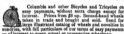

LAMPLUGH and Brown are making a luggage carrier for the handle-bar, which when not in use can be used for a leg rest for "legs over."

HILLMAN & Co. are out with a bicycle of the Rover type, although they still pin their faith to the Kangaroo.

SPINDLES with springs have been fitted to bicycles before now, but an improved method has been patented by a Sheffield firm, which consists of forming the spindle of the bicycle's front fork in such a manner as to enable a conical spiral spring to be placed around it. On the neck of the backbone a suitably shapen box is then fitted, which box completely surrounds and covers the spindle and spring, the top of the box resting on the top of the conical spring, and so forming a "socket head," touching the spindle only at bottom and top, and yielding downward to every inequality of the road surface. A similarly arranged spindle, spring, and box-head can be applied to the steering wheel of a tricycle, the steering bar or arm in any case being rigidly attached to the top of the spindle, while the backbone is attached to the box. — *Wheel World.*

JOE PENNELL and Philip Hamerton have been arrested in France as spies. They were on a sketching voyage on the Saone. Pending investigation, they were allowed to remain on their boat.

THE N. C. U. has decided against the push-off for tricycles.

TOMMY LANE's boy has won his first prize at the age of ten. He begins well.

THE Marlboro' Club Tandem is now constructed with a rod connecting the two handle-bars. This enables the rear rider to steer, for when he turns his bar he also moves the forward bar.

INDEED fortunate is the house which has little of a previous season's stock on hand, and few houses are ever in that prosperous condition. The Pope Manufacturing Company, of Boston, notwithstanding that it is the largest cycle house in the world, and consequently must carry an immense stock, has always been fortunate in not being obliged to carry over an abundance of any previous year's stock, and on the 1st of July of the present season there were not any Expert Columbias, Columbia Light Roadsters, nor Columbia Racers, of the pattern of 1885, in stock, the highest compliment which the wheelmen of America could pay these popular machines.

THE *Globe* sent a special reporter to New York to interview President Beckwith. The president refused to be drawn out.

WE made a call at the new rooms of the Springfield Bicycle Club last week, and found the club well quartered. The rooms occupy one entire floor of a large building on Main street. The front room is used as the parlor and reception room. In the centre is a heavy oak table, and on the walls hang many handsome engravings. Opening out of the parlor is a small directors' room, with cherry desk and engravings. The parlor is separated from the general reading-room by folding doors and portieres to match the window draperies. This room, which is for informal meetings of the club, is finished

in terra cotta and blue. The carpets of both the parlor and reading-room are of heavy brussels. The billiard room, which occupies the remaining space in the rear, is furnished with two tables, one for pool and one for billiards. There are also card tables in this room. Leading from the billiard room are coat and toilet rooms. Numerous trophies won by the club in former years hang on the walls and rest on the tables. The club has spent $1,000 to beautify the new house.

A. L. ATKINS, manager of the Columbia racing team, is off on a several weeks' vacation trip down Cape Cod way. Expect fish stories on his return.

BY the way, — why not send the Columbia team to Cape Cod? They could get plenty of sand down there.

PRESIDENT CLEVELAND and bride have promised to review the St. Louis wheelmen's torchlight parade, which is to be held next month.

CHICAGO wheelmen are boasting that they have now got the fastest track in the world. It is four laps to the mile, it is a dead level, with easy curves, and has a hard, smooth surface.

HENDEE has been presented with a handsome diamond stud by the Caledonian Club, in appreciation of his record of 2.34, made last week in connection with the series of sports held under the auspices of this club.

GETCHELL is suffering from a bad gash in his right thigh, the result of three headers at North Adams, 5 July.

IT is announced on the authority of the Springfield *Union* that eight of the best racing men of this country, amateurs and professionals, have pledged themselves to visit England next spring to participate in the racing events there, and return in time for the fall tournaments at Springfield and Lynn.

BURNHAM received a neat income from an accident insurance company, in the olden time, in the way of indemnities for injuries received by falling off his bicycle. The insurance company has lately refused to cover accidents resulting from racing, and Burnham is left to nurse his bruises without recompense.

WHAT's this? Here comes the *Bi. News* forward with the charge that our friends of the *World* who hate scissors, are cribbing their photo notes from an English paper without credit. Having lost their scissors, they probably use an axe.

FURNIVALL is repeating the successes of last year on the path. He is once more the one-mile champion of England, having won it 26 June, in a contest with Speechly and Illston.

IN a ten-mile team race between Oxford and Cambridge, contested 23 June, Oxford was the winner, making twenty-two points to fourteen for Cambridge. Gatehouse represented Cambridge and finished first. His presence seemed to ensure a victory, and Cambridge was backed by heavy odds.

RUDGE & Co. have built a Crescent tandem.

W. B. EVERETT & Co. have a ladies' S. S. on view.

THE mayor of Chelsea, his wife, the city treasurer, and the city engineer, are all active tricyclers.

THE English racers are using a number slip on their machines to carry the number of the rider. This is a step forward.

THE St. Louis illuminated parade committee, headed by J. S. Rogers, is at work preparing for the event.

THE *American Wheelman* bets a box of cigars that Corey can't ride Crank Hill. This will end in smoke.

A RACING circuit, to include St. Louis, Chicago, Detroit, and Cleveland, is one of the things talked about for the fall.

CHARLES WARE, of Marblehead, went to Montreal and won three races. He is a new rider, and may be heard from in the future.

HUNTER, of Salem, entered the Montreal races as a resident of Alberton, P. E. I., and claimed to be only temporarily a resident of the States. Perhaps he would have won a few races if he had dealt fairly.

A. T. LANE, who won the tricycle championship of Canada at the Montreal meeting, writes us that this was done on the anniversary of his introduction of the wheel into Canada. He first rode a 50-inch bicycle in Montreal on the first day of July, 1874.

OUR exchange editor came into the office one morning last week and exclaimed: "'S 'ot!" and looked ready to die. In a few minutes we were accosted by "Pen Syl" with the remark: "'S 'ot!" and we thought he was going to drop right down. "Daisie" was not far behind, and "'S 'ot!" was the first sound that emanated from her lips. "'S 'ot!" came like the gurgling of a black bottle in a dark closet from the throat of the racing editor. The fighting editor spoke as if he had just come from a representation of "L'Assommoir," for "'S 'ot!" was the shape which his morning salutation took. "5678," too, turned his attention to the weather, and ejaculated "'S 'ot!" and so the magic password floated from mouth to mouth, and "'S 'ot!" "'S 'ot!" "'S 'of!" reverberated from all the corners like the plunging of red-hot bars of iron into ice-water.

THE Pope Manufacturing Company is at work on a Cripper form of tricycle which they hope to have on the market in the fall.

FRED BELL, of Chelsea, tried to get ahead of a train at Mystic crossing, Charlestown, last Tuesday, but the gates came down and struck him and he was thrown over. He was picked up by the passengers in a horse car, that happened to be near at hand and taken home. It was found that his arm was broken.

BURNHAM starts this week for New Hampshire on tricycle. He will continue his training on the roads around Newmarket.

ONLY one official on the Common knew what a lap race was. Their specialty was the dinner at Parker's after the races.

Who climbed up Corey?
I, said the STAR,
With my Curved Handle Bar;
I climbed up Corey.

**And verily the STAR doth it every time. Read the Record, and see if it has n't
won every Corey Hill Contest, and then get one of**

W. W. STALL, 509 Tremont St., BOSTON, MASS.

THE Boston Club made about $600 at the cycleries.

H. W. HAYES, President of the Cambridge Club, is to be the new Chief Consul for Massachusetts.

WE have received from Dr. W. G. Kendall a number of views showing starts in the races at Boston and Lynn in May, and also the start in the Prince-Neilson and Woodside race of 5 July. They are very well executed, and will form a very attractive addition to our collection.

THE PATH.

NORTH ADAMS, July 13, 1886. — John S. Prince, the bicyclist, won a five-mile race with a horse at Hoosac Valley Park this afternoon. Time, 15.47. Purse, $200. Five hundred people witnessed the race, and about $500 changed hands on the result.

BINGHAMTON, 5 July. — The Binghamton tournament was a great success. The races were well contested, and there was much enthusiasm. The following is a summary of the races : —

Two Mile. — A. B. Rich (1), 5.56½; H. S. Kavanaugh (2), 5.57; J. R. Schlager (3).

One Mile Novice. — C. B. Kies (1), 3.04½; L. Davis (2), 3.05.

One Mile, N. Y. Championship. — J. R. Rheubottom (1), 3.05¾; H. C. Hersey (2), 3.06; A. B. Rich (3).

Half Mile, Boys. — Fred Bump (1), 1.43; Bert Warren (2); Bert Kenyon (3).

One Mile Handicap. — W. A. Platt, 11s. (1); C. E. Titchener, scratch (2), 2.55; W. H. Stone, 22s. (3). Titchener's mile was the fastest in the tournament.

Three Mile Handicap. — H. S. Kavanaugh, 75 yds. (1); A. B. Rich, scratch (2), 9.54; P. J. Duckelow, 90 yds. (3).

One Mile, Run and Ride. — W. H. Stone (1), 4.44½; C. J. Connelly (2).

Three Mile, 9.45 Class. — C. E. Titchener (1), 9.32⅗; H. C. Hersey (2), 9.33; P. J. Duckelow (3).

One Mile Consolation. — C. J. Connelly (1), 3.10; P. J. Duckelow (2).

One Mile Team Race. — Binghamton team, Titchener, Platt, Niles (1), 15 points; Genesee Club team, Connelly, Keis, and Montgomery (2), 6 points. Titchener finished first in 2.58.

A parade in the morning was participates in by two hundred wheelmen. The Wilked Barre Club was awarded the first prize for the finest appearing body in line.

The festivities of the day were pleasantly wound up by a miscellaneous entertainment at the Pioneer Rink that evening. After an elaborate drill, executed with neatness and precision by the Scranton Club, an exhibition of the "trick mule" bicycle was given, Captain Rice, of Syracuse, winning the prize for his skill in manipulating the machine.

MONTREAL, 1, 2, and 3 July. — The annual meeting of the Canadian Wheelmen's Association at Montreal was eminently successful. The meeting opened with a parade of wheelmen on Thursday, 1 July, in which one hundred and ninety men participated. The first day's races were as follows : —

One Mile for Amateurs who have never raced before. — Chas. Ware, Marblehead (1), 3.20½; D. Pollock, Montreal (2), 3.37⅗.

One Mile Championship — H. W. Clarke (1), 3.09½ Fred Foster (2), 3.09⅗.

Three Miles Roadster Machines. — T. Fane (1), 10.08½; J. H. Robertson (2).

Half Mile, Hands Off. — Chas. Ware (1), 1.43; D. B. Holden (2).

One Mile Tricycle Championship. — A. T. Lane (1), 3.51; G. M. Mothersill (2). This gives the Canadian record to Lane.

Five Mile Championship. — F. Foster (1), 18.56; J. R. Scales (2).

Three Miles. — H. W. Clarke (1), 10.4½; D. E. Hunter (2).

SECOND DAY.

Road Race to Lachine, 10 Miles. — F. Foster (1), 42; M. F. Johnson (2), 42.15; J. R. Scales (3), 42.30; T. Fane (4), 43.30; F. W. S. Crispo (5), 43.45.

Concert at Victoria Rink, fancy riding by Master Lane, and a slow race in which Mr. Williams took first prize, and Master Lane the second. Master Lane is a son of A. T. Lane, the popular bicycle agent of Montreal, and is but ten years old. Lester and Alden gave some trick riding and played a polo scratch.

THIRD DAY.

One Mile. — Chas. Ware (1), 3.23½; D. Pollock (2), 3.33¼.

Half Mile in Heats. — First heat, Fred Foster (1), 34⅘; J. H. Robertson (2). Second heat, H. W. Clarke (1), 1.30; D. E. Hunter (2). Final heat, H. W. Clarke (1), 1.30; Fred Foster (2); D. E. Hunter (3).

Five Miles. — Fred Foster (1), 17.10½; T. Fane (2), 17.25⅗.

Two Miles. — Chas. Ware (1), 6.47¼; N. L. Lusher (2), 6.49.

Three Miles. — Fred Foster (1), 9.55⅕; T. Fane (2), 9.55⅗. D. E. Hunter (3).

A. T. Lane ran a mile against time, to beat his record of Thursday (3.51), but the wind was against him and he finished in 3.52⅗.

CHICAGO, 5 July. — Races at Cheltenham Beach on the occasion of the annual meet of the Illinois Division.

One Mile, Novice. — C. B. Pierce (1), 301; J. M. Crennan (2).

One Mile, Chicago v. St. Louis. — A. A. Hart, St. Louis (1), 3.6¼; N. H. Van Sicklen (2).

Two-Mile Handicap. — J. P. Heywood, 10s. (1), 7.26¼; C. Pierce, 20s. (2); S. P. Hollingsworth, scratch (3).

Two Mile, 7.15 Class. — A. A. Hart (1) 6.24⅕; C. B. Pierce (2); S. P. Hollingswort. (3).

One Mile Tricycle, State Championship, — N. H. Van Sicklen (w.o.), 3.20.

One Mile, State Championship — J. P. Heywood (1) 3.1⅕; J. M. Crennan (2).

One Mile, 3.10 Class. — A. A. Hart (1), 3.11½; C. B. Pierce (2); W. H. Wylie (3).

Three Mile. — N. H. Van Sicklen (1), 10.9¼; S. P. Hollingsworth (2).

Five-Mile State Championship. — C. B. Pierce (1), 17.25; J. M. Crennan (2).

One Mile Handicap. — J. P. Heywood, scratch (1), 2.59; S. P. Hollingsworth, scratch (2).

One Mile. — N. H. Van Sicklen (1), by a claim of foul; A. A. Hart finished first in 2.55¾, but was disqualified.

One Mile Consolation. — W. S. Webster (1), 3.10⅕; C. S. Heywood (2).

JOLIET, Ill., 5 July. — *Road Race of Four and a Half Miles.* — Hicks (1); Strong (2); Sanders (3).

ROCKFORD, Ill. — *One-eighth Mile.* — Frank Ashton (1). *One Mile.* — Freeman Lillibridge (1), 3.12. *Five Mile.* — F. Lillibridge (1), 18.16.

BROOKLYN, N. Y., 5 July. — Races under auspices of the Nassau A. C. *Three Mile Handicap.* — P. H. Burnett, 275 yds. (1), 10.30⅘; E. C. Parker, 235 yds. (2), by 75 yds.; C. Lee Meyers, 200 yds. (3).

PHILADELPHIA, Pa., 5 July. — Races under the auspices of the Sons of St. George.

Two Mile Amateur. — P. Coningsby (1,) 14.2; G. Smith (2).

NEW YORK, N. Y., 3 July. — Races under auspices of the American Athletic Club.

Two Mile Handicap. — A. B. Rich, scratch (1), 6.45⅘; C. M. Phelps, 100 yds. (2) by five yards; P. M. Harris, Jr., 75 yds. (3).

BIDDEFORD, Me., 9 July, W. M. Woodside and Fred. Westbrook of Forepaugh's circus, raced on bicycles at the Biddeford Trotting Park, after the close of the circus performance. The match was for $500 a side, the distance one mile. Woodside won in three minutes fifty-nine seconds, beating Westbrook by one second. The match was private and witnessed by *attachés* of the circus principally.

HARTFORD, 8, 9 September; Springfield, 14, 15, 16, 17; Lynn, 23, 24, 25. A good circuit.

THE one-mile bicycle record for grass was made by J. H. Adams at the Ravensbourne sports on Saturday, 26 June, in England, 2.55⅘. Previous best, by H. L. Cortis, 2.56½.

THE chairmen of the various committees to have charge of the fall tournament of the Springfield Club are as follows: On racing, Sanford, Lawton; prizes, W. C. Marsh; advertising, H. E. Ducker; music and park, F. E. Ripley; tickets, W. H. Selvey; reception, I. A. Quimby; press, A. R. H. Foss; police, W. H. Jordan.

THE Boston Bicycle Club members are already devising plans for the annual 100-mile road race to occur next fall. This time care will be taken that the course is properly measured.

THERE will probably not be another race meeting of importance held on the Lynn track until the three days' tournament next September.

AT Long Eaton, England, 26 June, Cripps and Ratcliffe took the two-mile tandem record in 5.37⅘. On the same day Allard

covered a mile on a Marlboro' Club tricycle in 2.54.

THE Chicago Bicycle Club will hold a race meeting 31 July.

FURNIVALL was the hero of the day on Saturday, 26 June, when the one-mile championship, N. C. U., of Great Britain was run on the Jarrow track. The attendance was about 6,000. M. V. J. Webber and R. H. English were absent through indisposition. Speechly won his heat in 2.58¾; Furnivall won his heat in 2.47¼, and W. A. Illston won his in 2.49¼. Furnivall won in the second round by four yards in 2.43¾. In the final, Illston immediately cut out the running at a fast rate for a couple of laps, when Furnivall took a spell in front, but shortly after Speechly, with a lightning spurt, rushed to the head of affairs, and a desperate race ensued. Speechly continued to lead until one hundred yards from home; here Furnivall made his effort, which was a brilliant one, and gradually forging ahead, he won amid great cheering by three yards, Illston being about five yards away. Time, 2.46. The winner was hoisted shoulder high and carried into the dressing room, being cheered to the echo *en route*.

Furnivall rode with legs bandaged and threatening to give way at any time, and the mile was the fastest he ever rode.

F. J. OSMOND and S. S. Williams have taken the English record for two miles on an Invincible tandem. Time, 5.47¾.

JOHN LEE captured the two-mile Safety record of England at Long Eaton, 26 June, in 5.52¼.

SCHOCK wants to race for six days with any man in the world barring John S. Prince. He will wager $500 or $1,000, on the result.

THE CLUB.

THE annual election of the Rochester Bicycle Club resulted as follows : — President L. F. Featherly ; Secretary, R. A. Punnett ; Treasurer, W. Craib ; Captain, Chas. Ford ; Lieutenant, Albert Schirck ; First Guide, H. A. Zimmer ; Second Guide, W. P. Sweeney ; Bugler, B. L. Genther ; Executive Committee, Messrs. Lennox, Stinson, Klein. Featherly, Punnet and Craib.

THE members of the Springfield Young Men's Christian Association have formed a bicycle auxiliary with these officers : Captain, E. A. Jones ; Secretary, C. S. Cleaves ; Executive Committee, Charles K. Starr, H. S. Woffenden, and Charles A. Morgan.

THE following gentlemen compose the new board of officers of the Boscobel Bicycle Club of Lynn : President, E. N. Carthy ; Vice-President, S. Steele ; Secretary, E. A. Packard ; Treasurer, E. Truesdale ; Club Committee, J. T. Stevens, C. A. Saunders, W. L. Lewis, G. Sieson ; Captain R. J. Heren ; First Lieutenant, E. Truesdale ; Second Lieutenant, G. Sieson ; Color Bearer, H. Fisher ; Bugler, E. Packard ; Second Bugler, T. Stevens.

THE New South Wheel Club of Birmingham, Alabama, was organized 7 July, with the following officers : L. D. Aylett, President ; E. L. Rowley, Secretary and Treasurer ; J. W. Lutz, Captain.

COMING EVENTS.

JULY.

16 Friday. — Elwell's Blue Nose Tour starts from Boston for a two weeks' run down the St. John River.

20 Tuesday. — 50-mile road race for A. M. Hill medal, at New Orleans, La.

22 Thursday. — Annual races of the Genessee Club, Rochester, N.Y. Half-mile national championship.

23 Friday. — Races of the Trojan Wheelmen, at Rensselaer Park, Troy, N. Y.

31 Saturday. — Races of the Chicago Bi. Club, on the ball grounds. Entries close 24 July, to F. A. Ingalls, 189 Michigan avenue.

AUGUST.

3 Tuesday. — Clerical wheelmen's tour starts from New York City. Rev. Sylvanus Stall, Lancaster, Penn., promoter.

9 Monday. — Iowa division tour leaves Des Moines for five days' tour to Spirit Lake, Iowa, where fall meet will occur.

19 Thursday. — Annual meet and races of the Pennsylvania Division as guests of the Williamsport (Pa.) Bi. Club.

26, 27 and 28 Thursday–Saturday. — Race meeting of the Cleveland Bicycle Club.

28 Saturday. — Annual meet and races of the New Jersey division, at Millville, N. J.

SEPTEMBER.

3, 4 Friday, Saturday. — New York division meet and races, at Buffalo, N. Y.

6 Monday. — L. A. W. tour from Rochester, to end at Harper's Ferry on 16 September. Annual meet Ohio division, at Massillon, Ohio.

8, 9 Wednesday, Thursday. — Annual race meeting of the Connecticut Bicycle Club, at Charter Oak Park, Hartford, Conn.

9, 10 Thursday, Friday. — Annual tournament Berkshire County Wheelmen, at Pittsfield, Mass.

14 to 17 Tuesday to Friday. — Springfield Bi. Club's annual tournament, at Hampden Park, Springfield, Mass.

21, 22, 23 Tuesday–Thursday. — Bicycle races at Junction City, Kansas. Apply to Charles S. Davis, Junction City, Kansas.

23, 24, 25 Thursday–Saturday. — Fall tournament of Lynn Track Association, at Glenmere Park, Lynn, Mass.

ON THE ROAD THE COLUMBIAS ON THE PATH

Boston, July 6, 1886.

The records made and the prizes won by riders of COLUMBIAS during the season of 1885 are familiar to wheelmen.   Appended is a recapitulation of the more important victories for riders of COLUMBIAS during the opening of the present season.

SMASHED RECORDS ON COLUMBIAS.

GEO. M. HENDEE AT SPRINGFIELD,
July 5.

½-MILE (World's Record) . . . . 1.52.
1-MILE (World Amateur Record; Fastest Mile ever made in Competition) . . 2.34.

WM. A. ROWE AT LYNN,
July 5.

4 MILES (World's Record) . . . . 11.05.
5 MILES (World's Record) . . . . 13.57 2-5.
6 MILES (World's Record) . . . . 16.47.
7 MILES (World's Record) . . . . 19.38.
8 MILES (World's Record) . . . . 22.34 2-5.
9 MILES (World's Record) . . . . 25.18.
10 MILES (World's Record) 28.03 2-5

THE COLUMBIAS AT BOSTON,
May 29.

1-MILE L. A. W. BICYCLE CHAMPIONSHIP RACE . . . . . . A. B. RICH.
1-MILE L. A. W. TRICYCLE CHAMPIONSHIP RACE . . . . . A. B. RICH.

THE COLUMBIAS AT LYNN,
May 31.

1-MILE OPEN RACE . . . . W. A. ROWE.
3-MILE RACE, 9.45 CLASS . . . . CHAS. E. WHITTEN.
1-MILE RACE, 3.30 CLASS . . . . CHAS. E. WHITTEN.
5-MILE OPEN RACE . . . . GEO. M. HENDEE.
3-MILE HANDICAP RACE . . . . CHAS. E. WHITTEN.
5-MILE PROFESSIONAL RACE, AMERICAN CHAMPIONSHIP, JOHN S. PRINCE.
Six Firsts out of a possible Eight, and Two Seconds, won on Columbias.

THE COLUMBIAS AT NEW HAVEN,
June 11, 12.

1-MILE OPEN RACE . . . . W. A. ROWE.
3-MILE OPEN RACE . . . . GEO. M. HENDEE.
2-MILE HANDICAP RACE . . . . W. F. KNAPP.
20-MILE COLUMBIA CUP RACE . . . . A. B. RICH.
1-MILE RACE, 3.05 CLASS . . . . E. A. DEBLOIS.
5-MILE LAP RACE . . . . GEO. M. HENDEE.
½-MILE BOYS' RACE . . . . F. A. CLARK.
3-MILE OPEN RACE . . . . W. A. ROWE.
3-MILE HANDICAP RACE . . . . E. A. DEBLOIS.
Every Open Event won on Columbias.

THE COLUMBIAS AT LYNN,
June 17.

1-MILE NOVICE RACE . . . . S. L. TRUESDALE.
1-MILE OPEN RACE . . . . W, A. ROWE.
Time, 2.37 2-5.
2-MILE LAP RACE . . . . GEO. M. HENDEE.
2-MILE HANDICAP RACE . . . . F. S. HITCHCOCK.
1-MILE PROFESSIONAL TRICYCLE RACE, WORLD'S RECORD, T. W. ECK.
Time, .42 2-5.

CHAMPIONSHIPS ON COLUMBIAS,
Season of 1886.

1-MILE BICYCLE . . . . L. A. W. CHAMPIONSHIP.
1-MILE TRICYCLE . . . . L. A. W. CHAMPIONSHIP.
4-MILE BICYCLE . . . . N. A. A. A. CHAMPIONSHIP.
10-MILE BICYCLE . . . . L. A. W. CHAMPIONSHIP.

THE COLUMBIAS IN THE WEST.
THE RECORD BROKEN. — SPLENDID PERFORMANCE OF S. P. HOLLINSWORTH.

INDIANAPOLIS, IND., June 19. — S. P. Hollinsworth, of Russiaville, was wonderfully successful in his attempt to beat the long-distance amateur bicycle record of this country and Great Britain. He completed his task at Greenfield this morning at 4 o'clock, and in the 24 hours scored a total of 281 9-10 miles. His actual riding time was 21 hours and 28 minutes, 2 hours and 37 minutes being lost in eating and in being rubbed down. Heretofore the best American record was 259½ miles, made by Munger, of Detroit, at Boston, while the English record is 266. The best track record is 276. — *Special Despatch to the Boston Herald.*

This record was made on a 55-inch COLUMBIA LIGHT ROADSTER. — *Indianapolis Times.*

THE COLUMBIAS IN NEW JERSEY,
June 19.

25-MILE INTER-CLUB ROAD RACE . . . . E. H. VALENTINE.
On Columbia Light Roadster.

THE COLUMBIAS AT BROOKLYN,
June 19.

1-MILE NOVICE RACE.
2-MILE HANDICAP RACE.
3-MILE HANDICAP RACE.
2-MILE CHAMPIONSHIP RACE, BEDFORD CYCLE CLUB.
5-MILE NEW YORK STATE CHAMPIONSHIP RACE.
The above Events won on Columbias.

LONG-DISTANCE RIDERS ON COLUMBIAS.
Season of 1886.

AROUND THE WORLD (ON THE WAY) . . . . THOMAS STEVENS.
FROM NEW YORK TO SAN FRANCISCO (ON THE WAY), F. E. VANMERBEKE.
FROM NEW YORK TO SAN FRANCISCO (ON THE WAY), S. G. SPIER.
FROM NEW YORK TO SAN FRANCISCO AND RETURN (ON THE WAY),
GEO. B. THAYER, CORRESPONDENT OF THE HARTFORD "POST."

CATALOGUE SENT FREE.

THE POPE MFG. CO.

PRINCIPAL OFFICE, 597 WASHINGTON STREET, BOSTON.

12 Warren St., New York.   Branch Houses: 115 Wabash Ave., Chicago.

VOL. I., No. 17. BOSTON, MASS., 23 JULY, 1886. FIVE CENTS.

THE CYCLE

PUBLISHED EVERY FRIDAY BY ABBOT BASSETT, 22 SCHOOL ST., ROOM 19.

VOL. I. BOSTON, MASS., 23 JULY, 1886. NO. 17.

TERMS OF SUBSCRIPTION.

One Year, by mail, post-paid.........................$1.50
Three Copies in one order............................3.00
Club Subscriptions...................................1.00
Six Months...90
Single Copies..05

Specimen Copies free.

Every bicycle dealer is agent for the CYCLE and author-
ised to receive subscriptions at regular rates. The paper
can be found on sale at the following places : —
  Boston, CUPPLES, UPHAM & CO., cor. Washington and
School Streets. Tremont House news stand. At every
cycle warehouse.
  New York, ELLIOTT MASON, 12 Warren Street.
  Philadelphia, H. B. HART, 811 Arch Street. GEORGE
D. GIDEON, 6 South Broad Street.
  Baltimore, S. T. CLARK & Co., 4 Hanover Street.
  Chicago, W. M. DURELL, 115 Wabash Avenue. JOHN
WILKINSON & Co., 77 State Street.
  Washington, H. S. OWEN, Capital Cycle Co.
  St. Louis, ST. LOUIS WHEEL Co., 1121 Olive Street.

ABBOT BASSETT . . . . . EDITOR

A. MUDGE & SON, PRINTERS, 24 FRANKLIN ST., BOSTON

All communications should be sent in not later than
Tuesday, to ensure insertion the same week.

Entered at the Post-office as second-class mail matter.

THE *Bulletin* is exceeding wroth because
certain notices of the Racing Board have
been published in the CYCLE, and we get
an occasional slur which takes the form of
an assertion that this paper is the organ of
the Racing Board. We are not a little surprised that the Secretary-Editor should object to our use of the CYCLE and other papers in prosecuting the work of the League,
for they have often been used to good effect
and in a way impossible for us to use the
Bulletin. Nevertheless, no official notice
has been used that has not been sent first to
the *Bulletin*. In one instance it was found
necessary for the Chairman of the Racing
Board to warn wheelmen against entering
races which were to be held on a Friday afternoon in a New England city. He inserted an
official notice in the CYCLE, the Boston
Herald, and the Boston *Globe*. All three of
these papers were distributed in the city on
Friday morning, and the notice was read by
many. The same notice was sent to the
Bulletin, and it reached New England on
the Monday following, and without the other
papers the notice would have been worthless.
This is one of many instances where the
Racing Board has employed the outside press
in addition to the *Bulletin*. The Board is
very grateful to that press for its favor, and

very sorry that the Secretary-Editor should
seem to condemn what has been done.

THE Secretary-Editor publishes, 16 July,
an article that appeared many days ago
in the Springfield *Union*, and it calls upon
the CYCLE to reply to it. If the Sec.-Ed.
will turn to the *Bulletin* of 9 July, he will
find the reply to the article in an editorial of
his own. When a journal publishes first the
reply to an article, and then follows it up the
next week with the article itself, we cannot
find time to respond to a request for a reply
more than to ask the editor to consult his
own files (see *Bulletin*, page 27, central column, extract from *Globe*).

WHAT a number of new clubs are being
formed ! Evidently a reaction in favor of
small clubs with greater sociability is taking
place.

LAST winter the fine club-houses, and
superior facilities for entertainment afforded
by the larger clubs, attracted the suburban
riders ; but now that the riding season is in
full force, the advantages of belonging to a
club where all members are known to each
other, and where an "every-day sort of a
fellow" may hold a position, are the greater
attraction.

A CERTAIN large suburban club called a
two days' run, great fun being promised.
About six out of fifty members came to
time, and rode to the destination. We met
them on the road. Two riders first came in
sight. They were hot and dusty, and with
sleeves rolled up, and noses on wheel they
dashed by. Soon two more scorchers of
the same party came by, and shortly afterwards, during which time the two first men
must have been a mile ahead, the last two
came along, hardly able to climb a slight
grade, yet exerting themselves to keep up
with the leaders. Bicycle clubs are formed
to promote sociability.

THE letter from Robt. Todd comes in good
time. The position taken by the N. C. U.
does not surprise us in the least. It was to
be expected. But there are many in the A.
C. U. who have believed that their Union
would be recognized by the N. C. U. and
the L. A. W. ignored. All such will be
convinced of their error on reading Mr.

Todd's letter. It was only a few days ago
that an officer of the A. C. U. laughed at
the idea expressed by us that the N. C. U.
would not recognize the A. C. U. on the basis on which the Union was then working.

PRESIDENT BECKWITH ARRESTED.

DR. N. MALON BECKWITH was ar-
rested last Saturday on a charge of criminal
libel preferred by D. H. Renton, of 228 Broadway. Monday afternoon Edward F. Hill,
ex-chief consul of the New York State division, was arrested at his home in Peekskill,
the prisoners were taken before Justice of the
Peace Powers, of West New Brighton, S.
I., at which place Renton resides. President Beckwith was allowed to go on his own
arrived with his lawyer from Peekskill, the
justice could not be found, and Mr. Hill was
compelled to remain at Staten Island Hotel
until Tuesday morning, when he was also
allowed to depart on his own recognizance.
  The preliminary hearing is set down for
Friday. The charges of Mr. Renton are
based on his expulsion from the League for
conduct unbecoming a gentleman, and for
threatening to have an officer of the League
arrested. Last July, Renton, who has
gained some fame as a racing man, competed at a race given by the Scranton, Penn.,
Bicycle Club. Just after the races a communication was published in the *Bulletin*
calling upon racing men to be more particular in their dress on the race track. This
was written by Col. Geo. Sanderson, and it
was commented on by Editor Aaron, who
said it was timely, and that a reform was
needed.
  Though no names were mentioned, Renton
took it to himself, and has used the courts to
defend himself against what he considers a
slander. Editor Aaron was arrested in New
York on a charge of criminal libel, was tried
at West Brighton last September, and com-
promised by publishing a retraction and paying the cost of court and the fee of plaintiff's
counsel. At a meeting of the board of officers of the League, held in New York 22 February, charges were made against Renton
and he was expelled. That did not suit his
ideas of justice, and at another meeting of
the board held at Boston, 29 May, he peti-
tioned for a hearing, which was denied him,
his communication being laid on the table
without being read.

ADHESIVE Tire Tape is always ready for
business, only takes an instant to put it on,
and it will hold your tire in place until it can
be cemented. For sale by Howard A.
Smith & Co., Newark, N. J.

E. P. BAIRD won the Orange Wanderers'
ten-mile open road race held Saturday, 10
July, on a 53-inch Rudge Light Roadster.
Time, 36.51½.

LADIES' RIDE TO WORCESTER.

A RECENT issue of the Worcester *Gazette* had the following: "Two of the tandem tricycles, each ridden by a lady and gentleman, have been attracting a great deal of attention about the city since Monday evening. The parties riding them are Mr. and Mrs. Herbert Moulton of this city, and Mr. and Mrs. Charles Hopkins of Wellington. Mr. and Mrs. Moulton had their tandem tricycle last fall, but an accident disabled it, and new parts had to be obtained from England. They went to Boston for it, and in company with Mr. and Mrs. Hopkins rode from Medford to this city yesterday. These tandem tricycles are not common in this country, and they will continue to be scarce for some time to come, as for some reason the makers have cancelled all orders, and refuse to receive any new ones at present. Mr. Hopkins is of the opinion that these machines are to become very popular in the future. It sounds like a great talk for a lady to start out on a journey from Boston to Worcester, but the only drawback to the pleasure of the ride was the steep hills. On a level and smooth road like Park avenue the tandem machine glides along with an ease and grace that makes riding it a genuine delight. After riding from Medford to Worcester, after a rest and a good dinner, both parties went out and took a tour about the city, riding some distance on Park avenue, and Mr. and Mrs. Hopkins will return to their home in Wellington on their machine. The machine runs easier with its two riders than a single tricycle. Both ladies are enthusiastic, and will continue to enjoy the pleasure of riding in spite of the great amount of curiosity which they draw to themselves at present. R. E. M. Suverokrop rode his Cripper tricycle to Boston on Saturday, returning with the above party on Monday, and making one or two side trips during the time, covering over one hundred and fifty miles in the three days."

McCURDY'S RECORD.

MR. ALFRED A. McCURDY, mounted on a Star bicycle, started from the corner of Crescent and Moody streets, Waltham, at 30 seconds after 9 o'clock Monday morning, on an attempt to roll up over 281 miles within the ensuing 24 hours. The course had been carefully measured by four cyclometers, and the record of the lowest, 12½ miles, taken. Howard Carroll of the Lynn Cycle Club was the check at the corner of River street and Auburndale avenue, corner of Cherry and River streets, and corner of Waltham and River streets. The judges were G. F. Barnard, T. A. Carroll, and G. A. Downs. McCurdy rode a 51-inch Star racer, weighing 41 pounds. A Star roadster and an Apollo ordinary were kept ready for him in case of accident. He completed his first twelve and one half miles in fifty minutes. Fifty miles were covered in 3.32.3, and then he had dinner. He only took fifteen minutes for this, and seemed to get away in good spirits. He had good pacemakers, including Wm. A. Rowe, Drummond, Tracy of Waltham, Gordon and Wendell, Whitten and Sherman of Lynn. During the evening McCurdy exchanged his racer for the roadster, and at this time he began to fall behind the record. Dr. H. L. Jordan, of Waltham, was in constant attendance on the rider and attended to his diet.

The moon was up about 10 o'clock, but was so obscured by clouds that it did not do much good until about 12 o'clock. At the end of every lap, by Dr. Jordan's orders, he took one dessert spoonful of whiskey and half a glass of oatmeal water, and a lacto-peptine powder every time he took food. This was mixed with water or the boviline. A bismuth powder, carefully mixed, was given every second or third time. At 8.40 A. M., McCurdy arrived from his twenty-second trip with two hundred and seventy-five miles to his credit. He had then 21.20 to cover $6\frac{9}{10}$ miles and equal Hollinsworth's record. He was cheered to the echo as he went by the rooms, and a half dozen riders went to cheer him along at his best pace. But he was thoroughly tired and his speed was all gone. He could just go and that was all. He covered about four miles on the roads in the city during the intervening time, and finished in front of the club rooms at just 9.30. The whole course, with the additional part, will be carefully measured. If the measurement is found correct, he has failed by about two miles to equal the Western man's feat.

Following is a summary of the progress of the run:—

Distance.	Start.	Finish.	Elapsed time.	Rest.
12½ miles	9.00.30	9.50.00	49.30	....
25 miles	9.50.00	10.40.10	50.10	....
27½ miles	10.40.10	11.35.40	55.30	....
50 miles	11.35.40	12.33.00	57.20	15.20
62½ miles	12.48.20	1.52.00	1.04.20	....
75 miles	1.52.00	2.54.40	1.02.40	12.40
87½ miles	3.07.20	4.09.50	1.02.30	....
100 miles	4.09.50	5.28.10	1.18.20	10.50
112½ miles	5.39.00	6.39.00	1.00.00	....
125 miles	[illegible].39.00	7.43.00	1.04.00	28.45
137½ miles	8.11.45	9.13.30	1.01.45	....
150 miles	9.13.30	10.16.15	1.02.45	....
162½ miles	10.16.15	11.20.00	1.45.00	1.45
175 miles	11.20.15	12.28.00	1.07.45	....
187½ miles	12.28.00	1.29.45	1.01.45	12.15
200 miles	1.42.00	2.37.00	55.00	....
212½ miles	2.37.00	3.31.00	54.00	....
225 miles	3.31.00	4.25.30	54.30	2.32
237½ miles	4.28.00	5.25.00	57.00	2.00
250 miles	5.27.00	6.28.40	58.20	....
262½ miles	6.28.40	7.33.00	1.04.20	....
275 miles	7.33.00	8.38.40	1.05.40	....
278½, about	8.38.40	9.00.30	0.21.50	....

Riding time — 22 h. 29m. 55s.
Resting time — 1h. 30m. 5s.

F. W. PERRY'S RECORDS.

AFTER McCurdy had finished, Mr. F. W. Perry, of the Massachusetts Bicycle Club, started out on his 55-inch Apollo to break the twenty and twenty-five mile road records. He was supplied with pacemakers, and made a good run. The twenty-mile distance was marked off with great care. Perry scored as follows: twenty miles, 1.12.35; twenty-five miles, 1.32. Previous records: Eldred of Springfield, twenty miles in 1.19.50. Munger's record at New Orleans was 1.24.46¾ for twenty-five miles.

PATENTS.

LIST of patents for inventions in cycles granted this week.

H. Barrett & J. J Varley, London, Eng., elastic tire.

A. Coudyser, Hartford, Conn., polycycle.

J. N. Waite, Hartford, Conn., velocipede.

W. L. Fish, Newark, N. J., saddle.

L. E. Whiton, West Stafford, Conn., bicycle tire.

FROM A FEMININE POINT OF VIEW.

SHALL we remain in town or go into the country? This is a question that many wheelmen are now discussing, for it comes home to them with peculiar force. To go into the country means nine times in ten to surrender the wheel for a season, for country roads do not hold out inducements for the metallic pegasus.

No sensible person would make pretence of disbelieving that the country has some charms in summer; that it is a fine thing to lie under the pines and listen to the breeze as it makes each leaf a harp, to wander through green lanes, and all the rest of it; but equally true is it that to a right-thinking man the country's disadvantages often overbalance the advantages.

Two men could not be more differently constituted than Dr. Johnson and Charles Lamb, yet they agreed in thinking London to be the true paradise. From one point of view they were right. Whatever may be the disadvantages of the city, it is usually a concentration of the conveniences of life, while there are simple as well as creditable tastes which in the country it is almost impossible to gratify, at least without inordinate trouble and expense.

SOME of these tastes, it is true, are artificial, and yet by long use they have become secondarily natural, and are not to be lightly disregarded.

THE poet has said prettily enough, that "God made the country." Yet, in spite of the antithesis, it is equally true that God made the town; nor is it to be supposed that all the blessings of Providence stop with the grassy fields and the cabbage gardens.

IT is in the city that the man who has money, much or little, to spend, can spend it according to his tastes; can buy books, pictures, handsome raiment, and be wise and curious in his diet. It is in the city that he can see what it is quite out of his power to purchase; can view the best works of art; can hear the finest music; can always get the latest newspaper; in fact, can do a hundred and one things not possible under the greenwood tree.

IN the city man does not grow stagnant, lumpish, and somnolent, for he is kept upon the *qui vive* by constant contact with his neighbors, and by fresh reports coming almost hourly, through post or telegraph, from all parts of the world.

THESE are the things which the city-bred man misses when he goes into summer retreat, and their want to him is a real one.

I AM led to these remarks after talking with a number of friends who are giving up their annual trip to the country and taking their outing in piecemeal. They tell me they would rather stay about Boston, and make little day trips to this or, that place, constantly changing their scene and getting

a good deal out of their wheels. I like the idea very much, for, like Ixion, I am bound to the wheel.

I AM a convert to the handle-bar steering, and hope to ride nothing else in the future. I find that I can do more with a machine thus equipped than I ever was able to with the side steerers. I have been riding one of the new Marlboro' Club machines, and although it is geared very high, I have climbed hills on it that I have always walked before.

THE mounting and dismounting is a little awkward at first, but it is soon mastered and is after all no great objection. I was told that the vibration would be hard on the hands, but the makers have corrected this evil by the use of a spring which absorbs all vibration, and nothing of the kind is experienced.

I AM told that Mr. Gaskell is selling this machine in large numbers, and that no other bar-steering machine in the market so well supplies the demand for a ladies' machine as this does. Surely I have seen no other, and I hope to see the orders pouring in upon him so fast that other makers will take the hint and cater to the ladies' taste. The ladies are coming forward in large numbers, and their wants must be supplied.　　DAISIE.

THE COURIER SAFETY.

MANUFACTURED BY SINGER & CO., COVENTRY, ENG., AND IMPORTED BY W. B. EVERETT & CO., BOSTON.

THE rapid rise into popular favor of that class of bicycle known as the "Safety" is due to the fact that to a great many people there remains an impression that the ordinary bicycle is dangerous on account of the liability of its rider to fall over the handles, or, as it is called, " take a header." If this is the chief requirement of a safety bicycle, then most of the so-called safeties are certainly misnamed, seeing that their only claim to safety lies in their small wheels, which only reduce the height the rider has to fall, in case of an accident of that kind. An exception to the machines referred to is the Courier, from which a header is impossible. For some weeks past, I have, through the courtesy of the 'agents, W. B. Everett & Co., been experimenting with the machine, and much pleased am I with the result. In general outline it resembles the Rover pattern, only that the front wheel is the smaller of the two, being but 26 inches, while the rear wheel is 36. The ordinary bicyclist is, as a rule, " all over the road " upon mounting this machine, and it requires a few hours' practice before he can get used to the action, and some beginners may be inclined to refuse the Courier on account of its steering seeming strange at first, but I can tell them that it is very easily mastered in one ride. When once accustomed to it, however, its good features become more and more prominent, and its absolute immunity from headers undoubtedly earn for it the title of safety without qualification. Side falls are prevented by dropping the foot on the ground, and in case of the necessity for a quick dismount it can be done in an instant. It has no tendency to wobble from side to side as many of the

geared machines have, as no matter what pressure is put on the pedals, it does not affect the steering in the least, the rear wheel being the driver. It is the best hill climber I ever rode, and I have thoroughly tested it on that point. To those who love bicycling, and feel some objection to the risks accompanying the ordinary, I can recommend it. Its peculiar construction gives it numerous advantages. It is safe in every respect, — a header being impossible; and the rider being so near to the ground feels as secure as when upon his feet. For strength, durability, and general construction, the name of the makers, Messrs. Singer & Co., is a sufficient guarantee.　　GEORGE W.

BLUE NOSE TOUR.

THE Blue Nose tourists left Boston on Friday last, and are now wheeling in and about the land of codfish and potatoes. The following gentlemen make up the party: F. A. Elwell, E. G. Whitney, Sanford Lawton, J. E. Beal, G. E. Cane, W. H. DeGraaf, Charles B. Davidson, C. W. Griffith, F. W. Hanford, W. H. Selvey, D. E. Miller, W. C. Marsh, F. A. Lindsey, F. H. Messer, George R. Macausland, J. W. Macausland, Armand Wendell, C. A. Hazlett, H. M. Bennett, E. H. Elwell, F. L. Godetz, G. B. Morrell, J. B. Moore, W. R. Pitcher, W. H. Gray, F. J. Arnold, O. W. Temple, E. S. Kennard, and E. C. Tewksbury.

A DISPATCH from Grand Falls, N. B., 17 July, to the Globe, says : The "Blue Nose" bicycle tourists arrived here at six P. M. during a thunder storm. Owing to numerous delays the train was one hour late. The entire party numbers thirty-eight, and a more sociable crowd it would be hard to find. A most humorous incident occurred between Aroostook Junction and this place : Three of the wheelmen decided to ride on the cowcatcher of the engine for nineteen miles, and the heavy rain-storm coming up, there was no escape for them, and when they alighted at Grand Falls they were thoroughly drenched by the rain, and blacked with the soot from the engine. To-morrow will be passed in rowing on the river and sight-seeing about town.

To-DAY, 23 July, the schedule puts them at Fredericton. They leave 5½, John for Boston on the " Flying Yankee " 28 July.

CONNECTICUT CLUB.

THE Connecticut Bicycle Club of Hartford has adopted the following : —

Whereas, it is understood that steps have been taken by the officers of the L. A. W. to remedy the existing breach in the organization, caused by the decisions of the Racing Board, and the action of the Connecticut Club in taking the initiatory steps in leaving the L. A. W. was based solely upon dissatisfaction with such decisions and their injustice to racing men and clubs who give races;

Resolved, that the motion now before this club, striking out the L. A. W. clause from the club's by-laws, lie on the table until the next meeting.

KIRK COREY pushed his Rudge to the front in the one-mile bicycle race held at the 5th of July celebration in Brookline, Mass. It was on the same track that his brother Harry won his maiden race five years ago.

ACROSS THE CONTINENT.

MR. GEORGE B. THAYER, of Hartford, Ct.' a correspondent of the Evening Post of that city, is on his way across the continent. He started 10 April, and is probably by this time at Salt Lake City. His route so far has included the southern part of Connecticut, the bank of the Hudson from Tarrytown to Albany, the Erie Canal towpath, Niagara Falls, the lake shore to Cleveland, to Columbus, to Indianapolis and to Chicago. From Chicago he rode to Grinnell, Ia., from there to Omaha. He stopped at Denver and Colorado Springs, and then struck northwest to Fort Collins, Longmont, and Laramie. His expenses have so far averaged less than $1 a day. The bicycle which has withstood 2,500 miles of hard travelling has not broken in any part. Mr. Thayer is journeying wholly for information, experience, and pleasure.

RUSSIAN TOUR.

MR. JAMES RICALTON, the gentleman who has started on a tour through Russia in the interest of Outing, is a resident of Maplewood, near Orange, N. J., and an experienced traveller. Judging from the success of his past efforts, he bids fair to succeed in his attempt through Russia, and the articles from his pen and illustrations through his camera will add an additional feature to Outing.

He has travelled through Iceland, and is the first white man known to have reached the Geysers without a guide. Total cost of his Iceland trip was $200 from New York.

He has also gone through Brazil and for 1,800 miles up the Amazon. His desire was to travel and increase his store of knowledge, also to see how cheaply it could be done. This trip cost but $225, and while away he captured a young jaguar (a species of tiger), which he sold for $100, and it is said that this animal is now in the Zoölogical Garden at Philadelphia. On his trip up the Amazon he was accompanied by a young naturalist, whose desire was to secure specimens of birds. He killed one of a species never before seen, which is now at the Smithsonian Institute, Washington, D. C.

The combined boat and push cart with which Mr. Ricalton expects to reach Russia was made by himself during the past winter. It is ingenious, and will serve him, for a boat, tent, dark room for his photographing, kitchen to cook and eat in, — in fact, it is a house on wheels, as well as a boat when on the water. He carries a rifle, revolver, oil stove, condensed coffee and milk, etc.

NEW FACTORIES,

GORMULLY & JEFFERY have broken ground, and started work on their new factories, which, when completed the latter part of September, will form the largest and most complete bicycle manufacturing plant in the world, with a capacity of turning out seventy-five perfect bicycles a day, and will furnish employment for four hundred skilled mechanics. The new building will occupy as much ground as the present two, and will be five stories high, with a basement underneath, and will be joined to the present factories. The main floor will be taken up entirely by the offices and stock rooms, which former will be commodious and elegant. Full particulars as to detail will appear in

this paper at a later date. The growth of this firm has been phenomenal, and few believed a short time ago, when Gormully & Jeffery were advertising boys' bicycles on Canal street, that so few years of shrewd business tact and excellent mechanical management would find them at the head of the industry.

FROM THE N. C. U.

THE following communication has been received by the Chairman of the Racing Board:—

LONDON, July 6, 1886.

ABBOT BASSETT, Esq., Boston, Mass.

Dear Sir :— I have your letter of 16 June with accompanying paper. This should have been answered before, but that it was delayed in the delivery by the post-office authorities and delivered at the wrong address. I note the action taken by the L. A. W. with reference to the policy of the Racing Board. The National Cyclists' Union has, in the past, recognized the decisions of the L. A. W., and I think I may state that it proposes to do the same in the future, and that the Union will support you in every reasonable action which is taken for the purpose of purifying the sport.

I am, yours faithfully,
ROBERT TODD,
Sec. N. C. U.

THE CAPITAL CLUB IN HAGERSTOWN.

"L. W. S." tells the story in the *Evening Star* of a visit of the Capital Club, of Washington, to Hagerstown, Md. The initials will be recognized by all who know anything about the Club, for of that organization "L. W. S." is one of the bright particular stars. We have room for a few extracts only.

"The capacity of a spacious and elegant box car, tendered them by the B. and O. R. R. Company, was severely tested by the number of bicycles and tricycles belonging to the party; while the party itself scattered through the train in congenial groups, patronized the banana man and the illustrated papers, and sang club songs in a way which, to a cultivated musical ear, was simply unbearable. Now, for instance, there was 'Bottles.' 'Bottles,' as you know, is the proprietor of an alleged tenor voice, which, in a chorus, when it could n't be heard, would be listened to with pleasure; but his amateur assumption of the part of Nanki Poo to the accompaniment of rumbling wheels and rattling windows, was of such a character as to call forth a gentle hint that the club motto was temporarily *silentium audeamus.*

"It is difficult to give such hints without making them too obvious, and thus giving offence to the performer; but in this case a single application of a loaded satchel after the manner of an Indian club was found quite sufficient."

This little bit of description of the scenery met with *en route* is worthy the pen of Wm. Black:—

"We passed several fields in which things were growing; there were also trees covered with umbrageous foliage; the grass was of a bright green color mostly, and grew along the road and by the fences. Cattle grazed in the meadows and also lay in the middle of the road. There were plenty of stones to throw at them. Several variety of birds

were running an open-air concert in the leafy woods; all nature was bathed in sunlight and seemed to rejoice in her own loveliness. The temperature of the bath was about 118° F.

"Far off to the east the shadowy outline of the Blue Ridge was vaguely defined against the sky, which latter was of a deep blue color throughout its entire majestic concavity. There were no clouds to mar the perfect beauty of the celestial arch. We wished there had been. A tiny brook ran babbling between mossy banks, and murmuring its song of peace and happiness as it danced and sparkled in the sunlight on its way to the mighty ocean; it was not a large brook, but it ran directly across the road, and one of the boys took a header in trying to ride through it. (This is all there is to be about scenery: I have got in growing crops, grass, trees, birds, sunlight, sky, mountains, and brook, and that is about all the stock in trade the scenic word-painter ever has.)

"With a perfect roadbed, easy grades, and the genial influence of the sunlight, we sped onward at an average speed of 4½ miles an hour. Those who imagine that because a bicycle is capable of great speed, it is always pushed to its utmost capacity, have a very mistaken idea of the pleasures of wheeling on a hot day. Do you always drive your 2.30 trotter at *that* rate? We simply sauntered along at a restful pace, stopping occasionally at some weather-beaten pump for internal and external irrigation, or beneath some of these trees mentioned above, where the stray breezes might blow through our —— midst to effect a reduction of temperature in the well-known principle of evaporation.

"On reaching Falling Waters we halted to allow certain stragglers who had been overcome by the heat and too much water to overtake us. As we lay grouped picturesquely on the banks of the canal, we were marked as prey by a band of desperate characters of both sexes returning from Sunday school in a wagon, and who were anxious to obtain funds to procure an organ for that institution. When assailed by the pathetic entreaty of a pair of bright eyes, the owner of which personally presented a hat to the notice of each member, what man could be unkind? Excepting 'Rudy,' who, in a condition of mental syncope, put a cent into the hat and then endeavored to collect the change from a quarter which the recklessly extravagant X-man had inserted therein! It is pleasant to record that he did not succeed.

"It was considered fitting that our athletic figures should be perpetuated for posterity by means of the photographer's art, and so we all grouped ourselves in the open square beneath the broiling sunlight while five photographers discharged five cameras at short range. It is hard for one man to look graceful and 'pleasant' when exposed to one camera. It would take a treasury clerk to evolve the mathematical computation which expresses the labor required of 150 men to look pleasant for five of those instruments.

"The Hagerstown Club led the parade 23 strong—a fine body of men. They were followed by the McConnellsburg (Pa.), Williamsport, Martinsburg, Woodstock, Washington Cycle, District Wheelmen, Maryland, Baltimore, Westminster, and Capital Clubs. Altogether there were 155 wheelmen in line. The Capital Club appeared in line 36 strong, under command of Captain Olds and sub-

Captain Sharrets, and having Messrs. Hansmann and Church on a sociable, and Forney and Wagner on safeties. Mr. Hansmann officiated as bugler, with all the effect of a condensed Marine band.

"In the evening there was a banquet, after which the tables were cleared and the guests had settled back in that condition of anxious expectancy which always precedes an intellectual treat, when a startling whisper in our captain's ear soon created a scene of panic and consternation. The information that the 12-o'clock train left at 11 came rather late, but there was still time for a lightning transfer to the depot. A wild rush ensued. Those halls of dazzling light were deserted, and the orator, in a condition of mental and bodily preparation for his expected effort, was hurried along with the rest. The speech has never been delivered. The joke is rendered complete by the fact that the train did not leave until 12."

THE BONESHAKER CRAZE.

STAND aside you young fellows who now sit astride the bicycle and give an old fellow a chance to be heard. Don't think that you have all the fun nowadays, for although the old boneshaker used to rattle us about and play the mischief with our bones, we had a deal of fun with it, and the recollection of those days has a charm for us old fellows that you youngsters can little appreciate. I want to carry you back to December of 1868, and to a city a few miles from Boston. I picked up a hand-bill one afternoon and was told by it that a riding school had been opened in a certain hall, and that all could now have an opportunity to ride the velocipede. Having my curiosity aroused, I went to the hall that evening, and found upon entering that the floor had been cleared and covered liberally with a layer of sawdust. The velocipedes, six in number, stood at the upper end, and we were told that they were to be let to any one who desired to learn, for sixty cents an hour. The machine has been described so many times that I will not attempt it here; but I will say that many of the old boneshakers that are shown to-day were used in this country had no spring upon them whatever, the saddle being bolted on to the iron cross bar that connected the wheels. The tires were made of flat strips of iron, and in turning corners would cut up the floors of the halls so badly that sawdust had to be used to protect them. On payment of the required sum, we were entrusted with a machine, and were expected to master it ourselves, or with what assistance we could obtain from a friend. The correct way to learn, we were told, was to keep one leg on the floor, and so push the machine around the hall until we could gain control of it sufficiently to put both feet on the treadles. It was very ludicrous to see five or six men pushing these machines around and hopping on one leg, and it afforded unbounded merriment for the people who had paid their fifteen cents to see the fun. When a man was bold enough to ride ten feet with both feet on the treadles, he was greeted with great applause and laughter, and was considered quite a rider. In the course of a week there were quite a number of men who could ride fairly well, and they would have

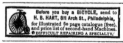

done very well, but there was always a new lot of beginners coming on to the floor, and this made constant fun for the spectators. After a while most of the young men had conquered the machine, and could ride with little difficulty. Then fancy riding and races were in order. Many were the disputes as to who was the best rider and the faster. One who could ride without hands, pedal with one leg, ride side saddle, or mount from the pedal, was considered a fancy and trick rider of considerable merit. To settle the numerous disputes as to which was the fastest rider, the proprietors advertised a race for the championship of the city, and invited the flyers to enter. For a curb a half-inch rope was nailed to the floor, about four feet from the sides of the hall, and there were thirty-six laps to the mile. The contestants rode one at a time, and the man who made the mile in the fastest time was declared the winner, and presented as an emblem of the championship with a silver cup, which had been bought at one of the numerous dollar stores which were so plenty at that time. The month of February saw the craze at its height. Every hall that could be had was transformed into a riding school; all sorts of artifices were resorted to in order to attract audiences. One party advertised a young lady rider, and presented a young man dressed in female attire, and so close was the resemblance that the trick was not discovered for some time. Walter Brown, the famous oarsman of his time, opened a school in Bowdoin square, of this city, and Horticultural Hall was transformed into a riding school, and it was at the latter place that the fast riders were wont to compete for championship honors. A fast rider in those days was one who could ride a mile inside of six minutes. In those races a competitor who could ride the whole distance without falling was almost certain to be the winner.

Races were advertised for the championship and $1,000, and the competitors were paid $10 a night for their part of the deception. I was one of a great many who thought there was a fortune in the machine, and went with a friend into the business. Sargent Bros. of this city were the agents for the machine, and so great was the demand for them that it was two weeks before we could be supplied. Procuring six machines at $75 each, we started for the western part of Massachusetts, and opened a riding school at North Adams, in the vestry of a church, on the 22d of February, 1869, Washington's Birthday. We were greeted with crowded houses, and often we were obliged to keep open all night, so great was the demand for the sport. And so we went on from one town to another until spring opened, and our hopes of wealth were dashed to the ground, for when the machines were taken on the road they were found to be practically useless, so that the craze died a natural death, and we started for Boston, where we disposed of our machines at the nearest junk shop for $5.00 a piece, and our dream was at an end.   HAWKSHAW.

AUTOMATIC STEERING.

[539.] — *Will automatic steering continue in vogue for next season ?* This is a question now asked by manufacturers and agents alike, besides raising the curiosity of many an anxious purchaser who desires to be " in fashion next time round."

There are a few interesting points worth calling attention to on this subject. What is automatic steering? Well, of course, it is greatly misnamed, but as generally accepted it means a *mechanical inclination to run in a straight line.* I think, however, I can point out a steering more nearly coming under the definition. It is a fact not generally known that the " Bicyclette," " Rover," " Premier," and other safeties of the new type may be made to possess one of the most perfect and beautiful achievements in the way of steering that can possibly delight the rider.

While experimenting with bicycles in 1875 — just eleven years ago — I was much struck with the difference *rake* made in affecting the steering of our then *only* popular velocipede, viz. the " high bicycle." I found that a forward rake at the top — the reverse of what is generally adopted — very materially interfered with the " art of balancing," and the machine seemed to positively object to go to the left when falling to the left, and *vice versa.* In the same way, an extremely " backward " rake would also put extra pressure on the hands, and manifest a tendency to interfere with the steering. Great was my joy, however, to find it possible to obtain a medium between these two extremes, where the machine would actually tend *to steer itself,* and finally I found that, at a certain rake, both *hands and feet* might be removed, and down an incline the machine would really both balance and steer without any touch or any attention whatever. No doubt, this knowledge is " old as the hills " *now,* but it was not *then.* Unfortunately it possessed no advantages for an ordinary bicycle rider. It was uncomfortable to ride down-hill with feet off and hands off too; but to my " safety " it was a perfect charm, and no more exquisite delight could be derived than to tread hard on a firm treadle without *side movement,* and find the machine positively *self-balancing and self-steering,* this, too, at any variable speed. A slight inclination of the body to the left, and the machine runs to the left — the same to the right — without any touch of the handles, or the hands being employed at all.

I have ridden on these machines *many miles, and over rough ground,* watching the beautifully sensitive and almost living motion of the steering handle unaided. This, then, to my mind, is " automatic steering " in the true sense of the word, and a severe sarcasm on those makers who actually introduced a bicycle *with a spring to tend to keep the steering straight.* The most ignorant boy rider knows well enough that to steer in a fixed straight line is to stop the balance, and any tendency to do so in a bicycle is to oppose the whole principle of the machine balance when in motion.

In view of these facts, how amusing it is to witness some riders without experience of the new " Bicyclette " style of safety. They grasp the handles with a grip which completely strangles the poor machine in its kindly intentions, and compels an erratic course through sheer ignorance of the beauty of its principle of construction, which I again declare to be nothing less than *self-balancing and self-steering* in these perfect machines.

Of course, two particulars are essential, — the centre-pin or socket must be quite free and oiled, and the rake slanting an inch or two, so that the weight of the wheel will turn itself in either direction, and bricks must be avoided on the road.

H. J. L., *in Cyclist.*

CYCLETS.

A LEAGUE blouse or touring jacket has been decided upon. It is of seersucker, and costs $5.00.

HERBERT W. HAYES has received his appointment as chief consul of Massachusetts, and President Beckwith has notified Massachusetts wheelmen that no other person should be recognized.

CYCLISTS who desire to ascertain the meaning of the words " gentleman amateur," are referred to our report of the races at East Saginaw. A Star rider, knowing the advantage he held in a safety race, offered to withdraw, but was persuaded to compete by the other three competitors. — *Journal.*

THE New York Division has got over a thousand dollars in its treasury, and there is not even a suggestion of a junket.

FRED JENKINS has had an operation performed on his eyes, which, if successful, will render it unnecessary for him to wear glasses. We hope to hear the best results.

ROWE, Hendee, Knapp, and Burnham cannot be promateurs under A. C. U. rules. It is very hard for us to see where the promateurs are to come from.

CHICAGO gave up its second tournament at Cheltenham Beach. They saw the folly of attempting too much at one time. The public will not go too often to bicycle races.

IT has come to be an attraction for a hotel if it is located where the roads are good. Wheelmen are good customers, and they won't go where they have to ride in sand.

ENGLISH law requires that women in factories may not work later than 10 P. M. As it is necessary for later work than this at the *Cyclist* office on mailing day, the male typos and the office hands wrap the papers after ten o'clock. Thus the law prevents the females from doing mail work.

MR. W. J. C. ELLIOT, a racing man of some repute in Melbourne, has just been successful in an action for an " interim injunction to restrain the Victorian Cyclists' Union from declaring him a professional bicyclist," and " to have the minute on the books referring to him cancelled." The Victorian definition is almost a fac-simile of the N. C. U., and makes especial reference to " other athletic exercises " as being amenable. — *Cyclist.*

IT is reported that L. D. Munger, the speedy road rider, now travelling through the Southern States in the interest of W. B. Everett & Co., has been paying too much attention to the best girl of a hot-blooded young Southerner, and that as a result the wheelman has been invited to fight a duel with real revolvers and genuine 32-calibre cartridges. — *Globe.*

" BI." — No, we don't know who you are. We wish we did. One who has done

done very well, but there was always a new lot of beginners coming on to the floor, and this made constant fun for the spectators. After a while most of the young men had conquered the machine, and could ride with little difficulty. Then fancy riding and races were in order. Many were the disputes as to who was the best rider and the faster. One who could ride without hands, pedal with one leg, ride side saddle, or mount from the pedal, was considered a fancy and trick rider of considerable merit. To settle the numerous disputes as to which was the fastest rider, the proprietors advertised a race for the championship of the city, and invited the flyers to enter. For a curb a half-inch rope was nailed to the floor, about four feet from the sides of the hall, and there were thirty-six laps to the mile. The contestants rode one at a time, and the man who made the mile in the fastest time was declared the winner, and presented as an emblem of the championship with a silver cup, which had been bought at one of the numerous dollar stores which were so plenty at that time. The month of February saw the craze at its height. Every hall that could be had was transformed into a riding school; all sorts of artifices were resorted to in order to attract audiences. One party advertised a young lady rider, and presented a young man dressed in female attire, and so close was the resemblance that the trick was not discovered for some time. Walter Brown, the famous oarsman of his time, opened a school in Bowdoin square, of this city, and Horticultural Hall was transformed into a riding school, and it was at the latter place that the fast riders were wont to compete for championship honors. A fast rider in those days was one who could ride a mile inside of six minutes. In those races a competitor who could ride the whole distance without falling was almost certain to be the winner.

Races were advertised for the championship and $1,000, and the competitors were paid $10 a night for their part of the deception. I was one of a great many who thought there was a fortune in the machine, and went with a friend into the business. Sargent Bros. of this city were the agents for the machine, and so great was the demand for them that it was two weeks before we could be supplied. Procuring six machines at $75 each, we started for the western part of Massachusetts, and opened a riding school at North Adams, in the vestry of a church, on the 22d of February, 1869, Washington's Birthday. We were greeted with crowded houses, and often we were obliged to keep open all night, so great was the demand for the sport. And so we went on from one town to another until spring opened, and our hopes of wealth were dashed to the ground, for when the machines were taken on the road they were found to be practically useless, so that the craze died a natural death, and we started for Boston, where we disposed of our machines at the nearest junk shop for $5.00 a piece, and our dream was at an end.   HAWKSHAW.

AUTOMATIC STEERING.

[539.] — *Will automatic steering continue in vogue for next season?* This is a question now asked by manufacturers and agents alike, besides raising the curiosity of many an anxious purchaser who desires to be " in fashion next time round."

There are a few interesting points worth calling attention to on this subject. What is automatic steering? Well, of course, it is greatly misnamed, but as generally accepted it means *a mechanical inclination to run in a straight line*. I think, however, I can point out a steering more nearly coming under the definition. It is a fact not generally known that the " Bicyclette," " Rover," " Premier," and other safeties of the new type may be made to possess one of the most perfect and beautiful achievements in the way of steering that can possibly delight the rider.

While experimenting with bicycles in 1875 — just eleven years ago — I was much struck with the difference *rake* made in affecting the steering of our then *only* popular velocipede, viz. the " high bicycle." I found that a forward rake at the top — the reverse of what is generally adopted — very materially interfered with the "art of balancing," and the machine seemed to positively object to go to the left when falling to the left, and *vice versa*. In the same way, an extremely "backward" rake would also put extra pressure on the hands, and manifest a tendency to interfere with the steering. Great was my joy, however, to find it possible to obtain a medium between these two extremes, where the machine would actually tend *to steer itself*, and finally I found that, at a certain rake, both *hands and feet* might be removed, and down an incline the machine would really both balance and steer without any touch or any attention whatever. No doubt, this knowledge is "old as the hills" *now*, but it was not *then*. Unfortunately it possessed no advantages for an ordinary bicycle rider. It was uncomfortable to ride down-hill with feet off and hands off too; but to my "safety" it was a perfect charm, and no more exquisite delight could be derived than to tread hard on a firm treadle without *side movement*, and find the machine positively *self-balancing and self-steering*, this, too, at any variable speed. A slight inclination of the body to the left, and the machine runs to the left — the same to the right — without any touch of the handles, or the hands being employed at all.

I have ridden on these machines *many miles, and over rough ground*, watching the beautifully sensitive and almost living motion of the steering handle unaided. This, then, to my mind, is " automatic steering " in the true sense of the word, and a severe sarcasm on those makers who actually introduced a bicycle *with a spring to tend to keep the steering straight*. The most ignorant boy rider knows well enough that to steer in a fixed straight line is to stop the balance, and any tendency to do so in a bicycle is to oppose the whole principle of the machine balance when in motion.

In view of these facts, how amusing it is to witness some riders without experience of the new " Bicyclette " style of safety. They grasp the handles with a grip which completely strangles the poor machine in its kindly intentions, and compels an erratic course through sheer ignorance of the beauty of its principle of construction, which I again declare to be nothing less than *self-balancing and self-steering* in these perfect machines.

Of course, two particulars are essential, — the centre-pin or socket must be quite free and oiled, and the rake slanting an inch or two, so that the weight of the wheel will turn itself in either direction, and bricks must be avoided on the road.

H. J. L., *in Cyclist.*

CYCLETS.

A LEAGUE blouse or touring jacket has been decided upon. It is of seersucker, and costs $5.00.

HERBERT W. HAYES has received his appointment as chief consul of Massachusetts, and President Beckwith has notified Massachusetts wheelmen that no other person should be recognized.

CYCLISTS who desire to ascertain the meaning of the words " gentleman amateur," are referred to our report of the races at East Saginaw. A Star rider, knowing the advantage he held in a safety race, offered to withdraw, but was persuaded to compete by the other three competitors. — *Journal.*

THE New York Division has got over a thousand dollars in its treasury, and there is not even a suggestion of a junket.

FRED JENKINS has had an operation performed on his eyes, which, if successful, will render it unnecessary for him to wear glasses. We hope to hear the best results.

ROWE, Hendee, Knapp, and Burnham cannot be promateurs under A. C. U. rules. It is very hard for us to see where the promateurs are to come from.

CHICAGO gave up its second tournament at Cheltenham Beach. They saw the folly of attempting too much at one time. The public will not go too often to bicycle races.

IT has come to be an attraction for a hotel if it is located where the roads are good. Wheelmen are good customers, and they won't go where they have to ride in sand.

ENGLISH law requires that women in factories may not work later than 10 P. M. As it is necessary for later work than this at the *Cyclist* office on mailing day, the male typos and the office hands wrap the papers after ten o'clock. Thus the law prevents the females from doing mail work.

MR. W. J. C. ELLIOT, a racing man of some repute in Melbourne, has just been successful in an action for an " interim injunction to restrain the Victorian Cyclists' Union from declaring him a professional bicyclist," and " to have the minute on the books referring to him cancelled." The Victorian definition is almost a fac-simile of the N. C. U., and makes especial reference to "other athletic exercises " as being amenable. — *Cyclist.*

IT is reported that L. D. Munger, the speedy road rider, now travelling through the Southern States in the interest of W. B. Everett & Co., has been paying too much attention to the best girl of a hot-blooded young Southerner, and that as a result the wheelman has been invited to fight a duel with real revolvers and genuine 32-calibre cartridges. — *Globe.*

" BI." — No, we don't know who you are. We wish we did. One who has done

so many favors for us as you have, should be known. We want to show you that we are appreciative. Use four parts lard oil and one part kerosene 160 test. For each pint of the oil add one ounce of camphor gum, dissolved in the kerosene before adding the lard oil.

THOMAS WARWICK & Son are making a new backbone, strengthened at the neck end, where breaks most frequently occur.

R. J. MECREDY won three championships of Ireland, at Ball's Bridge, 3 July. They were the one and four mile bicycle, and the one-mile tricycle events. We must surely have him over here this fall.

THE match between Wood and Howell is off on account of a disagreement regarding the track upon which it was to be run.

IT is rumored that Kennedy Child is on the way to America.

F. W. ALLARD, who was over here with the English racers last year, is being heard from on the track. He has won several races, a championship, and taken a few records already this year. He downed Furnivall and Gatehouse in the five-mile trichampionship.

THE Invincible bicycle has not taken many records since Cortis left the path, but now Speechly is bringing it forward.

MR. SAM PATTON is announced as temporary editor of the Bicycle South, vice W. W. Crane resigned.

THE New Orleans newspapers announce the safe arrival at Deming, N. M., of Van Meerbeke, the New York to San Francisco cycler. Date not given.

BARTON KEENE, class of '80, of the University of Pennsylvania, who recently lowered the college bicycle record by sixteen seconds, has gone to England to race with English collegians.

THE road record of the Star Club, of Cleveland, for six months ending 1 July, is as follows: Number of runs, 17; total mileage, 835; longest run, 152 miles; average, 49 miles; attendance, 125; average, 7. The largest individual records are: R. W. Wright, 2,030 miles, and H. E. Chubb, 1,850 miles.

NORTHAMPTON cyclists are trying for long distance records. Clarence Shearn's cyclometer registers 1,050 miles, and Harry Haven has ridden over 800 miles this season.

TWO Boston ladies, Misses Kendall and Jackson, will make a tricycle tour to New Haven, this week. They will ride by way of Providence.

MR. A. C. RICHARDSON, of Buffalo, has been riding about Boston and vicinity the past fortnight. He says the riding in Buffalo is far ahead of that which he finds in Boston, but once outside the city and Buffalo stock goes downward.

IT is expected that Massachusetts will have her quota of representatives filled at once. Among the names mentioned for members of the Board, are those of Elmer G. Whitney, Boston; W. M. Pratt, Brockton; J. S. Webber, Jr., Gloucester; Lincoln Holland, Worcester; A. W. Dyer, Lawrence, and John Amee, Cambridge.

KLUGE's fall at Lynn, Decoration Day,

has proved more serious in its result than was originally hoped and thought. — World.

We wonder how much of an injury Kluge would have sustained had it been as bad as they hoped it would be?

THE editor of our local contemporary is charged by the Republican with having described a beautiful river at Chicopee, which turns out to be a canal.

FURNIVALL is suffering from synovitis of both knees This is inflammation of the synovial membrane, which contains the synovial fluid that oils the knee joints. It is a dangerous disease, and if he does not rest he will be crippled for life.

MR. G. P. MILLS is on a run to John-o'-Groat's. He started Sunday, 4 July, and on Thursday he was well on his way, and thirty hours ahead of Lennox's record. He covered 473 miles in two and a half days.

F. W. BERRIDGE rode twenty miles on a Rover at Lillie Bridge, 7 July, in 58.59., and in the hour he ran twenty miles, thirty yards. This is 105 yards short of the American safety record.

THE Overman team, Ives and Rhodes, have gone to Springfield to train for the fall tournaments.

ALL rowing men will be interested in reading "Famous Oarsmen of the Tyne," by Aaron Watson, in Outing for July, from the fact of its treating of the first introduction upon English waters of the famous sculler Albert Shaw, then American consul at Manchester, England.

CHIEF CONSUL HAYES is off on a vacation. He will set the Massachusetts division in motion on his return.

THE Cambridge Club men are at Downer's. Many live there; others go down on Sunday.

GETCHELL is boarding at Swampscott, and getting in some training for the fall races.

THERE is an exodus of manufacturers in the direction of Europe. Good-by, gentlemen. Europe allows you to go abroad, but our rope ties us at home.

PRESIDENT BECKWITH has been making Hayes for Massachusetts while the sun shines.

WE had a look in at the rooms of the Wakefield Club this week, and found them very prettily quartered.

BETWEEN lists 43 and 44 of League applicants, there is a jump of ninety numbers. Why? Are large numbers desirable?

THE London editor of the Cyclist speaks in commendation of the iced lager at the "Gigshilleries." This must be English for "Ginslingeries."

AMONG the most successful pastors in Philadelphia, the following are enthusiastic riders of the bicycle: Rev. Wayland Hoyt, D. D., of the Baptist church; Rev. George K. Morris, D. D., and Rev. S. O. Garrison, D. D., of the Methodist church; Rev. J. C. Chapman, of the Reformed Presbyterian church; Rev. J. Henry Sharpe, D. D., Rev. C. C. Dickey, Rev. William L. Ledwith, Rev. William C. Rommel, and others of the Presbyterian church. For a minister to ride a bicycle is not so much of an inno-

vation, after all. It is decidedly more dignified and graceful than the riding of a horse, and there is no exercise more conducive to health. — Southwestern Observer.

W. H. LANGDOWN, amateur champion bicyclist of Australia and captain of the Pioneer Bicycle Club, of Christchurch, New Zealand, sailed Saturday for Springfield, and is expected to reach America about 20 Aug.

REV. J. HENRY SHARPE, pastor of the West Park Presbyterian Church, Philadelphia, an enthusiastic wheelman, and a member of the L. A. W., started on the 12th inst. for England, in company with Rev. Wayland Hoyt, D. D., pastor of the Memorial Baptist Church, Philadelphia. The two gentlemen will make a tour of the middle counties of England on their bicycles.

MR. R. P. GORMULLY, of Gormully & Jeffery, sailed for Europe, accompanied by his brother, the eminent Canadian barrister, on the Etruria, last Saturday, from New York. The large and rapidly growing business of this enterprising firm has demanded the arduous attention of its business head, so that Mr. Gormully was pretty well worn out, and compelled to take a vacation. He will be absent in the neighborhood of six weeks, most of which time will be spent in England. It would seem that most of our American manufacturers were in Europe this season. Mr. Gormully, however, will not spend any time among the English manufacturers, as the Gormully & Jeffery wheels are entirely manufactured and designed in this country.

THE Rudge took four prizes at the Montreal races, and three on Boston Common, 5 July.

AMERICANS are prone to boast loudly of what their men will do when the Englishmen come over here next fall and try to back up their assertions by reference to the remarkable times made of late by Rowe and Hendee, with the comment that the English men have never yet done anything so fast. This is all very well, but it should be remembered that in England they have no such tracks as the one at Lynn, and that in former years those English racing men who came here always succeeded in making faster time than they were ever able to do at home. — Globe.

No maker has yet given us an umbrella clip for the handle bar. And yet such a thing would have its uses. One of the Japanese umbrellas carried like a color staff would give a grateful shade during the hot days of August, and it would not take much wind. An enlarged color clip would do the business.

E. A. RICHWINE and W. T. Fleming, of the Pennsylvania Bicycle Club, rode to Luray Caverns, Va., and return, a distance of five hundred and eight miles, in ten days. They started on 1 July, and returned on the 10th.

THE finest country in the world for cycling is Japan. The roads are better than the trimmest paths of a park, and pleasant sights and sounds are on every side. Stevens will find this a very paradise after the abominable highways of China. Perhaps he will take a spin along the great wall, in which case his camera will have some interesting tales to tell. — Outing.

THERE are more of the American cycles

in actual use in the South than those of all other makes combined. Several of the largest clubs ride these wheels exclusively and take their club name from them. Gormully and Jeffery are the youngest in point of age of all the American manufacturers; but they know how to make bicycles and sell them.

IF Hendee's friends think he will break 2.25 before the season closes, Rowe's friends are not naming any particular time that they expect him to break, but they know that he can break Hendee. — *Lynn Bee.*

THUS goes on the war. In the fall the two men will come together. Better not prophesy unless we know. A great many things will occur before Hendee and Rowe race together.

S. G. WHITTAKER has joined the forces at the Coventry Cycle Agency, St. Louis, and is booming the trade in "Club" machines. The new house starts off with flying colors.

THE PATH.

NEWARK. — On Saturday afternoon, 10 July, the Orange Wanderers gave a ten-mile road race for the championship of Essex, Union, and Hudson Counties, N. J.

There were nine starters, viz. C. A. Stenken, W. P. Smith, and C. L. Meyers, of the Hudson County Wheelmen; F. D. Palmer and C. R. Hoag, Newark; E. B. Moore, Elizabeth; T. H. Burnet, Roselle Ramblers; F. B. Hallett, Orange; and E. P. Baird, Orange Wanderers.

The race was twice over the O. W.'s five-mile course, which is quite hilly, but in good condition after the morning rain.

At the start Stenken went to the front, with Baird close behind, the remainder of the field holding close to the leaders. This order was maintained for four miles, when in the most reckless manner Palmer spurted by Stenken and dashed into the little wheel of the latter's Star, throwing them both, and causing Meyers to fall over them. Hoag's tire on his little wheel came off, and he was compelled to stop shortly before the above accident, leaving but five men in the race. Smith led at the five-mile post, with Baird close behind. Four miles from home Baird began to do some fine work, and soon left Smith far behind.

The men finished in the following order: Baird, time, 36.51⅕; Smith, 37.24; Burnet, 38.51; Hallett, 38.51⅕; Moore, 41.03⅕. The race for third place between Burnet and Hallett was very close. In the absence of an authentic record of better than forty-two minutes, Baird's time stands as the American road record for ten miles. It is to be hoped that Baird, Stenken, and Hoag may be brought together again under more favorable circumstances.

WILMINGTON, DEL., 5 July. — Races run under auspices Wilmington Club.

One-Mile Amateur. — Chas. McCurdy (1), 4.07⅕.

Two-Mile Handicap. — H. B. Schwartz, scratch, 8.41.

One-Mile Amateur. — H. B. Schwartz (1), 3.22; C. McCurdy (2).

BROOKLYN, N. Y., 10 July. — Races under the auspices of the Brooklyn Athletic Association.

Three-Mile Handicap. — A. B. Rich, scratch (1), 9.43⅕; E. C. Parker, 275 yds. (2), by ten yds.; E. J. Halstead, 300 yds. (3), one yd.

TORONTO. — The Toronto (Ont.) Bicycle Club held a road race 10 July, the competitors being Fred Brimer, W. H. Cox, W. H. West, A. C. Bowers, W. H. Thomas, and W. Robins. The road being in such poor condition, croppers and falls were in order. Before one mile had been covered, Bowers had ran foul of a stone, and a most unpleasant fall, damaging his machine, bruising himself, and ruining his chances for first place, was the result. At the end of the second mile, Brimer, having recovered from the effects of a header, succeeded in capturing first place, which he held to the end of the race, winning in 34.30, with Brown second in 37.00, and West third, one half minute later.

BROOKLYN. — The second day's contest between W. M. Spencer, the cow-boy, with his horses, and W. M. Woodside and W. J. Morgan, the professional bicyclers, came to an abrupt termination on Tuesday of last week, at Washington Park, Brooklyn, the managers having satisfied themselves that it was a failure. At the close the scores were: Bicycles, 95 miles; horses, 92. The band quit work early in the afternoon. The best bicycle mile was 3.30, and the horseman's, 3.48.

THE five-mile tricycle championship of the N. C. U. was contested at Glasgow, 3 July. The men finished as follows: F. W. Allard (1), 20.42⅗; P. Furnivall (2); G. Gatehouse (3). Allard rode a Marlboro' Club.

H. A. SPEECHLY made a run for a record in a three-mile handicap at Crystal Palace, 3 July, and put the following new records on the English books: One mile, 2.34⅘; three miles, 8.20⅕. No official timer was present, but five watches were held on the rider, and agreed within one fifth of a second.

THE Berkshire County Wheelmen of Pittsfield have fixed upon 10 and 11 Sept. as the dates of their fourth annual tournament. This veteran organization does not propose to be behind the record of former years, and with a fine array of prizes, expect to attract a fine lot of riders for the following events, which will be run under L. A. W. rules: First day — One-mile novice, three-mile Berkshire county championship, one-mile invitation, five-mile record, professional; one-half-mile open, two-mile invitation, three-mile B. C. W. championship, five-mile handicap, open. Second day — One-half-mile invitation, three-mile professional, two-mile open, five-mile handicap, invitation; one-mile three-minute class, open; one-mile professional; three-mile record, invitation; five-mile record, open; one-mile consolation. Entries close 4 Sept. with W. S. Kells, secretary. The club now has forty-one members, and is in a very prosperous condition in every respect.

PITTSBURG is to have a grand race meeting, 18 Sept., at Exposition Park, under the auspices of the four clubs of that vicinity, the Keystones, Allegheny Cyclers, Sewickley Valley Wheelmen, and Pittsburg Wheelmen.

THE East Hartford Wheel Club has instructed its racing committee to arrange for a series of club races to be held once or twice a month.

AT a meeting of the directors of the Lynn Cycle Track Association, held last week, it was voted to raise both turns of the track one foot; also to dig up the homestretch a distance of fifteen feet from the curb, and the backstretch ten feet from the curb, and fill in with a mixture composed of clay and finely screened blue gravel. It is believed that a smoother surface will be thus secured, and that the track will be made somewhat faster than it now is.

THE CLUB.

THE District Wheelmen of Washington, D. C., elected the following officers for one year, 8 July: Ballard Morris, president; S. O. Edmonds, captain; George A. H. Mills, lieutenant; N. L. Collamer, secretary.

AT a meeting in Eliot Hall, Jamaica Plain, last week, thirteen gentlemen signified their intention to join a bicycle club if formed, and elected G. F. McCausland, president; J. Howard Edwards, vice-president; Edward J. Woodworth, secretary and treasurer; directors, president and secretary, and H. A. Cardinal, E. C. Chase, and C. A. Underwood. H. A. Cardinal, C. A. Underwood, and E. C. Chase were instructed to prepare a constitntion and by-laws, and to report at the next meeting.

THE following officers were elected by the Berkshire County Wheelmen at the semi-annual meeting, Tuesday, 6 July: President, E. H. Kennedy; vice-president, J. N. Robbins; secretary, M. S. Kelly; treasurer, H. G. West; captain, C. C. Kennedy; first lieutenant, W. H. Sheridan; second lieutenant, H. J. Grant.

COMING EVENTS.

JULY.

23 Friday. — Races of the Trojan Wheelmen, at Renssalaer Park, Troy, N. Y.

31 Saturday. — Races of the Chicago Bi. Club, on the bal grounds. Entries close 24 July, to F. A. Ingalls, 189 Michigan avenue.

AUGUST.

3 Tuesday. — Clerical wheelmen's tour starts from New York City. Rev. Sylvanus Stall, Lancaster, Penn., promoter.

9 Monday. — Iowa division tour leaves Des Moines for five days' tour to Spirit Lake, Iowa, where fall meet will occur.

14 Saturday. — Race meeting by Iowa division, at Spirit Lake.

19 Thursday. — Annual meet and races of the Pennsylvania Division as guests of the Williamsport (Pa.) Bi. Club.

26, 27, and 28 Thursday–Saturday. — Race meeting of the Cleveland Bicycle Club.

28 Saturday. — Annual meet and races of the New Jersey division, at Millville, N. J.

SEPTEMBER.

3, 4 Friday, Saturday. — New York division meet and races, at Buffalo, N. Y.

6 Monday. — L. A. W. tour from Rochester, to end at Harper's Ferry on 16 September.

Annual meet Ohio division, at Massillon, Ohio.

8, 9 Wednesday, Thursday. — Annual race meeting of the Connecticut Bicycle Club, at Charter Oak Park, Hartford, Conn.

10, 11 Friday, Saturday. — Annual tournament Berkshire County Wheelmen, at Pittsfield, Mass.

14 to 17 Tuesday to Friday. — Springfield Bi. Club's annual tournament, at Hampden Park, Springfield, Mass.

18 Saturday. — Races at Pittsburg, Penn.

21, 22, 23 Tuesday-Thursday. — Bicycle races at Junction City, Kansas. Apply to Charles S. Davis, Junction City, Kansas.

23, 24, 25 Thursday-Saturday. — Fall tournament of Lynn Track Association, at Glenmere Park, Lynn, Mass.

MISCELLANEOUS

Advertisements will be inserted in this column for one cent a word, including heading and address; but no advertisement will be taken for less than twenty-five cents.

BICYCLES. — Fair prices and spot cash paid for desirable second-hand wheels. BUTMAN & CO., 89 Court Street.

BICYCLES AND TRICYCLES received on consignment; no charges made when goods are furnished in exchange. BUTMAN & CO., Oriental Building, 89 Court Street.

FOR SALE. — One 54-inch, '86 pattern, Rudge Light Roadster; run ten miles, $120; guaranteed in perfect condition. Address Box 2571, Boston.

BICYCLES AND TRICYCLES. — 125 shop-worn and second-hand wheels now on exhibition. Stock constantly changing; no price list; correspondence and inspection invited; open Saturday evenings. BUTMAN & CO., Scollay Square, Oriental Building.

BICYCLES AND TRICYCLES. — Bargains for cash; wheels not sold on instalments nor rented. BUTMAN & CO., 89 Court Street.

BICYCLES AND TRICYCLES. — Specialty in furnishing new wheels for exchange. BUTMAN & CO., Scollay Square, Oriental Building.

RUDGE RACERS.
ATTENTION RACING MEN.

1 53 Rudge Racer, used twice,			.	$90.00.
1 54 " " used three times			.	90.00.
1 55 " " never used			.	90.00.
1 57 " " "			.	90.00.

Saddle on backbone, and all latest improvements. Apply early.

STODDARD, LOVERING & CO.,
152 to 158 CONGRESS ST., BOSTON.

ENGLISH RECORD ON AN
2.34 4/5. INVINCIBLE.

GIDEON & BROWN, American Agts.,
PHILADELPHIA.

HOLDFAST© TIRE CEMENT
PUT UP IN 2 OZ. STICKS
PRICE 20 CTS.
SENT POST PAID ON RECEIPT OF PRICE
= H. B. HART, 811 ARCH ST. PHILA. =

PATENTS

Secured on reasonable terms. Work reliable. Papers carefully and legally drawn. Special attention given to inventions in cycling by an experienced wheelman. Write for particulars.

N. L. COLLAMER · · · Patent Attorney,
WASHINGTON, D. C.

Who climbed up Corey?
I, said the STAR,
With my Curved Handle Bar;
I climbed up Corey.

And verily the STAR doth it every time. Read the Record, and see if it hasn't won every Corey Hill Contest, and then get one of

W. W. STALL, 509 Tremont St., BOSTON, MASS.

OIL IF YOU WANT THE BEST **ENAMEL**

———— THAT IS ————

THE FACILE

And if your local dealer does not keep it and will not get it, send direct to headquarters for it. It cannot be mailed; but six or more bottles of OIL, or four or more of ENAMEL, will be sent, carriage-paid, to any place east of the Rockies and having an express office, on receipt of the price.

If you want the best Duplicating Apparatus, Fountain Pen, Type-Writer, or Automatic Postal Scale — I SELL THEM.

If you want the Best Roadster Bicycle, suppose you send for Descriptive Price List, and look into the FACILE, which, by the way, is not a "new" machine but is proved by seven years' hard and increasing use, by all sorts of persons, under all sorts of conditions. It is greatly improved this year, and the price is reduced five dollars. Mention this paper, and write to

J. WILCOX, 33 Murray St., New York.   DOWNES & WOODWARD, Agents for Boston and Vicinity, 23 Water St.
AGENTS WANTED.

ON THE ROAD THE COLUMBIAS ON THE PATH

Boston, July 6, 1886.

The records made and the prizes won by riders of COLUMBIAS during the season of 1885 are familiar to wheelmen. Appended is a recapitulation of the more important victories for riders of COLUMBIAS during the opening of the present season.

SMASHED RECORDS ON COLUMBIAS.

GEO. M. HENDEE AT SPRINGFIELD,
July 5.

½-MILE (World's Record)	1.52.
1-MILE (World Amateur Record; Fastest Mile ever made in Competition) . .	2.34.

WM. A. ROWE AT LYNN,
July 5.

4 MILES (World's Record)	11.05.
5 MILES (World's Record)	13.57 2-5.
6 MILES (World's Record)	16.47.
7 MILES (World's Record)	19.38.
8 MILES (World's Record)	22.34 2-5.
9 MILES (World's Record)	25.18.
10 MILES (World's Record)	28.03 2-5

THE COLUMBIAS AT BOSTON,
May 29.

1-MILE L. A. W. BICYCLE CHAMPIONSHIP RACE	A. B. RICH.
1-MILE L. A. W. TRICYCLE CHAMPIONSHIP RACE	A. B. RICH.

THE COLUMBIAS AT LYNN,
May 31.

1-MILE OPEN RACE	W. A. ROWE.
3-MILE RACE, 9.45 CLASS	CHAS. E. WHITTEN.
1-MILE RACE, 3.20 CLASS	CHAS. E. WHITTEN.
5-MILE OPEN RACE	GEO. M. HENDEE.
3-MILE HANDICAP RACE	CHAS. E. WHITTEN.
5-MILE PROFESSIONAL RACE, AMERICAN CHAMPIONSHIP, JOHN S. PRINCE.	

Six Firsts out of a possible Eight, and Two Seconds, won on Columbias.

THE COLUMBIAS AT NEW HAVEN,
June 11, 12.

1-MILE OPEN RACE	W. A. ROWE.
3-MILE OPEN RACE	GEO. M. HENDEE.
2-MILE HANDICAP RACE	W. F. KNAPP.
20-MILE COLUMBIA CUP RACE	A. B. RICH.
1-MILE RACE, 3.05 CLASS	E. A. DeBLOIS.
5-MILE LAP RACE	GEO. M. HENDEE.
1-MILE BOYS' RACE	F. A. CLARK.
3-MILE OPEN RACE	W. A. ROWE.
3-MILE HANDICAP RACE	E. A. DeBLOIS.

Every Open Event won on Columbias.

THE COLUMBIAS AT LYNN,
June 17.

1 MILE NOVICE RACE	S. L. TRUESDALE.
1-MILE OPEN RACE	W. A. ROWE.
	Time, 2.37 2-5.
3-MILE LAP RACE	GEO. M. HENDEE.
2-MILE HANDICAP RACE	F. S. HITCHCOCK.
1-MILE PROFESSIONAL TRICYCLE RACE, WORLD'S RECORD, T. W. ECK. .	
	Time, .42 2-5.

CHAMPIONSHIPS ON COLUMBIAS,
Season of 1886.

1-MILE BICYCLE	L. A. W. CHAMPIONSHIP.
1-MILE TRICYCLE	L. A. W. CHAMPIONSHIP.
4-MILE BICYCLE	N. A. A. A. CHAMPIONSHIP.
10-MILE BICYCLE	L. A. W. CHAMPIONSHIP.

THE COLUMBIAS IN THE WEST.

THE RECORD BROKEN.—SPLENDID PERFORMANCE OF S. P. HOLLINSWORTH.

INDIANAPOLIS, IND., June 19.—S. P. Hollinsworth, of Russiaville, was wonderfully successful in his attempt to beat the long-distance amateur bicycle record of this country and Great Britain. He completed his task at Greenfield this morning at 4 o'clock, and in the 24 hours scored a total of 281 9-10 miles. His actual riding time was 21 hours and 23 minutes, 2 hours and 37 minutes being lost in eating and in being rubbed down. Heretofore the best American record was 259½ miles, made by Munger, of Detroit, at Boston, while the English record is 266. The best track record is 276.— *Special Despatch to the Boston Herald.*

This record was made on a 55-inch COLUMBIA LIGHT ROADSTER. — *Indianapolis Times.*

THE COLUMBIAS IN NEW JERSEY,
June 19.

25-MILE INTER-CLUB ROAD RACE	E. H. VALENTINE.
On Columbia Light Roadster.	

THE COLUMBIAS AT BROOKLYN,
June 19.

1-MILE NOVICE RACE.
2-MILE HANDICAP RACE.
3-MILE HANDICAP RACE.
2-MILE CHAMPIONSHIP RACE, BEDFORD CYCLE CLUB.
5-MILE NEW YORK STATE CHAMPIONSHIP RACE.
The above Events won on Columbias.

LONG-DISTANCE RIDERS ON COLUMBIAS.
Season of 1886.

AROUND THE WORLD (ON THE WAY) . . . . . . THOMAS STEVENS.
FROM NEW YORK TO SAN FRANCISCO (ON THE WAY), F. E. VanMEERBEKE.
FROM NEW YORK TO SAN FRANCISCO (ON THE WAY), S. G. SPIER.
FROM NEW YORK TO SAN FRANCISCO AND RETURN (ON THE WAY),
GEO. B. THAYER, CORRESPONDENT OF THE HARTFORD "POST."

CATALOGUE SENT FREE.

THE POPE MFG. CO.

PRINCIPAL OFFICE, 597 WASHINGTON STREET, BOSTON.

12 Warren St., New York.   Branch Houses: 115 Wabash Ave., Chicago.

THE CYCLE

PUBLISHED EVERY FRIDAY BY ABBOT BASSETT, 22 SCHOOL ST., ROOM 19.

VOL. I.   BOSTON, MASS., 30 JULY, 1886.   No. 18.

TERMS OF SUBSCRIPTION.

One Year, by mail, post-paid...........................$1.50
Three Copies in one order........................... 3.00
Club Subscriptions.................................... 1.00
Six Months.. .90
Single Copies... .05

Specimen Copies free.

Every bicycle dealer is agent for the CYCLE and authorized to receive subscriptions at regular rates. The paper can be found on sale at the following places: —

Boston, CUPPLES, UPHAM & Co., cor. Washington and School Streets. Tremont House news stand. At every cycle warehouse.

New York, ELLIOTT MASON, 12 Warren Street.

Philadelphia, H. B. HART, 811 Arch Street. GEORGE D. GIDEON, 6 South Broad Street.

Baltimore, S. T. CLARK & Co., 4 Hanover Street.

Chicago, W. M. DURELL, 115 Wabash Avenue. JOHN WILKINSON & Co., 77 State Street.

Washington, H. S. OWEN, Capital Cycle Co.

St. Louis, ST. LOUIS WHEEL Co., 1121 Olive Street.

ABBOT BASSETT . . . . . EDITOR

A. MUDGE & SON, PRINTERS, 24 FRANKLIN ST., BOSTON

All communications should be sent in not later than Tuesday, to ensure insertion the same week.

Entered at the Post-office at second-class mail matter.

THE Orange Wanderers are indignant at the attack made upon them by Karl Kron in the *Bulletin*. We think they are justly indignant, for nothing that they have done warrants the language used by the New York gentleman. Wheelmen in asserting their rights often forget that others have rights as well as themselves. The circumstances of this case go to show that the Orange wheelmen acted in a spirit of fairness towards those who use the highway, and were willing to put themselves to some inconvenience in the interest of the great public. Public safety will soon call for a lantern and bell after nightfall, and wheelmen will have to submit to highway regulations of this kind. Already laws of this kind have been passed in places near Boston, and we shall have more very soon. Karl Kron's intemperate language, if regarded, will lead to serious difficulties between wheelmen and town authorities.

v THE Racing Board has voted to approve the rules of the A. C. U., and now there can be peace between the two organizations. This does not mean that the League abandons racing, for those who want to, can still employ League rules. The A. C. U. has agreed to admit none but amateurs to amateur races, and this is all the League has ever asked of it. So long as amateurs are protected, it matters not to the League how many classes they divide all others into.

IT has not been strange that the non-wheel press has been full of idle gossip and false reports during the little discussion between the L. A. W. and A. C. U. It was to be expected. The wonder is that a great many of the foolish articles have been reproduced in the *Bulletin*.

THE *Bulletin* is printing very long articles to show that the circulation of that paper is larger than that of any wheel paper in America. No need to dispute this. The *Bulletin* has a very much larger circulation than the CYCLE. We wish we could say otherwise, but we can't.

THE clergymen start on their tour next Tuesday. We suppose they have given Satan such a drubbing that he will not get up while they are away. It is very certain that they will be in better condition to meet him on their return.

THE man who really enjoys wheeling is he who avoids its squabbles and strife, does not spurt, and never rides too far. —*Globe*.

WE are inclined to offer a very liberal reward for the man who can fill this bill. Tastes differ. It was only the other day that a wheelman said to us : " I tell you what it is, there is n't any fun in wheeling unless you can go it like jingo." And yet we believe this man " really enjoys " wheeling. We wonder if our contemporary ever saw a happy man. If not, we would like to show him a wheelman just in from a run, who has " broken up " every other member of his club.

THE League having given up all jurisdiction over road racing, there was a very unusual mingling of professionals and amateurs on the occasion of McCurdy's ride. We don't know that any harm was done, but it cannot occur again, for the A. C. U. will take up what the L. A. W. has abandoned, and men must keep to their own class in road racing as well as path racing.

MR. A. KENNEDY-CHILD, who was one of the first to discourage the times made at Springfield and elsewhere, arrived last Monday and intends to remain with us for a year, perhaps more. He will locate in Hartford, where he has friends. He appeared anxious to meet the editor of the late *Cyclist ana Athlete*, who promised him a coat of tar and feathers, as he never liked to disappoint any one, and was also anxious to pay his respects to Mr. Aaron, of the *Bulletin*. He speaks well of the League, and thinks they have made a mark by standing by their rules, and is apparently not in sympathy with the N. C. U. of England for their recent backdown in the amateur wrangle. —*Jenkins in Sporting Life*.

THE Racing Board, in formal resolution, date of 9 July, disclaims all jurisdiction over road racing, as it " cannot be practised save in defiance of law," and the League." is an organization formed to secure to wheelmen all their rights under the law." As the Board has heretofore neither recognized nor disclaimed road racing, this formal declaration was called for in view of the fast increasing popularity of this department of the sport, and the disclaimer seems just and what should have been expected. As far as its influence on road racing goes, however, that will probably be small. Road racing is so essentially an amateur pastime, a practical sport, so to speak, that brings out the qualities of the every-day rider and the every-day machine, that it is a particularly attractive one, and where roads may be obtained without conflicting with the laws, or arrangements may be made with the authorities, the races may continue to be held and the records broken, while yet not antagonizing the position that the Racing Board takes, or asking of it what it cannot consistently give. — *Providence Journal*.

THE promaturers are to be confined to races among themselves, but the Pope Manufacturing Company controls Rowe, Hendee, Knapp, and Burnham, undoubtedly the best men in America. These four men are not to be allowed to race against each other, but are to be scattered around at various meetings to down all comers from the ranks of rival manufacturers. It is tolerably certain that every promaturer race will fall to the lot of one of these men, and their less speedy rivals will be defeated time after time. It does not stand to reason that the employers of the defeated men will stand this state of affairs long, and in consequence they will withdraw their patronage. The only hope for this class that I can see at present is that some of the second-raters of last season will develop unexpected form, good enough to down the Pope Company and its flying employes, and this seems extremely improbable, as with the exception of the performances of Rowe, Hendee, and Knapp, we have heard of no startling time this season. If things continue as they have begun, the season of 1887 will find the four fast men forming " Promateur Class, Pope Manufacturing Company, managers and proprietors." —*Journal*.

THE vagaries of· bicyclers are extraordinary to the eyes of the non-wheeling citizen. It is not the fashion just now to be seen in knee breeches on ordinary occasions, and the schemes resorted to by out-of-town bicyclers to appear like other people on the streets, when they have come to town in cycling suits, are various and absurd. It is not an uncommon thing, among those who are in the intimacies of such things, to see a man wearing long trousers over his short ones.

But the most novel of all these methods of concealment that have come to the Historian's knowledge is that adopted by young Mr. Q——, of Waltham, who goes about these hot days wearing a long seersucker duster, that comes clear down to his heels, as a disguise. — *Record.*

THE wheeling mania seems to have a permanent hold in Hartford. Local wheelmen, particularly those of the new Hartford Wheel Club, are like the typical Irishman with the chip, always looking for a race. They have taken part in a number of races already, including a 20-mile road race of their own, the State road race of the same length, and the East Hartford spring meet. It is understood the Connecticut Bicycle Club will reserve one race for the Hartford Wheel Club at the big meet 8 and 9 September. But the riders cannot wait for that, and have races arranged at Charter Oak Park for Wednesday next. Half a dozen wheelmen on bicycles and tricycles can be seen speeding almost every evening at the park. Once a week also there is a miscellaneous gathering at the park of wheelmen from all the clubs within a radius of several miles, and there is some very good speeding. The women are riding a good deal this summer, though they prefer the cool evenings to the daytime. Several,tandems are owned here, and these, with the light special tricycles made at the Weed shops here, are the sorts most used.— *Springfield Republican.*

THE Coventry Machinists' Co. have come out with a new tricycle which·is thus spoken of by the *News:* We have been enjoying a ride upon a tricycle which the Coventry Machinists'.Co. have just made to the specification of a distinguished amateur. It differs but slightly from the standard pattern of the "Marlboro'" Club," but it is in these trifling details that the excellence of such a machine, for fast riding, consists. A twenty-four-inch steering wheel, combined with the coiled-wire springs on the fork ends, reduces the vibration wonderfully, and as the machine has full-sized rubbers in the hollow rims, the motion is exceedingly smooth and comfortable, albeit the low handles, full-length cranks, and sixty-inch gearing combine to make it essentially a tricycle for speed.

WILLIAM B. PAGE, of the University of Pennsylvania, high jumper and cyclist, arrived at Glens Falls, N. Y., 11 July, on his annual bicycling tour, which he proposes shall this season extend over a distance of two thousand miles. This is Mr. Page's fifth annual bicycle trip, and when he is completed he will have travelled nearly 7,000 miles. In 1882 he covered 260 miles ; in 1883, 200 miles ; in 1884, 1,400 miles ; and in 1885, 1,188½ miles. During four consecutive days of his last trip he made 398 miles, and on a single day 141 miles.

THE committee on the illuminated parade at St. Louis have wisely seen the advantage of making it the centre of a series of cycling events, and grasping the opportunity changed the date of the parade to Friday, 1 October, with a road race Saturday morning; races at Union Park Saturday afternoon, a concert and general good time in the evening, with a run to DeSoto the day following. The whole occasion to be a Western inter-State meet. With this idea the chief consuls of the Western States have been addressed by Chief Consul Rodgers.

MR. SUMNER B. ELY, of Chicago, and Mr. Harry Slade. of Quincy. started for a trip to Portland, Me., last Tuesday, on bicycles.

CONTRIBUTORS' CLUB.

" REPRESSIVE " LEGISLATION.

Editor of the Cycle: The Orange riding district is composed of the·city of Orange and the adjoining townships of East Orange, South Orange, West Orange, Bloomfield, and Montclair. In this district are about 100 miles of macadam roads, which offer to wheelmen very great advantages.

There have always been many cyclists in this district, but the past fifteen months have shown a remarkable growth in their number. This increase has been largely due to the opening of four stores dealing in wheels and their accessories, and to the activity of the local club. The dealers have rented cycles, taught numbers to ride, and sold dozens of machines. Beside these recruits, there are many who have hired bicycles and tandems occasionally, and so become more or less interested in cycling. The activity of the Orange Wanderers has resulted in doubling their club membership (now forty-six), and in a number of successful public entertainments. A new club, the East Orange Wheelmen, has also been formed.

Perusal of these facts will indicate that the riders living in the Orange district are now numbered by hundreds, while many others from the immediate vicinity, Newark, Elizabeth, etc., are constantly using our roads. This large number inevitably contains some persons not too careful of others' rights. It is noticeable here, as elsewhere, that there are some riders who often ignore the fact that others than themselves have any rights upon the road.

The Orange common council some time ago took into consideration an ordinance to compel cycles to carry lanterns after dark, and a bell or whistle at all times, in order to give notice of approach. When the Orange Wanderers learned that such action was certain to be taken, they decided to advocate it, in order to secure its passage in a reasonable form, and to put themselves on record as favoring suitable regulations. The club membership embraces business men, clerks, ministers, doctors, lawyers, and ladies. It is not·a youthful organization, and it is fully competent to judge of the necessities of its situation.

It seems hardly necessary to enter upon a

defence of the practice of carrying lanterns and bells. The simple fact that a cycle moves noiselessly, without giving warning of its approach, and so startles both pedestrians and horses when suddenly meeting or passing them, *especially at night*, is sufficient reason why lanterns and bells should be carried. It is perfectly preposterous to assert that other vehicles move without noise on macadam roads. Their approach is easily distinguished at a considerable distance. It is not pedestrians and teams, however, which *alone* may suffer. Accidents between wheelmen are constantly barely avoided, because cycles rush unannounced almost upon one another. I have seen accidents escaped by a hair's-breadth where the parties had no lanterns, which would not have been possible had they carried them.

A large proportion of our wheelmen are forced by their business hours to ride chiefly in the evening. Throughout the season, also, very many carriages are upon the road every night. It is consequently of the highest importance that such habits should be formed as will be most fair to all, and will reduce the possibility of accidents to a minimum.

Some wheelmen have comp'ained of the passage of an ordinance bearing upon cyclists. I fail to see the force of their objections. They have gotten used to riding in the dark themselves, and do not want to be forced to carry a light. But reflection will surely show them that they have a duty to perform to others, and that they must respect the rights of others if they in turn wish to have their own rights respected. It is certainly a common right of every one to have reasonable notice of the approach of every vehicle, and this cannot be given by cycles at night. unless a lantern is carried, and in the daytime a bell or whistle.

No one is more ready than I to demand for wheelmen their full rights, and no club will do more than the one of which I have the honor to be the executive officer, to maintain them. But I believe, with my club, that it is just as much our duty to secure fair play *from* wheelmen as fair play *to* wheelmen, and that by acting fairly toward others we shall best secure fairness toward ourselves.

The people of the Oranges are in every way favorably disposed toward cyclists, and few "road hogs" exist to annoy us. The ordinances passed by Orange and West Orange are not aimed at any rights, but are simply an attempt to protect non-wheelmen. I beg the cyclists of our vicinity to consider the matter in this light, and to act in accordance with the very simple requirements of the law.

There is no reason to suppose that strangers will be subjected to any undue annoyance. A kindly feeling exists toward wheelmen, and the police of the towns have often shown themselves to be considerate· and obliging. The question is a simple one of fair play. Cycles advance very rapidly and entirely noiselessly. All other vehicles make a considerable noise, which gives warning of their approach.

If one occasionally finds it necessary to run a short distance·upon a side path, it is proper that he should politely request pedestrians to give way, and not violently ring them off. But on the road, it is folly to try

to depend upon the voice, though of course it is sometimes best to use it. A bell or whistle is necessary.

When an educated man, presumably a gentleman, deliberately indulges in a violent attack upon a reputable organization, his conduct receives the contempt of all fair-minded men. When such a man not only makes an attack, but throws aside the habits of polite society, and even ignores common decency in the grossness of his language, he exhibits his character in a most unfavorable light. And the cause for all this is simply that the man does not approve of some action taken by the said organization, though it is none of his business at all. It is hardly necessary to add that the wishes of such a man need not be much respected.

A certain Mr. Lyman H. Bagg, known in the wheel press by the pen name of "Karl Kron," is such a person.

Mr. Bagg finds vent for his spleen in characterizing the action of the Orange Wanderers as "stupid betrayal;" "atrocious and unaccountable . . . act of treachery;" "unpardonable sin;" "accursed folly;" "intolerable effrontery;" and "a monumental blunder which is worse than a crime."

The Orange Wanderers care nothing for Mr. Bagg, or for any man capable of writing so vulgar a letter. They do, however, resent the use of the insulting language which characterized his attack on page 80 of the *Bulletin*. Every wheelman who is acquainted with the club knows the members full well as enthusiastic cyclists. Of course, the Orange Wanderers do not expect to have all wheelmen agree with them; but when they disagree, and publish their opinions, it is only fair to expect that ordinary courtesy will be shown.

Mr. Bagg tries to bolster up his attack by referring to what, he says, are the sentiments of their most experienced and distinguished member, L. H. Johnson.

I know Mr. Johnson as a gentleman, a fellow club member, and, I trust, a friend. It is somewhat singular that the assertion that he is "bitterly hostile " to the club's action should come first from a stranger and non-resident.

When the matter was discussed in club meeting, Mr. Johnson did not oppose it. I am not sure that he was in the rooms at the time, but if he was not, he was not farther off than down one flight of stairs at his office, and he certainly knew what was to be done. There was no dissenting voice on the motion.

I am loth to believe, under these circumstances, that Mr. Johnson has been correctly reported. The time for opposition was when the matter was being discussed. I cannot think that he, if opposed to it, would remain silent at the time, and afterwards attack his club.

Though, in Mr. Bagg's elegant language, the Orange Wanderers are but a " crowd of smooth-spoken camp followers," whom he wants to hold ▴ . . up to the lasting execration of every wheelman," we shall pursue our course as peacefully, and probably quite as prosperously, as heretofore.

LUTHER H. PORTER,
President Orange Wanderers.

16 JULY, 1886.

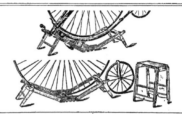

BICYCLE STAND AND CAMP STOOL.

PATENTED AND MANUFACTURED BY A. W. GUMP, DAYTON, O.

THE above cuts show the new bicycle stand and camp stool which has been patented by A. W. Gump, of Dayton, O.

As shown by the engraving, it can be used for holding the bicycle when not in use. The bicycle can be inverted when it is necessary to clean it, so that the wheels revolve, making it easier to remove mud and dirt. The bicycle stand can instantly be converted into a camp stool, or it can be folded into very small space. It is strong and light and holds the bicycle firmly. It is made of ash, varnished on the wood, and weighs five and one half pounds. It is easily adjustable to different sized bicycles.

The stand is meeting with popular favor, and it will undoubtedly have a large sale among riders and dealers. The manufacturers will supply it made of black walnut or other fine woods, and the trimmings can be nickel-plated. The clubs will probably go in for the better quality stands, and they will do for prizes.

THE JOHN O'GROATS' RECORD.

THIS record is coming down to very small figures. Now we have the eight hundred and sixty-one miles traversed by G. P. Mills, of the Anfield Bicycle Club, in five days, one hour and forty-five minutes, beating the best previous record by one day, six hours and forty minutes. He rode an ordinary bicycle, 53-inch Humber, with ball bearing head. Mr. Mills started from Land's End at midnight, 11 July, and helped on by pacemakers and fellow clubmen, he reached Edinburgh in three days. After leaving Perth he encountered a heavy wind, which blew against him till the finish, reaching John O'Groats at 1.45 on Saturday morning. Mills is not satisfied with this record, and says that if it had not been for wind, he would have made two hundred miles a day.

WILCOX'S RECORD.

GORMULLY & JEFFERY, Chicago, Ill.

Gentlemen: I have the pleasure to inform you that my champion and I have to-day covered the following distances in the following time, viz. : — Twenty miles in 1.15.; 3.; twenty-five miles, in 1.42.2. ; fifty-one miles, in 3.52, straight away, over a hilly road and a bad head wind, Messrs. Gleason and

Hutto, of Tipton ; Wainwright and Allen, of Noblesville, and Wilson and Huess, of Greenfield, acting as timers. The hundred miles were made in 9h. 10m. I believe that these records have never been touched by a heavy roadster, and you understand that the route was fifty-one miles long, not crossing a ten-mile stretch of perfect road. — Respectfully yours,

E. H. WILCOX.

INDIANAPOLIS, 17 July, 1886.

G. LACY HILLIER'S OPINION.

CHAIRMAN BASSETT, of the CYCLE, is having a hard time of it in America ; and if it will help him any in the lot he has chosen, he has the sincere sympathy of all right-thinking Englishmen, who can admire one man's efforts against the tide of popular feeling to keep some of the real meaning of " amateur " about the definition of a cycle rider. Mr. Bassett is being abused all round, as far as we can see, and any scribe who is hard up for a subject to write upon at once pounces on the unfortunate Chairman of the Racing Board, and does not rest till he has done his best to hold him in print up to the ridicule which touches the feelings so deeply of most men. Bassett, however, seems unaffected by these endeavors to turn him from the path of duty, and his list of suspends grows larger and larger. The respect we once felt for the American racing man gets less and less, and we wonder where sport and sporting instincts are going to in the gulf of time, and whether they will ever rise again to the respectable height they once occupied. People talk about the makers over here controlling the press ; but no one can say the English papers, as a rule, lose all respect for their principles by backing up a state of things such as this, which is rotten to the core. Looking at the various American papers, the CYCLE seems to us the only one which goes heartily against the makers' amateur, and we respect Chairman Bassett for having principles, and not being afraid to stick to them. — *Bicycling News.*

NOTES OF A CYCLIST.

THE new Rover looks like a better machine than the earlier ones. The frame appears more rigid and decidedly stronger. I believe it is also lighter, and it seems a trifle less sensitive. If it will stand the strain of steady work, it ought to become popular.

A MONTHLY bicycle paper is to make its appearance in San Francisco in August. It is to be called the *Pacific Wheelman.*

RHODE ISLAND wheelmen have been eating clams this week at Crescent Park, Providence. After they have finished eating, it is thought there will be shells enough to build a new road across the State.

"I. C. U. are getting the A. C. U. and the N. C. U. confounded," said Brown to a newspaper reporter. "L. A. W.! js that so ?" said he of the press gang. The future is full of promises for confusion in this matter, and the lay press will soon get into a horribly dazed state regarding the two unions.

THE New Orleans tourists, A. M. Hill, C. M. Fairchild, and H. W. Fairfax, have published a letter of thanks to the members of the League for the kindness and courtesy shown them during their trip. The letter concludes as follows : "To all of these clubs and gentlemen we tender our heartfelt thanks. They made our tour pleasant and enjoyable when otherwise it would have been most tedious."

LAST Saturday afternoon, George A., the twelve-year-old son of Howard Perley, a well-known citizen of Lynn, and Neil, a young son of S. Henry Kent. went to Nahant on their bicycles. A visit to Spouting Horn was proposed, where the two lads alighted and walked upon the rock. In some manner young Perley slipped from the rock into the ocean and was drowned. The body could not be found, the strong undertow at this point evidently carrying it far out into the sea.

THE Citizens' Club, of New York, held their monthly meeting last week, and about twenty put in appearance. One or two members were elected, and the by-laws changed to allow the tricyclers to have a lieutenant who takes care of his division while on a run. Mr. George Martin Huss was unanimously elected, and T. C. Smith was selected as captain in place of Simeon Ford, who recently resigned, owing to increased business cares that prevented his giving the proper attention to the office. Mr. Fred G. Bourne, who recently returned from the other side, where he had gone in search of health, was warmly received.

WILLIAM FORBES, of Morrisonville, Ill., is a wheelman of more than local celebrity. He is a somnambulist as well. A few nights ago he arose in his sleep, put on his hat and his night-clothes, bestrided his bicycle, and struck out at a prize-winning rate through the streets of the slumbering village. He was headed off by the night watchman, who was not afraid of ghosts on wheels. With difficulty he was awakened from his dream as the champion wheelman of the world.

JO PENNELL has been escorted across the French border and allowed to return to England. He was in prison for ten hours on one occasion, and a whole day on another. He is now free to use his pencil, and will probably tell us all about his prison life.

FRED T. SHOLES, of Cleveland, is on a wheel trip from New York to the Catskills.

THE INVINCIBLE

Has not a very long list of records to show; but as it is the BEST TRICYCLE MADE, it does not need them. Quarter-mile WORLD'S RECORD, 41 2-5s., was made on an Invincible. Send for Catalogue to

GIDEON & BROWN - - - Philadelphia, Pa.

THIS SPACE RESERVED

———— FOR ————

JENS F. PEDERSEN,

MANUFACTURER OF

MEDALS,

1 1-2 Maiden Lane - - - NEW YORK.

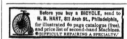

THE last candidate for popular favor which has reached this side is a beautiful crank machine called the Regent. It is a light roadster, — very light, in fact, for it weighs somewhat less than the Rudge, and about the same as the Humber Light Roadster.

IT is built by Trigwell, Watson & Co., of ball-bearing head fame, and of course has that valuable feature. It also has a new pattern direct spoke which does not screw into the hub. The spoke has a substantial head at the hub end, which keeps it firmly in place there, and is fastened at the rim with thread and nipple. The forks are full; the bar dropped at the ends, where it is curved slightly back, and has **T** handles. Backbone is oval; rubber seven-eighth and three-quarter, with very large surface exposed. Cranks with six-inch throw. Bown's bearings.

IT is a very rigid feeling machine, and quite taking in its lines. I shall be anxious to see how it stands road work. It looks as if it ought to do well with a good light rider.

. I HAVE become a thorough convert to the spade or **T** handle. I have recently put the former upon my light roadster, and I find them such· an improvement that I wonder how I ever got along without them. I shall certainly never have another wheel with anything else. They make my bars over thirty-one inches long, and I find that they are far more comfortable than any other length or style I have previously tried. For ordinary pear handles, I found twenty-eight inches to be a very good length, and thirty inches was too long. The grip on the spade handle makes the difference.　　　5678.

PATENTS.

CYCLING patents granted 21 July, 1886 : —
H. J. Lawson, Coventry, Eng., velocipede.

F. H. Stevens, Gloucester, Mass., oil can.
A. Vick, Mount Carmel, Conn., velocipede.

CYCLETS.

THE illuminated parade at St. Louis is set down for 1 Oct., and a very elaborate affair is promised.

THREE Providence wheelmen have been making a run to New York. They went through all right, but they tell great stories of walking through Rhode Island and Connecticut sand under the broiling rays of a not too frigid sun.

ANOTHER party of Providence wheelmen have ridden to Boston and gone on to New Hampshire. Why is it that the Providence men are leaving the State? Can the enforcement of the prohibitory law have anything to do with it?

W. M. WOODSIDE is to shortly attempt the feat of riding a bicycle twenty-one miles in an hour, at either Springfield or Lynn, Mass. "Woody" is reported to be in grand shape now. He is under the care of Wm. J. Morgan.

PRINCE writes us that he will soon try and put twenty-one miles into sixty minutes at Chicago. He has faith to believe that he can do it.

ENGLISH cycling firms have borrowed an American idea, and now the fences, rocks, and old buildings in the rural districts are ornamented with advertisements.

H. O. DUNCAN has won the championship of France over Terront and DeCivry. He made six and one quarter miles in 20.48.

PERCY STONE, of St. Louis, went down to Columbus and took in all the best prizes. Who says a rolling stone gathers no — prizes? Percy captured six firsts and one third prize. In the two-mile handicap, the limit man was given three hundred yards. Still Percy came in first by two hundred feet; made the first one half mile in 1.17, one mile in 2.52 ; two miles in 6.01.

A BOSTON wheelman rode on the sand from Crescent Beach to the Point of Pines last week. He said it was a harder job than a fifty-mile ride on the road.

THE Newburyport pike is now in fine wheeling order. We have n't had as much poetry written about this pike as has been put upon paper about the Lancaster pike, but we have an idea that there is a big field for poetry between Maplewood and Saugus.

NEW names are found on the championship list this year.

OYSTERS are to be avoided at present, but clams can be taken with impunity, likewise with melted butter.

THE Mayor, his wife, and the civil engineer of Chelsea, Mass., are all wheel enthusiasts. What a delightful town this should be ! For instance, if Mrs. Mayor should happen to wheel into a rut, and get a shaking up, Mr. Mayor could issue an order for the improvement of the street, which the civil engineer would be only too happy to carry out. — *Wheel.*

THE CYCLE entered the race for public favor with a heavy handicap, but in spite of his arduous duties on the racing board, Editor Bassett has managed to send his paper well to the front. — *Globe.*

IRELAND is to be represented at the Springfield tournament this fall by a specially imported team of racing men.

THE Lynn cycle track will be ready for use in a few days. It is said to be much faster than it was before the improvements.

T. L. INGRAM, the champion amateur of the Southern States, has retired from the path after four years of most successful racing.

MR. F. W. PERRY, of the Massachusetts Club, started Friday afternoon to wheel to the home of his parents in Bridgport, Ct., *via* Worcester, Springfield, Hartford, and New Haven. We imagine that it will be a peripatetic trip very largely.

THE League membership rolls were last week increased by the addition of 124 new names.

THE Worcester Bicycle Club has arranged for a field day, to occur in about three weeks.

IT is understood that L. D. Munger has retired from the racing arena for the rest of the season. His connection with W. B. Everett & Co. has ceased.

IT has not yet been decided whether or not the Boston Club will join the A. C. U,, but there is every reason to believe that it will. The previous vote was conditional upon an expense of $5 to join, but the club dues of the A. C. U. are $10.

MR. C. S. HOWARD desires us to state that he is no longer the Boston correspondent of the *Wheel,* and therefore should not be held responsible for what appears in the Boston letter.

McCurdy's course was measured carefully with a cyclometer, and proved to be $\frac{1}{16}$ of a mile over 12½ miles in two circuits. He made eleven double rounds, and is thus entitled to $\frac{6}{16}$ extra. Thus we have 275 miles plus 4 miles that he ran additional, and $1\frac{9}{16}$ for the overplus, or $280\frac{9}{16}$ miles in all. He made at the rate of about twelve miles an hour on the last few, and at the end ran up a long flight of steps as lightly as his attendants were able to. His friends claim that he was not so badly done up as has been reported.

A NORTHAMPTON man has invented a new cyclists' whistle, which he guarantees will produce a more fiendish noise than anything of the kind yet placed upon the market. It is a question whether this is· one of the things that " supplies a long felt want."

A CYCLE picnic was gotten up by a suburban club, last week. Ten bikes, eleven trikes, six tandems, eighteen males and fifteen females made up the party. Beautiful day, fine roads, shady trees, mirth and merriment, bountiful lunch, nothing left, safe return. " We 'll try it again."

BEFORE Rowe went into racing he was a good laster. This is why he is so good a long-distance man.

MRS. GARDNER's lodging-house at Springfield, has been enlarged preparatory to the reception of the racing men in the fall.

THERE will be a run of the Boston Club to Riverside, (Auburndale) on Sunday, starting from the clubhouse at 10 A. M. A picnic lunch will be served by the steward of the club, providing a sufficient number will attend. Ample opportunity will be afforded for boating, canoeing, and bathing.

AT the last meeting of the Northampton Wheel Club, C. H. Sawyer was elected second lieutenant and C. H. Johnson color-bearer. The club members voted to increase the annual dues to $6.00 a year, and to take immediate steps toward the renting and furnishing of club rooms.

CYCLERS who go into photography should remember that the amateur and professional line is very clearly drawn among the photographers. Those who sell photographs cannot be amateur photographers.

IT is said that the only time McCurdy smiled after his attempt on the twenty-four hour bicycle record, was when a Waltham maiden slapped him vigorously on the back and exclaimed : " You 're a daisy, old boy ; give me your hand." — *Globe.*

Up to the end of June, Van Sicklen led the members of the Chicago Bicycle Club in riding distance, having covered 1,562¾ miles, W. O. Mumford came next with 1,362 miles, and F. A. Ingalls third with 1,283½ miles.

The form of the *American Wheelman* will be changed with the next issue. In future it will be the same size and form as the *Wheelman's Gazette*. Typographically this will be an improvement.

C. D. Vesey, the racing man of Surrey, is now in Canada, and may pay a visit to the States. Vesey has been with us before, and has taken home a good deal of portable property in the form of prizes.

The five-mile L. A. W. championship, which was voted to the Connecticut Club, of Hartford, Conn., and declined when they decided to run under A. C. U. rules, has been located with the New York division, and will be run at the Buffalo races in September.

We have received the bound volume, No. 12, of the *Bicycling World* from the publishers.

Mr. and Mrs. Pennell's *Century* papers on tricycling in Italy are to be issued in book form, with the playful title, "Two Pilgrims' Progress from Fair Florence to the Eternal City of Rome."

Andrew Welton, of New Haven, intends to leave this week on a two weeks' trip to New York, thence up the Hudson to Albany, where he will strike the Erie towpath and follow it to Buffalo. From there he will proceed along the southern coast of Lake Erie, and through northern Ohio and Indiana to Chicago, his destination. Mr. Welton expects to accomplish this journey of over 1,000 miles in fifteen days. He will return by rail.

The second edition of the Essex County Handbook will soon be issued in an enlarged and improved form. George Chinn, of Beverly, is getting it out.

The Bluenose riders are back. Judging from the color of the noses that they have brought with them, the land is misnamed. One rider who has just come from Maine after a hard ride, says he is going to call the Pine Tree State the Land of Broken Noses.

A stock company is being formed in Troy, with a capital of $25,000, for the purpose of building a new quarter-mile board bicycle track, with an elegant grand stand and other conveniences, at Saratoga. Among the subscribers to the stock are members of the Troy Bicycle Club, W. M. Woodside and W. J. Morgan, the professionals. It is proposed to have the first races in August. Pools will be sold on all races.

Put a bicycle track down in Saratoga, and the young bloods will have one more thing to gamble on. Money changes hands freely in Saratoga.

T. G. Blinn, of the Highland Park Wheelmen, left Oakland, Cal., at 5 A. M. 9 July, bound for Santa Cruz. At 9 A. M. he took breakfast at San Jose, and then started over the Santa Cruz mountains, reaching the summit at noon; stopped there an hour for rest and lunch, reached Santa Cruz, via Soquel, at 6.10 P. M.; distance, ninety miles;

actual riding time, 11h. 10m. This is the first time that a wheelman has ridden from Oakland to Santa Cruz over the mountains in one day.

Wilford H. Barber is said to have beaten the world's unicycle record at Rochester, N. Y., 22 July, by making a mile in 3.51. Best previous record, 4.00, by N. E. Kaufman on same track.

In consequence of the disposition shown by certain bicycle riders to disregard the Philadelphia Park regulations, and the reasonable restraints of the law within the built-up portion of the city, the Association for the Advancement of Cycling has decided to lend its aid to prevent "coasting" and reckless riding in the Park, and excessive speed in riding around the City Hall.

The Massachusetts Club headquarters are at East Gloucester, at the Sea Shore House, kept by Mrs. D. C. Voss The house is situated at a fine beach, which offers excellent opportunities of bathing and fishing. The view from the house is unsurpassed. Situated opposite the entrance to Gloucester Bay, all the vessels entering or leaving the harbor can be seen; also the green heights of Magnolia, Norman's Woe, the scene of Longfellow's "Wreck of the Hesperus," can be seen from the piazza of the hotel. The following members of the club have been stopping there for the last two weeks where they have been having a grand time. Second lieutenant J. M. Burr, A. D. Salkeld, T. F. Salkeld, C. B. Goldthwait, E. R. Eaton, and S. R. Eaton. They had as their guests, last Sunday, Capt. A. D. Peck, Jr., W. M.-Farrington, Harry Salkeld, N. Ethier, and C. A. Collins.

The Iowa Division L. A. W. is looking forward to issuing a road map, or rather a series of road maps, of the riding districts of the State.

The case of D. H. Renton against Dr. Beckwith and E. F. Hill came up before Justice Alston last Friday, at Port Richmond, Staten Island, in a preliminary hearing. The witnesses for whom subpœnas were issued not being within reach of the process of law, an adjournment was taken till 22 September, when the case will come up again.

Investigation will reveal the fact that all the records of the present day are held by riders of wheels fifty-six inches or less in size.

Elmer G. Whitney is appointed a representative for Massachusetts.

THE PATH.

THE COLUMBUS TOURNAMENT.

The Southern bicycle tournament was held at Columbus, Ga., 15, 16, and 17 July. There were a number of visiting wheelmen in attendance from St. Louis, Memphis, Montgomery, Macon, and other cities. The attendance of spectators each day was very large. The races were good, and the Southern mile record, 2.56¾, was taken by P. W. Stone, of St. Louis.

FIRST DAY. 15 JULY.

One Mile Novice. — C. H. Dillingham (1), 3.26½; E. L. Pease (2); J. F. Barnett (3).

Half Mile Amateur. — R. H. Polk (1), 2.21; C. H. Dillingham (2).
Five Mile State Championship. — T. L. Ingram (1), 17.24½; C. T. Gurnsey (2).
Half Mile for Boys. — G. H. Mason (1), 1.48½; W. Bedell (2).
One Mile Handicap. — C. H. Dillingham, 250 yds. (1), 2.44; E. L. Pease, 250 yds (2); P. W. Stone, scratch (3), 2.56½.
Half Mile Amateur. — J. A. Lewis (1), 1.26.
Half Mile Handicap. — J. A Lewis (1), 1.26.
Quarter Mile Amateur. — Percy W. Stone (1), 40s.

SECOND DAY. 16 JULY.

Road Race. — P. W. Stone (1).
Two Mile Handicap. — P. W. Stone, scratch (1), 6.01; C. H. Dillingham (2).
One Mile State Championship. — T. L. Ingram (1), 3.02½; C. T. Gurnsey (2).
Half Mile Handicap. — C. H. Dillingham (1), 2.02½; R. H. Polk (2).
One Hundred Yards' Slow Race. — J. B. Whitlock (1), 4.05; C. H. Dillingham (2).
Three Mile Lap. — P. W. Stone (1), 9.57½; J. A. Lewis (2).
Trick and Fancy Riding. — C. H. Dillingham (1).
Half Mile Handicap. — Jno. A. Joseph (1), 1.22½; J. A. Lewis (2); C. H. Dillingham (3).

THIRD DAY. 17 JULY.

Hill Climbing Contest. — Percy W. Stone (1).
One Mile Handicap. — C. H. Dillingham (1), 2.56½; C. H. Dillingham (2).
Half Mile Professional. — Best two in three. Jno. M. Horton (1), 1.31¼, 1.24½; J. H. Polhill (2).
Half Mile Safety Handicap. — R. H. Polk (1), 2.04; C. H. Dillingham (2).
Half Mile Boys' Handicap. — A. Welborn (1), 3.12½; M. Brannon (2).
Ten Mile State Championship. — R. A. Brantley (1), 34.54; C. T. Gurnsey (2).
Half Mile Ride and Run. — C. H. Dillingham (1), 1.20½; C. Jackson (2).
One Mile Time. — C. H. Dillingham (1), 3.54; J. A. Lewis (2).
One Mile Professional. — J. H. Polhill (1), 3.08; J. M. Horton (2).
One Mile Handicap. — P. W. Stone (1), 2.56½; C. H. Dillingham (2).
Half Mile Star. — W. Cook (1), 1.46; C. G. Gauls (2).

The races were run under L. A. W. rules, and the tournament was a success in every way, and will probably become an annual fixture hereafter.

Indianapolis, 15 July. — Races under the auspices of the Indiana L. A. W. Division.

One-Mile Novice. — M. Goodwin (1), 3.11½; W. J. Dixon (2).
Five-Mile State Championship. — L. M. Wainwright (1), 17.03¾; S. F. Hollingsworth (2).
Half-Mile Heat. 1.40 *Class.* — H. Hulman (1), 1.27½; C. R. Crain (2), 1.35.
Two-Mile State Championship. — A. Hulman, 6.28½; W. McWorkman (2).
One-Mile, 3.30 *Class.* — A. Hulman (1), 3.33½; C. R. Crain (2).
One-Mile State Championship. — L. M. Wainwright (1), 3.10¾; H. Hulman (2).

One-Mile Handicap. — J. Zimmerman, 15 seconds (1), 3.15$\frac{4}{5}$; S. P. Hollingsworth (2).

Consolation Race. — L. J. Keck (1); A. B. Cosand (2).

WEST NEW BRIGHTON, N. Y., 17 July. — Races run under auspices of the Staten Island Athletic Club.

Two-Mile Handicap. — A. B. Rich scratch (1), 13$\frac{3}{5}$; E. J. Halstead, 225 yards (2), 14$\frac{3}{5}$.

EAST HARTFORD, 21 July. — Races under auspices E. H. Club.

One-Mile Handicap. — S. S. Terrill, 75, yards (1), 3.07.

Two-Mile Amateur. — H. E. Bidwell (1), 6.16; W. A. Prior (2). Bidwell continued to ride against time for five miles, and made the distance in 16 06$\frac{1}{5}$.

One-Half-Mile Amateur. — S. L. Forbes (1), 1.34$\frac{2}{5}$.

WINONA, MINN., 5 July. — *One-Mile Professional.* — Best two in three. First heat, Grant Bell (1), 3.12$\frac{2}{5}$; R. H. Spear (2), 3.13$\frac{1}{5}$. Second and last heat, Bell (1), 3.34; Spear, 3.34$\frac{1}{2}$.

One-Mile Amateur. — H. C. Schroeder (1), 3.13$\frac{1}{5}$; E. A. Savage (2).

Five-Mile Professional. — Grant. Bell (1), 18.01$\frac{2}{5}$; R. H. Spear (2).

Half-Mile Club. — J. R. Marfield (1), 1.30$\frac{1}{5}$.

Half-Mile Amateur. — H. C. Schroeder (1), 1.28; E. A. Savage (2).

One-Mile Club. — J. R. Marfield (1), 3.07$\frac{3}{5}$; J. J. Wilson (2).

CINCINNATI, O. — Races under auspices of the Avondale Club.

One-Mile Novice. — Frank Andress (1), 3.21$\frac{3}{5}$; M. J. Bell (2).

Two-Mile Amateur. — E. H. Croninger (1), 6.48$\frac{1}{4}$; D. Sammett (2).

Half-Mile Dash. — E. H. Croninger (1), 1.35.

One-Mile Amateur. — B. Burroughs (1), 3.06$\frac{1}{2}$.

Half-Mile Consolation. — T. Estabrook (1), 1.33$\frac{1}{2}$; T. Wayne (2).

ROCHESTER, N. Y., 22 July. — Races under auspices of the Genesee Club.

One-Mile Amateur. — H. S. Kavanaugh (1), 2.50$\frac{1}{2}$.

One-Mile Novice Heat. — H. J. Sinclair (1), 3.12 and 3.18$\frac{1}{2}$.

One-Mile 3.10 *Class.* — E. P. Cochrane (1), 2.58.

Half-Mile L. A. W. Championship. — C. E. Titchener (1), 1.20.

Two-Mile Western State Championship. — E. P. Cochrane (1), 6.25.

Boys' Quarter-Mile. — B. Kenyon (1).

Three-Mile Club Championship. — J. G. Elbs (1), 10.17.

One-Mile Handicap. — E. P. Cochrane, 60 yds. (1), 2.57$\frac{1}{2}$; A. B. Rich, scratch (2).

Five-Mile Amateur. — H. S. Kavanaugh (1), 15.54.

Consolation. — S. H. Rich (1), 3.11$\frac{1}{2}$.

Wilford S. Barber rode to beat the unicycle mile record, and succeeded, time 3.51, beating record by nine seconds.

TROY, N. Y., 23 July. — Races under the auspices of the Troy Club.

One-Mile Handicap. — H. S. Kavanaugh, scratch (1), 3.01$\frac{3}{5}$; A. F. Edmands, 50 yds. (2); A. P. Dunn, 50 yds. (3).

One-Mile Handicap Club Race. — A. F. Edmands, scratch (1), 3.08$\frac{3}{5}$; Smith, 75 yds. (2).

One Hundred Yards Dash. — T. Kennedy (1), 11$\frac{1}{2}$ s.

Half-Mile Horse and Bicycle. — 1st heat, W. J. Morgan (1), 1.30; 2d heat, W. J. Morgan (1), 1.32.

Five-Mile Horse and Bicycle. — Kittie F. (1), 16.32; W. M. Woodside (2), 16.35$\frac{1}{5}$.

WHEELING, W. VA. — W. D. Banker; of the Allegheny Cycle Club, won the thirty-mile road race, held at Wheeling, W. Va., 13 July, under the auspices of the Wheeling Wheelmen. L. E. Shoup, same club, won the fifteen-mile race. The course for the first race was from Wheeling to West Alexander, over the National road, and return, and the course for the second race from West Alexander to Wheeling. The road was rather muddy. Banker's time was 2h. 52$\frac{1}{2}$m. Shoup's time was 1h. 29$\frac{3}{4}$m. L. A. Bell was second and Charles Siddell was third.

JOHN S. PRINCE was defeated at Akron, O., 20 July, in a five-mile race for $100 by W. W. Richardson's trotting mare, Eva R. The mare won by half a second. Time, 16.09$\frac{3}{5}$. The track was sandy.

THE Capital Club held a five-mile race for the Flint cup and the district championship at Washington, 23 July. The contestants were Messrs. Philip Brown, Crist, Seufferle, and Barbour, all of the Capital Club. Brown won by a few feet, with Crist second.

THE fifty-mile road-race of the New Orleans Bi Club, which was fixed for the 20th inst., did not come off. After changing the date twice, and keeping the entries open for a month or more, but three men could be found who were willing to start. A day or two before the 20th, one of the three withdrew, and as it required three starters to make the race, and as no others were willing to attempt the run, the race was declared off. It is possible that if enough entries can be secured, the race may yet be run, sometime or other, just when nobody knows.

THE fifth annual tournament of the Scranton (Pa.) Club will be held at the Scranton Driving Park, 24 Aug.

THE Troy Bi Club will hold races 1 Sept. There will be nine open events.

THE Weedsport Bicycle Club will hold its third annual race meeting at Weedsport, N. Y., Thursday, 19 Aug. The races will be run under L. A. W. rules, and consist of the following events: Half-mile novice, one mile open, half-mile boys' race, one-mile 3.20 class; one-mile tricycle 100-yards slow race, one-mile club handicap, one-mile championship of Central New York, half-mile hands off, one-mile ride and run, three-mile lap race — L. A. W. members only, half-mile time race, time 1.40, and one-mile consolation. Entries close 17 Aug.; entry fee 50 cents for each event. For entries and further particulars address

H. E. RHEUBOTTOM,
Secretary.

FOREIGN RACING NOTES.

THE five miles tricycling championship Scotland was decided at Glasgow on 3 Jul The track was four laps to the mile. Furn vall, who was suffering from the effects of header, and who rode with knee bandage was beaten in the final. Summary — Fir heat — F. W. Allard, 16.24; George Gat house, by six yards. Second heat — P Fu nival, 18.32$\frac{3}{5}$; J. M. Inglis, by a yard. Fin heat — Allard, 20.42$\frac{3}{5}$; Furnivall, by si yards; Gatehouse, by a like distance.

THE first race for the fifty-guinea Irvin Challenge Cup — five mile tricycle — wa run at Lillie Bridge on 3 July, A. E. Langle winning in 16.27$\frac{3}{5}$; J. Lee, second.

W. F. BALL won the mile handicap a Leicester, on Saturday, 3 July, in brillian style, winning from the twenty-five yard mark, by ten yards, in 2.33$\frac{1}{5}$.

THREE Irish championships were decide at Dublin on the 3d, R. J. Mecredy winnin the one-mile tricycle in 3.14$\frac{3}{5}$, the mile bicycle in 2.47$\frac{1}{5}$, and the four-mile bicycle in 11 45$\frac{2}{5}$.

AT Leicester, Eng., 3 July, F. J. Lees won the mile handicap from the fifteen-yards mark in 2.36., and riding out the full distance, made the mile in 2.38., beating the record by 1$\frac{3}{5}$. Howell beat Wood in the five miles; time, 14.59.

Wheeling will not accept Hendee's record as an amateur one, and claims the world's amateur record for Speechly, at 2.34$\frac{1}{5}$.

TRADE NOTES.

COMING EVENTS.

JULY.

31 Saturday. — Races of the Chicago Bi. Club, on the ball grounds. Entries close 24 July, to F. A. Ingalls, 189 Michigan avenue.

AUGUST.

3 Tuesday. — Clerical wheelmen's tour starts from New York City. Rev. Sylvanus Stall, Lancaster, Penn., promoter.

9 Monday. — Iowa division tour leaves Des Moines for five days' tour to Spirit Lake, Iowa, where fall meet will occur.

14 Saturday. — Race meeting by Iowa division, at Spirit Lake.

19 Thursday. — Annual meet and races of the Pennsylvania Division as guests of the Williamsport (Pa.) Bi. Club.

Weedsport (N. Y.) Club races. Entries close 17 August. Address H. E. Rheubottom.

24 Tuesday. — Fifth annual tournament of the Scranton (Penn.) Club. F. C. Hand, Scranton, Penn.

26, 27, and 28 Thursday–Saturday. — Race meeting of the Cleveland Bicycle Club.

28 Saturday. — Annual meet and races of the New Jersey division, at Millville, N. J.

September.

1 Wednesday. — Race meeting of the Troy (N. Y.) Club, nine open races. R. S. Coon, Troy, N. Y.

3, 4 Friday, Saturday. — New York division meet and races, at Buffalo, N. Y. Five-mile L. A. W. championship.

6 Monday. — Grand tour of the L. A. W. from Niagara Falls and Buffalo, through Central and Southern New York, Virginia, and the Shenandoah Valley, winding up at Harper's Ferry, 18 September. Entries now open with the Marshals.

Annual meet Ohio division, at Massillon, Ohio, on invitation of Massillon, Canton, and Alliance Clubs. Apply to Jos. S. Meyer, Jr., 37 N. Market street, Canton, Ohio.

8, 9 Wednesday, Thursday. — Annual race meeting of the Connecticut Bicycle Club, at Charter Oak Park, Hartford, Conn.

10, 11 Friday, Saturday. — Annual tournament Berkshire County Wheelmen, at Pittsfield, Mass.

14 to 17 Tuesday to Friday. — Springfield Bi. Club's annual tournament, at Hampden Park, Springfield, Mass.

18 Saturday. — Races at Pittsburg, Penn.

21, 22, 23 Tuesday–Thursday. — Bicycle races at Junction City, Kansas. Apply to Charles S. Davis, Junction City, Kansas.

23, 24, 25 Thursday–Saturday. — Fall tournament of Lynn Track Association, at Glenmere Park, Lynn, Mass.

October.

1 Friday. — Illuminated parade of wheelmen at St. Louis, Mo. J. S. Rogers, care of *American Wheelman*, St. Louis.

1, 2 Friday, Saturday. — Interstate meet at St. Louis, Mo. Apply to J. S. Rogers.

MISCELLANEOUS

THE THIRD ANNUAL TOURNAMENT

OF THE

CONNECTICUT ✳ BICYCLE ✳ CLUB

Will be held September 8th and 9th, at Charter Oak Park, Hartford.

NOTICE THE PROGRAMME.

FIRST DAY, SEPT. 8.

1-Mile Bicycle, 3.10 Class ··········Amateur
1-Mile Bicycle, 2.40 Class ··········Promateur
3-Mile Open ··········Professional
1-Mile, A. C. U. ··········Championship
2-Mile Handicap ··········Amateur

FANCY RIDING.

1-Mile Tricycle, Open ··········Promateur
3-Mile Bicycle, Open ··········Amateur
10-Mile Lap Race ··········Promateur
1-Mile Team Race ··········Amateur

SECOND DAY.

1-Mile Bicycle ··········Hartford Wheel Club
3-Mile Tricycle, Open ··········Promateur
1-Mile Bicycle, Handicap ··········Professional
1-Mile Bicycle, Open ··········Amateur
1-Mile Bicycle, Open ··········Promateur
5-Mile Bicycle, Lap Race ··········Professional
2-Mile Tandem Tricycle ··········Amateur
5-Mile Bicycle, Open ··········Promateur
5-Mile Bicycle, State Championship ··········Amateur
Consolation Race.

Over $2,000 will be expended in prizes, and it will be the study of the managers to make these the most satisfactory races ever given by the Club.

Address, for Entry Blanks,

GEO. H. BURT, P. O. Box 414 · · · · HARTFORD, CONN.

Vol. I., No. 19.   BOSTON, MASS., 6 AUGUST, 1886.   FIVE CENTS.

THE CYCLE

PUBLISHED EVERY FRIDAY BY ABBOT BASSETT, 22 SCHOOL ST., ROOM 19.

VOL. I. BOSTON, MASS., 6 AUGUST, 1886. No. 19.

TERMS OF SUBSCRIPTION.

One Year, by mail, post-paid...........................$1.50
Three Copies in one order............................ 3.00
Club Subscriptions................................... 1.00
Six Months... .90
Single Copies.. .05

Specimen Copies free.

Every bicycle dealer is agent for the CYCLE and authorized to receive subscriptions at regular rates. The paper can be found on sale at the following places :—

Boston, CUTPLES, UPHAM & Co., cor. Washington and School Streets. Tremont House news stand. At every cycle warehouse.
New York, ELLIOTT MASON, 12 Warren Street.
Philadelphia, H. B. HART, 811 Arch Street. GEORGE D. GIDEON, 6 South Broad Street.
Baltimore, S. T. CLARK & Co., 4 Hanover Street.
Chicago, W. M. DURELL, 115 Wabash Avenue. JOHN WILKINSON & Co., 77 State Street.
Washington, H. S. OWEN, Capital Cycle Co.
St. Louis, ST. LOUIS WHEEL Co., 1121 Olive Street.

ABBOT BASSETT . . . . . EDITOR

A. MUDGE & SON. PRINTERS, 24 FRANKLIN ST., BOSTON

All communications should be sent in not later than Tuesday, to ensure insertion the same week.

Entered at the Post-office as second-class mail matter.

BLANKS for mail votes in the Board of Officers, L. A. W. have been sent out. It seems hardly necessary to discuss the questions at issue. They have been before the wheel world until they have been worn threadbare.

Call No. 1 calls for a change in the amateur rule, which will allow men who receive salaries for racing to compete as amateurs, and it also calls for the reinstatement of those men who have been declared professionals by the Racing Board. This vote is not now pressed by the friends of the racing men, for they have found in the A. C. U. an organization that will let the makers' amateurs race among themselves, and we think they are willing to let the League remain true to its amateur ideas.

Call No. 2 asks that the League give up all charge of the racing interests. The proposition is absurd. We have State Divisions of the L. A. W., and we have League clubs that wish to conduct amateur race meetings. Why should they not do this under League rules if they wish to ? Let the officers vote " yes " upon this question, and we shall see the New York Division, the California Division, and many others going to the A. C. U. for rules to run their meetings under.

To say that the racing interests have been a bone of contention in the past is not true. We have had many discussions over the amateur question, but they all concerned membership in the League. Discussions on racing matters have been confined to the Racing Board, and have not been public. So long as the League makes a man's amateur status requisite for membership, we shall have discussions in the future as we have had them in the past, and this will obtain whether there is a Racing Board or not. The proposition to abandon racing seems too absurd to call for extended comment.

WE have it on the authority of the highest officials in the A. C. U. that they do not wish the League to give up control of amateur racing, and we shall see many of these voting against the proposition. Since the call was made for these mail votes, the minds of a great many men have been changed.

IT has been our proud boast that wheelmen who have finished long-distance contests have been in fine condition compared to that of those who have engaged in prolonged walking feats. But it would seem that we are approaching the era when wheelmen will go to the very end of their rope, and give us just such exhibitions of exhaustion as the pedestrians have shown us. The recent John o'Groat's rides are cases in point. In the recent successful attempt of G. P. Mills to beat the record, the rider slept but six hours in the five days he was on the road, and during the latter half of the journey it was with extreme difficulty that he was kept awake. *Wheeling* says of this performance : " The riding of G. P. Mills, a youth of twenty summers, on the road, and of several very young fellows on the path, such as S. E. Williams, of the West Kent, brings into prominent relief the question of cycling in its relation to health. We cannot think that such a ride as that of Mills, however great the feat of physical endurance, is beneficial to the sport in the lessons it teaches. Granted that English bulldog pluck and stubborn resistance to the claims of nature carried him through : what has he gained ? A bubble reputation. And at what expense ? Let us all hope at none ; but the human frame is moulded on certain principles, and can no more stand a continued outrage to those principles than can any other organiza-

tion. Sooner or later, the strain must tell, and that especially in the case of a young man just entering upon the best years of his life. We repeat that we can see no good thing in these cruel rides, wherein heat and cold, storm and sunshine, hunger and thirst, want of sleep, bodily and mental trouble, all amalgamate in a horrible *mélange* barring the way to record, and refusing to yield until pierced by the frantic thrust of feverish ambition."

YACHTSMEN are now turning their attention to the question of an amateur rule in their sport. A noted yachtsman writing on this topic says : " So long as a sport is not a money-making affair and glory is the only incentive, so long will it remain in the hands of men who race to win, and so long will it be a ' square ' sport. It is true that there is no money in yacht-racing at present. The testimony of successful yachtsmen is unanimous that they spend more than they win in keeping their boats in condition. It is a cause for congratulation among yachtsmen that this is the fact. But what assurance have we that it will remain so ? Yachting is yet in its infancy. Not till last year was there anything like a general interest in the sport. This interest has lasted through the winter, and there are probably one third more people interested in yachting than there was a year ago. Yachtsmen pride themselves that there is something in yachting which keeps "these tricky fellows" out,—" it is an elevating sport," they say. Undoubtedly yachting, if entered into in the proper spirit, is an elevating sport. But, unless the history of other sports is misleading, the professionals will come in, and, instead of being themselves elevated, will drag the sport down to their own level. The prizes would be increased until there was money in it, races would be sold, and then yachting, as far as racing was concerned, could have no attraction for honest men. It is admitted that this is not the case at present, but it will assuredly result unless measures are taken for its prevention ; and it is much easier to keep the sport clean than it is to cleanse it after it has been dragged in the mire."

PRESIDENT BATES grumbles. He admits it. He would have radical changes made in the League management. He would have new laws made. And yet, after all, have we

not already just what the president wants us to have ? The Board of officers is a thoroughly representative body. It is made up much after the fashion of Congress, and each member represents a large constituency. Would it not be better to wisely carry out our present plan than to try others? True, the attendance at the officers' meetings is not very large, but it should be remembered that it is possible for nearly every member of the Board to be represented. Each representative can hold three proxies, and each chief consul can hold six. If the meeting is held in Boston, the California representatives can send their proxies with instructions, and their influence can be felt in every vote. Lack of interest on the part of League representatives has stood in the way of the effective working of the present system, and where there is a lack of interest there can be no good work. An agenda published at a reasonable time before the meeting would help matters along amazingly, and we believe it would lead to a more general use of proxies.

FROM A FEMININE POINT OF VIEW.

This is the season when the clergyman leaves his pulpit, the merchant his desk, and the artisan his bench. One and all they seek surf or shade, and leave the cares of business behind them. The clergyman closes the door of his chapel, or gets a friend to supply the pulpit, and the places of the others are filled as best they may be. The work of the world must go on, though the workers are at play.

I am going to have my pulpit supplied this week, and I have invited a few contemporary lady writers to speak for me. I will ask you to listen with patience to what my sisters have to say.

VIOLET LORNE IN BICYCLING NEWS.

The coming generation takes to wheels even earlier than in the schoolboy stage. One day last week, in Southampton High street, I saw a very pretty and novel combination of tricycle and baby carriage. Before the door of a shop stood a machine waiting for its owner, with a big square, brown basket slung at the back. The lid was propped open, and from within there smiled out one of the bonniest little child faces possible to fancy, — a wee mite of some two years old, wrapped up in fleecy coverings, and gazing out upon the surrounding world with a delighted pride in her position, very charming to witness. If Lewis Morris's exquisite little poem on the Italian organ-grinder's child " cradled in music " credited the little peasant baby with receiving an inspiration for a life of melody from the associations of its infancy, that wee girl in the brown basket may well be expected to grow up one of the women tricyclists of the future.

It is a great mistake to imagine one requires additional clothing in cycling. The reverse is the truth. One does not prepare oneself for the ball-room or the tennis-court by putting on extra warm garments, and why should one do so for riding, which involves an amount of violent exercise greater than either?

————

The C. T. C. flannel will make an excellent gown for all-round work and weather. I quoted, not long since, the experience of a Yorkshire lady who has found it most suitable and convenient. But let me counsel her to have the bodice made up on a thin cotton lining (it must certainly be lined, or it will neither fit nor wear well) ; one of those fine striped materials usually employed for dress-bodice linings will exactly answer her purpose. Additional warmth can always be secured by extra outside garments, if necessary.

————

If " C. S. F." is contemplating a new style of skirt, why trouble herself over the intricacies of kilted widths let in, either down the front or on either side ? These arrangements seldom either look or act well, and are apt to be clumsy and eccentric in finish. Why should she not at once adopt the simple kilted skirt, — a deep kilt from eight inches below the waist to the hem, — with kiltings of from one inch to two inches in width, according to her individual taste, and a sash drapery above and behind as a finish ?

————

If this skirt be well taped (two rows of strong, well-sewn tape), and made up on a foundation of gray cotton lining, I think I can venture to promise " C. S. F." that, after once riding in this particular make of tricycling gown, she will never voluntarily relinquish it for one less easy, less suitable, less convenient, or less pretty. As to the question about length, the skirt should be from two to three inches from the ground as the wearer is standing ; and I am sorry I cannot recommend any quick and easy way of fastening it up when compelled to dismount, for, according to my own experience, none such exists. A skirt long enough to require such adjustment is dangerous and ungainly, and to be shunned like the plague. With a skirt the length I have just recommended, there is no necessity for any shortening process, even in muddy weather.

————

Witness, again, a pretty little incident of a tricycling picnic when last those summer frivolities were in season. When Horace gallantly rushed to the assistance of Madge as she dismounted to push her " Salvo " up a heart-breakingly steep hill, in his ardor to seize the machine, she let loose before he could quite arrive on the spot, and he came into violent collision with its little back wheel, thereby abrading his ankle-bone, ruining his temper, and tearing his stocking. Did Madge deplore her carelessness, and reproach herself for the precipitation which was the real original cause of all his anguish? Not so. She only shrugged her shoulders expressively and resignedly at the rest of the party, and said, in the voice of her who is conscious of amiably enduring the hopelessly imbecile, " Dear me, how awkward ! I hope you have n't hurt the machine ! "

ROSE MEADOWS IN WHEELING.

An exchange says : " It is the height of immodesty to believe that tricycle riding is not ladylike and modest. A flowing skirt and the absence of hoops are all the necessary conditions, so far as the dress is concerned."

————

For my part, I quite agree with the author of these sentiments. Why should it be thought less ladylike for girls to tricycle than to ride a horse if they are so fortunate as to possess one ? Have we not our doctors' authority to go upon, as to the beneficial effects cycling has upon the health? I don't think there will be found one doctor in twenty who does not only allow it, but advises, recommends, and advocates it.

————

Even Mrs. Grundy is now coming round with regard to tricycling for ladies. Good! In a reply letter of hers to a friend, Kate Candor, she gives a reason for allowing her daughter to have a machine of her own. She says, " As you are doubtless aware, most of the desirable young men in this place are wheelmen, and were constantly getting up riding parties — or what they call *runs* — to which all the ladies who rode tricycles were invited. As Martha, poor girl, had no machine, she was left out in the cold, so you see we were *forced* to buy one for her." After all, Mrs. Grundy, you are not very strong-minded.

————

To any of my lady readers who have not yet decided on their costume for the season, the description of a dress I have just seen may be of use. The material is a fairly fine navy blue serge, not at all a heavy one. The skirt is in broad double box-pleats all round, of course not taped and without steels. There is an adjustable back and front drapery all in one, which could easily roll up into a very small parcel and be strapped on to the machine, though really for some people the dress would look very well without it. The kilting between the broad folds is full enough to allow of the wearer's sitting *in* it, and not *on* the pleats themselves, so that when riding, the skirt would appear the same length all the way round. I hope I have explained this quite clearly, as it is an important item.

IRIS IN RECREATION.

" Do you ride during this hot weather ? " we asked a lady only yesterday. " Oh, yes," was the reply, " we are out on the tandem every day after half-past four or five ; it is really cooler riding than staying in the house trying to keep cool." Let others prove the truth of these words, and see if the easy motion, the current of air thus created, and the gentle exercise of an early wheel ride, are not more comfortable conditions than can be found elsewhere. We grant that the heat of mid-day is for many injurious, and while one feels it less on a wheel than in walking, it yet often causes headache. For such there is the cool breezy morning, before the sun is high enough to be aught but agreeable in its heat and light, and again there are the two hours between sundown and dark, when riding will be found most delightful.

A word of warning, however, to such

would-be energetic sisters, — eat before riding. A glass of milk and a sandwich, if you can; at any rate, a sandwich. Don't try to ride for appetite, and come to the breakfast table pale and haggard, the appetite gone, with a headache, probably, in its place.

BLAIKIE says, " Any exercise that causes one to perspire freely a half hour a day, will reduce the weight." I have no comment to make on this other than to note, while it is perhaps unnecessary, that wheeling is such exercise as he describes, and that, to state it generally, women as a class need less fat and more muscle.

THANKS, ladies. My little congregation have enjoyed your words, and it may be that it may lead to a request for me to " exchange oftener."   DAISIE.

THE Cyclist reports that Howell completed a mile in 2.39⅔ at Leicester starting from a stool, a performance equal to about 2.36 push-off. Howell also did a half mile in 1.17, both of which performances are English records. These are two more for the Rudge Racer.

TWENTY-FIVE cents will buy a package of adhesive tire tape that is always ready for business, and will hold a loose tire in place until it can be cemented. For sale by Howard A. Smith & Co., Newark, N. J.

CONTRIBUTORS' CLUB.

AN AMATEUR GRUMBLE.

Editor of the Cycle: I rise to grumble. I desire to grumble a purely amateur grumble. I have examined the constitution and by-laws, and I think I have a constitutional right to grumble a strictly amateur grumble. The chair will please note that I don't engage in, or personally teach, grumbling as a means for attaining a livelihood, or for a stated bet, money prize, or for gate money; nor do I compete with professional grumblers; nor does anybody pay me wages, or pay my training expenses for grumbling; nor do I expect any reward, or remuneration, or prize other than the usual, regular, and long-established leather medal, against which there has never been any protest or decision.

I want my grumble to begin at the very beginning. I want to grumble at the primary constitution, and organization, and methods of the L. A. W. I believe that these have become such that grumbling is about the only legal practical privilege a member has left. I believe that all the troubles that have arisen, and all that threaten to arise, are directly due to the defects of the organic system. I believe the L. A. W. organization to be an impractical hodge-podge. I said so immediately after its second annual meeting, and I have been growing more and more convinced of it ever since. I think that what we need is a thorough, radical, and business-like reorganization.

The L. A. W. is now an organization practically governed by a bureaucracy, sometimes advised by a mass meeting of the wheelmen of the vicinage of the annual meet. Originally, the annual mass meeting held all power. But, through the inherent defects of the mass meeting system, this power has been gradually transferred to a bureaucracy. The primary defects of the mass meeting system are: 1. The annual meeting consists of the wheelmen of the immediate vicinity where it is held, reinforced by the scattering few who happen to have leisure and money to attend at their own expense from various distances. 2. It only holds a session of a couple or three hours, which is not even attended by all those who are at the meet. 3. There is nothing like systematic debate, careful consideration by committees, or pre-arrangement and orderly conduct of business. 4. The members who do attend the annual mass meeting have no real power. They can resolve and talk, but they cannot amend the constitution; they cannot settle the most important and most dangerous questions that arise. The members of the L. A. W., instead of governing, are governed, and are largely at the mercy of the boards and officers — the creatures of their own creating.

At the last meeting, the question of racing rules — the most important and most dangerous issue that has ever come before and threatened the very existence of the League — was decided, as I am informed, by a vote of less than one hundred members, in which the whole western half of the continent did not cast a solitary vote!

Now, no corporation does business that way. No government does. No organized great body in the United States does. The United States has a Congress. The States have Legislatures. Corporations all have regular delegate meetings.

I proposed four or five years ago, and I wish to renew the proposition, that the L. A. W. be so reorganized as to be governed by an annual congress of delegates, representing every State and part of a State, annually elected by the members, who shall sit and do business two or three days if necessary, who shall have their expenses paid, and who shall correspond to a State Legislature, or to the Congress of the United States, wielding the supreme legislative powers of the League. I propose that each State shall be entitled to at least one representative; that each State shall be entitled to one representative for each one hundred League members or over a moiety thereof; that the representative or representatives who actually attend from each State, shall be entitled to cast the full vote to which the State is entitled, — that is, one vote for each one hundred members, and one vote for exceeding a moiety thereof. I would give this annual congress power to alter the constitution in any respect by a two-thirds vote; power to amend any by-law by a majority vote; power to make or abolish any office, — in short, the supreme legislative powers of the League.

A fund not exceeding twenty-five cents annually per member of the whole League would pay the expense, the delegates to draw therefrom according to mileage; or else, a fund from each State more or less onerous, according to their distances from the place of meeting. But a distant State need not send more than one representative, with power to cast its full vote.

This congress, with a two or three days' annual meeting, being attended by delegates whose duty it would be to take part in its deliberations, would do the business of the League in an orderly, systematic, and thorough manner. All States and sections would be surely and equally represented. Its meeting would not be for fun, but for work.

I believe that, if the League had been so organized, it would have avoided or settled all the troubles which now beset it. I believe that, unless it does soon set up such an organization, it is threatened with further troubles which may cause serious defections from its ranks.

This grumble is brief. I have not time, nor you space, for details. But this mere suggestion of points is enough for a first heat. If anybody else goes for the leather medal, I have still wind for two more heats, and I depend upon you to see that I have fair play. Yours, with a sore head,
PRESIDENT BATES.

LANSING, MICH., July 19, 1886.

ELECTRIC TIMING.

PROF. C. H. McLEOD, of the McGill University, Montreal, P. Q., has invented an electrical timing apparatus, which has been tried and found practicable and accurate. A Montreal newspaper says : " An electric circuit is made, with connections at the starting and finishing points of a race. In races taking in a lap or more, the start and finish is at the same place, while in parts of a lap there have to be connections from every distance. The time is indicated on a chronograph formed of a cylinder (worked by a clock), which revolves at a uniform rate all through, the seconds being marked in waved lines, giving a distinct mark for each second. The start is made with a pistol, the discharge of which starts the clock, thus timing from the actual moment of sending the men off. In bicycle races the tape, or finishing-line, is about half an inch off the ground, each bicycle, as it goes over the line, causing a distinct mark to be made on the paper of the cyclometer, thus taking the exact time of every man in the race. In foot races the wire is breast-high, and the pedestrian himself breaks the current and stops the clock. The hundredth part of the second can be caught with this instrument, and properly handled, as it was by Professor McLeod and his assistant, it is infallible."

CANADIAN PROFESSIONALS.

At a meeting of the membership committee of the Canadian Wheelmen's Association, held at Simcoe, Ont., 27 July, five wheelmen, viz. Fred McMahon and H. Marlatt, of Simcoe, Sidney Dixon, Hagersville, and T. Walker and R. Hiscock, Caledonia, were deprived of their amateur standing for the taking part in a bicycle race held at Hagarsville, Ont., on 1 July, at which money prizes were offered. McMahon and Marlatt, being members of the association, were expelled. Amateur wheelmen are cautioned against competing with these riders in future.

PATENTS.

LIST of cycling patents issued 27 July. Furnished by N. L. Collamer, patent attorney, Washington, D. C. : E. G. Latta, Friendship, N. Y., velocipede ; Loyd & Priest, Harborne, Eng., tricycle.

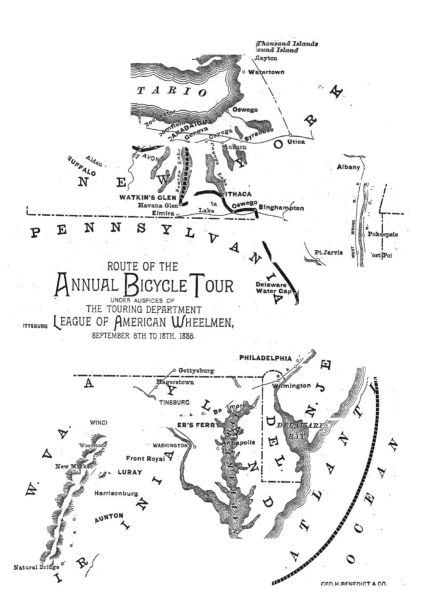

ROUTE OF THE
ANNUAL BICYCLE TOUR
UNDER AUSPICES OF
THE TOURING DEPARTMENT
LEAGUE OF AMERICAN WHEELMEN,
SEPTEMBER 6TH TO 18TH, 1886.

The Route.

Niagara Falls and Vicinity.
International Hotel.
Ar. from Chicago and
the West, Sept. 5th, 1886
M. C. R. R.

MONDAY, Sept. 6th.
Lv. Buffalo, 9 A. M
(Genesee Hotel.)
Lancaster,
Alden, 23 miles, dinner.)
Darien,
Batavia, 42 miles.

TUESDAY, Sept. 7th.
Lv. Batavia, 10:30 A. M
Stafford.
Le Roy, 10 miles, dinner.
Caledonia.
Avon, 29 miles.

WEDNESDAY, Sept. 8th
Lv. Avon, 9 A. M.
E. Avon.
Lima.
W. Bloomfield.
E. Bloomfield.
Canandaigua, 21 m 1ea.
Canandaigua Lake.

THURSDAY, Sept. 9th.
Lv. Canandaigua, 9 A. M.
Geneva, 22 miles.
Seneca Lake.
(Steamer.)
Dinner on board,
Watkins Glen.

FRIDAY, Sept. 10th.
Lv. Watkins Glen, 10 A. M.
Havana Glen.
Cayuta Lake, 10 miles, (dinner.)
Perryville.
Ithaca, 31 miles.
Aboard night train.
(Pullman sleeping cars.)
For New York.

SATURDAY, Sept. 11th.
Ar. New York, morning.
Wheels to Old Dominion Dock.
Grand Union Hotel.
Lv. New York, 3 P. M.
O. D. Steamship, "Guyandotte."

SUNDAY, Sept. 12th.
Atlantic Ocean.
Ar. Old Point Comfort, evening.
Hygeia Hotel.

MONDAY, Sept. 13th.
Norfolk and Vicinity.
Hampton Roads.
Lv. Old Point Comfort, 1:25 P. M.
Chesapeake & Ohio Ry.
Ar. Richmond, 6:15 P. M., (supper.)
Ar. Staunton, Va.

TUESDAY, Sept. 14th.
Lv. Staunton, 10:30 A. M.
Mt. Sydney.
Mt. Crawford.
Ar. Harrisonburg, 25 miles, 3 P.-M.

WEDNESDAY, Sept. 15th.
Lv. Harrisonburg, 9 A. M.
New Market, 19 miles, (dinner.)
Mountain Climb to
Luray Caverns.
Luray Inn, 36 miles.

THURSDAY, Sept. 16th.
Luray Inn and Cavns.

FRIDAY, Sept. 17th.
Lv. Luray, 8 A. M.
Milford.
Front Royal, 25 miles, (dinner.)
Stony Point.
Newtown.
Bartonville.
Kernstown.
Winchester, 45 miles.

SATURDAY, Sept. 18th.
Lv. Winchester, 9 A. M.
(Branch off to Martinsburg.)
Berryville.
Ford two streams.
Charlestown, 23 miles, (dinner.)
Ford one stream.
Harpers Ferry, 31 miles.
Lv. Harpers Ferry, 11:30 night, B.& O.
Ar. Chicago, Monday A. M.
Lv. Harpers Ferry, 4:26 A. M., B.& O.
Ar. New York, Sunday P. M.

WHEELMEN TRIUMPHANT.

WHAT may be regarded as a signal victory has recently been gained by the wheelmen of Sacramento. The riverside drive, a turnpike road skirting the river-bank, had, for a long time, been closed to wheelmen. A notice to the effect that bicycles and tricycles were not allowed on the road were posted above the gateway, and a belligerent old ruffian put in charge, who used the most offensive language to wheelmen who came to the gate, and, offering toll, asked to be allowed to ride on the road. In May last, the chief consul visited Sacramento, and, going to the toll-gate, had the same experience. At that time there was no organization among the Sacramento wheelmen. He returned to San Francisco, reported the matter to the National Headquarters of the League, and, under the direction of the L. A. W. officers, was preparing a course of action. Meanwhile, the wheelmen at Sacramento organized a club. It was composed of some of the best young men of the town. They selected as their president a Mr. Bennett, a gentleman of prominence in the community. The matter of opening the road to the wheelmen was agitated in one of the daily papers, and then a committee from the club called on the directors. They were pleasantly received, and the result of the interview was that the road was opened to all wheelmen, with toll fixed at ten cents. We compliment the Sacramento wheelmen on their wise and dignified conduct of this affair. We compliment the directors of the road on their gain of progressive ideas. They are men of experience in affairs, and no doubt fully realized that they had no power to expel wheelmen from their road, except by brute force, and that every time they exerted such force their servants became liable to arrest for assault and battery and they to a suit for damages in an action of tort. — *Ingleside.*

NEW HAVEN.

GEO. S. HICKOX, steward of the New Haven Orphan Asylum, had one of his legs broken by a fall from a bicycle, Friday, 30th ult.

A. M. KIRKHAM, who, with a companion, was coming down from East Rock Park last Sunday, was quite badly shaken up by a horse shying and jumping against his bicycle. The two riders passed on either side of the team, with the above disastrous result. Eight spokes of Kirkham's machine were broken, besides considerable bending of cranks, etc.

PRESIDENT FRISBIE, of the New Haven Club, is talking up a short run with some of the club-members for this week. They propose to go from over the following route, to Springfield, Pittsfield, Albany, and down the Hudson to New York.

BY a recent ordinance passed by both branches of the city government, the indiscriminate watering of the Telford pavements is done away with. The city has assumed control of this watering, and sprinkles the streets in the centre of the city three times a day during the very hottest of the weather, and twice at other times. The quality of the surface of the roadway is very much improved by this method.

THE mayor recommended to the road department the discontinuance of the laying of Telford pavements, which cost the property owner on streets where it is laid at least $1.75 per square yard, and the city proportionately, and the macadamizing of the streets as fast as possible at the expense of the city. Several miles of our streets have already been so treated, and give general satisfaction.

THERE seems now to be a good prospect that the Marlin Fire Arms Company of this city will make a tricycle, and possibly a bicycle, in the spring of 1887. Holders of various patents on both kinds of machines have been negotiating with the firm. The company themselves hold patents on the best friction clutch and ball bearings for machines that have so far appeared.

BICYCLE business is at almost a standstill just at present, few men wanting to ride during this hot weather. Neither of the six agents in town have done very much business except the Bicycle Supply Company, who have sold a great many Star machines. Quite a number of the older crank riders have bought the cart-before-the-horse style. Notably is this the case with those impetuous fellows who have been trying to keep in the front of the crowd on runs, and have inadvertently taken a bad header. For a scorching machine the Star seems to be at the head of the list.

MOST of our riders are making their plans for their vacations so that they can include the Connecticut Division meet at Hartford and the Springfield meet in the following week.

ST. LOUIS PARADE.

THE following is a programme of the three days of sport that St. Louis is preparing for wheelmen : Friday night, 1 Oct., grand illuminated parade ; Saturday morning, road race from Manchester to the city, eighteen miles, and a hill-climbing contest at Son-of-a-Gun ; afternoon, races at Union Park, with some Eastern flyers entered ; evening, sociable with music and light refreshments at some large hall. Sunday, run to DeSoto over the famous air-line route, the party to be divided into several sections under competent tour masters. This will afford visiting wheelmen a round of fun and amusement that is strictly in line with their sport. Beside this, there will be the magnificent exposition, the Gilmore band concerts, the parade of the secret societies, and scores of other entertainments that week, while the following week will come the grand St. Louis fair and Veiled Prophet's procession and ball. Prizes are to be offered for the best decorated machines of the various styles.

NEW YORK DIVISION.

AT a special meeting of the board of officers of New York State Division, held at the Grand Union Hotel, on Monday, 25 July, it was

Resolved, That it is the sense of the board that we are opposed to the proposed amendment : " That the League strike out from its by-laws all matters pertaining to racing, and confine itself to touring and legislative work, and such other matters as are deemed for the best interests of the wheelmen of America."

Resolved, That it is the sense of the board that we are opposed to striking from the by laws Section 3, Article II, and to striking out "Committee on Racing, to be called the Racing Board, in subsection *g*, Section 1, Article III," except the Racing Board, and Section 6, Article III, and Rule H, of the rules of the Racing Board ; and that the Racing Board be requested to reinstate all those men who failed to fill out the certificates furnished them by the Racing Board ; it being the intention of this Board to record itself against above proposed changes.

Resolved, That it is the sense of this Board that the action of the President of the League in removing the chief consul of Massachusetts be sustained.

CYCLETS.

A LONG LESSON.

Mv next-door neighbor a daughter has,
A maiden passing fair ;
And every day, as his door I pass,
I see her sitting there.

She takes an interest, this maiden good,
In the workings of my wheel ;
And every day, as a bicycler should,
Its mysteries I reveal.

I explain with care each complex part,
And she seems to comprehend ;
Yet every day we are losing heart
O'er the lessons which have no end.

It 's surely enough to discourage us both,
To find our work merely begun ;
And yet every day we grow more loth
To leave such a task undone.

And so, as we see that to finish indeed
Will take us the rest of our life,
To-day my neighbor's daughter agreed
To be *her* neighbor's wife.

C. E. TITCHENER is half-mile champion of the L. A. W. It is a fact worthy of notice that we hear little about the wheels ridden by the champions this year.

THE route of the L. A. W. and a map of the same appears in our issue this week. They tell their own stories more clearly than an elaborate article could set them forth.

THE Connecticut Bicycle Club is out with its full programme, and a very attractive one it is.

H. J. PAUSEY, an English manufacturer, took a header on the Ripley Road 18 July, and striking on the top of his head, was instantly killed.

Wheeling has sent out blanks asking for

an expression of opinion regarding the best six riders on the path and on the road (two classes) that the world has ever known. A number of answers have come in, and all place Cortis at the head of path riders.

THE *Cyclist* tells of a new sport engaged in by the ruralists. It consists in the collection right across the road of a ridge of stones about one foot high carefully masked with dust ; or it may take the form of a brick placed on the highway and artistically covered with a handful of new hay. When the game is ready, the merry villagers lie and wait for the first cycler who comes along, and in his tumble they get their pleasure.

A WRITER in *Harper's Bazar* says a good tricycling outfit, including the machine, will not cost less than from $120 to $150. He has not been there.

THE same writer says that the two-track tricycles are rapidly supplanting the three-track machines. Can it be that he writes from the neighborhood of Philadelphia ?

A NEWARK, N. J., genius has invented a bicycle alarm which, for novelty, at least, should take the prize. He calls it the " rattlesnake." It can be brought in contact with the spokes near the hubs by pulling a string which is attached to the handlebar, and it gives out a sound similar to an old-fashioned rattle carried by night watchmen.

THE Connecticut Bicycle Club will give for the A. C. U. championship an elegant trophy made by Elkington & Co., London, and imported by Shreve, Crump & Low, Boston.

THE Blue Nose tourists wore a badge for each tour they have attended. Mr. Elwell hid behind nine of them.

SACRAMENTO wheelmen are rejoicing that they have opened a turnpike formerly closed to them.

THE New Orleans *Picayune* of 23 July contains an extended account of the recent tour of the three New Orleans wheelmen from the latter city to Boston. It is quite interesting reading, and any one will be amply repaid for the outlay of five cents for a copy of the paper.

CHIEF CONSUL HAYES has called a meeting of the Massachusetts Division L. A. W. 11 August at Young's Hotel. The meeting will be for the purpose of organizing and electing officers to serve for the ensuing year.

AN amusing incident relative to Sunday riding is told by a member of the Chelsea Club. While several members of that club were returning from Gloucester, and passing through Medford, they were used as a practical example of the wickedness of young men by a preacher who was talking about the degeneration of the young man of the present age. As they rode by he said, " See there, those young men are going stright to h —." " No, we 're not," replies one, " we are going to Somerville." — *Globe.*

AN effort is to be made to have a parade of cyclists on the first day of the Hartford tournament.

DAN CANARY seems to have become as much attached to England as " Our Mary "

is. Mary will not come back for four years. Dan's engagements already extend far into 1887. He is shortly to make a tour on the continent, and at Christmas he will return to Manchester for a thirteen weeks' engagement at one of the pantomimes. He will be a feature of the West End Cycle Company's show in the early part of 1887.

AT the last meeting of the Lynn Cycle Club, a vote of thanks was passed to the Waltham Club members, who had extended so many favors to them during McCurdy's recent attempt to break the twenty-four hour road record.

A SPRINGFIELD clothier has put up a bicycle to be guessed for. The one who tells nearest to the number of beans in a bottle has the bicycle, and the award will be made at the Springfield tournament.

THE Providence *Journal* thinks Massachusetts has a fair share of the officers in the A. C. U., and suggests that it be called the M. C. U.

OUR friend Jenkins is going into racing as the manager of a track. Jenkins and Ducker will now be business rivals.

A CITIZEN of the United States, who recently arrived in Boston from a trip abroad, brought with him a tricycle, which he claimed to be exempt from duty as a personal effect. The collector, however, refused to admit it to free entry on the owner's admission that he had used it abroad but once. The case was appealed to the treasury department, which has sustained the claim of the importer that the machine had been in " actual use " abroad.

THE ministers are off. The start was made from New York on Tuesday.

NINETY-THREE applications for membership were enrolled on the L. A. W. list of 26 July.

COLONEL POPE and George H. Day will sail from England for home 10 August.

ON Saturday, 14 August, at 4 P. M., the Orange Wanderers will give a hill-climbing contest up Eagle Rock Hill. First prize to the rider making fastest time, and a prize to every one that gets up. Entries to E. P. Baird, Brick Church, N. J., close to August.

A CORRESPONDENT of the *Bulletin* wants the age limit of the League reduced. A reduction of two years would bring in a great many desirable members.

GEO. CHINN, of Beverly, Mass., has just issued the third edition of the " Wheelman's Hand Book of Essex County." It is a valuable guide to that locality, and as twenty cents will procure it, there should be a very large sale of it.

KLUGE has been riding a tandem about Orange, N. J. This looks as though he might be getting along.

A COASTING step for the Star is the latest novelty. It is fastened to the steering rod, and is made by H. A. Smith & Co., of Newark.

THE Fox grip rim used on the Royal Mail is voted a great success. With this rim in use one is saved the trouble of cementing his tire, for it never gets loose.

THE number of League members necessary for the appointment of a State representative will be increased from fifty to a hundred at the next meeting of the board of officers. At least a motion to this effect will be made.

KENNEDY-CHILD dropped in upon us last week and gave us the latest from the other side. He is not a little disgusted that men under the pay of makers are allowed to ride in amateur races in England, and says he is done with the sport so far as the legislative part is concerned. He thinks that not many amateurs will come to America this fall, though a number of professionals are to be here.

CAPTAIN PECK and three members of the Massachusetts Club rode to Worcester on Saturday and returned on Sunday. They were entertained by Worcester wheelmen.

CHARLES MARTIN and John Robinson, of the Massachusetts Club, rode in one day to Portsmouth and back from Boston last month. Robinson took a header on the way home, and lay in an insensible condition for two hours. The distance is 125 miles.

WE have received long communications from Karl Kron and Mr. E. J. Shriver, on the Orange bell and whistle ordinance, but lack of space forbids their appearance this week.

TAYLOR BOGGIS, of Cleveland, has decided to retire from racing. A fall on the track decided the question for him.

THE Cleveland and Detroit Club are arranging for an exchange of visits.

THE building of the Simmons Hardware Company, of St. Louis, collapsed last week. A large loss, including cycling goods, was the result.

CANADA will send Fred Foster to the fall tournaments. He will train at Springfield.

A LARGE number of Boston wheelmen went to Marblehead on Sunday to see the Galatea come in.

HOWELL had a bad fall while training last month, and broke his collar bone.

THE News is out with an attack on the value of the Springfield prizes. We believe Springfield did not state values last year.

THE Columbia team put in a week of clam eating at the Point of Pines after the 5th of July.

THE rocks in front of the Ocean House, at Swampscott, are peopled with wheelmen every Sunday.

CARDS were invented for the use of the insane, or rather to amuse a monarch who was insane, so we are told ; but, nevertheless, some otherwise very sensible men with fair average intellects seem to take no pleasure in life except in playing cards. They may ride down to a place of interest on their cycles, but there is a pack of cards in each multum, and when the ride is ended they pass the night in gambling. They may be "training" through the finest scenery in England, or elsewhere, but they never look at it so long as there is a pack of cards to be had and a spare cushion or newspaper to act as a table. We do not wish to be like the Pharisee and express pleasure that we are not as other men are, but we do fancy that the man who is not possessed of the gambler's spirit has much to be thankful for. — Wheel World.

THE following sketch of an occurrence about two years ago, illustrating Cola Stone's strong sense of humor, will be remembered by a number of old-timers.

Per custom, a crowd of his admirers sat one evening on the agency bench, each with a tall story to tell, the "agency kid," meantime, being sent on frequent trips to the "bakery" for "stuffed clubs," etc.

Arthur Young had a most interesting story to relate. The speaker grew tragic and spat tobacco juice in a rapid and reckless manner, while the boys' eyes fairly popped.

He was done. The crowd, heaving a united groan at the farce, had skipped out, while Cola, overcome by the ludicrous situation, jumped into the air with a yell, and came down on the agency desk with crushing effect. Next day Arthur received a bill reading : "To repair of desk, caused by bad joke, $3.50." — Journal.

IN response to queries about his book, "Ten Thousand Miles on a Bicycle," Karl Kron writes this column as follows : " Dear Sir ; I regret to inform you that I shall have to sweat through still a third summer to finish my task. I now have 650 pages in type, and the best I hope for is to publish in September."

—JOHN M. HATTLER, Charles H. Hoetsch, Levi Young, and Wm. M. Young, left Lyons, N. Y., 2 August, to ride to New York City, three hundred and fifty miles.

It is their first attempt at long-distance riding.

Newly Arrived Gentleman : " Whisht, Patsey ! Did yez see the bye goin' pasht alayin' on the top af a whale ? "

Patsey: My, but yer a gossoon ! The whale 's a Boy-sickel."

" A phwhat ? "

" A Boy-sickel. When I kim over they called thim a wheel-hossopede, an' sence the byes tuk to riden them its Boy-sickels they are. An' ef yees' desire to learn to ride wan, ye can begin be larnin' on the grindstone in me back yard. An' whin yes kin ride a grindstone along the top uv a rail fince, ye can tackle a Boy-sickel."—Spectator.

W. W. BERRY, captain of the Pittston, Pa., Bicycle Club, writes : " I received my 58-inch Rudge Light Roadster last Thursday. It is the finest machine I ever saw. It runs so easy I don't know I am pedaling half the time."

MESSRS. STODDARD, LOVERING & CO. wish to state that they are now prepared to fill orders for the American Rudge. They report the demand for this machine has been something extraordinary, and they have been taxed to their utmost to keep up with sales. The American riders are beginning to appreciate that they can get a first-class machine for in the vicinity of $110.

MR. H. M. SABIN, with Stoddard, Lovering & Co., took unto himself a partner for life on Monday last, and received from his friends in the Massachusetts Club an elegant dinner service.

THE twenty-mile L. A. W. championship has been located with the Winona Bicycle Club, and will be contested at the meeting of the Minnesota Division, L. A. W., to be held at Winona in September.

THE telephone man is going to talk to wheelmen. There ought to be a girl at the other end to make things seem natural.

F. R. BROWN, of Springfield, has been reinstated as an amateur wheelman by the Racing Board.

WHEELMEN who wish to have an enjoyable afternoon run are recommended to go to Allen's pond, at Newton, for a swim. This pond is the enlargement of the pure and never failing "Cheese Cake," near its source. It is secluded, fenced in, and sup-

plied with dressing rooms, swimming-post, spring-board, etc. The number of dressing rooms has been doubled, and the depth of the water increased six inches. Arrangements have been made by which the water can be drawn from the bottom during the day, thus raising the temperature several degrees. The sheet of water — 5,000 square feet — is divided by a floating boom into two parts for safety, and is from six inches to five and a half feet in depth. Bathers will wear tights or suits, and provide their own towels. Suits and tights, if marked, can be left in care of the attendants, for which a small charge will be made Strangers may similarly be furnished with tights, towels, etc. Open from 8.15 to 10.15 A. M., and from 5 to 7 P. M. for gentlemen. Arrangements for evening baths, with suitable illumination, can be made.

. THE clerical wheelmen started from New York Tuesday afternoon, on their tour up the Hudson and through central New York. Twenty clergymen were in the party, representing various denominations and States. The Citizens' Club, of New York, escorted the tourists through Central Park and to Yonkers. "Karl Kron" was along. The ride was delightful and thoroughly enjoyed. Others will join the party on the way to Poughkeepsie by the way of Tarrytown and Newburg, through the highlands of Hudson. Rev. Sylvanus Hall, of Lancaster, is commander, Rev. Irwin P. McCurdy, D. D., of Philadelphia, chaplain, and Rev. Howard H. Russell, of Oberlin, Ohio, quartermaster.

THE PATH.

THE Montreal Bicycle Club held their annual handicap road race to Valois, Can., 24 July. A half dozen started, and the contest over the uneven and arduous course resulted thus : W. D. Bohm, scratch, first, in 1.5.07 ; J. H. Robertson, scratch, second, by two seconds ; C. Pollock, 6.00, third ; G. Darling, 3.00, fourth.

ELMIRA, N. Y., 29 July. — The new four-lap track of the Elmira Bicycle Club was opened to-day. Attendance, good ; weather, warm ; track fair, but heavy in spots from heavy showers of the night before.
One-Mile Championship of "Southern Tier." — H. C. Hersey (1), 2.49 ; C. E. Titchener (2), by 10 yards.
One-Mile Handicap. — G. L. Davis, 18 seconds (1), 3.05 ; C. E. Titchener, scratch (2), 2.49.
The Elmira Club are justly proud of their new four-lap track, and they are going to hold a very large race meeting in September.

THE Harlem Wheelmen will hold their first annual race meeting on Saturday, 11 Sept., at the Manhattan Athletic Grounds, New York City. The events will be : One-mile novice, one-mile club championship, three-mile State championship, two-mile lap race, two-mile team race, two-mile handicap, one-mile 3.10 class, one quarter-mile one-legged, one half-mile without hands.

THE New Jersey Cycling and Athletic Association have secured the services of Mr. Frederick Jenkins as manager of their new grounds at Roseville Station, Newark, N. J. They will hold a three days' tournament on 30 Sept., 1 and 2 Oct. The track is said to be one of the finest in the country, and no expense will be spared to make the affair a huge success. Mr. Jenkins has had considerable experience with race meetings, and the successful League meet in New York in 1883 was largely due to his efforts. Full particulars will be published later, and the manager's address in Oraton Hall, Newark, N. J.

THE annual tournament of the Williamsport Wheel Club will be held at Old Oaks Park in conjunction with the meet of the Pennsylvania Division L. A. W., 19 Aug. As now arranged the programme is : One-mile dash, open ; half-mile ride and run ; half-mile club championship ; quarter-mile dash ; two-mile dash, open ; one-mile, L. A. W. State championship ; fancy and trick riding ; one-mile, hands off ; three-mile L. A. W. State championship ; one-mile, tug-of-war ; five-mile dash, open ; one-mile safety, open ; one-mile club race ; consolation race.

THE Keystone Bicycle Club, Pittsburg Wheelmen, Sewickley Valley Wheelmen, and Allegheny Cyclers, will hold their associated club race meeting 18 Sept., at Exposition Park track, Allegheny City, Pa.

THE last day of the State fair at Meriden will be devoted to bicycle racing this year. Prizes worth $600 will be offered, and the Meriden Wheel Club will have charge.

THE Lynn Cycle Club Track Association has been awarded the five-mile bicycle and one-mile tricycle A. C. U. championships.

FOREIGN RACING NOTES.

G. GATEHOUSE, amateur, rode two miles on a tricycle in 5.57¾ (best on record) at the Racing Cyclists' meeting in London, Eng., 15 July.

Wheeling says that the reported ride of one Berridge on a Rover Safety cannot be verified. It was claimed that he covered twenty miles within the hour, but no one can be found who saw him do it, nor does any one know of such a person.

MECREDY, of Dublin, won the twenty-five mile N. C. U. tricycle championship at Alexandra Park, 17 July.

FOR a sick man Furnivall is doing well. He is still on the track and winning victories.

THE CLUB.

THE semi-annual election of the Bay City wheelmen, held in San Francisco, Cal., 12 July, resulted thus : President, Edward Mohrig ; vice, R. M. Welch ; secretary, Emil F. Fahrbach ; treasurer, E. J. Schuster ; captain, Daniel O'Callahan ; first lieutenant, William Meeker ; second, Frank James.

DENVER has a club of ninety-three members. Fifty applications were received at the last meeting as the result of abolishing the initiation of five dollars for all applications made at this meeting.

THE New Britain Bicycle Club has elected the following officers : captain, Howard S, Hart ; first lieutenant, Elbridge N. Wightman ; standard-bearer, Fred Mills. The club has at present a membership of twenty-four members.

MISCELLANEOUS

The Cycle.

Vol. I., No. 20.   BOSTON, MASS., 13 AUGUST, 1886.   FIVE CENTS.

MARLBORO CLUB
TRICYCLE.

RECORD!

CHAMPIONSHIP!

F. W. ALLARD won the N. C. U. 5-Mile Championship on a Marlboro Club, beating Furnivall and Catehouse.

F. W. ALLARD takes the 1-Mile Tricycle Record (2.54), on a Marlboro Club.

COVENTRY MACHINISTS CO.

THE CYCLE

PUBLISHED EVERY FRIDAY BY ABBOT BASSETT, 22 SCHOOL ST., ROOM 19.

VOL. I.   BOSTON, MASS., 13 AUGUST, 1886.   NO. 20.

TERMS OF SUBSCRIPTION.

One Year, by mail, post-paid.............................$1.50
Three Copies in one order...............................3.00
Club Subscriptions.......................................1.00
Six Months...90
Single Copies..05

Specimen Copies free.

Every bicycle dealer is agent for the CYCLE and authorized to receive subscriptions at regular rates. The paper can be found on sale at the following places : —

Boston, CUPPLES, UPHAM & Co., cor. Washington and School Streets. Tremont House news stand. At every cycle warehouse.
New York, ELLIOTT MASON, 12 Warren Street.
Philadelphia, H. B. HART, 811 Arch Street. GEORGE D. GIDEON, 6 South Broad Street.
Baltimore, S. T. CLARK & Co., 4 Hanover Street.
Chicago, W. M. DURELL, 115 Wabash Avenue. JOHN WILKINSON & Co., 77 State Street.
Washington, H. S. OWEN, Capital Cycle Co.
St. Louis, ST. LOUIS WHEEL Co., 1121 Olive Street.

ABBOT BASSETT . . . . . EDITOR

A. MUDGE & SON, PRINTERS, 24 FRANKLIN ST., BOSTON

All communications should be sent in not later than Tuesday, to insure insertion the same week.

Entered at the Post-office as second-class mail matter.

THE regular fall meeting of the Board of Officers will be held at Buffalo, 3 September. We must confess we should like to have had it at another time and in another place. The fall meeting will be a very important one, and not less than a full day should be given to it. At Buffalo there will be the annual meeting of the New York Division and the big tournament. The programme for the division meeting calls for a business meeting in the forenoon, and the League meeting is down for the same time. We don't know how the meetings can be held so as not to conflict. But outside of this conflict in the time, there is the fact that the attention of those who go to Buffalo for the meeting will be distracted by the other events, and we do not believe that the time will be given to League work that its importance demands. The most unsatisfactory meetings that we have had, heretofore, have been those held at Philadelphia and Springfield on tournament dates. Then, as to Buffalo, it has been claimed that it is very central; so it is, but it is four hundred or more miles from everywhere.

THE little book by B. W. Potter, on "The Road and the Roadside," recently published, has a good many points of interest to wheel-men, and especially to those of Massachusetts, because it deals particularly with Massachusetts laws. We clip from it a few notes of general interest.

"THE difference in length between a straight and a slightly curved road is very small. Thus, if a road between two places ten miles apart was made to curve so that the eye could nowhere see farther than a quarter of a mile of it at once, its length would exceed that of a perfectly straight road between the same points, by only about one hundred and fifty yards."

"IT is an accepted maxim by road engineers that the horizontal length of a road may be advantageously increased, to avoid an ascent, at least twenty times the perpendicular height which is to be thus saved; that is, to escape a hill a hundred feet high, it would be proper for the road to make such a circuit as would increase its length to two thousand feet."

"TO drive a carriage or other vehicle on a public way at such a rate, or in such a manner as to endanger the safety of other travellers, or the inhabitants along the road, is an indictable offence at common law, and amounts to a breach of the peace."

"WHEN persons meet each other on a bridge or road, travelling with carriages or other vehicles, each person shall seasonably drive his carriage or other vehicle to the right of the middle of the travelled part of such bridge or road, so that their respective carriages or other vehicles may pass each other without interference; that one party passing another going in the same direction must do so on the left-hand side of the middle of the road. . . . By the travelled parts of the road is intended that part which is usually wrought for travelling, and not any track which may happen to be made in the road by the passing of vehicles."

"WHEN there is snow on the ground, and the movement of your sleigh is comparatively noiseless, don't drive on a public way without having at least three bells attached to some part of your harness. . . . You would be liable to pay a fine of fifty dollars for each offence." While this restriction exists concerning sleighs, does it not have a bearing upon the lamp and whistle question? The law steps in and compels the sleigh to carry a bell, because it is noiseless. The bicycle is just as noiseless as the sleigh. We think it hardly fair to say that an iron-tired buggy with an iron-shod horse makes as little noise as a bicycle.

"ANY traveller on the road, either riding or walking peaceably, who is suddenly assaulted by a dog, whether licensed or not, may legally kill him, and thus relieve his owner or keeper of a disagreeable duty."

A TANDEM ACCIDENT.

THE terrible accident to Mr. and Mrs. Rufus H. Stickney, of Somerville, which occurred Thursday night, of last week, near the Chestnut Hill reservoir, has carried sorrow into many homes in the city in which they resided, and has enlisted the sympathy of a large circle of friends in the cycling fraternity. A number of conflicting reports have been in circulation, but the following account of the accident has been furnished by Mrs. Stickney through a member of the family.

Mr. and Mrs. Stickney were making a short visit at the Woodland Park Hotel, Auburndale, and enjoying the fine riding to be found in that vicinity. Mr. Stickney went out to the hotel Thursday afternoon from business in Boston earlier than usual, and told his wife that they would have an early supper in order to enjoy a good run. Mr. Hopkins, of Wellington, was to go over and ride with Mr. Stickney later in the evening, but the threatening clouds kept him at home and also led to the speedy trip homeward, during which the accident occurred. They left the hotel on the machine at 6.30 o'clock, and had a pleasant run out to Chestnut Hill reservoir, around which they circled some time in the moonlight. About eight o'clock it began to cloud up and threaten rain, so they decided to hurry back to the hotel, and, in order to do so, took the shortest way, which carried them down the hill from the reservoir to Allston. It was very dark when they started, and the machine was not provided with a headlight. The riders coasted down the hill with considerable rapidity, Mrs. Stickney riding on the forward seat and managing the steering bar, with her husband behind her looking after the brake, which was a powerful one. While passing over the thoroughfare which leads down from the reservoir, no difficulty was experienced, but when the machine approached the junction formed by Winship street with Chestnut Hill avenue, Mrs. Stickney saw that they were crowding too near a cobble-stone gutter. She turned

the handle bar quickly, and this gave the machine such a swerve that the whole weight of the riders, two hundred and fifty pounds, at least, was thrown against one of the drivers, and it gave way, throwing them out. Mr. Stickney was lifted in the air and pitched bodily over his wife's head. His wife at the same instant was buried beneath the machine She was struck on the head by some portion of the tandem, but managed to free herself and go to the assistance of her husband, who was lying in a heap in the cobble-stone gutter. He was unconscious for the moment, but quickly came to his senses. On coming to, he immediately inquired of his wife the extent of her injuries. She, seeing that he was probably injured the most, made a passing comment about herself, and helped him to a seat on the curbstone. This was about 8.30, and a Mr. White who was passing came to the couple's assistance. Mr. Martin, a member of the Massachusetts Club, happened along at this time, and, calling him by name, inquired as to how he met with the accident. Mr. Stickney requested his friend to get his machine into the clubhouse, and, while giving him some directions, Mrs. Stickney fainted. Mr. Stickney told his friend to go to the engine-house near by and procure assistance for his wife. A chair was brought, and Mrs. Stickney was carried into the engine-house and placed upon a cot. Mr. Stickney was then assisted to the engine house by Mr. White, who inquired about his injuries. Stickney told him that he had hurt his arm badly, and White, thinking it might be broken, got him to put it about his (White's) neck, and in this way they walked to the house. On the way Stickney vomited blood, and this was his first indication that he was seriously hurt. On arriving at the engine house, Stickney, in his anxiety about his wife's condition, seemed to forget his own, which was gradually growing worse. He bathed his wife's temples and fanned her until she regained consciousness, and then his strength left him. He first felt a nausea in the stomach, and commenced vomiting, complaining all the time about his head. The calling of a doctor was suggested, but Mr. Stickney objected. His wife gave up her place on the couch and he was placed upon it. As he appeared to grow worse, a doctor was sent for, and one finally arrived. By this time the injured man was unable to speak, and he had to be constantly aroused to prevent his falling into a stupor. Morphine was injected, and a carryall was procured, and at 9.10 Mr. Stickney was placed in the carriage with his wife. He was in a semi-conscious state during the drive to the hotel, which occupied three-quarters of an hour. On arriving, he was placed on a cot in the parlor of the hotel, and Mrs. Stickney went upstairs to prepare the bed in her room for him. She was told that her husband would be brought up immediately, and as he did not come she flew down-stairs only to find that he had breathed his last. He had burst a blood vessel on the brain, the concussion resulting in his death. The scene which followed was heartrending. A telephone message was sent to the residence of Mrs. Stickney's father in Somerville, and Mr. and Mrs. H. F. Woods, intimate friends of the family, and Mr. Stickney's

sister drove out to the hotel, arriving there about one o'clock in the morning. Mrs. Stickney suffered severe scratches to her face and head, and injured her side, but it is nothing serious.

Mr. Stickney was twenty-nine years of age, and was an active representative of his father, Mr. Rufus B. Stickney, in the business at 205 State street. He had graduated at the Somerville High School, and entered the office of Stickney & Poor as a boy and had worked his way through, the various grades, until of late he had been placed in a position where much of the executive management of the entire business fell to his hands. Bright, smart, and energetic in business, he was also regarded as a faithful and good friend by his associates, and many words of highest eulogy for his excellent qualities are spoken by social acquaintances. He was greatly interested in bicycle matters, and was a member of the Massachusetts Club. His wife was formerly Miss Carrie E. Conant, of Somerville. He leaves no children.

The funeral took place at the residence of his father, Mr. R. B. Stickney, corner of Broadway and Sycamore street, Winter Hill, Somerville, Sunday afternoon. The house was crowded with relatives and friends, delegations also being present from the Massachusetts and the Somerville bicycle clubs, of which the deceased was an honored member.

Mr. Stickney was a great lover of flowers, and once remarked to his wife that when he died he wanted to be buried in these emblems of purity and love. His fondest desires in this direction were fully and most elaborately carried out. There were between thirty and forty magnificent set pieces of every conceivable design arranged tastefully about the casket, and the fragrance from a thousand roses permeated the house of mourning. The Massachusetts Bicycle Club's tribute was a very large tablet, knotted at the four corners with white silk ribbons, tying roses. Through the centre ran a broken column of white carnations in bas-relief. The Somerville Bicycle Club contributed a handsome standing star.

At the conclusion of the service the relatives followed the remains to the grave at Mt. Auburn, where the burial was private, the following named intimate friends of the deceased acting as pall-bearers: Messrs. S. T. M. Pennock, Jr., Frank W. Downer, Frank P. Tucker and F. H. Tilden.

WILKESBARRE PARADE.

THE lantern parade of the bicyclists of Wilkesbarre, Penn., and neighboring places, which took place 6 August, was one of the most brilliant spectacles of the illuminational sort that ever took place in that city. There were ninety-six wheels in line, and each had two, and some three and four lanterns of bright colors, and as they moved noiselessly along the asphalt the scene was almost spectral. The clubs represented were the Scrantons, fourteen men, under Lieut. F. B. Ward ; Kingstons, thirteen men, Capt. Chas. Morgan and Lieut. Harry Flannegan ; Wyomings, nine men, Capt. Pierce Tracy ; Pittstons, Capt. Wm. W. Berry, twenty men ; Ramblers of Wilkesbarre, sixteen men, Capt. S. A. Wheeler ; and Wilkesbarres, Capt. Jess. G. Carpenter, twenty-four men. The march was in every possible order.

BELLS AND WHISTLES AT ORANGE.

WE are snowed under this week. A perfect avalanche of manuscript has come to us relative to the Orange bell and lamp ordinance. If we were to print it all we should have to increase the size of our paper and exclude everything else. To print one and not all would work an injustice. We will try and give the gist of all.

Karl Kron complains that we have allowed a correspondent to use his family name in alluding to him. He says that he is and has been known to wheelmen as Karl Kron, and he wishes to be so called in the future. He claims the right to the privacy of his family name when not engaged in cycling affairs. He further claims that the harsh words he has uttered against Orange wheelmen were well deserved, since they have acted in a way to injure the cause of wheeling.

Mr. E. J. Schriver writes in reply to Mr. Porter. We extract the following : —

"As to the careless riders who make trouble, with or without cautionary paraphernalia, the established laws of the road will take care of them. Nothing would please me better than to see the best friend I have severely fined every time he indulges in riding on sidewalks, coasting hills with brake off, or reckless riding of any sort. Let the Wanderers expend their energies in seeing the general laws enforced, and they will gain just as much sympathy from the public ; but they must keep their hands off the rights of wheelmen, and not get up special enactments.

"This part of it they do not seem to consider at all ; and in fact the trouble is apparently that they look on the whole thing as a local matter in which a non-resident must not meddle, for, as Mr. Porter says, 'it is none of his business at all.' New Jersey, as we all know, is a foreign country, but Jersey men have been taken into the bosom of the League, and owe it to fellow-wheelmen that they should think twice before endangering our legal status. It is not only that the casual stranger who happens on Orange roads should not suffer because he may not agree with the Wanderers as to the necessity of carrying a tin kettle on his wheel, but a very dangerous precedent has been created. If, as you say, there are similar ordinances in Boston, then so much the worse for Boston [We said near Boston. — ED.] and its wheelmen who permit it. If there are local riders anywhere who cannot get along without these nonsensical toys, let them use themselves, but not force them on others. But even if they do get up a propaganda by means of town boards to compel outsiders to follow their habits, they have no right to do so in such a way as to make a distinction between cycles and other vehicles.

"If this now famous ordinance had required all vehicles to carry lamps at night, the only possible real danger would have been met, and no bad precedent created ; but as it stands, unless adjudged unconstitutional, it gives a warrant to other boards for requiring that cycles must be subjected to some other ridiculous regulation that does not apply to vehicles of all kinds, — regulations such as restricting to an impossibly slow gait, which would practically forbid wheeling altogether.

"As to day riding, the argument that cycles

make less noise than carriages is the sort of nonsense that one hears now and then from some backwoods farmer, but rarely from an experienced wheelman ; as well compel the driver of a sulky (which makes no more noise than a bicycle and less than most three-wheelers) to sound an alarm when he passes a beer-track or a steam roller, because his vehicle makes less noise ! If an accident occurs, the party to it who has shown negligence pays the penalty, and so it should be with wheelmen. Only enforce the established laws against your own careless or new members, gentlemen, of these over-scrupulous clubs, and you will not need new laws that separate you into a different class of travellers, and put you at the mercy of any ignorant constable you may run across."

Mr. L. H. Johnson's name has been brought into the discussion and he has been claimed by both parties to the controversy as a friend of their side. He writes to us and says, *inter alia* : —

" From the importation of the first bicycle into this country to the present day, there has been a ceaseless struggle on the part of wheelmen to maintain *equal* rights with other vehicles. 'As a precedent for this, we have had the impartial legislation of England, where cycles in no case are restricted beyond other· vehicles, and in many sections are allowed special privileges. The streets of London are open for unlimited cycling. One hour after sunset bicyclers must light their lamps ; *so must the cab-drivers*. A hansom driven at a rapid rate through Piccadilly without lights is dangerous ; so is a buggy on the unlit surface of Park avenue in the Oranges. All other vehicles (than cycles) do *not* make a noise which gives warning of their approach to other drivers ; any horseman will admit this.

Mr. E. J. Schriver of the New York Bicycle Club, expresses in a clear and dignified manner the views of many wheelmen, both resident and non-resident, on this subject. He makes the sound point of questioning the constitutionality of such an ordinance, and generously offers assistance, in a private letter to me, should an arrest furnish a test case. The New. York Club has by formal resolutions protested against the ordinance, and the action of the Orange Wanderers, and called on the League Officers to test the constitutionality of the ordinance.

PENCILLED PARAGRAPHS.

IT is amusing to read the anonymous sea story now running in *Outing* and then notice the author's illustrations with his name prominently attached to each. The articles are very interesting, however.

THE Connecticut Bicycle Club Race Committee has a large and elegantly designed challenge shield which will be offered as a prize at their tournament. This is the first prize of the kind in the country.

-. No one had a larger circle of friends in the Massachusetts Club, nor will any member be more sincerely mourned than poor Stickney.

A SORT of vague suspicion that there is some sort of a ring in the League, and that its headquarters are in New York, is creeping upon Massachusetts Division members.

SOME of the members of the Massachusetts Club are talking of getting that club to join the A. C. U. in a body.

RALPH P. AHL tells some rare old stories of the fun a wheelman can find in the French capital.

THE Lynn track has been lowered about three inches at the upper turn by assiduous scraping with a drag, and has been taken up and raised seven inches on the lower curvet This will enable the rider to carry his spurt clear around the turns, and will enable the racers to make better time.

THE next issue of the ·*Wheelman's Gasette* is the tournament number.

HARTFORD will makes its main effort in the one-mile A. C. U. championship, where the American cracks will compete.

THE Massachusetts Division is the deadest division in the country, and with its excellent roads, large membership, and past experience should do some work for itself in holding interesting meets, runs, races, and in publishing a complete road book and map of the State.

ONE ⁄member of the L. A. W. Racing Board says he had rather see one base ball match than see a dozen bicycle races, and yet he wonders why the racing men are pleased with the recent changes in the racing management.

OUR editor has neglected to state that " Daisie " is at Plymouth.

DETROIT will run its races under A. C. U. rules, and will endeavor to collect a large number of the promaters at its tournament.

IN a stop watch there are four chances to one that the time will be caught on the fifth seconds rather than on the even minutes, and yet the Lynn timers were only able to catch fifth seconds six times out of a possible thirty.

THE Lynn board of directors became so desperately in earnest about repairing their track in season, that the president and one of the board turned to themselves and handled the sprinkler and· the leveller with diligence and skill for two days.

THE question of records is a little mixed in some men's minds. The record sheet from ¼ to 20, made by Rowe last season, stands now as it did then (excepting Speechley's mile, if accepted) as the best amateur records. Rowe's and Hendee's new records stand on the promater part of the sheet, from ⅓ to 1 for Hendee, and from 2 to 10 for Rowe. Speechley's record, if accepted, will be the amateur world's record.

MCCURDY thinks there is no show for an American getting the twenty-four hour record on a fifty-mile course, unless he goes across and does it on English roads. He will try it there himself soon.

DEACON WILMOT, of the Bowdoin Square Baptist Church, which figures in the Downs affair, is the father of W. D. Wilmot, the fancy rider.

CLEVELAND makes a great talk about the pure amateur features of its tournament, and yet·they tried hard to get the promaters to attend.

THE Springfield Club rooms have now two home trainers, and races and records are all

the talk of the members, who spend half their time pegging away at the iron wheels.

THE Boston representative on the Blue Nose tour is reported as being a fine follower of Burchard during the trip, with the Romanism and Rebellion left out. See ? ⸣

THERE seems to be a general disposition among the officers to vote for the Ducker side of the Ducker-Beckwith question, with the understanding that his resignation shall follow the vindication.

CORCORAN, the old Harvard boat crew trainer, is handling Neilson and Foster of Toronto this season.

FRED. FOSTER, of Toronto, is going to be a hard nut for Rich, Valentine, Kavanaugh & Co. to crack this fall.

THE two Blue Nosiests that enjoyed the trip the best, and were freshest at the end, were Selvy and Miller, of Springfield, who rode nearly the entire distance in a canoe, with an Indian to paddle.

FRED. JENKINS has swung Newark into line alongside of Ducker, and our English friends will have a chance to try the American mettle at Roseville, in October.

WOODSIDE and Morgan arrived at Springfield on the 10th, and will train there for the fall tournaments.

THE Pope Manufacturing Company received for repairs last week an Expert Columbia which had been recently fished out of the hold of the Gate City in a somewhat rusty and demoralized condition.

PEN SYL.

DEATH OF MAJOR DURRELL.

MAJOR WILLIAM M. DURELL, widely known among the wheelmen of America, and Western agent of the Pope Manufacturing Company, died quite suddenly Wednesday morning, 4 August. Apoplexy was supposed to have been the cause. Major Durrell had been largely interested financially and otherwise in the athletic sports venture at Cheltenham Beach; and also in Duncan C. Ross. His friends were not quite satisfied with the physician's diagnosis of the cause of his death, and determined to investigate, and in this connection some startling facts have been brought to light. Apoplexy is conceded to be the cause of his death, but the apoplectic stroke is the direct result, so it is alleged by detectives who have worked up the case, of a brutal beating the major received in a sporting resort, where he had gone in company with Ross. Here he met Paddy Ryan, the pugilist, Harrison, the " Unknown," and numerous lesser lights in the sporting world. Numerous fights are said to have taken place during the evening between Ryan and Harrison, owing to a desire to settle old scores. Others were also drawn into the quarrels, and finally the fighting became so general that everybody was drawn into the *mêlée* for the love of a broil or for self-preservation. It is not known why the major was set upon, but be got away from the place at 10 o'clock and went to his home, where he complained to his wife of a severe pain in his head. A physician was at once called, and found that there was a pronounced determination of blood to the head. Fearing apoplexy, he adminis-

tered hypodermic injections. At 7 o'clock the next morning Mrs. Durrell was awakened by the heavy gasping of her husband. Before a physician could be summoned he was dead. An examination showed that the deceased had received numerous kicks and blows on the right side, extending from the shoulder to the hip; there were discolorations, the result of blows on the back, and that there was a large swelling on the neck, apparently caused by a blow or a kick. The friends of Major Durrell on hearing these facts immediately proceeded to investigate the matter, and what they have already learned has satisfied them that the deceased received the injuries which caused his death during the fight which occurred in the saloon and·in the alley adjacent, and in which Paddy Ryan, the pugilist, Harrison, the "Unknown." so-called, and others of that ilk were engaged. The major was a gentleman both by birth and education; had served in the Confederate army with distinction, and honorably earned his title. He also lost an arm in the service. He was known as a generous man, a true-hearted friend, and a genial companion.

NOTES FROM THE SOUTH.

THE annual races of N. O. B. C. are fixed for the 27th and 28th of the present month. The State and club championship will be contested for, and, as all the crack racing men of the club will enter, there will no doubt be some fast riding. The programme also includes tandem, tricycle, and safety races, all of which will prove a novelty, this being the first of the kind in this city. The races will doubtless be a success, as the boys will attempt to redeem the failure of their fifty-mile race.

LAST year the majority of the races, including the State championship, were won by Mr. E. P. Baird, now of the Orange Wanderers, but who at the time was in charge of an exhibit at the World's Exhibition in this city, and also a member of the local club. When he left for his home in the North, he carried the honors with him; this year, however, they will stay where they belong, at home.

As previously prophes'ed, the tandem becomes more popular. Two already in the city, and two more ordered.

It is extremely probable that within the next three months another club will be organized. There are already enough riders to warrant it, and almost every day brings more converts to the wheel.

THE New Orleans Bicycle Club is steadily increasing its membership, and there is talk of finding more commodious quarters. BI. NEW ORLEANS, 5 August, 1886.

FOUR first prizes were won on a Rudge racer in the Genessee tournament, held at Rochester, N. Y., on the 22d.

ON 4 July, H. O. Duncan won the championship of France, against all comers, on a 5>-inch Rudge racer.

WM. H. LANGDOWN.

WILLIAM H. LANGDOWN, the Australian bicycle rider, who is making a journey of sixteen thousand miles to participate in the Springfield tournament this fall, is a resident of Christchurch, New Zealand, and captain of the Pioneer Bicycle Club, of Christchurch. He is the amateur champion of New Zealand. He is also considerable of a long-distance rider. One of the longest tours yet accomplished in Australia was that of Mr. Langdown, who, in the early part of the season, started from Wellington, proceeded through the Manawatu gorge, and through some very rough country to Napier, on the east coast, thence crossing the ranges to Wanganui on the west coast. It was his intention to continue his journey by the west coast until reaching Wellington again, but, owing to his bicycle breaking down at New Plymouth, he had to abandon his intention. The time spent up to this point was about six weeks, and the distance covered was about six hundred miles.

NEW TRICYCLE RECORDS.

TOM BATTENSBY has taken all the English professional tricycle records to ten miles. The evening of Monday, 26 July, was fixed for the attempt, and the track was in grand order, although a strong wind made riding anything but easy. Punctually to time Battensby, on his "Crescent" racing tricycle, weighing forty-two pounds and geared to sixty-four inches, came up to the scratch, accompanied by Hawker. At the word "go". he was quickly under way, and finished his first quarter in 47s., his second quarter taking 44s. only. Riding wonderfully easy and carefully coached by Hawker and Farndon, Battensby reeled off the miles as follows : —

Mile.	Min.	Sec.
First	3	3
Second	6	9
Third	9	12
Fourth	12	18
Fifth	15	25
Sixth	18	35¾
Seventh	21	41
Eighth	24	48¼
Ninth	27	59
Tenth	31	2¼

There has been but one series of professional tricycle records, and those were made and held by Fred. Lees in May of 1884. It was an easy task to break the existing records, but Battensby wanted world's records, and got them above five miles.

A CYCLE FIRE ENGINE.

A NOVEL system of fire extinguishing has just been introduced by Mr. William Glenister, chief of the volunteer fire brigade, Hastings, and Mr. J. C. Merryweather, of London. The apparatus forms the subject of a patent. The new fire and life-saving machine consists of a tandem tricycle, with which are embodied the following: (1.) A hose wheel carrying a large quantity of specially constructed hose for winding in a small compass with all the attachment for working on to a fire from street hydrants. (2.) A light double pump fire-engine in collapsible cistern capable of throwing twenty-

five gallons per minute to be worked by two pumpers. (3.) A simple fire escape with descending ropes and bag. (4.) Pumping seats formed from the riders' seats. The machine is run at full bicycle speed by two men, and if desired, the treadles can be so disposed as to work the fire pumps, but for this a special gearing is required. For country districts and suburban towns this improved machine will doubtless be appreciated. — Engineering.

CONTRIBUTORS' CLUB.

LEARNING TO RIDE.

Editor of the Cycle: I send you the accompanying letter, which came into my possession, and which, as describing the experiences of a beginner on the tricycle, may have some interest, at least for your lady, readers, who cannot appreciate the "Amateur Question." L. W. SEELY, Capital Club.

Dear Mamie: We are still in the city trying to keep cool, with only moderate success. Uncle John promised to take me to the Catskills if I would remain here until the family left, and you may imagine I consented.

Cousin Tom says I 'll be sorry; that the isothermal line on which Washington is located runs directly to Galveston, Texas, and that as soon as the line is in working order, we shall receive hot weather directly from that point. Do you know what an isothermal line is?

Tom is a terrible tease, but then he is perfectly lovely about the summer opera and the tricycle, and the latter is what I wanted to tell you about. Of course Tom rides a bicycle; he calls it a "58-inch Apollo," and says it 's the best hill-climber made. I asked him how he knew, and he said there was scriptural warrant for the assertion ; and then he told me to look in the Bible and see what the bad little children desired the prophet Elisha to do. I looked, and all it said was, "Go up, thou bald-head." I don't see any sense in that, do you ? I told Tom so, and he said the spelling was changed in the modern version.

Well, Tom took me to a funny place, that looked like a miniature railway station, where there was a tall man of noble and commanding appearance, who sat at a desk and smoked. The railway station had a large back yard with high fences, and several gentlemen were learning to ride ever so many different kinds of bicycles, and constantly falling off. Tom spoke to the tall gentleman and I understood him to ask for a "crippler trike." I asked him what a crippler trike was, and he said I 'd find out if it upset with me.

Well, it seems that Mr. Owens did n't have one of that kind disengaged, so we took another called a "Victor." I took a lesson in the back yard, while all the gentlemen who were learning to ride stopped and looked on.

We took a beautiful ride afterward. The streets are perfectly lovely here, and as smooth as a floor, and we had a delightful time. I had no adventures, except that I ran into a lamp-post, and again into a policeman, who politely apologized to me for

being in the way. Tom would not let me go fast, although he says that with practice I can beat a street car on an up grade.

The ladies ride alone a great deal in Washington, so last Tuesday afternoon the idea seized me to go and get a tricycle and take a ride by myself. I said nothing to any one, and especially Tom, for I knew he would insist on going.

So I slipped out of the house and went to Mr. Owens, where I got the "Victor," and started out. I had no adventures until I reached K street, where I saw a bicycler approaching from the opposite direction. He had a very pretty uniform and a beautiful wheel, with which, nevertheless, he did not seem to be very well acquainted, for he wobbled terribly, and oscillated from one side of the street to the other. This confused me, and in my terrified efforts to avoid him, we collided with a perfectly awful crash. For an instant the air seemed to be full of bicycles and blue uniforms, but it cleared presently, and I found myself still seated on my machine, and looking at the wheelman who was picking himself up and looking ruefully at his bicycle. "The darned thing 's buckled," he said in quite a low and savage tone, as if he did n't mean me to hear. "I am very sorry," said I; "can I help you unbuckle it?" I did n't know what he meant, but it was easy to see that something had happened, for the wheel looked exactly like a figure 8.

Well, he tried to straighten out the wheel but could n't, and as an African with a pushcart happened along, he put the wheel on board and walked off, muttering something about "another bill for repairs."

Then an awful thing happened. Going down hill and finding a street railway at the bottom, I put on the brake and the tricycle stopped right on the track. The wheels settled down into the little hollows, and would n't move. I tried to push down the little button in the brake handle, but could n't, and there I sat in the hot sun and waited for something to happen. It happened pretty soon in the shape of one of those horrid little Belt Line cars, which was stopped by a desperate effort of the driver, just before running over me. I looked at the horse, and the horse looked at me. The driver looked at us both.

"Get that thing off the track," said he.

"I can't," said I.

"Well, you 've got to," said he; "I can't wait here all day."

"Come and help me then," said I.

"I can't leave my cash box," said he.

Then we looked at each other some more, while the horse tried to eat the rubber tire. Finally I asked him as politely as I could, if he would mind driving around, as it must be apparent to him that I could n't move the machine, which must leave enough wellnear as much as I do. He stared at me at first, and then swore softly to himself, jumped off the car, seized the tricycle, dragged it off the track, and then without a word of apology the horrid thing got on his car and

showed me all over it, and we had a lovely time, although he teased me terribly about it, and scolded me for going alone. I will write you about my wheeling adventures as fast as they occur.

Well, dear, I must close now, as Tom has just shouted up the stairs that it is time to start for the theatre. "Brace up, Dolly," is his elegant way of putting it.

Good-by, your loving　　　　DOLLY.

WASHINGTON, D. C., 26 July, 1886.

CYCLETS.

WHEELMAN'S CHORUS.

When the city man has finished his employment,
　　　　　His employment;
When anxiety and all its cares are o'er,
　　　　　Cares are o'er;
He devotes his mind to wheeling as enjoyment,
　　　　　As enjoyment;
And voteth all his business is a bore,
　　　　　Is a bore.
His feelings he 'll with difficulty smother,
　　　　　　— Cully smother;
When after all his daily toil is done,
　　　　　Toil is done;
Taking one consideration with another
　　　　　With another;
The wheelman's lot it is a happy one,
　　　　　Happy one.'
When the enterprising wheelist 's not a wheeling,
　　　　　Not a wheeling,
When the wheelman is n't occupied on wheels,
　　　　　— Plod on wheels,
He loves to saunter in the evening early,
　　　　　Evening early,
And listen to the distant village peals,
　　　　　Village peals.
When the tourist 's not engaged in his vocation,
　　　　　His vocation,
He loves to go a touring in the sun,
　　　　　In the sun,
Taking all things into due consideration,
　　　　　— Sideration,
The Wheelman's lot it is a happy one,
　　　　　Happy one.
　　　　　　　　ALF GIBSON.

KEEP your mouth shut while riding, and you will suffer little from thirst.

ONE of the Vanderbilt boys has purchased a tricycle and is 'riding it in England.

THE Coventry Machinists Company has taken up and will use Illston's self-lubricating chain for tricycles. It has marvellous strength, reduces weight and is very clean.

STENKEN, of Jersey, has been climbing Eagle Rock Hill.

PRESIDENT BECKWITH has appointed for Massachusetts the additional representatives recommended by Chief Consul Hayes: E. H. Foote, Somerville; A. W. Dyer, Lawrence; W. M. Pratt, Brockton; John Amee, Cambridge; Edward K. Hill, Worcester; J. S. Webber, Jr., Gloucester, and W. H. Emery, Roxbury.

LAST week Nelson L. Floden and E. M.

hopes to get his man sufficiently well to visit Springfield next month. Howell is making splendid progress.

THE League membership rolls were last week increased by the addition of eighty-five new names.

PRESIDENT BECKWITH is away on a month's vacation.

A WASHINGTON street dealer exposes in his window bark helmets for cylers' use. Would n't they attract the dogs?

THE H. B. Smith Machine Company has issued a lithograph hanger showing Chickering on a Star beating Old Father Time. The old man scythes for a victory, but the Star seems to get there.

BICYCLES must be made in pairs for every one has its felloe.

Two deep crosses filled with chalk have been cut in the grass on either side of the spot where Pausey, the English manufacturer, fell and was killed on the Ripley Road.

THE Springfield prizes which are being depreciated by the News are triple plate goods. We did n't suppose any one would think for a moment that they were solid silver. Any one who desires to present us with a silver service is hereby notified that we will be satisfied with triple plate.

IF the champion of Ireland will only come over we will Mcredy for him.

"THEY ran a cremation that time," said Arty. "What the deuce is a cremation?" asked Tim. "Why, a dead heat," said the manager, and then the crowd broke up.

WHEELMEN always make good bookkeepers. They know how to keep a balance.

THE CYCLE loses a warm friend in the death of R. H. Stickney. His was one of the first names to go on our list, and he persuaded many another to do likewise.

DON'T be afraid of your cap lining these hot days. Put some green stuff over your head and save a sunstroke.

MR. C. H. CROSBY, of Bangor, was one of the Elwell bicycle party and one of the contestants on the road from Westfield to St. John, a distance of fourteen and one-half miles. It was wet and rainy at the time, but, notwithstanding this, some great time was made, according to the newspaper reports. Mr. Crosby led until within a short distance of the finish, when he was passed by Mr. F. A. Lindsey, of Lynn, Mass., who, at the close, won by only twenty feet. The distance was made in 1. 5.

BOSTON wheelmen who find it too hot for road riding now spend their afternoons at the base ball grounds.

W. W. STALL has gone into photography. Having had no little success with the camera

THE THIRD ANNUAL INTERNATIONAL TOURNAMENT
— OF THE —

CONNECTICUT ✳ BICYCLE ✳ CLUB

Will be held at HARTFORD, Sept. 8 and 9.

CHARTER OAK PARK HAS BEEN GREATLY IMPROVED DURING THE PAST YEAR, AND IS NOW FASTER THAN EVER.

FIRST DAY.

Amateur One Mile, 3.10 Class. — First prize, gold medal; second, gold and silver medal; third, silver medal.

Promateur One Mile, 2.40 Class. — First prize, solid silver brush and comb; second, rifle.

Professional Three Mile. — First prize, cash, $75; second, $50; third, $25.

Promateur A. C. U. Championship. — First prize, an elegant silver shield; second, gold medal.

Amateur Two-Mile Handicap. — First prize, Columbia Light Roadster bicycle, presented by the Weed Sewing Machine Co.; second, diamond and ruby horse-shoe scarf pin.

Promateur One-Mile Tricycle. — First prize, spider scarf pin, diamond and sapphire; second, pearl-handled revolver.

Amateur Three-Mile Open. — First prize, diamond ring; second, solid silver shoe set in handsome plush case.

Promateur Ten-Mile Lap Race. — First prize, diamond ring; second, hall mirror of elegant design.

Amateur One-Mile Team Race. — First prize, handsome engraving; second, handsome engrave list.

SECOND DAY.

Amateur Hartford Wheel Club. — First prize, gold medal; second, silver medal.

Promateur One-Mile Open. — First prize, diamond stud; second, gold watch chain with charm.

Professional One-Mile Handicap. — First prize, $100 cash; second, $50; third, $25.

Promateur Three-Mile Tricycle. — First prize, fine alligator travelling bag, completely furnished; second, alligator travelling bag.

Amateur One-Mile Bicycle. — First prize, shot gun; second, pearl-handled revolver.

Professional Five-Mile Lap. — First prize, $100 cash; second, $50; third, $25.

Amateur Two-Mile Tandem Tricycle. — First prize, two gold-headed canes; second, two silver-headed canes.

Promateur Five-Mile Open Bicycle. — First prize, shot gun; second, fishing set, rod, basket, etc.

Amateur Five-Mile State Championship. — First prize, gold medal; second, silver medal.

In the Consolation Race there will be three prizes in keeping with the above list.

Over $2,000 has been expended in getting up the above list, and all the prizes are of the very best order.   Entrance fees, $1.00 for each event, except Professionals.

Address for Blanks, CEORGE H. BURT, Box 414, HARTFORD, CONN.

SEPTEMBER 30th, ——————— OCTOBER 1st and 2d,

ARE THE DATES FOR THE

FIRST ANNUAL CYCLING TOURNAMENT,
GIVEN BY THE

New ✳ Jersey ✳ Cycling ✳ and ✳ Athletic ✳ Association

ON THEIR THREE-LAP TRACK AT

ROSEVILLE STATION   - - - - -   NEWARK, N. J.

$2,000 IN PRIZES!

Address, for Particulars, FREDERICK JENKINS, Manager, Oraton Hall, Newark, N. J.

---

pedalling up Beacon Hill. One was a Boston girl, who was entertaining a young lady from Chicago. When they arrived at the top the Boston girl said, " The extraordinary exertion essential to the ascent has caused me excessive fatigue." When the Chicago girl joined her friend she exclaimed : " Great-Scott, but I 'm done up ! "

THE Pope Manufacturing Company will have the new racing tricycle on Cripper lines completed this month. A racing Safety will also be ready. The roadster Crippers will not come till much later.

SANDERS SELLERS, of Preston, Eng., the well-known amateur, who was the first in the

world to make the mile inside of 2.40, will participate in the American tournaments. He will find faster men this time.

McCURDY gave up his idea of going to Minneapolis on account of the restrictions which the recently adopted A. C. U. rules put upon the selection of a route. Hollingsworth's route would not do now.

GID HAYNES has returned from his several months' Western trip. He has seen a great deal and is ready to tell all about it.

GEORGE S. HICKOX, steward of the New Haven Orphan Asylum, had one of his legs

broken by a fall from a bicycle, Friday, 30 July.

REV. GARRETT BEEKMAN and his sons, Fred and Harry, made the journey of forty-seven miles from Boston to Sterling camp ground, on bicycles, the father riding a Facile machine, and the sons on Star machines. They left Boston Wednesday at 5.30 A. M., stopping in Framingham and other places, in all about three hours, and arriving at the camp ground at 3.40 P. M. Fred Beekman made a stretch of thirty miles up hill and down without dismounting from his machine. For almost the entire distance the bicyclists had to ride in the teeth of a strong wind,

HELLO!

RUDGE TELEPHONE MAN.

Mr. BASSETT:

I have just bought a RUDGE RACER from STODDARD, LOVERING & Co., and intend to enter at Hartford, Springfield and Lynn. Send me a copy of the latest rules at once.   How much are you paying for records this week?

I'm a "dandy," and my RUDGE RACER is a "daisy."

DRUMMOND, the pace-maker of ebony hue, is ambitious to do something for himself in the record-breaking line, and will soon make an attempt to capture a few road records to twenty-five miles.

THERE is a bear at Denmark, Me., that eats dogs. Every well-regulated city and town should have a vigorous, capable bear, with just such an appetite. — *Lewiston Me. Journal.*

THE clerical wheelmen arrived at Saratoga last Saturday. On Sunday they attended church, in a body, three times. They wore the regular cycling costumes, including the knee breeches, Monday morning a pleasant excursion was made on the wheel to some of the springs and the rough Woodlawn Park, after which they attended the Ministerial Association meeting. In the afternoon there was another spin to the lake and to the Grizer and Vichy Springs. The tourists are gaining in strength, weight, and endurance.

IF by any possibility mail vote No. 1 should prevail, the League would find itself in a very funny predicament, for the men who cannot be amateurs under A. C. U. rules could be so under League rules.

NOW, take a rest, for September is coming wherein you will do much work.

MRS. WELDON, an English lady, and member of the bar has taken to the tricycle, and the event is deemed to be important enough to call for long articles in the papers. She was induced to make a run against time on a race track at Coventry, and was timed a quarter of a mile for 1.52⅖.

THE fatal accident to the tricycle riders at Chestnut Hill is the first one we remember to have seen recorded from this style of wheel, and ten thousand riders might probably be taken over the same road without a recurrence of the casualty. The "laws of disorder" are mighty uncertain in their operation. — *Herald.*

A CORRESPONDENT wants to know what an "earth current" is. An earth current is that motion of the earth's surface which a bicycler encounters when he dismounts over the handle of his machine. — *Burlington Free Press.*

G. B. THAYER, the Connecticut wheelman, who started to ride across the continent is reported at Sacramento, Cal. Not a little of his prairie riding was in a train.

OUR gallery of photos has been increased this week by the addition of a fine picture of L. M. Wainwright, of Noblesville, Ind.

JOSEPH PENNELL and his wife are to make a tricycle trip through Spain, to gather material for another book, doubtless.

C. T. C. sends us what he calls a touring wrinkle: "Tourists are in this uncertain climate liable to be caught in a heavy shower at any time (more especially when a gloriously fine day is prophesied). A plan adopted by an Australian friend of mine might serve as a useful hint to those who may find themselves in a similar predicament. My friend was riding up country and suddenly, when some miles from any adequate shelter, was caught in a regular downpour; there being no one near, he immediately divested himself of *all* his clothes, packed them into the hollow of a tree close at hand, and enjoying a splendid *al fresco* shower-bath, calmly awaited the end of the shower, when he dried himself in the sun, and, donning his clothes, proceeded on his way rejoicing." — *Bi. News.*

THE *Herald* man, not the paper's cycling editor, is out with a suggestion. As it is rather unique in its way we will put it in without comment: —

"The fatal tricycle accident which took place at Brighton on Friday evening may be cited as proof that even this seemingly safe machine is one which may need readjustment in order to bring it into common use among the timid. There are certain degrees of danger in almost everything that we do, and one rarely passes a day without taking risks which may be attended with fatal results. But it does not on this account follow that it is not desirable to reduce these risks, by wise precautions, to their minimum. The tricycle is in process of development. It promises, both in consequence of safety and convenience, to in time supersede the bicycle; but unquestionably human ingenuity, if properly brought into play, can make it a safer machine than it now is, without lessening the merits that it already possesses. What is needed would seem to be the arrangement of the mechanism to such a way that a sudden arrest of motion will not necessarily cause the machine to make a complete somersault. Rather than have such a mishap it would seem to be desirable to have such an adjustment of parts that the arrested motion will find vent for itself in

breaking some central part of the machine, throwing the rider or riders directly forward but not in such a manner as to force them to land on their heads."

WE have been asked several times if promateur events can be run at meetings held under League rules. Certainly they can. Professional events have always been run at our race meetings, and there is no good reason why the new class of riders should not be provided for, if committees wish to have them. The League is working to keep men where they belong, and it matters not into what class racing men go, so long as they do not push themselves where they do not belong.

CHIEF CONSUL BIDWELL, of New York, was in Boston this week.

In the lantern parade at Wilkesbarre, four washboilers had been procured and were tied to four wheels ; two men followed, and lighting packs of fire-crackers in quick succession, threw them into the washboilers, where they cracked and banged in a most sonorous style. The fusilade was kept up for quite a while, and mixed with Roman candles and other pyrotechnics made a lively display.

COREY has got a telephone. Now you will hear from him.

HENDEE, Rowe, Knapp, and Burnham have got back to Lynn.

RIDE the Lillibridge saddle if you desire unalloyed comfort. If you prefer to be saddle sore, try some other kind of seat.

W. B. EVERETT & Co., made a big hit with the Straight Steering Trike. Every one sold advertises itself, and sells another.

THE PATH.

THE PATH.

WOODSTOCK, CAN. 27 July. — Races under the auspices of the Woodstock Club.
Half-Mile Amateur. — McKay (1), 1.27 ; Brader (2).
One-Mile Amateur. — H. Clarke (1), 2.50½.
Five-Mile Handicap. — Phillboy, 2⅞ laps (1), H. Clarke (2), 15.49.
YOUNGSTOWN, OHIO. — Races under the auspices of the Inter-State Bi. Association,
One-Mile Novice. — Wm. Connel (1). 3.18 ; Frank Goodrich (2).

Half-Mile Open. — Charles Brown (1), 1.26; J. B. Hilford (2).

Half-Mile, Inter-State Championship. — W. A. Crawford (1), 1.32$\frac{2}{5}$; W. L. Horner (2).

One-Mile Open. — Charles Brown (1), 3.51$\frac{4}{5}$; J. B. Hilford (2).

One-Mile Inter-State Championship. — W. A. Crawford (1), 3.5$\frac{3}{5}$; Charles Brown (2).

Two-Mile Open. — J. B. Hilford (1), 7.1; Charles Brown (2).

Two-Mile Inter-State Championship. — W. Crawford (1), Frank McCoy (2).

Two Mile Open. — Charles Brown (1), 2.54.

CHICAGO, ILL., 31 July. — Races under the auspices of the Chicago Clubs.

One-Mile Novice. — M. Bowbeer (1), 3.08$\frac{1}{2}$; Gus. J. Kluge (2); M. D. Wilbur (3).

One-Mile Tandem. — L. W. Conkling, and N. H. Van Sicklen; walk over, 3.24.

One-Mile Open. — Van Sicklen (1), 2.59$\frac{1}{2}$; W. S. Webster (2).

One-Mile Boys. — J. Levy (1), A. C. Field (2).

One-Mile Handicap. — Van Sicklen (1), 2.53$\frac{3}{5}$; E. Mehring (2), J. P. Heywood (3).

One-Mile 3.30 Class. — M. D. Wilbur (1), 3.05; F. E. Spooner (2).

Five-Mile Handicap. — Van Sicklen, scratch (1), 16.33$\frac{1}{5}$; W. S. Webster, 20 seconds (2), W. G. E. Pierce, 25 seconds (2); J. P. Heywood, 20 seconds (3).

THE Queen's County Agl. Society will hold its annual fair at Mineola, L. I., in September. The following bicycle events will be run: 21 September, two-mile race for residents of Queen's county; 22 September, mile heats, best two in three, open; 23 September, two-mile race open to all. Three prizes in each contest. Medals valued at $10, $7.00, $5.00. Entrance fee, $1.00, in addition to member's ticket of $1.00.

AT the fair of the Kansas Central Agricultural Society to be held at Junction City, Kan., 22 and 23 September, there will be races for wheelmen and a general meeting of the wheelmen of the State, when a League division will be formed.

THE Albany wheelmen, on 2 August, perfected arrangements for their annual tournament, which will occur at the grounds of the Ridgefield Athletic association on Saturday, 28 August. Committees were appointed with the following chairman: Entertainment and reception, Captain Hawley; track, Henry Gallien; printing and advertising, Frank Munsell; treasurer, Richard Robe; secretary, Thomas H. Clemishire.

THE EVENTS IN DETAIL.

The following interesting programme was arranged for the tournament:

1. Half mile dash, open, two prizes.
2. One mile novice race, open, medal and prize.
3. First heat of two mile team race between the Albany and Troy Bicycle Clubs and the Trojan and Albany Wheelmen.
4. Five mile open race, two prizes.
5. One mile club championship for a medal.
6. Three mile championship New York State division L. A. W.
7. Second heat of team race.
8. One mile time race, to beat 3.40, open, medal and prize.
9. Five mile handicap club race, medal and prize.
10. Consolation race, one-third of a mile for League pin and prize.

The cinder track which is in charge of Manager Charles Weaver, of the Grounds is one-third of a mile, and very fast. A new covered grand stand has been erected, and every arrangement made for the comfort of visitors. Entrance fees to each open race have been placed at one dollar, and may be sent to Captain H. E. Hawley. Every effort will be made to make the tournament a grand success, and a very large attendance is expected.

THE Boston Bicycle Club's annual 100-mile bicycle road race will be run 27 September, at 11 A. M., over a course of fifty miles. There will be two classes, amateurs and promateurs, and the race will be run under A. C. U. rules. First and second prizes will be given. Entries should be sent with $1 to R. J. Tombs, captain, 36 St. James avenue, on or before 25 September at noon.

AN attractive programme has been prepared for the annual Meet of the New Jersey State Division, L. A. W., under the auspices of the Millville Bicycle Club. at Millville, 28 Aug. The events are: One mile, novice; one mile, State championship; one mile, boys under 16; one mile, 3.00 class; quarter mile; one mile, 2.55 class; three-mile lap; five mile, State championship; one mile, open; one mile, consolation. An entrance-fee of $1, returnable to starters, will be charged each race.

THE climbing contest up Eagle Rock Hill, under the auspices of the Orange Wanderers, has been postponed to 14 Aug. The race will start promptly at 4 P. M., and will be open to all L. A. W. members. The competitor making the fastest time will be awarded first prize, while a suitable trophy will be given to every rider who succeeds in reaching the top without a dismount.

RACING entry blanks for September races recently sent out by the Connecticut Bicycle Club omitted the price for promateurs. Fees for promateurs and amateurs are the same, $1 for each event.

JOHN S. PRINCE is in Minneapolis, Minn., and from that place he issues a challenge to race Fred Merrill, the Pacific coast champion, ten miles, allowing the Californian one quarter of a mile start, the race to be for $250 a side, and to take place at Minneapolis.

THE Dorchester Bicycle Club will hold a fifteen-mile club race and a fifty-mile road race about 1 Oct., over fast courses, and it is expected that all the crack riders will be there.

THERE will be five races for promateurs at the Pittsfield tournament.

THE A. C. U. ten-mile bicycle and the one-mile tandem championship will be run at Springfield this fall.

THE race meeting of the Connecticut Club, of Hartford, comes first on the docket of the large fall tournaments. The club is already receiving entries for the events, and they bid fair to have an array of racing men greater than ever before. They will actually spend $2000 in prizes.

FRED WOOD won the twenty-mile championship at Leicester, 24 July, in 1.5.17. J. Bird second and A. Hawker third. There were nine starters. Howell had twice won the belt, valued at £40, and his accident prevented his competition and the probable victory.

ALLARD rode a mile on a trike, 24 July, in 2.55$\frac{4}{5}$, making the first quarter in 43s., against a strong wind.

THE Detroit Bicycle Club will give a race meeting Saturday, 21 Aug., for amateurs and promateurs. Races will be run at "Bicycle Park" the track being in excellent condition.

THE CLUB.

CLINTON, Mass., Bicycle Club. — At semi-annual meeting held 2 August, following officers were elected: President, Geo. B. Jackson; captain, I. M. Cunningham; sub-captain, C. F. Martin; secretary-treasurer, E. A. Evans; color bearer, H. E. Giles; bugler, H. F. Lord; club committee, W. H. Jackson, F. B. Evans, with first three above named officers. Thirty active members, majority belongs to L. A. W.

THE Hyde Park Ramblers have elected these officers: President, Theodore Walters; captain, H. S. Peare; lieutenant, Archie Samson; color bearer, J. Wallers; secretary and treasurer, C. B. Bird.

COMING EVENTS.

AUGUST.

14 Saturday. — Race meeting by Iowa division, at Spirit Lake.
Hill-climbing contest of Orange Wanderers, at Eagle Rock Hill.

19 Thursday. — Annual meet and races of the Pennsylvania Division as guests of the Williamsport (Pa.) Bi. Club.
Weedsport (N. Y.) Club races. Entries close 17 August. Address H. E. Rheubottom.

21 Saturday. — Races at Detroit, Mich.

24 Tuesday. — Fifth annual tournament of the Scranton (Penn.) Club. F. C. Hand, Scranton, Penn.

27, 28, Friday, Saturday. — Annual races of the New Orleans (La.) Club.

26, 27, and 28 Thursday–Saturday. — Race meeting of the Cleveland Bicycle Club.

28 Saturday. — Annual meet and races of the New Jersey division, at Millville, N. J.
Races of the Albany Wheelmen, at Albany, N. Y.

SEPTEMBER.

1 Wednesday. — Race meeting of the Troy (N. Y.) Club, nine open races. R. S. Coon, Troy, N. Y.

3, 4 Friday, Saturday. — New York division meet and races, at Buffalo, N. Y. Five-mile L. A. W. championship.

6 Monday. — Grand tour of the L. A. W. from Niagara Falls and Buffalo, through Central and Southern New York, Virginia, and the Shenandoah Valley, winding up at Harper's Ferry, 18 September. Entries now open with the Marshals.
Annual meet Ohio division, at Massillon, Ohio, on invitation of Massillon, Canton, and Alliance Clubs. Apply to Jos. S. Meyer, Jr., 37 N. Market street, Canton, Ohio.

8, 9 Wednesday, Thursday. — Annual race meeting of the Connecticut Bicycle Club, at Charter Oak Park, Hartford, Conn. Entries to Geo. H. Burt, Box 414, Hartford, Conn. Close 1 September.

11 Saturday. — Races of Harlem Wheelmen, at Manhattan Grounds, New York. Entries close 4 September, to F. L. Bingham, 49 Rose street, New York.

10, 11 Friday, Saturday. — Annual tournament Berkshire County Wheelmen, at Pittsfield, Mass.

14 to 17 Tuesday to Friday. — Springfield Bi. Club's annual tournament, at Hampden Park, Springfield, Mass.

18 Saturday. — Races of Associated Clubs at Allegheny City, Penn.

Races of Passaic County Wheelmen, at Clifton, N. J.

21, 22, 23 Tuesday–Thursday. — Bicycle Races at Junction City, Kansas. Apply to Charles S. Davis, Junction City, Kansas.

Races at Queen's County Fair, Mineola, L. I.

23, 24, 25 Thursday–Saturday. — Fall tournament of Lynn Track Association, at Glenmere Park, Lynn, Mass.

27 Monday. — Annual 100-mile race of Boston Bicycle Club. Entries to R. J. Tombs, 36 St. James street.

30 Thursday. — First day of tournament of New Jersey Cycling and Athletic Association, at Roseville Station, Newark, N. J. Apply to Frederic Jenkins, manager, Oraton Hall, Newark, N. J.

OCTOBER.

1 and 2 Friday, Saturday. — Second and third days of tournament at Newark. Apply to Fred Jenkins.

1 Friday. — Illuminated parade of wheelmen at St. Louis, Mo. J. S. Rogers, care of *American Wheelman* St. Louis.

1, 2 Friday, Saturday.— Inter-State meet at St. Louis, Mo. Apply to J. S. Rogers.

MISCELLANEOUS

Advertisements will be inserted in this column for one cent a word, including heading and address; but no advertisement will be taken for less than twenty-five cents.

S. S. — We want you to know that our straight steerer is the best machine on the market. We are now filling large orders. Our Apollo, still holds the road record for twenty and twenty-five miles. W. B. EVERETT & CO., Berkeley square, Boston.

AMERICAN. — This is our name, and the machines we make are worthy of it. GORMULLY & JEFFERY, Chicago, Ill.

WANTED. — To sell a few more Marlboro Club machines. We have been driven to supply the demand, but we are now catching up. COVENTRY MACHINISTS COMPANY, 239 Columbus avenue, Boston.

WANTED. — Fifteen wheelmen or more to get their machines repaired at my repair shop. Especially the more. W. W. STALL, 509 Tremont street.

BICYCLES. — Fair prices and spot cash paid for desirable second-hand wheels. BUTMAN & CO., 89 Court Street.

BICYCLES AND TRICYCLES received on consignment; no charge made when goods are furnished in exchange. BUTMAN & CO., Oriental Building, 89 Court Street.

FOR SALE. — One 54-inch, '86 pattern, Rudge Light Roadster, run ten miles, $110; guaranteed in perfect condition. Address Box 2571, Boston.

BICYCLES AND TRICYCLES. — 125 shop-worn and second-hand wheels now on exhibition. Stock constantly changing; no price list; correspondence and inspection invited; open Saturday evenings. BUTMAN & CO., Scollay Square, Oriental Building.

BICYCLES AND TRICYCLES. — Bargains for cash; wheels not sold on instalments nor rented. BUTMAN & CO., 89 Court Street.

BICYCLES AND TRICYCLES. — Specialty in furnishing new wheels for exchange. BUTMAN & CO, Scollay Square, Oriental Building.

WHEELMEN, ATTENTION.

A Hydrometric Paradox.

The favorite run from Boston through Brighton, Newton, Newtonville and West Newton, to the Woodland Park Hotel is TEN miles.

A bath or swim in Allen's charming pond of pure running water (with every bathing and dressing convenience), will make the return run one of EIGHT miles. Try it.

Everything necessary provided for 15 cents.

JAMES T. ALLEN.

N. B. — Private entrance to pond midway between West Newton and the Hotel, off Washington Street, opposite Greenough.

The Road Book of Boston and Vicinity

CONTAINS all important routes around Boston, details of road surface and turnings, copious and interesting notes, many new points reached.

PRICE, 15 CENTS.

A. L. ATKINS, care of Pope Mfg. Co., Boston.

PATENTS

Secured on reasonable terms. Work reliable. Papers carefully and *legally* drawn. Special attention given to inventions in cycling by an experienced wheelman. Write for particulars.

N. L. COLLAMER - - - Patent Attorney,

WASHINGTON, D. C.

LONG BRANCH DISTRICT TELEGRAPH AND MESSENGER CO.

GEO. N. CURTIS, Prest.   J. W. CURTIS, Sec'y and Treas.

CENTRAL OFFICE, WEST END POST OFFICE BUILDING,
OPEN DAY AND NIGHT.

Long Branch, N. J., July 22 1886

The Pope Mfg Co.
Boston Mass.

Dear Sir

After an experience of three years in the use of your Bicycles in our service I can say that they give very general satisfaction; and for the prompt collection and delivery of telegrams, and messages of various kinds, are indispensable. Our messengers seem to take to them naturally and become expert-riders in a few days   Very respy PJ Casey

m. McGrane

The Cycle.

VOL. I., No. 21. BOSTON, MASS., 20 AUGUST, 1886. FIVE CENTS.

MARLBORO CLUB

TRICYCLE.

RECORD!

CHAMPIONSHIP!

F. W. ALLARD won the N. C. U. 5-Mile Championship on a Marlboro Club, beating Furnivall and Gatehouse.

F. W. ALLARD takes the 1-Mile Tricycle Record (**2.54**), on a Marlboro Club.

COVENTRY MACHINISTS CO.

239 Columbus Avenue, Boston.

THE CYCLE

PUBLISHED EVERY FRIDAY BY ABBOT BASSETT, 22 SCHOOL ST., ROOM 19.

Vol. I. BOSTON, MASS., 20 AUGUST, 1886. No. 21.

TERMS OF SUBSCRIPTION.

One Year, by mail, post-paid...........................$1.50
Three Copies in one order.............................. 3.00
Club Subscriptions.................................... 1.00
Six Months.. .90
Single Copies... .05

Specimen Copies free.

Every bicycle dealer is agent for the Cycle and authorized to receive subscriptions at regular rates. The paper can be found on sale at the following places :—

Boston, Cutter, Upham & Co., cor. Washington and School Streets. Tremont House news stand. At every cycle warehouse.

New York, Elliott Mason, 12 Warren Street.

Philadelphia, H. B. Hart, 811 Arch Street. George D. Gideon, 6 South Broad Street.

Baltimore, S. T. Clark & Co., 4 Hanover Street.

Chicago, W. M. Durell, 115 Wabash Avenue. John Wilkinson & Co., 77 State Street.

Washington, H. S. Owen, Capital Cycle Co.

St. Louis, St. Louis Wheel Co., 1121 Olive Street.

ABBOT BASSETT . . . . . Editor

A. Mudge & Son, Printers, 24 Franklin St., Boston

All communications should be sent in not later than Tuesday, to ensure insertion the same week.

Entered at the Post-office as second-class mail matter.

Believing that those who read the papers wish first of all to be entertained ; and believing that variety, the spice of life, is essential to the best entertainment ; and believing that discussions of the amateur question and League politics have ceased for the nonce to afford entertainment, we are going to give our readers a little change. It is warm weather, and light reading is in demand. We are going to give you a story or two. In this issue we have drawn upon a contemporary for a story, but next week we shall give you something new. A well-known writer for the wheel press has furnished us a story which is exceedingly interesting, and it will appear next week. Look out for it. It will be called " The Cycler's Story."

In the last issue of the *Bulletin*, Mr. Miller, of the Racing Board, rebukes the editor for allowing such articles as he has lately seen fit to publish, to appear in its columns. He concludes what he has to say as follows :

" As a member of the Racing Board, I can assure you that the first word has yet to be mentioned in that Board toward the relinquishment of its powers over the race path to the A. C. U. or any other organization, and that any suggestion toward that end by

the press are worthy only of being cast into your 'official' waste-paper basket, instead of encumbering the columns of our valued journal with such worthless chaff ! "

The A. C. U. does not ask to have the League abandon racing, in the first place ; and in the second, the Racing Board could not so commit the League if it wanted to.

Some one, who signs himself " Charter Oak," writes to the *American Wheelman* and gives what he calls a *true* account of the meeting of Messrs. Bassett and Ducker at Springfield. We were going to lift it and italicize the true statements in it, but on looking it through we found just about ten words in the whole article that . were true. The writer gave a column and a quarter of chaff, only ten words of which were true.

Many amateur wheelmen are laying plans for racing with and against professionals. They claim that their amateur standing will not be affected, because the League disclaims jurisdiction over road events. They forget that the A. C. U. has jurisdiction over road racing, and that the officers of that organization will not let the amateur rule be broken on the road. Any rider who is declared to be a promateur or professional by the A. C. U. will be so regarded by the L. A. W. The League has no jurisdiction over running and jumping, but if the N. A. A. A. A., which has, should declare a man to be a professional runner or jumper, the League could not accept him as an amateur wheelman.

FROM A FEMININE POINT OF VIEW.

The terrible accident that occurred in Allston recently has carried grief to many hearts outside the immediate circle of friends and acquaintances in which the afflicted parties move. Our hearts go out in kindly sympathy to the noble woman who has been bereft of her chosen life companion, and I know that I speak for a large number of wheelwomen when I say that her grief has been shared by them, and that they have sorrowed with and for her in the days of agony.

Nothing that we can say will restore to her the one that has gone, nor will it compensate in any manner for what she has lost, but it is gratifying at such times to be assured that we are held in grateful remembrance, and our burden becomes the lighter. And so let me speak for my lady readers and assure our friend that our sympathy is with

her, and more deeply felt than words can express.

I want to suggest a little trip a-wheel for those venturesome spirits who like to seek out new fields of exploration. I have been enjoying the cool breezes and delightful air of that quaint little town on the South Shore where the Pilgrim Fathers found a home. I did not take my wheel with me, and regretted it every minute of the time that I was there.

I would not advise the ladies to go to Plymouth awheel unless it be on a tandem with a gentleman, for there is no little sand along the South Shore and with a single tricycle there would have to be a good deal of pushing. Bicyclers have visited the ancient town on many occasions, I was told, but the natives have yet to see a lady riding in the place.

A pleasant trip could be made by taking a wheel on board the steamer which arrives at Plymouth at noon and remaining over a day, using the time in riding about. Or a good deal could be done in a single day, for the steamer stops over for two hours, and in that time many of the attractions could be viewed.

I don't think I need tell what there is at Plymouth ; for the Rock, the great statue of Faith, and the famous collection of curious and ancient relics, are known the wide world over. The roads are good, though there are several hills to climb.

I am in receipt of a letter from a lady rider who has had an unpleasant experience in a storm. She was caught in a smart shower, and was miles away from any habitation. In consequence, she arrived at her destination in a very damp and bedraggled condition. And now she suggests a cycling cape of gossamer to be used on such occasions. I do not believe in rubber garments for riding. Had our friend been clad in rubber she would have been as moist from perspiration as she was in this case from the rain, and she would have suffered more inconvenience, I do not doubt, for rubber prevents the escape of all that should go forth from the body when one is unusually active, as she is in riding. If we get caught in the rain it is much better to get a drenching than to wear waterproof clothing, but we must be careful to make a change of clothing as soon as we get to shelter. Daisie.

The Committee on Rules and Regulations of the L. A. W. will submit a new rule at the Buffalo meeting, which shall provide that the officers shall be elected by the membership at large in general meeting. This is as it should be. There must be something to awaken an interest in that meeting.

BIKE AGAINST STRIKE.

On the 15th August, 187' the quiet little town of N—— was aroused by the news that the workers of the Regent Iron Works were on strike. For some time past there had been great discontent amongst them, but none had dared to rebel openly. The head of the neighboring iron works had slightly raised the wages of his men, and those at the Regent Works wanted a corresponding rise in theirs. This they had been promised they should have at the end of November. But this did not suit them, and one of them, named Bill Barker, had gone so far as to send a threatening letter to Mr. Cross, the head of the works, for which he was imprisoned. On coming out of prison, he at once began to stir his comrades to action, and the strike was the result. As he was known to be a most desperate fellow, it was greatly feared that he and his workers would not stop at words. On the night of the 14th they had held a meeting at a brick kiln, not far from the town, and the next morning two men who were known to be against the movement were found dead, one in the kiln, and the other in a ditch close by. The town was all in a ferment, the shops were shut, and most people were afraid to go out of doors. At that time there was staying at the Bull Inn a gentleman who was making a tour in that part of the country, on a bicycle, named George Dundas. He had only arrived the night before this strike was known, and as he had sometimes stopped there before, he was not a stranger to the majority of the inhabitants. After breakfast, on the morning of the 15th, having nothing to do for an hour or two, he went out to have a stroll round the town, to see anything there was to see, and to buy a few things he needed. He had bought all he wanted, and seen everything worth seeing, and was returning home to the inn by an out-of-the-way lane, when a little ragged lad stepped out of the hedge, and after looking suspiciously around, came up to the cyclist, and said, in a low frightened voice, —

" Please are you Mr. Dundas, sir ? "

" Yes, my lad ; what can I do for you ? "

For a second or two the boy did not speak, but glanced at the hedges and trees as if he feared a lurking enemy ; then he said —

" You know about the strike, sir ? "

" Yes, I do ; why ? "

" 'Cos they be going over ter Cross — Mr. Cross, I mean — this morning."

" Going over to Mr. Cross, my boy ; well, what of that ? "

" Why, they 're going ter fire the house, sir."

" What ! "

" They 're going ter fire the house. I heard Bill Barker say that he 'oped ter be able ter break the old un's 'ed — that's Mr. Cross."

" When did they start ? "

" 'Bout 'arf-past ten o'clock, sir."

George glanced at his watch — it was then 11.35 — and putting it back in his watch-pocket, said, —

" How far is it to Mr. Cross's ? "

" 'Bout ten miles, sir. Oh ! sir, don't you think you could ride to him on your bisocle, sir ? "

" On my machine ? — well, so I could. What time do you say they started ? "

" 'Arf-past ten, sir."

" Half-past ten — ten miles. Well, I can but try. I'll go at once ; good-bye, my boy. You will see me again before long. Good-bye ! "

" Good-bye, sir, don't breathe a word ter any one ; Bill 'ud break my 'ed."

" I won't you may be sure. Good-bye ! "

George hurried off to the Bull ; took off his waistcoat and hat, brought out his machine — a 58. " Interchangeable " — got on, and was off. The roads were dry and hard, and the day was a splendid one. A very slight wind was blowing from the right, but only just enough to keep the day fresh. He soon got away from the town and into a hard sandy road, with hedges each side, as most of the roads in those parts have. As it was not a market-day there were very few people on the road, and only two vehicles were passed the whole way. So intent was he upon his ride that he did not notice the rate at which he was travelling ; and it seemed only a minute or so when he passed the " Wheat Sheaf," which he knew was just five miles from N——. A group of rustics outside, thinking he was on a race, cheered lustily. It was a race ; but what for ? No paltry prize. On him and his machine depended the lives of a whole household of harmless people. Directly in front was the long and steep Redstowe Hill. He put on the speed, rushed at it, and for a time went up pretty fast, but soon relapsed into one steady grind. The monotonous rise and fall of the pedals, the sight of the wheel under him slowly travelling round, the hedges and stones passing gradually away behind him, all tended to make the pace unbearable to one whom twenty miles an hour was the pace he wished for. At last the top was reached. The road the other side was first a very steep hill, then a slightly down course for about one mile, and finally a straight level run to Mr. Cross's house. Dundas could see the country for miles every way, and looking about on all sides, could perceive no traces of the strikers. At first the hill was so steep he thought he should be obliged to dismount, but by the aid of back pedalling and a strong brake, he was enabled to descend at a moderate pace. When about half way down he glanced to a field on his left, and — oh, how his heart jumped ! — there were the enemy. They were still a good way off, and were not walking in a straight line, but in a slanting direction, so that they must strike the road about a mile in front. If he could pass that point before they reached it, he was safe ; if not who could tell what would happen ? The hedge each side was pretty high, so that by leaning over the handles he was concealed from their view, but further on it was barely four feet. He rode slowly till the low hedge was reached, and then put on the speed and dashed into the open. He had not gone many yards before there came a shout from the left, of " There 's some one on the road ; " followed by another of " At him, boys ; if he passes the game 's up." All began to run, and it was clear that unless he put on more speed, they would be into the road before he passed. The road was wide, in splendid condition, and he was riding slightly down hill. The pace increased, his feet could scarcely keep pace with the treadles ; the wheels looked spokeless, except from above, where the only signs of

their having spokes was that near the rim a sort of silvery sheen denoted where they were whizzing round and round. This could not last much longer. He felt as if his thighs had been seized in an iron grip, and there held. The men were within a hundred feet of the road, — one was far in advance of the rest ; a glance showed that he was Bill Barker, the leader of the strike. On he came ; he leaped the hedge ; the machine passed like a flash ; a howl of rage and disappointment arose from the strikers as Bill Barker fell with a dull thud into the road, a foot or so in the rear of the bicycle. Now all the danger was over, all he had to do was to ride on. Could he do this ? The excitement of the last ten minutes had been so great that he had not noticed how fatigued he was ; but now came the reaction. He turned the corner, and about a quarter of a mile distant, saw the house of Mr. Cross. His head swam ; hedges, house, trees, and fields all seemed to dance before him in one mazy galop. The gates which faced the road were shut, but on calling out they were opened, and telling the man to close them again, he shot through and rode up to the house. Sitting down on the grass he explained to Mr. Cross the circumstances of his ride. The house was barricaded at once, and all the servants and people about the house told off to various posts. George had dinner and a short nap, and by 5 o'clock felt all right again.

The besiegers had surrounded the house ; and the head gardener, who had been imprudent enough to look out of a window, had been shot at. All the household were in a state of great anxiety, as it was well known that, though the house was large and well built, it was not sufficiently strong to stand the repeated attacks of nearly two hundred men. At 8 p. m. one door had been burst in and several shots fired through the opening, but the place was quickly blockaded again. It was clear that unless help arrived soon all would be over. A conference was held in the drawing-room, and after a good bit of talk George asked how far it was to the barracks.

" A good eight miles," answered Mr. Cross.

" Have you any oil ? "

" Yes, plenty ; why, what for ? "

" I 'm going to try to ride to the barracks," quietly answered George.

" Why, man, the fellows are all round the house, and it 's beginning to rain ; we shall have a regular hurricane shortly. I should not think of letting you go." So saying, Mr. Cross departed to look after the defenders.

George was soon left alone in the room with Mr. Cross's eldest daughter, a pretty girl of seventeen years, who had all of a sudden taken great interest in him.

" Miss Cross, I 'm going to ask a favor of you," said George, " will you do it ? "

" What is it ? I 'll do it if I can."

" Do you know where the keys of the gates are kept ? "

" I do."

" Well, will you unlock them for me ? "

" I will, if you will promise me that when you reach the barracks you will stay there, and not attempt to get back to-night."

" I promise," replied George, and off he went to get his machine ready. After he

had oiled it, he brought it round to the gates and waited for them to be opened. It was then that he saw for the first time what a night it was. As yet it had not rained much, but there was a regular gale blowing, and far away to the east the dull rumble of the thunder was to be plainly heard, while occasionally a faint long flash was seen in the same direction. He had not to wait long, for in a few minutes the gates were opened by the young lady herself. After bidding her good-bye, he got on and was off on his midnight ride. He saw nobody about till he had got well out of the avenue, when on turning the corner in the road he came upon six men seated under a tree round a large turf fire. A shout was raised as he passed, and a voice cried out, "Quick, Ned, bring round the grey mare, he's off to Kilrush." George had gone about a mile on the road when, some distance behind, he heard the clattering of mounted men, no doubt his pursuers. "Now for a struggle," thought he.

At a quarter past 2 A. M., the officers and men of the barracks at Kilrush were aroused by hearing two shots fired, seemingly coming from the main road. Most of them turned out to see the cause, and heard far away the dull thud, thud, thud, of horses. urged at full speed along a clayey road, Knowing that something must be up, several officers strolled along the road in the direction of the noise. They were walking in the road, listening to the sounds coming nearer, when something was seen a few yards in front, and a bicyclist passed by them going at a tremendous pace; and shortly after came two mounted men, apparently in hot pursuit. They passed without noticing the officers, who immediately began to run towards the barracks as hard as they could go.

At the barracks the excitement was intense, several men being mounted in readiness for any emergency. It could now be seen that it was a man on a bicycle, and two following on horseback, that were nearing the entrance. When within about thirty feet, the pursuers stopped, took aim with their pistols, two shots were heard, and, with a cry of pain, the cyclist threw up his arms, the machine rolled unsteadily across the road, and a cry of "Good God! he's down," arose from the assembled soldiers, as rider and machine came down with a crash in the midst of them. George Dundas had completed his ride; he had reached Kilrush.

In broken sentences he informed the garrison of the state of affairs at Mr. Cross's, and then became unconscious; but his friends were saved.

For six weeks George Dundas lay between life and death in a state of delirium. All the while he was nursed chiefly by the Cross family. People called all day to inquire how he was getting on. Nothing was done to his machine, but it was placed in the barracks, covered with mud and blood (for George had been hit in the right side, and had bled profusely), and with the saddle torn from end to end by a shot. Some six months after the event, there appeared in the Dublin *Chronicle* the following paragraph:—

Married, on the 4th inst., by the Rev. P. O'Garth, at St. Patrick's, Dublin, Mr. G. Dundas, son of Mr. Dundas, of the firm of Collins, Dundas & Co., bankers, of London, to Miss L. Cross, eldest daughter of Mr. Cross, of the Regent Iron Works, Connemara. Erin go bragh."

The little boy who had given George the information was not forgotten, and never had cause to repent meeting him on the day of the strike. Barker and three others were caught and tried, and the last that was heard of them was that they were working in government service in the neighborhood of Portland.

After he was married, George often used his machine, and had plenty of adventures, but he always owned that never in his life did he ride like he did when he rode "Bike against Strike." — *Wheel World.*

McCURDY'S RECORD.

At the close of McCurdy's attempt to beat the twenty-four hour record at Waltham, on 19 and 20 July, it was announced that he had failed, having covered about 280 miles, cyclometer measurement. The route was remeasured with a cyclometer and resulted in increasing his distance to 280 4/10 miles. On Monday, 9 Aug., McCurdy had the course surveyed by Edward S. Smilie, surveyor of Newton, who makes the distance covered by McCurdy at Waltham, 286.559 miles. Mr. Smilie furnishes a complete and minute table of all the distances. A summary of his measurements shows that the long course covered by McCurdy twenty-two times was actually 12.822 miles in length, making 282.084 miles. In addition, the Lynn man covered a short course once of 4.475 miles, making the grand total, as above stated, 286.559.

UP EAGLE ROCK HILL.

Out of seven entries for the Orange Wanderers' hill-climbing contest, last Saturday, only four started. They were John A. Wells, on a 51-inch Star; C. H. Chickering, on a 42-inch Star; C. L. Myers, on a Columbia Light Roadster; and E. P. Baird, on a Royal Mail. A good many wheelmen were present, and lined the road from start to finish.

The hill is 1 3/8 miles long, but as there is a level stretch near the foot, the start was made on it, at Harrison avenue, making one mile to be ridden. The grade grows steeper as you ascend, and varies from about one foot in fifteen to one in eight, with a soft spot near the top.

Wells was the first man off. He rode easily and completed the ascent in twelve minutes. Five minutes later, Chickering started with a rush and finished in nine minutes. Myers rode half way, and Baird nearly reached the top.

THIRST AND DRINKING IN HOT WEATHER.

So far as the mere sensation of thirst is concerned, there can be no question that it is a mistake to drink too much or too frequently in hot weather; the fluid taken in is very rapidly thrown out again through the skin in the form of perspiration, and the outflow being promoted by this determination towards the surface, a new and increasing demand for fluid follows rapidly on the successive acts of drinking and perspiring, with the result that "thirst" is made worse by giving way to it. Meanwhile, it must not be forgotten that thirst is nature's call for fluid to replace that lost by cutaneous exudation in warm weather; and if the demand be not met, what may be regarded as the residual fluid of the tissues must be absorbed or the blood will become unduly concentrated. Now this absorption of the residual fluid of the tissues has the obvious drawback of taking into the blood in a concentrated instead of a dilute form the products of disassimilation, together with the absorption of some excrementitious matters which would probably not be taken up at all if the blood were not abnormally dense. It is necessary to recognize that harm may be done by a process of self-poisoning with excrementitious matter, retained or taken up in default of an adequate supply of fluid in the form of drink to dilute and wash it away. There is, moreover, another disadvantage of the non-drinking method of suppressing thirst. It is especially needful for the preservation of health that the metabolism on which normal nutrition depends should be rapid and free in hot weather. If the organic temperature is, or more accurately, if the several and complementary temperatures of the organism are, to be maintained at the health point, tissue change must be favored, and such modifications of body heat as may be effected by flushing and evaporation must be facilitated. In short, if we refuse to drink when we are thirsty simply because we shall thirst again, we are imposing a restraint on the activities by which nature is endeavoring to preserve the health. We venture to hope that those who are zealously urging the policy of refusing to quench their thirst in this hot weather because "drinking makes people more thirsty," will reconsider their policy from the physiological standpoint, and that they will recognize that to thirst and drink, and perspire and drink again, are the natural steps in a process by which Nature strives to maintain the integrity of those organic changes which the external heat has a tendency to impede. The natural and true policy is to supply an adequate quantity of fluid without excess. Therefore, do not abstain from drinking, but drink slowly, so as to allow time for the voice of Nature to cry "Enough." There is no drink so good as *pure* water. For the sake of flavor, and because the vegetable acids are useful, a dash of lemon juice may be added with advantage. The skin should be kept fairly cool, so that a sufficient quantity of the fluid taken may pass off by the kidneys. — *Lancet.*

The following is the new definition recently adopted by the English Amateur Athletic Association: "An amateur is any person who has never engaged in, nor assisted in, nor taught any recognized athletic exercise for money, or who has never, either in public or in private, raced or exhibited his skill for a public or for a private stake, or other remuneration, or for a purse or for gate money, and never backed or allowed himself to be backed either in a public or private race."

The Cycle and "Wheelman's Reference Book" will be sent to any address for $1.65.

THE STAR'S WORLD'S RECORD!

McCURDY'S COURSE.

———286.559 Miles in 24 Hours.———

THE LONG COURSE.

Starting Point, Moody Street.

Crescent to Adams Street..................	695 feet.
Across Square............................	155 "
On Crescent and Derby to Cherry Street....	7,907 "
Cherry to River Street...................	1,977 "
River Street to Auburndale Avenue........	686 "
Auburndale Avenue to Lexington Street....	4,529 "
Lexington Street to River Street.........	3,720 "
River Street to Auburndale Avenue........	2,774 "
River Street to Cherry Street............	686 "
River Street to Waltham Street...........	980 "
Waltham to Crafts Street.................	3,539 "
Crafts Street to Watertown Street........	4,400 "
Crafts Street to Washington Street.......	2,253 "
Crafts Street, from Washington Street to Watertown Street..................	2,253 "

Watertown and Waltham Streets to River Street	6,595 feet.
River to Cherry Streets..................	980 "
River, from Cherry Street to Auburndale Avenue	686 "
On Auburndale Avenue....................	4,529 "
On Lexington Street.....................	3,720 "
On River Street........................	2,774 "
River Street to Cherry Street............	686 "
River Street to Waltham Street...........	980 "
Waltham Street to Crafts Street..........	3,539 "
Waltham Street and Extension to Lowell Street	4,457 "
Lowell Street to Pine Street.............	1,318 "
Pine Street to Starting Point............	884 "
	67,702 feet,

OR 12 $\frac{822}{1000}$ MILES.

ON THIS CIRCUIT McCURDY MADE 22 LAPS.

Newton, Aug. 9, 1886

Having measured the above distances, I hereby certify that they are correct.

E. S. SMILIE, Surveyor.

THE SHORT COURSE.

Crescent Street to Adams Street..........	695 feet.
Adams Street to Brown Street.............	2,113 "
Brown Street to Moody Street.............	764 "
Moody Street to Crescent Street..........	2,451 "
Moody Street to Felton Street............	1,020 "
Felton Street to Prospect Street.........	2,875 "
Prospect Street to Main Street...........	1,759 "
Main Street to Moody Street..............	2,532 "
Moody Street to Felton Street............	623 "

Moody Street to Crescent Street..........	1,020 feet.
Crescent Street to Adams Street..........	695 "
Adams Street to Brown Street.............	2,113 "
Brown Street to Moody Street.............	764 "
Moody Street to Crescent Street..........	2,451 "
Crescent Street to Adams Street..........	695 "
Around the Park at Adams Street..........	363 "
Crescent Street to Starting Point........	695 "
	23,628 feet,

OR 4 $\frac{473}{1000}$ MILES.

Newton, Aug. 9, 1886.

The short lap made by McCurdy to complete distance. Having measured the above distances, I hereby certify that they are correct.

E. S. SMILIE, Surveyor.

CONTRIBUTORS' CLUB.

THE ORANGE ORDINANCE.

Editor of the Cycle: Please allow me one word.* Those who have attacked the Orange Wanderers on account of their connection with the Orange ordinance, requiring lights and bells, have generally based their attacks on the theory that the Wanderers *originated* the ordinance.

That theory is false.

The Wanderers did not originate either of the ordinances. They knew that they were in contemplation by the authorities, and as they, as a club, approved of the principle involved, they passed their resolutions.

LUTHER H. PORTER,
President Orange Wanderers.

CYCLETS.

MY WHEEL.

ROLL on, roll on, O wheel, bright and new,
Roll on, the sheltered roadways through,
Roll, roll, past meadows, morning sweet,
Each lur'a glad sights thy rider's eyes to greet,
Your polished metal glist'ning in the morning sun,
As sped we swiftly by the varied landscapes, all as one.

Roll swifter, wheel, for the moon is high,
And towards shelter weary birdies fly,
There to rest their tired pinions as they sing,
Praise to their Maker, 'ere again they wing.

O wheel, a friend both tried and true,
For such to me indeed are you,
I would not bring our journey to an end,
But darkness lowers. See to the West the sun descend;
Though when with thee I seldom weary grow;
O wheel, I now must bid thee, roll slow.   R. G. B.

WHY is the sum that men are taxed to join the League like a baby? Because its a precious little.

"SEE here, what's this new society?" said Brown to Jones. "Which one?" inquired his friend. "Why, Smith used to put ' L. A. W.' after his name, and then he put 'C. T. C.' and now I have got a note in which he puts down ' R. S. V. P.'"

PENNSYLVANIA paragraphers say that Massachusetts has been foremost in every row that has occurred in League affairs.

A WHEELMAN never gets so well up in the world as he does when he has taken a header. He is generally aching then. See?

FRIENDS of the late Major Durell say that the story circulated by the *Inter Ocean* regarding the bar-room quarrel is not true; that Durell was not present at the fight, and that it is not known how he received the bruises.

WHEEL papers have not done guessing at the true inwardness of the meeting of chiefs at Springfield. We have to smile at the results.

THINK of a Boston club calling a run to Music Hall. This is what the Massachusetts Club did and it was a success. Music, beer, ice cream, etc., etc.

SPRINGFIELD has received assurances that a large English contingent will come over, under the lead of Harry Etherington.

THE League has now a membership of 9,383.

THE New York Division has made a change in the time for its meeting. It will be in session during the evening of 3 Sept., and leave the day open for the meeting of the League officers.

FROM all that we can learn, Boston will not be very well represented at the fall meeting in Buffalo. We have yet to discover an officer that will go on.

EVERY wheelman who went on the Blue-Nose tour rode on a Star. The machine had two wheels of equal size, and was propelled by steam down the lake.

THE Chelsea Cycle Club members are having a good deal to say about the excellence of a fish dinner, served to them at the Putnam House at Revere Beach. The ordinary fish dinner has usually a very small complement of swimming fish, and a very large proportion of the sedate clam.

SOME very entertaining bits of Oriental life and manners will be found in Thomas Stevens' narrative of his experience among the nomad Koords, as detailed in August Outing. It is striking to note the keen interest that these wild herdsmen take in learning the probable chances of hostility, at some future date, between their deadly enemy, the Muscovs and the Inglisis.

"ATKIN'S Wanderer's" is what the *American Wheelman* calls the Columbia team.

GIDEON, of Philadelphia, has been on a vacation over the handle bars. He went over at a 2.28 clip, and kissed the earth with all the enthusiasm of youth.

RUMOR, which is always very busy just before a big race meeting, tells us that Rowe and Burnham have been making some fast time on the track at Springfield. Rowe is credited with a mile in 2.29½, and Burnham covered the same distance in 2.32. Burnham also made two miles in 5.18¾.

THE fast men are a good deal like a music teacher just now, for they are beating time.

LAMSON, of Portland, photographer, made some very pretty pictures of the Blue-Nose tourists. Mr. E. G. Whitney, of the tourists, has favored us with a very nice one.

"BOYD," — The L. A. W. will have little, if anything, to do with the racing men who come over from England. They are booked for the A. C. U. tournaments, and if they race with promateurs they will be dealt with by the A. C. U. We believe the A. C. U. intends to act squarely, and they can be trusted to deal with the English contingent.

THE Massachusetts Division has agreed to pay the expenses of a lawsuit brought by a Newton wheelmen to maintain his rights on the highway. A legal advisory board will be established by the officers.

THE *American Wheelman* is out in its new dress, and looks as fresh as a daisy, while its reading matter has lost none of its old-time sparkle.

PHILADELPHIA is arranging for another race meeting. It will be held on the gilt-edge amateur basis.

THE Yost and McCune Safety will not be put on the market this year.

THE English papers will disallow McCurdy's record for 287,879 miles, because it was made over a short course, but they will oblige us by showing rules to compel a man to take a longer one. In the absence of rules, the record is as much worthy of acceptance as any that England has given us. If it is urged that a more creditable one has been made in England over a longer course, we can only say that America cannot give us such roads as England has for a long course, and few will doubt that McCurdy did more work than the English record holder did.

THE *Herald* had a very good cut of Chief Consul Hayes last Sunday. The average newspaper cut is a poor thing, and when we do get a good one, it is brilliant by contrast.

THE Fitchburg band has been engaged for the Springfield tournament.

THE telegraph operator at Marblehead employs the wheel in the delivery of telegraphic messages.

GASKELL is going into training, and will ride in the fall races.

LANGDOWN, the Australian champion, has arrived in San Francisco.

WOODSIDE is down for an attempt to ride twenty-one miles in the hour on 28 August, and he will endeavor to get special sanction from the A. C. U. to allow Hendee and Rowe to race against him.

THE English riders who have accepted Springfield prizes without a murmur, and who talk of trying for some more, are now discrediting them in their own country. We don't think England will make out much of a case if it tries to show that better prizes are given at races in England than are given in America. And, moreover, we hope the amateur inclined press will not condemn inexpensive prizes.

THE following have been appointed a special committee to count the mail vote now pending before the L. A. W. board of officers: John A. Wells, chief consul, Pennsylvania; Eugene M. Aaron, secretary-editor; Ed F. Burns, representative, New Jersey. The vote closes August 28, at noon, and the result will be reported in the issue of the *Bulletin* for September 3.

JENKINS alludes in a familiar way to "Jim" Stickney who lately met with an accident. The friends of Rufus Stickney never heard him called "Jim."

JOHN S. PRINCE is in Minneapolis, Minn., and from that place he issues a challenge to race F. T. Merrill, the Pacific coast champion, ten miles, allowing the Oregonian one quarter of a mile start, the race to be for $250 a side, and to take place at Minneapolis.

JENKINS says he never won a prize at Springfield. He forgets the editor's race which he and "we" won from Editor Aaron by default, and he should remember that Editor Aaron gave him a dinner in payment. The dinner was as expensive as it pretended to be.

MR. FOWLER, of the Pope Manufacturing Company, is at work on the company's calendar for 1887, and he tells us that it will beat the record and go far ahead of the one from which wheelmen are now tearing leaves.

RUDGE TELEPHONE MAN.

HELLO, MR. BASSETT.

Can you tell me what constitutes a straight Amateur? I have just sent my entries for the **Hartford Meeting**, the **8th, 9th,** and **10th** of **September,** to Mr. Geo. Burt, and I just want to say, that **Stoddard, Lovering & Co.** don't lend or give me my **RUDGE RACER,** my **"Uncle"** don't pay my expenses, and my **"Grandmother"** don't care a rap how I spend my time.

WHAT'S THE MATTER WITH ME?

FRED E. VAN MEERBEKE, *en route* on a bicycle from New York to San Francisco *via* New Orleans, reached Tucson, Arizona, on the 4th inst., after being on the road ninety-six days. He has had a hard time through the dry regions. The distance travelled to date by country roads is 3,066 miles. He left Tucson on the 7th inst., going *via* Los Angeles and Oakland, expecting to reach the Golden Gate by the 25th inst.

IT is rumored that the dealers in lamps and bells will not object to a few more just such ordinances as that which the Orange city fathers have passed.

A SPRINGFIELD clothier has put up a bicycle to be guessed for. The one who tells nearest to the number of beans in a bottle has the bicycle, and the award will be made at the Springfield tournament. — *Cycle.* Of course some Boston man will win. — *Wheel.* Oh no! It takes a New York man to find out what's in a bottle.

RHODE ISLAND wheelmen will tour to Newport, 24 August, and make a day of it at this charming watering place.

PERCY STONE leaves Saturday night for Lynn, Mass., where he will go into strict and systematic training for the Hartford and Springfield tournaments. We will now have an opportunity of seeing just what he can do with careful training, something he has never had before. I have great faith in Percy and believe that he will acquit himself well, even with the flyers. At short distances he has done the quarter mile in less than 38, the half in 1.17, and the mile in less than 2.47; he has an excellent spurt, and his good work in the fifty-mile road race shows that he is gaining in endurance. — *St. Louis Spectator.*

IN the opinion of many, the L. E. C. W. has, in the recognition of the professional as a worthy member, set the older and more powerful organization an example which it will do well to follow. — *Bulletin.*

WE are very glad to note that the story of Major Durell's death is pronounced untrue. Private letters state that there were no bruises of any kind on his body, and therefore he could not have been injured as reported.

FRED MILLER of East Boston, while riding a bicycle near Spot pond, Sunday, was thrown from his machine down a steep embankment. Both of his arms were rendered useless. He also received severe injuries to his body. The bicycle was badly wrecked.

PHILADELPHIA has, in the person of William Fleming the greatest long-distance rider in America, and probably, when the road conditions are taken into consideration, the greatest in the world. Mr. Fleming has a record of over 5,000 miles in one riding season, all of which were made, not by persistent travelling over a short stretch of choice road, but by long tours over the diversified highways of the South and West. He has introduced the wheel into localities where its appearance was as great a curiosity to the inhabitants as is Stevens' bicycle to the dwellers in the Orient. He is a typical American of the "leather-stocking" build, gaunt and tireless, and is a member of the Pennsylvania Club. — *Philadelphia Press.*

G. B. THAYER writes to *Ingleside* of his trip across the country. He says: "I rode over a thousand miles the first three weeks, and many a day made seventy to seventy-five miles: The whole distance I travelled on the wheel was 3,056 miles ; on the cars about 1,800 miles ; and afoot, climbing mountains in Colorado and the Yosemite, would nearly, if not quite, make the total number of miles travelled during the trip 5,000. The cost, including every expense whatsoever, has been $120, so that it has averaged but little over a dollar a day."

WILLOW COTTAGE, Magnolia, has been appointed a League hotel. The terms will be two dollars per day or fifty cents a meal. The hotel will be open through the fall riding season. Wheelmen can depend upon considerate attention.

THERE is a good deal of complaint arising from the action of wheelmen who go to hotels in large numbers and fail to behave themselves. At some of the North Shore houses wheelmen are in very bad odor.

A MEETING of the Massachusetts Division officers was called for the 10th. Our notice was made out for the 11th, and so we remained contentedly at home on the 10th, while on the 11th we engaged with Representative Harris in a hunting match about the city to find the meeting. There was no quorum on the 10th, but those who did put in appearance talked over various matters informally, and it was agreed to call a general meeting of the Division at an early date.

THE National Association has adopted the following rule, to take the place of Article VI. of The Laws of Athletics : *Timekeepers.* — Each of the three timekeepers shall time every event, and in case two watches agree, and the third disagree, the time marked by the two shall be the official time. If all three watches disagree, the time marked by the watch giving the middle time shall be the official time. If there should be but two timekeepers, and their watches do not agree, the time marked by the slowest watch shall be the official time. Time shall be taken from the flash of the pistol.

THIS is essentially the League rule, with the addition of a provision for the use of two watches.

WHEELMEN are like tailors — when they have climbed a hill ; they make pants.

A COLORED "gemman" from New York City dropped into Stone's place a few days ago and hired a crank. Not long after, he returned with a wagon load of bicycle parts. Of course he blamed the roads. — *Critic.*

AMERICAN wheelmen are very confident that the English riders will be beaten this year. But then, "Nothing is certain" ; but if nothing is certain, how can it be certain that nothing is certain?

SOME one has been telling a contemporary that wooden wheels are coming in for tricycles. We have seen a wooden wheel for a tricycle and it scaled three and a half pounds without a tire. We shall soon tell our readers about a wooden wheel tricycle that weighs not over fifty pounds and sells at a figure much lower than any machine now on the market.

THE Massachusetts Club is going to the dogs. They will see them at the Ashmont Kennels on Saturday.

"MEN often jump at conclusions," says the proverb. So do dogs. We saw a dog jump at the conclusions of a wheelman the other day. It was a great feat.

THE Canadians are very much exercised that Hunter entered the Montreal races as a Canadian, but Hunter says he did so by advice of Secretary Gnaedinjer.

THERE is no truth in the report that the duffers will train on ketch up for the fall tournaments.

THE Invincible took the gold medal at Vienna Exhibition.

A MEETING of manufacturers and others interested in opposing the claims made by Mr. William Bown, in reference to the manufacture of ball bearings, will be held at the Grand Hotel, Colmore-road, Birmingham, on Tuesday, 10th August, at 3.30 o'clock. — *Wheeling.*

ALBIN, the trick rider, who visited America a few years ago, riding a bicycle eight feet high, is dying of consumption and is in reduced circumstances. A subscription has been started for him in England.

Wheeling believes that waiting races and a large "gate" are incompatible. A scorching gait brings the best gate.

ALPHABET WEBBER says that his prizes won at Springfield were just what they were represented to be, and that he was and is satisfied with them.

AND now it is the proper thing to look up a cycler's relations, to see if rich relatives stand ready to pay expenses. Perhaps makers may hire men to parade as rich uncles.

THE important part which can be played by brown paper when a touring cyclist gets wet, is apt to be forgotten. An ounce of practice is, however, worth a ton of theory, and we can personally bear testimony to the fact that on having to resume our wet clothing to return home from Gigg's Hill, some hours after the Ripley Road club handicap last week, we were entirely saved from a chill by a judiciously-placed layer of ordinary brown paper. — *Cyclist.*

OUR contemporaries are making merry with what they call our "patent" trowsers. We have nothing to say, yet, about the "unmentionables," but we do desire that our friends will not credit us with the stupid idea that knee breeches are immodest. When we think that to be so, we shall organize a crusade against them, and we certainly shall not wear them as we do now.

AND now they talk of building a cycle track on the Great Eastern. This will be one of the novelties that the world will talk about and let severely alone.

AN English lady in the Fulham district wears a divided skirt and rides a Humber tricycle. This is a record that America will allow England to keep.

MILLS made his famous ride to John o' Groats without a spring. If the journey could be taken without a fall it would be well.

THE new track at Coventry, Eng., is turning out records very fast.

Wheeling thinks the N. C. U. should give up its jurisdiction over road racing just as the League has.

JENKINS has put a "derick" on to his name to give it a hoist.

JOHN KEEN has been doing some more racing against horses. On 2 August he competed with three of them for twenty miles, and came off victor by twenty yards.

WE have received a very fine photo of the Winona Club's track at Winona, Minn. It was taken by Chas. A. Tenney, of Winona.

It is very evident that the boys wish to show the track rather than themselves, for every man in the foreground is back to the camera, and in several cases they are hidden behind umbrellas.

EASTERN men are prone to present a very broad front to the camera, and few are found looking at anything else when a camera is turned on. The West has sent us an object lesson.

OUR gallery of photographs is growing very fast. We have room for more, and should be glad to receive the phiz of any and all wheelmen, or views of cycling places.

McCURDY has established his claim for a record much better than any that has been made before. We presume there are none who will say that a survey is less reliable than a cyclometer. The *Star* can rightfully claim the world's record.

LOOK out for our new story which will appear next week.

IVES and Rhodes have returned to Springfield to train, not liking the condition of the Lynn grounds.

PRINCE and Eck are to race at North Adams, 28 August. Eck will ride in half-mile heats against horses, and Prince will ride ten miles against two horses, a fresh horse every five miles.

THE Lynn Club have a scorcher's run to Gloucester on Sunday next.

ROWE made a third of a mile in 49 seconds on the bicycle at Lynn Saturday, which is at the rate of 2.27, for the mile.

THE *Southern Cycler* has been sold to the *American Wheelman* of St. Louis.

THE timers of Hanlan's late record at Worcester, only varied five seconds or so from each other. What would we poor cyclists think if we had such timers at a record breaking, and would n't it rejoice the soul of G. L. Hillier if we did?

F. T. MERRILL, professional champion of the Pacific Slope, is in town with his family, and will start in training soon.

THE PATH.

BY final vote of the Pennsylvania Racing Committee, the following championship races for Pennsylvania have been assigned as stated : Quarter mile to New Castle Bicycle Club; half mile and five mile to Pittsburg combined clubs ; one mile and three mile to Williamsport Wheel Club ; two mile to Scranton Bicycle Club. This leaves the ten mile still open.

THE Orange Wanderers will hold the initial race meeting on the new track at Roseville, 4 September.

THE East Hartford track is to be raised eighteen inches, and widened about four feet. In the centre a ball field will be laid out, and a nine has been formed, with H. E. Bidwell as captain.

F. S. BUCKINGHAM has just lowered the tricycle records a notch. At Torquay, on Monday, 2 August, he made two miles in 5.52¾ and three miles in 8.55¾.

CON DWYER, the Australian champion, on 18 June, covered a mile in 2.38¾. He rode a Club racer.

AN amalgamated cycle handicap was run in England at the Guildford camp. Bicycles, tricycles, and safeties ran in the race. It was won by a bicycle rider from the ninety-yard mark.

ENGLEHART made a run for a record on a Kangaroo, at Coventry, 29 July. He made time as follows : Quarter, 42; half, 1.22 ; three quarter, 203 ; mile, 2.45. These are claimed to be world's records, but they are not. The American records are much better. They beat the English records, however.

F. S. BUCKINGHAM made a new record at the three quarter mile distance on a tricycle, at Coventry, 26 July last. Time, 2.11; previous record, 2.12.

Now that Howell is ill, Wood is winning all the English championships. Howell had his turn at the business when Wood broke his arm two years ago.

THE Queen's County Agricultural Society offer the following premiums for bicycle riding, to be competed for, at the fall fair, to be held at Mineola, 21, 22, 23, 24, September. 1886. First prize, $10, medal ; second prize, $7.00, medal ; third prize, $5.00, medal.

Tuesday, 21 September, 2 o'clock, P. M., two-mile race, open to all residents of Queen's County. Wednesday, 22 September, at 2 o'clock, P. M., mile heats, best two in three, amateurs, open to all competition. Thursday, 23 September, at 2 o'clock, P. M., two-mile race, open to all competition. Entrance fee, $1.00, in addition to members' ticket. Five to enter, three to start. Entries close Saturday, 11 September, 8 P. M., at the society's office, Mineola, or will be received at any time previously by the secretary, Jacob Hicks, Old Westbury, Queens County, L. I.

COMING EVENTS.

AUGUST.

21 Saturday. — Races at Detroit, Mich.

24 Tuesday. — Fifth annual tournament of the Scranton (Penn.) Club. F. C. Hand, Scranton, Penn.

27, 28, Friday, Saturday. — Annual races of the New Orleans (La.) Club.

26, 27, and 28 Thursday–Saturday. — Race meeting of the Cleveland Bicycle Club.

28 Saturday. — Annual meet and races of the New Jersey division, at Millville, N. J.

Races of the Albany Wheelmen, at Albany, N. Y.

Woodside's run for a record of twenty-one miles in the hour.

SEPTEMBER.

1 Wednesday. — Race meeting of the Troy (N. Y.) Club, nine open races. W. M. Thiessen, 556 Fulton street.

3 Friday. — Fall meeting of officers, L. A. W., at Buffalo, N. Y.

3, 4 Friday, Saturday. — New York division meet and races, at Buffalo, N. Y. Five-mile L. A. W. championship.

4 Saturday. — Race meeting of Orange Wanderers, and opening of Roseville track.

6 Monday. — Grand tour of the L. A. W. from Niagara Falls and Buffalo, through Central and Southern New York, Virginia, and the Shenandoah Valley, winding up at Harper's Ferry, 18 September. Entries now open with the Marshals.

Annual meet Ohio division, at Massillon, Ohio, on invitation of Massillon, Canton, and Alliance Clubs. Apply to Jos. S. Meyer, Jr., 37 N. Market street, Canton, Ohio.

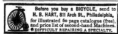

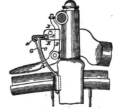

VOL. I., No. 22.   BOSTON, MASS., 27 AUGUST, 1886.   FIVE CENTS.

THE CYCLE

PUBLISHED EVERY FRIDAY BY ABBOT BASSETT, 22 SCHOOL ST., ROOM 19.

VOL. I.   BOSTON, MASS., 27 AUGUST, 1886.   NO. 22.

TERMS OF SUBSCRIPTION.

One Year, by mail, post-paid..........................$1.50
Three Copies in one order............................ 3.00
Club Subscriptions................................... 1.00
Six Months... .90
Single Copies.. .05

Specimen Copies free.

Every bicycle dealer is agent for the CYCLE and authorized to receive subscriptions at regular rates. The paper can be found on sale at the following places : —

Boston, CUPPLES, UPHAM & CO., cor. Washington and School Streets. Tremont House news stand. At every cycle warehouse.

New York, ELLIOTT MASON, 12 Warren Street.

Philadelphia, H. B. HART, 811 Arch Street. GEORGE D. GIDEON, 6 South Broad Street.

Baltimore, S. T. CLARK & Co., 4 Hanover Street.

Chicago, W. M. DURELL, 115 Wabash Avenue. JOHN WILKINSON & Co., 77 State Street.

Washington, H. S. OWEN, Capital Cycle Co.

St. Louis, ST. LOUIS WHEEL Co., 1121 Olive Street.

ABBOT BASSETT . . . . . EDITOR

A. MUDGE & SON, PRINTERS, 24 FRANKLIN ST., BOSTON

All communications should be sent in not later than Tuesday, to ensure insertion the same week.

Entered at the Post-office as second-class mail matter.

CHIEF CONSUL CHASE, of the Rhode Island Division, L. A. W., has issued a card which reads as follows : —

A party of wheelmen dining recently at Coles Hotel, Warren, conducted themselves in such an unbecoming manner, that complaint has been made to the landlord. As the party contained a number of the members of the L. A. W., it seems best to remind such League members as need the notice, that in the by-laws is a section that reads as follows :

Art. V. Sec. 5 (b). A member may be expelled on account of conduct unbecoming a gentleman, etc.

When hilarity and fun is carried beyond a certain point, it becomes ungentlemanly. The wise cycler knows when to stop; those who do not, are not desirable League members, as they disgrace the whole organization.

We are glad to note the card, though we regret that it was called for. There has been too much of this kind of thing in other places besides Rhode Island. Down on the North Shore the landlords are getting to be disgusted with wheelmen, for they have been the victims of boyish pranks too often. We have heard on several occasions lately that the guests of Gloucester hotels have been unable to sleep when a party of wheelmen was at the hotel, and we have not felt that the cause was being benefited.

MR. HILLIER is still in doubt regarding American records, and he refuses to credit them. Before Mr. Hillier can qualify as a doubter, he should remove the doubt which has been thrown upon his own records for fifty-three and fifty-four miles, and he

should also show good reason for accepting the tricycle records of Lowndes, which were shown to be no records on the evidence of Hillier himself, but which were used by our doubting friend after a lapse of time had caused many to forget his testimony.

MILK has always stood the friend of wheelmen, and when it proves false, upon whom or what can we place our trust. A well-known Boston club has always pursued a consistent policy on the milk question, and there has been some talk among its members of adopting a cow as a design for the club badge, but now that a shadow of suspicion has been thrown upon this innocent and exhilarating beverage, we cannot tell to what we are coming. The papers tell us that forty guests at a hotel were recently made very sick by drinking " pure fresh milk," and only the other day a baby was drowned in a tank of sour milk. It might not be a bad idea for some one of the cycling associations to appoint a committee whose duty it would be to regulate the milk supply.

IF it costs $10,000 a year to run a yacht, and if there is a fascination about the sport that draws to it men who are not able to afford the expense as well as those who are, it may be that a stigma will be thrown upon yachting even worse than that which rests upon some of the less expensive sports.

YACHTSMEN race for glory, not for gold. But if we can judge by the money outlay indulged in by yachtsmen, there would be little temptation to them in a purse. It used to be said of Rothschild that there was little sport for him at cards. Any loss he made would not hurt him, and it was of no great object for him to win. There is no honor to be gained at cards.

On their recent trip from Philadelphia to Lake George, certain members of the Pennsylvania Bicycle Club replied to all questions by handing out a bit of pasteboard two and a quarter inches square, on which was printed the following : " 'A fool can ask more questions than a wise man can answer,' hence this." Then followed the name of the towns on their route; and on the reverse side was printed : " We are : C. A. Roberts, W. A. Stadelman, F. H. Lippincott, H. L. H. Hall, W. D. Sapples, H. L. Roberts, T. A. Bradley, Albert Kohler, C. T. Harvey, A. F. Lewis, H. A. Lewis. All members of the Pennsylvania Bicycle Club, of Philadelphia, Pa. Leaving Philadelphia, Saturday, 10 July, 1886." — *L. A. W. Bulletin.*

To complete this, all those persons who were met and asked regarding roads, routes, etc., should have been furnished with similar cards. It would be a good idea under this system of things to supply local consuls with cards to be handed to the wandering wheel-

men, who go to them for information. Wheelmen are too often annoyed by questions from rustics and from the curious, but it is not a sign of good breeding to respond with an insult. We are all more or less dependent upon one another in this world, and the man who asks questions generally gets along at the head of the procession. The Philadelphia boys did a smart thing, perhaps, but smart things are not always in keeping with the acts of a gentleman.

THE Connecticut Club adopts the A. C. U. rules, believing them in many ways superior to those of the L. A. W. — " H." *in Gazette.*

We wish " H." would go further and tell us some of the " many ways " in which the rules of the A. C. U. are superior to those of the L. A. W. The fact is, the rules are virtually the same. If the Connecticut Club had run its tournament under League rules, it might have had the three classes of races just as it now proposes to, and it could have had the League championship. By running under A. C. U. rules it gets the A. C. U. championship. It is merely a question of championships, and the club would seem to prefer that of the younger association to that of the elder.

IT would seem to be no more than justice that the State officials should be allowed mileage when they attend the meetings of the division board of officers. A case in point is that of Massachusetts. The meetings of the division are always held in Boston, and it is right that they should be, for in this way can the greatest number be accommodated. But it is not to be supposed that the Western members will always be present at the meetings. It would call for an expenditure of time and money that few could afford. The Springfield boys, and Kendall, of Worcester, generally come down to the meetings, but they do it at great personal sacrifice. If we are to have important meetings, there should be a good attendance, and the men who give their time to the League should not be expected to pay their railroad fares.

A COLLECTION of letters from the files of manufacturers would make interesting reading, if good judgment was used in the selection. One that should find its way into such a

Hampden Park, Springfield, Mass., U.S.A., September 14, 15, 16, and 17, 1886.

FIFTH ANNUAL TOURNAMENT OF THE SPRINGFIELD BICYCLE CLUB.

OFFICIAL LIST OF RACES AND PRIZES.

FIRST DAY—TUESDAY, SEPTEMBER 14.

EVENTS.	CLASSES.	WHEELS.	CONDITIONS.	FIRST PRIZES.	SECOND PRIZES.	THIRD PRIZES.
1-mile	Promateur	Bicycle	World's Championship, 1st heat.			
1-mile	Amateur	Bicycle	Novice.	Vase Lamp, hammered copper and	Scarf Pin, diamond setting.	Fancy Inkstand, gold and oxidised.
10-mile	Promateur	Bicycle	A. C. U. Championship.	A. C. U. Gold Medal. [oxidized.	A. C. U. Gold Medal.	A. C. U. Gold Medal.
5-mile	Professional	Bicycle	Handicap.	$100 Cash.	$50 Cash.	$40 Cash.
1-mile	Promateur	Bicycle	World's Championship, 2d heat.			[qué, gold lined.
5-mile	Amateur	Bicycle	16.30 Class.	Gold Watch, open face.	Vase Lamp, gold and Silver.	Smoking Set, hammered and appli-
1-mile	Professional	Tricycle	Open.	Gold Watch, open face.	Ewer, antique brass, embossed.	Opera Glass, pearl mounted.
3-mile	Professional	Bicycle	Open.	$62.50 Cash.	$37.50 Cash.	$25 Cash.
1-mile	Promateur	Bicycle	World's Championship, 3d heat.			
1-mile	Amateur	Tandem	A. C. U. Championship.	Two Gold Medals.	Two Silver Medals.	

SECOND DAY—WEDNESDAY, SEPTEMBER 15.

EVENTS.	CLASSES.	WHEELS.	CONDITIONS.	FIRST PRIZES.	SECOND PRIZES.	THIRD PRIZES.
1-mile	Promateur	Bicycle	World's Championship, 4th heat.			
5-mile	Amateur	Bicycle	Lap.	Gold Watch, open face.	French Clock, with bronze figure.	Glass Vase, decorated gold stand.
6-mile	Professional	Bicycle	Handicap.	Diamond Stud.	Gold Watch, hunting case.	Silver Chronograph Watch.
3-mile	Professional	Tricycle	Open.	$62.50 Cash.	$37.50 Cash.	$25 Cash.
1-mile	Promateur	Bicycle	World's Championship, 5th heat.			
5-mile	Professional	Bicycle	Lap.	$62.50 Cash.	$37.50 Cash. [breech-loader.	$25 Cash.
3-mile	Promateur	Bicycle	Lap.	Gold Watch, hunting case.	Stevens Shot-gun, double-barreled,	Silver Chronograph Watch.
5-mile	Professional	Bicycle	Handicap.	$62.50 Cash.	$37.50 Cash.	$25 Cash.
1-mile	Promateur	Bicycle	World's Championship, 6th heat.			[tern.
3-mile	Amateur	Tricycle	Open.	Gold Medal.	12 Silver Knives, renaissance pat-	Traveling Clock, and case.

THIRD DAY—THURSDAY, SEPTEMBER 16.

EVENTS.	CLASSES.	WHEELS.	CONDITIONS.	FIRST PRIZES.	SECOND PRIZES.	THIRD PRIZES.
1-mile	Promateur	Bicycle	World's Championship, 7th heat.			
3-mile	Amateur	Bicycle	Open.	Gold Medal.	French Clock, with bronze figures.	Gold Watch Chain.
10-mile	Promateur	Bicycle	Lap.	Diamond Stud.	Gold Watch, hunting case.	Gold Watch, hunting case.
1-mile	Professional	Bicycle	Open.	$80 Cash.	$30 Cash.	$20 Cash.
1-mile	Promateur	Bicycle	World's Championship, 8th heat.			
5-mile	Amateur	Bicycle	Open.	Tea Set, 6 pieces, satin embossed.	Stevens Sporting Rifle.	Stevens "Hunter's Pet" Rifle.
3-mile	Promateur	Tricycle	Open.	Gold Watch, hunting case.	Diamond Stud.	Gold Watch Chain.
3-mile	Professional	Bicycle	Handicap.	$50 Cash.	$30 Cash.	$20 Cash.
1-mile	Promateur	Bicycle	World's Championship, 9th heat.			
3-mile	Professional	Tricycle	Handicap.	$62.50 Cash.	$37.50 Cash.	$25 Cash.

FOURTH DAY—FRIDAY, SEPTEMBER 17.

EVENTS.	CLASSES.	WHEELS.	CONDITIONS.	FIRST PRIZES.	SECOND PRIZES.	THIRD PRIZES.
1-mile	Promateur	Bicycle	World's Championship, 10th heat.			
3-mile	Amateur	Bicycle	9.45 Class.	Gold Watch, open face.	Carving Set, renaissance pattern.	Gold Cuff Buttons, stone settings.
3-mile	Promateur	Bicycle	Open.	Diamond Stud.	Complete Fishing Outfit.	Water Set, silver, gold lined.
10-mile	Professional	Bicycle	Open.	$120 Cash.	$60 Cash.	$60 Cash. Fourth, $30 Cash.
3-mile	Promateur	Bicycle	World's Championship, 11th heat.			[and oxidised.
5-mile	Amateur	Bicycle	Handicap.	Diamond Stud.	Scarf Pin, diamond setting.	Biscuit Jar, decorated china, gold
3-mile	Promateur	Bicycle	2.40 Class.	Gold Watch, open face.	Pedestal Lamp, antique brass, tulip	Gold Watch Chain.
5-mile	Professional	Bicycle	Open.	$100 Cash. [Medal.	$60 Cash. [globe.	$40 Cash.
1-mile	Promateur	Bicycle	World's Championship, final heat.	Winner last heat, Gold Watch and	Winner fastest heat, Fine Gold	[Fifth, Lakin Cyclometer.
1-mile	Amateur	Bicycle	Consolation.	Gold Watch Chain.	Stevens Bicycle Rifle. [Watch.	Seal Ring. Fourth, Traveling Bag.

ENTRIES CLOSE SEPTEMBER 7, 1886.

All Events have three Prizes, where there are four or more starters. Entry Forms, Blanks, List of Prizes, etc., will be furnished upon application to SANFORD LAWTON, Secretary Springfield Bicycle Club, Springfield, Mass., U.S.A.

budget would be that which was recently received by a well-known manufacturer from the secretary of a club just formed. The writer notified the maker that a club had been organized, but had not selected a name. He said that the boys were very anxious to call the club by the same name as that of the maker's bicycle, and they would do this, if he, the maker, would furnish a League uniform to each member. He hoped to have an early reply to his communication, for, in case the offer was not accepted, the club wished to make it to another manufacturer. Present indications point to the club paying for its own uniforms.

ENGLAND cannot cope with the makers' amateur question; the law of libel is too stringent over there. But America can and will. The English riders who come over this fall will be obliged to go into promateur races, or stay off the track. They belong with Rowe, Hendee, and the others. They have been guilty of the same violation of the amateur rule that our riders stand charged with, and they will not be allowed to capture easy victories in competition with our amateurs.

THE A. C. U. has voted to recognize the action of the L. A. W. in disqualifying those men who have forfeited their amateur status. All such will be barred from amateur events under A. C. U. rules. The Union has decided to enforce its rules to the letter, and will take up the case of the tandem riders who made a record on the road last week, and disqualify all the amateurs who were engaged therein.

THE letter from Robert Todd, Esq., sets at rest the question of sanction by the N. C. U. for English amateur riders to compete with our promateur class. No such sanction will be given. Those riders who come to America and ride with any but amateurs will be promptly disqualified by the N. C. U. The A. C. U. will not allow the English riders to compete in amateur events, for under the rules of the Union there are few who can do so, since all, or nearly all, will receive expenses.

JUST what the difference is between a cycling press man who puffs a machine for "ads.," and an ordinary wheelman who rides for the same purpose, is a little difficult to understand. — World.

There is no great difference between the man who is hired by a maker to ride a machine for advertising purposes, and the man whom he hires to run a paper in his particular interest.

NOT all who apply to the Racing Board for reinstatement get their requests granted. Whittaker, Illston, Adams, Hitchcock, and others have been told, "We had rather not."

No bare legs at any race meeting held under L. A. W. rules. Next thing in order will be that all contestants must wear cutaway coats, silk stockings, and stovepipe hats. — *Springfield Gazette.*

LEAGUE rules never proscribed bare legs, and they do not now. The only regulation of this kind that we have heard of was made by the Springfield Bicycle Club several years ago. The ink is hardly dry on the paper of the *Gazette* wherein bare legs were condemned and tights recommended. The above criticism comes from a queer source.

A NUMBER of these men, who are proud to be known as "makers' amateurs," though the term "makers'" serf is much better suited to their present condition, are now, it is said, dependent on the salaries and fees they derive from certain manufacturers. If their "manager" takes snuff, they needs must sneeze. — *E. M. Aaron, in Bulletin.*

Is every man who works for a living a "serf"? He must do his employer's bidding or quit the service. Under this process of reasoning there are many "serfs" in America. We submit that the term is not merited. The makers' amateurs are no longer masquerading. They have come out openly and declared that they are paid for riding, and that they prefer to make their living in this way rather than at the desk or bench. When they were pretending to be what they are not, we took up the cudgels against them, and did not cease fighting until they changed their policy. They have made a change in their policy, and it is only fair that they should be given a chance to show the world what can be done by the class of riders that chooses to elevate itself above the common run of professionals. We are well aware that the term "serf" was used by Mr. Aaron to strengthen an argument made to show that the makers' amateurs should not be reinstated, but there was no need to use the offensive epithet, and he would have done better had he said that the makers' amateurs do not ask nor want to be reinstated, nor do they think they ought to compete with amateurs.

IF we are to have war in the camp, let us not wage it against the men who have gone from us. Let us rather bend our energies to send over to them these men who still remain with us without right or title to the name of amateur.

WHEELMEN have not done for Brother Jonathan what the followers of other sports have done. We have seen our English

friends go home laden with the spoils of victory each year, and the Yankee ensign has always trailed in the dust. It has not been so in yachting, in rowing, in pedestrianism,— no, nor in sparring. We are going to correct this state of things next month, for we venture the prediction that our boys will show their back wheels to English riders. We have never been hopeful before, but this time our confidence is unbounded. At the same time we have in mind the remark of a backwoods philosopher, who said: "A man is never so apt to be mistaken as he is when he is dead sure of a thing."

THE CYCLER'S STORY.

BY COLIN GRAY.

THEY came up with him on the road, and he told them his story on the rocks at Nahant.

It was a perfect day that Sunday, and everything in nature conspired to tempt wheelmen to take to the road. The warm rays of the sun were tempered by cooling breezes from the Northwest, and the roads were well packed down, the result of recent rains.

The Chelsea Club, led by Captain Frost, turned out in large numbers, and set their faces in the direction of the North Shore, intending to stop at Swampscott, Salem, Marblehead, or Nahant, as the fancy of the members dictated, or the incidents of the day swayed their inclinations.

Arriving at the Sunnyside, a halt was called, and the riders refreshed themselves with water from the spring, and cream pie from the larder of the hostelry. It was here that the heavy member of the club joined them. He had started later than they, and moreover, was mounted on a three-wheeler. After this the pace was slow, for, although the riders wanted to spurt along the levels or race with the horsemen, the captain would not allow the club to run away from the heavy member. An informal vote was taken over the cream pie and water, and it was decided that Nahant should receive a visit from the club as soon as their wishes could take them to the rocky peninsula, always remembering that the heavy member was to regulate the pace.

Their route lay through Lynn to the beach, past the Indian camp where the son of the forest drives sharp bargains with the summer residents, exchanging baskets and gewgaws for hard dollars, and where soap and water are among the neglected luxuries; thence along the narrow isthmus and over Little Nahant to the greater Nahant beyond. It was on the peninsula that the club came up with Herbert Nickerson, of whom we shall hear more presently. The freemasonry of the wheel led to a speedy acquaintance without the formality of an introduction, and he was soon riding along in friendly intercourse with the club members.

Those of you who have been to Nahant know well the natural beauty of the place, and they know that fleet-winged time does not lag when one is stretched out at full length on the rocks surveying the delightful ocean view spread out before him. The wheels of the club rested against the huge bowlders just after noon of the day whose history I am writing, and the mem-

bers were lying about in picturesque positions. It was the heavy member who started
him off, and he did it by asking some com-
monplace question about the wheel. "That
wheel is my savior!" exclaimed the newly-
found friend, "and I would n't part with it
for untold wealth. It saved my life, and it
proved the best medicine I ever took."

There was a blank look on the faces of
the club, for they did n't comprehend the
meaning of his words.

"You don't quite understand what I
mean, I see," said Nickerson, "and so I 'll
tell you all about it. It 's a long story, but
we are not pressed for time, and I want to
have you know what the bicycle has done
for one poor fellow, who is deeply grateful
and does not hesitate to call it his savior."

And then he told us his tale : —

CHAPTER I.

"It was in the summer of the year, —
well, never mind the exact year; it can
easily be fixed when I say it was a very hot
and close summer time. Boston literally
broiled, and those who could afford the time
and the money to get out of it, did so as
soon as they could.

"We were already in the second week of
the long vacation, but as yet I had not been
able to arrange my work so as to take advantage of it. I toiled on at the office,
scarcely able to breathe, and devoutly
wished that I was either tramping the New
Hampshire hills, or drinking in the invigorating air of Magnolia or Manchester-by-
the-Sea. I had been overworked, and consequently was in that condition of both
mind and body which may be most fitly described by the expression 'dried up.'

"I had had some very heavy cases, which,
with the exception of one, I had successfully
carried through.

"The one I lost I had, however, taken
the most trouble with. It was from the first
a most hopeless and unpromising affair, and
when it was first submitted to me, I advised
that it should be dropped. In an after consultation, however, I was so pressed that I
consented to accept a brief for the plaintiff.

"There was just one possibility of success, but I had never any great hope, and
so I told my client. The action was for
the restitution of some property which had
been, it was alleged, illegally willed away.

"My client was a tall, gaunt, hollow-eyed
man. I do not think he thought of anything else; he seemed to eat the subject, to
drink it, and to sleep it. He carried about
with him continually various documents relating to it. Most of these were concealed
in his hat, and from their having been often
fingered, and from the character of their
abiding-place, they had assumed a very
grimy, greasy aspect.

"So soon as I consented to take the
brief, he used to address letters to me upon
the case, — long, rambling letters, of sometimes four or five pages of foolscap. They
were written with a formal margin, where
appeared an abstract of each paragraph in
red ink.

"As time went on, my client used to way-
lay me. I would find him waiting for me
when I got to my office in the morning. I
told him sharply that I could not see him,
and that I was too busy to talk with him, to
all of which he would reply that 'it did not

matter; he would wait.' And wait he did,
for when I went out, — it did not in the least
matter how long I had been in, — he was
patiently waiting for me, with a look of resigned suffering on his face.

"For one or two days I missed him, to
my great relief; and when on the third day
he did not make his appearance, I began to
hope that he had ceased to bother me. On the
fourth day, as I was coming out of the court-
house, the officer on duty at the door informed me that a young lady had been inquiring for me.

"Such an unusual and out-of-the-way circumstance made me ask somewhat incredulously : —

"'For me?'

"'Yes, sir; she said she had a letter for
Mr. Nickerson.'

"'Why did she not give it to my clerk at
the office?'

"'I wanted her to do so, but she would
not; she said she must not deliver it to anybody else.'

"'What was she like?'

"'Well, sir, you can judge for yourself,
for here she comes.'

"From the direction of the door I saw
the slight figure of a girl coming toward me.
Her carriage was very graceful and not
without a certain dignity. She was clad
entirely in black, with the exception of a
something of a white gauzy material round
her throat. I had only time to note further
that she wore a thick veil over her face, and
then she had reached the steps on which I
was standing.

"'This is Mr. Nickerson,' said the officer.

"She turned toward me, and I could see the
outlines of an oval face and the flashings of
a pair of bright eyes behind the veil.

"'I was directed to give you this,' she
said in a soft, silvery voice; and she put
into my hand a long blue envelope, the very
sight of which sent a shudder through my
frame. There was the direction, in the distinct but formal and crabbed writing of my
client: 'To Herbert Nickerson, Esq., at-
torney-at-law,' etc. etc.

"'Stay one moment,' I said, when I had
recovered from the temporary distraction
caused by the sight of the envelope. 'Stay,
there may be an answer'; and I feigned an
extraordinary interest in the contents of the
envelope, for the purpose of entering into
conversation with its fair carrier.

"'There is no answer,' she said, I
thought, with a half sigh. Then she turned
away and walked off with a quick step.

"My first impulse was to run after her and
learn something more of her, but the sense
of the ludicrousness of a sedate member of
the bar running in the street after a young
woman struck me at once; and so I solemnly looked at the documents in the envelope, conscious that I had better keep up
my dignity before the officer. Then I
shook my head gravely, and slowly walked
away. In my hasty glance at a letter enclosed with one of the interminable epistles
my curious client had favored me with, I
learnt that he was ill, but that he hoped to
resume communications with me in a few
days.

"It was with some interest that I looked
out during the next few days for my client.
I saw him not, and other matters drove all
thoughts of him and his messenger out of

my head. He turned up, however, one day,
and as I was not particularly busy at the
moment, I condescendingly listened to him,
and even perused with what interest I could
assume one of his greasy documents. An
anxious smile lit up his hollow eyes, and
played about his worn mouth as I did so. I
saw he was delighted at my awakened
interest in his case.

"Presently I asked: 'Is your daughter
quite well?'

"He looked at me with a vacant expression,
as of a man suddenly pulled back into a
world he disliked from one in which he delighted, and paused for a moment. Then
he went on reciting a table of degrees of
consanguinity, of which he was never weary,
and which I had interrupted.

"As the day of the trial approached he got
more and more importunate. He spent his
days in trying to get at me, and I should say
wasted most of his nights in writing to me.

"It need hardly be said that this wretched
importunate suitor worried me dreadfully.
He had a distinctly depressing effect upon
me, and I found that after coming across
him I was quite nervous.

"The day of the trial came. I laid great
stress upon the point of law which I considered gave us a chance, but the judge
overruled me, and that very early fell to the
ground. The trial was, however, brought
unexpectedly to a conclusion for the want of
a link in the chain of evidence.

"I was sorry that we had not been successful, but I devoutly thanked my stars that at
least I would be haunted no longer by such
a client; and so I went down to the office in
high spirits the next morning; but my flow
of spirits departed and my feet dragged
heavily as I saw the long black figure to
which I had got so accustomed waiting in
its usual place. For a moment or so I was
in despair; then I made up my mind that
I would stand no more of these proceedings;
they were affecting my health and my professional reputation. So I walked firmly up
the steps, acknowledging somewhat stiffly
the 'Good-morning' given me.

"'If you will come into my office, I will
see you,' I said, and he meekly followed me in.

"'It is very fortunate,' he said.

"'I am very sorry,' I replied, 'but I do
not think that we should by any possibility
have won.'

"'I have spent the last three years of my
life,' he went on, 'in getting all these details,
and I have put all my money into it, and now
it is all lost.'

"'I am very sorry,' I repeated, looking
up in his face.

"He took no notice of my remark, but
stretched out his long arms toward me, and
clasping his hands as if round an imaginary
neck, he said in a hoarse, hollow voice which
trembled with rage : —

"'But I will have my revenge.'

"Involuntarily I started back and congratulated myself that it was not my neck that he
had between those long fingers. I edged
toward the bell to call in my clerk, when the
fingers relaxed, and he turned slowly away,
put on his hat and made for the door. Before he left the room he turned to me and
said solemnly : —

"'Mark me, I will yet have revenge,' and
then he disappeared.

(To be continued.)

SANDERS SELLERS has cabled that he will not come to America this year. He has important examinations to take and cannot leave.

CHARLES RICHARDS DODGE has been piloting a party of the Capital City boys down through the North Shore.

THE A. C. U. admits neither professionals nor club members. If a man belongs to a club, he cannot join the Union unless his club does. Only the unattached can join as individuals.

W. B. EVERETT will sail for England on 4 September.

PROBABLY the most unique feature of the St. Louis illuminated carnival will be the St. Louis Bicycle Brass Band. It is the only one of its kind in the world, numbering thirteen with the drum major.

MR. DUCKER, in the *Bulletin*, advises League members to vote "no" on the mail-vote questions relating to the amateur law. The A. C. U. no longer desires that the League should give up racing.

HARRY PARKS, a boy sixteen years old, recently rode down nineteen steps of the flight in front of the Capitol building here (Washington) on a Standard Columbia bicycle. To show how easy it was, he rode down eleven more times the same evening. The little wheel gave out from under him on his last trip.

IT will not be very long before we see record-breakers at the dime museums. If there is a public desire to see a man who has jumped off a bridge, why not to see a man who has ridden three hundred miles in a day? Dime museum men, please take notice.

THE Hartford hackman who ran down Mr. E. Y. Judd, of the Connecticut Club, paid ten dollars fine and costs of arrest and conviction of assault for his carelessness.

SMALL boy examining a cyclometer on a bicycle : "Say, cully, dat's one of them things dat tells yer how fast yer goin'." Second urchin, evidently mistaking it for a compass : "No, 'tain't, neither. It tells yer where yer are when yer lost."—*Gazette*.

A CORRESPONDENT suggests that wheelmen show us how fast they can ride between Boston and New York. Let each rider choose his own route and get there as quickly as possible. He thinks that this will develop the best road between these points if nothing else. Which maker will send a man out to give us the Boston to New York record ? We already have had competition for the record from Philadelphia to New York.

THE glass manufacturing firm of Whitall, Tatum & Co., whose factory is at Millville, N. J., at the request of its employees, has built a shed where the bicycles may be safely stowed during working hours. The members of the firm say that bicycles are useful to them for bringing them promptly to their work at the appointed hour. — *Gazette*.

HARTFORD men are claiming that their city is the place where the pipe of peace is smoked each year. "H." says in the *Gazette* : "Hartford, you know, comes first after the summer's rest, and here friend and foe meet together, shake and make merry, and go away without a 'foe' in the crowd.

It was most beautiful to see, last year, how certain brethren of the cycling quill, who during the preceding season had vituperated each other with extreme viciousness, become chatty, confidential, and friends forever after. Here old sores heal. Have any of late felt the mighty smite of Aaron's rod ? If they can catch him at Hartford, they will speedily resolve that the chastening was merited, and the blows governed by a wise hand and discerning spirit ; or, they will never believe that they were smitten at all." All right ! We 'll all go to Hartford ! A lot of us will have to do some tall smoking this year.

H. F. SEIFERTH is to be editor of the *Bicycle South*.

NEW ORLEANS has a "light" ordinance, which requires light vehicles as well as cycles to carry a light after dark, but it seems to be enforced only against cycles.

CAPT. PECK, of the Massachusetts Club, tells us that a run to Allen's swimming bath for a swim is about as enjoyable an outing as can be arranged.

MR. HENRY W. WILLIAMS, ex-president of the Massachusetts Bicycle Club, has been obliged to give up cycling for a time on account of a serious affection of the left eye. He has been unable to ride since the latter part of June, but having undergone a painful operation upon the eye, confidently hopes to be able to mount his wheels during the fall of this year. He is still under treatment.

THE Pope Manufacturing Company will have a tent on the grounds at Springfield, and will welcome all visitors. Accommodations will be furnished for correspondence, etc. etc. An office will be opened at the Massasoit House as well.

THE Massachusetts Division, L. A. W., meets at Young's Hotel on Saturday evening. A full attendance is desired. We are going to do great things, so be on hand. Perhaps Consul Hayes will cut a watermelon.

WM. H. LANGDOWN, the amateur champion of New Zealand, has arrived in Springfield after a journey of 1,600 miles. He was met at the depot by President Ducker and members of the club. He left home 15 July. He scales 165 lbs. and stands five feet 8¼ inches high. He will be the guest of the Springfield Club during his stay in America.

POLLS for the mail vote close at Philadelphia on Saturday, at noon. Send on your vote if you have not already done so.

G. LACY HILLIER publishes a *fac simile* of a forged letter containing his signature. We know of a letter written by this illustrious individual, which is not a forged one, asking that his expenses be paid to attend a certain meeting, which was refused.— *Gazette*. This is a serious charge. Will Mr. Hillier meet it ?

SPRINGFIELD will distribute a large number of watches this year. There is less silverware than last year, and the selection has been made with a view to have articles which will be useful and of value to young men. Seventy five hundred dollars was at the disposal of the committee, and $2,700 has been used for purses in the professional

races. The prizes for the one-mile race for the world championship, while given in the list for the first day, will not be decided until the last, as two heats will be ridden each day. The man who goes into the races and comes out without a watch will have made very bad time.

KNAPPY came down to the track the other day with a bit of a cold. He showed it in his voice. "Come, young fellow," said Asa, "you must n't talk hoarse around here ; this is n't a trotting track." And then Harry brought out his camera and took a photograph of the joke.

THE A. C. U. executive has voted to recognize the action of the L. A. W. in disqualifying the racing men, and all such cannot enter amateur events under A. C. U. rules.

THE Star people will have a tricycle on the track at the fall races that promises to beat everything on three wheels. Kluge will ride it.

BURLEY AYERS thinks the strong road rider should have as much honor as the fast track rider. The world, however, likes to see competition, and the speediest man or thing gets the applause every time.

THE Goodman brothers of Hartford have been awarded the score card privileges of all the great race meetings.

THE A. C. U. will not allow Rowe or Hendee to make pace for Woodside in his attempt to cover twenty-one miles within the hour.

"THAT machine 's a centre-gear," said the clerk to an inquirer. "A cent a gear ? Then it must be worth about two cents," answered the customer. The clerk explained.

THE Connecticut Division of the League will have a parade on the morning of the first day of the races. The matter of having a parade has been carefully weighed, and the desire for one seemed to be so general that it has been decided to have one. The indications are that this parade will be the largest ever given in Connecticut, and that the representation of clubs all over the State will be excellent.

A MAN who called himself a count hired two tricycles of W. B. Everett & Co., last month, — one for himself and one for his valet. He failed to return the wheels. He was found later and arrested. The wheels were returned. The count proved a no-'count sort of a fellow.

KNAPP, of the Columbia team, is going to name his wheel "Cleveland." He says that Cleveland always wins, and, moreover, he came from Cleveland.

MINNEAPOLIS is to have another six-day race. It will be managed by T. W. Eck, and contested in November. It is hoped that the foreign riders will go in.

A GOOD road runs one hundred and twenty-five miles from Chicago to Janesville, Wis. Western wheelmen are talking of road races thereon.

THE position made vacant by the death of Major Durell has been filled by the Pope Manufacturing Company, who have selected

for the position Mr. R. D. Garden, a gentleman well known in various parts of the country. Mr. Garden is an athlete of some repute, and was formerly a member of the New York Athletic Club. He has been in the Boston office for some months past.

MR. R. P. GORMULLY, of Gormully & Jeffery, sailed from Liverpool for New York, 21 Aug.

A QUESTION that has been agitating French cyclists for the past few months is the employment of velocipedes in time of war. It has been announced that a squad of cyclists were attached to one of the German army corps, and, under the ægis of the Union Velocipedique de France, a request was addressed to the minister of war for permission to organize a squad of cyclists to operate with the troops in the autumn manœuvres. The cyclists offered to place themselves for the time under military regulations, pay, food, accommodation, and discipline, believing that their services would be found welcome for the conveyance of orders, despatches, etc. Some delay occurred in the receipt of a response, but at last the answer arrived with the permission of the minister of war for two cyclists to follow the operations under the direction of the brigadier, and for their services the sum of two francs, forty cents, a day was offered.

THE Citizens' Club have had a stirring time with their road officers. The resignation of Capt. Ford caused a general move-up of the junior officers, but, of course, as no one could hold two offices at once, the lieutenants were forced to resign and take their chances of promotion. This, of course, delayed the matter of a vacancy for a month, and at the last meeting A. E. Paillard was elected first lieutenant to fill the place of T. C. Smith, who had been elected captain. As Mr. Paillard formerly held the office of first color-bearer, he of course resigned, and so another vacancy was in order. The new wheel-room, which now extends the full depth of the lot, gives great satisfaction. It is 20x40 feet, lighted by two skylights, and the floor is lined with concrete, making a serviceable and clean room. A tool bench has been put up at one end and the members can hammer away to their heart's content and try all sorts of improbable experiments. — *Jenkins in Sporting Life.*

WE have been asked to draw attention to the racing costumes of some of the men now on the metropolitan path, and though we do not wish to mention names, we trust that several riders whom we could name if it were necessary, will take the hint that public feeling is against their appearance in costumes more suitable for bathing, than racing before an assemblage of both sexes. — *Wheeling.*

A SUBSCRIPTION is being raised in Ireland to pay the expenses of an Irish team to Springfield. The Springfield club has put itself down for $150.

AN English firm has made a tricycle for racing which has a forty-inch wheel on one side and a thirty-six-inch on the other. It is claimed that this will take the curves easily, and will go well enough on the straights.

TRIGWELL and Watson, of London, have

put upon the market a non-vibrating handle bar. A joint is made in the bar midway between the handle and head, and here the bar is imbedded in rubber and allowed play.

I ATTENDED a meeting of the executive committee of the Illuminated Parade, this week. They are getting along swimmingly. Letters were read from wheelmen all over the country, asking for information as to rates for transportation, hotels, etc , and the places they were to be assigned in the parade. A good amount of business was gotten through with, and the indications are that the parade will be a large success, as everybody seems to be willing to put their shoulder to the wheel. The procession will probably consist of the mounted police, the bicycle brass band, of fourteen pieces (on wheels), the demon drill squad, the flambeau division, and a bicycle and tricycle division, the fireworks being probably sent off from the latter. Many of the wheelmen have already hit upon novel ideas for the decoration of their wheels. Any one who will send to W. M. Brewster, 305 Olive street, will receive suggestions for decorations. Edward R. Stettinius has been chosen grand marshal, and Ab. Lewis captain of the Flambeau division. — *Spectator.*

THE Coventry track bids fair to give Springfield a pull. The English records are flying fast, and very soon we may expect our own to be touched. We do not find that the English officials are any more strict than our own, and we do not see that they give us any more reliable records than we make over here.

Wheeling puts it down as a fact worthy of note that a manufacturer entered one of his racing men in a race without consulting the rider.

RICHARD GARVEY is at San Diego, Cal., managing a stage route and a mine. We all remember Dick Garvey, and it would n't be a bad idea for some of us to go out and ride on his stage.

A CINCINNATI paper has offered a medal to be contested for by local wheelmen.

THE A. C. U. is sending out blank certificates which they require racing men to sign. These call for a statement regarding the status of the signer. The Union proposes to classify all men now on the path.

COL. ALBERT A. POPE and Mr. George H. Day arrived in Boston on the Cunard steamship "Pavonia," on Saturday last. The gentlemen have been absent about two months. They visited England and France.

THE Massachusetts Club is planning for a series of Saturday evening entertainments, to begin early next month.

THE other day a Boston reporter told a wheelman that Dick Howell was dead. He did it to see how far the story would go. It went quite far enough to satisfy him.

WHEN Americans beat the Englishmen at cycling, perhaps the great public will get up as much interest in our sport as they now show in yachting. It pays to win.

MR. GULICK, of the L. A. W. Committee on Rights and Privileges, will take steps at an early day to test the Orange ordinance which compels cycles to carry lights.

A TEST case has been started in North Carolina. Two young wheelmen have been

arrested for riding bicycles on the turnpike, and the L. A. W. will defend them. The case will come up next month. The League has secured some of the best legal talent in the State.

A NEW JERSEY man has built a tricycle twenty-seven feet high. He will use it to go to vessels in distress, propelling it through the breakers, and taking off passengers and cargo. Two men will drive it, and the builder has no fear that the breakers will throw it over. We are glad to know that the money spent upon this thing will go into the hands of deserving mechanics.

LACY HILLIER says he has finally decided not to come to America this fall.

AT the meeting of English manufacturers held to take concerted action towards contesting the Bown patent, a guarantee fund was started, and a committee of three was appointed to canvass the trade with a view to its increase.

THE English wheelmen are talking of starting a guarantee fund for legal expenses in proceedings against the makers' amateurs.

A FREIGHT car struck a passenger car on the Albany Railroad last Saturday. If the blow had come three feet forward of where it did strike, the A. C. U. would now be in mourning for its president. Mr. Ducker has carefully preserved pieces of wood from the wreck.

THIS is the way the jockey encourages his trotter in a race : " Up-ah-r-r-r-r-r-rooph ! " While the pedestrian's trainer yells : " Go arne, Dinney, oure father's eye is on you ! " And the professional trainer of wheelmen ejects one stentorian " Ah ! " that frightens everybody in the neighborhood, and quickens the spurting cyclist at least ten seconds in a mile.

FRIAR'S POINT, Miss., has organized a bicycle club, the only one within a radius of fifty or a hundred miles.

CHARLES WIESINGER, of Adrian, Mich., started to ride from Michigan to New York on a 54-inch Apollo bicycle. He arrived safely at his journey's end, and came to Boston, where he spent a few days.

ONE of the favorite beverages of the New Orleans wheelmen is a glass of seltzer sweetened with raspberry or some other fruit syrup. It is known at their rendezvous as a "bicycle punch."

SOME few months ago Mr. F. W. Perry, of the Massachusetts Club, had his Apollo bicycle stolen. He made a strong effort to recover it, and although in his search he found several other stolen machines, his own was not discovered. Last week W. B. Everett & Co. received a letter from a Lowell wheelman who wished to have the handle-bar to his machine altered. He said it had too low a drop and spade handles. The firm knew at once that this must be Perry's wheel, for no other machine had been sold fitted in this way. Mr. Gilligan was at once sent to Lowell, and he identified the machine at once. It was in the hands of a party who had bought it of a pawnbroker. The thief took it to Lowell and pawned it. Moral : It is well to have your machine a little different from the standard pattern.

HURRAH FOR LYNN!

First Grand International Fall Tournament

OF THE

LYNN CYCLE CLUB TRACK ASSOCIATION,

At LYNN, MASS., September 23, 24, and 25, 1886.

A. C. U. RULES TO GOVERN.

$5,000 in Prizes! Races for Amateurs, Promateurs, Professionals. $5,000 in Prizes!

BEHOLD THE GRAND LIST OF RACES AND PRIZES!

FIRST DAY, THURSDAY, SEPTEMBER 23.

1-Mile Novice, Bicycle, Open, 1st, Gold Medal; 2d, Gold and Silver Medal; 3d, Silver Medal.
2-Mile Amateur Bicycle, 5.45 Class, 1st, Fruit and Flower Stand; 2d, Silver Revolving Butter Dish; 3d, Silver Bell Spoon Holder, gold lined.
1-Mile Promateur Bicycle, Open, 1st, Snowflake Silver Embossed Tea Set; 2d, Silver Engraved Ice-Water Set; 3d, Cake Basket, hammered, Venetian chased, gold lined.
3-Mile Professional Bicycle, Handicap, 1st, $60 Cash; 2d, $40 Cash; 3d, $20 Cash.
2-Mile Amateur Tricycle, Lap, 1st, Base Parlor Lamp, gold and oxidized; 2d, Silver Vase, gold inlaid and oxidized; 3d, Russia Leather Satchel.
10-Mile Promateur Bicycle, Lap, 1st, Fine Gold Watch, stem-winder; 2d, Silver Festoon Chased Tea Set; 3d, Gold Watch Chain.
1-Mile Amateur Bicycle, Open, 1st Silver Water Set, snowflake chased; 2d, Silver Vase, gold and oxidized; 3d, Gold Watch Chain.
5-Mile Professional Bicycle, Lap, 1st, $75 Cash; 2d, $50 Cash; 3d, $25 Cash.
3-Mile Promateur Bicycle, Handicap, 1st, Silver Tilting Water Set, gold ornamentation; 2d, Clock, Persian chased, appliqué, candelabra, plaqué; 3d, Pair Pearl Opera Glasses.

SECOND DAY, FRIDAY, SEPTEMBER 24.

1-Mile Professional Bicycle, Open, 1st, $50 Cash; 2d, $30 Cash; 3d, $20 Cash.
1-Mile Promateur Tricycle, A. C. U. Championship (time limit, 3m. 5s.), 1st, A. C. U. Gold Medal; 2d, A. C. U. Gold Medal; 3d, A. C. U. Silver Medal.
10-Mile Amateur Bicycle, Lap, 1st, Lynn Prize Cup; 2d, Dessert Set, coral rose, glass and silver; 3d, Nut Bowl, gold lined, oxidized finish.
5-Mile Promateur Bicycle, Handicap, 1st, Gentleman's Fine Gold Watch; 2d, Épergne, engraved, oxidized, gold finish; 3d, Snowflake Chased Tilting Ice-Water Set, gold lined
1-Mile Amateur Bicycle, 3.06 Class, 1st, Fishing Set; 2d, Cake Basket, gold lined, oxidized finish; 3d, Fine Russia Leather Satchel.
5-Mile Professional Bicycle, Lap, 1st, $75 Cash; 2d, $50 Cash; 3d, $35 Cash.
1-Mile Amateur Bicycle, A. C. U. Championship (time limit, 3m. 30s.), 1st, A. C. U. Gold Medal; 2d, A. C. U. Gold Medal; 3d, A. C. U. Silver Medal.
3-Mile Promateur Bicycle, Lap, 1st, Double Walled Silver Ice-Water Urn; 2d, Shot Gun, double-barreled, breech-loader; 3d, Silver Watch.
5-Mile Amateur Bicycle, Handicap, 1st, Centre Piece and Fruit Dish, Crystal Dishes; 2d, Flower Stand, cut glass, gold, oxidized finish; 3d, French Pearl Opera Glasses.

THIRD DAY, SATURDAY, SEPTEMBER 25.

1-Mile Promateur Bicycle, Open, 1st, Lynn Prize Cup. (Special Prize for Record.) 2d, Base Lamp, gold inlaid and oxidized finish; 3d, Diamond Breast Pin.
3-Mile Amateur Bicycle, 9.10 Class, 1st, Base Lamp, gold and silver and hammered; 2d, Vase, gold finish; 3d, Gentleman's Gold Ring.
2-Mile Professional Bicycle, Lap, 1st, $50 Cash; 2d, $30 Cash; 3d, $20 Cash.
3-Mile Amateur Tricycle, Lap, 1st, Photographer's Outfit; 2d, Silver Watch; 3d, Fishing Set.
5-Mile Promateur Bicycle, A. C. U. Championship (time limit, 15m.), 1st, A. C. U. Gold Medal, diamond setting; 2d, A. C. U. Gold Medal; 3d, A. C. U. Gold and Silver Medal.
1-Mile Amateur Bicycle, Lap, 1st, Fruit Dish, rich cut glass, gold, oxidized; 2d, Cigar Box, oxidized; 3d, Gentleman's Gold Chain.
10-Mile Professional Bicycle, Lap, 1st, $100 Cash. ($50 extra for Record.) 2d, $50 Cash; 3d, $25 Cash.
3-Mile Promateur Bicycle, Handicap, 1st, Handsome Oil Painting; 2d, Silver Cashmere Band Tea Set; 3d, Dessert Set, coral rose and glass.
1-Mile Amateur Bicycle, Consolation, 1st, Half dozen Napkin Rings, gold ground, satin case; 2d, Silver Watch; 3d, Russia Leather Satchel.

ENTRIES CLOSE SEPTEMBER 16.

All Events have Three Prizes where there are four or more starters. Entry Forms, Blanks, List of Prizes, etc., furnished upon application to E. M. BAILEY, Secretary Lynn Cycle Track Association, LYNN, MASS.

SEPTEMBER impends.

LET us call it the tournamonth.

IT is the month of months for wheelmen.

IT gives us beautiful weather for riding, and it gives us the big race meetings.

THE tournament managers have, however, given us little time to ride in this year.

WE hope to be around, and if we can squeeze a little fun into the month of hard work, we shall surely do it.

WE have often wondered if wheelmen wouldn't like to alter Dr. Watts on "Heaven," and call it a place where racing never stops, and meetings never end. What a place that would be for the makers' amateurs.

THE makers' amateurs have been pretty well abused of late, but American wheelmen are going to entrust to them the duty of maintaining America's glory on the path. We think they will do it.

WE went down to Lynn last week to see the boys ride, and we have a good report to make. They are riding in most excellent form.

WE are not going to tell you the time they made, for we don't know. The coachers and trainers keep that to themselves, and they work things so that outsiders can't get the time.

AT one point in the Lynn track there is an old broom stuck up, and the end of a house comes in at a convenient place. These are points used by the timers for starting the men, and if by any possibility the starting-points should be guessed, an outsider could hardly tell the final point. We did n't see any watch nor hold one, but we believe the boys went as fast or faster than three minutes to the mile.

IF John Bull beats Jonathan, he will have to go as fast or faster than three minutes to the mile.

THEY have got one of Victoria's subjects down at Lynn. His name is Fred Foster, and he comes from Canada. He is subject to the Queen, but we are going to put down his victories as American for all that. He is only a foster-child.

GETCHELL goes down to Lynn from Cambridge every morning, and returns at night, giving several hours each day to training. If Getch. gets a prize this fall, it can be well said that it was earned.

HENDEE and Knapp ride in couples, while Rowe goes around the track with Neilson. Burnham chooses Crocker for a mate, and that little bunch of riders going about together is made up of the pure amateurs.

THE Springfield Bicycle Club will repeat its excellent minstrel entertainment two evenings during the tournament. The boys are now reading up for new jokes.

THE Springfield track is now the centre of great attraction, and the boys are making good reports of themselves.

PERCY STONE has arrived and is now a member of the Victor team.

THEY tell of marvelous performances on the part of Rhodes and Ives, both of whom have run a mile inside of 2.33.

WOODSIDE is also riding wonderfully well, and the twenty-one miles an hour has got to go on record.

LANGDOWN, the New Zealander, is looked upon as a surprise party of the future. He is a little stiff yet from his journey, but promises well. The boys have been to walk with him, and they say if he can ride as fast as he can walk, he will go well to the front.

THE entrants for the international championship must have a record of 2.45, and to enable candidates to get such a record, a special record-breaking meeting will be held at Springfield, 4 September.

THE prizes for the promateurs and professionals at Springfield are of like value. The amateur prizes are of less value.

A TELEGRAM has been received announcing the death, 21 August, from typhoid fever, of Geo. E. Weber, the famous Star rider. This is a great blow to the racing interests of the sport, as well as to the many friends of Mr. Weber.

RATES from Boston to Buffalo for Officers' meeting, $8.52. To be had at Fitchburg office, 250 Washington street.

EVERY one should have his machine in the best possible condition. This can be done by using a bottle of Ardill's Liquid Enamel, price 75 cents. Stoddard, Lovering & Co., agents, 152-8 Congress street, Boston.

CONTRIBUTORS' CLUB.

BELLS IN NEW ORLEANS.

Editor Cycle : — As there is quite a controversy going on in your columns on the subject of cycles being compelled by law to carry lamps and bells, this communication may not be amiss. Down here (New Orleans) we have had a law of the same kind in operation for some time past, and though there was a feeble kick at first, the kickers, in common with the rest of us, gracefully gave in without causing trouble.

From actual experience, I can testify that the carrying of a lamp or bell is little or no hindrance whatever, and in face of the fact that other vehicles are compelled to do likewise, at least as to the lamp, it is but fair that cycles should do as well. I might add, however, that the bell is of little service, there being but little occasion to use it ; still, it once in a while comes in handy.

It seems to me that to take the matter into court would but endanger the cause of wheeling generally. Better submit to the law. It is but just.　　　　BI.

FROM ROBERT TODD.

LONDON, 12 August, 1886.

ABBOT BASSETT, ESQ.,

Chairman Racing Board L. A. W.,

BOSTON, MASS., U. S. A.

Dear Sir, — I duly received your letter of 27 July, with reference to the position taken up by the L. A. W. and the A. C. U. towards each other, and towards amateur riders. I have thought it best to publish your letter for the information of English riders. It is by your letter made perfectly

clear that the N. C. U. cannot consent to English amateur riders competing against the pro-amateurs of the A. C. U., a class against whom the amateurs of the L. A. W. would not be allowed to compete.

Believe me,

Yours very faithfully,

ROBERT TODD,

Hon. Sec.

ELECTRIC TIMING.

THE timing at Springfield will be done by electricity. A wire will be stretched across the path two inches beyond the tape, and one inch high. As the wheel passes over this a circuit will be closed and the time recorded. Regular time-keepers will be employed in addition to the mechanical apparatus. There will be a similar wire at the quarter pole for timing the quarter-mile distance. Electric bells will be placed at the handicap marks along the track, and as the pistol is fired these will be rung from the scratch at the moment the pistol is fired. The rider will get his signal to go before he gets the report of the pistol.

A big clock will be placed in front of the judges' stand, on which will be recorded the time in minutes and seconds of each quarter and half mile. By this means people in the grand stand will be enabled to see how fast the men are riding, and moreover, the time for the quarter will have been announced before the men have reached the half-mile. In addition to this, previous to the starting of each event, there will be displayed on a large board the best recorded time for the event about to be run, thereby enabling the spectators to know, at the finish of the race, whether or not the record has been broken.

THE TANDEM RECORD.

ABOUT ten days ago Harry Corey, of the Massachusetts Club, thought it would be a good idea to make a twenty-four tandem tricycle record on the road, and Mr. Ducker, president of the American Cyclist Union, was notified that an attempt would be made by himself and Mr. W. H. Huntley, of the Nonantum Club, of Newton. Neither of the above-named gentlemen had been in training, with the exception of three days before on a Rudge Humber tandem which they intended to use. It was their idea simply to make a record for the time being, and if it was beaten they would try it later on. Precautions were taken by the various members of the Nonantum Club, including J. H. Lewis, vice-president of the A. C. U., to carefully check the cyclometer and attend to the riders during their rests. The tandem was fitted with 42-inch driving wheels and geared to fifty-five inches. It weighed about one hundred pounds.

At precisely two o'clock they started from Newtonville, with Drummond and Doane in charge as pacemakers. They first went to West Newton over across Centre street to Crafts, down Crafts to Washington, thence to Babcock street, Allston, *via* Newton and Brighton, returning through Babcock street, Brighton, to Chestnut Hill Reservoir, round the Reservoir, down Chestnut Hill avenue to Brighton, through Newton to West Newton, and then back to Newtonville, arriving at 3.55 ; distance ridden, 24⅜ miles. Time for

Adjustment in Height in Front.   Adjustment in Length.   A Comfortable Coasting Plate.
Adjustment in Height in Rear.   Adjustment in Width.   A Bifurcated Seat.

THE LILLIBRIDGE SADDLE

Is the only one having any of these Points; is the only one that can be changed in Shape or Position at all; is the BEST and CHEAPEST; is adapted to all makes of Bicycles. Special Styles for the Safeties and Star.

Price, Nickelled, $5.00.   Price of oiled Spring, with Straps, etc., for Old Saddles, 75 Cts.

FREEMAN LILLIBRIDGE, Rockford, Ill.

THE BOSTON BICYCLE SHOE.

The Perfect Shoe for Cycling.

Hand-sewed, hand-made, first-quality stock and warranted in every respect. Every pair of our No. 1 Boston Sporting Shoes is marked inside, "Boston: Strickland & Pierce, Hand-Sewed," and is stamped "Patent" on the bottom. None others are Genuine. Bicycle, Base Ball Sprint Running, Pedestrian, Gymnasium, La Crosse and other shoes. Prices and rules for self-measurement sent on application.

STRICKLAND & PIERCE,

156 and 156½ Summer Street,

BOSTON.

SAFE, PRACTICAL and FAST.

NO HEADERS OR DANGEROUS FALLS.

Best Road Record for 50 and 100 Miles.
World's Safety Records from 1 to 20 Miles.
First American Machine to make more than 20 Miles within the Hour.
Three L. A. W. Championships for 1885.
Won all Hill Climbing Contests, both as to Speed and Grade.
Won all the First Premiums, when in Competition, since 1881.
NEW CATALOGUE READY.

H. B. SMITH MACHINE CO.

Smithville, Bur. Co., N. J.

THE AMERICAN CHAMPION, CHALLENGE, SAFETY AND IDEAL.

The above Machines have been awarded First Prize at the New Orleans Exposition, and the Champion holds the World's Long Distance Record. They Run Easy; Sell Easy; Repair Easy; and the Prices are Easy. They are the best. These are the only Machines of high grade sold at a medium price. It will pay you to examine them, or send two-cent stamp for Catalogue and Prices. We also have a large stock of Children's Machines at very low prices. First-class Repairing and parts for repairing. All kinds of Machines constantly on hand; also Sundries.   Discount to the Trade. Call or write to the New England Headquarters.

MURRAY'S, 100 SUDBURY STREET, BOSTON, MASS.

HOLDFAST TIRE CEMENT
PUT UP IN 2 OZ. STICKS.
PRICE 20 CTS.
SENT POST PAID ON RECEIPT OF PRICE
H. B. HART, 811 ARCH ST. PHILA.

LYRA BICYCLICA:

SIXTY POETS ON THE WHEEL.

By J. G. DALTON.

Much enlarged second edition. One hundred and sixty filled pages, elegantly bound. In boards, 75 cents; flexible, 40 cents; sent post-paid. This is the standard and only book of thorough-going cycling verse, and comparable in art to none but the first-rate poets. No reading cyclist should overlook it. Old edition, 20 cents. For sale at CYCLE office.

JOHN HARRIOTT,

MEDALS and BADGES,

BICYCLE CLUB PINS OF EVERY DESCRIPTION.

DESIGNS ON APPLICATION.

433 Washington Street (Cor. Winter Street,) Boston, Mass.

DAYTON BICYCLE STAND and CAMP STOOL.

Prepared by A. W. GUMP, Dayton, Ohio.

It can be used as a stand, converted into a stool, used for cleaning, or folded into small space. It is adjustable to any size bicycle. Weight, 5¼ pounds.
Price, $3.00 each.

BEFORE YOU BUY A BICYCLE, send stamp to A. W. GUMP, Dayton, Ohio, for List of New and Second-hand Machines.

HELLO, MR. BASSETT!

RUDGE TELEPHONE MAN.

I see that **Huntley** and **Corey** have made 202 miles in 24 hours on a **RUDGE HUMBER TANDEM.** Well, that's not bad, you know. I've got one of the same machines, and I tell you it is great. It catches the girls every time. Guess they think I am about right up to date.

twenty-five miles, 1 h. 57 m. They stopped four minutes for refreshments, and with the same pacemakers started at 3.59 P. M., and after circling Washington Park, they rode through Walnut street to Newton Centre, round the Lake, up Highland avenue to Needham, returning *via* Highland avenue to Beacon street, up Beacon street to Sign Boards, and returning to Walnut street, then to Newtonville. Distance, 26⅝ miles; time of arrival, 6.04 P. M.; total, 50½ miles; time for fifty miles, 3 h. 59 m. Stopped twenty-four minutes, and started at 6.28 P. M., with Kirk Corey and H. A. Fuller as pacemakers. They took the Newtonville course through Waltham, Auburndale, and West Newton, then back through Newtonville, Brighton, and Allston, circling the Reservoir, and returned to Newtonville by West Newton, arriving at 9.17 P. M. Distance, 29⅜ miles; total distance, 80⅞ miles. They rested ten minutes and started at 9.27, with McCurdy and Ellison in charge. They rode over the Needham course as before specified, and returned to Newtonville at 12.20 A. M. Distance, 25⅜ miles; total, 106⅛ miles. Rested twenty minutes and started at 12.40 A. M., and started over the Newtonville course, with Drummond and Kirk Corey in charge, returning at 1.23 A. M. Distance, 7⅛ miles; total, 113¼ miles.

Stopped five minutes, and started at 1.28 A. M., with Fuller and Kirk Corey, who attended in charge, and rode over the Brighton and Allston course, returning to Newtonville, arriving at 4.30 A. M. Distance, 22½ miles; total, 135⅝ miles. Stopped thirty-seven minutes and started at 5.07 A. M., with McCurdy and Williams in charge. Rode through Waltham, West Newton, and Auburndale, returning to Newtonville at 6 A. M. Distance, 7⅛ miles; total, 142⅞ miles. Stopped two minutes and started at 6.02 A. M., with Drummond and Williams, over the Needham course, returning at 9.18 A. M. Distance, 26¼ miles; total, 169⅛ miles. Stopped twenty-two minutes and started at 9.40 A. M., with Sidwell and Porter, over the Newtonville course, returning at 10.20 A. M. Distance, 6⅜ miles; total, 175½ miles. Stopped seven minutes and started at 10.27 A. M., with Sidwell and Marple in charge, over the Brighton and Allston course, returning, *via* Newton Centre to Newtonville, at 12.47 P. M. Distance, 18¼ miles; total miles, 194. Stopped three minutes and started at 1 P. M., with Drummond and Williams in charge. Went through Waltham, returning, *via* West Newton, to Newtonville at 1.52 P. M. Distance, 8¼ miles; total, 202¼ miles for the twenty-four hours.

Had it not been for the severity of the weather through the night, which stiffened Corey's muscles, a higher record would have been made; but being on the front of the tandem, and the night being very cold, he got the full benefit of the dampness and wind.

Both riders feel confident that they can make close on to two hundred and fifty miles, and will probably try it again later on if a suitable time can be found.

They will attempt some of the shorter records very soon, and feel confident they can make fast time.

A few days before the race, they rode ten miles in forty-four minutes. The tandem used was a Rudge Humber, similar to the one Jos. Pennell, the author of the articles in the *Century Magazine*, "A Canterbury Pilgrimage," used during his tour in Italy.

ENGLISH RECORDS.

AT the Coventry track, on Friday, 6 August, Englehart made a run for a safety record on a Kangaroo. He made the following records: two miles, 5.37; that beats English record, but is behind the American. Three miles, 8.27; four miles 11.14; five miles, 14.01⅕. The three-mile time beats the world's safety record. The four-mile time beats the world's safety record and the English record of the ordinary bicycle, which was 11.24. The five-mile time beats the amateur record for the world on any kind of machine, but is behind Rowe's promateur record of 13.57⅘.

At the Coventry track, on Friday, 6 August, F. S. Buckingham make a run for a tricycle record. He succeeded in scoring the following times. Those marked with an asterisk are best English record. The American record was not touched:—

MILES.	M.	S.	MILES.	M.	S.
¼	0	43⅘	2¾	*8	29⅕
½	1	26⅗	3	*9	17
¾	*2	11	3¼	*10	6
1	2	56	3½	*10	56
1¼	3	44⅗	3¾	*11	44⅗
1½	4	32⅘	4	*12	34
1¾	5	20	4¼	*13	22⅗
2	6	6⅗	4½	*14	11
2¼	*6	53⅘	4¾	*15	0
2½	*7	40⅗	5	*15	40⅘

A run for a record was made at Paignton, on 4 August. Fenlon, Ball, and Buckingham (on his safety) did the running. The records were not touched till the eighth mile, when Fenlon knocked a fifth of a second off English's record of 23.28⅕, making the fraction three fifths. At the eleventh mile the English records began to fall and were broken by Fenlon, with one exception, to twenty-five miles. Rowe holds world's records to twenty miles, and these were not touched, but above the twenty miles the English hold the world's records, and the times below take this record:—

MILES.	OLD.	NEW.
11	0 32 16⅕	0 32 19⅗
12	0 35 14⅘	0 35 15
13	0 38 12⅕	0 38 16
14	0 41 8⅕	0 41 26
15	0 44 5⅕	0 44 29⅗
16	0 47 7⅕	0 47 26
17	0 50 11⅕	0 50 22
18	0 53 11⅕	0 53 20
19	0 56 15	0 56 15
20	0 59 16⅗	0 59 6⅕
21	1 2 27⅕	1 3 45⅕
22	1 5 31⅕	1 6 51⅕
23	1 8 35⅕	1 10 9⅕
24	1 11 40⅗	1 13 26⅕
25	1 14 38	1 16 41⅕

One hour, 20 miles, 380 yards.

G. P. MILLS, the English rider, who made so much fame in his John-o'-Groat's ride, has just put up the English twenty-four hour bicycle record to 273 miles.

THE greatest safety for night riding is a thorough *reliable* lamp. The celebrated "King of the Road" has the above quality in a very marked degree. Stoddard, Lovering & Co., 152 and 158 Congress street, Boston.

THE PATH.

NEWCASTLE, PA., 19 Aug. — Races under the auspices of the Newcastle Club.

One-Mile Novice.—C. D. Pierce (1), 3.20⅗; L. N. Crawford (2). *Half-Mile Open*,—S. P. Hollingsworth (1), 1.27⅘; C. M. Brown (2). *One-Mile* 3.10 *Class*,—C. M. Clark (1), 3.35⅘; Elder Morehead (2). *One-Mile Open*,—C. M. Brown (1), 2.59⅘; S. P. Hollingsworth (2). *Two-Mile Open*,—C. M. Brown (1), 6.54; S. P. Hollingsworth (2). *One-Mile* 3.00 *Class*,—S. P. Hollingsworth (1), 3.09⅘; W. A. Crawford (2). *Quarter-Mile*,—L. A. W. Pennsylvania State Championship, C. M. Brown (1), 42 s.; W. S. Crawford (2). *Boys' Quarter-Mile*,—F. Johnson (1), 1.03; L. Seckler (2). *Two-*

Miles 2.30 *Class,* — S. P. Hollingsworth (1); Banker (2).

WILLIAMSPORT, PA., 19 Aug. — Races under auspices of the Pennsylvania Division, L. A. W. — *One-Mile Novice,* — A. Monnies (1), 3.08¾; J. B. Nallen (2). *Half-Mile Ride and Run,* — N. R. Hubbard (1), 2.05 ; J. B. Nallen (2). *Half-Mile Williamsport Club Championship,* — J. W. Rowman (1), 1.23. *Quarter-Mile Heat,* — H. C. Hersey (1), 39¼ ; W. J. Wilhelm (2). *Two-Mile Amateur,* — C. W. Hank (1), 6.36. *One-Mile State Championship,* — J. R. Shlager (1), 2.47. *One-Mile Hands Off,* — B. Brown (1), 3.23¼. *Three-Mile State Championship,* — J. R. Shlager (1), 9.22 ; W. J. Wilhelm (2). *One-Mile Team,* — Scranton team (1), 2.48¾. *Five-Mile Lap,* — W. J. Wilhelm (1). *One-Mile Club,* — E. L. Sheffer (1), 3.08¼. *One-Mile Consolation,* — E. Gohl (1), 3.02.

WEEDSPORT, N. Y. — Races under the auspices of the Weedsport Club.

Half-Mile Novice, — L. W. Putnam (1), 1.35 ; W. B. Perry (2). *One-Mile Open,* — J. R. Rheubottom (1), 2.58 ; E. H. Gamble (2). *Half-Mile Boys,* — Bert Kenyon (1), 2.17 ; Henry Brewster (2). *One-Mile Handicap,* — J. R. Rheubottom, scratch (1), 3.04½ ; L. W. Putnam, 100 yards (2). *One-Mile 3.20 Class,* — B. A. Pratt (1), 3.20¼ ; W. B. Perry (2), W. F. Herring (3). *One-Mile Central N. Y. Championship,* — C. E. Titchener (1), J. R. Rheubottom (2). *One-Hundred Yards Slow,* — J. R. Rheubottom (1), 1.56 ; J. G. Elbs (2). *Half-Mile Hands Off,* — J. R. Rheubottom (1), 1.42 ; J. G. Elba (2). *One-Mile Tricycle,* — W. F. Herring (1), 4.46¼ ; J. R. Rheubottom (2). *One-Mile Ride and Run,* — W. H. Stone (1), 4.42½ ; John G. Elbs (2). *Three-Mile Lap,* — C. E. Titchener (1), 9.44, 24 points ; J. R. Rheubottom (2), 18 points. *Half-Mile,* 1.40 *Class,* — W. H. Stone, 1.40 ; C. J. Connelly (2). *One-Mile Consolation,* — F. L. Dunbar (1), 3.44 ; E. J. Rice (2).

THE Ilderan Bicycle Club, of Brooklyn, will hold a twenty-five-mile road race for the club championship on 13 Sept. A score or so of members have entered, and first and second are to be rewarded with gold medals, while the first six will constitute the team to represent the club in the New York and New Jersey road race in November.

IN the competition for the twenty-five-mile amateur bicycle championship of Victoria, on the Warehousemen's Ground, Melbourne, 10 July, Con Dwyer was credited with lowering the record for twenty-five miles to 1h. 15m. 1⅘s. Maltby and Rollinston, the American cyclists, have been giving exhibitions of trick-riding at Botany, near Sydney, their feats causing something of a sensation.

THE North Attleboro' Club will hold a race meeting 15 Oct.

THE first prize in the five-mile race at the Orange Wanderers' Cycling Tournament, 4 Sept., is a Beeston Humber Racing Bicycle, value $150, donated by Llewellyn H. Johnson, Humber & Co.'s United States agent. So desirable and valuable a trophy will undoubtedly attract a large field of flyers and add greatly to the interest of the meet.

DENVER is at last to have a race-course worthy of her wheelmen. Arrangements have been perfected by the Colorado Wheel Club, whereby the exposition half-mile track will be put in first-class order for bicycle racing, a grand stand and dressing rooms built, and everything done to make an attractive place. The track will be forty feet in width, and the fastest one in the West.

THE Massachusetts Club will hold a series of road races the latter part of September.

THE Farmers and Mechanics Association will hold bicycle races at their fair to be held in North Attleboro', 14 Sept. The races will be managed by the Columbia Bicycle Club of North Attleboro'.

A CABLEGRAM from Berlin, on 16 Aug., says : " The races for the bicycle and tricycle championships of Europe took place to-day. The bicycle race was won by Hale of Gainsborough, and the tricycle race by Kidierlen of Delft."

As predicted early in the season, the Buffer Saddle has had a most flattering run, and it well deserves it. Stoddard, Lovering & Co., sole United States agents, 152-8 Congress street, Boston.

COMING EVENTS.

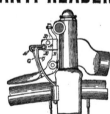

The Cycle.

Vol. I., No. 23.   BOSTON, MASS., 3 SEPTEMBER, 1886.   FIVE CENTS.

THE MARLBORO' TANDEM.

The Latest! The Fastest! The Best!

"OUTING," for May, says—"The 'Marlboro' Tandem is in every way the greatest advance for 1886."

Runs on Three Wheels only. Patent Automatic Steering.

The Coventry Machinists Co., Ld.

239 COLUMBUS AVENUE - - - - - - BOSTON.

THE CYCLE

PUBLISHED EVERY FRIDAY BY ABBOT BASSETT, 22 SCHOOL ST., ROOM 19.

VOL. I.   BOSTON, MASS., 3 SEPTEMBER, 1886.   NO. 23.

TERMS OF SUBSCRIPTION.

One Year, by mail, post-paid.................................$1.50
Three Copies in one order...............................3.00
Club Subscriptions......................................1.00
Six Months..90
Single Copies......... 05

Specimen Copies free.

Every bicycle dealer is agent for the CYCLE and author-
ized to receive subscriptions at regular rates. The paper
can be found on sale at the following places : —
Boston, CUPPLES, UPHAM & CO., cor. Washington and
School Streets. Tremont House news stand. At every
cycle warehouse.
New York, ELLIOTT MASON, 12 Warren Street.
Philadelphia, H. B. HART, 811 Arch Street. GEORGE
D. GIDEON, 6 South Broad Street.
Baltimore, S. T. CLARK & CO., 4 Hanover Street.
Chicago, W. M. DURELL, 115 Wabash Avenue. JOHN
WILKINSON & CO., 77 State Street.
Washington, H. S. OWEN, Capital Cycle Co.
St. Louis, ST. LOUIS WHEEL CO., 1121 Olive Street.

ABBOT BASSETT · .   .   .   .   EDITOR

A. MUDGE & SON, PRINTERS, 24 FRANKLIN ST., BOSTON

All communications should be sent in not later than
Tuesday, to ensure insertion the same week.

Entered at the Post-office as second-class mail matter.

OUT of a membership of over 1,400, there
were but fourteen members of the Massachusetts Division present at the annual
meeting on Saturday night. But it was a
representative gathering, and it is safe to
say that these fourteen would have swayed
the legislation if there had been three hundred present. And yet, we have no rings in
the Bay State.

THE L. A. W. should be severely criticised for offering special sanction to the
coming over of these English amateur professionals. — *Herald.*

THE L. A. W. has not offered to sanction
the racing of amateurs with promateurs. It
can do no such thing under its rules. The
N. C. U. has, however, a special clause in
its amateur rule which allows for the special
sanction of "mixed" races, and international comity calls for the respect of such
action on the part of the L. A. W., should
the N. C. U. think best to employ this
clause of its rules. We do not hesitate to
say that we should prefer to see the English
riders come over with sanction to ride in
promateur races, rather than have them
come over as amateurs with carefully concealed business relations, and go into amateur races.

IF the Galatea should carry home the
America's cup, we don't believe that Lieut.
Henn will take it to a silversmith to find its
real value. Yachtsmen have not come to
that yet.

THE Massachusetts Division has appointed a committee on Rights and Privileges. It is proposed that the legal rights
of wheelmen shall be maintained on the
highways. From what we know of the
committee, sidewalk riders will get little
sympathy. It may be that they will attend
also to the rights and privileges of pedestrians on the sidewalks.

AT the Buffalo meeting, L. A. W., many
important changes will be made in the By-
Laws of the League. Among these changes
a very important one is that which restores
to the membership at large the right to elect
the president and vice-president. It has
been claimed that the Board of Officers is a
more representative body than the general
assembly ; but when clubs can send their
proxies by fifties to the general meeting, a
very general expression of opinion can be
called out. The change, which will allow
large State divisions to provide for the election and apportionment of Representatives
and the Chief Consul, is a good one, and will
work to the advantage of the League in many
ways.

THE CYCLE clipped the account of the
Stickney accident and got it wrong. — *World.*

THE CYCLE did no such thing. Had we
done this, we should have said that Mr. Stickney was taken to the *Woodlawn* Park Hotel,
and that the tricycle struck the curbstone.
These mistakes were made by the daily press,
and faithfully reproduced in the *World* and
other papers. The CYCLE gave the only
correct account of the accident that has been
published, and it was made up as a result of
a consultation with friends of the deceased and
with those who saw the accident.

THE Boston correspondent of the *Bulletin*
tries to be funny at the expense of truth. He
reports that two members of the Massachusetts Division Board of Officers failed to
attend the meeting of that body, because they
could not find the room where the meeting
was to be held ; and he says that of the two
parties, those who were at the meeting, and
those who failed to find the room, one
" waited in the parlor, and the other tarried

---

at the bar." If there were a grain of truth
in this, it might be funny ; but it is not true,
and the writer knows that it is not.

THE cyclists of England are not the only
doubters. In a recent interview L. E. Myers
said to a reporter : " When our English
cousins heard about their records having
been knocked into the shade, they merely
laughed, and called it ' American bounce '
All of the English authorities said it was
just possible that the tracks were short, or
the people who held the watches did n't know
their duty." Myers has been over, and they
doubt no longer. We 'll have to send some
of our fast cyclers over.

KARL KRON is much incensed that we did
not give him two or three columns of space
to say what we condensed into ten lines.
In his passion he has sent his letter to a
contemporary, with a two-column criticism of
our course. We feel sure that we shall have
the gratitude of our readers, for the infliction
we have saved them. Boiled down articles
find favor at the CYCLE office.

WE were in error in stating that an ordinance requiring a bicycle to carry a light was
on the books of a city near Boston. We
referred to Newton. The city clerk has
furnished us with the ordinance relative to
highways, and we find that the section relating to cycles reads as follows : —

" SEC. 19. No bicycle or tricycle shall
be propelled upon any street or way, unless
provided with a bell, to be rung when approaching any person ; and neither shall be
propelled upon a sidewalk."

The penalty affixed to this is a fine of not
less than one, nor more than twenty dollars.

SOME one has said that " all literature is but
the turning of one bottle into another." There
are few papers that can live without their
exchanges, and it is only fresh young editors
that pretend they do. No cycling paper has
been drawn upon more freely than the CYCLE.
It was only the other day that our contemporary the *World* took a poem from our
columns and printed it without credit ; and
the little poem " Wheel Ethics," which first
saw the light with us, has been reproduced
several times, credited to another journal
that took it from us without credit. These
things do not trouble us much, and we don't
care to bore our readers with the details of
the credited and uncredited articles which
appear in other journals. Veteran journalists

always know a fresh editor by the frequency with which he cries that he is being robbed, and they may well laugh at the editor who says he can get along without exchanges. The CYCLE always gives credit when it thinks credit to be due.

THE Board of Officers has given a decided negative to the questions propounded in the mail vote. There is no wavering in their decision. By a very large vote, they say that the amateur rule shall remain as it is ; that Rule H shall remain, and that the League shall not give up racing. They voted eighty-five negatives and fifteen affirmatives. They also sustained the action of President Beckwith in removing Mr. Ducker by a vote of ninety to ten. The Board of Officers has faith in the Racing Board.

THE CYCLER'S STORY.
BY COLIN GRAY.
CHAPTER II.

" At last, with a feeling of intense delight and satisfaction, I saw the possibility of getting away from Boston. Where should I go ? I received a letter from my dear friends the Willoughbys, who had taken an old house in the mountain regions of New Hampshire during the temporary absence of the owner, and were hospitably bent on filling it with guests. Florence Willoughby was my cousin, and before she married the wealthy son of a wealthy stockbroker, we used to 'spoon' a good deal. 'Do come,' she pleaded in her letter of invitation, 'for in order to make up for past unkindness and neglect on my part'—these last few lines were expressively underlined—' I mean to introduce you to an old school-fellow of mine—such a darling girl, and as good as she is lovely, and I shall expect you to marry her ; for I feel it is my mission to provide you with a wife. It is quite time, sir, you were settled.'

"I could not help heaving a sigh as I thought of dear little Flo', and how happy we could have been. I think she liked me a little bit until the other fellow made his appearance. I liked the phrase 'the other fellow' ; it eased my mind to think of him in that form : but I decided to accept the invitation for all that.

"I duly arrived at the house of my good friends, having been met at the depot by a servant of the family, and driven over. My welcome was a very warm one. I had not seen Florence for four years, and really she had grown so plump and matronly, that I hardly recognized in her the slender young lady who used to hang on my arm, or languidly ask me to pick up her fan. ' The other fellow' was, I soon discovered, a hearty generous man, and he appeared to be as delighted to see me as if he had known me all my life.

" That night at dinner, I laughingly asked Florence when the 'dear darling girl' referred to was to make her appearance. With a roguish shake of the head she informed me that Lucy would not arrive for a day or so,—that she had lately lost her father by death.

" 'Indeed, I am sorry for that,' I answered in a conventionally sorrowful tone, though I am bound to confess I did not care a jot about it. I did not know either Lucy or her father ; and, besides, Lucy was a name I detested.

" The village where I had temporarily cast my fortunes was situated not far from a well-known show-place, a mountain gorge spanned by a bridge, which, by reason of its daring construction, was familiarly known as the Devil's Bridge.

" This spot was so close, that the noise of the falling water could be heard quite distinctly from the house. I never shall forget the curious sensation there came over me, as I leaned over the parapet and looked down into the seemingly unfathomable abyss. My head, unused to such sights, swam, and my nerves, probably unstrung by my late application to work, positively gave way, and for a moment or two I felt quite giddy. Florence noticed this, and in some alarm pulled me back by the tails of my coat, though I do not think I was in any danger of falling.

" 'What a place to fall down !' I said, when I had recovered my mental balance.

" 'Yes, indeed !' said my host ; and then, to turn the conversation, he promised that a few days' hill-climbing would soon take all nonsense out of me, and that when I got back to Boston I should not know what a nerve was.

" Tired with an all-night journey, I was not sorry to retire at a very early hour to bed that night.

" It is not easy to change one's habits all at once. I was a late bird, like most bachelors, and thought the best time for enjoyment between eleven and one. When I had to go to my room, I found the excitement of saying ' Good-Night' and of making arrangements for the next morning had effectually driven off my drowsiness, and I did not care in the least to go to bed. It was bŷ ten o'clock I found, so I lit a cigar, softly raised the window, and threw myself into a lounge-chair by it.

" It was a beautiful night ; the full harvest moon had risen, and flooded all with her mellow light. Just the suspicion of a mist lent a gauzy effect to the surroundings. Not a sound could be heard save that made by the plashing of the cascade under the Devil's Bridge in the distance. When I recognized it, my thoughts turned to the afternoon visit, and I could not help wondering how it would look under the moonlight. My next thought was, why not go and see? Why not ? My window was only an easy height from the ground, and I could easily get back again. Not a soul was about. I could get away unobserved ; the night air would do me good, and I should just have time to finish my cigar in the going there and back.

" In a moment I had put on my hat and was out on the green-sward. How delicious the soft, cool air was ! I leisurely strolled into the lane that led to the gorge and turned in its direction.

" How glorious it was ! The moon tipped every little bit of projecting rock with silver. As I looked over the parapet into the gorge, the sense of unfathomableness did not take possession of me as it had in the afternoon ; on the contrary, I seemed to be looking down into a sort of fairy bower, for the crossing branches and leaves formed a silver tracery, under which there was a soft gossamer cloud, which seemed a fitting bed for elves.

" I was looking down at this, when I felt a hand laid upon my shoulder. Looking hastily up, I beheld a long lank figure, with a cadaverous face, that I remembered only too well, though I had ceased to think about it. I saw my curious client ! 'What brings him here in this place and at this time ?' I wondered. I must confess a very unpleasant sensation came over me as I recognized him.

" ' Do you remember me ?' he asked in his usual hollow voice.

" 'Certainly,' I replied, holding out my hand with an affectation of politeness. ' How do you do ?'

" 'Do you remember our last interview ?'

" 'I do.' As I said this I seemed to feel a distinctly cold something trickle down my back.

" 'Revenge I must have, and revenge I will have !' As he hissed out these words he put his face close to mine, and I saw the same strange bright look in his eyes that I had seen in my chambers that day, only it was intensified by the moonlight.

" 'Ere I had time to utter a syllable, he added : ' But before I have had my revenge I seek a solution of the mystery. It lies down there,' and he nodded in the direction of the gulf. 'You understand me ?'

" I nodded my head vehemently and smiled in a more ghastly manner than before, though I was calculating in my mind whether, if it came to a trial of strength, I could master him.

" ' It is you must unfathom this mystery.'

" 'I ! Why?'

" 'Because you are profound ; you understand the law and its tangles ; because you are my counsel and my case is in your hands ; the fee is in your pocket now.'

" I was glad to find that, as he talked, he receded backwards, and I trusted that we should soon be clear of the dangerous gorge. On level ground I felt I should have more chance in the event of a struggle ; one little gap in the railings safely passed, and I should be all right. We had reached this gap when, with superhuman strength, he sent me spinning from him, and I fell through it into the dreadful gulf ! I seemed to fall miles ; I fell really only a few yards. Putting out my hands, instinctively I clutched a projecting ledge of the rock and found myself hanging by my arms, my whole weight held up by the strength of my fingers. With what despair I held on, and yet with what electric rapidity it flashed through my mind that only a few seconds could I thus support myself ! What could I do ? Nothing but expend my strength in a despairing cry for help, in the hope that it would be heard by the inmates of the house. This I gave, and I can hear now the echoes in that fearful depth mocking my despair ; they seemed all around me — now close to me gurgling in my ear, and now dying away in a sort of chuckle down below. Then I began to economize my strength, by giving each of my fingers a rest in turn, but I found at last, after what seemed an age of torture, that my powers were giving way, and my senses were leaving me. I was about to resign myself to fate when I saw lights above

me, and heard the welcome voice of my friend Willoughby. Strong arms reached down to me and lifted me up, and I remember no more.

"When I next opened my eyes, it was in the room I had so incontinently left that dreadful night. This fact did not come to me all at once, but very slowly. I found, too, that I could not raise my arm, and I could feel that I had much less hair on my head than usual. Then I made out two figures, — one a quaint old woman in a wonderful cap of snowy whiteness, and a red shawl upon her shoulders; the other a young woman in black, with a bunch of white daisies at her throat. I recognized her at once. It was the beautiful messenger who brought me the letter from my client. Her's was an oval face of exquisite beauty, and a pair of eyes were fringed with long black lashes; all this I took in, also by slow degrees. Then the elderly woman came forward and uttered an unintelligible ejaculation, at which the younger woman hurriedly left the room only to return in a few minutes with my friend Willoughby, who exclaimed in his bluff way: ' Welcome back, old fellow! now you 'll be up and around again in a very short time. You 've had a hard siege of it.' Then Florence, claiming a cousin's privilege, bent over me and kissed my forehead, and I heard her whisper, ' Thank Heaven!'

"A week passed before I became strong enough to sit up. One day I sat propped up in bed with pillows. Lucy — yes, I called her Lucy, and rather liked the sound of the name — was sitting opposite to me, reading. During a pause, I asked suddenly: — 'Why did you take such an interest in me? You were my nurse, I hear.'

"'Well, I had been used to nursing, and I felt handy to it, Mr. Nickerson. I have had, unfortunately, a great deal of it to do.'

"I looked at her black dress, and then I remembered what Florence had said on the night of my arrival, about the ' dearest girl' having recently lost her father. She raised her eyes to mine for a moment, and a strange thrill went through me. They seemed to remind me of something in the past. Before I could, however, think it out, she said : —

"'Florence is, you know, an old schoolfellow, and as I have no home now, she has insisted upon my taking up my abode here, and I was glad to be of service to her.' Besides —'

"'Besides what?'

"'I felt it a matter of duty as well to you, see,' she went on, with heightened color and in answer to my inquiring look.

"'It is, I believe, partly owing to my poor dead father that you have suffered so.'

"'Your dead father, Lucy?' I asked incredulously, yet with a nervous excitement ; 'is he dead, then?'

"'Compose yourself. My poor father, your unhappy client, died a few days after the case was decided. The loss of it broke his heart.'

"'Died! Then who was that I met on the Devil's Bridge that night?'

"'No one.'

"'But that dreadful face?'

"'All the result of an overworked mind. Your cry alarmed the house, and you were found hanging from your bedroom windowsill, with your feet barely six inches from the ground.'

"For a year I was not allowed to work. The doctor told me that I must have exercise and plenty of it. That I must not work all the time, and he wound up by saying, ' Get a bicycle and ride it or you won't live three years. Well, I took his advice, and here I am, perfectly restored to health. I ride every day. It interferes somewhat with my business, but it gives me health. Do you wonder that I call it my savior?' There are other kinds of exercise I know, but I never should have the patience to keep up practice at a gymnasium or at any of the many sports. The fun of wheeling kept me to it and it gave me back the health that I had lost."

"'What became of Lucy?' do you ask? ' Oh, she 's all right! and when she writes a visiting card, she puts down my name with a ' Mrs.' before it.'"

CYCLETS.

DAISIE has sent us a charming little story, which will appear next week.

IT is stated on good authority that several Boston ladies are riding Singer's Straight Steerer without a divided skirt. We have not seen them, and we take the statement as we do our corn, with a grain of salt.

GETCHELL met with a bad fall at Lynn last week, and suffered severe bruises.

PROVIDENCE is a city under the prohibitory law. Can it be wondered, then, that a party of Providence wheelmen out on a cruise should want to run aground on Rumstick Neck.

THEY were on the piazza of a hotel at Newport, and Jones was talking with a pretty girl. "Let 's go and see the Galatea," said Barnes. "Oh, no, I prefer the gal at here," said Jones.

CHAS. WEISINGER, who started to ride from Adrian, Mich., to Boston, stopped at New York, and came to Boston by boat. A telegram from home announcing the death of a relative put a sudden end to his journey. He remained in Boston a day or two and returned to his home last week. He reports a good ride, interspersed with the pleasures and the hardships incident to such a trip.

THEY tell us that the Puritan is good for "running and reaching." Well, a great many of our racing men are good for running and reaching the tape first.

OF all the flowers that bloomed in the spring, the Mayflower has proved the best. She is not a trailing arbutus, however, but one of our beauties nevertheless.

DAN CANARY, who astonished thousands of spectators with his seemingly impossible cycling performances at the Charter Oak Park meeting last year, will be succeeded this season by the double acrobatic riders of the Star machine, Lester and Alden, whose feats, though perhaps not more difficult than Canary's, are very wonderful to behold, and decidedly novel.

Outing has arranged with the Connecticut Bicycle Club for facilities for taking photographs and sketches of the coming tournament, and will publish an illustrated account of the parade and races.

NEW ORLEANS now has two clubs : the N. O. Bicycle Club, and the newly organized Crescent Wheelmen.

ST. LOUIS will be ready with her invitation at Buffalo. She wants the League meeting very badly. Can it be that she has heard that it cost the Massachusetts Division only twenty-seven cents?

Wheeling puts this down as the gist of the position of the N. C. U. on the amateur question. "Our promateurs are not as other people's promateurs are. They 're English, you know — quite English."

HARRY LEEMING says that Furnivall is bound to make a mile in 2.25 before he gives up his hunt for records.

THE Salvation Army has purchased three Marlboro' tandems, which will be ridden during a campaign in the north of England. They are all fitted with sockets for carrying banners.

THE tandem drove the sociable out, and now comes a one-track sociable, which the Englishmen are riding, and they say it 's the best yet.

THE Cyclist has proposed that letters of machines put a trade-mark on their wheels which should be known in the trade. It is thought that this plan will lead to the recovery of many stolen machines. The idea will no doubt be adopted and put in practice.

CABIN JOHN BRIDGE adventurers will, now take their places with the barrel men of Niagara and the cranks of Brooklyn Bridge.

D. G. BIGGS, of Louisville, Ky., U. S. A. has invented a "balance power gear " for bicycles, which the Bicycling World illustrates. It is practically Grey's hand-power gear applied to a bicycle, and is precisely the same as a gear shown at the Stanley Show of 1880, by a French firm — we think Clément and Cie. — Cyclist.

THE Bicycling News for 20 August has portraits of the English champions for 1886, — Furnivall, Mecredy, Allard, and Fenlon.

THE Cyclist employees have been holding their annual "wayzgoose." That 's the horrid name they give to a picnic over there.

MR. BOWN publishes a list of those whom he has licensed to use his ball bearing, and says he shall sue all who use it without authority.

FRANK EGAN writes to an exchange, and says that the cigarette girls will next appear on wheels. Heaven save the mark! Let the boys look at them at their desks and on the ball field, but keep them off the wheel.

R. H. ENGLISH was down for a race with Fred Wood on 28 August, but the riders had a disagreement, and the race was given up.

THE Natural Bridge has been added to the programme of the League tour. The hop at Watkins' Glen is promised to be a "daisy" affair.

L. E. HICKOK is riding a bicycle on a business trip through New England. He represents Wilcox & Howe, of Birmingham, Conn. He dropped in on us the other day, and said that he had gained three days in time over the cars, and his expenses had been very much less. The firm gets the bene-

Hampden Park, Springfield, Mass., U.S.A., September 14, 15, 16, and 17, 1886.

FIFTH ANNUAL TOURNAMENT OF THE SPRINGFIELD BICYCLE CLUB.

Who Takes 'Em ? Who Takes 'Em

OFFICIAL LIST OF RACES AND PRIZES.

FIRST DAY—TUESDAY, SEPTEMBER 14.

EVENTS.	CLASSES.	WHEELS.	CONDITIONS.	FIRST PRIZES.	SECOND PRIZES.	THIRD PRIZES.
1-mile	Promateur	Bicycle	World's Championship, 1st heat.			
1-mile	Amateur	Bicycle	Novice.	Vase Lamp, hammered copper and	Scarf Pin, diamond setting.	Fancy Inkstand, gold and oxidised.
10-mile	Promateur	Bicycle	A. C. U. Championship.	A. C. U. Gold Medal. [oxidised.	A. C. U. Gold Medal.	A. C. U. Gold Medal.
5-mile	Professional	Bicycle	Handicap.	$100 Cash.	$60 Cash.	$40 Cash.
1-mile	Promateur	Bicycle	World's Championship, 2d heat.			[qué, gold lined.
3-mile	Amateur	Bicycle	16.80 Class.	Gold Watch, open face.	Vase Lamp, gold and Silver.	Smoking Set, hammered and appli-
1-mile	Promateur	Tricycle	Open.	Gold Watch, open face.	Ewer, antique brass, embossed.	Opera Glass, pearl mounted.
3-mile	Professional	Bicycle	Open.	$62.50 Cash.	$37.50 Cash.	$25 Cash.
1-mile	Promateur	Bicycle	World's Championship, 3d heat.			
1-mile	Amateur	Tandem	A. C. U. Championship.	Two Gold Medals.	Two Silver Medals.	

SECOND DAY—WEDNESDAY, SEPTEMBER 15.

EVENTS.	CLASSES.	WHEELS.	CONDITIONS.	FIRST PRIZES.	SECOND PRIZES.	THIRD PRIZES.
1-mile	Promateur	Bicycle	World's Championship, 4th heat.			
1-mile	Amateur	Bicycle	Lap.	Gold Watch, open face.	French Clock, with bronze figure.	Glass Vase, decorated gold stand.
5-mile	Promateur	Bicycle	Handicap.	Diamond Stud.	$37.50 Cash.	Silver Chronograph Watch.
3-mile	Professional	Tricycle	Open.	$62.50 Cash.	$37.50 Cash.	$25 Cash.
1-mile	Promateur	Bicycle	World's Championship, 5th heat.			
3-mile	Professional	Bicycle	Lap.	$62.50 Cash.	$37.50 Cash. [breech-loader.	$25 Cash.
5-mile	Promateur	Bicycle	Lap.	Gold Watch, hunting case.	Stevens Shot-gun, double-barreled,	Silver Chronograph Watch.
3-mile	Professional	Bicycle	Handicap.	$62.50 Cash.	$37.50 Cash.	$25 Cash.
1-mile	Promateur	Bicycle	World's Championship, 6th heat.			[tern.
3-mile	Amateur	Tricycle	Open.	Gold Medal.	12 Silver Knives, renaissance pat-	Traveling Clock, and case.

THIRD DAY—THURSDAY, SEPTEMBER 16.

EVENTS.	CLASSES.	WHEELS.	CONDITIONS.	FIRST PRIZES.	SECOND PRIZES.	THIRD PRIZES.
1-mile	Promateur	Bicycle	World's Championship, 7th heat.			
3-mile	Amateur	Bicycle	Open.	Gold Medal.	French Clock, with bronze figures.	Gold Watch Chain.
10-mile	Promateur	Bicycle	Lap.	Diamond Stud.	Gold Watch, hunting case.	Gold Watch, hunting case.
1-mile	Professional	Bicycle	Open.	$50 Cash.	$30 Cash.	$30 Cash.
1-mile	Promateur	Bicycle	World's Championship, 8th heat.			
5-mile	Amateur	Bicycle	Open.	Tea Set, 6 pieces, satin embossed.	Stevens Sporting Rifle.	Stevens "Hunter's Pet" Rifle.
3-mile	Promateur	Tricycle	Open.	Gold Watch, hunting case.	Diamond Stud.	Gold Watch Chain.
1-mile	Professional	Bicycle	Handicap.		$30 Cash.	$30 Cash.
1-mile	Promateur	Bicycle	World's Championship, 9th heat.			
3-mile	Professional	Tricycle	Handicap.	$62.50 Cash.	$37.50 Cash.	$25 Cash.

FOURTH DAY—FRIDAY, SEPTEMBER 17.

EVENTS.	CLASSES.	WHEELS.	CONDITIONS.	FIRST PRIZES.	SECOND PRIZES.	THIRD PRIZES.
1-mile	Promateur	Bicycle	World's Championship,10th heat.			
3-mile	Amateur	Bicycle	9.45 Class.	Gold Watch, open face.	Carving Set, renaissance pattern.	Gold Cuff Buttons, stone settings.
3-mile	Promateur	Bicycle	Open.	Diamond Stud.	Complete Fishing Outfit.	Water Set, silver, gold lined.
10-mile	Professional	Bicycle	Lap.	$120 Cash.	$90 Cash.	$60 Cash. Fourth, $30 Cash.
1-mile	Promateur	Bicycle	World's Championship,11th heat.			[and oxidised.
3-mile	Amateur	Bicycle	Handicap.	Diamond Stud.	Scarf Pin, diamond setting.	Biscuit Jar, decorated china, gold
1-mile	Promateur	Bicycle	2.40 Class.	Gold Watch, open face.	$60 Cash. [globe.	Gold Watch Chain.
5-mile	Professional	Bicycle	Open.	$100 Cash. [Medal.	Pedestal Lamp, antique brass, tulip	$40 Cash.
1-mile	Promateur	Bicycle	World's Championship, final heat.	Winner last heat, Gold Watch and	Winner fastest heat, Fine Gold	[Fifth, Lakin Cyclometer.
1-mile	Amateur	Bicycle	Consolation.	Gold Watch Chain.	Stevens Bicycle Rifle. [Watch.	Seal Ring. Fourth, Traveling Bag.

ENTRIES CLOSE SEPTEMBER 7, 1886.

All Events have three Prizes, where there are four or more starters. Entry Forms, Blanks, List of Prizes, etc., will be furnished upon application to SANFORD LAWTON, Secretary Springfield Bicycle Club, Springfield, Mass., U.S.A.

fit of the saving in expenses, and he gets a good time.

A MEETING of the board of Officers' League of Essex County Wheelmen was held at Salem last week. George Chinn of Beverly, R. H. Robson and A. N. Webb of Salem, were appointed a committee to arrange for a meet of the League on Saturday, 9 October. The sentiment of the meeting was in favor of holding a race meet on that date in Lynn, if satisfactory arrangements can be made with the Lynn Cycle Track Association.

THE California Division will meet at San Francisco 9 Sept. The three-mile National championship will be contested at that time.

JACK PRINCE expresses himself as very sorry that Howell is out of condition. He wants to meet and down the great Englishman, but he sees no great honor in beating a sick man.

AN English wheelman took a header the other day, and was immediately surrounded by a curious crowd. He took of his hat and passed it around, soliciting aid to repair damages. The crowd dispersed.

IT may be that the Lynn Cycle Club will locate its proposed new clubhouse at the corner of High Rock and Grover streets, as the suggested North Common street lot is too expensive, costing $6,000. The club wants to expend about $5,000 in a house and lot.

"BICYCLES! Bicycles!" Nay, to shun laughter,
Try cycles first, and *buy* cycles after;
For surely the buyer deserves but the worst
Who would buy cycles, failing to try cycles first! — *St. Nicholas.*

DR. KENDALL has had a photograph taken of himself on a bicycle with his pup "Bess" running by his side. It should ornament the title-page of Will Carleton's "Betsey and I are out."

LANGDOWN will ride a Columbia. The peculiar persuasive powers of Manager Atkins are best shown by the action of these men who come to us from abroad, and go right on to Columbias. Foster, of Canada, was riding a Columbia three days after he struck the Lynn track, and his English wheel was laid aside.

WE can go down to the Hartford races in the morning and get back the same night, if we don't care to stay over. The 9 o'clock train will land us in Hartford in plenty time for dinner.

THE man who will furnish ham sandwiches to the visitors at the Hartford races is named Bacon. We trust he will put plenty of meat between the bread, and not try to save his bacon.

WHITTAKER has been very much troubled about his disqualification. He says there is no one to race with in St. Louis if he cannot be an amateur. He can now race with Percy Stone.

A WESTFIELD rider is running up a road record in competition for a cyclometer. He has already ridden six thousand miles. We understand that this and all the other Westfield records are made on a smooth road around a park, and that the riders keep up their speeding far into the night. Last year Goodnow took the prize in this way, covering five thousand and fifty miles.

MR. SANFORD LAWTON once more becomes secretary-treasurer for Massachusetts. The Division members had an idea that it would be a good thing to have chief consul and secretary-treasurer in the same city, but they did n't want to give up Lawton.

LAST year Massachusetts had seven hundred members in the League. Now she has fourteen hundred and ten, — a good percentage of increase. She has nine representatives, and she is entitled to five more.

THE Massachusetts Division has got $928.76 in its treasury, and it proposes to have a good road book, cost what it will. The Old Bay State got out the first book of this kind, and pointed the way for other divisions to go. We think she may give them another pointer soon. She has been left behind in the matter of road books, but mark our words, she will not stay there.

THE League Meet cost the Massachusetts Division the enormous sum of twenty-seven cents!

AT the parade of the Connecticut Bicycle Club at Hartford, 8 and 9 Sept., prizes will be offered — (1) to the club parading the largest number of uniformed riders; (2) to the club presenting the finest appearance; (3) to the club parading the largest proportion of its membership. All wheelmen in the State, whether members of the L. A. W. or not, are invited to take part in the parade.

WE are hearing of some wonderful practice times at Lynn and Springfield. It should be remembered that these performances are done with flying starts.

THE London cycling papers announce that after Bob English has competed in the fifty-mile N. C. U. championship race, he is to turn professional and arrange for a race with Fred Wood.

THE efforts of the riders at the Saturday races to deceive the handicapper, brought down on their heads the indignation of the audience several times. It was perfectly clear that no man was doing his best.

MORGAN gave a banquet to the officers of his race meeting at Springfield last Saturday.

THIS is about the way the racing men are doing a mile at the Springfield track: Rowe, 2.27⅗; Hendee, 2.30; Knapp, 2.32⅖; Burnham, 2.32⅖; Adams, 2.32⅘; Rhodes, 2.33; Kluge, 2.38; Ives, 2.38; Langdown, 2.39; Haradon, 2.45.

A TALL hat gives the head an air-cushion protection. So says a wheelman. Then we must wear them. A pitcher's mask will save a scraped nose. Let's wear it. Cricket leggins will save our shins. Put them on. And, by the way, why not get a suit of armor?

THE status of Mr. Corey has been discussed pretty freely in the papers of late. And now Mr. Corey says he makes no claim for a record, and that he regards his ride on the tandem with Huntley as a private trial. He wrote the A. C. U. officials regarding the trial, but they sent back word that his arrangements were not satisfactory, and that no record would be allowed under the conditions proposed. He tells us that the A. C. U. does not regard the ride as a public one, and says they will not proceed against him.

HUNTLEY will make an attempt to beat McCurdy's record over the same course. He will ride a 54-inch Rudge Light Roadster, and will make no claim for a record, since the course is not such as the A. C. U. prescribes. He hopes to make more miles than did the Star rider.

AND now Corey and Kennedy Child will run for a road record, on a Rudge Humber tandem. England and America on one machine. They will give us a good record, but will it be the best?

FRED WOOD sailed for America on the "Germanie," 26 August, and Howell left on the "Arizona," 28 August. Howell will be accompanied by W. B. Atkins, who is his father-in-law, and landlord of the Red Cow.

STODDARD, LOVERING & CO. have received a large invoice of the Crescent tricycles, and sold all but two.

GORMULLY & JEFFERY are already at work on novelties for next year. They intend to add a number of machines to their present line. A. W. Gump, of Dayton, Ohio, who is well known as the largest dealer in second-hand machines in this country, has declared in favor of the American Safety; *vide* his testimonial in the Gormully & Jeffery advertisement on another page. This speaks well for that machine.

IN *Wheeling's* quest for the six best path riders, Cortis and Furnivall led with thirty-eight votes. The list had besides the names of Speechly, English, Webber, and Keith Falconer. A good list; but if it were possible to put these men in competition with an American team, does any one think that Rowe and Hendee would come in seventh or eighth man?

IN Mr. Todd's report of the last N. C. U. meeting, he says: "With reference to the correspondence which had taken place between Mr. Ducker, president of the A. C. U., Mr. Bassett, chairman of the Racing Committee of the L. A. W., and the secretary of the N. C. U. (of which a copy is sent herewith), the executive resolved: That under no circumstances will permission be given by the N. C. U. to any English riders to compete in America against any class of riders except such as are recognized by the L. A. W. as amateurs, as distinguished from pro-amateurs and professionals; the N. C. U. recognized the two latter classes as being in fact professionals."

WE have served as referee at very many tournaments where George Weber has been on the track, and we never knew him to protest a rider but once. At that time he came to us, and said that two riders had crowded him off at the upper turn and prevented his winning the race. He entered his protest and turned to go away, but had not gone ten yards, when he came back and said, "I guess I'll withdraw that protest; I don't believe they meant to do it; and besides, I don't want to go back on the boys."

AT Springfield on Saturday three men went on to the track to run a half-mile race. One was on a Star, one on a Columbia racer, and a third rode a roadster. When they were on the back stretch, the Star man jumped on his pedals and laid over for a spurt *à la* Kluge; but he did n't spurt. He went over the handle-bar, turned a complete

somersault, and the two others piled up on top of him. There was a very large pile, made up of assorted bicycles and men, right on the track. Instead of mounting again, each man went to the grass and began making an inventory of his bruises. Asa Wendell ran across the field and picked up the Columbia man and put him on his machine, and he was the first at the tape.

WEBER, or "Star" Weber, as he was familiarly known, complained of lassitude a month ago, when beginning to train for the fall tournaments. He was taken off the track by advice of a physician, and treated for malarial fever. After apparent improvement he returned to the track, and a relapse set in, which did not at first seem to be serious, but resulted fatally. He was a great favorite, and no rider had more pluck, endurance, persistence, and staying powers, nor was a fairer or squarer rider. He was to have appeared in the coming one-hundred-mile road race, and it was expected that he would have left all world's records in the shade. — *Ex.*

THE Hartford Wheel Club will be represented in the tug-of-war race, by DeBlois, Harding, and Fahy, all of whom are in active training at Charter Oak Park and doing remarkably good time. H. E. Bidwell, the East Hartford flyer, is now at Cleveland, participating in a two days' meet there. His mile in 2.44¾, on a road machine at Springfield, just prior to his departure, justly warrants his friends in predicting a "clean sweep" for him West. He will ride in all amateur events at Hartford. — *Censor.*

WE may be accused of want of patriotic feeling because we write strongly on this subject, but we will risk that in the firm assurance that we are doing right in calling attention to the hypocrisy of the Union's attitude. It is a patent fact to all who know anything of the racing life of to-day, that numbers of amateurs have their expenses paid by makers, and their machines supplied to them, The same thing is done in America. There, however, the A. C. U. boldly divides these men from the pure amateurs, and constitutes of them a promateur class. The English legislature, which knows perfectly well that the men they call "English amateurs" are exactly on the same footing as the American promateurs, pretends that the two sets of men differ, which pretence we deliberately characterize as absurd, indefensible, and unworthy of a great association. — *Wheeling.*

A PARTY of twenty-eight bicycle riders from Providence and vicinity, with their machines, enjoyed all night Tuesday of last week on the beach at Rumstick Neck. They landed there about ten o'clock in the evening, and left for home about five o' clock the next morning. They were all on a small steamboat, and the boat had run aground and was stuck hard and fast, and that is how they came to be there. The fog was so thick that if the boat had not stuck in the mud she might have stuck in the fog before she got home, so that it did not make much difference anyway. The parties were members of the State Division of the L. A. W., headed by Chief Consul Chase. They had started off with the original intention of having a run at Newport, but the Newport

experience, considered purely as an experience, pales into insignificance when compared to that part of the programme on Rumstick Neck which was not announced in advance.

THE BICYCLE THAT JACK MADE.

(A MODIFIED VERSION OF AN OLD STORY.)

THIS is the bicycle that Jack made.

This is the lathe all polished and true,
For the bicycle that Jack made.

This is the steel properly "tempered" thröugh,
Which was put in the lathe, all polished and true,
That finished the work, kept under-weighed
For the bicycle that Jack made.

This is the iron, "carbonized" and clean,
That was "blown" in the "converter" and "puddled" to steel,
That made the metal properly "tempered" through,
Which was put in the lathe, all polished and true,
That finished the work, kept under-weighed
For the bicycle that Jack made.

This is the ore, gathered out of the pit,
Which was melted in a furnace, blazingly lit,
That made the iron, "carbonized" and clean,
Which was "blown" in the "converter" and "puddled" to steel,
That made the metal properly tempered through,
Which was put in the lathe, all polished and true,
That finished the work, kept under-weighed,
For the bicycle that Jack made.

This is the chemical of formula O₂ Fe₂,
Which combines in atoms of twenty-eight times two,
That formed the ore, gathered out of the pit,
Which was melted in a furnace, blazingly lit,
That made the iron, "carbonized" and clean,
Which was "blown" in the "converter" and "puddled" to steel,
That made the metal properly "tempered" through,
Which was put in the lathe, all polished and true,
That finished the work, kept under-weighed,
For the bicycle that Jack made.

This is the gas oxygen — that you cannot see
Which proportions with iron in atoms three,
To make the chemical of formula O₂ Fe₂,
That combines in atoms of twenty-eight times two,
To form the ore, gathered out of the pit,
Which was melted in a furnace, blazingly lit,
That made the iron, "carbonized" and clean,
Which was "blown" in the "converter" and "puddled" to steel,
That made the metal properly "tempered" through,
Which was put in the lathe, all polished and true,
That finished the work, kept under-weighed,
To complete the bicycle that Jack made.

Wheeling Annual.

MARK TWAIN AS A WHEELMAN.

AMONG the hundreds of enthusiastic wheelmen in Hartford, says an exchange, are several clerical gentlemen, one of them the rector of the Church of the Good Shepherd, Rev. J. H. Watson, who does his marketing, visits his parishioners, and performs all his perambulatory duties as a man and a minister — except, perhaps, attending funerals — upon his bicycle. Rev. Charles E. Stowe is an expert rider, and Rev. J. H. Twitchell, pastor of the Asylum Hill Congregational Church, bestrides a wheel. The latter does it with fear and trembling. His friend, Samuel L. Clemens, better known as Mark Twain, undertook to ride a bicycle at about the same time that his pastor began, and, like him, is not happy in the sport. The teacher of Mr. Clemens during the first weeks of his wheeling tells this story of him : —

Mr. Clemens objected to assuming a costume suitable to the exercise, and one day started out to ride, wearing a long linen

duster over his clothes. His teacher gently suggested that it might be inconvenient. Mr. Clemens thought not. The young man feared a fall, but Mark Twain said that he would risk it. They had not gone four rods from home, however, when he began to revile the flapping thing, and in less than ten minutes the skirt was caught upon the wheel and carried up into the fork of the wheel, and instantly the author of "Innocents Abroad" lay upon his face in the dirt, with the machine clattering about his ears. His companion alighted and ran to help him. The scope and volume of vituperation that smoked up through the spokes of that wheel are said to be unrepeatable by persons less gifted in the language than the victim. He was rescued from the machine, and crawling to his feet, said with stifled fury, "Wait a minute." Taking his knife from his pocket, the amateur wheelman opened it, and with fierce determination cut the superfluous length from the linen coat until it took on the semblance of a butcher's short frock, and then remounting his machine with the assistance of his trainer, he said : "Now, I'll buy a Norfolk jacket, as I should have done before." Which he did. But he has never entirely conquered the skittish wheel.

NEW YORK DIVISION.

THE New York State Division, under the able management of its chief consul, George R. Bidwell, takes a front rank in advancing cyclers' interest here. Prominent among the moves to be made is an attack upon the park commissioners in their political stronghold in the State capitol at Albany. A bill will be introduced there in the coming session compelling the commissioners, and all others who pretend to control traffic over public or park roadways, to admit cyclers upon the same basis as other vehicles. This is a move in the right direction. While examining into the law in this matter, Chief Consul Bidwell has discovered that there exists one which compels township and county officials to place signboards at the junction and crossing of all county roads, under penalty of fine for not doing so. Local consuls will be instructed to call the attention of their town and county officials to this law, and to take steps to rigidly enforce it, by which means the opening wedge may be inserted that will ultimately result in better roads and attention to same from the parties holding offices for that purpose. — *Egan in Journal.*

ENGLISH CHAMPIONSHIPS.

THE English championships for 1886 have resulted as follows : —

The one-mile amateur bicycle championship was run on the Jarrow track, Newcastle-on-Tyne, on Saturday, 26 June, and was won by P. Furnivall in 2.46. Silver medals were won by H. A. Speechly, W. A. Illston, J. E. Fenlon, and C. E. Harling for beating the time standard, 2.48. The five-mile amateur bicycle championship was run at the Recreation Grounds, Long Eaton, on Saturday, 24 July, and was won by P. Furnivall in 14.44¼. Silver medals were won by W. A. Illston, G. Gatehouse, E. Hale, and H. Wade for beating the time standard, 15m. The twenty-five mile amateur bicycle championship was run at the Recreation Grounds, Weston-super-Mare, on Whitsun

HURRAH FOR LYNN!

First Grand International Fall Tournament

OF THE

LYNN CYCLE CLUB TRACK ASSOCIATION,

At LYNN, MASS., September 23, 24, and 25, 1886.

A. C. U. RULES TO GOVERN.

$5,000 in Prizes! Races for Amateurs, Promateurs, Professionals. $5,000 in Prizes!

BEHOLD THE GRAND LIST OF RACES AND PRIZES!

FIRST DAY, THURSDAY, SEPTEMBER 23.

1-Mile Novice, Bicycle, Open, 1st, Gold Medal; 2d, Gold and Silver Medal; 3d, Silver Medal.
2-Mile Amateur Bicycle, 5.45-Class, 1st, Fruit and Flower Stand; 2d, Silver Revolving Butter Dish; 3d, Silver Bell Spoon Holder, gold lined.
1-Mile Promateur Bicycle, Open, 1st, Snowflake Silver Embossed Tea Set; 2d, Silver Engraved Ice-Water Set; 3d, Cake Basket, hammered, Venetian chased, gold lined.
3-Mile Professional Bicycle, Handicap, 1st, $60 Cash; 2d, $40 Cash; 3d, $20 Cash.
2-Mile Amateur Tricycle, Lap, 1st, Base Parlor Lamp, gold and oxidized; 2d, Silver Vase, gold inlaid and oxidized; 3d, Russia Leather Satchel.
10-Mile Promateur Bicycle, Lap, 1st, Fine Gold Watch, stem-winder; 2d, Silver Festoon Chased Tea-Set; 3d, Gold Watch Chain.
1-Mile Amateur Bicycle, Open, 1st Silver Water Set, snowflake chased; 3d, Silver Vase, gold and oxidized; 3d, Gold Watch Chain.
5-Mile Professional Bicycle, Lap, 1st, $75 Cash; 2d, $50 Cash; 3d, $25 Cash.
3-Mile Promateur Bicycle, Handicap, 1st, Silver Tilting Water Set, gold ornamentation; 2d, Clock, Persian-chased, appliqué, candelabra, plaque; 3d, Pair Pearl Opera Glasses.

SECOND DAY, FRIDAY, SEPTEMBER 24.

1-Mile Professional Bicycle, Open, 1st, $50 Cash; 2d, $30 Cash; 3d, $20 Cash.
1-Mile Promateur Tricycle, A. C. U. Championship (time limit, 3m. 5s.), 1st, A. C. U. Gold Medal; 2d, A. C. U. Gold Medal; 3d, A. C. U. Silver Medal.
10-Mile Amateur Bicycle, Lap, 1st, Lynn Prize Cup; 2d, Dessert Set, coral rose, glass and silver; 3d, Nut Bowl, gold lined, oxidized finish.
5-Mile Promateur Bicycle, Handicap, 1st, Gentleman's Fine Gold Watch; 2d, Épergne, engraved, oxidized, gold finish; 3d, Snowflake Chased Tilting Ice-Water Set, gold lined
1-Mile Amateur Bicycle, 3.05 Class, 1st, Cake Basket, gold lined, oxidized finish; 3d, Fine Russia Leather Satchel.
5-Mile Professional Bicycle, Lap, 1st, $75 Cash; 2d, $50 Cash; 3d, $25 Cash.
1-Mile Amateur Bicycle, A. C. U. Championship, 1st, A. C. U. Gold Medal; 2d, A. C. U. Gold Medal; 3d, A. C. U. Silver Medal.
3-Mile Promateur Bicycle, Lap, 1st, Double Walled Silver Ice-Water Urn; 2d, Shot Gun, double-barreled, breech-loader; 3d, Silver Watch.
3-Mile Amateur Bicycle, Handicap, 1st, Centre Piece and Fruit Dish, Crystal Dishes; 2d, Flower Stand, cut glass, gold, oxidized finish; 3d, French Pearl Opera Glasses.

THIRD DAY, SATURDAY, SEPTEMBER 25.

1-Mile Promateur Bicycle, Open, 1st, Lynn Prize Cup. (Special Prize for Record.) 2d, Base Lamp, gold inlaid and oxidized finish; 3d, Diamond Breast Pin.
3-Mile Amateur Bicycle, 9.10 Class, 1st, Base Lamp, old silver and hammered; 2d, Vase, gold finish; 3d, Gentleman's Gold Ring.
2-Mile Professional Bicycle, Lap, 1st, $60 Cash; 2d, $30 Cash; 3d, $20 Cash.
3-Mile Amateur Tricycle, Lap, 1st, Photographer's Outfit; 2d, Silver Watch; 3d, Fishing Set.
5-Mile Promateur Bicycle, A. C. U. Championship (time limit, 15m.), 1st, A. C. U. Gold Medal, diamond setting; 2d, A. C. U. Gold Medal; 3d, A. C. U. Gold and Silver Medal
1-Mile Amateur Bicycle, Lap, 1st, Fruit Dish, rich cut glass, gold, oxidized; 2d, Cigar Box, oxidized; 3d, Gentleman's Gold Chain.
10-Mile Professional Bicycle, Lap, 1st, $100 Cash. ($50 extra for Record.) 2d, $50 Cash; 3d, $25 Cash.
3-Mile Promateur Bicycle, Handicap, 1st, Handsome Oil Painting; 2d, Silver Cashmere Band Tea Set; 3d, Dessert Set, coral rose and glass.
1-Mile Amateur Bicycle, Consolation, 1st, Half dozen Napkin Rings, gold ground, satin case; 2d, Silver Watch; 3d, Russia Leather Satchel.

ENTRIES CLOSE SEPTEMBER 16.

All Events have Three Prizes where there are four or more starters. Entry Forms, Blanks, List of Prizes, etc., furnished upon application to **E. M. BAILEY,** Secretary Lynn Cycle Track Association, **LYNN, MASS.**

Monday, 14 June, and was won by J. E. Fenlon in 1.19.29⅗. Silver medals were won by B. Ratcliffe, G. Gatehouse, W. Terry, D. Belding, C. E. Masters, and R. H. English for beating the time standard, 1h. 20m. The one-mile amateur tricycle championship was run at the Recreation Grounds, Weston-super-Mare, on Whitsun Monday, 14 June, and was won by P. Furnivall in 3.5⅗. Silver medals were won by A. E. Langley and John Lee for beating the time standard, 3.5. The five-mile amateur tricycle championship was run at the Hampden Park track, Glasgow, on Saturday, 3 July, and was won by F. W. Allard in 20.42⅗. A silver medal was won by G. Gatehouse for beating the time standard, 17m. The twenty-five mile amateur tricycle championship was run on the Alexandra Park track, London, on Saturday, 17 July, and was won by R. J. Mecredy in 1.55.40⅗. The time standard, 1h. 30m., was not beaten. The fifty-mile amateur bicycle championship was run at Lillie Bridge, 14 August, and was won by J. E. Fenlon in 2.47.21¼. The time standard, 2h. 50m., was beaten by seven riders.

JOHN-O'-GROAT'S HANDICAP.

A HANDICAP run to John-O'-Groat's has been instituted and started. G. P. Mills and Alfred Nixon started Sunday, 15 August, at midnight on tricycles; Lennox started on a bicycle twenty-fours later, and T. R. Marriott started on a safety at 6 A. M. Tuesday. The *News* of Friday, 20 August, has news of the riders. Lennox, Marriott, and Nixon are out of the race, and Mills is well on his way and eighteen hours ahead of the record. He expects to get to John-O'-Groat's in 5 days, 23 hours. The record is 6 days, 15 hours, 22 minutes.

THE VICTOR TEAM.

THE following idea of American promateurism is not evolved from our own imagination, but is the statement made to us by Mr. A. H. Overman himself, who is at the present time in Europe. Upon asking him his opinion of the recent separation of the makers' men, he said: "Yes, we have a class now of promateurs, but they ought to be professionals, for they are professionals, nothing more and nothing less. The definition is absurd. Now, my company has four men in training for the Springfield meeting, where they will be put up to ride against Pope's men. We have the best trainer in America looking after them. We pay him solely to train and look after these riders; they do nothing else but ride, and are entirely in his hands, and take their regular exercise two or three times a day, as he decides. He keeps a record of their performances, which I can see at any time, and they are looked after with the greatest of care. So far as they are concerned, we pay them a salary and defray all expenses for them. They do nothing for a living but ride, and are neither more nor less than professionals. So far as we are concerned, it makes no difference to us what they call themselves. We are having them trained in the hope of securing world's records. It is the records we want, and we care nothing whether the men are amateurs, promateurs, or professionals." This will give an idea of what the promateur really is; and if any one can after this, say that the men ought not to be professionals, he must be hopelessly wanting in common sense. The only equivalents in England are our leading professionals, Howell and Wood, who, like the American promateurs, are retained, paid, and trained by the makers of the machines they ride. — *Cyclist.*

CABIN JOHN BRIDGE.

A WASHINGTON wheelman has been riding his wheel along the stone coping of Cabin John Bridge. This coping is 200 feet long and about a foot broad, and is bevelled on the two upper edges for an inch or two. On the inside of these walls is the solid roadway above the duct. On the outside is a perpendicular descent of about 125 feet in the centre of the bridge, and no less than 75 feet at either abutment. This foolhardy feat had its natural result in finding an imitator, and on Sunday last Will Robertson of the Capital Club did the same thing, and put a finishing touch to the performance by riding on the big wheel with his little wheel in the air over a good stretch. This thing should be stopped before there are broken necks.

MASSACHUSETTS DIVISION COMMITTEES.

CHIEF CONSUL HAYES has appointed the following committees for the next year: —

Racing — Abbot Bassett, chairman; C. S. Howard, Boston; C. L. Smith, Cambridge.

Touring — W. O. Green, Holyoke, chairman; E. K. Hill, Worcester; A. D. Peck, Jr., Boston.

Finance — J. Fred Adams, Haverhill, chairman; A. L. Bowker, Cambridge; F. P. Kendall, Worcester.

Rules and Regulations — W. I. Harris, Boston, chairman; A. S. Parsons, Lexington; E. H. Foote, Somerville.

Legal Advisory Board — Charles E. Pratt, chairman; W. S. Slocum, J. S. Dean, all of Boston.

The special committee on Signboards and Stencils, and the construction of the same, Messrs Hill and Tolman, of Worcester, was reappointed.

AN AIR CUSHION ON THE HEAD.

CHIEF CONSUL HAYES, of Massachusetts, has received a letter containing a suggestion which we take great pleasure in placing before our readers. Here it is: "A recent accident to a wheelman has suggested to me the use of the high silk hat worn by fox hunters as a means of escape from the danger attending a header. I once was much given to the sport, and, of course, occasionally got a cropper, but never with much injury by reason of landing on an air cushion which the hat practically becomes when brought in sudden contact with any obstacle. The only possible objection is, perchance, the additional exposure of so large a head-gear to the wind; but if a life will occasionally be saved, it certainly is worth considering." We have never gone over the handles and struck on an air cushion, as the writer claims to have. A tall hat illustrates as much as anything else the total depravity of inanimate things, and we have noticed that when a man falls down, his tall hat is never inclined to pilot his head to the ground. It generally goes off in another direction, and if it does take the same course with the head, it reaches the ground far in advance. This is observation, not experience. Nevertheless, if wheelmen desire to adopt the plug hat, we shall offer no objection.

D. H. RENTON'S CASE.

WE had a call last week from Mr. Chas. D. Renton, of New York. He is the father of Mr. D. H. Renton, who was expelled from the League, and he is assisting his son in his suit against President Beckwith and Mr. Hill, formerly of the membership committee. He tells us that his side of the case has never been put before the cycling world, and regrets that wheelmen have so strong a prejudice against him and the cause he is championing. He claims that it was agreed in the settlement whereby Secretary Aaron was allowed to pay costs and go free in the suit for criminal libel, that his son was not to be expelled from the League. He tells us that, after that settlement, he and his son had dropped the whole matter, and had determined to do nothing more in the way of proceedings against those who were responsible for the publication of the reports regarding young Renton's dress at Scranton. Then came the February meeting of the Board of Officers at New York, when D. H. Renton was expelled from the League, because, as it was stated, he had written a threatening letter to a League officer. Mr. Renton denies that such a letter was written, and he challenges its production. He says he has tried to get a hearing for his boy, but has been unable to, and his only redress can be had in the courts. At Boston a letter from his son was refused a reading. He says he shall push the cases now in the courts, and shall sue the League for damages later. The facts in the case will all come out in court, and meanwhile he asks a suspension of judgment on the part of the cycling world.

THE PATH.

WORCESTER, 7 Aug. — Races under the auspices of the Worcester Club. — *One-Mile Novice.* — C. H. Morse (1), 3.22⅗. *Five-Mile Club Championship*, — G. A. Booker (1), 18.09. *One-Hundred Yards' Slow*, — F. W. Bassett (1). *One-Mile Tricycle*, — R. E. M. Surerkrop (1), 4.20⅗. *Three-Mile Open to Worcester County*, — W. W. Windle (1), 11.29. *One-Mile Handicap*, — C. H. Morse (1), 3.16. *Half-Mile Consolation*, — G. F. Warren (1), 1.37⅗.

TORONTO, CANADA, 21 Aug. — Races under the auspices of the Toronto Club. *One-Mile Open Class*, — first heat, F. G. Brimer (1), 3.20; W. Shepard (2); second heat, — W. H. West (1), 3.22; C. L. Macnab (2); final heat, — Brimer (1), 3.12; Shepard (2). *Two-Mile Handicap Open*, — W. S. Campbell (1), 6.19; T. Fane (2). *One-Mile Open*, — H. Davies (1), 2.58¼; H. Clarke (2). *Five-Mile Open*, — W. S. Campbell (1), 17.16¼. *Two-Mile Club Championship*, — M. F. Johnston (1), 6.38. *Half-Mile Club Handicap*, — F. J. Brimer 20 yards (1), 1.29; M. F. Johnston, scratch (2). W. H. Barber attempted to break unicycle record and failed; time, 4.06.

RUDGE TELEPHONE MAN.

HELLO, MR. EDITOR!

I hear that **HOWELL,** with his **59 RUDGE RACER,** sailed last Saturday for this country. Well, if **RICHARD** gets in good shape, he 'll make it lively. By the way, can you tell me who 's champion of America just now? After **HOWELL** goes back to England, there 's always somebody who claims the title. Speak up, gentlemen; I 've got my finger on my chestnut bell.

DETROIT, MICH., 21 Aug. — Races under auspices Detroit Club. *Thiee-Mile Club Championship*, — F. X. Spranger (1), 11.20⅕. *One-Mile Professional Handicap*, — J. S. Prince, scratch (1), 3.16; T. W. Eck, 90 feet (2). *One-Mile Open*, — S. P. Hollingsworth (1), 3.05⅕; Munger (2). *Half-Mile Amateur*, — S. P. Hollingsworth (1), 1.30⅕. *Five-Mile Professional Handicap*, — J. S. Prince, scratch (1), 18.03⅕; T. W. Eck, 250 yards (2). *One-Mile Club Championship*, — F. X. Spranger (1), 3.15⅘; Park (2).

CLEVELAND, OHIO. — Races under the auspices of the Cleveland Club.

FIRST DAY.

One-Mile Novice. — W. H. Wylie (1), 3.02⅕; F. E. Ranney (2).

One-Mile Tricycle State Championship. — K. A. Pardee (1), 3.14⅘; G. Collister (2).

Half-Mile Θpen. — A. B. Rich (1), 1.21⅕; W. E. Crist (2).

Two-Mile, 6.30 *Class.* — G. H. Terry (1), 6.15; F. X. Spranger (2).

One-Mile Tandem. — J. T. Huntington and G. Collister (1), 3.06; E J. Douhet and W. D. White (2).

One-Mile Open. — A. B. Rich (1), 2.53½; W. E. Crist (2).

Half-Mile, 1.30 *Class.* — P. S. Brown (1), 1.26⅗; F. E. Ranney (2).

Five-Mile State Championship. — K. A. Pardee (1), 17.09⅕; G. Collister (2).

Quarter-Mile Open. — H. S. Kavanaugh (1), 40⅗; H. E. Bidwell (2).

One-Mile Tricycle Open. — A. B. Rich (1), 3.17: K. A Pardee (2).

One-Mile Handicap. — G. H. Terry, 10 seconds (1), 2.58; J. T. Huntington (2).

SECOND DAY.

One-Mile Open. — Second heat, H. E. Bidwell (1), 2.53⅘; H. S. Kavanaugh (2).

One-Mile Amateur. — F. X. Spranger (1), 2.54⅘; F. E. Ranney (2).

Two-Mile State Championship. — J. T. Huntington (1), 6.15⅘; K. A. Pardee (2).

Half-Mile Handicap. — W. E. Crist, cot, ten yards (1), 1.18⅗; A. A. Hart, twenty-five yards (2).

One-Mile Tandem. — Huntington and Collister (1), 3.04⅕; Rich and Rheubottom (2).

One-Mile Open. — H. E. Bidwell (1), 2.53⅘; H. S. Kavanaugh (2).

Quarter-Mile 45 *s. Class.* — G. H. Ferry (1), 40⅗: P. S. Brown (2).

Two-Mile Lap. — H. S. Kavanaugh (1), 5.57½; A. B. Rich (2).

One-Mile Tricycle Handicap. — K. A. Pardee, forty yards (1), 3.10; A. B. Rich (2).

Half-Mile Open. — A. B. Rich (1), 1.19⅕; W. E. Crist (2).

One-Mile Three Minute Class. — K. A. Pardee (1), 3.04½; P. S. Brown (2).

THIRD DAY.

One-Mile 3.10 *Class.* — F. X. Spranger (1), 2.55; G. H. Terry (2).

One-Mile State Championship. — K. A. Pardee (1), 2.56⅘; J. T. Huntington (2).

Two-Mile Handicap. — A. B. Rich, scratch (1), 5.47⅗; S. P. Hollingsworth, 50 yards (2).

Half-Mile Tricycle Open. — A. B. Rich (1), 1.34⅘; K. A. Pardee (2).

One-Mile Handicap. — P. S. Brown, scratch (1), 2.54⅗; W. H. Wylie, fifteen yards (2).

Five-Mile Lap. — H. S. Kavanaugh (1), 5 points; S. P. Hollingsworth (2).

Quarter-Mile Open. — J. R. Rheubottom (1), forty seconds; C. E. Titchener (2).

One-Mile Open. — Final heat, A. B. Rich (1), 2.54; J. R. Rheubottom (2).

One-Mile Lap. — H. S. Kavanaugh (1), fifteen pts.; C. E. Titchener (2), eleven pts.

One-Mile Consolation. — W. C. Herring (1), 2.59; E. J. Douhet (2).

CARTHAGE, OHIO, Aug. 18. — Races under the auspices of the Hamilton County Fair: —

Two-Mile Amateur. — T. Belding (1), 7.35¼; T. Wayne (2).

Half-Mile Amateur. — C. T. Easterbrook (1), 1.37¼; Chas. Croninger (2).

One-Mile Amateur. — C. Croninger (1), 3.36; F. Andrews (2).

Five-Mile Amateur. — Ed. Croninger (1), 19.32; E. Mulhauser (2), 21.00.

Two-and-One-Half-Mile Amateur. — D. J. Sammett (1), 9.16.

SCRANTON, PA., 24 Aug. — Races under the auspices of the Scranton Club. *Two-Mile State Championship*, — J. R. Schlager (1), 6.10½; J. B. Nallin (2). *One-Mile Novice*, — E. Siebecker (1), 3.01½; H. C. Wallace (2). *One-Mile Open*, — C. E. Titchener (1), 2.46½; E. P. Baird (2). *One-Mile Club Championship*, — J. R. Schlager (1), 2.51¾; A. Monies (1). *Half-Mile Boys*, — E. M. Coursen (1), 1.41¾. *Three-Mile Handicap*, — C. E. Titchener (1), 8.59; John S. Kulp (2). *One-Mile Lap*, — Nallin (1), 4.22½. *One-Mile Consolation*, — Stone (1), 3.23½.

SPRINGFIELD, MASS., 28 Aug. — Races promoted by W. J. Morgan. *Half-Mile Boys*, — First heat, Chas. King (1), 2.32⅗; A. Jones (2); 2d heat, King (1), 1.37⅗; Jones (2). *Quarter-Mile Velocipede*, — M. Hayes (1), 1.16; W. Smith (2).

F. F. Ives' attempt to beat without hands record of 2.58⅘. W. Rhodes, pacemaker. The attempt was successful; time, 2.44⅘.

Five-Mile Horse v. Man. — Horse Propeller (1), 16.25⅕; W. J. Morgan (2), 16.29.

C. E. Kluge endeavored to beat the Star record for one mile of 2.41; time, 2.49⅕.

Woodside's attempt to beat the professional five-mile record of 14.23⅗; Morgan, pacemaker; 1st mile, 2.42; 2d, 5.27⅕; 3d, 8.15⅖; 4th, 11.04⅘; five miles in 13.50⅕, beating the record by 33⅗ seconds.

One-Mile Promateur. — C. Kluge (1), 2.49⅕; Adams (2).

W. A. Rhodes' attempt to lower the world's five-mile record of 13.57⅗: 1st mile, 2.36⅗; 2d, 5.19; 3d, 8.01⅕; 4th, 10.48⅘; five miles. 13.30, beating Rowe's record at Lynn by 27⅗ seconds.

One-Mile Professional Handicap. — Woodside scratch (1), 2.40; Morgan, 25 yards (2).

PHILADELPHIA has a new three-lap day track at Olympia Park. A race will be held there 6 Sept.

THE Rhode Island Division will hold a race meeting at Narragansett Park on Tuesday, 21 Sept. The members recognize that the date will conflict with the big race meetings, and they will endeavor to have no more than a little home affair of their own. Nevertheless, the Providence boys know how to make home affairs interesting.

AT the last meeting of the Board of Officers of the New Jersey Cycling and Athletic Association, it was unanimously decided to add another top-dressing of fine clay and gravel. This will make the track some seconds faster, and equal to any in the country. The Delaware, Lackawanna and Western have decided to stop all trains at the gates upon tournament days, which will be a great convenience to those going out from the city. The ball games every Saturday are attracting a large attendance, and it looks as if the grounds would be a very paying investment.

THE Dorchester Bicycle Club has arranged for its annual fall road races, which are to take place Saturday, 9 Oct. The races will be 15 miles, 6 miles, 3 miles, and 1 mile, and will be started from the corner of River and Washington streets, at 2 P. M.

KLUGE, the Star rider, won a three-mile handicap from Munger at Chicago, 22 Aug., in 9.45; Van Sicklen won a three-mile race in 10.07¾, and a five-mile race in 16.30.

PRINCE won a mile handicap from Eck at Detroit, 21 Aug., in 3.16, the latter being given 90 feet start in his tricycle. He also won a five mile race in 18.03½, conceding Eck 250 yards.

THE Ilderan Bicycle Club of Brooklyn will hold a twenty-five-mile road race for the club championship on 13 Sept. A score or so of members have entered, and first and second are to be rewarded with gold medals, while the first six will constitute the team to represent the club in the New York and New Jersey road race in November.

A. R. COLEMAN won the one-hundred-mile bicycle road race at Red Bank, Thursday, in 9 h. 53 m. John B. Bergen and T. S. Rockwell, the other starters, dropped out.

THE Berkshire County Wheelman of Pittsfield, at their tournament, 10 and 11 Aug., will race under the rules of the American Cyclist Union, instead of the L. A. W., as heretofore announced, and entries will close 6 Sept.

PRINCE and Eck raced with horses at North Cambridge on Saturday. The track was very rough and the horses won. Prince was thrown and hurt his knee, and Eck retired early in the race.

THE Pope cup goes next to Indianapolis, to be run for at the race meeting of the I. A. C., held 28 Sept.

NEW RECORDS.— Long Eaton, England, 25 Aug. George Gatehouse, on a tricycle: quarter mile, .40; half, 1.19; three quarter, 2; mile, 2.41⅘.

Percy Furnivall, on a bicycle: quarter, .37; half, 1.15½; three quarter, 1.51½; mile, 2.30.

Sidney Lee, on a tricycle: fifty miles on the road, 3.9.15.

THE CLUB.

THE Crescent Wheelmen of New Orleans, La., organized 24 August with the following officers: President, S. H. Plough; vice-president, P. M. Hill; secretary-treasurer, R. G. Betts; captain, A. P. Wolfe.

ABOUT a dozen bicyclists met 27 August, and organized under the name of the Wanderers' Club. The following named officers were elected: Walter Gardner, president; Fred A. Fisher, vice-president; Joseph Lufkin, secretary and treasurer; Daniel McPhee, captain.

COMING EVENTS.

SEPTEMBER.

MISCELLANEOUS

GRAND BICYCLE MEET

AT THE SIXTEENTH ANNUAL EXHIBITION AND FAIR OF THE

FARMERS' AND MECHANICS' ASSOCIATION,

Under the Auspices of the **COLUMBIA BICYCLE CLUB,** of North Attleboro', Mass.

On TUESDAY, SEPT. 14, at 11 O'CLOCK.

The Track, a Half-Mile one, has lately been put in first-class condition, and is, without doubt, one of the fastest in New England. L. A. W. Racing Rules to govern the following events:

1. HALF MILE, OPEN.
2. ONE MILE, NOVICE.
3. THREE MILES, LAP.
4. ONE MILE, HANDICAP, BOYS UNDER 18.
5. ONE MILE, OPEN.

6. ONE MILE, 3.30 CLASS.
7. ONE MILE, CLUB HANDICAP.
8. TWO MILES, OPEN.
9. HALF MILE, HANDICAP, BOYS UNDER 15.
10. TWO MILES, TEAM RACE (three men each Team).

VALUABLE PRIZES IN EACH EVENT.

Boys entering must state fastest time ever made in a race. Entrance fee, 50 cents. Close Sept. 11. Entry Blanks and List of Prizes furnished on application by

O. W. CLIFFORD,

COLUMBIA BICYCLE CLUB - - - - - - - **NORTH ATTLEBORO', MASS.**

SPECIAL ANNOUNCEMENT
No. 1.

The COLUMBIA SAFETY,

Which was recently placed upon the market, has received a recognition from Wheelmen beyond our most sanguine predictions for its reception.

THE HANDSOMEST SAFETY.

THE LIGHTEST SAFETY.

THE ONLY SAFETY
WHICH IS
Self-Adjustable to any reach of Rider.

We have now a stock of these machines sufficient to immediately fill orders of any reasonable size.

SPECIAL ANNOUNCEMENT
No. 2.

The unprecedented demand for the

KIRKPATRICK SADDLE

has heretofore this season rendered it extremely difficult, often impossible, to fill orders from old Columbia riders and owners or dealers of other makes of machines with a degree of promptness satisfactory to us. It is with pleasure that we announce a

LARGE STOCK

of these saddles ready for immediate shipment.

CATALOGUE SENT FREE.

THE POPE MFG. CO.,
597 Washington Street, Boston.
12 Warren Street, New York. } Branch Houses, { 115 Wabash Avenue, Chicago.

The Cycle.

VOL. I., No. 24.   BOSTON, MASS., 10 SEPTEMBER, 1886.   FIVE CENTS.

THE CYCLE

PUBLISHED EVERY FRIDAY BY ABBOT BASSETT, 22 SCHOOL ST., ROOM 19.

VOL. I.   BOSTON, MASS., 10 SEPTEMBER, 1886.   No. 24.

TERMS OF SUBSCRIPTION.

One Year, by mail, post-paid.............................$1.50
Three Copies in one order............................... 3.00
Club Subscriptions...................................... 1.00
Six Months.. .90
Single Copies........... .... .05

cycle warehouse.

Specimen Copies free.

. Every bicycle dealer is agent for the CYCLE and authorized to receive subscriptions at regular rates. The paper
can be found on sale at the following places : —

Boston, CUPPLES, UPHAM & Co., cor. Washington and
School Streets. Tremont House news stand. At every
cycle warehouse.

New York, ELLIOTT MASON, 12 Warren Street. .
Philadelphia, H. B. HART, 811 Arch Street. GEORGE
D. GIDEON, 6 South Broad Street.
Baltimore, S. T. CLARK & Co., 4 Hanover Street.
Chicago, W. M. DURELL, 115 Wabash Avenue. JOHN
WILKINSON & Co., 77 State Street. ·
Washington, H. S. OWEN, Capital Cycle Co.
St. Louis, ST. LOUIS WHEEL CO., 1121 Olive Street.

ABBOT BASSETT   .   .   .   .   EDITOR

A. MUDGE & SON, PRINTERS, 24 FRANKLIN ST., BOSTON

All communications should be sent in not later than
Tuesday, to ensure insertion the same week. ·

— *Entered at the Post-office as second-class mail matter.*

THE Racing Board is roundly denounced
by our local contemporary. It has been
doing this thing for a long time past. The
influence of the journal is shown by the
votes of confidence obtained by the Board.
Unanimous in general meeting, eight to one
in mail vote.

THE creation of the promateur as a recognized type and the general upsetting of
racing matters is really all the Racing Board
has accomplished. It has not done any
good to the sport. We defy any one to
show that the Board has benefited cycling.
— *World.*

IT has substituted honesty on the path
for subterfuge. The Board of Officers has
said that this is a good thing for cycling, by a
vote of about eight to one. We are very sorry
to see our contemporary on such unstable
ground as it is now treading. It is putting
forth ideas originally held by the A. C. U.
members, but they have found them falla-
cious and given them up.

A CONTEMPORARY says : " It takes a club
to kill a crank." We have generally found
that cranks flourish in wheel clubs. There
is no club, no matter how seclusive, but one
old crank is there ; there is no scheme so
crazy or delusive whose introduction cranky
will not dare.

A TANDEM EPISODE.

BY DAISIE. .

" COME, Guy, wake up ! Don't let your
thoughts run away with you altogether.
You don't seem to be aware that you 've got
a companion to-day, and that it 's your duty
to be sociable. You 've been completely
oblivious to everything around you for the
last half hour." So spoke Mr. John Jones,
who occupied the rear seat of a tandem behind Mr. Guy. Atherton, who was in charge
of brake and tiller in front. They were
bowling along a level stretch of road in
Eastern Massachusetts, and while the rear
rider was alive to everything going on about
him, his friend seemed deeply absorbed in
his own thoughts, which, if outward evidences were to be relied upon, were not of
the most pleasant kind.

" I beg ten thousand pardons, my dear
boy," answered Guy. " I am not indifferent
to your presence, but I 've got a knotty
social problem to solve, and it 's troubling
me. I am going to take you into my confidence, for I shall probably need your assistance to mature a little plan I have in mind.
Wait till we get over this hill. By George,
that was a teaser, but she went up. There 's
nothing like a tandem for hills."

" Yes, that was a tough one, but we 're
going to have a good coast to make up for
the climb. There are downs as well as ups
in a cycler's life. But let me into your
scheme. Count on me to help you out in
anything outside of matrimony. If there 's
a woman in your plan, I am committed
against it. I am too much of a bachelor to
have anything to do with the petticoat
brigade."

" It savors a little of that, I must confess,"
returned Atherton, laughingly ; " but you
need have no fears for yourself. You recol-
lect Miriam Ryder, my cousin, and also my
father's ward ? She is spending her vacation at our house, and it was she that suggested to me the plan I am about to divulge to
you. She came dashing into the room where
I sat, last evening, with an open letter in
her hand — the very personification of indignation — exclaiming, —

" ' How unfortunate, Cousin Guy, it is to
be rich and handsome ! I fully intend, when
I get emancipated from school, and seriously
think of marrying, of changing my name,
donning some simple garb, and going into
the country to earn my living by my own
exertions.'

" ' Well, cousin mine,' said I, smiling at
her enthusiasm, ' what do you propose to
effect by your rustic simplicity ? '

" ' Why, win a husband by my own merits
— not by my pretty face, name, or fortune.
One of my schoolmates writes me of a
friend of hers who has been a wife but a
year, whose liege lord told her unblushingly
that it was her beautiful face and fortune
that he wedded — not herself. Now, Guy,'
continued Miriam, seriously, ' have a care

that you do not win a wife through either of
these mediums, or through the romance of
your name, particularly.' "

" So you are going to try some such ruse,
Guy, my boy ? " said Jones, laughingly ; " and
pray tell me in what way I can be of assistance to you. But wait till we 've inter-
viewed that pump over there. I 'm dying
with thirst. I can see an empty tomato can
on top of the pump. The villagers have
probably had too many dippers stolen, or
else they carry impecuniosity to the extent
of making every one furnish his own dipper.
Some good Samaritan has made up for the
delinquencies of the town and given us a
tomato can. Here 's to the health of the
hero of the tomato can. May he never know
thirst except when I am around to invite him
to drink."

Having refreshed themselves at the village
pump, our travellers resumed their journey,
after satisfying the curiosity of a passer-by,
who wanted to know how much the tandem
cost, whether it would go as fast as a bicycle,
whether it was not hard work, etc. etc. It
was not long before the conversation began
from the point where it was broken off.

" You were asking me to tell you how you
could assist me," resumed Guy. " I will do
so. You know how often you have laughed
at your plain, unromantic name — Mr. John
Jones ? Well, I have a fancy to borrow it
for a while, and lend you my fortune, with
the name Mr. Guy Atherton, as a passport
into some fair lady's favor ; and as you profess yourself impregnable to their battery of
charms, you will be in no danger, while I
wish simply to be Mr. John Jones, with no
pretensions above a fair share of agreeable-
ness, and a tolerably good-looking phiz."

" A new kind of sport that will be, Guy.
Beats cycling all hollow. But where do you
propose to go with your new name ? "

" I 'm going on a long run into the country,
and I 'm going to take you with me. You
shall occupy the back seat of the tandem,
and we 'll explore new fields. You can afford
it, for you know you 've got a fortune now.
We 'll start out in search of adventure. Perhaps we will do some gunning and some
shooting, and perhaps —."

" Yes," said Jones, interrupting him,
" perhaps you will find some bright, particular star, and think to wed it. But do not
count on my doing the same thing, for you
know I decided long ago to lead a life of
single blessedness."

" Do not be *too* sure, my dear fellow ; you
may even get ahead of me, for perhaps you
will get a little of my nature along with
your new title. But do you like the plan ? "

" Very much ; it will be a pleasant change
from city life and drudgery. But when do
you propose to go ? "

" Next week," said Atherton ; " for I am
heartily tired of pleas, writs, courts, and, in
fact, everything that pertains to a lawyer's
life. We 'll take along a couple of valises,
and run across the country by easy stages.

We ought to cover fifty miles a day at least."

Nestled lovingly beneath the sheltering arms of many a noble elm and chestnut tree, was the quiet village of Woodville, with its picturesque scenery of vine-wreathed cottages and bright-flowered gardens ever tempting the passer-by to stop and admire. Standing coquettishly by itself, on the banks of the beautiful stream which wound quietly through the village, was the residence of Mr. Whiting, the wealthiest citizen in the place. Becoming weary of mercantile life, he had left the city, and had chosen Woodville as his permanent home; but being naturally of an active disposition, could not content himself without some excitement. He accordingly purchased a small manufacturing establishment about two miles from the village, riding out every day to attend to his business.

He had just returned from the factory, and was seated in his great arm-chair on the piazza, enjoying the luxurious coolness of the evening, when his youngest daughter Belle, a wild, joyous, madcap creature, came dashing up the gravel walk, and throwing her arms around his neck, exclaimed,—

"Oh, papa! won't it be jolly? We are to have our picnic the day after to-morrow! I have just been to see Jennie Cary, and she tells me that there are two arrivals in our quiet little place. Only think, papa!" said Belle, without stopping to take breath, "two gentlemen from the city,—a Mr. Jones and a Mr. Atherton! And they rode here on a tricycle. Both on one machine. And they wear knickerbocker trousers. And Jennie says they're just too lovely for anything. And she says she 's going to ride the tricycle. And one man told her it was a ' daisy,' and the other called it the name of a sewing machine, a Weed, or a Grover and Baker, or a Singer, or something like that, and — and I 'm so glad."

"Well, my little wildfire, why does it please you so much? Are you going to take them by storm? Or do you want me to buy you a tricycle just like theirs?"

"Why of course we 're going to take them by storm! Can't you see what an attraction they will be at the picnic? All the girls are set by the ears, and they are putting extra ribbons on their bonnets and new lace on their dresses in honor of the two strangers. I have already sent them invitations by Jennie, who has been introduced to them by her uncle who keeps the hotel. And only think, they say they will get the hotel appointed a league hotel, and then all the wheelmen will come this way to stop there. Won't it be jolly? But you must let me go now, papa, for I want to carry the good news to Ellen and mamma."

"Why, Bell! what a looking creature you are!" said both ladies in the same breath. "Your curls are flying in all directions, and your face is as red as red can be!"

"Oh, Ellen dear! pray spare your lecture for another time. I 'm not in a receptive mood. I want to give out. I 've got something delightful to tell you." And she told them the story that she had but just given to her father, reproducing it as nearly as it is possible for an enthusiastic girl to duplicate a narrative when she is full of excitement over it.

"Only just think, Nell! Guy Atherton — what a delightfully romantic name! It 's enough to provoke a mash with any girl. I 'm head-over-heels in love with him already. Are n't you caught a little, too, Nell?"

"Hush, Belle! How can you behave so? And do give up that dreadful slang. I don't see where you can learn it. I have very little interest in these young men, and I can't see that it adds to their charms that they ride on a velocipede. I have generally found that riders of bicycles are not sufficiently careful of their apparel to appear in the presence of ladies. What is the other gentleman's name?"

"That 's just like you, Nell; you can't see that a gentleman can be a gentleman unless he wears a dress suit. As for me, I never look at the togs. I 'm generally too much taken up with the wearer. What 's the other fellow's name? Listen to it, and don't let it throw you over! It 's Jones. Jones in all its glaring simplicity and plainness. And a splendid looking fellow he is too, Jennie says."

"I dare say you 'll think him splendid, Belle, just because he carries about such a dreadfully plain name. It 's just like you to do that. But I shall detest him. I never could endure so hideous a cognomen. Mrs. Jones, indeed! No, I thank you!"

"One of them is quite wealthy, Jennie says, and I suppose you will make attacks upon his heart at once," said Belle, teasingly.

"I presume it is Mr. Atherton," said Ellen. "But whom have you invited to your picnic?"

"Oh! all the girls, which will be two for every gallant. Girls are a drug in this place and young men are at a premium. If a girl can get half a fellow it 's the better half."

"You have not invited Clara Morgan, surely?" cried Ellen.

"Surely I have. I would n't slight her for the world,—she is my best friend."

"Are you not ashamed of yourself?" returned Ellen, poutingly; and, running to Mrs. Whiting, she exclaimed, indignantly: "Mamma, Belle should not be permitted to behave as she does. She has invited these gentlemen to meet Clara Morgan, a factory girl. I shall die of mortification."

"Not yet, Nell, my love; don't die this evening; wait till some other evening, for Jennie is coming to call with the gentlemen this P. M. So put on your best dress-up smile for the occasion, and perhaps you 'll make a good impression on the knights of the knickerbockers."

Evening came and with it came the tandem tourists. The invitation to attend the picnic was accepted with many expressions of gratitude. The wheelmen said they would ride their machines, and would not object to giving a few lessons in riding to the ladies of the party while they were on the way to the grove. Belle was in her brightest of spirits, and kept the company in good humor with her quick repartees and lively sallies. Wheeling and wheelmen was the principal topic of conversation, and Belle expressed an earnest desire to learn to ride at once.

"What name is your vehicle denominated?" asked Ellen, with that preciseness to which she was inclined.

"It 's a Springfield tandem made by Singer," answered Mr. Atherton, formerly Mr. Jones ; for we must now follow their example and make a change in names.

"Well, if it 's made by a Singer, I suppose it 's a base concern," cried Belle, anxious to get in her little joke.

"I perceive the tenor of your remarks," said Guy, taking her up, " but it 's a double, not a treble."

"Oh, I see!" said Belle, "a sort of duet."

"Yes, we can do it every time," answered Guy.

"I never knew that this was the part of the country where chestnuts grew, but I feel as though I was among the nut trees," put in Jones. And this stopped them.

That night when the girls were preparing for bed they were a little confidential, as all girls are at this trying time.

"I like Mr. Jones the best. But such a name, — I would never marry him!" said Nell.

"Do not trouble yourself to win him," said Belle, laughing, " for he is poor, Jennie tells me, — as poor as the traditional church mouse. Atherton is my fancy of the two, but I hate rich folks. Besides, he is a professed and practising bachelor."

The sun beamed with unwonted brightness the morning for their picnic. Belle was up early, dancing around as gay and happy as the birds.

Not so Nell ; she was sullen and dispirited, because Clara Morgan was to be of the party, for although Clara was poor, she was fair and beautiful, winning all hearts by her gentle, artless manners, and Nell feared her as a rival.

"You will go, Clara, my pet, won't you?" said Mrs. Morgan, tenderly.

"I do not care about it, dear mamma, for Ellen Whiting will spoil all my pleasure, as usual ; but as Belle insists upon my going, I will."

"What a contrast there is between those two girls!" said Mrs. Morgan. "I think Belle will try and make it pleasant for you."

"Most certainly, mamma ; but you seem so feeble, my mind will wander back often to you."

"Oh, dear sister!" said Louise, a bright-eyed, laughing creature, of about ten years of age, "you must certainly go, and I will stay and nurse mamma. I can take care of her, so don't you be afraid."

"I know you will, my pet," said Clara, kissing her ; "and perhaps I had better go, though I scarcely know how to leave my work for a day."

"My poor child," said Mrs. Morgan, wiping away a tear, " what a weary life is yours!"

"Oh, never mind, mamma," returned Clara, cheerfully; "I am getting along nicely, and shall be able to keep Johnny in school another quarter. But I must hurry, or I shall be late."

The place selected for the picnic was about a mile from the village, on the banks of a beautiful stream ; and so all of the party walked, save only those who rode on the tandem. There were two ladies to each gentleman, en route every one of the girls had to ride the machine on the front seat, while Jones or Atherton rode behind

and gave instructions. There was much riding up and down the road on the machine, and it is a fair estimate that the tandem covered five miles in going the mile to the grove.

The day passed pleasantly and quietly away at first, nothing occurring to damp the happiness of the gay party except the ill-concealed chagrin and sarcastic expressions of Ellen, because Clara was not slighted by the gentlemen, as she had hoped. Its peace was disturbed somewhat, however, at about 4 o'clock, when a scream of pain was heard, and Belle came bounding in terror to where the company was seated, exclaiming : —

"Oh, dear! She's killed! I know she's killed! Come quick some of you and get her out! She's under the machine and she can't get up! Come quick!"

They all rushed at once to the spot indicated, Jones reaching it first. There the condition of things told the story. Belle and Clara had slipped aside with an idea to have a ride on the tandem all by themselves. They had ridden a short time, had lost control of the machine, and had run down an embankment. Belle had escaped unhurt, but Clara lay under the machine in a faint. It took but a moment for Jones to remove the tandem, and, taking Clara in his arms, he bore her to the river's bank, laving her temples until she revived sufficiently to realize her situation. Blushing deeply, she thanked her friends for their kindness, and attempted to rise, but could not stand, for her ankle was sprained. She begged to be taken home at once, but as she could not walk, she must be carried. This was a matter easily arranged. The tandem was uninjured, and Clara was placed on the front seat with her foot on the rests, and Jones, taking the rear seat, proceeded to pedal her home. The distance was not great, and very soon Clara was at home under the careful nursing of her mother, and Jones had returned to the party for another passenger. But the incident had destroyed all interest in the picnic, and when he got back they were ready to go home. Jones invited Belle to take the vacant seat on the tandem. This did not altogether please Atherton, who felt that he should be the one to ride with the lively girl in whom he had taken a decided interest. but Jones wanted to talk about Clara. His interest in the young lady had become very keen, and like all people who find themselves in this condition of mind, he wanted to talk it over. Belle was not the one to refuse to talk with him, and this he knew well enough when he asked her to ride.

"I feel so condemned for asking dear Clara to ride with me," said Belle, starting the conversation just in the way Jones wanted her to. "Her suffering will not be light; she will be so troubled, too, that she cannot attend to her work."

"Why does she work in the factory? — is there nothing else she can do? She seems far too fragile and delicate for great labor."

"Because necessity compels it. She was taught our village school for several previous summers, but through the machinations of an enemy, she was this year deprived of it.

"O yes," returned Belle ; "but she could not think of leaving her invalid mother for a single night."

"She has no father, then?" said Jones, much interested.

"No ; he died about three years since, and Clara by her own exertions has supplied the wants of the family, since she has a younger brother and sister whom she insists upon keeping in school. Their little cottage is their own, but still it is very hard for them to get along."

"She is certainly a noble girl, and should be honored both for her independence and tender interest in her family. I shall certainly call in the morning and extend my sympathy. Will you accompany me, Belle?"

"I will with. pleasure," replied Belle, pleased with Mr. Jones' approbation of Clara.

They had now reached the home of Belle, and she alighted from the machine with many expressions of thanks for the ride.

"Why, my little gazelle," exclaimed Mr. Whiting, who was in his accustomed seat on the piazza, "what has happened? Have you lost your heart to-day, and found none in compensation?"

"No, no, dear papa; my heart is unchanged as yet ; but I was thinking of our dear Clara. She fell from the tandem and sprained her ankle."

"I am sorry for her," said Mr. Whiting, feelingly, "for she is a lovely girl."

"I am not sorry," said Ellen, who had just parted with Atherton at the gate, "only that it gives her that attention from the gentlemen which she so coveted. She is an artful, intriguing girl, and I firmly believe she did it on purpose."

"Hush, hush, my child!" said Mr. Whiting. "Such a remark is unworthy any one."

"You should be ashamed of such a thought, even," said Belle, indignantly. "She would despise intrigue in any form. I think her the loveliest girl our village boasts."

"Except one," thought Atherton, gazing admiringly upon Belle. He had returned with Ellen's parasol unperceived by the girls, but just in time to hear what they were saying of Clara. Nell had made a deep impression upon him, and he had resolved to see her often, while in Woodville ; but her malicious, ungenerous remarks about Clara had unmasked her, and broken the charm with which she was fast binding him, placing Belle in her stead.

"Are you not very lonely, Clara?" said our friend Jones, as he was sitting for the sixth evening in the neat little parlor of Rose Cottage (a name given to Clara's home by Belle). "You must nurse your lame foot tenderly, that you may be able to attend a sailing party which we have in view for next week. I shall have to leave your pleasant little village soon, much to my regret."

"I should be very lonely, but Belle has been often with me through the days, and you have been very kind to deprive yourself of the pleasant companionship of your friends to relieve the tedium of my evenings?"

"It has been no deprivation. I crave no

"for your sweet society through life to share alike my joys and sorrows? Will you not be my partner on the tandem through life?"

"Oh! my friend," said Clara, smiling through her tears, "your words have made me infinitely happy; but I could not leave the precious charges here given unto my care by a dying father. I love you more than I can tell you, but I cannot leave my feeble mother."

"Nor need you, dearest; we can labor together for them, surely, if we love each other."

"But if I say yes, must I go through life with you on a tandem? Would it not be better to go hand in hand? I don't want you to follow me, nor do I want to go behind. Can't we travel side by side?"

"If you'll say 'Yes,' I'll get a sociable and we'll go side by side, I don't want to give up the tandem, but I must have my companion."

"Your'e a silly boy. You need n't give up the tandem. We'll journey in company if you insist upon it."

The irrepressible Belle burst into the room at this moment, and with a woman's instinct she saw what was going on.

"I hope I don't intrude. If I do I'll go away. But I've got some news for you. Now, don't you say a single word, Mr. Atherton, for I want to be the first to tell it. What do you think, Clara? this man has persuaded me to accept him. I told him that I liked him well enough, but I detested his money. I want to live in a cottage and pay for all of it. He says he's going to will his money to unfortunate wheelmen who take headers ; says he'll found a special hospital for them. Won't that be jolly? Shall I take him, Clara? I've told him I would; but if you object, I'll take it all back."

"Why, you madcap darling," said Clara, "of course you must have him. I want you to be real happy, and I want your congratulations, for I have agreed to ride a tandem through life with Mr. Jones."

"You have! Why, isn't that too awfully nice for anything? I'll make Atherton give you all his money to set you up in life with. Mr. Atherton, you may give your check-book to Mr. Jones."

A quiet smile came over the faces of both gentlemen, and then Belle demanded an explanation. The secret came out ; and it is unnecessary to say that all parties were satisfied to have things in their normal state.

And so there were two weddings in Woodville, — two weddings and a combination tour. It was altogether a novel ceremony, for the two bridal parties drew up to the church door on tandems, and they left the holy edifice and started off upon their machines followed by the cheers of friends and the customary old shoes.

WHY is a colored professional cycler like the rubber you use for erasing ink marks? Because he is an "inky racer" (ink eraser).

WHY does a hub lamp remind one of the trial of a murderer? Because when on being "examined" it is found "wicked" enough

Hampden Park, Springfield, Mass., U.S.A., September 14, 15, 16, & 17, 1886.

FIFTH ANNUAL TOURNAMENT OF THE SPRINGFIELD BICYCLE CLUB.

OFFICIAL LIST OF RACES AND PRIZES.

FIRST DAY—TUESDAY, SEPTEMBER 14.

EVENTS.	CLASSES.	WHEELS.	CONDITIONS.	FIRST PRIZES.	SECOND PRIZES.	THIRD PRIZES.
1-mile	Promateur	Bicycle	World's Championship, 1st heat.			
1-mile	Amateur	Bicycle	Novice.	Vase Lamp, hammered copper and	Scarf Pin, diamond setting.	Fancy Inkstand, gold and oxidized.
10-mile	Promateur	Bicycle	A. C. U. Championship.	A. C. U. Gold Medal. [oxidized.	A. C. U. Gold Medal.	A. C. U. Gold Medal.
5-mile	Professional	Bicycle	Handicap.	$100 Cash.	$60 Cash.	$40 Cash.
1-mile	Promateur	Bicycle	World's Championship, 2d heat.			[gué, gold lined.
5-mile	Amateur	Bicycle	16.30 Class.	Gold Watch, open face.	Vase Lamp, gold and Silver.	Smoking Set, hammered and appli-
1-mile	Promateur	Tricycle	Open.	Gold Watch, open face.	Ewer, antique brass, embossed.	Opera Glass, pearl mounted.
3-mile	Professional	Bicycle	Open.	$62.50 Cash.	$37.50 Cash.	$25 Cash.
1-mile	Promateur	Bicycle	World's Championship, 3d heat.			
1-mile	Amateur	Tandem	A. C. U. Championship.	Two Gold Medals.	Two Silver Medals.	

SECOND DAY—WEDNESDAY, SEPTEMBER 15.

EVENTS.	CLASSES.	WHEELS.	CONDITIONS.	FIRST PRIZES.	SECOND PRIZES.	THIRD PRIZES.
1-mile	Promateur	Bicycle	World's Championship, 4th heat.			
5-mile	Amateur	Bicycle	Lap.	Gold Watch, open face.	French Clock, with bronze figure.	Glass Vase, decorated gold stand.
5-mile	Promateur	Bicycle	Handicap.	Diamond Stud.	Gold Watch, hunting case.	Silver Chronograph Watch.
3-mile	Professional	Tricycle	Open.	$62.50 Cash.	$37.50 Cash.	$25 Cash.
1-mile	Promateur	Bicycle	World's Championship, 5th heat.			
3-mile	Professional	Bicycle	Lap.	$62.50 Cash.	$37.50 Cash. [breech-loader.	$25 Cash.
5-mile	Promateur	Bicycle	Lap.	Gold Watch, hunting case.	Stevens Shot-gun, double-barreled,	Silver Chronograph Watch. ·
3-mile	Professional	Bicycle	Handicap.	$62.50 Cash.	$37.50 Cash.	$25 Cash.
1-mile	Promateur	Bicycle	World's Championship, 6th heat.		[tern.	
3-mile	Amateur	Tricycle	Open.	Gold Medal.	12 Silver Knives, renaissance pat-	Traveling Clock, and case.

THIRD DAY—THURSDAY, SEPTEMBER 16.

EVENTS.	CLASSES.	WHEELS.	CONDITIONS.	FIRST PRIZES.	SECOND PRIZES.	THIRD PRIZES.
1-mile	Promateur	Bicycle	World's Championship, 7th heat.			
3-mile	Amateur	Bicycle	Open.	Gold Medal.	French Clock, with bronze figures.	Gold Watch Chain.
10-mile	Promateur	Bicycle	Open.	Diamond Stud.	Gold Watch, hunting case.	Gold Watch, hunting case.
1-mile	Professional	Bicycle	Open.	$50 Cash.	$30 Cash.	$30 Cash.
1-mile	Promateur	Bicycle	World's Championship, 8th heat.			
5-mile	Amateur	Bicycle	Open.	Tea Set, 6 pieces, satin embossed.	Stevens Sporting Rifle.	Stevens "Hunter's Pet" Rifle.
3-mile	Promateur	Tricycle	Open.	Gold Watch, hunting case.	Diamond Stud.	Gold Watch Chain.
1-mile	Professional	Bicycle	Handicap.	$50 Cash.	$30 Cash.	$30 Cash.
1-mile	Promateur	Bicycle	World's Championship, 9th heat.			
3-mile	Professional	Tricycle	Handicap.	$62.50 Cash.	$37.50 Cash.	$25 Cash.

FOURTH DAY—FRIDAY, SEPTEMBER 17.

EVENTS.	CLASSES.	WHEELS.	CONDITIONS.	FIRST PRIZES.	SECOND PRIZES.	THIRD PRIZES.
1-mile	Promateur	Bicycle	World's Championship, 10th heat.			
3-mile	Amateur	Bicycle	9.45 Class.	Gold Watch, open face.	Carving Set, renaissance pattern.	Gold Cuff Buttons, stone settings.
3-mile	Promateur	Bicycle	Open.	Diamond Stud.	Complete Fishing Outfit.	Water Set, silver, gold lined.
10-mile	Professional	Bicycle	Lap.	$120 Cash.	$90 Cash.	$60 Cash. Fourth, $50 Cash.
1-mile	Promateur	Bicycle	World's Championship, 11th heat.			[and oxidised.
3-mile	Amateur	Bicycle	Handicap.	Diamond Stud.	Scarf Pin, diamond setting.	Biscuit Jar, decorated china, gold
1-mile	Promateur	Bicycle	2.40 Class.	Gold Watch, open face.	Pedestal Lamp, antique brass, tulip	Gold Watch Chain.
5-mile	Professional	Bicycle	Open.	$100 Cash. [Medal.	$60 Cash. [globe.	$40 Cash. [Fifth, Lakin Cyclometer.
1-mile	Promateur	Bicycle	World's Championship, final heat.	Winner last heat, Gold Watch and	Winner fastest heat, Fine Gold	Seal Ring. Fourth, Traveling Bag.
1-mile	Amateur	Bicycle	Consolation.	Gold Watch Chain.	Stevens Bicycle Rifle. [Watch.	

ENTRIES CLOSE SEPTEMBER 7, 1886.

All Events have three Prizes, where there are four or more starters. Entry Forms, Blanks, List of Prizes, etc., will be furnished upon application to SANFORD LAWTON, Secretary Springfield Bicycle Club, Springfield, Mass., U.S.A.

CYCLETS.

CYCLING.

I AM a slave to cycling,
    I bow to its every behest;
    I yield to the spell
    That I love so well,
When I mount my wheel at even,
    And ride toward the glowing West.

I am a friend to cycling,
    I work for it many an hour.
        When the gleaming day
        Has faded away,
I tell of its wondrous virtue,
    I sing of its mighty power.

I 'm a lover of cycling.
    I have pledged my troth to my wheel;
        It 's mine forever,
        It fails me never,
    It holds in its flying circle
    Joy none but the cyclers feel,

I 've pledged my life to cycling,
    'T is the greatest blessing of man;
        Wherever I rove,
        Wherever I move,
    I dwell on its endless blessings,
    .I do for it all I can.   L. H. P.

CYCLING QUOTATIONS.

The bugles sound the call. — *Scott.*
We seem to cut the wind. — *Hood.*
But oh ! the road is very hard. — *Burns.*
Enough of climbing toil. — *Wordsworth.*
But steep and flinty was the road. — *Scott.*
We came down a foul hill. — *Shakespeare.*
Go paddling, paddling through the wet. — *Hood.*
Summer will come again, and summer sun, — *Hood.*
Merrily, merrily, whirled the wheels. — *Longfellow.*
Swiftly turn the murmuring wheel. — *Wordsworth.*
The folded gates would bar my progress now. — *Cowper.*
To wheel about, loug as the summer lasted. — *Words-*
worth.

Flying from London smoke and dust annoying. — *Hood.*
Still, all day, the iron wheels go onward. — *Elizabeth B.*
Browning.

Descending now, but cautious lest too fast,
    . A sudden steep. — *Cowper.*
Turns with less noisy wheels to the roadside
And passes gently by. — *Wordsworth.*

Take the lead and then keep it;
    That is, if you can. — *Ingoldsby.*
Hence the declivity is sharp and short,
And such the reascent. — *Cowper.*

    Adjust the unimpaired machine,
    To wheel the equal dull routine. — *Burns.*

Though, like a demon of the night,
    He passed and vanished from my sight.
                            — *Byron.*

To make a tour and tak' a whirl,
    To learn *bon ton,* an' see the worl'. — *Burns.*

How oft upon yon eminence our pace
Has slackened to a pause. — *Cowper.*

    See, see ! he 's off the saddle !
    He headlong tumbles. — *Tannahill.*

And many a joke, and many a song,
Gaed round while wheels were busy rinning.
                            Robert Nicoll.

Turn, turn, my wheel ! turn round and round,
Without a pause, without a sound. — *Longfellow.*

And the wheels how they spin,
How the dirt, right and left, o'er the hedges is hurled. —
                            Thomas Noel.
If aught obstruct thy course, yet stand not still,
But wind about till thou hast topped the hill — *Denham.*

He is mounted; he rides up the street. — *Scott.*
I love the sport well ; but I shall as soon quarrel with it as
    any man in England. — *Shakespeare.*
Th' alert and nimble motion of those joints that never tire.
                            — *Cowper.*
As if a wheel had been in the midst of a wheel.
                            — *Ezekiel x. 10.*
Then may I set the world on wheels. — *Shakespeare.*
Be warned by me, then; they that ride so, and ride not
    warily, fall into foul bogs. — *Shakespeare.*
Mounted upon a hot and fiery steed, which his aspiring
    rider seemed to know. — *Shakespeare.*

WE are at Hartford. We shall be at
Springfield in the sweet by and by.

THE CYCLE printers made a good show
in the labor procession.

JOHN BULL will have no victories to crow
over·this year.

NEW-YORKERS are already bringing forward candidates for the League presidency
next year. They are all residents of Manhattan. New York always was modest, and we
can well believe she would like to keep the
first office in the gift of wheelmen forever,
Perhaps the West would like a chance at
the.prize.

AND now the Boston ladies are talking of
a repetition of the North Shore trips, which
were so successful last year. We expect to
see a larger turnout this year, for the number of lady riders·has increased very largely.

CHARLES FRAZIER is expected to make
his appearance on the track once more this
fall. He has had a long vacation, which he
has employed in the machine shop and in the
forest shooting bears and things.

WITH a desire to correct records this fall,
the Pope Manufacturing Company has in-
vested $350 in a watch. Now let a good
man hold the watch, and away for the records.

EDITOR AARON has not been without his
troubles. Ever since his advent in Buffalo
Aaron has been shadowed by two suspicious
looking strangers, who, he supposes, are
emissaries of Renton, the self-appointed
Nemesis of the League officials. Fearing
some scheme is in process to put him in
durance just as he is about to start for home,
the crafty editor has given out that he will
visit Niagara to-morrow, but ere this sees
the light of type the editor will have skipped
far beyond the reach of Renton and his myr-
midons. — *Herald.*

WHAT is the difference between a first-
rate hub lamp, and a stout and healthy
vagrant ? One is a trusty lamp, the other a
lusty tramp.

WE don't believe there was any necessity
for fear on the part of Mr. Aaron. Mr.
Renton assured us last week that he was on
friendly terms with the gentleman, and that
he had no idea of troubling him again. The
affair between them was adjusted, and satisfaction was expressed by both parties.

GIRLS think wheeling inimical to love ;
but what did Carlyle say ? ' " The British
Isles contained thirty odd millions of inhabitants, and the majority were fools," and
the census has proved the feminine gender
to be the majority.

THE *Irish Cyclist and Athlete* thinks the
I. C. A. should not recognize Sunday racing.
It says that most of the members are Catho-
lics, and that this sect does not consider indulgence in such an amusement on Sunday
to be sinful, but the effect of racing on Sunday would be to destroy the character of the
day as a season of rest, and it would be made
a day of toil.

ROBERTSON is going across Cabin John
Bridge on the coping once more, and will be
photographed in the act.

THERE is a story of antiquated complexion
which tells of a man who never found anything to satisfy him down· here below.
When he died he took ·his disposition with
him, and in the upper world he was as unhappy as he was below. He even found
fault that his halo did n't fit him. We know
an editor that will kick up a jolly row if he
ever gets a halo, for there are nine chances
in ten that he won't be satisfied with it.

WHY may a bi. be termed an inebriate ?
Because the spokes are " tight," the saddle
" screwed," the head a little " loose," while
the machine itself cannot stand without· support.

H. A. C. — Such things do not trouble
us. The young man has been instructed by
his principal to crush the CYCLE out of existence. He was ordered to do it in three
months, but he failed to do this, and is still
at work. Meantime the CYCLE is flourish-
ing. We know very well that the young
man does not mean what he says, but he
must take opposite ground to that taken by
us, and this accounts for many queer no-
tions he has put forth. Thanks for what
you say, but we don't care to publish the
letter. The course of the paper is gaining
friends for us every day.

STODDARD, LOVERING & CO. tell us that
they have a telegram from Howell to the
effect that he will not be in America this fall.

H. S. OWEN, of Washington, is in England, and the *Cyclist* reports a call from
him.

G. P. MILLS, whom we ·reported on his
way to John-o'-Groat's last week, is reported
at that noted cabin, and says he has beaten
Marriott's tricycle record ·by twenty-nine
hours, making the distance in five days, ten
hours.

ENGLISH residents of Calcutta introduce
a novelty into pony racing which makes no
end of sport. They make a man keep a
cigar in his mouth through the race, and he
must smoke it enough to keep it alight. A
novice at this business generally finds his
stomach full of smoke at the close, and they
play the joke on the greenies.

WHEN is a wheelist like a bad pen ? When
he spurts.

THE League officers have asked manufacturers to adopt a universal thread for nuts
and bolts. A good idea. We don't believe
much in the efficacy of such resolves, except
that they are one of the forces that go to
shape public opinion, and public opinion
always brings a bow from manufacturers.

WHAT is the difference between a convicted thief and a bicyclist who has had a
spill ? One is a fel-on, the other 's fell off.

ROSEVILLE TOURNAMENT PROGRAMME.

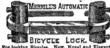

As usual, the Fitchburg band will give a concert on Monday évening before the Springfield tournament, on Court square.

THE Lynn Cycle Club, at a meeting held Friday evening, voted to defer action concerning a clubhouse until next spring. The location will probably be corner of High Rock and Grover streets.

THE Cleveland Bicycle Club will lose considerable money by its recent races, owing to the small attendance. Not over eighteen hundred people attended in three days, when they had near three thousand in one day last year.

Is it not a confession of weakness when a newspaper devotes columns of space to the criticism of its contemporaries? Men do not cry unless they are hurt. The CYCLE is causing many of its contemporaries to shed tears. It goes steadily ahead despite the stones that are being cast at it.

THE committee to count the recent mail vote at Buffalo, reported, on the vote to change the constitution, yeas, 19; nays, 81; on vote to request the Racing Board to rescind Rule H, yeas, 21; nays, 78; on the vote to reinstate certain expelled racing men, yeas, 15; nays, 85; on the vote to abolish all reference to racing in the League by-laws, yeas, 15; nays, 85; on the vote to sustain Henry E. Ducker's appeal against the decision of President Beckwith in removing him from the office of chief consul of Massachusetts, yeas, 9; nays, 87.

THE annual illumination of Charles River was down for Thursday evening of this week. This event always draws wheelmen, and the clubs nearly all called club runs to Waltham and Auburndale to take in the brilliant affair. There is an old proverb which refers to persons who have not the activity to set the river on fire. The residents along the border. of the Charles are not inactive, and if the river is not set on fire, it looks to be aflame, and looks go a great ways.

THERE is a difference of opinion regarding the recent correspondence between Robert Todd, Esq., and the chairman of the Racing Board. The World, in its usual spirit of hostility to the latter official, says: "We are not at all surprised that the N. C. U. will not grant special sanction to the visiting Englishmen after reading Bassett's letter to Robert Todd. Ducker would do better to let Bassett alone and manage his own affairs. Ducker evidently thought that Bassett would write a helping letter. If he did, he made a mistake. The whole thing was foolish."
The Wheel says: "The chairman of the Racing Board and the president of the A. C. U. endeavored to persuade the N. C. U. to allow Englishmen to compete with our promateurs without affecting their standing at home." The chairman of the Racing Board was not asked to write a helping letter, nor was he requested to use any effort to get the Englishmen over. He was asked to explain the position of affairs over here, and this he did as clearly as possible. Having explained this, the way was clear for the A. C. U. to prefer requests.

A WESTERN man was the second wheelman up Corey Hill. Three Westerners are

the only riders who have dared to coast Mt. Washington on ordinaries. A Western man won the Big Four Century against all the Eastern cracks, and the writer of the above "went broke" against him. A Western man was the only one who rode the entire distance on the Big Four tour, rain or no rain, mud or no mud. A Western club introduced electric timing. A Western man, at the head of the touring and transportation departments, has done the most practical work of the League. A Western man would have been president of the League to-day had he not withdrawn from the race. A Western paper ran the most successful and best arranged road race in the country. A Western division inaugurates the campaign for better roads. The biggest and best tours of the country have been arranged and carried out by Western men. It is true we do not run as big tournaments, or as big rows, as the East; but we do our proportionate share of the work. — American Wheelman.

It was old Mr. Samson, we believe, who lost his strength when he lost his hair. Things work differently nowadays. W. C. Herring, of New York, went to the Cleveland races with a full beard. This he wore the first two days, and he won nothing but the title "whiskers." On the third day he appeared with a smooth face and won the consolation race. It has not transpired if there was a Delilah in the case.

THE Massachusetts Club has arranged for a hare and hounds race. The hare will be let loose at 3.15 on Saturday afternoon, 18 September, and the hounds will start five minutes later. The scorchers are getting ready.

NEXT Monday Huntley will make an attempt to beat McCurdy's feat in his twenty-four hours ride. On the same day Corey and Kennedy-Child will ride a tandem for a record, so they say.

THE secretary of the League made a report at Buffalo showing the following condition of things in the League's numbers and finances: The total membership of the League is 9,676, a gain of fifty per cent in the one year; cost of the League bulletin for 17 weeks, 160,650 copies, $4,914.96; receipts, $4,324.88; net cost, $590.08, a cost of 19 cents per member. The last balance on hand, per treasurer's and secretary's reports, is $1,757.60.

THE League Bulletin does not pay expenses. The CYCLE has paid its expenses, and something handsome besides. That's where we beat the Bulletin. In the matter of circulation, we do not beat the Bulletin.

AND now State divisions of the League can arrange their wn affairs and elect their representatives and chief consul in the manner they think. best. So said the officers at Buffalo.

ST. LOUIS is happy. It has been decided that the League will meet in that city next May, and her cup of happiness is running over. Wonder if they'll take the parade to De Soto or over Son-of-a-Gun.

THE officers did well to postpone action on the by-laws till the spring meeting. It was a mistake to call the fall meeting at Buffalo, and it would have been a greater mistake had they done anything of importance.

ONE of our boys came near making a professional of himself while at Clarkesville. A crowd had gone to take a look at a pretty tough hill, and some one suggested that M—— could not climb it, and offered to bet the party that he could n't; the bet was made and money put up. M—— started down the hill with his machine; as soon as he was out of hearing, the chief consul, who was present, called the bet off, and stated his reasons for doing so, saying that if the bet stood he would have to declare M—— a professional, or rather report it to the board. At the same time he wanted to see M—— climb the hill. Everything was made satisfactory at the top of the hill by the time M—— started. Away he came, and seemed to mount it with ease. When he dismounted some of the boys thought they would see what he would say, and told him he was now a professional. His face a few seconds before was all smiles, now it was as long as your arm. He didn't know what to say. and on being told that the bet had been declared off by the chief consul, he once went to him and expressed his most hearty thanks for what he had done, and said that he had not once thought of the consequences. A good laugh was had at his expense, and a big watermelon at the expense of the party who would have lost had the bet not been declared off. — Memphis Cor. Journal.

THE World charges the Racing Board with keeping the foreign amateurs away from America. How does it account for the absence of the professionals? Howell, Duncan, De Civry, DuBois, Lees, and English were to come. The latter will be a professional hereafter; and having announced his intention to race in America hereafter, he could meet him in America if he was disposed to come.

POT-HUNTERS it seems, are unknown in Italy at present among cyclists, if we can judge by the report in " The Cyclist" of the recent races in Genoa, where colored flags were presented to the winners instead of our more substantial prizes. This will cause a thrill of joy to enter the breast of A. W. Rumney if he still holds the same opinions concerning laurel wreaths, etc. We also notice that the riders in a procession which took place before the race meeting all wore large bunches of flowers, which they eventually split up into smaller bunches and distributed to the different ladies present. — News.

A VERY pleasant incident occurred at the Cleveland tournament. After J. R. Rheubottom, of Weedsport, N. Y., had won the open quarter race in dashing style, Referee Sholes called him to the stand and said: "Mr. Rheubottom, it has come to our knowledge that you have recently left the ranks of the single bicyclists, and as a token of their esteem and good wishes to yourself and wife, the boys ask me to present you with this as a fine for your act," handing out of the stand a very handsome chased silver tray, pitcher, and goblet. "Rheuby," as the boys call

HURRAH FOR LYNN!

First Grand International Fall Tournament

OF THE

LYNN CYCLE CLUB TRACK ASSOCIATION,

At LYNN, MASS., September 23, 24, and 25, 1886.

A. C. U. RULES TO GOVERN.

$5,000 in Prizes! Races for Amateurs, Promateurs, Professionals. $5,000 in Prizes!

BEHOLD THE GRAND LIST OF RACES AND PRIZES!

FIRST DAY, THURSDAY, SEPTEMBER 23.

1-Mile Novice, Bicycle, Open, 1st, Gold Medal; 2d, Gold and Silver Medal; 3d, Silver Medal.
2-Mile Amateur Bicycle, 5.45 Class, 1st, Fruit and Flower Stand; 2d, Silver Revolving Butter Dish; 3d, Silver Bell Spoon Holder, gold lined.
1-Mile Promateur Bicycle, Open, 1st, Snowflake Silver Embossed Tea Set; 2d, Silver Engraved Ice-Water Set; 3d, Cake Basket, hammered, Venetian chased, gold lined.
3-Mile Professional Bicycle, Handicap, 1st, $60 Cash; 2d, $40 Cash; 3d, $20 Cash.
2-Mile Amateur Tricycle, Lap, 1st, Base Parlor Lamp, gold and oxidized; 2d, Silver Vase, gold inlaid and oxidized; 3d, Russia Leather Satchel.
10-Mile Promateur Bicycle, Lap, 1st, Fine Gold Watch, stem-winder; 2d, Silver Festoon Chased Tea Set; 3d, Gold Watch Chain.
1-Mile Amateur Bicycle, Open, 1st, Silver Water Set, snowflake chased; 2d, Silver Vase, gold and oxidized; 3d, Gold Watch Chain.
5-Mile Professional Bicycle, Lap, 1st, $75 Cash; 2d, $50 Cash; 3d, $25 Cash.
3-Mile Promateur Bicycle, Handicap, 1st, Silver Tilting Water Set, gold ornamentation; 2d, Clock, Fv Kan chased, appliqué, candelabra, plaque; 3d, Pair Pearl Opera Glasses.

SECOND DAY, FRIDAY, SEPTEMBER 24.

1-Mile Professional Bicycle, Open, 1st, $50 Cash; 2d, $30 Cash; 3d, $20 Cash.
1-Mile Promateur Tricycle, A. C. U. Championship (time limit, 3m. 5s.), 1st, A. C. U. Gold Medal; 2d, A. C. U. Gold Medal; 3d, A. C. U. Silver Medal.
10-Mile Amateur Bicycle, Lap, 1st, Lynn Prize Cup; 2d, Dessert Set, coral rose, glass and silver; 3d, Nut Bowl, gold lined, oxidized finish.
5-Mile Promateur Bicycle, Handicap, 1st, Gentleman's Fine Gold Watch; 2d, Épergne, engraved, oxidized, gold finish; 3d, Snowflake Chased Tilting Ice-Water Set, gold lined
1-Mile Amateur Bicycle, 3.05 Class, 1st, Fishing Set; 2d, Cake Basket, gold lined, oxidized finish; 3d, Fine Russia Leather Satchel.
5-Mile Professional Bicycle, Lap, 1st, $75 Cash; 2d, $50 Cash; 3d, $25 Cash.
1-Mile Amateur Bicycle, A. C. U. Championship (time limit, 2m. 50s.), 1st, A. C. U. Gold Medal; 2d, A. C. U. Gold Medal; 3d, A. C. U. Silver Medal.
5-Mile Promateur Bicycle, Lap, 1st, Double Walled Silver Ice-Water Urn; 2d, Shot Gun, double-barreled, breech-loader; 3d, Silver Watch.
3-Mile Amateur Bicycle, Handicap, 1st, Centre Piece and Fruit Dish, Crystal Dishes; 2d, Flow 2 Stand, cut glass, gold, oxidized finish; 3d, French Pearl Opera Glasses.

THIRD DAY, SATURDAY, SEPTEMBER 25.

1-Mile Promateur Bicycle, Open, 1st, Lynn Prize Cup. (Special Prize for Record.) 2d, Base Lamp, gold inlaid and oxidized finish; 3d, Diamond Breast Pin.
2-Mile Amateur Bicycle, 9.10 Class, 1st, Base Lamp, gold, silver and hammered; 2d, Vase, gold finish; 3d, Gentleman's Gold Ring.
2-Mile Professional Bicycle, Lap, 1st, $50 Cash; 2d, $30 Ca-h; 3d, $20 Cash.
3-Mile Amateur Tricycle, Lap, 1st, Photographer's Outfit; 2d, Silver Watch; 3d, Fishing Set.
5-Mile Promateur Bicycle, A. C. U. Championship (time limit, 15m.), 1st, A. C. U. Gold Medal, diamond setting; 2d, A. C. U. Gold Medal; 3d, A. C. U. Gold and Silver Medal
1-Mile Amateur Bicycle, Lap, 1st, Fruit Dish, rich cut glass, gold, oxidized; 2d, Cigar Box, oxidized; 3d, Gentleman's Gold Chain.
10-Mile Professional Bicycle, Lap, 1st, $100 Cash. ($50 extra for Record.) 2d, $50 Cash; 3d, $25 Cash.
3-Mile Promateur Bicycle, Handicap, 1st, Handsome Oil Painting; 2d, Silver Cashmere Band Tea Set; 3d, Dessert Set, coral rose and glass.
1-Mile Amateur Bicycle, Consolation, 1st, Half dozen Napkin Rings, gold ground, satin case; 2d, Silver Watch; 3d, Russia Leather Satchel.

ENTRIES CLOSE SEPTEMBER 16.

All Events have Three Prizes where there are four or more starters. **Entry Forms, Blanks, List of Prizes, etc., furnished upon application to E. M. BAILEY, Secretary Lynn Cycle Track Association, LYNN, MASS.**

him, took the present in one hand, his racing cap in the other, and looked around in a dazed way. Then he gasped and said: "Boys, I 'm overcome," and lifted the silver in his hand and bowed to his wife, who sat blushing in the stand. There is quite a story about Rheuby's marriage. He and pretty Miss Ingram of Weedsport started out with their minds made up to take in the Cleveland tournament and get married. On Friday morning he called on George Collister and asked him to do him and Miss Ingram a favor. What was it? Get them married. And Collister left everything else to do the work, got the license and Squire Peck, and the ceremony was performed in the hotel parlor.

THE Springfield Bicycle Club has preferred the following request to the A. C. U., and it has been submitted to a mail vote of the officers: The Springfield Bicycle Club contemplate giving at their coming tournament 14 to 17 Sept., a world's champion one-mile race, in which may be entered amateurs, promateurs, and professionals, each class to be kept distinct, till by competition the contestants have been narrowed down to the winner of a final heat, in each class, leaving the question of superiority to be decided between the winning amateur, promateur, and professional. We desire the sanction of the American Cyclists' Union allowing these three representatives of the three classes to compete in a final heat, and with that end in view would request you (the secretary) to obtain for us, if possible, permission to allow them — the winners — to enter for the race mentioned.

ON Saturday afternoon, 29 Aug., the yacht Edith, containing Charles S. Willis and four others, while sailing in the harbor, was run down by the steamer Chatham, of the Baltimore Line, and Mr. Willis was drowned. He was one of the founders of the Suffolk Wheel Club, and was vice-president of the club at the time of his death. He was an open-hearted, jolly fellow, much liked by his associates, and leaves a large circle of friends to mourn his untimely end.

"SHOULD cyclists ride on Sunday? is a question which sadly troubles some minds. Of course the unvarying strictness of Sabbatarianism will at once reply in a dignified and unmistakable 'no;' and I am bound to say that fellows who can ride during the week evenings and on Saturday afternoon will do well to rest on the Sabbath. But those who toil unceasingly from morn till dewy eve maintain that they do no harm by Sunday runs, since they cause no one else to work, and their own effort in riding a machine is much less than that of walking. They say also that pure worship is not confined to time or place, but springs from the heart, and that although they hear no 'parson pray and preach,' yet they attend a grand church, the roof of which is God's great blue sky, and the choir His vast throng of tiny feathered songsters, who seem ready to burst with their rapturous notes of praise. As the devout Sunday cyclist rides through the fresh sweet air, he forgets the cold, dreary earth, and seems quite near to heaven. There is a sermon, too, written in every fragrant flower and stately tree, and the text is 'God is love,' a sermon never deep or dry or dull, but fresh

with heavenly inspiration and infinite delight." — *Christian Commonwealth.*

DR. BLACKHAM introduced the following resolutions at the Buffalo meeting: —

Whereas, The League regards pure amateurship as a qualification for membership, and therefore should have full control of the question of amateurism.

Resolved, That the League hereby reasserts its supreme and sole jurisdiction over cycling athletics in the United States.

Resolved, That it refuses to acknowledge any division of this jurisdiction.

Resolved, That the Racing Board and Membership Committee be instructed to ignore any action or pretended action on the part of any other organization claiming to affect the amateur standing of any wheelman, for acts done or committed to be done in connection with cycling in the United States, nor shall the record of such action be deemed even as collateral evidence in cases before the Racing Board or Membership Committee.

Resolved, That if any wheelman has been suspended or expelled by our Racing Board or Membership Committee on account of any pretended action of any other organization, they are hereby restored to full and unblemished amateur standing.

The resolutions were tabled by a vote of 42 to 19.

OUR correspondent, "J. Parke Street," has our congratulations. He is back from his wedding trip and settled down to business.

THE cycle speeds away, away;
No eagle through the skies of day,
No wind along the hills can flee
So swiftly or so smooth as thee.

THE fall races will bring out very prominently the tactics of the manufacturers' racing team. The men have not been carefully trained for the purpose of beating each other.

TANDEM tricycles are popular among the members of the Salvation Army in England. Report comes to the effect that recently two sisters and two brothers were expelled from the army because they were found guilty of racing on the Sabbath for a bottle of gin. — *Globe.*

R. H. JAMES, of the Buffalo Bicycle Club, has covered 3,500 miles on his wheel so far this season, and expects to bring it up to 5,000. President Churchill has made 2,000 miles, and C. G. Gething and C. W. Adams have each covered 1,500 miles.

THE furniture and effects of the Faneuil House have been sold under the hammer.

THE Massachusetts club is at work laying out a course for its annual road races.

ON Friday afternoon of last week, Mr. H. D. Corey, with Mr. A. Kennedy-Child, rode a private road trial for ten miles on a tandem. The course comprised the well-known Newtonville circuit. The time was a few seconds less than forty-one minutes.

THE fourth annual meeting of the Minnesota Division, which is to be held in Winona, 22 and 23 Sept., promises to bring together the largest number of wheelmen ever assembled in the Northwest. Among the special features of the meet will be the hill-climbing contest up Beck's Hill, on the outskirts of Winona. The hill is eight hun-

dred feet long and sixty-seven feet high, with a grade, in places, of one foot in eight. No bicyclist has ever succeeded in riding his wheel from the bottom to the top.

THE lady tricyclists of Chelsea have a run every Saturday afternoon, and they are seldom without gentlemen friends in their train. One veteran bicycler of the lovely suburb can never be induced to mount his wheel for a run with the boys, but he always goes out with the ladies.

FROM the rules of the American Cyclists' Union just to hand, we learn that that body divides the country into five districts for legislative purposes, and that District No. 1 is to be known as the Eastern District, composed of the New England States *and the Dominion of Canada.* The italics are ours. We were always under the impression that Canada was governed, from a cycling point of view, by the Canadian Wheelmen's Association, and we have just been told by a prominent member of that association that it is perfectly independent of the United States and the L. A. W. For our own part, we protest against *the annexation of Canada by the United States.* What do our Canadian brethren of the wheel say? — *Cyclist.*

J. C. GARROOD, of Boston, and C. W. Hamshaw, of Blue Springs, Mo., have taken out patents for velocipedes.

THE Newcastle (Penn.) Club has hired grounds wherein will be facilities for tennis, base ball, and cycling. A little Keystone State town can do this, but Boston, with a big B, cannot. If not, why not? We never could account for the thusness of this thus.

THE coach and cart I like nor loathe,
Extremes are suited not for all;
On steely car, unlike them both,
I surest sit and fear no fall.
This is my choice; for me I feel
No ride is like the quiet wheel.

KNAPPY says he is not going to call his bicycle "Cleveland." He wants it to run on the surface, and if it cleaves land it will not do this. This cuts us up.

WHEN this you see, at the races, we are looking at the races. Next week we 'll tell what there befell the men who sought first places.

THERE will be few, if any, English amateurs in the fall races. And yet we think there will be large crowds at the races.

THE white dove of peace does not rest in the camps of the racing men. There is want of harmony in the Columbia team, and it is doubtful if all who have trained in that grand aggregation will go into the races.

A WHEELMAN at Crescent Beach introduced a new idea for the sea bathers. He rode his wheel up and down the beach into and out of the water. He was thrown over a number of times by the breakers, but he seemed to consider this a part of the fun. His antics drew a large crowd, and we imagine that is what he was aiming at. We have not heard how long it took him to get his machine in order after its bath.

"How did you hurt your nose?" said Mr. Munnybags to his bookkeeper. "Taking a trial balance, sir." "How in the name of all that 's figurative could you hurt yourself taking a trial balance?" "It was on a bicycle, sir."

DUNCAN tells the *Cyclist* that he is too busy to come to Springfield.

A PECULIAR handicap sweepstake race of one mile is to come off among three members of the Ixion Club, Messrs. Harris, Herring, and Squire. The two last recently had a match race for a handsome gold medal given by the loser, which proved to be Herring, and out of this has grown the present match. Harris is to allow both Herring and Squire seventy-five yards in the mile, and the winner is to receive as trophies the wheels of the other two. This is certainly a novel, and not likely to become a common style of racing. — *Cor. Journal.*

THE Pope cup is going into Van Sicklen's neighborhood. Van has two wins already. The cup may find a home in Chicago.

"THE tricycle is coming rapidly into favor, and will be the favorite of the ladies, and of such men as are too old, too timid, or too weak to ride the bicycle . . . ' but for the young, active, and enterprising of *mankind*, the bicycle is the ideal steed. . . . It is the coming horse for doctors and for patients." — George E. Blackham, M. D., in *Pope's Calendar.* We have seen the Doctor on a wheel just twice, and each time he was on a tricycle. Which can he be, old, timid, or weak?

At the Buffalo meeting a report was read from the Executive Committee. It was presented by Mr. Gulick. It was a long document, and recited the facts learned by the committee in regard to the secretary's office. An expert accountant had made a thorough examination of the office, and on his report the Executive Committee based their conclusions. The business of the office was found to be in a very loose condition, the books kept not being of a nature to enable any correct statement of affairs without much labor. Otherwise everything was in order, and all the money was accounted for. Mr. Veazie, the accountant, had, at the direction of the committee, organized a new and perfect system of accounts, by which the status of the division could be discovered at short notice, and the system was now in use and working very satisfactorily. The committee and secretary both recommended that the League should be incorporated.

M. J. LOWNDES, the well-known tricycler, of Coventry, has been arrested for bigamy. He has beaten the record, having taken more wives than is customary, and his name is on the record book of the police court.

ALF FLETCHER, of England, has made a new bicycle record for the road,— fifty miles in 3.9.56¼. He also scored 265¼ miles in 24 hours.

WE have received a very unique photo from Dr. Kendall. It shows the Boston Bicycle Club in the water at Allen's baths. There is a good exposure of head and shoulders. Otherwise the boys are enveloped only in the water.

"EVER had a cyclone here?" asked a Kansas man who was visiting a country aunt in the East: "A cyclone? Oh, yes," said his aunt. "Deacon Brown's son brought one from Boston a spell ago, but law! he could n't ride it. Tumbled off every time he tried."

When Samil Lambik courting went
Of little Ado Skrig,
He asked if she preferred assent
To tricycling or gig?

Miss Ado pursed her pretty lips,
And looked uncommon sly —
Thinking, perhaps, of moonlight trips,
Said, "You may have a Tri."

Oh! those who "Kiss and never tell,"
May kiss without much trouble;
And Samil said, "Oh, very well!
I 'd better have a double."

And, by-the-by, that double Tri.
Made many pleasant trips,
And very many times, — oh, fie!
Miss Ado pursed her lips.

THE SONG OF THE SHIRT.

WHAT size, sir?" said the Tottenham House young man.

"Well, I wear a fifteen collar," I replied; "but will it shrink?" I added, with an affectation of innocence.

"Oh! no, sir, it 's well shrunk, and we always make them an inch bigger in the collar to allow for a little shrinkage."

"Well, I think I 'll take a seventeen inch."

"Seventeen inch!!! you will find it much too large, sir; that with the extra inch will be eighteen."

"Never mind, I 'll try and bear it," I added, determined to profit by experience, and completed the purchase and departed.

I took that white flannel shirt home, and also an early opportunity of trying it on. It reached below my knees, hung in luxuriant profusion around me, and my neck looked like a prospective telegraph post ere the earth is filled into the hole.

"I guess," thought I, "if this blamed thing *don't* shorten sail next washing day, I shall have no alternative but to devote it to the embellishment of ' the unfortunate noble man at large.'" I tried various expedients, but with little success; and finally braced up the collar with the necktie, took a double reef in each arm, selected my most capacious pants, and then reckoned I could brave it out if the boys did let on any.

After a ride or two, I sent it to the wash. The old lady said she only took sacks on contract; she kept her word; on contract she did it, for when it came back it was several sizes smaller.

"Shure it 's an illigant shirt," said I, and for the first and last time felt satisfied with my purchase, it fitted so beautifully. The result of its next visit to the benign female who disassociates our linen from " matter" out of place," was calculated to fill me with grief. I could only just get the collar to button, the arms with the reefs shaken out, barely reaching my wrists, and the skirts were alarmingly curtailed.

Wash No. 3 necessitated the introduction of a large triangular piece of new material in the collar behind, the wristbands would n't fasten, and when in the saddle I no longer sat on the tail. The result of its fourth visit to the laundry was that I decided to inhabit that shirt no more — necessity had more to do with this resolve than I care to admit — so I handed the garment over to my eldest boy.

With becoming pride he went off boating in it, had an upset, and when he reached home it took us ten minutes to extract our son and heir from that shirt — it fitted him tighter than his skin. His brother inherited it, but happening to get caught in a thunderstorm, it foreclosed on him like a mortgagee, and we had to cut the stitches to disinter our progeny.

"Now you see," said my wife, "that I *am* right when I say that clothes *do* get too small for the children, and it is n't that they outgrow them. It 'll do for baby now."

"Well, well, don't give him his bath in it, or it *will* do for baby.'"

Next time it was was washed I had to give it to my daughter as a frock for her doll, but she tells me jerseys and such tight dresses are not fashionable.

"Warranted well shrunk." The words of that "pushing young particle" come back to me when I think of my ample acquisition of last spring.

But what has become of the balance of that white flannel shirt? — *Wheeling.*

WASHINGTON IS NO MORE.

When Washington was president,
As cold as any icicle,
He never on a railroad went,
And never rode a bicycle.

He read by no electric lamp,
Nor heard about the Yellowstone;
He never licked a postage-stamp,
And never saw a telephone.

His trousers ended at his knees,
By wire he could not snatch dispatch;
He filled his lamp with whale oil grease,
And never had a match to scratch.

But in these days it 's come to pass,
All work is with such dashing done —
We 've all those things; but then, alas! —
We seem to have no Washington.

— *Brooklyn Eagle.*

In the steamer, O my darling! when the fog-horns scream and blow,
And the footsteps of the steward softly come and softly go;
When the passengers are groaning with a deep and sincere woe,
Will you think of me and love me as you did not long ago?

In the cabin, O my darling! think not bitterly of me; .
Though I rushed away and left you in the middle of our tea;
I was seized with a sudden louging to gaze upon the damp, deep sea —
It was best to leave you then, dear; best for you and best for me. — *Texas Siftings.*

A "COMPOSITOR" DOG.

"WHAT kind of a dog is that you have?" asked the editor, addressing the foreman of the composing room.

"I call him a compositor dog," was the answer.

"It 's a name I invented myself," said the foreman, as he helped himself to a cigar from the editor's box.

"Why do you apply the name to him? What resemblance does a dog bear to a compositor, or *vice versa*?"

"Well, this dog is a setter."

Then the editor, with a melancholy look, turned to complete his article on "the lesson of the great strikes." — *Boston Herald.*

AT the Cleveland tournament resolutions of respect were passed to the memory of the late George Weber.

NOTES FROM THE SOUTH.

To better accommodate its increasing membership and consequent demand for more space, the N. O. B. C. has decided to erect a clubhouse of its own. The site has been selected, and work will probably be commenced within the next few weeks.

THE new club, the Crescent Wheelmen, are progressing nicely, and expect to be established in permanent quarters during next week. Though but two weeks old this club has already created a watchfulness on the part of its elder sister, the New Orleans Club, which, for some time past, has been in a somewhat drowsy state, but now that a competitor has made its appearance, it (the N. O. B. C.) is fully awake and beginning to hustle. So much for a little friendly rivalry.

YOU must know that we have no race track in this city suitable for cycles, and that our late races were run on a public thoroughfare. The need of a track and grand stands, however, was so thoroughly demonstrated that it is quite likely that ere another year will be have both. Your correspondent is informed that a certain individual of this city has the matter under consideration with every likelihood of carrying out the plan.

MR. R. C. CHAPMAN, of Charleston, S. C., is expected here next week. He is touring through the Southern country, having left Charleston on his bicycle on the 19th ult. Presume he has no regrets at escaping the little shock which upset that place a day or two since.

THE New Rapid is making a bid for Southern favor this year, an agent for that machine having recently been appointed here.

NOTHING has been heard recently from the projected tournament in Vicksburg, which was to occur next month, so presume it has fallen through, or if not, Mr. Bruce should let us hear something further.

BI.

NEW ORLEANS, 3 Sept. 1886.

THE PATH.

BUFFALO, N. Y. — Races under the auspices of the N. Y. State Division, L. A. W.

One-mile novice. — H. D. Kittenger (1), 3.00¼; Will G. Schack (1), 3.01½.

Three-mile handicap. — H. P. Davies, 150 yards (1), 8.58¼; Dukelow, 150 yards (2).

Half-mile State championship. — H. S. Kavanaugh (1), 1.21; C. A. Glanz (2). W. F. Barker, of Rochester, made a mile on the unicycle in 3.37½.

One-mile City of Buffalo championship. — C. A. Glanz (1), 2.55½; J. B. Milley (2).

Two-mile State championship. — H. S. Kavanaugh (1), 6.01¾; W. S. Campbell (2).

One-mile 3.10 class. — A. M. Montgomery (1), 3.08¾; P. J. Dukelow (2).

Five mile L. A. W. championship. — S. P. Hollingsworth (1), 15.23¾; H. S. Kavanaugh (2).

One-mile tricycle State championship. — A. E. Schaaf (1), 4.15; W. S. Campbell (2).

One-mile consolation. — E. P. Cochran (1), 3.05.

The timers were not well up in their business, and there was much confusion in this respect.

TROY, N. Y., 1 Sept. — Races under the auspices of the Troy Club.

One-mile novice. — J. W. McKee (1), 3.12¾; B. Billings (2).

Two-mile tricycle Co. championship. — A. F. Edmans (1), 6.37¾; G. R. Collins (2).

Half-mile dash. — J. R. Rheubottom (1), 1.28¾; H. P. Cole (2).

One-mile for Star wheels. — A. L. Arthur (1), 3.57; B. Billings (2).

Two-mile open. — J. R. Rheubottom (1), 6.12¾; A. F. Edmans (2).

One-mile 3.15 class. — G. R. Collins (1), 3.12¾.

Three-mile open. — E. P. Baird (1), 9.54¾; A. F. Edmans (2).

Two-mile team. — Albany v. Troy; Troy (1).

One-mile open. — E. P. Baird (1), 3.10; G. R. Collins (2).

Three-mile club championship. — J. R. Rheubottom (1), 10.49¾; A. F. Edmans (2).

One-mile consolation. — T. W. Roberts (1); 3.24¾.

NEW ORLEANS. — Annual races of the Louisiana Division, L. A. W., at New Orleans, 26 and 27 Aug.

FIRST DAY.

One-mile N. O. B. C. championship. — C. B. Guillotte (1), A. M. Hill (2), W. L. Hughes (3). Time, 3.10.

This was a magnificent race, being a constant struggle from start to finish. Guillotte and Hill both spurted for all they were worth about one hundred yards from the line, the former winning amid great excitement by half a wheel.

One-mile tandem. — C. H. Fenner and W. L. Hughes (1), B. C. Rea and C. B. Guillotte (2) 4.03.

Rea and Guillotte were well in the lead, when they took a bad side fall, losing the race and bruising themselves somewhat.

One hundred yards slow race. — Won by H. M. Marks in two straight heats.

Quarter-mile, hands off. — B. C. Rea (1), A. M. Hill (2) ; 49 seconds.

Quarter-mile dash. — W. L. Hughes (1), A. M. Hill (2) ; 41 seconds.

SECOND DAY.

One-mile division championship. — A. M. Hill (1), C. B. Guillotte (2) ; 3.23¼.

Guillotte rode against the advice of his friends, he being stiff and sore from his fall of the day before, but he nevertheless

pushed Hill hard, the latter winning by a bare six feet. W. L. Hughes was in this race, but took a header at the quarter mile.

One-mile handicap. — Geo. T. Guedry (34 yards), 1; H. M. Marks (194 yards), 2; B. C. Rea (scratch), 3; T. M. Hill (34 yards), 4.

One-mile time race (3.54). — A. A. Ruhlman, 3.52; H. M. Marks, 3.51.

Five-mile handicap. — A. M. Hill (scratch), 1; Geo. E. Guedry (424 yards), 2; 20.01$\frac{1}{5}$.

Guillotte started in this race, but his bruised leg gave out on the fourth mile.

Quarter-mile safety. — Walk-over for C. H. Fenner, Guillotte, who was also entered, being unable to ride.

Quarter-mile consolation. — T. M. Hill (1), Geo. Sentell, Jr. (2), H. H. Hodgson (3).

ROSEVILLE, N. J. — Races under the auspices of the Orange Wanderers, 4 September: —

Three-mile N. J. Championship. — J. B. Pearson (1), 9.07$\frac{1}{5}$; E. P. Baird (2).

One-mile Novice; first heat. — E. M. Smith (1), 3.14$\frac{3}{5}$; E. R. Lamson (2).

Second heat. — H. Wolcott (1), 3.08; H. Caldwell (2).

Final heat. — E. M. Smith (1), 3.09; H. Wolcott (2).

One-mile Hudson County Wheelmen. — C. A. Stenken (1), 3.12$\frac{1}{5}$.

One-third-mile Dash. — A. B. Rich (1), 56$\frac{3}{5}$; P. Brown (2).

Two-mile Tandem Tricycle. — G. M. Gideon and A. G. Powell (1), 6.35$\frac{1}{5}$; A. B. Rich and E. Valentine (2).

Five-mile Scratch. — A. B. Rich (1), 15.26$\frac{3}{5}$; W. E. Crist (2).

One-mile Orange Wanderers. — H. H. Wells (1) 3.34$\frac{1}{5}$; A. E. Cowdrey (2).

One-third-mile, Boys under Fifteen. — W. Willetts (1), 1.10$\frac{3}{5}$; G. Case (2).

One-mile Dash — A. B. Rich (1), 3.10$\frac{1}{5}$; P. Brown (2).

Three-mile Lap Race. — A. B. Rich (1), 9.18$\frac{1}{5}$, 57 points; C. R. Hoag (2), 49 points.

One-mile Consolation. — E. Valentine (1), 3.06$\frac{1}{5}$; E. C. Parker (2).

AT Long Eaton, 21 August, Percy Furnivall ran a mile in competition in 2.35$\frac{1}{5}$. His quarter was made in thirty-eight seconds, and his half in 1.16. Best American quarter, American, 35$\frac{1}{5}$; promateur, 36$\frac{3}{5}$. Best American half-mile, American, 1.12$\frac{1}{5}$; promateur, 1.13$\frac{3}{5}$; English record, quarter, 38$\frac{3}{5}$; half, 1.15$\frac{3}{5}$.

AT Long Eaton, 23 August, Furnivall made his mile in the following times: one quarter, 37$\frac{3}{5}$; one half, 1.16; mile, 2.34$\frac{3}{5}$. Later he made the three quarters in 1.53$\frac{1}{5}$, and the mile in 2.32$\frac{2}{5}$. Gatehouse rode a tricycle, and cut the following records: five miles, 14.57 (16.19); ten miles, 29.49$\frac{3}{5}$ (32.33$\frac{3}{5}$); twenty miles, 1,0.21$\frac{1}{5}$ (1.8.42).

THE Coventry track has also been giving us new records. At a race meeting, held 21 August, F. W. Allard ran a mile on a tricycle in 2.46$\frac{3}{5}$ in a trial heat, and then topped that with 2.45$\frac{1}{5}$ in the final. Best American amateur time, 2.53$\frac{1}{5}$; professional, 2.49$\frac{3}{5}$. The same day Engleheart gave us a new bicycle record for three miles of 8.16. Rowe's record is 8.07$\frac{2}{5}$, and the best English record is 8-20$\frac{3}{5}$.

FURNIVALL has been after the mile record again, and scored 2.32$\frac{2}{5}$. Last year Furnivall said to us, when we asked him to give us a good mile at Springfield, "It's no use trying; I can't do better than 2.47 if I do my best." We thought then that he would show better than his figures if any man forced him up to a 2.40 gait, and he is giving us very fair figures this year.

E. B. TURNER and Sidney Lee have gixen us a tandem road record of 3.9.55$\frac{1}{5}$. They did it on 21 August, on the Great North Road.

WHEN accidents threw Stenken, Myers, and Hoag out of the ten-mile road race given by the Orange Wanderers, six weeks ago, the success of Baird was not generally regarded as conclusive, for many believed that Stenken could defeat him. So it came about that a new race for the four above-named men was arranged under the joint auspices of the Hudson County Wheelmen and the Orange Wanderers.

Only Stenken and Baird appeared Tuesday, 31 August, at seven A. M., the time set for the race over the Irvington course. The macadam was in poor condition, owing to the recent dry weather, and fast time was impossible.

The men were started at 7.42 with Stenken in the lead for the first quarter mile. At that point Baird passed him, and was never caught. The time was, Baird, 37.1$\frac{1}{2}$; Stenken, 38.57.

The Irvington course is a hard one, having very little level riding on it, and four hard hills each way.

Baird rode a 53-inch Rudge and Stenken a Star.

THE following programme of events has been arranged for the Roseville tournament, although subject to change before closing of entries: —

First day, 30 September. — One-mile novice, bicycle; two-mile amateur, bicycle, 5.45 class; one-mile promateur, bicycle; three-mile professional, bicycle lap; two-mile amateur, tricycle; one-mile promateur, tricycle; ten-mile professional, bicycle; three-mile promateur, bicycle lap race; three-mile amateur, bicycle handicap.

Second day, 1 October. — One-mile amateur, bicycle lap; three-mile promateur, bicycle handicap; five-mile professional, bicycle; two-mile amateur, tandem tricycle; three-mile amateur, bicycle; ten-mile promateur, bicycle; one-mile professional, bicycle handicap, one-mile amateur, bicycle, three-minute class; two-mile promateur, tricycle.

Third day, 2 October. — One-mile professional, bicycle; two-mile amateur, tricycle handicap; five-mile amateur, bicycle scratch; one-mile promateur, bicycle handicap; five-mile professional, bicycle handicap; five-mile promateur, tandem; one-mile amateur, bicycle; five-mile promateur, lap; one-mile amateur, bicycle; consolation.

COMING EVENTS.

SEPTEMBER.

10 Friday. — Annual tournament Berkshire County Wheelmen, at Pittsfield, Mass.; two days.

11 Saturday. — Races of Harlem Wheelmen at Manhattan Grounds, New York. Entries close 4 September, to F. L. Bingham, 49 Rose street, New York.

10, 11 Friday, Saturday. — Annual tournament Berkshire County Wheelmen, at Pittsfield, Mass.

13 Monday. — Road race of Ilderan Bicycle Club, of Brooklyn, N. Y.

14 Tuesday. — Races at Cortland, N. Y., by Cortland Co. Cyclists Club.

Races at Farmers' and Mechanics Fair, No. Attleboro', Mass.

14 to 17 Tuesday to Friday. — Springfield Bi. Club's annual tournament, at Hampden Park, Springfield Mass.

18 Saturday. — Races of Associated Clubs at Allegheny City, Penn.

Races of Passaic County Wheelmen, at Clifton, N. J.

Fall race meeting of K. C. W., at Brooklyn, N. Y. Entries to C. Schwalbach, 124 Penn street, Brooklyn. Close 11 September.

Races at So. Worcester, Mass.

21 Tuesday. — Races by R. I. Division, at Providence, R. I.

21, 22, 23 Tuesday–Thursday. — Bicycle races at Junction City, Kansas. Apply to Charles S. Davis, Junction City, Kansas.

Races at Queen's County Fair, Mineola, L. I.

22, 23, Wednesday, Thursday. — Races of the Winona (Minn.) Club, and meet of Minnesota Division, on the 22d, five-mile N. W. championship; 23d, twenty-mile L. A. W. championship.

23, 24, 25 Thursday–Saturday. — Fall tournament of Lynn Track Association, at Glenmere Park, Lynn, Mass.; three days.

27 Monday. — Annual 100-mile race of Boston Bicycle Club. Entries to R. J. Tombs, 36 St. James street.

Races by Indianapolis (Ind.) A. A. Address C. F. Smith, 114 No. Penn street, Indianapolis, Ind.

28 Tuesday. — Kansas L. A. W. division meet and races, Junction City, Kan.

Second day of Indianapolis races. Pope Cup race.

30 Thursday. — First day of tournament of New Jersey Cycling and Athletic Association, at Roseville Station, Newark, N. J. Apply to Frederic Jenkins, manager, Oraton Hall, Newark, N. J.

OCTOBER.

1 and 2 Friday, Saturday. — Second and third days of tournament at Newark. Apply to Fred Jenkins.

1 Friday. — Illuminated parade of wheelmen at St. Louis, Mo. J. S. Rogers, care of *American Wheelman*, St. Louis.

1, 2 Friday, Saturday. — Inter-State meet at St. Louis, Mo. Apply to J. S. Rogers.

MISCELLANEOUS

The Cycle.

Vol. I., No. 25. BOSTON, MASS., 17 SEPTEMBER, 1886. FIVE CENTS.

TRIGWELL'S BALL-BEARING HEAD

Is enough in itself to determine one in favor of the

ROYAL ✠ MAIL!

The Only Wheel having this Head.

WE ARE RECEIVING THE HIGHEST TESTIMONIALS.   **TRULY THE WHEEL OF THE YEAR.**

Genuine Trigwell Ball-Bearing Head used on the Royal Mail.

The rigidity of a bicycle and the freedom in steering is increased to such an extent that hills can be surmounted with far greater ease, and rough roads traversed with considerably less discomfort. A Ball Head will not require lubricating or adjusting more frequently than ONCE EVERY ONE THOUSAND MILES.

The invention was awarded the Silver Medal at the Inventions Exhibition, 1885, by a jury of experienced and practical riders.

The One Hundred Mile Race of the London Bicycle Club, from Bath to London, was won on a bicycle fitted with this Head, in 7 hours 33 minutes, against a strong head-wind for at least a third of the distance, with heavy rain falling for six hours.

TESTIMONIALS.

Mr. FURNIVALL says:

The Ball-Bearing Head has quite surpassed my expectations. Its advantages for road riding are greater than one would believe possible without a practical experience of them. I will never have another bicycle without a Ball Head.

Mr. HAWLEY, Hon. Sec. of the L. B. C., says:

My bicycle was ridden about 4,000 miles last year, during which time the Ball Head was only adjusted three or four times. I certainly think this is a distinct advance in cycle manufacture.

Mr. HY. HERBERT, Clarence, B. C., says:

I cannot speak too highly of the Patent Ball-Bearing Head, which is really everything that can be desired for rigidity and ease of steering.

From "WHEELING," 1 Sept., 1886:

We seldom remember such unanimity as prevails with reference to the Ball-Bearing Head of Messrs. Trigwell, Watson & Co. Not a man who has tried it is there who does not swear by it as the greatest thing in bicycle manufacture of the day.

A Trigwell's Patent Ball-Bearing Head was fitted to the machine of Mr. Mills, on which he made the existing record (bicycle) for the Land's End to John o' Groat's ride, though he rode another machine not fitted with this head when he made the twenty-four-hour record. The longer ride, however, was by far the best test for this well-appreciated head-piece, whose merits are so pronounced that no bicyclist should be without it.

Mr. HARRY JONES, of the Haverstock C. C., says:

My record last year amounted to 8,241½ miles. I have ridden over some of the roughest roads through nearly every county in England and Wales, and can say that some of the grass roads traversed in Lincolnshire, etc., would have been quite unridable with the ordinary head; but in this, and where any delicate steering is required, I have found the Ball-Bearing Head invaluable, and also a great assistance in hill climbing. I have ridden it over 1,000 miles without oiling, and only adjusted it three times during the year, and the wear is imperceptible.

Mr. SHIPTON, Sec. to the C. T. C., says:

My views as to the merits of your new Ball-Bearing Head are pretty fully expressed in the C. T. C. Gazette for October last, to which you are at full liberty to make reference. The eulogium then bestowed I cannot but confirm by the light of more recent experience. To put it briefly, I consider the Ball-Bearing Head to be the most valid of all the modern-day improvements, and I would not be without it for twice its cost.

We have Royal Mails, either with Old Pattern Head and Cemented Tire, or Ball Head and Cemented Tire, or Ball Head and Grip-Fast Tire.

THE WHEEL OF WHEELS!

In Selecting a Wheel, Get the Latest Improved.

The Excellence of the Royal Mail Bicycle is Too Well Known to Need Description.

We take Other Wheels in Trade, and can Allow More Now for Old Wheels than able to in the Spring.

TRY A ROYAL MAIL.   *A FEW SECOND-HAND ONES IN STOCK.*

SEND FOR CIRCULARS.

WM. READ & SONS, Sole American Agents, 107 Washington St., Boston.

THE CYCLE

PUBLISHED EVERY FRIDAY BY ABBOT BASSETT, 22 SCHOOL ST., ROOM 19.

Vol. I.   BOSTON, MASS., 17 SEPTEMBER, 1886.   No. 25.

TERMS OF SUBSCRIPTION.

One Year, by mail, post-paid.........................$1.50
Three Copies in one order.............................. 3.00
Club Subscriptions..................................... 2.00
Six Months... .90
Single Copies.. .05

Specimen Copies free.

Every bicycle dealer is agent for the CYCLE and authorised to receive subscriptions at regular rates. The paper can be found on sale at the following places : —
Boston, CUPPLES, UPHAM & CO., cor. Washington and School Streets. Tremont House news stand. At every cycle warehouse.
New York, ELLIOTT MASON, 12 Warren Street.
Philadelphia, H. B. HART, 811 Arch Street. GEORGE D. GIDEON, 6 South Broad Street.
Baltimore, S. T. CLARK & CO., 4 Hanover Street.
Chicago, W. M. DURELL, 115 Wabash Avenue. JOHN WILKINSON & CO., 77 State Street.
Washington, H. S. OWEN, Capital Cycle Co.
St. Louis, ST. LOUIS WHEEL CO., 1121 Olive Street.

ABBOT BASSETT . . . . . EDITOR

A. MUDGE & SON, PRINTERS, 24 FRANKLIN ST., BOSTON

All communications should be sent in not later than Tuesday, to ensure insertion the same week.

Entered at the Post-office as second-class mail matter.

WITH all due respect for our friend Dr. Blackham, of Dunkirk, we must say that the resolutions introduced by him at Buffalo are decorated with more "unwisdom" than anything that we have seen from his pen.

"*Whereas,* The League regards pure amateurism as a qualification for membership, and therefore should have full control of the question of amateurship."

From this we conclude that the Doctor would have the League assert jurisdiction over walking, running, jumping, skating, rowing, etc. Perhaps the walkers, runners, jumpers, etc., would object. All government rests upon the consent of the governed.

"*Resolved,* That the League hereby reasserts its supreme and sole jurisdiction over cycling athletics in the United States."

From this we conclude that the Doctor wishes the League to take jurisdiction over professional and promateur races. He starts out with the assertion, which no one will gainsay, that the League admits none but amateurs, and yet he would have it take up, make laws for, and control classes of men who cannot join the League. Perhaps these men will object. What will the Doctor have us do then?

"*Resolved,* That it refuses to acknowledge any division of this jurisdiction."

Not even to the extent of letting go its control of road racing. The Doctor would have the League indorse the breaking of laws in the land. The League must assert jurisdiction over every phase of the sport. It must take up road racing and foster it by giving it countenance.

"*Resolved,* That the Racing Board and Membership Committee be instructed to ignore any action or pretended action on the part of any other organization claiming to affect the amateur standing of any wheelman, for acts done or committed to be done in connection with cycling in the United States, nor shall the record of such action be deemed even as collateral evidence in cases before the Racing Board or Membership Committee."

The Doctor would allow a man to compete with a professional or for a money prize at a meeting held under C. T. C., A. C. U., or N. A. A. A. A. rules, and would have the action of those societies ignored if the man was disqualified.

"*Resolved,* That if any wheelman has been suspended or expelled by our Racing Board or Membership Committee on account of any pretended action of any other organization, they are hereby restored to full and unblemished amateur standing."

The resolutions were tabled by a vote of 42 to 19. The officers did well. Such action, if taken, would have been ineffective and decidedly unwise. Underneath these resolutions can be plainly seen the Doctor's hostility to every organization contemporary with the League in which cyclers have an interest. He thinks the League should do everything, and sees no necessity for the existence of any other wheel organization. We disagree with him. The world is large and there is much work to do. There is always room for workers. We recognize very clearly that the League cannot do everything, and we see a field for the labors of every society that has come into existence. If there is no work to be done, or if they are incapable to do it, these organizations will find it out quickly enough. We have no sympathy whatever with the spirit of antagonism which comes out at intervals from a few individuals, who persist in seeing an enemy in every new organization that springs up. If any or all of these can do good for the cause, let no man try to bid them stand aside.

Wheeling, about the brightest of our English contemporaries, is in favor of the abolition of the amateur definition. It says : "The whole sentiment of amateurism is to our minds visionary and impossible," and further goes on to show that wheelmen are not of the moneyed class, but of the plain, ordinary people, who know the respective value of pounds, shillings, and pence, and the empty title of amateur. There is sound truth in this, and *we have been brought to realize how absurd the rule is, that is clung to so fondly, by its enforcement.* Dr. Blackham's stock is looking up. — *World.*

There can be no mistake in this. The oldest cycle journal in America comes out boldly in opposition to the amateur law. We are glad to know where to place the journal. And yet we can believe the amateur law will stand.

IF, as the *World* says, the whole sentiment of amateurism is visionary and impossible, and if the amateur rule is absurd, then are the 25,000 C. T. C. men, the 10,000 L. A. W. men, the 10,000 N. A. A. A. A. men, and the thousand upon thousands of other amateur athletes, mistaken. Why does not the editor become a professional? This is a very queer platform for the organ of the C. T. C. to stand on.

WE have a private letter from Mr. G. Lacy Hillier in which he asks us to deny, in the most positive manner, that he asked Mr. Ducker to pay a portion of his expenses to America. He denies that Mr. Ducker has any such letter as he says he has, unless it be a forgery, and he adds that should he choose to come to America, he is amply able to pay his bills, and moreover, he can come out as the representative of Iliffe & Son with all expenses paid at any time.

THE "makers' amateur" war in England has been reopened, and this time the N. C. U. means business. Mr. E. Hale (champion of Europe), E. Oxborrow, and A. P. Engleheart, have been permanently suspended, and R. V. Asbury has been suspended till further notice, for non-payment of entrance fees. Here's to the success of England! May she clear the board and relegate the suspects to the class where they belong.

Wheeling roundly denounces the N. C. U. for not granting sanction to the English amateurs to race with our promateurs. But

where is Harry? He did n't want sanction, did he?

THE PRIZE THEY RACED FOR.
BY COLIN GRAY.

It was a noble mansion before which he stopped, and alighting from his wheel, he leaned it against an arbor and approached the door: He was met by a servant.

"Is my sister at home?"

"Miss Hamilton is at home, sir. She is in the dining-room."

At half-past 6 o'clock every night, Mr. Hamilton asked the same question precisely, and received precisely the same answer. He had reduced his living to a system, and could tell to the fraction of a second just when to arrive at his home. He had made it a practice to take a spin upon his wheel every day after office hours, and his runs were so well timed that half-past 6 always saw him at his door. Leaving his wheel to the care of a servant, he sought his own room and quickly changed his riding suit to one more fitting the dining-room. On this evening he was a little more particular than usual; after dinner he was going with his sister to a lawn party, and he was a trifle nervous under Madge's bright eyes. "She sees everything," he mentally complained, "and I would rather wear a tight coat than have her twit me about a loose one." So he took pains with his toilet and was rewarded by a pleasant little nod of approval. He was a good-looking fellow, and men don't object to be told so, even by the women of their own family.

"We may as well have dinner, Jack; aunt has gone to Dr. Harwood's; she will not be at home till late."

So dinner was served; and after it, as Madge sat with her cup of coffee in her hand, she said: "Jack, come to the fire half an hour; I want to talk to you."

"And I want to talk to you, Madge. I heard something last night that annoyed me extremely."

"At the bicycle club, of course."

"Yes, at the club."

"I thought you only talked about bicycle subjects there?"

"As a general thing, we don't; but Karl Potter had heard something about you he thought it right to tell me."

"Something disagreeable, of course. People never 'think it right' to tell pleasant things. Well, what was it?"

"You know Edgar Sterling and Grant Digby?"

"Why, yes, I know them as athletic young men who are much interested in bicycle racing. I know that they have competed with each other many times; and I know that their friends all say that it is hard to tell which is the fleetest rider. I distinctly remember being present at several races when they have competed, and I suppose I have shouted in a very unlady-like way when one has beaten the other. Add to this that they are both in the habit of calling upon me, and you may judge whether I know them or not."

"They are lovers of yours?"

"They are among the list."

"I thought myself that they were favored visitors."

"My dear Jack, don't pretend to think about things too high for you."

"They, at any rate, think so."

Madge's face flushed angrily. "How do you know that?"

"Karl Potter told me so."

"Don't speak in enigmas, Jack, please. They always put me in a passion. How can Karl Potter know anything about either Grant Digby or Edgar Sterling? He is not in their set at all. I don't believe they ever speak to each other."

"Dame Rumor has a voice for every one."

"You don't mean to say, Jack, that you have been guilty of listening to what Dame Rumor says, especially when she talks about your sister? Upon my word, I believe that bicycle club is a perfect school for scandal."

"Don't be so scornful, Madge; I consider myself under great obligation to Karl for telling me. I know it was hard for him to do it, for men do not carry the words of Dame Rumor directly to those against whom they are addressed unless they want to do a friendly act."

"Very well; what does rumor say? I have made up my mind for something spiteful, and so you need not fear giving me the story just as it came to you."

"You shall have it Madge. Do you remember the day I took you to the club races? And have you forgotten how keenly you were interested? And I want you to concentrate your mind upon one race in particular. It was the one in which Sterling and Digby were the only competitors. Don't you remember how surprised you were that there were but two men in the race? And can't you recall how you applauded when the men came down the home stretch for the finish?"

"I remember very well, you know; there is no need for you to recall the incident; I was very much interested."

"Do you know what the prize was in that contest?"

"Oh, yes! it was a diamond ring. Mr. Digby showed it to me after the race. You remember that he won it. Mr. Sterling was close behind, and Digby only won by an inch they said at the time."

"Yes, the published prize was a diamond ring, but the prize they were striving for was yourself, Madge Hamilton. The scoundrels! I have a great mind to horsewhip them."

"Indeed! Keep your temper, Jack, and go on."

"They made a bargain in the tent before the race. They had been talking it over before. It was agreed that the one who won the race should have the first chance to propose for your hand. Then they went around and hired the other men to stay out of the race so that it should be confined to those two alone. It was further agreed that if Digby won your consent, he was to pay Sterling twenty-five thousand dollars as soon as possible after his marriage, and if Sterling won, he was to give Digby a like sum. Sterling is in a financial difficulty, and he wants to get out of it with the money obtained in this way. Is it not enough to drive a fellow to extremities? I've a good mind to shoot them on sight."

"Don't lose control of yourself, Jack! You see how cool I am. I don't propose to let the thing disturb me in any way. The fellows are no worse now than they were before, only they are found out. I will take care of myself, never you fear. They shall

propose to me and carry out their plan just as they have laid it out. I can hardly believe that Edgar Sterling entered into the bargain without compunctions."

"It was Digby who made the proposal. Sterling hesitated at first, but I imagine he is in a desperate strait at present, and willing to do almost anything to extricate himself from trouble."

"Certainly he is. What is a poor girl's name or happiness or honor, compared with the annoyance of pressing creditors?"

"Don't look that way, Madge darling, or I know I'll shoot the fellows. I only meant to warn you. I wish anything less than the whole truth would have done it."

"It would not; women judge men by themselves,—that is where we go wrong. Please leave this affair in my hands. I will bring it to a satisfactory solution, never you fear."

Madge was putting the finishing touches to her toilet as she said these words, and it was not long after that she left her house on her brother's arm on the way to the lawn party. It was one of those midsummer affairs held on the expansive lawn and the wooded portions of a large estate on the outskirts of the city. The grove was hung with Chinese lanterns and the lawn was brilliantly lighted. Booths were erected all about, and bands of music lent their sweet strains to the occasion. The brilliant costumes of the ladies gave a charm to the scene and the soft warm air made the evening out-of-doors one of exquisite pleasure. There were rustic seats under the foliage and along the borders of the lawn, and these were populated by the elderly guests, and those at remote distances were patronized by the lovers and friends of more youthful years.

Grant Digby and Edgar Sterling were crossing the lawn when they chanced to pass a booth in which were seated Jack Hamilton and his sister. She bowed to them with a smile so subtle and comprehensive that each was certain it was his specially.

"Did you notice how she smiled at me?" said Grant, posing himself gracefully.

"I thought it was at me," answered Edward sulkily.

"No; it was at me. I shall go and speak to her when we turn back."

"Madge divined this, and she sent her brother away with a message to pretty Maud Gaylord. So Grant had the ground to himself, and very safe ground he felt it to be.

Then Edgar made his effort, and was equally satisfied. There was something about Madge's manner to him delightfully shy and yet encouraging. For the first time in twenty years he kept his opinions to himself. "Grant," he mentally commented, "is terribly conceited, and may have deceived himself. If I am not a favored lover, I think Madge Hamilton is treating me badly."

And so thinking of Madge as likely to become his own, he began to feel the outrage of such a bargain as he had entered into. He could hardly bear to look into the young, candid face and think of his shameful little plot against this girl's money.

When Grant and he again talked over the matter, he ventured to suggest that they should each consider the bargain as to Miss Hamilton void, and leave themselves unfettered in the race. But Grant would hear of no such withdrawal. "The race," he said, "rests with you and me, Edgar. I am

sure of it. Marriage will break up our friendship; it can't help it, old boy; and whichever of us is left will need solid consolation. If you succeed, you will have to cut me in a short time, and the money will give me a new start in a new life. If I succeed, all the same we shall drift apart; and it would be a real comfort to me, in such case, to feel that at least I had been able to put you easy in money matters."

And Grant's manner was so grand and pathetic that Sterling felt it impossible to urge further a subject which Grant spoke of as "any way a great trial, and almost like the burial of a twenty years' friendship."

The next morning, in answer to Madge's request, Maud Gaylord came to spend the day at the Hamilton's. Madge had chosen Maud for a confidant, and for excellent reasons. Maud had a very large visiting list, she was dangerously sarcastic, and never spared friend or acquaintance, for a witticism. A report finding its medium through Maud would go into the world with a spice of ludicrous bitterness that no one else could give it. And also it would go in a dangerous kind of incognito, and would only become more widely known in consequence of the unobtrusiveness of its progress.

So about eleven o'clock Maud came chirping in, full of news as to the people she had met, and the engagement of "that poor little mouse, Jennie Billings, to Jacob Cutting. He 'll eat her up in a year, Madge," she said, with a laughable grimace; "that is, he 'll eat her bonds up. Oh, dear! how hard it is for a girl with money to be decently loved?"

This was just the opening Madge wanted. "She was so wretched, and needed some one to open her poor heart to;" and Maud was at once sympathetic and delightfully anxious. What a study her queer little face was, with its twinkling eyes and tight-drawn lips, as she listened to Madge's story! And what a revelation of womanly temper there was in the small nervous hands, and the restless movements of her prettily bowed and sandaled feet! Now, Maud, I have told you all. If you were I, what would you do?"

"I should crucify them — socially, I mean; fix them up with hair-pins, as it were. Put the story into their cups, dear — tea cups and wine cups. It will make their drinking disagreeable enough, I 'll warrant you. There are hundreds of young men just as mean and heartless and contemptible, dear; and every one of them will be 'dreadfully shocked' at the found-out fellows."

Madge had asked the two racing cyclists to call; and it had been agreed between them that Edgar should leave first, and that, all else being favorable, Grant should put his fortune to the test. They were annoyed at finding Maud sitting with Madge, but it was probable that Maud would leave after lunch.

Somehow Edgar Sterling imagined Madge's manner so peculiarly kind to himself, that he — finding a moment's opportunity to speak to her unnoticed — asked for an interview that night at eight, and received a gracious assent. Then, according to agreement, he went away before Grant Digby; and Maud, guessing what Grant had come for, left the room "to send a mes-

sage," and so gave the young gentleman the opportunity he sought.

Madge heard his poetic, passionate confession with a good deal of assumed feeling, but declared she could not at once answer so important a question.

"Would Mr. Digby call the following day at twelve o'clock?"

And as Maud entered just at that moment, and there was a most aggravating mocking smile on her face, Grant hurriedly took his leave, with all his hopes as yet uncertain.

He put on a brave face, however, to Sterling. But Sterling's hopes rose on Grant's delay. He thought it likely that Madge had purposely put off answering Grant until she heard what his reasons were for desiring an interview. She must have suspected them, and if this was the case, it was indeed a strong foundation for his hopes. So he heard Grant's account of his interview, but said nothing of his own appointment.

At eight o'clock he kept it, and found Madge just ready to leave the house. "She was going to a dinner party, but would be happy to give Mr. Sterling a few minutes." He was glad the agony was to be short. He said in a few plain words what he wanted to say, and said them in such a straightforward, honest manner, that Madge was almost sorry she could not believe a word of them. She pointed out the fact that her friends were waiting, the necessity of being careful in such decisions, and asked him to call for an answer next day at half-past twelve.

"Half-past twelve," thought Sterling; "Grant's appointment was twelve; evidently she means to refuse him;" and his own hopes rose still higher. That night Grant noticed that he seemed strangely averse to talk. He did not know that Sterling was arranging his prospective new life, and absolutely considering how he was to escape paying such a shameful "debt of honor" as would soon be due his friend from him.

True, he did not indulge the thought many minutes at a time, but it was there, just as it had been also in Grant's heart, in the same kind of dim, dumb way. Only Grant had at once solved the problem in a manner Sterling never thought of: "I shall lay the blame on Madge, and tell Edgar she watches her gold like a dragon."

A little before twelve the next day Grant went to his appointment, and his friend almost immediately followed him. He did not expect, of course, to meet Grant there; he would have got his dismissal and left. However, not only was Grant in the parlor, but also that tormenting Maud Gaylord. The two gentlemen looked at each other, but there was nothing now to be done but accept Madge's invitation to lunch, and wait for their opportunity.

Maud seemed that day to be possessed by a thousand malicious little sprites, and Grant and Sterling winced again and again under her sharp, subtle innuendoes. Her mirth, though mocking, was infectious, and by the time lunch was over, the whole party were in a mood of very unnatural and rather unpleasant exaltation. Madge showed it in her glowing cheeks, and in a certain set, proud manner. The company having re-entered the parlor after lunch, Madge

brought out a card table and laid upon it a pack of playing cards and a cribbage board.

"What are you going to do, Madge?" said Maud, her eyes filled with curiosity.

"I am going to play you a game of cribbage for a husband. If I win, I shall accept one of these gentlemen, and you must take the other. The one that wins has the first choice. Shall I shuffle?"

"I protest," said Sterling, "against such a mockery of the most solemn affair of life."

"Just hear him!" screamed Maud, laughing still more excitedly. "Pray, Mr. Sterling, did you ever hear of two gentlemen riding a race for a lady's hand and fortune?"

"And agreeing to console each other with twenty-five thousand out of the bank account?"

"Young ladies," said Mr. Sterling, "if any men have done what you say, they richly deserve your mockery; they must have been conceited fools to enter into such a plot."

"Gentlemen, I hope you will let the world know what you are racing for in the future, and if perchance a lady's hand and fortune is at stake, I trust she will be consulted in the matter, for it may be then, as it is now, that the prize goes to neither." And Madge ceremoniously bowed them into the hall, from whence they soon found their way into the street.

"Where are you going?" said Sterling, fiercely.

"I am going to New York at once."

"You can go to Timbuctoo if you like; I shall stay here; and I shall like to see the man, or the woman either, who will twit me about Hamilton's sister."

"A very rude, insolent girl, I think."

"She is nothing of the kind. She is a noble girl, — a sight too good, if she had not a penny, for such sneak thieves as you and me. There, Grant, keep out of my sight. We may as well part here as anywhere." And Sterling strode off in a towering passion with himself, and looked so formidable and black for weeks afterward that no one cared to speak of "that good thing about Hamilton's sister" in any place where he would be likely to hear of it.

Madge never saw him, and rarely heard of him. Indeed, he gave himself up, with all the passion of his nature, to money-making. On the whole, her revenge had not given her any pleasure; she found out, when anger was over, and love could obtain a hearing, that she had really liked Edgar, and her heart began sadly to make excuses for him.

One day, three years after their unpleasant parting, her brother said to her, "Madge, you were very nearly losing $100,-000, — would have done so but for — Edgar Sterling."

Madge blushed vividly, and looked up eagerly at her brother.

"That 's so," said Jack; "he knows everything about stocks and shares that can be known, and he brought me information which saved you a clear $100,000. I must say he spoke in a very manly, honest manner."

"Of the past?"

"Yes. He out with everything, and asked my pardon; said he could not do it for very shame until he had been able to prove his regret. He had been watching

HURRAH FOR LYNN!

First Grand International Fall Tournament

OF THE

LYNN CYCLE CLUB TRACK ASSOCIATION,

At LYNN, MASS., September 23, 24, and 25, 1886.

A. C. U. RULES TO GOVERN.

$5,000 in Prizes! Races for Amateurs, Promateurs, Professionals. $5,000 in Prizes!

BEHOLD THE GRAND LIST OF RACES AND PRIZES!

FIRST DAY, THURSDAY, SEPTEMBER 23.

1-Mile Novice, Bicycle, Open, 1st, Gold Medal; 2d, Gold and Silver Medal; 3d, Silver Medal.
2-Mile Amateur Bicycle, 5.45 Class, 1st, Fruit and Flower Stand; 2d, Silver Revolving Butter Dish; 3d, Silver Bell Spoon Holder, gold lined.
1-Mile Promateur Bicycle, Open, 1st, Snowflake Silver Embossed Tea Set; 2d, Silver Engraved Ice-Water Set; 3d, Cake Basket, hammered, Venetian chased, gold lined.
3-Mile Professional Bicycle, Handicap, 1st, $60 Cash; 2d, $40 Cash; 3d, $20 Cash.
2-Mile Amateur Tricycle, Lap, 1st, Base Parlor Lamp, gold and oxidized; 2d, Silver Vase, gold inlaid and oxidized; 3d, Russia Leather Satchel.
10-Mile Promateur Bicycle, Lap, 1st, Fine Gold Watch, stem-winder; 2d, Silver Festoon Chased Tea Set; 3d, Gold Watch Chain.
1-Mile Amateur Bicycle, Open, 1st Silver Water Set, snowflake chased; 2d, Silver Vase, gold and oxidized; 3d, Gold Watch Chain.
5-Mile Professional Bicycle, Lap, 1st, $75 Cash; 2d, $50 Cash; 3d, $25 Cash.
8-Mile Promateur Bicycle, Handicap, 1st, Silver Tilting Water Set, gold ornamentation; 2d, Clock, Parisian chased, appliqué, candelabra, plaque; 3d, Pair Pearl Opera Glasses.

SECOND DAY, FRIDAY, SEPTEMBER 24.

1-Mile Professional Bicycle, Open; 1st, $50 Cash; 2d, $30 Cash; 3d, $20 Cash.
1-Mile Promateur Tricycle, A. C. U. Championship (time limit, 3m. 5s.), 1st, A. C. U. Gold Medal; 2d, A. C. U. Gold Medal; 3d, A. C. U. Silver Medal.
10-Mile Amateur Bicycle, Lap, 1st, Lynn Prize Cup; 2d, Dessert Set, coral rose, glass and silver; 3d, Nut Bowl, gold lined, oxidized finish.
5-Mile Promateur Bicycle, Handicap, 1st, Gentleman's Fine Gold Watch; 2d, Epergne, engraved, oxidized, gold finish; 3d, Snowflake Chased Tilting Ice-Water Set, gold lined.
1-Mile Amateur Bicycle, 3.05 Class, 1st, Fishing Set; 2d, Cake Basket, gold lined, oxidized finish; 3d, Fine Russia Leather Satchel.
5-Mile Professional Bicycle, Lap, 1st, $75 Cash; 2d, $50 Cash; 3d, $25 Cash.
1-Mile Amateur Bicycle, A. C. U. Championship (time limit, 2m. 50s.), 1st, A. C. U. Gold Medal; 2d, A. C. U. Gold Medal; 3d, A. C. U. Silver Medal.
3-Mile Promateur Bicycle, Lap, 1st, Double Walled Silver Ice-Water Urn; 2d, Shot Gun, double-barreled, breech-loader; 3d, Silver Watch.
8-Mile Amateur Bicycle, Handicap, 1st, Centre Piece and Fruit Dish, Crystal Dishes; 2d, Flower Stand, cut glass, gold, oxidized finish; 3d, French Pearl Opera Glasses.

THIRD DAY, SATURDAY, SEPTEMBER 25.

1-Mile Promateur Bicycle, Open, 1st, Lynn Prize Cup. (Special Prize for Record.) 2d, Base Lamp, gold inlaid and oxidized finish; 3d, Diamond Breast Pin.
3-Mile Amateur Bicycle, 9.10 Class, 1st, Base Lamp, cold silver and hammered; 2d, Vase, gold finish; 3d, Gentleman's Gold Ring.
2-Mile Professional Bicycle, Lap, 1st, $50 Cash; 2d, $30 Cash; 3d, $20 Cash.
3-Mile Amateur Tricycle, Lap, 1st, Photographer's Outfit; 2d, Silver Watch; 3d, Fishing Set.
5-Mile Promateur Bicycle, A. C. U. Championship (time limit, 15m.), 1st, A. C. U. Gold Medal, diamond setting; 2d, A. C. U. Gold Medal; 3d, A. C. U. Gold and Silver Medal.
1-Mile Amateur Bicycle, Lap, 1st, Fruit Dish, rich cut glass, gold, oxidized; 2d, Cigar Box, oxidized; 3d, Gentleman's Gold Chain.
10-Mile Professional Bicycle, Lap, 1st, $100 Cash. ($50 extra for Record.) 2d, $50 Cash; 3d, $25 Cash.
3-Mile Promateur Bicycle, Handicap, 1st, Handsome Oil Painting; 2d, Silver Cashmere Band Tea Set; 3d, Dessert Set, coral rose and glass.
1-Mile Amateur Bicycle, Consolation, 1st, Half dozen Napkin Rings, gold ground, satin case; 2d, Silver Watch; 3d, Russia Leather Satchel.

ENTRIES CLOSE SEPTEMBER 16.

All Events have Three Prizes where there are four or more starters. Entry Forms, Blanks, List of Prizes, etc., furnished upon application to E. M. BAILEY, Secretary Lynn Cycle Track Association, LYNN, MASS.

your interests, and hoped you would look over his fault."

"I suppose a good action ought to cancel a bad one."

"I think so, Madge, especially when a fellow makes no excuses, but frankly admits he was to blame, and does his best to show his sorrow. I cannot see my way to write him down an enemy any longer; can you, Madge?"

And Madge, in a very soft, irresolute fashion, said simply "No."

Six months afterward the president of a famous down-town bank sent hurriedly over to Sterling's office. He wanted to see him at once on important business.

"Gone to Europe, sir," was the answer.

"He was married yesterday."

"Married! I thought he hated women. Married! To whom?"

"To Jack Hamilton's sister, — the prize he raced for."

CYCLETS.

THE STROLLER.

BY PRESIDENT BATES.

Pleasant it is, when days are long,
And winds are light and warm,
To wander from the busy throng,
Where the woods are sweet with song,
And bees hum faintly all day long,
By many a fertile farm.

My lazy feet alternate play
The languid pedals round;
My wheel rolls carelessly away
Wheresoe'r my fancies stray,
Almost as easily as they,
As they, without a sound,

Far off the ribboned roadway shuns
And leaves the town behind,
In stony grays, and dusty duns,
Where the winding river runs
And sparkles under summer suns,
Just dimpled by the wind.

And farther on my way I take
By many a curving reach,
Where the light ripples of the lake
All his reedy marshes shake,
And squirrels steal, their thirst to slake,
Along the pebbly beach.

Or where tall pines, beside the sea,
In columned aisles arise;
And the wood-spirit in each tree
Sighs and breathes melodiously,
And stirs and struggles to go free,
With inarticulate cries,—

Full of unutterable things,
In a confused refrain,
As, when a wind-harp shakes its strings,
Faint a phantom syren sings,
And melancholy music brings
Strange fancies to the brain.

Forgetful of the noisy street,
And all its sweating tide,
I watch the zephyr's airy feet
Ripple down the bending wheat:
Unmindful of the drowsy heat,
Light-clad and cool I ride,—

Till in the sunset's rosy deep,
Fades the still afternoon;
Till twilight stars begin to peep,
Wandering winds are all asleep,
And o'er the tree-fringed eastern steep,
Up soars the yellow moon.

When in the fruity autumn time,
In crimson, gold, and green,
The year puts on its perfect prime,
Morning meadows white with rime,
Up many a toilsome hill I climb,
That overlooks the scene.

In that bright, tonic atmosphere
To labor is to play;
Pleasure grows vigorous and severe,
Firm of hand, of vision clear;
And health, and strength, and courage cheer
The sunshine of the day.

From the wood silences around,
With fine, attentive ear,
The falling dead leaves rustling sound,
Through the morning calm profound,
And ripe nuts dropping to the ground,
And running rills I hear.

I hear the squirrels' pattering feet,
Run swift from tree to tree,
Of unseen wings the airy beat,
Sudden warblings, wild and sweet,
And faint, and far, and incomplete,
The soft wash of the sea.

A little fingering on the sight,
The scene I resurvey;
Then, swift as skimming swallows' flight,
Poised as skilfully and light,
Fly down the long slant of the height,
As airily as they.

Pleasant it is to wander far
In chase of childhood's dream,
Beyond our known horizon's bar,
Guided by a falling star,
To strange, new lands, whose wonders are
Lit by its mystic gleam.

Or, where sage manhood's rainbow ends,
To seek the fairy gold,
That generous Nature lightly lends
Freely to her faithful friends—
The fresh, bright vigor that she blends
Through all her heat and cold.

And thus, through sunny solitudes,
We stroll—my wheel and I—
Where Nature shows her secret moods,
In elusive interludes;
Where neither greed nor pride intrudes,
And life is not a lie.

We are at the Massasoit, Springfield. We hope our readers will get a good paper.

Last week we were away, and we did n't leave enough copy to fill out. We fear that some fine specimens of the castanea crept in without due credit. Charge it to the devil. A newspaper always goes to that individual if the editor is not on the lookout.

Two well-known cycling lights were very conspicuous by their absence from Hartford. Where were Ducker and Jenkins? Don't let it occur again.

Cycling journalists are not very terrible fellows when they get together, though they do dip their pens in gall for the benefit of one another occasionally. A group of such fellows was noticed at the rooms of the Connecticut Bicycle Club on the night of the first day of the tournament. There was Howard, of the *Globe*, Morse, of the *Herald*, Priall, of the *Wheel*, Myers of *Outing*, Aaron, of the *Bulletin*, Collins of *Recreation*, and "H." besides ourselves. The group was discussing the contents of the refreshment table.

Two new tricycles appeared on the track at Hartford. They were the Victor and the Columbia, and both were modeled after the Cripper.

Corey ordered for two persons at Hartford. He could n't satisfy his stomach on a single portion. And he is in training, too.

The Pope Manufacturing Company is building a very large fireproof storehouse at Hartford.

The *Wheelman's Gazette* says that the Englishmen are afraid to come over. There may be truth in that.

A great many papers are openly declaring that Messrs. Rich and Van Sicklen are not pure amateurs. These things are easily said. We know something whereof we speak, and we do not hesitate to say that those men will stand any investigation that can be made. Justice to them demands that the scribes cease their attacks, or else prove what they say.

The date of the Boston road race has been changed from 27 September to 2 October.

A correspondent who writes for a decision, says : "It has been claimed by some parties that a man is forever debarred from entering a class race if he wins either of the first three positions, though his time may be slower, if the winner's is faster, or equal." The claim is not a good one. The rule says plainly that *he* must have won one of the first three positions in the same or better time than the class under consideration.

The Springfield *Union* is down on cur dogs, and it says that owners should not take them to the races, but should leave them at home. It does not say what good they are at home, though.

When Sellers made a mile at Hartford in 2.39, the audience was wild with enthusiasm. Cheers rent the air, and sober men lost control of themselves. Hendee scored a mile in 2.38¾, and the crowd thought it was a loafing race.

Kennedy-Child, he of the "silver tongue," made the announcements to the crowd at the Hartford races.

The Pennsylvania Club has adopted a uniform made of cloth like that used by the League. It is gray in color and does not fade. The League cloth is being condemned by many who say that it turns red in the sun.

R. P. Gormully has returned from Europe.

The Star took its name because the crossed spokes formed a star in the centre. The Columbia racing wheel now has the same kind of a star, and it is brought out distinctly by the use of nickel plate.

Colonel Pope has waked up. He has lost his Knapp.

Secretary Aaron is coming to Boston to climb Corey Hill. He tells us that John A. Wells climbed it last May, and thought it not so hard as Ford's Hill, Philadelphia; and as Mr. Aaron has been up Ford's, he thinks he can down Corey.

THE Ohio Division comes out unanimously for Kirkpatrick as the next President of the League.

THE annual meeting of the Ohio Division, L. A. W., was held on Monday, 6 Sept., at Massillon. Chief Consul Kirkpatrick made a long address, giving the history of the division for the past year, and citing several cases where effective measures have been taken to secure the rights of cyclers. He concluded as follows : "In closing, I can only urge you to greater activity in increasing your membership, and earnestly fulfilling any duties that may devolve upon you. Avoid all strife. Seek only for the common good. Let no one-horse rival association cause you for a moment to lose your implicit confidence in the tried and true League of American Wheelmen, — an organization that, as the years go by, shall continually increase in effectiveness until she shall be the wonder of the world, and we shall proudly tell the coming generation of wheelmen how we were among its founders and early supporters."

A. B. RICH says he is going to Indianapolis to get another chance at the Pope cup. He thinks he cannot afford to let Van Sicklen take the cup. He is credited with one victory for the cup, and has received his souvenir medal. The Racing Board L. A. W. entered an official protest with the Pope Manufacturing Company against the entry of this victory, but it was ignored. The races at New Haven were not run under League rules, and the rules governing the contest for this cup provide that it shall always be run for at meetings held under League rules.

LANGDON appeared at Hartford in a suit of olive trimmed with blue. His dress was as conspicuous as any that Woodside ever wore.

WOODSIDE and Morgan are going to England to try their fortunes against the English on their own tracks.

IT is said that England will move on the works of the makers' amateurs. This has been said many times, but they don't move.

IT is not generally known, perhaps, that the Springfield Bicycle Club never has dealings with the racing Englishmen themselves, whether professionals or amateurs, but simply negotiates with British cycle makers for the appearance of their best men, and these firms send such riders as they choose. But the makers' amateurs seem to have decided that they prefer to maintain allegiance to the N. C. U. rather than stand by their contract with the manufacturers. — *Springfield Republican.*

MR. H. S. POTEROUS, the Opera Block jeweller, of Denver, Col., has donated a handsome diamond medal, valued at $150, to represent the championship of Colorado, and to be raced for every year under the auspices of the Colorado Wheel Club, until won three times by some one of the contestants.

THE Weed Sewing Machine Company is putting up a lot of houses for its operatives at Hartford. They are very fine structures.

"H." INVITED newspaper men to Hartford, and suggested that it was a good place to wind up their quarrels. The men who met there never had any quarrels. If they had them, they were forgotten at Hartford.

FOUR members of the Chelsea Club stopped for a drink at the Swampscott town pump last Sunday. Two of them used 47-inch and the others 52-inch wheels. The 52-inch men thought it would be a good joke to ride away with the smaller machines while their owners were hunting up something more palatable than cold water, so off they rode to Salem. The short fellows were obliged to mount the big wheels, and a hard time they had pushing them along. The jokers, however, fared but little better, and in future will be more careful about playing their pranks. — *Globe.*

THAT portion of the press that has favored the A. C. U. have been making much of the fact that several races lately held under the L. A. W. rules were financial failures. This proves nothing. The Pittsfield races under the A. C. U. rules were financial failures, and we don't think Hartford made much money. The rules have nothing to do with the success or failure of the meets.

W. W. STALL will take views at the Lynn races. Orders will be received by him at Lynn, and he will have the pictures on sale afterwards.

MR. W. H. HUNTLEY started out to beat the twenty-four hour record on Monday last. He selected the course over which McCurdy made his record, and covered eleven laps. He had a serious fall on the first lap, and received injuries which gave him trouble during all his subsequent ride. His effort was brought to an abrupt and painful ending at eleven P. M., after he had gone one hundred and forty miles. When turning the corner of Derby street and Cherry, he was thrown from his wheel by a stone, thought to have been purposely placed in the road by some one interested in preventing him from accomplishing his feat. He received bad contusions about the head and face, one eye being closed, and the arm injured in the beginning of the race again suffered severely. The police are seeking the perpetrator of the outrage, for whose apprehension a reward will probably be offered.

As a result of the Hartford races, Rowe will, in future, swell around with a diamond ring and a diamond stud ; Hendee will go around with a shot-gun looking for the men who dare to call him a professional ; Ives will arrange his toilet with a silver brush and comb, and defend himself with a revolver ; Crocker will go for protesters with a rifle ; Hart, of New Britain, will ride a Columbia Light Roadster ; Burnham will sport a scarf pin and alligator travelling bag ; Foster will wear a diamond ring ; Rich will put on his shoes with a silver shoe horn and button hook ; Rhodes will gaze at his sweet face in a mirror and go fishing ; Gaskell will drive away advertising agents with a revolver ; and Crist and Brown will promenade Washington streets with gold-headed canes.

THE Hartford Club gave Fred Wood a gold medal for his brilliant record.

AN associated press dispatch from Ithaca, N. Y., dated to Sept., says : About twenty members of the League of American Wheelmen, who started from Buffalo on the 6th for Harper's Ferry, on their annual tour, arrived here at seven o'clock to-night. In descending the steep hill leading to the village, two of the party — Warner and Dakin — took headers. Warner received a ghastly cut under the chin, and was severely jarred. Dakin struck on the right side of his forehead, sustaining concussion of the brain, and, possibly, fracture of the skull. Dakin now lies in an unconscious and critical condition. The remainder of the party, with the exception of one or two who will stay here to care for the injured, will leave for New York to-night.

THE League of Essex County Wheelmen held its eighteenth annual meet in Salem, Saturday forenoon, and then rode to Lynnfield. About twenty members assembled on Salem Common and rode away. A few more joined the party at Lynnfield. In the afternoon there were games of base ball, foot ball, etc. A very enjoyable day was passed.

LOST IN RUSSIA.

MR. RICALTON, the adventurous explorer, who was sent out to the Arctic Ocean in May by *Outing*, in order to make a journey on a three-wheeled machine from Archangel straight through Russia to Crimea, has not been heard from since leaving New York. His friends are very anxious on his account, and it is feared that the Russians may have treated him as they did Thomas Stevens on his bicycle, only a little more effectively. Mr. Ricalton had with him a photographic apparatus, with which he intended to illustrate a series of articles in *Outing*, and it is quite likely that this instrument was the excuse for his arrest.

HOLLINGSWORTH, the hardy road-rider from the Hoosier State, won a five-mile race at the recent Buffalo meet. The prize was a diamond collar button. When the gem was presented to him, he innocently exclaimed : "Why, what can I do with this ? I never wear a white shirt." — *Globe.*

DR. TYLER handicapped the Hartford racers.

HARTFORD gave us some new promateur tricycle records.

IN yachting circles England condemns America for using racing machines. In the wheeling world, England used racing machines long before America did.

CYCLING PATENTS.

C. E. Courtney, Union Springs, N. Y., velocipede.

H. J. Curtis, Hartford, Conn., tricycle brake.

J. A. Lakin and C. J. Emerson, Jr., Westfield, Mass., cyclometer.

J. M. Martin, New Haven, Conn., clutch for tricycles.

D. H. Rice, Brookline, Mass. (2), clutch and wheel.

W. M. Wilson, Philadelphia, Pa. velocipede wheel.

FROM A FEMININE POINT OF VIEW.

NOT only the weather, but the country, just now seems to be in an exceptionally cheerful and beneficent mood. Something in the golden air, the bountiful harvest, the coming home after the summer's holiday, and settling down to the routine of duty again, has worked together to bring all the kindly influences of human nature uppermost, and to put gloom and bitterness out of sight for a season.

WE are in the midst of the month of months for wheelmen. There is a mellow richness in the opening month of Autumn which is suggestive of the best fruits of the season of warmth which has preceded it.

THE same month which gives to us the juicy and delicious products of our orchards, makes all external nature redolent of a richness and color which delight the eye and elevate the mind. There is a freshness and crispness in the air which gives new life to the system that has been made languid by summer heats; the blood courses more quickly through the veins, and the whole nature is conscious of a more vigorous and abounding vitality.

I AM writing now in Nature's studio, far removed from the haunts of men. I am sitting alone on a great rock which overlooks a wide expanse of territory, and no human being is in sight. Can it be wondered, then, that my thoughts take a turn in the direction of a glorification of nature? My ride has taken me fifteen miles from my home, and I sit with note-book on knee and pencil in hand to give vent to the enthusiasm of the moment.

WHAT can be finer than the scene stretched out before me? It is an ideal September landscape, with its varied hues, the rich brown of the hill and meadow contrasting so finely with the bright colors of the leaves as they set the woods aflame. The flowers give to the scene a gorgeousness unknown to the painter's canvas. The golden rod and the aster gleam brightly in the fields; the lady's slipper shows its yellow clusters amid the grass, and the frost flower adds its bluish purple to the hues that glorify the landscape.

THE thought of the wintry coldness and desolation that must follow this warmth and richness of color should make us appreciate more keenly the short-lived splendors of the scene, and invest September with a fascination appropriate to its fleeting glory.

I HEAR the notes of preparation for the fall runs, and already plans are being laid for days of outing at the North Shore and elsewhere. There were gay times last year, and I do not doubt we shall see them repeated the present and the coming month.

WE are not a little dependent upon the gentlemen for the arrangement of these trips, and just now we find our lords and masters carried away with ideas about racing and the tournaments. Oh, well! The races are soon over with, but the touring possibilities are forever with us. I hope to tell the ladies very soon of events to come which will be of interest to them.

"MERRIE WHEELER" and her spouse have been telling of a wonderful run they made on a tandem to see the yacht race at Marblehead. I don't know the statistics in detail, but they accomplished their journey in quicker time and with greater pleasure than had they taken the train.

MY friend Maud, the enthusiast, has had another tricycling experience which is worthy of note. She has been spending the summer at the beach, and occupied a cottage with an elderly lady and her daughter. One night the lady was taken dangerously ill and it was necessary to summon a doctor. The nearest physician lived in a town three miles distant, and the road to it lay across the marshes. As may be readily seen, it was not an inviting road for a lone female to take after midnight, and there are few who would venture it on foot. But Maud had her tricycle with her, and is moreover a brave little body, and she volunteered to go for the doctor. The ladies would not hear to the proposition at first, but their necessities were great, and they yielded. Maud mounted her machine and spun over the deserted highway without a fear. She reached the doctor's house in safety, told her errand, and pedalled home in the wake of his carriage. That is all. You will say that is not much to tell of, and I shall perhaps agree with you. The point of the story lies in the fact that Maud did in a tricycle what she would have been incompetent to do without it; for knowing the character of the road, I venture to say that few women would venture to traverse it alone at midnight. Maud says she would not have dared to.

I HAD a little adventure the other day that gave me not a little amusement. It put the politeness of a gentleman to a severe test, and he proved equal to the occasion. Riding along, I came to a cross street from which there emerged a bicycler going at a very fast pace. We should have struck each other had he not jumped from his machine to avoid it. He was thrown down, but not hurt. Rising, he came to me with hat in hand and said: "Madam, I beg your pardon. I don't know which of us is to blame, but I'm in too much of a hurry to investigate. If it was my fault, I hope you will excuse me. If it was your fault, don't mention it." And he mounted his machine and hurriedly rode away.

THE Chelsea ladies are out on the road a great deal lately. Many new riders have come in this year and they are full of enthusiasm. I note that the ladies have adopted a club color, and their ribbons and tape trimming are of uniform shade. With true feminine instinct, a bright ribbon hangs on the head of the machine. Do I like this? I said that true feminine instinct dictates the action, and I am feminine.

DAISIE.

LONDON, 25 Aug., at Holy Trinity Church, Marylebone, Miss Edith Harris, to W. McCandlish, editor of *Wheeling*. Congratulations and best wishes.

MCCANDLISH, of *Wheeling*, hits the nail on the head when he says the English amateur ranks contain no better men, socially or morally considered, than Rowe, Hendee *et als.*

MR. JOHN H. CUNNINGHAM, Westminster, Md., writes: "The 54-inch American Rudge received all O. K. It is a beauty. In my experience of six years, the American Rudge is the most reliable wheel on the market to-day. It gives splendid satisfaction."

THE PATH.

PITTSFIELD, 10 Sept. — Races under the auspices of the Berkshire County Wheelmen.

One-mile novice, — T. H. Livermore (1), 3.22$\frac{1}{2}$; F. H. McKee (2). *Three-mile Berkshire County championship*, — H. Lee (1), 10.26; W. H. Sheridan (2). *One-mile promateur*, — W. A. Rowe (1), 2.48; C. E. Kluge (2). *Five-mile professional lap.* — Woodside (1), 15.37$\frac{1}{2}$; Crocker (2), Neilson (3). *Half-mile open*, — E. A. DeBlois (1), 1.29; W. H. Langdown (2). *Two-mile promateur*, — Geo. M. Hendee (1), 6.07$\frac{2}{5}$; Ives (2), Kluge (3). *Three-mile B. C. W. Club championship*, — H. J. Grant (1), 10.16; Sheridan (2). *Five mile handicap*, — E. B. Smith, 650 yards (1), 16.33; DeBlois (2), Ware (3).

SECOND DAY.

Half-mile promateur, — Burnham (1), 1.21$\frac{1}{2}$; Kluge (2). *Three-mile professional*, — Neilson (1), 9.11; Woodside (2). *Two-mile open*, — Foster (1), 6.12; Kavanaugh (2). *Five-mile promateur handicap*, — Ives, 150 yards (1), 17.02$\frac{2}{5}$; Rowe, scratch (2); Burnham, 75 yards (3). *One-mile three-minute class*, — W. H. Langdown (1), 3.04$\frac{2}{5}$; Ware (2). *One-mile professional*, — H. J. Crocker (1), 2.59; Woodside (2), Neilson (3). *Three-mile promateur lap*, — Hendee (1), 9.56$\frac{2}{5}$; Stone (2), Kluge (3). *Five-mile open*, — Foster (1) 16.41$\frac{1}{5}$; Langdown (2). *One-mile consolation*, — Brown (1), 3.25; Crist (2).

NEW YORK. — Races under the auspices of the Harlem Wheelmen.

One-mile novice, — Final heat, Joseph W. Whitson (1), 3.25$\frac{3}{4}$; H. Vanderlinden (2). The latter fell at the finish, throwing Whitson, but neither were seriously injured. *One-mile club championship*, — J. W. Powers, Jr. (1), 3.18$\frac{4}{5}$; E. J. Halsted (2). *Three-mile State championship*, — A. B. Rich (1), 11.02$\frac{1}{4}$; A. F. Edmans (2). *Two-mile record*, — A. B. Rich (1), 1$\frac{1}{2}$ miles. *Four hundred and forty yards one-legged race*, — E. J. Halsted (1), .59$\frac{1}{2}$; Edmans (2). *One-mile 3.10 class*, — Final heat, E. J. Halsted (1), 3.28. *One-mile Morrisania Wheelmen championship*, — W. A. Carpenter (1), 3.45; H. B. Hanford (2). *Two-mile handicap*, — Final heat, A. F. Edmans, 125 yards (1), 6 40$\frac{1}{2}$; C. R. Hoag, 40 yards (2). *Half-mile without hands*, — A. F. Edmans (1), 1.42$\frac{1}{2}$; T. W. Roberts (2).

The closing event was the most interesting race of the day. It was a team race between the Harlem and Kings County Wheelmen. A. B. Rich and E. Valentine won for the Brooklyn team. The prize was a very large silver cup.

ROSEVILLE TOURNAMENT PROGRAMME.

HARTFORD, CONN., 8 and 9 Sept.— Fall tournament of Connecticut Bicycle Club. Summary of races: —

One-mile Amateur, 3.10 class. — W. L. Prior (1), 2.53¾; H. S. Hart (2); Wm. Harding (3); Chas. W. Ware (4); E. B. Smith (5). H. L. Burdick, of Albany, D. C. Pierce, of Brockton, C. D. Heath, of Lee, Eugene Valentine, of New York, and Chas. Ware, of Marblehead, were protested in this race on the ground that they had records better than 3.10. Pierce and Valentine did not appear. Heath and Burdick admitted the records and were barred. Ware denied that he had such a record and rode under protest.

Leader.	Miles.	M.	S.
William Harding	¼		40½
William Harding	½	1	24¾
William Harding	¾	2	14
W. L. Prior	1	2	53¾

One-mile Promateur, 2.40 class. — F. F. Ives (1), 2.54¼; Horace Crocker (2), 2.54½; Percy W. Stone (3); C. P. Adams (4); C. E. Kluge (5).

Leader.	Miles.	M.	S.
F. F. Ives	¼		54
C. E. Kluge.	½	1	36½
C. E. Kluge	¾	2	19
F. F. Ives	1	2	54¼

Three-mile Professional. — Fred Wood (1), 8.59½; W. M. Woodside (2), 8.59¾; R. Neilson (3); John S. Prince (4); C. F. Frazier (5).

Leader.	Miles.	M.	S.
R. Neilson	1	3	01
Robert James	2	6	06½
F. Wood	3	8	59½

Quarters, first mile: 46, 1.33½, 2.18½.

One-mile Promateur, A. C. U. Championship. — Geo. M. Hendee (1), 2.38¾; W. A. Rhodes (2), 2.50½; C. P. Adams (3). Best record for track: —

Leader.	Miles.	M.	S.
Adams	¼		37¼
Hendee	½	1	19
Hendee	¾	2	01
Hendee	1	2	38¾

Two-mile Amateur Handicap. — H. S. Hart, 200 yards (1), 5.41¼; E. A. DuBlois, 60 yards (2), 5.41¾; Fred Foster, 15 yards (3); A. B. Rich, 15 yards (4); W. E. Crist, 30 yards (5); E. B. Smith, 200 yards (6); H. L. Burdick, 75 yards (7); C. D. Heath, 60 yards (8); P. S. Brown, 30 yards (9); C. W. Ware, 150 yards (10); Gaskell was put down for scratch man, but he did not start. No full-mile time was taken.

Leader.	Miles.	M.	S.
William Harding	½	1	13
William Harding	1	2	44
Howard S. Hart	2	5	41¼

One-mile Promateur Tricycle. — E. P. Burnham (1), 3.09½; F. F. Ives (2), 3.10; C. E. Kluge (3). The times made in this take the promateur tricycle record.

Leader.	Miles.	M.	S.
E. P. Burnham	¼		56
E. P. Burnham	½	1	45¼
E. P. Burnham	¾	2	34
E. P. Bnrnham	1	3	09½

Three-mile Amateur. — Fred. Foster (1), 9.15; A. B. Rich (2), 9.15¼; E. A. DuBlois (3); P. S. Brown (4); W. H. Langdown (5).

Leader.	Miles.	M.	S.
Langdown	1	3	15
Langdown	2	6	30
Foster	3	9	15

Quarters, first mile: 46¼, 1.37, 2.29, 3.15.

Ten-mile Promateur Lap. — W. A. Rowe (1), 30 57½, 38 points; W. A. Rhodes (2), 31.05, 32 points; P. W. Stone (0), 6 points; C. E. Kluge (0), 3 points. Four starters and two at the finish.

Leader.	Miles.	M.	S.
W. A. Rowe	1	2	58
W. A. Rowe	2	5	57
W. A. Rowe	3	9	02
W. A. Rowe	4	12	11½
W. A. Rhodes	5	15	16½
W. A. Rowe	6	18	26
W. A. Rhodes	7	21	37
W. A. Rowe	8	24	43
W. A. Rowe	9	27	53½
W. A. Rowe	10	30	57½

Quarters, first mile: 46½, 1.33, 2.21, 2.58.

Summary of points: First man counts four; second man counts three.

Rowe.	Rhodes.	Stone.	Kluge.
4	3	2	1
4	3	2	1
4	3	2	1
4	3	—	—
3	4	6	3
4	3		
3	4		
4	3		
4	3		
4	3		
—	—		
38	32		

One-mile Team Race. — Hartford Wheel Club (1), 11 points; East Hartford Wheel Club (2), 10 points. DeBlois, of the H. W. C., finished first in 2.50½; Bidwell, of the E. H. W. C., was second. There were six entries, and the first man scored six points. The points were made as follows: H. W. C., 6, 4, 1 = 11; E. H. W. C., 5, 3, 2 = 10.

SECOND DAY.

One-mile Handicap, Hartford Wheel Club. — G. C. Dresser, 170 yards (1), 2.41¾; E. A. DeBlois, scratch (2), 2.42½; G. C. Pratt, 170 yards (3); H. H. Chapman, 170 yards (4); Wm. Harding, 50 yards (5); M. A. Norton, 200 yards (6); H. K. Lee, 200 yards (7); Henry Goodman, 170 yards (8). DeBlois' time by quarters: 38½; 1.20¼; 2.3¾; 2.42½.

One-mile Promateur. — W. A. Rowe (1), 2.40; F. F. Ives (2), 2.41½; P. W. Stone (3); W. A. Rhodes (4); C. E. Kluge (5); C. P. Adams (6).

Leader.	Miles.	M.	S.
Charles P. Adams	¼	0	40
Charles P. Adams	½	1	21½
C. E. Kluge	¾	2	07¼
W. A. Rowe	1	2	40

Three-mile Professional Handicap. — F. Wood, scratch (1), 2.33; R. A. Neilson, 25 yards (2), 2.33¼; W. M. Woodside, 15 yards (3); W. J. Morgan, 110 yards (4); R. James, 25 yards (5); F. T. Merrill, 125 yards (6); C. F. Frazier, 60 yards (7). The fastest time ever made in competition.

Three-mile Promateur Tricycle. — E. P. Burnham (1), 9.30½; F. F. Ives (2), 9.31. As there were but two starters, a time limit was fixed. The officials notified the men that there would be but one prize unless 10.05 was beaten. All the promateur tricycle records to three miles fell to Burnham in this race: —

Leader.	Miles.	M.	S.
E. P. Burnham	1	3	11
E. P. Burnham	2	6	30
E. P. Burnham	3	9	30½

Quarters, first mile: .50, 1.37, 2.24, 3.11.

One-mile Amateur. — A. B. Rich (1), 2.46½; H. W. Gaskell (2), 2.48; C. D. Heath (3). Brown, Crist, and Foster collided and fell.

Leader.	Mile.	M.	S.
Charles D. Heath	¼		44
Charles D. Heath	½	1	22¼
Charles D. Heath	¾	2	03
A. B. Rich	1	2	46½

Five-mile Professional Lap. — W. M. Woodside (1), 15.59, twenty-three points; R. A. Neilson (2), 15-59¼, seventeen points; W. J. Morgan (3), sixteen points. Five starters. Summary of points.

Woodside.	Neilson.	Morgan.	Wood.
5	4	2	3
4	3	2	5
4	3	5	2
5	3	4	—
5	4	3	10
—	—	—	
23	17	16	

Two-mile Amateur Tandem. — Crist and Brown (1), 5.58¼; Bidwell and Jackson (2), 6.22. Only two men came to the scratch. They were told that the race must be won in 6.10 or no prize.

Leader.	Miles.	M.	S.
Bidwell and Jackson	¼	0	44¾
Crist and Brown	½	1	29¾
Crist and Brown	¾	2	14
Crist and Brown	1	3	
Crist and Brown	2	5	58¼

Five-mile Promateur. — G. M. Hendee (1), 16.7½; W. A. Rhodes (2), 16.10½; E. P. Burnham (0).

Leader.	Miles.	M.	S.
W. A. Rhodes	1		
W. A. Rhodes	2	6	12½
W. A. Rhodes	3	9	31¾
W. A. Rhodes	4	12	55
G. M. Hendee	5	16	07½

Quarters, first mile: 42¾, 1.27, 2:12, 2 59½.

Five-mile Conn. Championship. — H. S. Hart (1), 17.08; E. A. DeBlois (2), 17.8½; Wm. Harding (3); W. L. Prior (4).

Leader.	Miles.	M.	S.
William Harding	1	3	26
E. A. DeBlois	2	6	46¾
William Harding	3	10	11
William Harding	4	13	50¾
H. S. Hart	5	17	08

Quarters, first mile: 56, 1.46, 2.50.

One Mile Consolation. — W. H. Langdown (1), 3, 4; C. D. Heath (2), 3, 9; E. B. Smith (3); D. C. Pierce (4); H. K. Lee (5); Charles Lee Myers (6).

NOTES.

The tournament was a success. The absence of the English riders was not seriously felt.

Lester and Alden gave exhibitions of fancy riding each day. They used the Star machine and wooden buggy wheels.

England was represented on the Board of Officials in the person of A. Kennedy-Child.

Secretary-Editor Aaron was present each day on the judges' stand, and was as conspicuous as it is possible for such a little fellow to be.

The grand stand was a scene of great beauty. Hartford has more pretty girls to the square inch than any city in America, always excepting Boston, of course.

The clubhouses were opened each evening, and the festive punch bowl was set out. The punch was very good, so we were told.

The "boys" are not slow to give names to visiting wheelmen. The New Zealand was called the "Cannibal," and Merrill, of Oregon, was the "Pacific Slop."

Fred Wood makes friends wherever he goes, and his great record of 2.33 was received with loud applause.

The "Duffers'" races, so called, are always the most interesting of such occasions. The State championship created more enthusiasm than any event of the tournament, and Hart, the winner, was carried to his tent on the shoulders of his friends.

Langdown came 16,000 miles, and won the consolation race. He needed consolation, if aby one did.

The defeat of Rich, by Foster, was one of the interesting events of the tournament. These two were looked upon as the rivals for first honors in the amateur events of the fall tournaments.

Our old friend Gaskell made one of his old-time spurts, and took second place in a race, the second day. He was on a Columbia racer.

The storm of the second day deprived the audience of the pleasure of seeing Rowe run a mile against time. He was down for this on the programme of the second day, but when the time came for the event, the track was soft and muddy and he did not run.

Knapp has withdrawn from the Columbia team and gone to Denver.

The crowds expected to see Rowe and Hendee in competition, and there was much dissatisfaction that they did not meet. They had no intention of meeting.

Hendee likes to be one-mile champion. Having been barred from that place in the L. A. W., he has taken it in the A. C. U.

Postponements of the trotting meeting had deferred its end until Saturday, and the club did not have sufficient time to prepare the track. It was in fair condition only.

The parade on the morning of the first day was quite successful, 211 wheelmen being in line. The Connecticut Club turned out 26 men, Hartford Wheel Club 49, East Hartford 24, and Danbury, Bridgeport, New Haven, Bristol, Winsted, and Springfield sent delegations. There were fifty unattached men in line. The parade was under the chief marshalship of Chief Consul Charles G. Huntington. The prizes for the parade were awarded as follows: For the club with the largest number of men in line, first prize, Hartford Wheel Club. For best appearance, the Poquonnock Club. For the best proportionate representation, the Waterbury Club. For the largest non-league organization, the East Hartford Club.

Crocker was protested by Kluge, on the ground that he was a professional. He offered in evidence that Crocker was a paid trainer and coacher for Burnham. This was clearly established and Crocker was disqualified. As he had not entered for any of the professional races, he was thrown out of the tournament.

Cycling journalism was represented by Charles Lee Myers of *Outing* and *Recreation*. He won no prizes.

It was very evident that Frazier was in too fast company. We seldom saw him come in last in the old days. He may come up yet.

The timing was done by Col. Henry Kennedy, F. G. Whitmore, George Best, and E. Y. Judd.

Prince is having a Columbia racer set up for his use at Springfield.

Ware was protested in the 3.10 class race on the ground that he made a mile at Boston, 5 July, in 1.55. The best mile time made in Boston on that day was 3.15, and Ware's time was 3.20. Ware's best time at Montreal was 3.20½.

The rain of the second day came at a very bad time, for it poured down in torrents just before the races were advertised to commence, and many were kept at home.

Mr. George H. Day, of the Weed Sewing Machine Company, hired the upper story of the judges' stand for the second day, and filled it with ladies and gentlemen.

Stephen Terry, Esq., took a party of newspaper men about Hartford the second day and showed them the sights. They were Editor Aaron, of the *Bulletin*, Mr. C. S. Howard, of the *Globe*, and "We."

The amateur photographer was on hand. Mr. W. W. Stall, of Boston, secured a number of views of the starts, and Mr. C. L. Myers, of New York, also took a number.

The Hartford boys are generous hosts, and they did their "greatest utmost" to make everybody happy. The happiness was at its height with some of the guests at about midnight on the first day.

THE Pittsfield races gave us a few surprises. Neilson and Crocker won over Woodside; and Ives, with a handicap of 150 yards, beat Rowe.

Special dispatch to CYCLE. San Francisco, 10 Sept.—Three-mile National Championship won by F. D. Elwell, Bay City Wheelmen, 9.46; R. M. Welch, Chief Consul.

FRED LEES won the 10,000 metre (about 6¼ miles) race at Christiania, Norway, 29 August, in 18.10¼, beating with all the other competitors world's record at this distance, 18.26. The winner defeated Du Bois by half a second. Fenlon won the amateur international events, 1,609 metres and 10,000 metres.

DAN G. KIRSHBAUM, of Burlington, Ia., writes: "I have just returned from the Iowa Division tour, from Des Moines to Spirit Lake, a distance of 211 miles, and can say that the Rudge Light Roadster stands the racket as well, if not better, than the heavier machines. I have had my wheel for nearly a year, and have not paid out a cent for repairs."

ENGLISH RECORDS.

THE English record sheet is being revised very rapidly, and scarcely a week passes that we do not see new figures taking the place of the old. Our latest English exchanges give us the following: Long Eaton, 24 August, Gatehouse on a tricycle against time, — Quarter, .40s.; half, 1.19; three quarters, 2 minutes; mile, 2.41⅗; beating all records. Afterwards he made a flying quarter in 36⅘.

LONG EATON, 24 August. — Percy Furnivall against time on a bicycle. Quarter, .37; half, 1.15⅘; three quarters, 1.51⅕; mile, 2.30; breaking all records. Afterwards a flying quarter in 35⅕ seconds.

SURBITON, 28 August. — Annual fifty-mile championship of Surrey Club. A walk-over for C. Potter. Records broken from twenty-eight miles up as follows: —

28	1	27	55⅘	40	2	7	48⅗
29	1	31	9⅘	41	2	11	9⅕
30	1	34	22⅘	42	2	14	28⅖
31	1	37	38⅘	43	2	17	49⅕
32	1	41	2⅕	44	2	21	14⅕
33	1	44	20⅕	45	2	24	28⅖
34	1	47	41⅕	46	2	27	53⅗
35	1	51	6⅘	47	2	31	13⅕
36	1	54	29⅖	48	2	34	44⅗
37	1	57	58⅕	49	2	38	17
38	2	1	18⅗	50	2	41	40⅗
39	2	4	36⅕				

Record for two hours, thirty-seven miles, 1,010 yards. Best previous fifty-mile record, 3.11.15.

LONG EATON, 26 August. — George Gatehouse against time on a tricycle. The following record was made. All the times above one mile beat the record.

MILES.	TIME. M. S.	EACH MILE. M. S.	PREVIOUS RECORD. H. M. S.
1	2 50⅕	2 50⅕	0 2 41⅗
2	5 37⅖	2 47⅕	0 6 17
3	8 30⅘	2 53⅖	0 9 38⅗
4	11 26⅘	2 56	0 13 3
5	14 27⅗	3 0⅘	0 16 19
6	17 25⅗	2 58	0 19 35
7	20 16⅘	2 51⅕	0 22 54
8	23 15⅘	2 59	0 26 9
9	26 25⅖	3 9⅗	0 29 23
10	29 26⅕	3 0⅘	0 32 33⅗
11	32 24⅗	2 58⅖	0 37 26
12	35 24⅕	2 59⅗	0 40 51
13	38 24⅘	3 0⅗	0 44 19
14	41 23⅘	2 59	0 47 45⅗
15	44 23⅘	3 0	0 51 4
16	47 16⅗	2 52⅘	0 54 34
17	50 18⅕	3 1⅗	0 57 58
18	53 22⅕	3 4	1 1 35
19	56 15⅘	2 53⅗	1 5 11⅗
20	59 10⅗	2 54⅘	1 8 42

Records for one hour, twenty miles, four hundred and sixty yards, six inches.

COVENTRY, 27 August. — A. P. Engleheart against time on a safety. The times are best on record for England, but they do not equal the American record except for the twenty miles. Weber's record for twenty miles is 59.46.

MILES.	M.	S.	MILES.	M.	S.
¼	0	46⅗	10	29	55⅗
½	1	27	11	32	52
¾	2	10	12	35	54
1	2	54	13	38	55
2	5	50⅖	14	41	54⅖
3	8	48	15	44	55
4	11	47	16	47	53⅖
5	14	46⅗	17	50	48
6	17	48⅖	18	53	44
7	20	51	19	56	39
8	23	53	20	59	27
9	26	54⅖			

BIGGLESWADE, 31 August. — Sidney Lee against time, on the road, riding a tricycle. Five miles, 16.50; ten miles, 34.34; twenty miles, 1.8.15; fifty miles, 3.9.15. The machine, a Beeston Humber, weighed thirty-six pounds, and was geared to sixty-four inches.

W. A. ILLSTON made a flying quarter mile at Jarrow, 28 Aug., in 34⅘. This beats Furnivall's Long Eaton record.

TWENTY miles in the hour on a tricycle is now an accomplished fact.

MORRIS and Taylor, of England, have made twenty miles on a tandem in 1.00.52⅘.

TWENTY miles in the hour has been ridden on a tricycle by G. Gatehouse. See record elsewhere.

LENOX, who started from Land's End to make a record to John o' Groat's, was run down by a drunken trooper and seriously injured.

THE North Road Cycle Club organized a mixed road race for 100 miles, and run it on the Great North Road 28 August last. The tricycles started at 11.20 A. M., the tandems at 11.25, and the bicycles, ordinary and safety, at 11.30. E. Hale, on a Premier safety, finished first, in 7.3.44. J. H. Adams and R. V. Asbury, on a tandem, were second, in 7.29.5. Nobbs, on an ordinary, was third. Sidney Lee was the first tricycler to arrive, and his time was 8.29.48. The best bicycle record is 6.39.5, and the tricycle record is 7.35.

COMING EVENTS.

SEPTEMBER.

18 Saturday. — Races of Associated Clubs at Allegheny City, Penn.

Races of Passaic County Wheelmen, at Clifton, N. J.

Fall race-meeting of K. C. W., at Brooklyn, N. Y. Entries to C. Schwalbach, 124 Penn street, Brooklyn. Close 11 September.

Races at So. Worcester, Mass.

Races of Owl Cycling Club at Chicago, Ill.

21 Tuesday. — Races by R. I. Division, at Providence, R. I.

Races of Wyoming (Pa.) Wheelmen, at Ag'l Fair.

21, 22, 23 Tuesday–Thursday. — Bicycle races at Junction City, Kansas. Apply to Charles S. Davis, Junction City, Kansas.

Races at Queen's County Fair, Mineola, L. I.

22, 23, Wednesday, Thursday. — Races of the Winona (Minn.) Club, and meet of Minnesota Division, on the 22d, five-mile N. W. championship; 23d, twenty-mile L. A. W. championship.

23, 24, 25 Thursday–Saturday. — Fall tournament of Lynn Track Association, at Glenmere Park, Lynn, Mass.; three days.

27 Monday. — Races by Indianapolis (Ind.) A. A. Address C. F. Smith, 114 No. Penn street, Indianapolis, Ind.

28 Tuesday. — Kansas L. A. W. division meet and races, Junction City, Kan.

Second day of Indianapolis races. Pope Cup race.

30 Thursday. — First day of tournament of New Jersey Cycling and Athletic Association, at Roseville Station, Newark, N. J. Apply to Frederic Jenkins, manager, Oraton Hall, Newark, N. J.

OCTOBER.

1 and 2 Friday, Saturday. — Second and third days of tournament at Newark. Apply to Fred Jenkins.

1 Friday. — Illuminated parade of wheelmen at St. Louis, Mo. J. S. Rogers, care of *American Wheelman*, St. Louis.

1, 2 Friday, Saturday. — Inter-State meet at St. Louis, Mo. Apply to J. S. Rogers.

2 Saturday. — Road races of Dorchester Club.

Annual 100-mile road race of Boston Bicycle Club.

MISCELLANEOUS

Advertisements will be inserted in this column for one cent a word, including heading and address; but no advertisement will be taken for less than twenty-five cents.

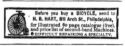

The Cycle.

Vol. I., No. 26.   BOSTON, MASS., 24 SEPTEMBER, 1886.   Five Cents.

THE CYCLE

PUBLISHED EVERY FRIDAY BY ABBOT BASSETT, 22 SCHOOL ST., ROOM 19.

Vol. I.   BOSTON, MASS., 24 SEPTEMBER, 1886.   No. 26.

TERMS OF SUBSCRIPTION.

One Year, by mail, post-paid...........................$1.50
Three Copies in one order..............................3.00
Club Subscriptions......................................1.00
Six Months...90
Single Copies..05

Specimen Copies free.

Every bicycle dealer is agent for the Cycle and authorized to receive subscriptions at regular rates. The paper can be found on sale at the following places:—,

Boston, Cupples, Upham & Co., cor. Washington and School Streets. Tremont House news stand. At every cycle warehouse.

New York, Elliott Mason, 12 Warren Street.

Philadelphia, H. B. Hart, 811 Arch Street. George D. Gideon, 6 South Broad Street.

Baltimore, S. T. Clark & Co., 4 Hanover Street.

Chicago, W. M. Durell, 115 Wabash Avenue. John Wilkinson & Co., 77 State Street.

Washington, H. S. Owen, Capital Cycle Co.

St. Louis, St. Louis Wheel Co., 1121 Olive Street.

ABBOT BASSETT . . . . Editor

A. Mudge & Son, Printers, 24 Franklin St., Boston

All communications should be sent in not later than Tuesday, to ensure insertion the same week.

Entered at the Post-office as second-class mail matter.

The Springfield tournament has once more passed into history, and left its lessons behind. What are these lessons? Let us take counsel together and see.

First of all, it is generally admitted that the promateur class will have a very short existence. There are but few riders in its ranks, and it gains few converts. There will be but two classes of riders in the very near future.

Open races must go, and men who are fair competitors, one with another, must be brought together by a system of handicapping or classification. The clubs that hold race meetings must bring about this change.

Springfield is no longer the only place where one can see a large field of the best riders. New York wheelmen have now a Roseville, and Boston has the Lynn track. We did not see, as in former years, large delegations from these cities. Cycle racing will soon be reduced to a business basis, and big booms can no longer be expected.

It is not necessary to have the Englishmen at the tournaments to make them a success. Springfield and Hartford have shown us that we can succeed without them.

Championship races, with two starters, are a mistake. Neither man desires to make the pace, and all the men say that the one who does so rides to lose.

Classification will put men of equal, or nearly equal, powers together. At Springfield there were many men in the open races that had no possible chance to win, and they merely encumbered the track. Merrill, Morgan, and James would give us a good race if pitted against one another, but they were over-matched in races with Wood, Woodside, and Neilson from scratch, and they seldom finished. Such men as Hall, Myers, and Langdown had no chance with Rich, Foster, and Crist, and their presence on the track only increased the liability to accident. Class races will settle this thing.

We have no faith in the efficacy of the rule which imposes a fine of ten dollars on men for loafing, and we believe it should be used only in flagrant cases, and then the men should have warning. The rule was used at Springfield in one case without warning. There was no excuse for the exhibition which Neilson and James gave, and after that, the riders in the championship were notified that they must make the mile in less than three minutes or be fined. With men who are obliged to qualify for a race with a record of 2.45, a limit of three minutes is not a hardship, and this will give them ample opportunity for tactics.

On general principles, however, we do not believe it is fair for the referee to tell the men how to run their race. As many races are won by the head as by the legs, and competitors should be allowed to ride as they please within certain limits. Those limits should be carefully drawn by the referee, and therefore one more reason for a careful choice of this official is added, to those which already exist. We believe, however, that a time limit would work to better advantage than the fine.

The time limit was used to good advantage at Hartford and Springfield. When the number of starters was equal to the number of prizes, and one man had a walkover, the referee put a time limit within which the last man must come in order to get his prize. This made a fast race, and it

saved a loafing exhibition by the weaker riders, who would otherwise be sure of a prize.

Our thanks are due the Springfield Club for courtesies extended, and for very many friendly and generous acts.

Dr. Blackham replies to what we said anent his resolutions. We still contend that our interpretation of them was a fair one from the text, and we do not think that they bear out what he says that he intended they should. Had he put his ideas before the Board just as he puts them in his letter to us, we should have offered no opposition, but should have said the question is a fair one, and the Board had better decide it. We cannot see behind the words of the Doctor's resolutions the ideas that he gives us in his letter published this week.

CYCLETS.

The records were too low to be disturbed much.

The tournaments have showed us a good crop of amateurs thus far.

The Holly Springs (Miss.) *South* is publishing a series of interesting papers descriptive of Europe and its peoples by a correspondent who is doing that country on a bicycle.

Messrs. Hemingway and Persons, two Jackson, Miss., bicyclists, recently rode from that place to West Station in the same State, a distance of sixty-eight miles, in some eight or ten hours. Any one who is at all acquainted with Southern roads knows that this is a good day's travel.

Herbert S. Owen, of Washington, has returned from his English tour.

Thomas Stevens has arrived at Delhi. He must be passing a Delhightful time.

Joseph Powell, of Smithville, N. J., met with an accident, 8 Sept., in a race at Freehold. A policeman's horse became frightened, and ran on to the track just in front of Powell, as he was finishing a race. Both men and the horse were thrown, and seriously injured.

F. B. Collins, of the Brooklyn Bicycle Club, made a road record of two hundred and two miles in twenty-four hours, on 11 September.

Frazier is to go to England along with Morgan and Woodside. They will try the English cracks on their own tracks.

The *Cyclist* has no idea that England will make an intermediate class of riders.

The meet of the California Division was eminently successful. There was a parade

and races. Over a hundred wheelmen, representing nearly every city on the coast, rode in the line to the park. During the races in the afternoon, Mr. F. E. Van Merbeeke, who recently rode from New York to San Francisco, was introduced to the audience, and gave an exhibition ride around the park.

BEFORE the New Zealander is Lang down this way, we 'll teach him to ride fast.

AT the September meeting of the Orange Wanderers, held last week, certain resolutions were offered, asking for the repeal of the Orange and West Orange ordinances, and proposing others in their places. These resolutions were rejected by a decisive majority. As the club, however, is not, and has never been, perfectly satisfied with the form of the ordinances, it was voted to record its disapproval on its minutes. It was also ordered that a committee be appointed to prepare resolutions to be presented at the October meeting of the club, looking toward the modification or amendment of the ordinances.

HAL GREENWOOD, of St. Louis, Mo., has been playing with Corey Hill. He rode up and coasted down, and then repeated the performance three times. Then he went over and rode up the other side once or twice for the fun of the thing. He showed Doane, of Dorchester, how to do it, and then Doane climbed the hill.

THE Capital Club, of Washington, has issued a pamphlet containing the history of the club, the rules, list of officers, etc.

STALL tells us that the picture of the cycling journalists at Springfield was a failure. So many good-looking men, the camera could n't take in at one time.

BABY, the French tricyclist, has ridden a distance of 1,056 kilometres or 660 miles in 5d. 1oh. 17s.

WM. STARLEY, of England, has made a tricycle with 96-inch wheels. Mr. Sturmey has ridden it, and says it runs easily and goes up hill with very little exertion for the rider.

HOWELL will try for some records on the Coventry track. He is in prime condition, and will no doubt show us some good figures. Fred Lees has gone to Norway.

THE readers of the C. T. C. *Gazette* are exchanging ideas regarding the best means to employ to rid themselves of the 'nuisance of barking and biting dogs. A Mr. Shea suggests a mammoth torpedo whose explosion will frighten any cur out of a seven weeks' growth, and he adds that it will not make a small boy happy if used against him. H. N. Green condemns the ammonia squirt suggested by a previous writer, says he is a friend of the dogs, and threatens to sue any wheelman that attacks a dog with the squirt. Another writer thinks torpedoes would do, and still another suggests blank cartridges.

THE new badge of the C. T. C. is an exact copy of the League badge with a change of initials. The *Gazette* says: "Those of our readers who are conversant with matters Transatlantic will recognize in the new badge illustrated upon another page a striking resemblance, as far as the front is concerned, to those of the League of American Wheelmen and the Canadian Wheelmen's

Association. The similarity is intentional, and is a complimentary acknowledgment of the fact, that starting into life much later than the C. T. C., and consequently possessing the benefit of other people's experience, both the bodies referred to had the good taste to adopt a design — a flying wheel — truly symbolical of the sport. Although the new badge is sufficiently significant to be at once recognized by the *cognoscenti*, it is not so unblushingly candid that our members will object — as they have occasionally in the past — to become walking advertisements among the general public for the club's sake."

CAPT. CHARLES E. GATES, of the Chautauqua *Wheelman*, Gerry, N. Y., has completed his long tour from western New York to Lake Minnetonka, Minn., and is now stopping with his brother, O. S. Gates, at Excelsior, Minn. He started 2 July, and stopped off four weeks at different places on the road to visit friends and take in some of the cities. The wheel ridden throughout the trip was a 48-inch Star, weighing forty-five pounds, which was rather light for such roads as he toured over. The routes were accurately preserved, and will appear in the New York and other State books. Total distance ridden by wheel, 1,060 miles; by cars, 250, and but few miles of walking.

HOWARD S. HART, of New Britain, son of William H. Hart, president of the Stanley Works, won first prize in the two-mile bicycle race at Hartford, second in the one-mile and on Thursday took first prize in the five-mile, all of course, being in the amateur classes. When he went home to New Britain, Thursday evening, there was a great turnout of his friends. The met him at the depot with a carriage and a band, put him into the carriage with the wheel he had won for one of his prizes on Wednesday, and escorted him home in triumph, with much burning of rockets and Roman candles and much cheering.

A NEW danger has been added to touring, if we are to judge from a communication which has been received by us from an East London rider. This gentleman, touring with a friend on a tricycle, recently put up at an inn at Chatham for the night, where they were well housed and treated; but on going to the stables next morning, where the machine had been left, they found that some persons had, in the night, abstracted all the balls from their main bearings. A looker-on, of hang-dog aspect, suggested that a "pal" of his had some little steel balls which he thought might fit in the bearings; but the cyclists thinking that probably he himself, or his "pal," was the miscreant, decided to do without them, "even if they had to wheel the machine home." This brings matters back to the old coaching times, when "pals" of peripatetic highwaymen hung about inn yards and pulled lynch pins out of post-chaises. Since the foregoing experience, the above-mentioned tourists have always left their tricycle over night at the nearest railway cloak-room. All the same, the proprietor of the stables where they left their machine was responsible for the damage. — *Cyclist.*

GEO. DAKIN, who fell at Ithica, has so far recovered from his injuries, that he has returned to his home in Buffalo.

AT the Cleveland races, George Collister and J. T. Huntington broke the one-quarter and one-half mile tandem record, on a Rudge Humber tandem, making the one-quarter in 43½ sec., and the one-half in 1.24.

MR. W. B. SAYLOR, of Bordentown, N. J., writes: "Received the American Rudge yesterday morning, in good condition, and I, as well as my customer, like it better than any I have yet seen."

DOGS.

A PERSON who takes a dog to a bicycle track renders himself liable to nothing less than downright manslaughter. And a heavy penalty should be inflicted upon any individual whose carelessness or thick-headedness causes him to let a dog loose on a track where racing men are at practice. Saturday afternoon, as Heath of Lee was coming down the straight, a dog crossed the track directly in front of his wheel. Fortunately he was riding a Star; otherwise he would have received serious if not fatal injuries. The front wheel struck the dog a terrible blow in the neck, which caused the machine to sway and wobble all over the track. Heath showed himself possessed of good staying powers, and was able to prevent a bad fall, controlling his machine long enough to enable him to strike on his feet. The small wheel had been knocked badly out of gear, and the whole machine badly wrenched. Just behind Heath at the moment of the accident was Percy Stone, who, by what seemed a miracle, succeeded in safely dodging both the dog and Heath. Following Stone were Frazier, Merrill, Woodside, Hall, and several others who had time enough to slow up and avoid bad headers. Had the men been bunched as closely as a few minutes previously, and going at the same rate of speed, nothing could have prevented a most terrible accident, as all would have gone together in a heap. Everybody who saw the accident was highly incensed, and all expressed a wish that the machine had killed the dog. It was noted that the animal immediately disappeared from view. One wheelman was so indignant that he remarked that if he had had a pistol with him, he would have immediately shot the dog. Had he done so, nobody would have blamed him. Only a wheelman can realize the helpless position in which a rider is placed under the circumstances. Going at full speed, if anything crosses his path there is no averting the consequences, which involve possible loss of life, and at the least, serious injury. Persons who own dogs, and do not know enough to leave them at home when visiting a bicycle track, ought to be made to realize that they are jeopardizing human life by so doing. One terrible accident would, of course, open their eyes. But that is learning the lesson at too great a cost. There seems to be no remedy for such cases. The managers of the Springfield tournament have every year forbidden the admission of dogs to the park during racing. But some people, who have more regard for their pets than for the lives of human beings, persist in bringing them to the park, avoiding detection by hiding them in their carriages. The animals eventually get restless and uneasy, and their owners, careless of consequences, let them out to

roam the grounds at will. It would be advisable for the proper authorities to sanction the shooting of any dog seen on the park during the progress of a race. The people can aid the managers by heeding their request to leave their pets at home; but they won't do it, and therefore it seems that summary measures for the suppression of this nuisance would be not only expedient, but justifiable. — *Springfield Union.*

BOTH Mr. B. B. Ayers, tourmaster of the L. A. W., and Mr. G. R. Bidwell, the chief marshal, will use Rudge light roadsters on the L. A. W. tour. Of the sixteen officers of the tour, nine of them are mounted on their Rudge light roadsters.

JOHN'S HOLIDAY TOUR.
(Wheel World.)

YOUNG Mr. John Williamson, who lived with his mother at Daisy Villa, was as pleasant a young cyclist as you would come across in a good day's ride anywhere. He was a young man of a quiet and retiring temperament, and, indeed, in the neighborhood of his mother's residence, the aforesaid Daisy Villa, it was currently reported that half a pound of the best fresh or a quarter of "real Dorset" would not have melted if placed within his mouth. As to the truth of this assertion we cannot vouch, never having tried the experiment; but though a quiet young man, John was by no means a sham cyclist; indeed, he had on one occasion ridden forty-five full miles in the day on his tricycle.

John was also a great man at the church, and at Sunday-school treats, concerts, picnics, magic lantern entertainments, and penny readings he was all there, and every one allowed that in handing round tea, cutting bread and butter or cake, and managing the children, John had but one rival; that rival was one of the opposite sex — Miss Florence Lord, twenty, pretty, and accomplished, and, as the vicar said, "the right-hand man of their church." When an old servant of the church retired from active service, who but Miss Lord collected enough to present him with a handsome testimonial to make glad his heart in his days of ease? If an old lady required piloting to church, or expressed a desire to journey up to London, who but Miss Lord was good enough to take charge of her? and in twenty other departments she was equally invaluable. In short, Florence Lord was the soul of the circle in which she moved. She was the leader of the ladies, John headed the gentlemen.

Strange as it may seem, though they were often brought into close proximity in the course of their duties, they were never much of friends. John was by no means a ladies' man, and somehow or other in that particular young lady's presence was quieter than ever. But still waters run deep, and let me whisper a secret, — John was in love with her; he had been from the first time he met her. It was a clear case of love at first sight.

The manner of their first meeting was this: A grand bazar was held at the church, and John — who had only recently moved into the neighborhood — went on the last evening it was open. He was walking round the hall, looking about on all sides, when a young lady of prepossessing appearance (as the newspaper reports say) came up and asked him to take a share in a raffle for a — baby's cradle, which she held in her arms. Reader, can you imagine what a shock this invitation gave to the sensitive nerves of our friend John? He politely declined to take a chance of securing the valuable prize, and the young lady, who was, of course, no other than Miss Florence Lord, went away to pounce upon some other probable investor.

When John became attached to the church, and occasionally met Miss Lord there, she would often call this little incident to his mind. For instance, at the time of decorating the church for Christmas, John, on the top of a tall pair of steps, said to Miss Lord, who was passing below with a large armful of evergreens, " Miss Lord, might I trouble you to pass me up that hammer?"

"I've a good mind not to," said she — "you would n't go in for my raffle."

Gradually, as their vocations brought them more together, John and the young lady got to be better friends, and by the time he had escorted her home from church several times, and from one or two parties, they quite understood one another. She was keen enough to perceive that under his quiet manner he had many sterling qualities, and he admired the young lady for — well, he did not know what in particular — just because he was in love with her, perhaps. But " he never told his love," and one day, on coming back from his Easter holidays, he wished he had. Miss Lord had gone away with a wealthy family in the country. John made many endeavors to ascertain where she had gone, but was unable to find out. His interest in the church declined from that day, and although he still went on with his Christian duties there, he lacked the fire of old.

Miss Lord had gone, and she had taken John Williamson's heart away with her.

One evening, some months after, when John came home from business, his mother said, as she carved the meat-pie for him, "When are you going to take your holidays?"

John, with his mouth full of pie, replied that he had that day fixed to go in three weeks' time, but where he was going to he had not the slightest idea. The year before he had been to a quiet little watering-place on the South coast, and would in all probability have gone there again had his mother not suggested his making a tour on his tricycle. This was quite a new idea, and John required some little time to thoroughly weigh the *pros* and *cons*.

"The only drawback I can see," said thoughtful Mrs. Williamson, " is the danger of damp sheets. If you do go, John, be sure you sleep between the blankets."

John promised, and at the same time sent his plate up for another help of pie.

"And," continued Mrs. Williamson, "mind what water you drink when you are out. Perhaps you had better get a pocket filter; and be sure and not to drink when you are hot."

And so she went on, until John suggested she should save up her cautions till he had finally settled whether he would go or not. All next day at the office, he was thinking the matter over, and making calculations as to the probable cost per day, etc., and by the evening he had quite decided to go.

"Well, my dear," said his mother, "what are you going to do?"

John replied that he had decided to go, and produced his calculations, etc., which mother and son went into at once. That finished, John went out and borrowed an armful of maps and road books to sketch out his course by. He had got a fortnight at his disposal, and proposed to do about forty miles per day for the first three days down to a well-known seaside resort, stay there a week or so, making runs in the neighborhood, and then ride back.

(To be continued.)

DR. BLACKHAM SPEAKS.

Editor CYCLE: — I am not insensible to the compliment of having two thirds of your first page devoted to my demolition. I object, however, to some of your conclusions as not being justified by anything contained in the resolutions you so sharply criticise.

1st. Your conclusion that the doctor would have the League assert jurisdiction over walking, running, jumping, etc., is erroneous. I have no desire to see the League take note of these matters, and purposely limited the jurisdiction to "cycling athletics in the United States." This does *not* mean that the League should take jurisdiction over professional races. It never had such jurisdiction and has no business with it anyhow. As to the promateurs — so called — I have nothing to say. Either a man *is* an amateur, or he is *not*. If he is not, the League has nothing to do with him save to keep him from contaminating the League amateurs.

Your statement that " the doctor would have the League indorse the breaking of the laws of the land," is unworthy of you, as you know it is not true. The League has no more to do with road racing that it has with burglary or petty larceny. If the League does not see fit to expel men for the former kind of law-breaking, as it doubtless would for either of the two latter forms, — it can just ignore it, refuse to enter records for it, and treat competing with or pace-making for a professional on a road race same as if it were a private trial, *i. e.* pay no attention to it at all.

Yes, " the doctor would allow a man to compete with a professional or for a money prize at a meeting held under C. T. C. or A. C. U. or N. A. A. A. rules, and would have the action of these societies ignored if the man was disqualified. Just exactly so if the meeting took place in the U. S. A. If in England or any of the British possessions then the action of the C. T. C. or N. C. U., or other British society, would be of effect. But all this does not say that our Racing Board should not take cognizance of such acts on the part of cyclers if done here. It could still take up each of these cases and suspend or expel just as if the A. C. U. or N. A. A. A. was not in existence. My only contention is that it should not be bound nor influenced by their action. I have no objection to the N. A. A. A. legislating for runners, jumpers, skaters, stand-on-their-headers, and all sorts and conditions of amateur circus actors, so long as it don't interfere with the cyclers, or as the League quietly ignores such interference if attempted.

I am equally well pleased to have the A. C. U. legislate for the non-amateur cyclers, but I don't want the League to surrender its

jurisdiction over an amateur, and thus deprive him of the benefits of League membership at the bidding of, or because of any action of, the A. C. U.

What I aim at in these resolutions is simply that the League shall assert its rights over its own membership, try any cases of violations of its laws with its own tribunals, and not deprive a man of his rights as a League member upon the say-so or action of a society to which the said member may never have given his adhesion.

GEO. E. BLACKHAM, L. A. W. 464,
Representative for N. Y.
DUNKIRK, N. Y., 18 Sept., '86.

MEMPHIS.

I WILL begin my letter by saying to the many readers of the CYCLE, who live in this city and the South, that they hear from me quite often, at least once a month, and I hope they will use their influence to induce their fellow-wheelmen to subscribe for it.

* * *

Do you know, Mr. Editor, that the CYCLE is the best liked of any of the cycling weekly papers? The subscribers and non-subscribers are always asking for the CYCLE; if it's a day behind, the first question you get the CYCLE?" The CYCLE is also looked on as *authority* here, on any and all matters pertaining to the wheel.

* * *

MEMPHIS feels highly honored, and that deservedly so. The Springfield Bicycle Club asked their president, W. L., Surprise, to act as one of the judges at their coming tournament. It is regretted both by the club and Mr. Surprise that his business would not admit of his absenting himself so long from the city.

* * *

BEFORE this reaches the eye of the public, the great Springfield tournament has come and gone, and with it, no doubt, all the records, at least a majority. The Columbia team are said to be in great shape, and the fight between them and the Overman team will be watched with interest. Which shall it be,— Rowe, Hendee, Knapp, Ives, or Rhodes? This is the all-absorbing question down this way.

* * *

AT a meeting of the Memphis Cycle Club, held Tuesday, 14 Sept., six wheelmen applied for membership, and it is thought that as many more will come into the folds of the club. They have now in prospect the building of a track in a convenient locality, and the fitting up of a club room, which is situated on Adams street, a good thoroughfare, and leads to good roads and pikes in every direction, the streets being paved with macadam now. In the rooms the club proposes to have racks for wheels, locked, a pool table, and other items of interest, which tend to draw the members together during the winter months, having on their tables all the cycling papers and illustrated weeklies. This is the idea as given by the president, and it is hoped they will be carried out.

* * *

THE matter of street pavements is being brought before the public through the columns of the daily *Appeal*. A few days since quite an article appeared, and with it also appeared the letter as published lately in the Philadelphia *Ledger* by Mr. M. C. Meags. The city government is now laying a patch of granite pavement for an experiment, and the only hope of our riders is that they will tear up Main and Second streets and relay them with granite instead of the horrible cobble-stone. I see from the *Bulletin* one of the Chicago riders don't like to ride on granite. My dear sir, it would be a great boon to us to have a good granite pavement on our principal thoroughfares; so, Brother Kennington, you can imagine what we must have, when we say a good granite pavement is so far superior to our cobble-stone, that the former would run like your asphaltum, while the latter would jolt your eye-balls out.

* * *

I WISH to quote at random from a letter received by your correspondent, who went from here by train to Cincinnati, and then intended to wheel to Massillon, Ohio. He says: ". . . We expect to make Springfield to-morrow, about seventy-four miles. The boys tell us that the roads are good, even better than those that they have shown us (around Cincinnati). If they are any better, I don't see how I can stop at Springfield, for nothing short of one hundred and fifty miles will satisfy me. . . We have met a number of the (bicycle) boys, and two of them were out with us yesterday, William Haven and Dave Sammitt. They downed us on the hill climbing. These boys can climb mountains, I believe. The pikes are fine, but I never saw the like of hills. . . . When we started out yesterday, S— (a Memphis lad) took a big header, going down a steep, rocky hill. The boys advised him to dismount, as they did; S— thought would show them how to ride, but he only succeeded in showing them how to take a first-class header. . . . We leave to-morrow (28) for Massillon."

CYCLOS.

MEMPHIS, TENN., 15 Sept. 1886.

MR. HILLIER REPLIES.

THE American Cycle says: "Mr. Hillier is still in doubt regarding American records, and he refuses to credit them. Before Mr. Hillier can qualify as a doubter he should remove the doubt which has been thrown upon his own records for fifty-three and fifty-four miles, and he should also show good reasons for accepting the tricycle records of Lowndes, which were shown to be no records on the evidence of Hillier himself, but which were used by our doubting friend after a lapse of time had caused many to forget his testimony." We were not aware that any-doubt existed concerning the 53 and 54 mile records. The records in question were made in a match carefully checked, clocked by G. P. Coleman, passed by the Records Committee of the N. C. U., and if we are rightly informed, they are tabulated by Mr. Ducker in his recent Annual or Handbook, and no one to our knowledge has ever had a word to say against them. So we can only suppose that they are questioned for the sake of questioning. This does not worry us, as questioning will do them good. As to such ancient history as the Lowndes ten-mile tricycle record, its accuracy was never questioned, but the point was raised as to whether a professional pace-maker who helped

Lowndes had vitiated not the record but the amateur status of the record-maker. The N. C. U. took no action, and Lowndes' record passed into the books, where it remained until Gatehouse erased it.—*Bi.News*.

THE *World* of 29 Jan. 1886, says of the 53-mile record: "In all the published reports of the event in which the record was made, including that of the paper of which Hr. Hillier was editor, the time was given as 3.3.26. We have heard no reason assigned for a change in the time first reported, but in all the compilations of best times on record by the English press, the record is given as we have it, 3.2.50, and the N. C. U. accepts these figures." The time for 54 miles was reported as 3.7.29, and the tables at the end of the year set it down as 3.6.15. We have asked the English papers repeatedly to explain this change in the figures, but they have failed to do so. (Cyclist, Vol. VI, Page 971.) We throw no doubt on the record. We have asked why the change was made, and Mr. Hillier has failed to answer. Regarding the Lowndes record, Mr. Hillier said in the *Tricyclist* (Vol. II, Page 15): "If the trial was a public one, then Mr. Lowndes infringed the law (Amateur) both in letter and in spirit, by allowing a professional to ride with him. If, on the other hand, the trial was a private one, then no law has been broken; but at the same time, the record cannot be claimed as a public record, and must therefore be put in the same category as the fine private performances of Cortis, Buckley, Whatton, and others, which, though most fully authenticated, cannot be put in the record books for the above reason." Mr. Hillier intimates that the protest against the amateur status of Mr. Lowndes was disallowed because Lowndes would not claim the record, but regarded the trial as a private one. There was no question but that Robert James, a professional, made the pace for Lowndes, and it is a matter of record that Lowndes did not claim the record for fear of losing his status. Why, then, did the N. C. U. enter the records on its books? If they are records, they must be in the professional tables. They cannot exist as amateur records. We still contend that the matter has not been explained.

ST. LOUIS.

OF course you have heard of our "Nocturnal Illuminated Wheelmen's Parade," which occurs on 1 October. The air is full of it here. Let me tell you what was done at the rally, attended last Thursday night by one hundred and fifty local wheelmen. Chairman Cooke's opening address was followed with an oration by Flyingstart Hicks, which had the usual effect of convulsing the crowd, convincing them that success was already secured, and in fact getting them into a state of inflation perfectly appalling. It is now pretty certain that St. Louis will place three hundred men in line. A large fenced enclosure opening upon the asphaltum at 20th and Pine streets has been secured for the week previous to the event, where machines can be kept and decorated. Starting there, the route will wind about the concrete surfaces, then making the usual round of the brilliantly lighted main thoroughfares, 4th street and Broadway, the granite pavements of which will be unsprink-

led; thence back to the asphaltum and disband. Police protection will be amply provided by a platoon of mounted reserves in the van and foot police at the sides. The parade, in charge G. M. Stettinius and aids, will be formed in about this order: After the police the St. John (Mich.) Bicycle Brass Band, 13 men; Missouri Club Flambeau Battalion; Missouri Bicycle Club, in uniform of white flannel; St. Louis Demon Drill Squad, composed of ten riders in Mephistophelean costume, who will form a square about two small trick riders, called the "little devils." A constant shower of sparks will fall upon the red suits of the squad, which Grand Marshal Stettinius claims will excel anything of the sort ever attempted. Next in order will come the Ramblers, Eurotas, Stars, and unattached, in two divisions. which will be intersected by the Humpty Dumpty squad; the Rambler Flambeau Battalion bringing up the rear. Presuming that the minimum number of riders will be three hundred, the parade will stretch to ten squares in length. The general basis of illumination will be a T-shaped upright attached to the head of the wheel, embellished to suit the fancy of the rider; though there are a number of ingenious schemes which have not yet been unfolded, especially those for the adornment of tricycles.

All else is at a practical standstill. Every wheelman in town is in the parade, heart and soul, and a like feeling prevails in Kansas City, where a circular has been issued bearing the legend, "Ho for the St. Louis Wheelmen's Carnival!" Our latchstring is out long and strong, and the slight favor of helping to enlarge the parade will be reciprocated next day by a howling time in the way of road and track racing and a biquet at night, and we will scare you to death on Sunday by showing you the little hills on the De Soto road.

We are kicking violently out here against the present mode of obtaining League uniform. We want them made here instead of New York, and we want the Division secretary to issue the certificate of membership required;

For things have come to a terrible pass
When a man can't wallop his own jack—.

GAS.

OHIO AND THE LAW.

FROM Chief Consul Kirkpatrick's address we extract the following to show what has been done by the Ohio Division to secure the rights of wheelmen: "Four distinct towns in this State have been the subjects of ordinances prohibiting or greatly restricting the use of bicycles on their streets. Under the direction and by the assistance of your officers, the local members of the Division have in each and every case secured the withdrawal of the said ordinances.

"In the town of Lockland a suit was threatened last December growing out of the scaring of a team by one of our members. A course of action was laid out by your proper officers, the result being that the suit was never filed. The fact that the League would back and protect the individual member, together with citations of decisions, convinced the plaintiff that he had no case.

"Later in the year a suit was entered against a member at New Philadelphia. Suit for damage was brought in the amount of $5,000. The division at once took up the case, the result being that the petition of the plaintiff was denied, and he thrown in the cost for his pains.

"About the first of July, the chief of police of the city of Cincinnati issued an order prohibiting bicycling within the corporation. A meeting of the local members was at once called, and the officers of the Division, learning of the meeting, were promptly on hand. A committee had already conferred with Mayor Smith, who at once conferred with the chief of police. The result was that during the meeting the mayor came in and advised that the whole matter was a mistake and a misunderstanding, and that wheelmen should have the same rights in the future as they had enjoyed in the past, — the same rights as other vehicles.

"Only a week ago yesterday a member of my own club riding in the western portion of our city passed a group of drunken toughs. Just after he passed them, one of the group seized the backbone of his wheel, and by shoving it sidewise, threw wheel and rider violently to the ground. The father of the wheelman, with our local club, at once took up the matter, had him arrested, and the next day in police court he was fined $10 and costs, $15.40 in all, to stand committed until the fine was paid.

"In not every one of these cases did the League show itself, but in reality it was back of them all. Had there been no such organization as the League of American Wheelmen, these ordinances and rulings would now be in force against us. Our own self-interest, then demands, of us unswerving loyalty to such an organization."

• THE Los Angeles *Express* of 28 Aug., says: Fred E. Von Meerbeke, the youthful New York Knickerbocker who left his native city on 1 March for a trip to San Francisco by way of New Orleans, arrived in Los Angeles yesterday afternoon. He is only twenty years of age, and is the youngest rider for a long distance in the United States. When he left New York his weight was one hundred and thirty-five pounds, and is now one hundred and thirty-one and one half. The run to New Orleans was made in forty-seven days, twelve days' time being lost on account of rains, the average day's journey being forty miles. He remained in the Crescent City fifteen days, and then started for California by way of Houston, San Antonio, El Paso, and Tucson, reaching the latter place 7 Aug. From Yuma he had to ride about one hundred miles on the train, on account of the water that caused the washouts still being in the road. Leaving San Gorgonia on Sunday, Colton was reached that night, and the trip from Spadra to this city made between 6.30 A. M. and 12.30 P. M., of Monday. The average daily distance travelled since leaving New Orleans, has been thirty-three miles. During the trip he estimates that he has walked one fourth of the entire distance. He was given one hundred and fifty days in which to reach San Francisco, and has still forty-nine days in which to finish. The return trip will be made by rail. During the trip thus far he has worn out seventeen steel balls in the bicycle, six pairs of pants and five pairs of shoes. Blue overalls and canvas shoes are worn. A similar trip was made to Denver last year, and next year, in company with a brother, Mr. Von Meerbeke expects to go to Europe and make a tour of the Continent.

THE bicycle tournament this week has fairly divided the honors of public local attention with the State convention. A most noticeable feature of the races was the character of the audience. The horse races drew as big a crowd on the big day as the bicycle races on the first day, but there was a vast difference in the character of the crowd. The cyclists had more women than men on the grand stand, and the people were all from the best of the city. The unfortunate weather of the second day has made the tournament a loss to the Connecticut Club rather than a gain, and strengthened the feeling that before another tournament is given there must be a good half-mile track in the city, and easy of access, and more than all, one not cut up and cuppy because of previous use for horse racing. — *Hartford correspondent Springfield Republican.*

THE PATH.

SPRINGFIELD, 21 Sept. — Races under the management of W. J. Morgan (2).

Five-mile Professional. — Chas. Frazier (1), 16.06; W. J. Morgan.

Quarter-mile Dash to Beat Record. — R. Neilson (1), 39s.; W. M. Haradon (2).

Eight-mile, Man v. Horse. — Horse Propellor (1), W. M. Woodside (2).

A five-mile race was also run between the above parties with the same results.

PROVIDENCE, 21 Sept. — Races under the auspices of the R. I. Fair.

One-mile State Championship. — E. Buffum (1), 3.10½; M. W. Turner (2).

Half-mile (under eighteen years). — H. Wilmarth (1), 1.26½; J. E. Tweedy (2).

One-mile Open. — F. B. Brigham (1), 3.10; H. Wilmarth (2).

Half-mile without Hands. — F. B. Brigham (1), 1.36½; E. S. Hutchins (2).

Three-mile State Championship. — E. Buffum (1), 10.39; H. G. Wilks (2).

One-mile for Stars. — James E. Dawson (1), 3.25½; C. M. Keep (2).

SPRINGFIELD TOURNAMENT.

TUESDAY, 14 SEPTEMBER.

One-mile Promateur, — First Heat of World's Championship.

Leader.	Miles.	M.	S.
C. E. Kluge	¼	39	
C. E. Kluge	½	1	18
W. A. Rowe	¾	1	57⅗
W. A. Rowe	1	2	38
C. E. Kluge (2)	1	2	40⅖

One-mile Novice, —

Leader.	Miles.	M.	S.
Wm. Harding	¼		41⅖
Wm. Harding	½	1	25⅘
Wm. Harding	¾	2	7⅕
Wm. Harding	1	2	51⅗

F. W. Fahy (2), 2.55⅗; Henry Goodman (3); H. H. Chapman (4).

Ten-mile Promateur A. C. U. Championship, —

Leader.	Miles.	M.	S.
C. P. Adams	¼		54⅕

C. P. Adams	¼	1	39
C. P. Adams	¾	2	27⅗
C. P. Adams	1	3	18⅗
C. E. Kluge	1½		
C. E. Kluge	2	6	27⅕
W. A. Rhodes	2½		
W. A. Rhodes	3	9	09⅗
W. A. Rhodes	3½		
W. A. Rhodes	4	12	04
W. A. Rhodes	4½		
W. A. Rhodes	5	15	05⅕
W. A. Rhodes	5½		
W. A. Rhodes	6	18	04⅗
W. A. Rhodes	6½		
W. A. Rhodes	7	21	07
G. M. Hendee	7½		
G. M. Hendee	8	23	51⅗
G. M. Hendee	8½		
G. M. Hendee	9	26	40
G. M. Hendee	9½		
G. M. Hendee	10	29	28⅕

Percy W. Stone (2), 30.19; W. A. Rhodes (3).

Five-mile Professional Handicap,—

Leader.	Miles.
F. T. Merrill, 440 yds.	¼
F. T. Merrill	½
F. T. Merrill	¾
F. T. Merrill	1
C. F. Frazier, 300 yds.	2
C. F. Frazier	3
C. F. Frazier	4
R. A. Neilson, 100 yds.	5

W. M. Woodside, 30 yds. (2), 14.36; H. Crocker, 100 yds. (3); F. T. Merrill, 440 yds. (4); C. F. Frazier, 300 yds. (5); W. J. Morgan, 250 yds. (6).

Wood started at scratch and finished two miles. He was timed as follows: ¼, 38⅗; ½, 1.20; ¾, 2.1⅗; mile, 2.46⅕; two, 5.53⅘. Woodside was clocked after Wood retired, as follows: Three, 8.22; four, 11.49⅕; five, 14.36.

One-Mile Promateur, Second Heat of Championship,—

	Miles.	M.	S.
E. P. Burnham	¼		48
E. P. Burnham	½	1	36⅕
E. P. Burnham	¾	2	23⅘
E. P. Burnham	1	3	02⅘

F. F. Ives (2), 3.03⅗

Five-mile Amateur, 16.30 class,—

	Miles.	M.	S.
E. B. Smith	¼		49⅘
E. B. Smith	½	1	36
E. B. Smith	¾	2	22⅘
E. B. Smith	1	3	11⅗
E. B. Smith	2	6	20⅕
E. B. Smith	3	9	21⅗
C. D. Heath	4	12	17
H. S. Hart	5	15	2⅕
H. L. Burdick (2)		15	03

P. S. Brown (3); A. F. Edmans (4); W. H. Langdown (5); C. D. Heath (6).

One-mile Promateur Tricycle,—

	Miles.	M.	S.
E. P. Burnham	¼	1	1⅗
E. P. Burnham	½	1	51
E. P. Burnham	¾	2	38⅘
E. P. Burnham	1	3	18⅕
F. F. Ives (2)		3	18⅗

C. E. Kluge (3).

Three-mile Professional,—

	Miles.	M.	S.
C. F. Frazier	¼		49⅗
C. F. Frazier	½	1	38⅕
C. F. Frazier	¾	2	24⅗
C. F. Frazier	1	3	14⅗
W. J. Morgan	2	6	8⅗
R. A. Neilson	3	9	01

Woodside ties Crocker (2), 9.1⅕; C. F. Frazier (3); Fred Wood (4); W. J. Morgan (5); F. T. Merrill (6).

One-mile Promateur,—Third Heat of World's Championship.

Leader.	Miles.	M.	S.
Percy W. Stone	¼		57
Percy W. Stone	½	1	48⅕
Percy W. Stone	¾	2	37⅗
Percy W. Stone	1	3	17⅘
C. P. Adams (2)		3	18

One-mile Amateur Tandem,—A. C. U. Championship.

Leader.	Miles.	M.	S.
Crist and Brown	¼		*41⅕
Crist and Brown	½	*1	21⅗
Crist and Brown	¾	†2	1⅘
Crist and Brown	1	†2	43⅕
Rich and Foster (2)		‖2	45⅗

Huntington and Collister (3)

* Best American record. † Best World record. ‖ Ahead of previous world's record.

One-mile Professional,—Fourth Heat in World's Championship.

Leader.	Miles.	M.	S.
R. James	¼	1	37⅗
R. James	½	2	58⅕
R. A. Neilson	¾	3	37⅕
R. A. Neilson	1	4	19⅗
Robert James (2)		4	20⅕

The men were fined $10 each by the referee for loafing.

Second Day.

Wednesday, 15 September.

All the riders were notified by the referee at the outset, that any championship heat that was run in slower time than three minutes, would be considered a loafing race, and fines would be imposed.

One-mile Professional,—Fifth Heat in World's Championship.

Leader.	Miles.	M.	S.
W. M. Woodside	¼		38⅕
W. M. Woodside	½	1	16⅗
Fred Wood	¾	1	56⅗
Fred Wood	1	2	32⅗
W. M. Woodside (2)		2	36

Fred Wood's mile is the fastest ever made in competition.

One-mile Promateur,—Sixth Heat in World's Championship.

Leader.	Miles.	M.	S.
G. M. Hendee	¼		37⅕
G. M. Hendee	½	1	14⅗
G. M. Hendee	¾	1	53⅗
G. M. Hendee	1	2	35
W. A Rhodes (2)		2	43

Five-mile Amateur Lap,—

Leader.	Miles.	M.	S.
A. B. Rich	½	1	20⅗
H. W. Gaskell	1	2	47⅕
A. B. Rich	1½		
Fred Foster	2	5	50⅕
H. W. Gaskell	2½		
H. W. Gaskell	3	8	46⅗
H. W. Gaskell	3½		
P. S. Brown	4	11	55⅗
H. W. Gaskell	4½		
H. W. Gaskell	5	15	03

F. Foster (2), 15.03⅕; A. B. Rich (3); P. S. Brown (4).

Rich (1), 111 points; Gaskell, (2) 89 points; Fred Foster (3), 74 points; P. S. Brown (4) 66 points.

Three-mile Professional Tricycle,—

Leader.	Miles.	M.	S.
R. James	¼		52⅗
H. G. Crocker	½	1	40⅗
H. G. Crocker	¾	2	26
H. G. Crocker	1	3	15⅕
H. G. Crocker	1½		
T. W. Eck	2	6	26⅕
T. W. Eck	2½		
H. G. Crocker	3	*9	41⅗

T. W. Eck (2), 9.45⅗; R. James (3).

There were but three starters and three prizes. The referee notified the men that the last man must finish in 9.50 or less, or forfeit a prize.

Five-mile Promateur Lap,—

Leader.	Miles.	M.	S.
W. A. Rowe	½		
W. A. Rowe	1	2	47⅘
W. A. Rowe	1½		
W. A. Rowe	2	5	42⅗
W. A. Rowe	2½		
W. A. Rowe	3	8	39⅗
W. A. Rowe	3½		
W. A. Rowe	4	11	37⅘
W. A. Rowe	4½		
W. A. Rowe	5	14	35

W. A. Rhodes (2), 14.36; F. A. Ives (3).

Rowe (1), 50 points; Rhodes (2), 34 points; Ives (3), 30 points.

One-Mile Professional.—Seventh Heat in World's Championship:—

Leader.	Miles.	M.	S.
J. S. Prince	¼		44⅘
H. G. Crocker	½	1	23⅗
H. G. Crocker	¾	2	4⅕
J. S. Prince	1	2	44⅘
H. G. Crocker		2	45

Three-mile Amateur Tricycle,—

Leader.	Miles.	M.	S.
H. W. Gaskell	¼		52
H. W. Gaskell	½	1	43⅗
H. W. Gaskell	¾	2	28
H. W. Gaskell	1	3	15
H. W. Gaskell	1½		
H. W. Gaskell	2	6	47⅘
J. T. Williams	2½		
A. B. Rich	3	9	57
H. W. Gaskell (2)		9	59⅗
J. T. Williams (3)			
Fred Foster (4)			

Three-mile Professional Handicap,—

Leader.	Miles.	M.	S.
F. T. Merrill, 250 yards	¼		
F. T. Merrill, 250 yards	½		
F. T. Merrill, 250 yards	¾		
F. T. Merrill, 250 yards	1		
C. F. Frazier, 150 yards	2		
Fred Woods, scratch	3	8	36⅘
W. M. Woodside, scratch (2)		8	37

R. A. Neilson, 50 yards (3).

Wood's time, Quarter, 42; half, 1.20⅗; three quarter, 2.04; mile, 2.40; two, 5.44⅗.

Five-mile Promateur Handicap.—W. M. Haradon, 550 yards (1); P. W. Stone, 350 yards (2); C. E. Kluge, 300 yards (3); G. M. Hendee, scratch (4), 14.17⅗; F. F. Ives, 150 yards (5); C. P. Adams, 200 yards (6).

Hendee's time: Quarter, 40⅗; half, 1.21; three quarters, 2.01⅕; mile, 2.44⅗; two, 5.35⅕; three, 8.28⅗; four, 11.19⅗; five, 14.17⅗.

Three-mile Professional Lap,—

Leader.	Miles.	M.	S.
W. M. Woodside	¼		42⅗

F. Wood	½	1	18
F. Wood	¾	2	02⅗
F. Wood	1	2	41
W. M. Woodside	2	5	36
R. A. Neilson	3	8	37⅗

C. Frazier (2), 8.39⅗; W. M. Woodside (3).
Woodside (1), 32 points; Neilson (2), 26 points; Frazier (3), 25 points.

THIRD DAY.

Rain caused a postponement of the races from Thursday, the 16th, to

FRIDAY, 17 SEPTEMBER.

One-mile Professional,—Eighth Heat of World's Championship.

Leader.	Miles.	M.	S.
Fred Wood	¼	1	9⅕
Fred Wood	½	2	9
Fred Wood	¾	3	5⅘
R. A. Neilson	1	3	46⅖
F. Wood (2)		3	46⅘

A loafing race. The referee declared it no race, and imposed a fine of $10 each. The race was run over again as follows:—

Leader.	Miles.	M.	S.
R. A. Neilson	¼		46
R. A. Neilson	½	1	21⅗
R. A. Neilson	¾	2	2
F. Wood	1	2	44⅕
R. A. Neilson (2)		2	44⅗

Three-mile Promateur Tricycle,—

Leader.	Miles.	M.	S.
E. P. Burnham	¼		40⅕
E. P. Burnham	½	1	24⅘
E. P. Burnham	¾	2	10
E. P. Burnham	1	2	56⅕
C. E. Kluge	2	5	57⅖
E. P. Burnham	3	8	56⅖
F. F. Ives (2)		8	56⅗
C. E. Kluge (3)			

Five-mile Amateur,—

Leader.	Miles.	M.	S.
H. W. Gaskell	¼		51⅕
C. L. Myers	½		1.42
C. L. Myers	¾		2.32
H. S. Kavanaugh	1		3.25
H. S. Kavanaugh	2		6.57⅗
H. S. Kavanaugh	3		10.21⅘
W. E. Crist	4		13.38
W. E. Crist	5		16.26
A. B. Rich (2)			16.26⅗

H. W. Gaskell (3); Fred Foster (4); E. A. DuBlois (5); H. S. Kavanaugh (6).

One-mile Promateur,—Ninth Heat in World's Championship.

Leader.	Miles.	M.	S.
G. M. Hendee	¼		43⅖
G. M. Hendee	½	1	25
G. M. Hendee	¾	2	7⅕
W. A. Rowe	1	2	44⅗

G. M. Hendee (2) 2.44⅘.

One-mile Professional Handicap,—

Leader.	Miles.	M.	S.
W. M. Woodside, 20 yards,	¼		43
W. M. Woodside, 20 yards,	½	1	22⅖
W. M. Woodside	¾		
W. M. Woodside, 20 yards,	1	2	34⅖

W. J. Morgan, 120 yards (2), 2.35; F. T.

A. B. Rich	½	1	28
H. S. Kavanaugh	¾	2	14⅘
H. S. Kavanaugh	1	2	57⅖
H. S. Kavanaugh	2	5	53⅗
Fred Foster (tie)	3	8	40⅕

W. E. Crist (tie) 8.40⅕; A. B. Rich (3); E. A. DuBlois (4); H. S. Hart (5); H. S. Kavanaugh (6); H. W. Gaskell (7).

One-mile to run off above Dead Heat,—

Leader.	Miles.	M.	S.
Fred Foster	¼		58⅕
Fred Foster	½	1	50⅖
W. E. Crist	¾	2	36
Fred Foster	1	3	11

W. E. Crist (2), 3.11⅖.

Ten-mile Promateur Lap,—

Leader.	Miles.	M.	S.
P. W. Stone	¼		58⅖
W. A. Rowe	½	1	36
W. A. Rhodes	¾	2	22
W. A. Rowe	1	3	2⅗
W. A. Rowe	2	6	10
W. A. Rowe	3	9	11⅖
W. A. Rowe	4	12	8⅖
W. A. Rhodes	5	15	8⅕
W. A. Rowe	6	18	18⅖
W. A. Rowe	7	21	29⅖
W. A. Rowe	8	24	40
W. A. Rhodes	9	27	46
W. A. Rowe	10	30	44

W. A. Rhodes (2), 30.44⅕; C. P. Adams (3).
W. A. Rowe, 118 points; W. A. Rhodes, 88 points; C. P. Adams, 69 points.

One-mile Professional,—

Leader.	Miles.	M.	S.
J. S. Prince	¼		46⅘
F. T. Merrill	½	1	33
W. M. Woodside	¾	2	11
W. M. Woodside	1	2	46

R. A. Neilson (2), 2.46⅘; Fred Wood (3); C. F. Frazier (4); J. S. Prince (5); F. T. Merrill (6).

Three-mile Professional Tricycle Handicap,—

Leader.	Miles.	M.	S.
T. W. Eck, 100 yards	¼		
T. W. Eck	½		
T. W. Eck	¾		
H. Crocker, scratch	1	2	55⅘
H. Crocker	2	*6	03⅘
H. Crocker	3	*9	10

T. W. Eck (2), 9.35; W. J. Morgan, 100 yards (3).
Crocker's quarter miles were: *39, *1.22, 2.07⅗, 2.55⅘.

*Best American professional record.

FOURTH DAY.

SATURDAY, 18 SEPTEMBER.

Three-mile Amateur, 9.45 Class,—

Leader.	Miles.	M.	S.
W. M. Harding	¼		45⅕
W. M. Harding	½	1	27⅖
W. M. Harding	¾	2	13
W. M. Harding	1	2	58⅖
W. M. Harding	2	6	13
H. L. Burdick	3	9	20

P. S. Brown (2), 9.21; W. M. Harding

W. M. Woodside	3	8	55
W. M. Woodside	4	12	1⅗
C. F. Frazier	5	15	7⅖
W. M. Woodside	6	18	22⅖
W. M. Woodside	7	21	34⅕
W. M. Woodside	8	24	42⅖
W. M. Woodside	9	27	52⅖
W. M. Woodside	10	31	19⅖

C. F. Frazier (2), 31.20; H. G. Crocker (3); W. J. Morgan (4).
W. M. Woodside (1), 138 points; C. F. Frazier (2), 120 points; H. G. Crocker (3), 99 points; W. J. Morgan (4), 74 points.

Three-mile Promateur,—

Leader.	Miles.	M.	S.
F. F. Ives	¼		43
F. F. Ives	½	1	24
W. A. Rhodes	¾	2	7⅖
W. A. Rhodes	1	2	48⅕
G. M. Hendee	2	5	57⅗
G. M. Hendee	3	9	2⅕

F. F. Ives (2), 9.32⅗; W. A. Rhodes (3); C. P. Adams, (4); C. E. Kluge (5).

Three-mile Amateur Handicap,—

Leader.	Miles.	M.	S.
G. R. Collins, 250 yds.	¼		
G. R. Collins	½		
G. R. Collins	¾		
G. R. Collins	1		
W. M. Harding, 150 yds.	2		
W. E. Crist, 40 yds (1)	3		
H. S. Hart, 50 yds. (2).			
F. Foster, scratch (3)		8	38⅗
E. A. DuBlois, 30 yds. (4).			
H. S. Kavanaugh, scratch (5).			
H. W. Gaskell, scratch (6).			
W. M. Harding, 150 yds. (7).			

One-mile Sanctioned Professional and Promateur,—

Leader.	Miles.	M.	S.
W. A. Rowe	¼		43⅕
W. A. Rowe	½	1	27⅕
W. A. Rowe	¾	2	28
W. A. Rowe	1	3	8⅗
Fred Wood (2)		3	9⅕

Men fined $10 for loafing.

One-mile Professional,—

Leader.	Miles.	M.	S.
R. A. Neilson	¼		47
R. A. Neilson	½	1	31⅗
R. A. Neilson	¾	2	20
R. A. Neilson	1	2	58⅗
J. S. Prince (2)		2	59

One-mile Promateur 2.40 Class,—

Leader.	Miles.	M.	S.
E. P. Burnham	¼		51⅗
E. P. Burnham	½	1	36⅕
E. P. Burnham	¾	2	12
Percy Stone	1	2	51
E. P. Burnham (2)		2	51⅘

F. F. Ives (3).
C. P. Adams (4).
W. M. Haradon (5).
C. E. Kluge (6).

Five-mile Professional,—

Leader.	Miles.	M.	S.
W. J. Morgan	¼		53⅖
W. J. Morgan	½	1	41⅖
W. J. Morgan	¾	2	30⅖

One-mile Tandem Handicap,—

		M.	S.
Collister and Huntington, 5s..	$\frac{1}{4}$		41
Crist and Brown, scratch.....			40$\frac{3}{5}$
Crist and Brown.............	$\frac{1}{2}$	1	19
Collister and Huntington.....		1	25$\frac{1}{5}$
Crist and Brown.............	$\frac{3}{4}$	2	3
Collister and Huntington.....		2	15
Crist and Brown.............	1	2	48
Collister and Huntington.....		3	20$\frac{1}{5}$

One mile against Time,—

Leader.	Miles.	M.	S.
G. M. Hendee...............	$\frac{1}{4}$		38$\frac{1}{5}$
G. M. Hendee...............	$\frac{1}{2}$	1	15$\frac{3}{5}$
G. M. Hendee...............	$\frac{3}{4}$	1	52$\frac{1}{5}$
G. M. Hendee...............	1	2	31

Paced by Burnham, Adams, and Rowe. Best promateur record for a mile.

Consolation Race. — One mile,—

Leader.	Miles.	M.	S.
G. R. Collins...............	$\frac{1}{4}$		48
G. R. Collins...............	$\frac{1}{2}$	1	33$\frac{3}{5}$
G. R. Collins...............	$\frac{3}{4}$	2	21
E. A. DeBlois...............	1	3	1$\frac{3}{5}$

A. F. Edmans (2) 3.1$\frac{4}{5}$; E. B. Smith (3); G. R. Collins (4).

NEW RECORDS.

First Day.

American Amateur Tandem,—

Leader.	Miles.	M.	S.
Crist and Brown.............	$\frac{1}{4}$		41$\frac{1}{5}$
Crist and Brown.............	$\frac{1}{2}$	1	21$\frac{4}{5}$
Crist and Brown.............	$\frac{3}{4}$	*2	1$\frac{3}{5}$
Crist and Brown.............	1	*2	43$\frac{1}{5}$

American Promateur Safety,—

	Miles.	M.	S.
C. E. Kluge.................	$\frac{1}{4}$		*39
C. E. Kluge.................	$\frac{1}{2}$	*1	18
C. E. Kluge.................	1	*2	40$\frac{4}{5}$

Second Day.

American Professional Tricycle,—

Leader.	Miles.	M.	S.
H. G. Crocker...............	3	9	41$\frac{3}{5}$

Third Day.

American Promateur Tricycle,—

Leader.	Miles.	M.	S.
E. P. Burnham...............	$\frac{1}{4}$		40$\frac{1}{5}$
E. P. Burnham...............	$\frac{1}{2}$	1	24$\frac{3}{5}$
E. P. Burnham...............	$\frac{3}{4}$	2	10
E. P. Burnham...............	1	2	56$\frac{1}{5}$
C. E. Kluge.................	2	5	57$\frac{2}{5}$
E. P. Burnham...............	3	8	56$\frac{2}{5}$

American Professional Tricycle,—

Leader.	Miles.	M.	S.
H. G. Crocker...............	$\frac{1}{4}$		*39
H. G. Crocker...............	$\frac{1}{2}$	1	22
H. G. Crocker...............	2	6	3$\frac{4}{5}$
H. G. Crocker...............	3	9	10

Fourth Day.

American Amateur Tandem,—

Leader.	Miles.	M.	S.
Crist and Brown.............	$\frac{1}{4}$		*40$\frac{2}{5}$
Crist and Brown.............	$\frac{1}{2}$	*1	19

American Professional Safety,—

	Miles.	M.	S.
C. F. Frazier...............	5	15	7$\frac{2}{5}$
C. F. Frazier...............	10	31	20

* World's records.

Positions Won.

The following table shows the positions won by the men at Springfield. The letter x indicates that they entered a race and did not finish. In the case of the tandem riders each man of a team is given the position won.

PROFESSIONALS.

W. M. Woodside ($511.25), 1, 1, 1, 1, 1, 2, 2, 2, 2.
R. A. Neilson ($295), 1, 1, 1, 1, 2, 2, 2, 3, 3, x, x.
Fred Wood ($182.50), 1, 1, 1, 2, 3, 4, 5, x, x.
H. G. Crocker ($256.25), 1, 1, 1, 2, 2, 3, 3, 4, 4.
J. S. Prince, 1, 2, 5, 5, x, x.
T. W. Eck ($75), 2, 2, 2, x.
C. F. Frazier ($175) 2, 2,, 3, 3, 4, 5, 6, x.
W. J. Morgan ($85), 2, 3, 4, 6, 6, x, x, x.
Robert James ($25), 2, 3, 3. 4, x, x, x, x, x.
F. T. Merrill ($20), 3, 4, 6, x, x, x, x.

PROMATEURS.

Wm. A. Rowe, 1, 1, 1, 1, 1.
George M. Hendee, 1, 1, 1, 2, 4.
E. P. Burnham, 1, 1, 1, 2, x.
P. W. Stone, 1, 1, 2, 2, x.
W. M. Haradon, 1, 5.
W. A. Rhodes, 2, 2, 2, 3, 3, x.
F. F. Ives, 2, 2, 2, 2, 3, 3, 5, x.
C. E. Kluge, 2, 3, 3, 3, 5, 6, x, x.
C. P. Adams, 2, 3, 4, 4, x, x.

AMATEURS.

W. E. Crist, 1, 1, 1, 1, 2, x.
A. B. Rich, 1, 1, 2, 2, 3.
P. S. Brown, 1, 1, 2, 3, 4, x.
Fred Foster, 1, 2, 3, 3, 4, 4.
E. A. DeBlois, 1, 4, 4, 5, x, x.
W. M. Harding, 1, 3, 7, x.
H. S. Hart, 1, 2, 5, x.
H. L. Burdick, 1, 2.
H. W. Gaskell, 2, 2, 3, 6, 7.
A. F. Edmans, 2, 4, 4, x.
J. T. Huntington, 2, 3.
G. H. Collister, 2, 3.
F. W. Fahy, 2.
Henry Goodman, 3.
J. T. Williams, 3.
E. P. Smith, 3, x.
G. R. Collins, 4, x.
H. H. Chapman, 4.
W. H. Langdown, 5.
H. S. Kavanaugh, 5, 6, 6, x.
C. Lee Myers, x, x, x.
H. J. Hall, Jr., x, x.
C. D. Heath, x, x.

NOTES.

Springfield luck and Springfield pluck succumbed to Mother Rain for a day, but came out all right.

Frazier, the Star man, gave us a few of his old-time spurts, but he could n't hold them.

The Columbia team carried away the lion's share of the prizes, but this was expected, as they were the lions.

Stall was very busy with his camera. He took views of the different teams, of the officials, the newspaper men, etc.

Percy Stone was generally admired for his fine riding. The ladies especially were delighted.

Neilson and James paid $10 each for the privilege of riding a mile slower than 4.19.

Hendee wore a pink suit in place of his customary suit of solemn black.

American wheels took nearly all the prizes.

The officials were as follows: Referee, Abbot Bassett, of Chelsea; judges, A. Kennedy-Child, of London, Eng.; W. V. Gilman, of Nashua, N. H.; F. A. Elwell, of Portland, Me.; C. A. Hazlett, of Portsmouth, N. H.; clerk of the course, D. Edgar Miller; assistant, H. B. Wadsworth; timers, O. N. Whipple, George C. Robinson, and Ethan C. Robinson; starter, C. E. Whipple; scorers, George S. Miller, J. Fennessy, and Arthur B. Wassung.

The Pope Manufacturing Co. and the Overman Wheel Co. had tents on the ground, and welcomed wheelmen, many of whom took advantage of the opportunity to write letters, smoke pipes, etc.

Henry Sandham, the famous artist of *Harper's Weekly*, was busily at work sketching the various scenes during the meet.

Neilson did some brilliant work, and so did Woodside. Fred Wood finished behind both.

The rule giving the referee power to fine men for loafing was used for the first time, but only in flagrant cases. The contestants in the world's championship were notified that a mile made in more than three minutes in so important a race would be considered loafing. The A. C. U. got a snug sum for its treasury.

Mr. J. E. Saville, of the Massachusetts Club, persuaded the Boston & Albany R. R. to make a special rate to Springfield. They sold a round trip ticket for $3, but the fact was not generally known, and few purchased the tickets.

When Hendee was defeated by Rowe, the ladies in the grand stand shed tears.

The officials at Springfield know their duties. The same parties have served in the same positions for three years, and things run very smoothly.

Fred Wood was sick. We believe Rowe can beat him, and would like to see them meet on equal terms. Rowe was a little out of condition the night previous to the great race.

The minstrel show was a success. The music was of a high order, and the fun was genuine. Sanford Lawton was interlocutor, and C. H. Parsons and D. E. Miller were with the end men. The private boxes were kindly placed at the disposal of the officials of the races.

Springfield audiences ask too much of the racing men, and the hissing habit is growing upon them very fast.

Neilson and Woodside carried off the honors in the professional races.

Everybody will want to get some of Stall's pictures. He took a full length view of the Secretary-Editor.

There were few falls this year. Burnham lost control of his machine and fell once, and Harry Hall broke a fork and fell, bringing Charles Lee Meyers down with him. Neither of the men were injured.

Springfield papers charge Hendee's defeat to the fact that he cut the pace for Rowe all the way around. He did this because the grand stand hissed when the men started off leisurely, and Hendee could n't stand that sort of thing.

Kluge made world's records for a safety as follows: Quarter, 39 sec.; half, 1.18; mile, 2.40$\frac{4}{5}$.

Rowe's record of a mile in 2.41 made last year, still stands as the best amateur mile ever made at a Springfield tournament.

Secretary Aaron and Mr. C. D. Renton had a consultation at Springfield. The latter wants the former as a witness.

"And lo! a little child did judge them."

Lewis T. Frye, who surrendered the mile championship to Hendee, was on hand. He says that the men don't have to work so hard as in the early days of racing.

The club took $400 less for the privilege of selling tonic beer on the grounds, than they could have taken for a rum privilege. No intoxicants were sold.

Neilson's backer made a bet of ten to one on Fred Wood in a race which Neilson won.

The club room was open night and day, and visitors were made welcome to its hospitalities.

The electric timing was used at the quarter pole only. It could not be made to operate over so long a tape as was necessary at the home stretch.

Record-breaking was postponed until after the tournament.

Mrs. Stall, of Allston, Mrs. Akin, of Cohoes, and Miss Ives, of Meriden, were the only lady tricyclists from beyond the borders of Springfield.

The Overman and Pope tents were popular resorts. They had free pipes and tobacco laid out. Now, if some dealer will lay out free ice-cream and lemonade, he will draw a bigger crowd.

Jack Prince was in trouble over his machine. He paid $140 cash for a new racer, but his employers would n't let him ride it.

Stone and Prince withdrew from the finals in the championship.

The old skating rink, where in 1883 the cycle exhibition was held, has now become a theatre. "Chestnuts" was on the boards, and many wheelmen visited the place.

Frank White, of Spalding & Brother, showed us a new Humber safety of exceeding beauty, and very light. The wheels were of equal size, and the machine weighed forty-eight pounds.

A. T. Lane, of Montreal, who first introduced the Kangaroo to Springfield, was on hand this year with a Premier safety.

Crist and Brown are Capital (Club) riders.

Fred Jenkins was on hand the second day looking after the interests of Roseville.

Yost and McCune have their safety on view. They now call it the Springfield Roadster.

Willie Haradon, who has been asking for reinstatement as an amateur by the League, with a good chance of getting it, could not wait and give up the Springfield tournament, and now his chances are very poor.

No victories gave greater pleasure to the audience than those which Herbert Gaskell won.

The bar-keeper at one of the hotels took a tandem that had been left with other wheels in the corridor, and inviting a friend to go for a ride, they took the machine out for a midnight wheel about Springfield. It was brought home in an express wagon, and the hotel will pay for it in many ways.

The racing men used to be content with one riding suit. Now they have two or three, and make a change for every race.

NEW YORK, 18 Sept. — Races under the auspices of the King's County Wheelmen.

Two-mile Team. — A. B. Rich and E. Valentine (1).

One-mile Novice. — C. F. Pray (1), 3.09⅘.

One-mile Lap. — A. B. Rich (1), 2.57⅕.

Two-mile Handicap. — J. W. Powers, Jr., 200 yards (1), 5.56⅘.

Three-mile Handicap. — A. B. Rich, scratch (1), 9.29⅘.

One-mile Club for Novices. — L. P. Webber (1), 3.19⅘.

One mile, 3.10 Class. — S. H. Rich (1), 3.08.

Five-mile scratch. — S. H. Rich (1), 18.40⅘.

One-mile Consolation. — E. C. Parker (1), 3.16⅖.

Two-mile Team. — King's County Wheelmen (1), 38 points; Harlem Wheelmen (2), 32 points.

SAN FRANCISCO, CAL., 9 Sept. — Races under the auspices of the California Division L. A. W.: —

One mile, Novice. — F. E. Browning (1), 3.05⅗; D. W. Donnelly (2).

Three-mile National L. A. W. Championship. — F. D. Elwell (1), 9.46⅗; S. F. Booth, Jr. (2).

Five-mile Handicap. — R. W. Turner, scratch (1), 17.25; A. S. Ireland (2).

One-mile State Championship. — F. D. Elwell (1), 3.16⅗; S. F. Booth, Jr. (2).

Two-mile Handicap. — F. E. Browning, 100 yards (1), 6.24⅗; S. F. Booth, Jr., scratch (2).

One-mile Consolation. — C. A. Biederman (1), 3.29½.

NO. ATTLEBORO', 14 Sept. — Races under the auspices of the Farmers' and Mechanics' Association.

Half-mile Open, — F. G. Gibbs (1), 1.29½; H. Wilmarth (2).

One-mile Novice, — W. L. Brown (1), 3.18¾; M. D. Livingston (2).

Three-mile Lap, — D. C. Pierce (1), 14 points; F. W. Perry (2), 12 points; F. G. Gibbs (3), 10 points.

One-mile Handicap, Boys under 18 years of age. — H. Wilmarth, 35 yards (1), 3.07½; H. Moore, 35 yards (2).

One-mile Open, — F. B. Brigham (1), 3.06¼; D. C. Pierce (2).

One-mile 3.30 Class, — W. L. Brown (1), 3.11¼; W. W. East (2).

One-mile Club Handicap. — J. E. Doran, 165 yards (1), 3.08⅘; F. B. Brigham (2).

Two-mile Open. — H. Wilmarth (1), 6.33¼; D. C. Pierce (2). The bell was rung at the wrong time. F. G. Gibbs took the signal, made a spurt, finished the lap ahead and stopped. The others went on for another lap and finished out the race. The officials say they notified the men on the track that there was another lap, but Gibbs says he did not get the word, and thinks he ought to have the race.

Half-mile Handicap, Boys under 15 years of Age. — W. Franklin, scratch (1); Frank P. Bonnett, 50 yards (2).

Two-mile Team Race, — Brockton Club (1), 57 points; Columbia (2), 54 points.

GREENSBURG, IND., 4 Sept. — Races under the auspices of the Greensburg Club.

Three-mile Open. — H. Hulman (1), 9.34; L. W. Wainwright (2).

One-mile Open. — L. W. Wainwright (1), 3.01; F. Belding (2).

Half-mile Decatur Co. Championship. — O. G. Miller (1), 1.44.

BRATTLEBORO', VT., 2 Sept.—Races under the auspices of the Vermont Club.

Three-mile Club Championship. — S. W. Kirkland (1), 11.04½.

One-mile Novice. — W. Sanderson (1), 3.03.

Half-mile State Championship. — S. W. Kirkland (1), 1.37.

Two-mile Handicap. — E. B. Smith (1), 8.02.

One-mile State Championship. — R. Andrews (1), 3.06¼.

Three-mile Handicap. — E. B. Smith (1), 10.59.

One-mile Open. — R. Andrews, 3.03½.

One-mile Consolation. — E. H. Atherton (1), 3.26 ; Capt. F. F. Reid rode a half mile on the unicycle in 1.57½.

ALL the arrangements have been completed for the three days' mammoth tournament of the New Jersey and Athletic Association, at their new grounds, at Roseville, N. J.

The track, which is a three lap, is in perfect condition, and no falling off of speed being necessary, owing to the raised corners, and with an exceptionally long homestretch, offers great opportunity for fast time, which the record breakers will not be slow to accept. All the competitors in the Springfield, Hartford, and Lynn tournaments, Hendee, Rowe, Ives, Kluge, Neilson, Crocker, Prince, Wood, Woodside, Frazier, Rich, Foster of Canada, Adams, and other fast men from all parts of the country. They all express their intention of putting a few records to their favor, and besides the regular races, several of them, notably Hendee, Woodside, Wood, and Rowe, will make special attempts against the existing times. Roseville is located on the outskirts of the city of Newark, and is thirty minutes from New York. Trains can be taken from the foot of either Barclay or Christopher street ferries, and all trains stop there at the grounds. Wheels will be carried free in the baggage car. Tickets, the regular price of which are fifty cents, will be sold at Delaware, Lackawana and Western stations, allowing. besides admission to the grounds, the excursion to Roseville and return, for sixty cents. Seat in uncovered stand, twenty-five cents extra ; reserved seat in grand stand, fifty cents extra. Upwards of ninety-five trains run between New York and Roseville daily, and all stop at the grounds during the tournament. Many parties have been, and are now forming, for a tour to the meeting, and to sample the famed roads of the Oranges. The roads stretch around in every direction from the track, and every opportunity is offered visiting wheelmen to ride over the superb roads during the morning, and form a good idea of the beautiful scenery, and unsurpassed residence section, attending the races in the afternoon, to witness the records go. All conveniences have been fitted up for the participants in the events, in the way of dressing rooms, shower baths, etc., under the grand stand, and the entrance thereto is directly opposite to the finish. As the programme is a varied one, including bicycle, tricycle, and tandem races, for amateurs, promaters, and professionals, no lack of variety can be claimed. The prizes are valued at two thousand dollars, and consist of medals, cash for professionals, and highly ornamental and useful articles.

IN the six-day professional bicycle race at Troy, N. Y., 4–9 Oct., the winner will receive $800 in cash and a championship belt. The following riders have entered up to date : Robert James, England ; W. M. Woodside, Minneapolis ; W. J. Morgan, Chicago ; Charles Frazier, Smithville, N. J. ; T. W. Eck, Minneapolis ; Mlle. Louis Armaindo, Montreal, Can., and Fred Merrill, Portland, Or.

THE annual fall road races of the Massachusetts Bicycle Club will take place 16 October, over courses yet to be determined upon. Although the programme has not been fully arranged, it has been decided that there shall be one open bicycle race of 25 or 30 miles, for amateurs, besides club bicycle and tricycle races of about 13 and 15 miles respectively. Three prizes will probably be offered in each race. As the arrangements now stand, none but amateurs will be allowed to compete in any of the races. All entries should be addressed to Captain Peck, 152 Newbury street, Boston, on or before 13 October.

THE Columbia Bicycle Club of No. Attleboro' will hold a race meeting 16 Oct. A fine programme is promised. A list of events will be published later.

COMING EVENTS.

MISCELLANEOUS

Lightning Source UK Ltd.
Milton Keynes UK
UKHW022001140119
335570UK00011B/517/P